RIMBAUD

'Robb rescues his subject from the generations of romantics, academics and intellectual fashion-mongers who have recast him down the years in images to suit themselves. This is a wonderfully deadpan Rimbaldian version for the post-modern age'
Hilary Spurling, *Daily Telegraph*

'[*Rimbaud*] is as fascinating, funny and illuminating as Robb's previous lives of Balzac and Victor Hugo. He is one of the very best biographers working today'
Mark Sanderson, *Time Out*

'Graham Robb's *Rimbaud* demythologizes the subject while leaving quite intact the magic of the art'
Julian Barnes, *Observer*, Books of the Year

'Clearly undaunted, Graham Robb – the author of acclaimed biographies of Balzac and Victor Hugo – now goes the distance with this more dangerous, even demonic subject . . . Robb tells this coruscating and enigmatic life story with intelligence, compassion, and a healthy dose of scepticism. He lets Rimbaud breathe'
Charles Nicholl, *Literary Review*

'Graham Robb, whose biographies of Balzac in 1994 and Victor Hugo in 1997 are triumphs of scholarship, now produces the best biography of Rimbaud'
'Editors' Choice', *New York Times*

'At once affectionate and unfooled . . . it is Robb's happy achievement to "allow Rimbaud to grow up"'
Alan Jenkins, *Financial Times*

'An exemplary biography'
Paul Bailey, *Daily Telegraph*, **Books of the Year**

'The single best work to read about this haunting and haunted poet'
Richard Howard, *New York Times*

'Robb offers a lucid and engaging account of a truly extraordinary life. His book is sure to gain Rimbaud still more admirers – while hopefully also prompting them to delve further into his incomparable and beguilingly beautiful poetry'
Economist

'Unfailingly good; a calm, sceptical eye turned on a turbulent life'
Philip Hensher, *Observer*, **Books of the Year**

GRAHAM ROBB was born in Manchester in 1958. He has published widely in nineteenth-century French literature: his highly acclaimed adaptation of Claude Pichois and Jean Ziegler's biography of Baudelaire appeared in 1989, his biography *Balzac* in 1994, and his *Victor Hugo* – winner of the Royal Society of Literature Heinemann Award and the Whitbread Biography Award – in 1997. He lives in Oxford.

Also by Graham Robb in Picador

BALZAC
(1994)

VICTOR HUGO
(1997)

Graham Robb

RIMBAUD

PICADOR

First published 2000 by Picador

This edition published 2001 by Picador
an imprint of Pan Macmillan Ltd
Pan Macmillan, 20 New Wharf Road, London N1 9RR
Basingstoke and Oxford
Associated companies throughout the world
www.panmacmillan.com

ISBN 0 330 48803 1

A CIP catalogue record for this book is available from
the British Library.

Typeset by SetSystems Ltd, Saffron Walden, Essex
Printed and bound in Great Britain by
Mackays of Chatham plc, Chatham, Kent

Contents

List of Illustrations ix

INTRODUCTION xi

PART ONE (1854–1871)

1. BAD BLOOD 3

2. FILTH 15

3. 'PERFECT LITTLE MONSTER' 26

4. 'MAD AMBITION' 33

5. CONVICTIONS 46

6. TOUR DE FRANCE 56

7. NEEDFUL DESTRUCTION 64

8. THE SEER 81

9. DEPARTURE 96

CONTENTS

PART TWO (1871–1874)

10. 'NASTY FELLOWS' 109

11. SAVAGE OF THE LATIN QUARTER 120

12. 'MLLE RIMBAUT' 131

13. DOGS 145

14. SONGS OF INNOCENCE 154

15. 'THE GOOD DISCIPLE' 163

16. FUGITIVES 172

17. UNDERWORLD 183

18. PAGAN 195

19. HOUSEHOLD IN HELL 207

20. 'NO SERIOUS MOTIVE'? 214

21. HARVEST 227

22. '*MÉTROPOLITAIN*' 237

PART THREE (1874–1880)

23. PIGEONS 253

24. PHILOMATH 262

25. MR HOLMES 276

Contents

26. John Arthur Rimbaud 287

27. Explosive 298

PART FOUR (1880–1891)

28. Empires 309

29. The Unknown 318

30. 'Poor Arthur' 330

31. Paradise 338

32. Abdo Rinbo 352

33. Guns for Africa 362

34. Horror 371

35. Profit 383

36. At Home 393

37. 'Odious Tyranny' 404

38. Opportunities 414

39. 'Ferocious Invalid' 425

40. Maritime 435

Epilogue 441

CONTENTS

APPENDICES

I. Family Tree 448

II. Poems by Rimbaud published in his lifetime 450

III. Historical Events 452

IV. Maps 454

V. French Texts 456

NOTES 473

SELECT BIBLIOGRAPHY 511

INDEX 531

List of Illustrations

MBCM – *Musée Bibliothèque de Charleville-Mézières*
BNF – *Bibliothèque Nationale de France*

Section One

The River Meuse at Charleville. *(MBCM)*

Rimbaud's sketch of a weeping woman.

The farmhouse at Roche. *(MBCM)*

Arthur at the Institut Rossat in 1864. *(MBCM)*

Arthur and Frédéric, First Communion. *(MBCM)*

5, Quai de la Madeleine. *(MBCM)*

Ernest Delahaye as a young man. *(MBCM)*

Georges Izambard. *(MBCM)*

Vitalie Rimbaud. *(MBCM)*

Mézières after the Prussian bombardment. *(MBCM)*

Rimbaud in October 1871, by Carjat. *(MBCM)*

Rimbaud in December 1871, by Carjat. *(MBCM)*

Paul Verlaine, *c.* 1869.

Stéphane Mallarmé.

Théodore de Banville, by Nadar. *(BNF)*

Charles Cros, by Nadar. *(BNF)*

Ernest Cabaner, by Manet. *(Musée d'Orsay)*

Edmond Lepelletier, 1880, by Thiriat. *(BNF)*

Mathilde Verlaine after her divorce. *(Bibliothèque Doucet)*

'Coin de table', by Fantin-Latour. *(Musée d'Orsay)*

Rimbaud, September 1872, by Régamey. *(MBCM)*

Rimbaud and Verlaine in London, by Régamey. *(MBCM)*

Rimbaud's poem on the Imperial Prince, in Régamey's album. *(*Verlaine dessinateur, *by Régamey, coll. Auberge Verte)*

34, Howland Street.

8, Great College Street.

Germain Nouveau. *(MBCM)*

'Portrait of the Frenchman Arthur Rimbaud, wounded after drinking by his close friend, the French poet Paul Verlaine. From life by Jef Rosman', Brussels, 1873. *(MBCM)*

Section Two

Rimbaud's letter to Delahaye from Stuttgart, 5 March 1875. *(coll. Jean Hugues, BNF)*

The *Prins van Oranje*, on which Rimbaud sailed to Java. *(Historical department, Royal Netherlands Navy)*

'Le nouveau Juif errant', by Delahaye, 1876. *(MBCM)*

'Les Voyages forment la jûnesse', by Verlaine, 1876. *(MBCM)*

Alfred Bardey. *(MBCM)*

La Maison Bardey at Aden. *(MBCM)*

Rimbaud in Harar, 1883. *(MBCM)*

Rimbaud in Harar, 1883. *(MBCM)*

Coffee merchant in Harar, by Rimbaud. *(MBCM)*

Makonnen, Governor of Harar, as a young man.

Menelik II, Emperor of Ethiopia. *(MBCM)*

Danakil warriors. *(coll. César Tian, MBCM)*

'Donna abissina', by Ottorino Rosa, showing Rimbaud's companion from 1884 to 1886. *(O. Rosa, L'Impero del Leone di Giuda, 1913)*

Rimbaud's house in Harar from 1888, by Ottorino Rosa. *(O. Rosa, L'Impero del Leone di Giuda, 1913)*

The poet of 'Voyelles', by Luque, 1888. *(BNF)*

Verlaine at the Café François Ier, c. 1890, by Dornac. *(BNF)*

Rimbaud's trunk. *(MBCM)*

Rimbaud's sister Isabelle, late 1890s. *(MBCM)*

Introduction

'Every being seemed to me to be entitled to several *other* lives.'

('Délires II', *Une Saison en Enfer*)

UNKNOWN BEYOND THE AVANT-GARDE at the time of his death, Arthur Rimbaud (1854–1891) has been one of the most destructive and liberating influences on twentieth-century culture. He was the first poet to devise a scientifically plausible method for changing the nature of existence, the first to live a homosexual adventure as a model for social change, and the first to repudiate the myths on which his reputation still depends.

Rimbaud's abandonment of poetry in his early twenties has caused more lasting, widespread consternation than the break-up of the Beatles. Even in the mid-1880s, when the French Decadents were hailing him as a 'Messiah', he was already several reincarnations from his starting-point. He had travelled to thirteen different countries and lived as a factory worker, a tutor, a beggar, a docker, a mercenary, a sailor, an explorer, a trader, a gun-runner, a money-changer and, in the minds of some inhabitants of southern Abyssinia, a Muslim prophet.

Rimbaud is largely responsible for what we now think of as the rebel artist – 'the poet of revolt, and the greatest of them all', said Albert Camus.[1] The poems he left behind like unwanted luggage turned out to be literary time-bombs: 'Le Bateau ivre' ('The Drunken

Boat'), the enigmatic 'Voyelles' ('Vowels') sonnet, *Une Saison en Enfer* (*A Season in Hell*), the prose *Illuminations* and some strangely unfamous masterpieces, like the Proustian 'Mémoire' and the obscene, pre-Freudian parodies of the *Album zutique*.

In his posthumous career as Symbolist, Surrealist, Beat poet, student revolutionary, rock lyricist, gay pioneer and inspired druguser, Rimbaud has been treated by four generations of avant-gardes as an emergency exit from the house of convention. 'All known literature', according to Paul Valéry, 'is written in the language of *common sense* – except Rimbaud's.'[2]

It is ironic that the experiments Rimbaud referred to as his 'verbal alchemy' have helped to establish the idea that literary texts should be studied in clinical isolation from the unprofessional muddle of a life. His most spectacular influence has been on writers, musicians and artists who considered his life an essential part of the work: Pablo Picasso, André Breton, Jean Cocteau, Allen Ginsberg, Bob Dylan and Jim Morrison, who is sometimes said to have faked his death in Paris and followed Rimbaud to Ethiopia.

Unlike so many privately respectable anti-heroes, Rimbaud led an exemplary life. The list of his known crimes is several times longer than the list of poems published by Rimbaud himself. Between the time when he first ran away to Paris (1870) and the last recorded sign of interest in his own poetry (1875), the longest texts in his *Correspondance* are the letter in which he described his plan for becoming a 'seer' by means of a 'long, immense and rational *derangement* of *all the senses*', and his statements to the Brussels police after he was shot by his lover, the poet Paul Verlaine.

The first biographical text devoted to Rimbaud – apart from adulatory school reports – was written on that occasion by a police constable:

> In morality and talent, this Raimbaud [*sic*], aged between 15 and 16, was and is a monster. He can construct poems like no one else, but his works are completely incomprehensible and repulsive.[3]

Since then, opinions have been almost uniformly extreme:

> 'An angelic mind that was certainly illuminated by heavenly light.'
> – PAUL CLAUDEL[4]

'The originator of modern prose rhythms, and the basis from which all speculations of the kind have arisen.' – EDITH SITWELL[5]

'A "spirit" of the highest rank in the body of a vicious and terrible child.' – JACQUES RIVIÈRE[6]

'A veritable god of puberty.' – ANDRÉ BRETON[7]

'The first poet of a civilization not yet born.' – RENÉ CHAR[8]

'A superior mental degenerate with the added complication, during the period of literary production, of toxic delirium.' – DR E. JACQUEMIN-PARLIER[9]

'Constitutional psychopath.' – DR J. H. LACAMBRE[10]

'The first punk poet.' 'The first guy who ever made a big women's liberation statement, saying that when women release themselves from the long servitude of men they're really gonna gush. New rhythms, new poetries, new horrors, new beauties.' – PATTI SMITH[11]

As some of these quotations suggest, Rimbaud's poetry is not just a powerful mental stimulant; it also provides a fertile medium for fantasy and delusion. The great demystifier of bourgeois literature and society has been smothered in myth. Even now, the vast confabulation of the Internet is spreading Rimbaud legends more rapidly than ever, attaching him to more recent vagrants and visionaries like Bruce Chatwin and Kurt Cobain.

The reverential tone was set immediately after Rimbaud's death. Horrified to see her brother depicted in the newspapers as a smutty, homosexual terrorist, Isabelle Rimbaud devoted herself to the task of cleaning up his reputation: 'How likely is it', she wondered, 'that a boy aged between 15 and 16 could have been the evil genius of Verlaine, who was eleven years his senior?'[12] The hagiography by her husband, Paterne Berrichon, which he almost called *La Vie charmante d'Arthur Rimbaud*, is often derided but remains surprisingly influential.

One of the starting-points of this biography was the discovery that Rimbaud's image is still a faint reflection of the evidence. Isabelle Rimbaud's fabrications were exposed long ago, but heart-warming phrases are still quoted from letters which are known to have been forged or expurgated.

Many biographers of Rimbaud obviously preferred the sentimental, schoolboy adventure stories of Rimbaud's early memorialists to the poet's own savage cynicism. The colonial past became a pretext for nostalgia, and Rimbaud's face was erased to the prepubescent blank of Hergé's Tintin, parading its spurious innocence in a world of crafty natives.

For many readers (including this one), the revelation of Rimbaud's poetry is one of the decisive events of adolescence. Unlike other such events, it appears to entail, not a loss of innocence, but a realization that innocence has far more possibilities than previously supposed. Such readers inevitably have an interest in keeping Rimbaud young, and perhaps, as Evelyn Waugh implied in the opening lines of *Scoop* (1938), the life of Arthur Rimbaud is not an adult subject:

> While still a young man, John Courteney Boot had, as his publisher proclaimed, 'achieved an assured and enviable position in contemporary letters'. [. . .] He had published eight books – beginning with a life of Rimbaud written when he was eighteen, and concluding, at the moment, with *Waste of Time*, a studiously modest description of some harrowing months among the Patagonian Indians.[13]

I have tried at least to allow Rimbaud to grow up. Having once ignored his post-poetic life in a spirit of textual purity, I found the investigation of his years in Arabia and Africa an enlightening and exhilarating journey. This period of his life turns out to be an important chapter in the history of the Scramble for Africa. It also retrospectively illuminates his writing. Like all great poets, Rimbaud was a brilliant manipulator. Anyone who first read his poems as the oracular burblings of a naturally inspired 'seer' can only profit from the knowledge that, apart from Victor Hugo, no French poet of the late nineteenth century had a greater impact on imperial politics or earned more money.

*

MY OWN EXPERIENCE of urban and rural East Africa has been less useful in writing this book than the 'rugged reality' of literary research. It is too easy to remain attached to old images and ideas when the mind is preoccupied with phrase-books, timetables, mosquito nets and water purification tablets. Nothing can replace the brutal shock of verifiable information: rediscovered letters, accounts of other travellers in an Abyssinia that no longer exists, the untold horror stories of Rimbaud's business deals, and the charting of his explorations in one of the world's largest remaining *terrae incognitae*.

The biographies of those who set off in search of Rimbaud, and even tried to live his life, are significantly identical in their conclusions to the romances of desk-bound biographers. Rimbaud road books belong to a separate sub-genre. This biography is not intended as a pedantic substitute or a medically tested antidote. The best, like Alain Borer's necromantic meditations or Charles Nicholl's more gritty, lyrical homage, *Somebody Else: Arthur Rimbaud in Africa, 1880–91*, are literary works in their own right.

Exposing myths and correcting misapprehensions is a pleasant but ultimately futile and even self-deluding activity. In the Hall of Mirrors of Rimbaud's reputation, there are at least as many Rimbauds as there are personae in his work. As Rimbaud scholars continue to demonstrate, with an annual average of ten books and eighty-seven articles, his poetry is not the literary equivalent of a live concert but a complex, almost pathologically ambiguous body of work. Unlike many of his contemporaries, Rimbaud is not remembered for moral witticisms that produce a general murmur of agreement but for enigmatic slogans that support a huge variety of interpretations: 'Real life is absent'; 'I is somebody else'; 'Love must be reinvented'; 'The time of the *Assassins* is upon us', which Henry Miller associated with millennial chaos and nuclear war;[14] and 'a rational *derangement* of *all the senses*' – often quoted without the 'rational'.

*

SINCE THE LAST full biographies of Rimbaud – Pierre Petitfils (1982) and Jean-Luc Steinmetz (1991) – a great deal of new information has come to light, some of it in the 1998 Drouot auction[15] when one of Rimbaud's schoolboy letters was sold for 3.5 million francs. The principal innovations, however, lie in the interpretation and chronology of the crucial moments of Rimbaud's life: his anarchist activities, his relationship with Verlaine, his explorations and gun-running expeditions, and his financial, political and religious interactions with the slave societies of the Horn of Africa.

I have not found the Rimbaud I expected to find, nor did I expect to spend as much time working on this book as Rimbaud spent producing four small bodies of work each of which represents a different stage in the history of modern poetry. My only regret is that it did not take twice as long. Rimbaud gave up writing poetry, but few people, having acquired the taste, ever give up reading it.

*

IT MIGHT REASONABLY be asked why this 450-page reconstruction of Rimbaud's life ends in a rubble-strewn hinterland of notes, especially since the book is designed to be read with only one bookmark. The notes are intended to support statements, to facilitate further research, and to acknowledge the fact that every biography is a collaboration. The notes and bibliography, in other words, are an extension of the acknowledgements.

The following people offered information or helped with questions which ranged from the small and tedious to the vast and unanswerable: Damian Atkinson, Jean-Paul Avice, Michel Brix, Elizabeth Chapman, Mastan Ebtahaj, Philip Gaskell, André Guyaux, James Hiddleston, Steve Murphy, James Patty, Claude and Vincenette Pichois, Raymond and Helen Poggenburg, John Wagstaff and Phil Whitaker. I am grateful to the staff of the Taylor Institution Library, the Modern Languages Faculty Library (Oxford), the Bodleian Library, the Public Record Office, the Bibliothèque Nationale de France and the Musée Arthur Rimbaud in Charleville.

Tanya Stobbs and Peter Straus at Picador, Starling Lawrence at Norton, Helen Dore, and my agent, Gill Coleridge, helped to make the telling of Rimbaud's life an incongruously happy experience.

Stephen Roberts read what was supposed to be the final version and illuminated several dark areas.

Margaret's treasured comments were my principal ulterior motive for writing this book.

GRAHAM ROBB   Oxford, 1999

Part One

(1854–1871)

1

Bad Blood

'I have never belonged to this race.'

('Mauvais sang', *Une Saison en Enfer*)

MOST ROMANTIC POETS practised surgery on their family trees, grafting on aristocrats and lopping off nonentities. Rimbaud pulled his tree up by the roots and heaved it on to a rubbish heap of ancient, faceless idiots:

> If only I had antecedents somewhere in French history!
> But no. Nothing.
> It is quite clear to me that I have always belonged to an inferior race. [. . .] The only time my race rose up in revolt, it was to go pillaging.[1]

Rimbaud was thinking of his own name. At various times, a *ribaud* (from *rimbaldus*) had been a prostitute, a libertine, a thuggish fornicator, a soldier who signed up only for the loot.[2] Many of his contemporaries would have considered this a fair description of the poet: Rimbaud by name, *rimbaud* by nature.

Three years before Rimbaud was born (20 October 1854), Napoleon III founded the Second Empire with a coup d'état and legitimized it by harking back, architecturally and administratively, to Ancient Rome. Rimbaud, who witnessed the fall of the Empire and dreamed of ideological steamrollers flattening society itself, harked back a little further:

I have the bluish-white eyes of my ancestors the Gauls, their small brains, their clumsiness in battle. I find my dress as barbaric as theirs. But I do not butter my hair.[3]

This worthless inheritance, according to *Une Saison en Enfer*, also included idolatry, love of sacrilege, extraordinary ineptitude in simple daily tasks, the full range of vices – 'especially deceitfulness and sloth' – and, to go with them, 'no moral sense'.

This is the self-portrait of the poet who became one of the most influential artistic gurus of the twentieth century: a one-man, alternative *comédie humaine*. The story told in the following pages will inevitably magnify the individual. It belongs to an ancient, optimistic genre, originally devised for mythological heroes and founders of religions. But it should be said that beyond these thickly carpeted chapters lies the great outdoors of Rimbaud's work, and that this unusual individual is also, by his own admission, a face in the undescribed crowd: a 'yokel' stranded in a landscape of factories and office buildings, a 'pagan' damned by the god of an imported religion, a 'negro' without a history.

*

THE HAPLESS SERFS and witless iconoclasts of *Une Saison en Enfer* are more particularly identifiable, in Rimbaud's mental world, as the family of his mother, Vitalie Cuif. The Cuifs were probably descendants of the Remi tribe, which gave its name to Rheims. For centuries, they had tilled the stony fields of the Attigny district on the border of the Champagne and the Ardennes. They emerge, dimly, into recorded history towards the end of the eighteenth century. In 1789, the Revolution caused some Church property to fall into the hands of the poet's great-great-grandfather. Gradually, he pieced together a small estate, including several farms. Rimbaud's sardonic comment on the rise of the bourgeoisie -- a history of the nineteenth century in half a sentence – suggests that he did after all have some precise knowledge of his forebears: 'families like mine, which owe everything they possess to the Declaration of the Rights of Man'.[4]

Rimbaud's mother, Vitalie Cuif, was born in 1825 and grew up in the middle of distant horizons. On a small lump in the landscape, the stolid, grey farmhouse built by her grandfather seemed to block the muddy lane that ran through the hamlet of Roche.[5] It commanded a monotonous view of fields and tree-lined streams. The Germans used it as an observation post in the First World War. Even in peacetime, its barred windows and fortress-like courtyard seemed to brace themselves against attack; but the only incursion of history into Vitalie's early life was the construction of the Ardennes Canal which severed the ancient road from Rheims – the road that had once enabled Julius Caesar to pacify Rimbaud's barbarian ancestors.

Vitalie was only five years old when her mother died. Almost before she learned to read, she was a mother to her two brothers and a wife to her father. M. Cuif was forty-one but never remarried. Vitalie was a powerful support, and perhaps, over the years, a peculiar relationship developed. A psychoanalyst has detected traces of incest,[6] and it does seem a desperate convenience to attribute her phenomenal capacity for not showing affection to 'natural disposition'. But whatever damage was done, its causes have disappeared with the seasons that marked out her life. She spent her first twenty-seven years cleaning, mending, helping with harvests, feeding the animals and her family, and saving up for a marriage that became increasingly unlikely.

After the bleak winter of 1851–2, old M. Cuif decided that it was time to retire and to take his daughter to market. They moved to the prosperous town of Charleville, twenty-five miles to the north, on a bend of the river Meuse. It boasted some impressive monuments – an Old Mill that looked like part of a château, a declamatory town hall, and the vast, cobbled Place Ducale, a dumpy and distended version of the Place des Vosges in Paris. Everything exuded confidence and steady profit. Across the bridge lay Charleville's older sister, the medieval citadel of Mézières. From the other bank, the town was overlooked by a low, shrub-covered hill known as Mount Olympus.

M. Cuif and his daughter took a south-facing apartment above a bookshop (which still exists) at 12 Rue Napoléon (now Rue Thiers), the busy main street that leads to the Place Ducale. On market days and Sunday mornings, the neighbours saw a thin, stony-faced girl with the hands of a peasant and the bearing of a bourgeoise. A fortress of rectitude, besieged by a mysterious enemy.

One brother, Félix, had been in trouble with the courts for an unknown reason and ran away in 1841 to fight in Algeria. The younger brother, Charles, was a drinker, slowly returning to the sods on which the family had built its fortune. While Charles and Félix organized their lives around alcohol and army discipline, Vitalie took to religion – a pitiless, Jansenist form of Christianity that demanded hard work with no guarantee of reward. Religion filled the gaps in her routine and gave her an exact, unvarying measure of other people's worth. 'The people who should be sent packing', she told her daughter many years later, 'are those who do not believe in God, because they have neither heart nor soul and should be sent off to live with the cows and the pigs, who are their equals.'[7]

No picture of Vitalie Cuif has survived, except perhaps a sketch by her second son, Arthur. It shows a stiff, skeletal figure of harsh, black lines, bent in grief or racked by migraine, severely buttoned, its hair bound tightly in a net. Vitalie was never described by anyone of her own generation, and she tends to appear in a dark, antediluvian light. This may not be entirely misleading; but the fact, for instance, that she once had herself lowered into the family vault to ensure that the niche for her corpse had been properly constructed does not necessarily denote a grim, suspicious personality. It may simply indicate previous experience of Charleville stonemasons.[8]

The most durable image of Mme Rimbaud is the ambiguous Impressionist tableau in her son's poem, 'Mémoire' – a Grim Reaper with a parasol and walking-shoes, bisecting the horizon:

> Madame is standing up too straight in the meadow
> nearby, where the threads of toil snow down, a parasol
> in her fingers, trampling the umbels, too haughty for her;
> children reading in the flowery green
>
> their book of red morocco!*

*

* For the French texts of verse poems by Rimbaud quoted in this biography, see Appendix V.

[6]

ALHOUGH VITALIE'S social life was confined to church, shopping and occasional games of whist, she somehow managed to meet a French army officer in 1852. Vitalie was twenty-seven, the officer was thirty-eight. Perhaps she and her father had gone to hear the military band that played in the Place de la Musique (now Square de la Gare) – the 'niggardly lawns' of Rimbaud's poem 'A la musique', 'where everything is well-behaved, the flowers and the trees':

> The song of trombones makes the soldiers feel romantic –
> Very naive – smoking the better brand of cigarette,
> Fondling babies to seduce the maids . . .

On the other hand, brother Félix might have met Captain Rimbaud in Algeria and painted a flattering picture of his sister: a hard-working, blue-eyed girl who kept an immaculate house and was in line for a handsome inheritance.

The potential husband was Frédéric Rimbaud, the son of a farmer's daughter and a master tailor from Dôle in the Juras.[9] He had volunteered in 1832 at the age of eighteen, rose through the ranks and distinguished himself as a Chasseur in the barbaric con-quest of North Africa. Since 1847, he had spent more time black-ening paper than slaughtering Bedouin tribesmen. He was put in charge of the Arab Bureau in the small Algerian outpost of Sebdou. His predecessor had just been massacred by horsemen led by Lieu-tenant Rimbaud's chess partner, the chief of the local tribe. At Sebdou, Rimbaud collected taxes, dispensed justice and acted as a kind of military anthropologist: learning about native culture, the better to repress it.

In 1852, he was promoted to the rank of Captain in the 47th Regiment and left the Sahara desert for the cold, damp and undan-gerous Ardennes. The only known image of him is a second-hand description of a half-remembered portrait: fair hair, blue eyes, full mouth, average height. But we do know that he wore a long mous-tache and a pointed beard since these were compulsory in the Chasseurs.[10]

For Vitalie, allowing herself to be courted by Captain Rimbaud was almost a rash, romantic act. He had nothing to offer but his salary, some personal effects and a clean record. The marriage contract, drawn up on 3 January 1853, was the fruit of calm reflection. Vitalie's assets – land and money totalling 140,000 francs* – are described, not as a dowry, but as the bride's 'personal fortune'.[11] No man was going to nibble at her savings. The Captain obtained permission to marry and the wedding took place on 8 February 1853 in Charleville.

Captain Rimbaud consummated the marriage, left for his regiment in Lyon, and, for the next seven years, saw his wife about as often as a bull sees a field of cows. A son, Frédéric, was born exactly eight months and three weeks after the wedding. The following year, Captain Rimbaud's leave was commemorated in the same fashion. On 20 October 1854, at six in the morning, a second son was born above the bookshop in the Rue Napoléon.[12] At 5 o'clock that afternoon, his grandfather and the bookseller from downstairs went to the town hall and had him inscribed in the register as 'a child of the male sex': Jean-Nicolas-Arthur Rimbaud. He was baptized a month later.

There is a story, told by those who believed that Arthur Rimbaud belonged to a race of superior beings, that he was on the road within minutes of birth. The midwife returned with the swaddling clothes to find the baby heading for the exit, eyes wide open and, even more remarkable, chortling to itself.[13]

The first plausible sign of independent activity gives no hint of supernatural origins. Arthur was supplied with linen and a cradle and put out to nurse in a family of nail-makers at Gespunsart, seven miles away, near the Belgian border. Mme Rimbaud turned up one day for a surprise inspection and was horrified to see the workers' baby resplendent in the clothes provided for Arthur. Meanwhile, a smutty, naked thing was grovelling happily in an old salt chest. It was eventually proved to Mme Rimbaud that this was what her baby wanted.[14]

The fact that Mme Rimbaud remembered this incident is more significant than the incident itself: the sight of little Arthur spurning the benefits of his station in life. For Mme Rimbaud, everything was

* For approximate modern equivalents, multiply by 3 (for pounds sterling) or 4.8 (for US dollars).

an omen. The ignoble uncles cast a long shadow. Perhaps, like them, her child was not inherently bourgeois.

*

IT WAS BECAUSE of the uncles that most of Arthur's early childhood was spent on the farm at Roche. Charles Cuif had finally been forced into a semblance of activity. He took a wife in February 1852. Vitalie left the running of the farm to her brother, and he celebrated his independence by devoting himself to drink. Whenever a tradesman came to the door, Charles would invite him at gunpoint to join him in refreshments until both men were completely paralytic. Anyone who declined the invitation was given a taste of buckshot. His wife packed her trunk and returned to her village. One day in 1855, the sun-scorched veteran returned from Algeria and turfed his brother out. 'The African', as Uncle Félix was known in the village, ran the farm until December, when, for an unknown reason, he died.

Vitalie now took over, and held the farm in such a tight fist that it became extremely difficult to manage. Tenant farmers came and went, exasperated by pernickety conditions and the steely blue eye that had memorized every fence-post and furrow. The house was said to contain an iron chest full of gold coins.[15] 'It is good to give alms', Mme Rimbaud later told her daughter, 'but wisdom tells us that we should give away only part of our surplus.'[16]

From time to time, a wine-sodden Uncle Charles came staggering into the farmyard, looking for work. Vitalie would ask to see his papers as if he were a stranger, then send him on his way. Uncle Charles spent the next fifty-eight years wandering the hedgerows of the Ardennes, a part-time labourer and a full-time embarrassment. He died in a convent in 1924 'with the comforts of religion' and the greater consolation, a few moments before death, of a litre of red wine.[17]

It was at Roche – three miles from the nearest café – that Captain Rimbaud came to know his wife: the chill, rasping voice, the infectious gloom, the crushing conviction that people should be as hard on themselves as she was on herself. Captain Rimbaud had inadvertently joined a new regiment. He began to look forward to the end of the holidays and the comparatively benign regime of army life.

In September 1856, having survived trench-digging in the Crimea, a bout of cholera and a month-long march across Europe, Captain Rimbaud left his regiment on the road to Paris and braced himself for a visit to Roche. Nine months later, in June 1857, a third child was born: Vitalie. She died in July, thus earning herself a special place as her mother's favourite child. Invisible in the normal light of day, Mme Rimbaud's tenderness blossomed in the tomb. The most touching passages of her later correspondence concern the exhumation of her second daughter when the family vault was rearranged: an appalling description of the greasy scraps of corpse and hairy scalp which she lovingly gathered up in her arms.[18]

Two months later, Captain Rimbaud was back to supply a replacement, then shot off again to Grenoble. Vitalie II was born punctually the following June. She first enters the family history two years later, when the four-year-old Arthur supposedly offered her to the bookseller downstairs in exchange for some coloured prints in his window.[19] The nice idea of trading in a family member for some *objets d'art* suggests that Rimbaud himself was the source of the tale.

The register of births in Charleville continued to keep step with the leave roster of the 47th Regiment. After supervising the harvest of 1859, Mme Rimbaud travelled to Sélestat near Strasbourg (her first trip beyond the Ardennes) and returned, pregnant, to the Rue Napoléon, where the landlord asked her to pack her bags and leave.

The dubious assertion that has become embedded in the Rimbaud legend is that the landlord was alarmed by the relentless proliferation of Rimbauds: it was a simple matter of space. But why could he not have waited until the lease expired two months later at the end of the year? Surely the death of Mme Rimbaud's father in 1858 had freed up a room or two? This sudden eviction of the pregnant mother probably had more to do with her notorious ability to antagonize neighbours.

The family camped until Christmas at the Hôtel du Lion d'Argent in the centre of Charleville. The search for new lodgings produced nothing better than an apartment at the north end of the Rue Bourbon – a dingy street of low houses with yards that smelled of rotting cabbages and cesspits, teeming with undesirables.[20] Mme Rimbaud set up her bourgeois outpost in the proletarian mire and gave birth to another daughter, Isabelle, on 1 June 1860.

Rimbaud's earliest memory dates from this difficult period, his sixth year. Like all earliest memories, it has a magnetic, three-dimensional quality – a single episode into which other, less innocuous scenes have insinuated themselves. Here is the story as Rimbaud told it to his schoolfriend, Ernest Delahaye:

> He remembered a conjugal altercation involving a silver bowl that stood on the sideboard. The use to which the bowl was put made an indelible impression on him. His father snatched it up in a rage and flung it on to the floor, where it bounced and made a musical sound. Then he replaced it on the sideboard. His mother, in the same lofty manner, took the resonant object, made it execute the same dance, then picked it up immediately and set it back carefully in its proper place. This was how they emphasized their arguments and asserted their independence. Rimbaud remembered the incident because it caused him great amusement and perhaps made him a little envious: how he would have loved to send the beautiful silver bowl spinning himself![21]

This splendid example of screen memory seems to have been Rimbaud's only clear recollection of his father. The image is as rich and concise as a poem or a dream: his parents engaged in a curious, ritualistic activity with a valuable, hollow object that bounces up and down and arouses feelings of envy in the son. Somewhere in this scene lies the irreversible catastrophe of childhood. From then on, the silver bowl was to remain firmly in its place.

Several reasons have been found for the rift between Rimbaud's parents, most of them implausible and all of them unprovable. References to Captain Rimbaud's drunkenness, idleness and atheism are based on nothing more substantial than a poor opinion of French army officers, as Colonel Godchot pointed out in 1936. And it seems unfair to attribute to Rimbaud Sr the mental illness later diagnosed in his son as 'dromomania' or 'ambulatory paranoia'[22] (a chronic case of the fidgets) simply because he belonged to a regiment.

It is more likely that the Captain's virtues were to blame. In his spare time, he was an avid compiler and annotator. He wrote enormous commentaries on army affairs (now lost), including a dissertation on military speeches, ancient and modern. His African reports show a real talent for describing the most unusual and horrific events in dry, analytical prose. The ravages of locusts, the duplicity of Arab diplomats, the attacks of tar-coated camels set on fire by suicidal tribesmen, are all treated with the same unruffled pen. He also produced a compendium of Arab jokes and a parallel-text translation of the Koran. Had these works been published, they might have earned him a serious reputation as an orientalist. This apparently fruitless scribbling must have eaten into the time he could have spent on the farm. In Mme Rimbaud's mind, anything that verged on the literary was flimflam and hypocrisy. 'I am not writing to wish you a Good New Year', she told her daughter Isabelle in 1906. 'It's futile. Actions are everything.'[23] Only the Captain's epic *Correspondance militaire* found favour: it was written on large sheets of paper which proved to be just the thing for wrapping up vegetables.[24]

The marriage was doomed from the beginning: a wife who felt violently uncomfortable whenever her views were questioned, and a husband whose favourite spare-time activity was textual analysis. A few visits in seven years, interspersed with five pregnancies and the Crimean War, were unlikely to iron out the differences.

One day in September 1860, Captain Rimbaud left to join his regiment in Cambrai. He never returned. Arthur was about to celebrate his sixth birthday. His mother was thirty-five. She was unhappier than she had ever been, marooned in a seedy neighbourhood with four demanding children and an excruciating personality: a combination of intransigence and acute awareness of what other people were thinking. To lose a husband while he was still alive was an unmentionable humiliation. She decided that from now on she would be known as 'Widow Rimbaud'.

Rimbaud often evokes this abandonment in his poetry. Like any personal disaster, it was not the event of a single day but the atmosphere of a whole life. The surprise is that the loss is invariably depicted through the mother's eyes and presented as something like the ache of sexual deprivation:

> The regret of thick, young arms [. . .]
> The gold of April moons in the heart of the sacred bed!

> ('Mémoire')

And yet she wants, she wants, her soul in distress,
Her head in the pillow, dented by stifled cries,
To prolong the final flashes of affection,
And drools . . . – Darkness fills the houses and the yards.

('Les Premières communions')

All that remained of the Captain – apart from his children – was a pile of manuscripts and a Bible-sized book full of annotations: an 878-page *Grammaire Nationale*, the sort of gargantuan summary of rules that seems to impress on its reader the obvious fact that no single human being can ever master anything so complex and devious as a language. The volume has survived. On the title-page, Captain Rimbaud has written, 'Grammar is the basis and foundation of all human knowledge' – a tantalizing axiom which his son must often have pondered. At an unknown date, Arthur inserted a slip of paper into this paternal monument. It bore the word ABRACADABRA and an explanatory note, 'To keep away fever'. Later, he came up with a more practical motto and inscribed it carefully above his father's phrase:

Have whichever thoughts you like,
But think carefully before you speak.[25]

Mme Rimbaud settled into her misery like an old woman taking to her bed. It was now that her character solidified into the intimidating grey tower known to literary history as the mother of Arthur Rimbaud. According to one of his contemporaries, she had 'a rather refrigerative appearance'.[26] She was never known to laugh or even smile. Descriptions written decades later still convey a sense of childish fear. Early this century, grizzled peasants at Roche, intercepted on their way to the beetroot field, remembered being chased from the doorstep by a sour-faced woman who threatened them with 'the galleys'. The Rimbaud children were said to have a slightly cretinous appearance, like beaten animals. Sympathy was expressed for the departed Captain.[27]

For Frédéric and Arthur, the final disappearance of their father meant more frequent smacks on the head. Any child would search itself for guilt, and Mme Rimbaud did nothing to dispel their doubts.

A conviction formed like a scar. She had 'sacrificed' her certain happiness with the Captain for the sake of her children, and the children would have to work very hard indeed to pay off the debt.[28]

Meanwhile, a vast Empty Quarter had opened up in Arthur's mind – the world into which his father had disappeared, taking with him the answers to questions as yet unformulated.

In their anxious search for origins, Romantic works like Rimbaud's are detective novels written by the unwitting perpetrator of the crime. Rimbaud was to become an unusually intrepid investigator, with an astonishing memory for the fantasies, or the facts, that might one day form a picture of the truth:

> Sometimes I thought of my father:
> In the evening, the card-game, the conversation turning naughty,
> The neighbour, and me, told to go away, the things I saw . . .
> (For fathers are disturbing!) and the things I thought of! . . .
> His knee, that sometimes fondled; his trousers,
> And that gap my finger itched to open . . .[29]

2

Filth

'the miserable incidents of my childhood'

('Ouvriers', *Illuminations*)

AFTER THE CAPTAIN'S desertion, Mme Rimbaud almost managed to be two parents at once. Frédéric and Arthur were
subjected to the usual array of punishments, dispensed with unusual
regularity: temporary starvation, isolation and sudden physical pain.[1]
They were often smacked, in public, by the hand that had reaped
harvests and driven cattle to the milking-sheds. When Rimbaud
depicted the 'seven-year-old poet' with a 'brow full of eminences', he
may have been referring, not only to phrenological signs of genius or
to pimples, but also to the marks of his mother's love.

On Sundays, according to the same poem, he was forced to 'sit,
pomaded, on a mahogany stool', reading 'a Bible edged in cabbage
green'. The Communion picture shows Arthur's hair shining with
the grease that signified cleanliness. Comparing the photograph with
later pictures of his electric shock of hair gives some idea of the
adhesive force of this pomade – a permanent firm hand pressing on
the scalp.

As long as they stayed in the working-class Rue Bourbon, Mme
Rimbaud felt that her children were in danger of contamination. Like
a family photo album assembled by a blackmailer, 'Les Poètes de sept
ans' records some of the perils of living with the plebs:

> His only playmates were those
> Puny, bare-browed kids whose eyes had run
> On to their cheeks, who hid their thin, yellow fingers,
> Black with smut, in antiquated clothes that stank of shit,
> And who talked with the sweetness of idiots!
> And if his mother panicked when she caught him
> Being nice to filth, his pity fed on her amazement –
> As it should . . . She had the blue eyes of the liar!

The child's defiance and the detection of hypocrisy in the mother's blue eyes – the same colour as his own – certainly date from the period in which the poem was written (Arthur's sixteenth year); but the images belong to the Rue Bourbon. This list of 'favourite things' is also a list of Mme Rimbaud's reasons for wanting to move: the pungent urchins, the 'black men, returning in smocks to the suburb', and the strapping eight-year-old girl next door who used to pounce and sit on him until he sank his teeth into her buttocks ('for she was never wearing drawers').

> Then, bruised by her fists and her heels,
> He'd take the smell of her skin back into his room.

At a time when pestilential odours were thought to be carriers of depravity as well as disease, and when respectability entailed a constant war on smut, a foul stench could have the fragrance of forbidden fruit. These memories of the 'seven-year-old poet' may not be genuine snapshots of the past, but they do commemorate the discovery of the world within and the uncontrollable rabble of sensual impressions. Somewhere in the mind was a private room with a lock on the door – a place of sudden relaxations:

> [. . .] In summer
> Especially, dull and subdued, he persistently
> Locked himself up in the cool of the latrines.
> And there at peace, he thought, opening his nostrils wide.

*

IN OCTOBER 1861, just over a year after the final disappearance of Captain Rimbaud, Arthur's universe suddenly expanded. He and his brother were sent as day-boys to a nearby school.

The Institut Rossat[2] looked like any other building in the street: a dark green door in the Rue de l'Arquebuse. Inside, a dim vestibule gave no hint that this was about to become one of the most up-to-date schools in the country, with laboratories and workshops. It would even have its own steam forge. Religious education was to be replaced by horticulture and mechanical engineering.

After a glimpse of stuffed birds and a skeleton on the right, the hallway opened on to a tight, rectangular courtyard. Its walls were painted a colour which a former pupil identified as 'corpse yellow'. On the far side, three steps led down to the art room. The wall on that side appeared to have been attacked by a virulent fungus: it was traditional for pupils to smash their inkwells against it on prize days. In a second quadrangle, which was too small for football, 300 boys played marbles under the windows of tenements that would have been called slums had they been for domestic use. When it rained, they huddled together under an open wash-house like passengers waiting for a train. The classrooms were damp and stale, crowded with massive wooden desks, rutted by years of doodling. If the environment had reflected its pedagogical aims, the Institut Rossat would have been preparing its pupils for a life in prison. It was Arthur's first taste of freedom, a haven of filth that seemed to collude in its own decay:

> In the gloom of musty-papered corridors he passed,
> Sticking out his tongue, both fists clenched
> Around his groin, watching spots under his eyelids.

Arthur's rebellion – suggestively summarized in these lines from 'Les Poètes de sept ans' as masturbation, insubordination and hallucination – took the form of academic excellence. In his three and a half years at the Institut Rossat, he won thirteen prizes and eleven merits. Shortly before his tenth birthday, he was tottering home with a pile of books presented to him for coming top in Latin grammar and translation, French grammar and spelling, History and Geography, Classical recitation and reading. He also won a merit in Arithmetic. These were not rewards for original thought. They showed simply that Rimbaud minor was better than anyone else in his year at ingesting and regurgitating the facts and precepts bequeathed by the past. Apart from his prizes, all we know about him in 1861–4 is that he was short, but able to defend himself in a fight, and remarkable for his pale blue eyes, said to be quite beautiful but strangely difficult to look at. They were so often likened to the sky that this must have been a genuine impression rather than a literary cliché.

Blue eyes excepted, none of this appears to match the infant rebel of 'Les Poètes de sept ans'. But the stern little face in a photograph of messily arranged Rossat boys in the autumn of 1864 does seem to have slipped out from between the lines of Rimbaud's poem:

> All day long, obedience oozed from every pore – a highly
> Intelligent boy; and yet, dark twitches flashed across his face
> And seemed to prove the pungent hypocrite within.

In the photograph, Arthur sits to the left of brother Frédéric, looking like a recently punished child, fists hidden by his *képi*, glowering at the lens; a living reproach, or a living self-reproach. This is the picture of a child who could find nothing in himself to match what his mother called love. The sense of his own hypocrisy was to stay with him like a tell-tale smell, just as the inquisitorial voice of Mme Rimbaud helped to give his later poems their characteristic, argumentative tone:

> [. . .] that awkward boy,
> Such a stupid little beast,
> Must never for a moment cease
> To scheme and to deceive
>
> Like a Rócky Mountain cat,*
> And to stink up every sphere!³

*

IN THE EARLY 1860s, the inhabitants of Charleville often saw a strange procession passing through the town.⁴ In front, two little girls held each other by the hand; then came two slightly older boys, also holding hands. They clumped along in big shoes, wearing old-fashioned clothes, very clean, tidy and silent, trying to ignore the

---

* 'Un chat des Monts-Rocheux': a non-existent species. 'Rocheux' is an allusion to the hamlet of Roche.

sarcastic remarks of passers-by. They were followed, at a distance that never varied, by 'Widow Rimbaud', heading for church or bent on the purchase of some vegetables.

Home was now 13 Cour d'Orléans, a brighter, more respectable area. But there was to be no backsliding. Brute discipline would turn them into useful citizens, even if it meant cutting them off from the rest of society. After school each day, Frédéric and Arthur were met by their mother and marched home where their sisters had the job of supervising their homework.[5] Any unauthorized activity was reported to Mother, who would then set extra homework. Before supper, the boys recited their Latin prose. Mme Rimbaud followed in the book, understanding just enough to know when they strayed from the text. A mistake meant bed without supper.

In April 1865, despite Arthur's satisfactory progress, Mme Rimbaud suddenly decided to transfer her sons to the municipal Collège de Charleville. She might have been concerned at the lack of religious instruction or, more likely, developed a suspicion that Arthur was not being stretched. There were also some worrying reports about the Institut Rossat. M. Rossat had been inviting liberal thinkers to give talks in Charleville and was even offering 'public lessons' to workers. He was suspected of promoting 'intellectual emancipation'. The effect of these 'advanced ideas' was soon apparent: pupils from the Institut were spotted drinking beer in cafés and smoking cigars on the public promenade.[6]

The Collège de Charleville was environmentally similar to the Institut Rossat but less cramped since it was less popular. It stood next to the tanneries by the river Meuse, on the edge of the Place du Saint-Sépulcre. Mothers had been known to stalk out of the building, vowing never to entrust their child to such a cesspit. 'Awful smells', according to a ministerial report, 'originating in the latrines, permeate the classrooms'. But improvements had been promised: general refurbishment, a new headmaster, and two clerics on the teaching staff.[7]

Rimbaud minor quickly made his mark at the Collège de Charleville. While Frédéric plodded along at the bottom of the class, Arthur, who was eleven months younger, was catapulted into the year above by an astonishing piece of homework which his fellow pupils remembered for years to come.

He had condensed 'ancient history' into a single piece of prose so beautifully written that it was shown to the whole school as a model to be imitated and admired. Arthur went straight from *septième* to *cinquième* and into the hands of M. Pérette – the sort of teacher who thrives on his pupils' ignorance.

Headmaster Desdouest, an impressive, eloquent man of extraordinary hats and moon-like face, was already dreaming of future glories. Arthur Rimbaud would put the Collège de Charleville on the map. M. Pérette, however, was determined to be unimpressed. By producing relentlessly impeccable work, Arthur Rimbaud was impeding the normal ebb and flow of error and improvement. The boy was a statistical obscenity; in addition to which, he had a shifty-looking smile. 'Call him intelligent as much as you like', M. Pérette told the headmaster, 'he'll come to a sticky end'.[8]

The tetchy M. Pérette has often been praised for his foresight, but the same thing was said to so many pupils that if teacher expectations were as influential as they are thought to be, Rimbaud's entire generation would have come to a sticky end. Rimbaud actually heard his inglorious demise predicted far less frequently than his fellow pupils. The only misdemeanour to report from his first years at the Collège de Charleville is not the act of a degenerate. A *surveillant* called Poncelet confiscated 'a tiny notebook' containing Arthur's draft of an adventure story 'set among the savage tribes of Oceania'.[9] This must have been one of the stories which his sister Isabelle remembered, inspired by *Robinson Crusoe*, Fenimore Cooper, Jules Verne and, according to one of his classmates, the popular translation of Speke and Grant's *Discovery of the Source of the Nile*:

> He used to entertain us throughout the long evenings by reading us his fantastic voyages to strange, unknown lands [. . .] Naturally, these were merely the amusements of a child. As soon as he had written them and read them out, they would be torn up and lost . . .

This euphemistic use of the passive suggests that Mme Rimbaud would have approved of the *surveillant*: 'Her principles', says Isabelle, 'made it impossible for her to encourage Arthur's literary efforts.'[10]

The skimpy file of school records and anecdotes would leave a very hazy picture of Rimbaud at the end of his childhood were it not for the survival of what looks at first like an ordinary exercise-book. On closer inspection, this small bundle of paper has the magical effect of revealing Arthur Rimbaud for the first time in the act of creation.

The document consists of a few ink-spotted sheets, held together by a pin. It is known rather portentously as the 'Cahier des dix ans', though it almost certainly dates from Rimbaud's eleventh year: allusions to Alexander, Darius and 'their cronies' and to 'that filthy language', Greek, indicate the syllabus of the Collège de Charleville.[11] Most of the sheaf is taken up with lines and homework – a fluent translation of some Cicero, the story of Adam and Eve in Latin, a smattering of venerable facts ('The Nile, with its floods, is the benefactor of Egypt') and some fragments of arithmetic ('If 20 litres cost 3,250, how much do 7 decilitres cost?'). Areas of scrawl and a tendency to write without punctuation or accents suggest a child with little time to waste. He signs himself 'Rimbaud Arthur de Charleville', which is the form his name would have taken in the prize lists of regional academic competitions. But any suspicion that these are the jottings of a teacher's pet is dispelled by a 750-word story, written, presumably, while he was pretending to do his homework.

The tale sets off along the broad path of cliché with a neo-classical evocation of twilight. The sun sets, the ferns bend their verdant brows before the freshening breeze, and the narrator drifts off beside a stream:

> I dreamed that I was born in Rheims in the year 1503. [. . .] My parents were not very rich but they were very respectable. Their only property was a little house which had always belonged to them and which was in their possession twenty years before I was born, plus a few thousand francs and in addition to that the small sums which came from my mother's savings.

This was obviously a child who had been impressed with the importance of domestic economics.

Two hundred words into the story, the narrator is already on his third genre – classical description, historical novel, and now realistic family drama:

My father was an officer in the King's armies.* He was a tall, thin man with black hair, and beard, eyes and skin [*sic*] of the same colour. Though he was nearly 48 or 50 you would certainly have thought him 60 or 58. He was fiery and hot-headed, often in a temper and unwilling to suffer anything he did not like. My mother was quite different: a calm and gentle woman, easily alarmed, she nonetheless kept her house in perfect order. She was so calm that my father used to tease her like a young girl.† I was the favourite. My brothers were not as brave as I even though they were bigger. I was not very fond of studying – learning to read, write and count. But decorating a house, tending a garden or going shopping – that was fine, I liked doing that.

Most autobiographies are testaments to the power of self-deception, but the ruses of an eleven-year-old are revealingly inept. Arthur's slightly shop-soiled fantasy of home is quite apparent. Mme Rimbaud's obduracy is turned into a virtue, while the angry black father comes in for some heartfelt criticism: his presence in the tale coincides, significantly, with the clumsiest syntax. A passage of broken phrases mentions the toys and sweets the father used to promise his son if he finished his sums. ('But I never could.') Then comes a torrent of consciousness which is as eloquent in its way as a picture of the schoolboy squirming at his desk, prematurely worried about the future:

> Despite that, my father sent me to school as soon as I was ten. What's the point, I said to myself, of learning Greek and Latin? I don't know. There's no call for it. What do I care if I pass? What's the point of passing examinations? There's no point, is there? Yes there is. People say you can't get a job unless you've passed. But I don't want a job. I'm going to be a *rentier* [a man of private means]. Even if you do want a job, why learn Latin? No one speaks that language. Sometimes I see some Latin in the newspapers but I'm not going to be a journalist, thank God.
> [. . .] And are we quite certain that the Latins ever existed? Perhaps

* Here, a footnote anachronistically places the father in the Cent-Gardes, which was the personal guard of Napoleon III.

† This is unclear in the original: the construction appears to compare the father to a young girl.

it's a made-up language, and even if they did exist, why can't they leave me to be a *rentier* and keep their language to themselves? [. . .]

Ah *saperlipotte de saperlipopette*! *Sapristi*!* I'm going to be a *rentier*. It's not much fun sitting on your backside all day long on a bench. *Saperlipopettouille*!

To get a job as a bootblack you have to take an exam because the jobs people give you are either as a bootblack, a swineherd or a ploughman. Thank God, I don't want to do that. *Saperlipouille*!

And on top of that you're paid with a slap in the face. People call you a beast, which isn't true, little nipper, etc. Ah! *saperpouillotte*!

To be continued soon.

By the end of the episode, sixteenth-century Rheims looks much like nineteenth-century Charleville. Rimbaud significantly sympathizes with the junior urban proletariat, the butt of adults' insults and aggression. To an eleven-year-old schoolboy with a furiously disinfecting mother, scraping the mud off adults' boots must have seemed the epitome of all professions. Perhaps Mme Rimbaud had told Frédéric – who was already showing signs of downward aspiration – that even swineherds had to pass examinations. Arthur, by contrast, has identified the key to freedom in the modern world: he wants to be a capitalist and a saver like his mother, not a soldier like his father. Neither is he going to devote himself to school work, which is seen here as an extension of the father's tyranny. Yet the story itself shows that intellectual pursuits already have an urgent appeal.

The other intimate section of the notebook is a little gallery of seven rough sketches purporting to illustrate the 'Pleasures of Youth'.[12] They show the Rimbaud family going about its daily self-destructive business. Two boys on a sinking boat cry for help. The 'Queen of the Northland' (one of Arthur's sisters) is about to have a sledging accident. A chair supporting a wobbly girl hangs from a door-knob. ''Old on wiv yer 'and!' her brother urges her in a northern accent. 'Agriculture' shows the children flapping their arms in amazement at a huge, fleshy thing protruding from a flower-pot. Religion is represented by two kneeling sisters handing a doll to their brother, who is dressed as a priest. Caption: 'Got to get it baptized'.

* Local colour: roughly equivalent to 'Gadzooks!'

In 'The Siege', a mother, a father and two sons stand at a window, hurling an assortment of missiles at a crowd in the street below. A man in a top-hat is saying, 'A complaint will have to be made.' Finally, as if to explain this constant state of imminent catastrophe: a woman sits weeping while a man – or a boy – strides away like someone escaping from the scene of a crime. Is this Captain Rimbaud leaving home, or Arthur following his example?

'The Siege' can be interpreted as an allegory of the Rimbauds' relationship with Charleville society. For mysterious reasons, perhaps not unconnected with men in top-hats making complaints, Mme Rimbaud was about to move again, to 20 Rue Forest. But the sinking boat was drawn from real life: a tanner's skiff that was moored to the riverbank opposite Mount Olympus. Ernest Delahaye, the son of a widow who ran a grocery store in Mézières, had seen Arthur and his brother playing quietly in the boat on their way to school. It was their only unsupervised moment. They pushed off with their feet until the chain jerked taut, felt the current take hold, then stared at the river flowing past, before pulling the boat back in and running off to school.

According to Delahaye, the Rimbaud brothers looked like little businessmen: bowler hats and umbrellas (though the school was less than 700 yards away), white collars, black jackets and slate-blue trousers cut by Mme Rimbaud from such a gigantic bolt of cloth that Arthur's legs were still slate-blue when he left for Paris six years later. Delahaye had met the elder Rimbaud in German class and in the corridor outside, where Frédéric was often sent to stand, according to pedagogical logic, for failing to keep up with the others. He first knew Arthur as the stick that was used to beat Frédéric: teachers asked why he couldn't be as clever and as studious as his brother. 'Who's this Arthur?' asked Delahaye. 'Arthur?' replied Frédéric. 'He's brilliant!'[13]

It was hard to make the acquaintance of the young genius. Even after Mme Rimbaud stopped picking him up from school, Arthur hurried straight home every day with Frédéric. Attempts to bully him had faltered at a faintly mocking smile and an air of impenetrable reserve. He was curiously indifferent to marbles, stamps and recreational violence. It was said that Arthur Rimbaud had already devoured hundreds of books. Verlaine's claim that Rimbaud had read all of

French poetry by the age of fourteen is slightly over-enthusiastic,[14] but the 'Cahier des dix ans' does show an unusual familiarity with several forms of fiction. He was known as a boy who took his own thoughts very seriously. One day, as they trooped out of chapel, some of the older pupils gathered round the font and started splashing each other with holy water. Rimbaud flew at them in a rage, punching and biting until the teachers intervened. This earned him the name *'sale petit cagot'*[15] ('sanctimonious little so-and-so'), but it seems to have enhanced his reputation as a committed intellectual.

Even his teachers found his silence unnerving. They peered into the all-absorbing tunnel to see whether anything was about to come out. A teacher called Lhéritier was asked to give Rimbaud extra tuition to prepare him for the regional examinations. M. Lhéritier prided himself on his matey relations with the boys, but his usual trick of defacing a porcelain figure that stood on his desk failed to break the ice, as did the more dangerous device of claiming to have written a poem in honour of Orsini, the man who had recently tried to blow up Napoleon III on the steps of the Opera. Rimbaud smiled politely and looked embarrassed.[16] Apparently, the adult world had no surprises for him. He was used to living with a human time-bomb that reprimed itself after every explosion.

When Delahaye finally managed to engage Rimbaud in conversation, some time in 1866, he proved to be worthy of his reputation. He already had an intellectual history. The 'sanctimonious' phase must have lasted a few weeks at most. Since then, he had discovered Romantic literature and was something of an expert on the plays and poems of Victor Hugo. But even Hugo was old hat. Delahaye had been amazed to learn that one of his classmates 'disapproved' of the *coup d'état* of 1851 which brought Napoleon III to power. Far from being shocked, Rimbaud already had a firm opinion of his own: 'Napoleon III should be sent to the galleys!'[17]

Sending people to the galleys was one of Mme Rimbaud's favourite notions. She had already mentally depopulated a large part of Charleville; but she had certainly never thought of applying the expression to the French Emperor. Delahaye felt a surge of excitement: 'God! What would happen next! . . .' Charleville suddenly seemed a very small place.

3

'Perfect Little Monster'

'Did I not *once* have a nice, heroic, legendary youth to record on sheets of gold?'

('Matin', *Une Saison en Enfer*)

A NEW TEACHER'S first impression of Arthur Rimbaud:

Small and timid [. . .], a little stilted and ingratiating. His fingernails were clean, his exercise books spotless, his homework amazingly correct, his marks scholastically impeccable. In short, he was one of those exemplary, perfect little monsters, a prime specimen of the *bête à concours*.* This was the face he always wore in the classroom. No doubt it was the involuntary effect of habit rather than hypocrisy.[1]

In 1870, Rimbaud would describe a classroom in terms which suggest that his stand-offishness was not just the result of being two years younger than his classmates. In his mother's mind, little boys were dirty animals, not much better than the livestock at Roche and considerably less useful. Her son took a similar view:

The pupils were like fat sheep sweating in their filthy coats, slumbering in the stench-laden asthmosphere† of the prep room, under the gaslight, in the stale warmth of the stove![2]

---

* 'Prize animal', reared to pass examinations.

† Sometimes corrected to 'atmosphère', but surely a deliberate mistake.

One of these ruminants – a boy named Jolly – wrote to his brother on 26 May 1868 with a piece of news which seems to confirm the teacher's assessment. The 'perfect little monster' had struck out on the road to glory:

> You probably know the Raimbaults [*sic*]. One of them (the one who is now in *troisième*) has just sent a letter consisting of 60 lines of Latin verse to the little Imperial Prince on the occasion of his First Communion. He kept it all a great secret and didn't even show his poem to the teacher. The result was that he made some grammatical errors and some of the lines were faulty. The Prince's tutor has just replied, saying that the little his Majesty was touched by the letter and that since he too was a schoolboy, he willingly forgave him his faulty lines. That taught our Rimbaud a little lesson for trying to show off his skill. The headmaster did not congratulate him.[3]

The snide comment at the end of Master Jolly's letter reflects the common view of Arthur Rimbaud: admiration for his intellectual prowess and a mute antipathy to his cold eyes and the thin smile that seemed to tax his face muscles.

When it was revealed in 1930 that Rimbaud, the avant-garde hero, had sent a Communion ode to the son of Napoleon III, some conservative critics declared that Rimbaud had been a natural Catholic and imperialist and had simply sulked himself anarchic. The notion that the grammatical strictures of a royal tutor turned him into a revolutionary says more about academic vanity than it does about Rimbaud's intellectual development. The ode itself has never turned up in the Imperial archives. It was probably lost when the Tuileries Palace was burnt to the ground in 1871, but the fact that the tutor ungraciously picked holes in the ode, combined with the fact that Rimbaud was spectacularly good at Latin, suggests that his tribute was not entirely devoid of insulting ambiguities. This was not the only time that Rimbaud ridiculed an institution and sought its approval at the same time.

Rimbaud's thoughts begin to make themselves heard more clearly towards the end of 1868. Amazed by his Latin homework, the form master sent a particularly fine example to the *Moniteur de l'Enseignement Supérieur*. This was a journal which allowed the

regional education authority to pat itself on the back by publishing
the most exquisite pieces of homework produced under its jurisdiction. The lines by which 'Rimbaud Arthur, day-boy at the Collège
de Charleville' brought honour on his school were supposed to be a
development, in Latin hexameters, of Horace's ode, 'Descende
caelo . . .'.

In Rimbaud's hands, the ode was a page of raw material waiting to
be remodelled. His opening remarks on despotic teachers 'crucifying'
their pupils bear no relation to the original text; nor does the
assertion that Apollo had etched on the author's brow with sacred
flame 'TU VATES ERIS': 'Thou shalt be a poet (or a seer)'.[4] Some
unusual items of vocabulary show that Rimbaud had managed to
obtain a copy of Catullus, who was emphatically not on the syllabus.[5]
He used it to give a powerfully erotic depiction of the mind-
enhancing warmth of Mother Nature, the divine antidote to academic
enslavement.

This perfect, irreproachable insolence – pasting his own face on to
a portrait of Horace – shows something more complex than furtive
rebellion. Rimbaud was practising a kind of super-obedience, developing his anti-academic theme in a manner that was calculated to win
academic acclaim. It never occurred to his teachers that the pupil
who succeeds by identifying the aims and methods of the education
system is also the pupil most likely to reject the system altogether.

*

THE ODE IN the *Moniteur de l'Enseignement Supérieur* was the first in
a string of victories which make Rimbaud's school career, as far as it
went, one of the most glittering in French literature. In 1869, he won
first prize in the regional examination with a Latin poem on Jugurtha.
The enemy of Rome was compared to Abd-el-Kader, the hero of
Algerian nationalism and one-time scourge of the French Army (and
of Captain Rimbaud). It is tempting to assume that Rimbaud was
being subversive; but if his allusion to Algeria's 'happiness under
French domination' was a cynical joke, as some have claimed, no such
thought would have occurred to the examiners. In Rimbaud's poem,
Abd-el-Kader is urged to 'yield to the new God', Napoleon III:
'Napoleo! proh Napoleo! [. . .] "Cede novo, tu, nate, Deo!"' In any

case, by the time Rimbaud wrote his poem, Abd-el-Kader was an ally of France. Rimbaud's aim was not to score a political point and win the admiration of future readers. His aim was to win the competition.

While brother Frédéric saw school as an unpleasant illness from which he would inevitably recover in his late teens, Arthur treated it as a profession. In order to gain access to forbidden authors like Catullus, he started his own business: for a small commission, he offered to buy books for the boarders. He would go to the bookshop in the house where he was born, take whichever book he wanted on credit, read it in bed without cutting the pages, then return it the next day and exchange it for the book he was supposed to have bought in the first place. Result: money in his pocket and knowledge of illicit literature.[6]

The legend of the poet who scorned the regular pay-cheque for the sake of Art is an insult to Rimbaud's ingenuity. In the prison economy of school, he was the alternative supplier. A black market in homework sprang up and appeared for a time to raise the general academic standard. Rich pupils who were also lazy or incompetent hired Arthur Rimbaud to write their Latin homework for them.[7] In Mathematics class, he quietly produced several slabs of Latin verse on the same subject. Each piece of homework had its own distinctive style, tailored to the customer. When they read out their ghost-written homework in class, dim-witted pupils sounded like ridiculously brilliant parodies of themselves.

None of these counterfeit pieces has survived – with the possible exception of a Latin poem in the *Moniteur de l'Enseignement Supérieur* by an otherwise unremarkable pupil in Rimbaud's class called Alfred Mabille. But a similar sort of exercise can be detected in Rimbaud's early poems: his skilful imitations of contemporary poets could easily be read as a one-man anthology of mid-nineteenth-century French poetry.

This parasitic service industry feeding on the education system is a splendid achievement for a child of fifteen. Rimbaud had a keen eye for the needs of the market and a firm grasp of self-advertisement. The memoirs of his classmates show that he already had that combination of theatricality and indifference which tends to create a legend. Every month brought a new Rimbaud story. Sometimes, he wrote the same piece of homework in three languages: French, Latin and Greek, all in verse. In Mathematics, he handed in poems instead of equations. Following the example of his father's annotated *Grammaire Nationale*, he presented his form master with a detailed list of stylistic errors in Boileau's *L'Art poétique* (1674)[8] – generally held to be the last word on proper poetic practice. In this, he was three years ahead of the leading virtuoso poet of the day, Théodore de Banville, whose *Petit traité de poésie française* (1872) would codify the precepts of the *l'art pour l'art* school and recast Boileau as a ham-fisted ignoramus.

For Rimbaud, the Collège de Charleville was a stage. In the six-hour regional *concours* of 1869, which he won, he appeared to sleep at his desk from 6 to 9 a.m., writing nothing. A nervous inquiry from the headmaster produced the information that Rimbaud had missed breakfast. The concierge was sent for a basket of food. Rimbaud ate slowly, then bent over his desk and handed in his poem on the stroke of midday, faultless and complete. The headmaster was still marvelling at this feat forty years later.[9]

Strangely, Rimbaud appears to have said nothing about his most impressive achievement. One of his poems had appeared in a 'real' journal: the *Revue pour tous*, guaranteed to be safe on any coffee-table. 'Les Étrennes des orphelins' ('The Orphans' New Year's Gift') was submitted in time for the appropriate issue (2 January 1870). It was a thoroughly competent, tear-jerking tale in French alexandrines. Though it appears in most editions as Rimbaud's first poem, it was obviously the masterpiece of his early manner, the only survivor of several trial runs.[10]

> Your heart has understood: these children have no mother.
> No mother in the home! – and the father's far away! . . .
> [. . .] The little ones are all alone in the frozen house -
> Four-year-old orphans. In their mind, by degrees,
> A cheerful memory awakes . . .

The two orphans, abandoned at Christmastime, are visited in their sleep by an angel. On waking, they are overjoyed to discover their mother's funeral wreath. (Evidently, they mistake the wreath for a Christmas present, though this is far from clear on a first and even on a second reading.)

Apart from the hallucinatory touch of a womb-like sideboard with its keyhole in which 'one seemed to hear a distant sound', Rimbaud's first known French poem is a kit assembly of lines from his favourite poets: the domestic, sentimental Hugo, the picturesque, anthologizable Baudelaire, and some popular poets – now utterly forgotten – who worked themselves up into a studiously emotional state over grandmothers, spinning-wheels, firesides and sickly children. This Victorian taste for chocolate-box winsomeness was to stay with Rimbaud for a surprisingly long time. He might even have thought he was achieving a similar effect in later poems which seem too sarcastic or intellectual for pathos.

At the age of fifteen, Rimbaud had more admirers than friends, but his skill as a writer made him a valued member of the institution, the apple of several paternal eyes which were, on the whole, willing to go blind if the prize pupil neglected Mathematics, read unsuitable books, grew his hair or, on one occasion, threw his dictionary at a classmate. Frédéric, who had been blamed for a drawing of the history master taking a bath 'without a vine-leaf', owed his continued presence at the Collège to his little brother. He was judged to be 'lazy and of bad character', but the headmaster was 'inclined to be indulgent', as the school inspector reported:

> The brother of this day-boy is the best pupil in the school – young Raimbaud [*sic*], one of our prize-winners. His departure would no doubt follow the expulsion of his brother and be a most regrettable loss to the school.[11]

The first signs of open subversion in Rimbaud's work actually betray a desire to confirm his place in school society. In an attempt to convince the Imperial authorities of its fearless conservatism – and perhaps to make a saving on teachers' salaries – the Collège de Charleville had formed an alliance with the seminary next door. Older boys who were studying for the priesthood now shared lessons with the 'rabble' from town. Each classroom became a junior model of the French parliament: a tense *ménage* of repressive clerics and reforming liberals.[12]

This exercise in cohabitation emphasized what until then had been trivial differences. The seminarists became more snobbish and unctuous; they took to carrying snuff-boxes and analysed their teachers' lessons for ideological incorrectness. The secular pupils became more profane, smoked cigarettes, and expressed atheist and liberal ideas. There is something of this unholier-than-thou attitude in Rimbaud's early verse: 'Les Premières communions', in which the young communicant complains that her flesh still 'crawls with the putrid kiss of Jesus', or the masturbating *abbé* of 'Le Châtiment de Tartufe', 'slobbering the creed from his toothless mouth'.

As the only boy who could beat the seminarists in academic combat, Rimbaud became the champion of the Collège. Without him, prize-giving would have been an annual humiliation. In 1869, he carried off eight first prizes, including the prize for Religious Education. He also covered himself in glory by embarrassing the history teacher, an *abbé* from the seminary. What, he asked, was the Church's view of the Wars of Religion, the Saint Bartholomew's Day Massacre and the Inquisition?[13] His first prize in History was obviously well deserved. In 1870, perhaps not surprisingly, his prize-list (seven firsts) was blotted by a lowly '4th merit' in History. Rimbaud was rapidly outgrowing the curriculum. A phrase in one of his essays had sent a little shock-wave through the school: 'Marat and Robespierre, the young await you!'[14]

The young would not have long to wait.

4

'Mad Ambition'

'I feel there is something in me . . . that wishes to rise . . .'

(Rimbaud to Théodore de Banville, 24 May 1870)

TWO WEEKS AFTER Rimbaud's poem appeared in the *Revue pour tous*, a new teacher arrived at the Collège de Charleville. Georges Izambard was only twenty-two years old. He had taught at a school in Victor Hugo's old home in Paris, and he had some odd ideas about teaching: he thought that boys could learn without being bored. The headmaster briefed him on arrival. He was to be entrusted with a pupil called Arthur Rimbaud – something of a swot, but a valuable asset to the school. As a special case, Rimbaud should be allowed to read anything he liked.[1]

The prize pupil turned out to be two quite different people. In class, he was a 'hermetic and reticent' little gentleman who never blotted his copybook. Outside, he was a 'true intellectual', 'vibrating with lyrical passion' and two complementary ambitions: to become a poet and to escape from his mother.[2]

Every day, Izambard found Rimbaud waiting for him after school with neat copies of his poems. The first poem was 'Ophélie'. An astonishing piece of work for a fifteen-year-old, it showed a rare ability to draw surprise effects from monotony and to infuse conventional phrases with real sentiment.

> On the calm, black wave where the stars are asleep,
> White Ophelia floats like a great lily,

Floats very slowly, lying in her long veils . . .
– In the distant woods the cries of hunters can be heard.

'Ophélie' used to appear in anthologies as one of Rimbaud's three or four best poems. Critics admired it, not as a typical Rimbaud poem, but as the result of a careful shopping expedition, a consumer's ode which pays a heavy tribute to the culture of its time. Its 'debts' are all quite evident: a poem by Banville, a painting by Millais and, apparently – rather than *Hamlet* – a theme set for homework by the Latin master. The self-conscious grandiloquence of the last stanzas makes the ominous thought seem relatively innocuous: the idea that the dreamer will be incapacitated by her visions.

Sky! Love! Liberty! What a dream, poor Lunatic!
You melted into it like snow in the fire:
Your great visions strangled your voice
– And the dreadful Infinite deranged your blue eyes!

Izambard was thrilled to have discovered a 'first-rate cerebral mechanism';[3] but he never pretended to have recognized Rimbaud as a future poet. Writing verse was a normal adolescent activity and could not form the basis of a sensible profession. Arthur Rimbaud was a brain bound for academic glory – a brain that demanded to be fed. Izambard lent him books from his own collection, which Rimbaud returned almost immediately, read and digested. His first known letter is a request to Izambard to lend him three books: *Curiosités Historiques*, *Curiosités Bibliographiques* and *Curiosités de l'Histoire de France* – the alternative curriculum. 'I shall come and fetch them tomorrow, at about 10 or 10.30. I shall be much obliged. They would be very useful to me.'

Some of Rimbaud's reading list can be reconstructed from his early texts. Fuelled by Hugo's *Notre-Dame de Paris*, the poems of Villon and a 'medieval' play by Banville, he produced a fashionable, Olde Worlde ballad about skeletons dancing on a gibbet ('Bal des pendus'), and a long passage of mock old French ('Lettre de Charles d'Orléans à Louis XI') which shows him absorbing the vocabulary of an entire period as if it were simply a matter of picking up a tune.

'Ophélie' was followed by another anthology piece: a poem on summer evening walks, written in early spring. Its closest relative is

Victor Hugo's poem on a dawn walk to his daughter's grave. Unlike Hugo, Rimbaud allowed himself to be distracted by his body:

> On fine summer evenings, I shall walk along paths,
> Prickled by wheat-stalks, trampling the fine grass,
> Dreaming, and feeling its coolness on my feet.
> I shall let the wind wash through my hair.
>
> I shall not speak, I shall not think,
> But endless love will rise up in my soul,
> And I shall go far, far away like a gipsy,
> Through the countryside – happy as with a woman.

This tiny poem, which expands like a mirage on a sea of silence, is a notable achievement in mid-nineteenth-century French verse, an unusual escape from the thud of rhetorical machinery. The theme of blissful unconsciousness seems to bear out Izambard's contention that Rimbaud wrote poetry in order to relax from the daily grind of school;[4] but the most remarkable thing about these early poems is their *un*autobiographical nature. Rimbaud was treating French poetry as a private boudoir, dressing himself in different genres, inspecting his development in other poets' mirrors.

*

RIMBAUD'S MAIN SOURCE of models was a prestigious anthology called *Le Parnasse contemporain*, which first appeared in 1866. It was published in instalments, some of which Rimbaud had managed to smuggle into his secret store in the attic.

In literary history, the 'Parnassian poets' are a sprawling constellation of lower-magnitude stars with which the dishevelled comets and dazzling supernovae of Hugo, Baudelaire and Mallarmé were briefly associated. It can be seen as a reaction to the failure of Romantic socialism in June 1848 and the subsequent triumph of the bourgeois Second Empire. Its watchword was 'impassivity' – the opposite of 'inspiration'. Strict, formal perfection was held to be the guarantee of aesthetic excellence. Themes tended to be exotic and conveniently unpolitical. It is partly this rejection of modernity that gives the beautifully calculated poems of the school's acknowledged leader, Leconte de Lisle, a haunting dullness. But as Rimbaud's wily imitations were to show, the stern slopes of Parnassus rose steeply from an interesting swamp of repressed emotions.

The attachment to formal correctness had an obvious appeal, both for the pupil who enjoyed school exercises and for the poet who wanted to try out different disguises. It also happened to be the case that anyone who wanted to see their work published in a prominent literary review would do well to sound as Parnassian as possible. Just as 'Les Étrennes des orphelins' had been prepared as bait for the *Revue pour tous*, '*Credo in unam*' was designed to be snapped up by the second volume of *Le Parnasse contemporain*, now approaching its final instalment.

'*Credo in unam*' (later titled 'Soleil et Chair') was a long, excited ode on the popular theme of a pagan Golden Age, when Man, his perceptions undimmed by 'pale Reason', sucked happily at the 'blessèd teat' of Nature: 'When one lies in the valley one can feel / That the earth is nubile and brimming with blood.' This pre-Christian paradise is contrasted, in the usual way, with the present age of puny, factory-warped serfs.

Rimbaud sent his poem, not to the lofty Leconte de Lisle, but to the smiling face of Parnassus, Théodore de Banville, who liked young poets, reviewed in liberal newspapers, and had been a close friend of Baudelaire. Rimbaud's letter was dated 24 May 1870. His handwriting ran in straight lines, but with a delicate spindrift of tails. He included his poems on Ophelia and summer evenings, claimed to be seventeen years old (he was fifteen and a half), and expressed himself in a curious mixture of juvenile enthusiasm, journalistic pastiche and innuendo:

> Two years from now, or perhaps in a year, I shall be in Paris. – *Anch'io*, gentlemen of the press, I shall be a Parnassian!* – I feel there is something in me . . . that wishes to rise . . . – I swear, dear Master, that I shall always adore the two goddesses, Muse and Liberty.
>
> Please do not turn up your nose at these lines . . . You would make me mad with joy and hope if, dear Master, you could *obtain* for the poem '*Credo in unam*' a small place among the Parnassians . . . I would

---

* A conventional reference to Correggio, seeing Raphael's 'Saint Cecilia': '*Anch'io sono pittore!*'

appear in the last series of *Le Parnasse*: it would be the poets' Creed!
. . . Oh mad Ambition!

Then he copied out his poems and, changing to the Olympian
style of Victor Hugo, made a final appeal in the postscript:

– I am unknown; what does it matter? Poets are brothers. These
lines believe; they love; they hope, and that is all.
　　Dear Master, help me. Raise me up a little. I am young. Hold out
your hand to me.

Banville kept the poems and probably sent one of his polite notes
of encouragement; but there was no room for an unknown provincial
schoolboy in *Le Parnasse contemporain*.

Rimbaud was undeterred. In any case his poem showed that he was
already outgrowing the Parnassians. Lines like 'Ape-like men who fell
from their mothers' vulvas' were not the sort of thing one expected
from a rosy young poet. Izambard was almost anxious with admiration. 'The Parnassian school had amused him for a moment, but –
pshaw! – three months later, he talked of it only with the bitterness
of a disappointed lover.'[5]

Having improved his technique by imitating Parnassians, Rimbaud
now set off down the path of deliberate destruction that was to
produce some surprising discoveries. The first sign of his new manner, in the early summer of 1870, was an irregular, lopsided sonnet
in which the Parnassian ideal of pagan beauty underwent a revolting
transformation. Instead of Aphrodite rising from the waves, a large,
bovine woman emerged from a green tin bath, 'Hideously beautiful
with an ulcer on the anus'.

Like Marcel Duchamp's moustache on the Mona Lisa, Rimbaud's
ulcer on the goddess of Beauty signals a sense of estrangement from
the classical past and the end of a kind of innocence.[6] Rimbaud was
going through poetic puberty at an alarming speed. In July, he
presented his teacher with a short story which seemed to belong to a
different tradition altogether – a tradition that was preserved, not in
books, but on lavatory walls. Izambard found it 'childish, stupid and
filthy'.[7] Many editions of Rimbaud's work omit it altogether or
relegate it to the back room of an appendix.

Un Cœur sous une soutane ('A Heart – or, in slang, 'Penis' – under a

Cassock') is the tale of a pusillanimous young priest who falls in love with a certain Thimothina – a hairy, flat-chested individual who sounds suspiciously unfeminine: 'I sought your breasts in vain', writes the narrator. 'You don't have any. You disdain those worldly ornaments.'

Like most of Rimbaud's satirical work, *Un Cœur sous une soutane* occupies an ambiguous zone. It can be read as a puerile farce, a political satire or as a sarcastic treatment of adolescent sexuality: 'I took a stuffed chair, reflecting that one part of myself was about to impress itself on some embroidery that Thimothina had probably made herself.' 'These socks I have been wearing for a month, I told myself, are a gift of her love.' It can also be read as a pre-Freudian analysis of the language of a group – the pseudo-religious jargon of the Charleville seminarists and the early French Romantics: milksops and pederasts, in Rimbaud's view, whose 'mysterious effluvia' and 'gentle zephyrs' are symptoms of what would now be called an anal obsession.

Rimbaud was testing the limits of Izambard's open mind. So far, the new teacher had proved to be an ideal older brother – someone who would give criticism and affection without expecting much in return. Would he still be a friend when he saw the inside of his pupil's mind?

But Rimbaud was also thinking of his earlier self, the 'sanctimonious little so-and-so'. Writing allowed the mind to act upon itself. He was already revising his first poems, subjecting himself to the same parodic treatment. His annotated copy of *Le Parnasse contemporain* (which he later gave to a friend)[8] shows that, instead of imitating poems he admired, he tended to remodel poems which had struck him as unusually clumsy or inane. In a piece by the forgotten Mme Blanchecotte, the line, 'My last chagrin wore heavily on me' was changed to 'My last *chignon* . . .'. Another alteration had God bestowing gifts on 'his pale human seal' ('*phoque*' instead of '*race*').

When it was applied to his own poems, the same device produced a kind of instant originality: even the blandest lines came out sounding like sudden illuminations. 'Fine summer evenings' became '*blue* summer evenings', while the 'flowering lotus' of '*Credo in unam*' turned into a mysterious '*chattering* lotus'. These little tricks are significant precursors of a new aesthetic age, when the final work emerges from the destruction of its earlier drafts, incongruous and evocative.

At school, too, Rimbaud was becoming almost dangerously proficient. The April 1870 issue of the *Moniteur de l'Enseignement Supérieur* was practically a special Arthur Rimbaud number. It contained four pieces of work. One was a daring French verse translation of some Lucretius – daring, because Rimbaud had taken the new translation of *De natura rerum* by the Parnassian, Sully-Prudhomme, copied out the appropriate passage, improved it with a few tasteful changes, and handed it in as his own work, thereby sneering at his teachers and winning their praise at the same time. The theft went undetected until 1932.

The other notable piece was criminal in a different sense: a Latin adaptation of a French text on Jesus in his father's workshop. The set passage coyly compared a trivial carpentry wound to the blood of the Passion. Rimbaud's version has been described as 'pious', 'irreproachable' and 'edifying'.[9] In fact, as George Tucker has demonstrated, it shows a remarkable grasp of Latin sexual innuendo. Jesus Christ labours with a heavy tool, pushing it to and fro until he spatters himself with blood, and receives the loving attentions of his mother.[10]

There is a thin line here, as in *Un Cœur sous une soutane*, between parody and self-analysis. Even if Rimbaud was amusing himself by imagining a passionate, incestuous relationship between the Virgin Mary and her son, he was also experimenting with the chaotic power of language: a few ambiguities, and the whole picture could change like a landscape clouding over. Perhaps he was beginning to reflect on the nature of his mother's iron-fisted affection. It is unfortunate that Ernest Delahaye remembered only the first and last lines of a narrative poem which Rimbaud showed him in 1870:

> A brunette, she was 16 when she married.
> . . . .
> For she's passionately in love with her 17-year-old son.[11]

*

BY NOW, Mme Rimbaud had realized (to quote 'Les Poètes de sept ans') that 'the soul of her child' was 'a prey to repugnant things'. One day, his security measures failed and a compromising object came to light. On 4 May 1870, with long, lunging downstrokes that suggest an unusually durable nib, she carved out a letter to M. Izambard:

> Sir,
>
> I am extremely grateful to you for everything you are doing for Arthur. You lavish advice on him and you set him extra homework. These are attentions to which we are not entitled.
>
> But there is one thing of which I cannot approve and that is, for instance, the reading of a book like the one you gave him a few days ago (Les Misérables, V. Hugot [*sic*]). You must know better than I, Sir, that one should take great care in choosing books that are to be placed in the hands of children. For that reason, I thought that Arthur must have got hold of the book without your knowing. It would certainly be dangerous to allow him to read such things.

Les Misérables was 'dangerous' because, as Mme Rimbaud reminded Izambard in a meeting arranged by the headmaster, Victor Hugo was an enemy of Church and State who had quite properly been thrown out of France.[12] Since *Les Misérables* was on the Index of Proscribed Books, she had probably not read it, but she would have known that its hero was an escaped convict, not unlike the itinerant Uncle Charles. It would soon be too late to stop the rot. Arthur was already in the habit of talking to strange men he met on the road – navvies, quarrymen and vagrants. Even when they were drunk, he told Delahaye, they were 'closer to Nature' and more truly intelligent than the educated hypocrites of his own class.[13] These were men who, like Captain Rimbaud, could set off down the road and never come back.

A passage of *Une Saison en Enfer* suggests that these western nomads were role models and objects of fantasy for Rimbaud far more than any writer. His mother was obviously right to be worried:

> When I was still a child, I admired the intractable convict on whom the prison always closes. I visited the taverns and the furnished rooms he was said to have sanctified by his presence. *With his mind*, I saw the blue sky and the flowery toil of the fields. I sniffed out the fate that

dogged him in the cities. He had more vigour than a saint, more common sense than a traveller, and himself, himself alone!, to witness his glory and his reason.

Mme Rimbaud was not alone in fearing subversive influences. On 19 July 1870, the Government of Napoleon III seized on a feeble pretext and declared war on Germany. Victory, it was assumed, would be swift and total. The whole country – including disaffected republicans – would be united in a spirit of self-righteous belligerence. The Empire would be saved.

That summer, the inhabitants of Charleville stood on their doorsteps, cheering the brave soldiers as they set off for certain victory at the front with cries of 'To Berlin!' Brother Fred was inspired to go and drink beer at the enemy's expense. He marched off without saying goodbye, managed to get himself enrolled in a regiment, despite being under age, and spent the next few months trapped by the Prussian army in Metz.[14]

Arthur found his militaristic brother contemptible. He had already refused to wear the new military school uniform, and when his fellow pupils pompously announced their intention to donate the money for their prize books to the war effort, he refused to cooperate.[15] This was a serious blow since Rimbaud was the only pupil in his year who won prizes. He did however agree to sell his books to the highest bidder.

For Rimbaud, this gung-ho chauvinism was a nationwide epidemic of smug provincialism. Any poet, it seemed to him, should be opposed to the Empire. This is why Delahaye had been able to win his confidence by crossing the Belgian border, entering a café and memorizing passages of the latest *Lanterne*[16] – the pocket-sized newspaper in blood-red covers that was banned in France for fomenting revolt and turning Napoleon III into a cartoon idiot. *La Lanterne* was written by a man who lived in Brussels in the home of Victor Hugo: proof that Romantic literature could still throw bombs at the establishment.

The bookshops of Charleville were a poor source of subversive literature. Rimbaud put his talent to work and wrote a saucy, song-like poem on a canoodling boy and girl ('Trois baisers'), which he sent to the savage satirical magazine, *La Charge*. The poem was printed on 13 August 1870 and earned him a free subscription.[17]

When war was declared, he added the blunt, slangy rhetoric of republican propaganda to his literary arsenal and devoted two poems ('Le Forgeron' and 'Morts de Quatre-vingt-douze') to the heroes of the French Revolution, those 'million Christs with soft, dark eyes'.[18]

Since it seemed a foregone conclusion that France would crush the enemy within a few weeks and consolidate the Empire, these poems were unlikely to be the shortest route to a literary career; but then, when he finally reached Paris – which he intended to do, he told Izambard, even if it meant 'dying on a heap of stones' on the way – the ideal society of 'brother' poets would surely accept him for what he was.

The 1869–70 school year ended in splendour and misery. Rimbaud came top once again in the regional examination, this time with a piece on 'Sancho Panza mourning his dead ass' (unpublished because of the war and now lost). Prize-giving on 6 August was largely a matter of the local bourgeoisie cheering Arthur Rimbaud. But Izambard was not there to see his pupil sneer at the applause. He had left on 24 July for his aunts' home in Douai. Rimbaud was anticipating a long and thirsty summer.

Fortunately, Izambard had told his landlord that Rimbaud should be given the key to his apartment. Every day, he went to sit in Izambard's pool of books like a parched sponge. By the time he wrote to his teacher on 25 August, he had sucked up the entire library and was already re-reading books which had not seemed particularly interesting the first time.

The brevity of Rimbaud's work tends to conceal this encyclopedic urge, which makes him a close literary relative of Balzac. The idea was not to accumulate knowledge at a steady pace but to exhaust the entire field as quickly as possible, even if it ended in a spasm of rejection. A few weeks later, he found the perfect image for his work in an essay by Montaigne and began to recite it to anyone who cared to listen:

> The poet, seated on the Muses' tripod, furiously pours out all that comes into his mouth, like the gargoyle of a fountain, and there escape

from him things of diverse colour, contrary substance, and interrupted flow.

It was a good description of his letter to Izambard. The envelope was marked 'Very urgent':

Sir,

You're lucky you don't live in Charleville any more! My native town is not the least in stupidity among all the little towns of the provinces.* I have no more illusions on that score. [...] It's a horrible sight – retired grocers dressing up in uniform. They're wonderfully dashing, those solicitors, glaziers, tax-collectors and cabinet-makers, all the pot-bellies patrolling ['*qui font du patrouillotisme*'] at the gates of Mézières. My fatherland is rising up! Personally, I prefer to see it sitting down. Don't stir yourself, that's my motto.

I'm disoriented, sick, enraged, stupid and dazed. I was hoping for sunbathing, endless walks, some rest, journeys, adventures – gipsying about. I was especially hoping for some newspapers and books. – Nothing! Absolutely nothing! The post has stopped sending things to booksellers. Paris is really treating us shabbily: not a single new book! Death! For newspapers, I'm reduced to the honourable *Courrier des Ardennes*. [...] It sums up the aspirations, desires and opinions of the population. You can just imagine! Bloody marvellous! . . . Exiles in our own land!!!

After painting this energetic picture of frustration, Rimbaud copied out a large piece of glutinously sentimental verse by Louisa Siefert about a childless young woman. One line was singled out for admiration: 'My life, at eighteen years, contains a whole past'. 'It's as beautiful as the lamentations of Antigone in Sophocles', he commented, impressively erudite. (In fact, he found the remark in the editor's preface and copied it word for word.)

He had also read 'a very bizarre and funny' book of poems by a young Parnassian, Paul Verlaine – a poet who was not afraid to break the longest-standing rules of French verse. Verlaine's *Fêtes galantes* contained the first example Rimbaud had ever seen of an alexandrine in which the caesura was straddled by a word – analogous to a sudden,

* Cf. Matthew 2:6: 'And thou Bethlehem [. . .] art not the least among the princes of Juda.'

fleeting change of time-signature.* Strange things were happening in
the literary capital . . .

    Au revoir. Send me a 25-page letter – poste restante – and make it
snappy!

A. Rimbaud

An enigmatic postscript hinted at an escapade: 'Soon I'll be
sending you revelations on the life I'm going to lead . . . after the
holidays . . .'

*

A DAY OR two later, Rimbaud gathered up some books and took
them to a secondhand dealer. This time, instead of exchanging them
for new books, he asked for cash and returned home, determined and
inscrutable.

Meanwhile, the retired grocers of Charleville were becoming less
enthusiastic about their 'patriotrolling'. Retreating soldiers were
straggling into town, survivors of the most inept military campaign
in modern French history. The Collège de Charleville was converted
into a hospital. The weather was fine, but there was the sound of
distant thunder. Eleven miles to the east, at Sedan, the ailing Napoleon III was watching the Prussian artillery through a haze of gun-
smoke and opium. His beautiful army was being destroyed. At
Charleville station, travellers were informed that the Prussians had
removed sections of track to the south. Anyone wishing to reach Paris
would have to take a train in the opposite direction as far as Charleroi
in Belgium and then change to the Saint-Quentin line.

On 31 August, while Mme Rimbaud sat at her window staring at
the muddied streets in a state of arrested panic, the train from
Charleroi was crossing the plains of northern France. In a third-class
carriage, a small boy was hiding under the seat, watching out for the
ticket inspector. With his last francs, he had bought a ticket for Saint-
Quentin; but the train had passed through Saint-Quentin station
hours before. It had now reached the 'military zone', where the roads

---

* The rule required a clear break after the sixth syllable. Verlaine's offending line
was, 'Et la tigresse épou | vantable d'Hyrcanie'.

were cluttered with cartloads of furniture and families heading west, abandoning their villages to the enemy.

Soon, the train would be entering the gravitational field of the huge urban sprawl, the inexhaustible fount of books and newspapers, the city where poets lived.

5

Convictions

'I am not a prisoner of my reason.'

('Mauvais sang', *Une Saison en Enfer*)

A T THE Gare du Nord, Rimbaud crept out of his carriage and joined the crowd that was heading for the barrier. A few yards in front of him he could see the Parisian traffic passing in the square.

Two men in railway uniform asked him for his ticket. He was taken to one side and searched: a suspicious little figure with long hair and grubby but respectable clothes. He had an accent that might be foreign. His pockets proved to contain incomprehensible notes, written in lines of different length. The story that he was suspected of espionage may well be true. Reports were coming in all the time of attempted coups and political agitators returning from abroad. Five days after Rimbaud's arrest, Victor Hugo arrived at the same station, but with a first-class ticket and a cheering crowd at the exit. Hugo and his republican supporters were believed to have formed an alliance with the Prussians. The ticketless boy, who came from a region that was now in enemy hands, might be part of an avant-garde.

Giving his age as seventeen and a half might have been a good idea professionally (in three different poems written around his sixteenth birthday, Rimbaud implied that he was seventeen); legally, it was suicidal. Anyone over the age of sixteen convicted of *vagabondage* was liable to six months in jail.[1]

Rimbaud watched the upper storeys of apartment blocks fly past the grill in the back of the police wagon – the famous 'salad basket' he had read about in _Les Misérables_. It trundled down the boulevards to the centre of Paris, crossed the Seine and came to a halt in the courtyard of police headquarters. He was marched into an office, interrogated by the desk sergeant, then deposited in the prison yard while his file began its administrative journey.

Business was brisk in the last days of the Empire. Rimbaud found himself surrounded by criminals with time on their hands – pimps, pickpockets and anarchists. Something unpleasant certainly occurred – perhaps just 'the ritual beating-up', as Izambard claims. But Izambard had a tendency not to want to believe Rimbaud's tales of life in the wild. Rimbaud's claim that he 'had to defend his virtue' against improper advances is entirely credible.

Finally, he was led before the examining magistrate and answered the questions that were put to him with such 'ironic disdain' (according to Rimbaud)[3] that he seemed to have his heart set on prison. Since the boy had no money and was unable to give an address in Paris, the magistrate had no choice but to send him to Mazas.

Rimbaud's tantalizing tour of Paris now continued east, along the Rue Saint-Antoine, towards the Place de la Bastille and the proletarian suburbs. Eventually, the 'salad basket' arrived at a building which Thomas Cook's _Guide to Paris_ pointed out to tourists as a 'gloomy and repulsive-looking' monument.[4] The brick walls of Mazas prison loomed over a sunless district of factories and slums. The flagship of the French penal system, Mazas was divided into single cells so that men whose crimes were of 'essentially different moral character' would not rub shoulders.[5] Evidently, the idea had not yet caught on at the Préfecture de Police.

Rimbaud was stripped, shaved, measured (5 feet 4 inches) and ordered to the showers while his clothes were fumigated. Then he was marched through a series of doors and locked into a cell. It contained a gas lamp, a table and a stool, two mess tins, a water bottle, hooks from which a hammock was hung at night, and the latest sanitary appliance: 'an odourless toilet fitted with a ventilator' – a stern contrast to the pungent latrines of home. Meals arrived in metal trucks which ran on a little railway.

Several days passed. With the country close to collapse, juvenile vagrants were not an urgent priority. Rimbaud wrote home, but the letter never arrived. Communications were suddenly interrupted. The Emperor had surrendered at Sedan, the day after Rimbaud's arrest. The Prussian army was marching on Paris.

In the streets outside, modern France was being born. On 4 September, a moderate republican government was entrusted with the job of defending what was left of France from the victorious Prussians. The word 'imperial', in Rimbaud's letter to Izambard, suggests that he knew nothing of these events. The only sound that reached him from the outside world was the clattering of trains on the nearby railway viaduct.

Paris, [Monday] 5 September 1870

Dear Sir

I have done what you advised me not to do: I left my mother's home and went to Paris! Arrested as I left the train for having no money and owing the railway thirteen francs, I was taken to the Préfecture and I am now waiting to be sentenced at Mazas! Agh! – *I place my trust in you* as in my mother. You have always been a brother to me and now I am asking urgently for the help you offered. I have written to my mother, to the imperial prosecutor and to the police superintendent at Charleville. If you don't hear from me on Wednesday, before the train that goes from Douai to Paris, *take that train and come here to claim me either by letter or by going to see the prosecutor* and pleading with him, *vouching for me* and *paying my debt! Do what you can*, and when you get this letter, write, *I order you*, yes, *write to my poor mother* (5, Quai de la Madeleine, Charlev.) *to comfort her. Write to me* too. Do your utmost! I love you like a brother and I shall love you like a father.

Greetings.

Your poor
Arthur Rimbaud

At the bottom of the page, a tiny postscript contained the main point of the letter, perhaps even the object of the whole adventure. He knew that in a milliner's shop in Douai, 100 miles to the north, three kind sisters lived with the orphan they had raised as their own son – Georges Izambard: 'And if you manage to set me free, you'll take me back to Douai with you.'

'Poor Arthur Rimbaud' had an oddly aggressive way of being pitiful. With its bullish demands, its detailing of the precise manner in which help was to be offered and its avoidance of the word 'please', Rimbaud's letter to Izambard gives a vivid image of his upbringing: any affection was inextricably bound up with coercion. The sharpness of his self-analysis is one of the delights of his poetry. In life, it took the form of emotional blackmail: Rimbaud was holding interviews for a 'father'. Izambard, who had already had a taste of Mme Rimbaud's temper, was to write to Arthur's mother and 'comfort' her . . .

A money-order arrived from Izambard. The vagrant was escorted to the station and put on the train to Douai. That afternoon, in a quiet, affluent street in the northern town, Izambard's 'aunts' opened the door to a grim-faced figure with very large feet and hands: a silent, dishevelled and smelly little boy. Even in its recently shaved condition, his scalp may have supported a sufficiently large population of lice to justify the operation described in the poem, 'Les Cher-cheuses de poux' ('The Lice-Seekers'), which Izambard associates with his aunts; but the poem was written several months later and there is no good reason to demand its biographical means of support. It is enough to know that Rimbaud enjoyed being fussed over by friendly women for the first time in his life.

He swore like a prisoner, ate like a pig, never passed the salt and never said 'thank you', but three weeks later, Izambard would find a short poem, gouged with a pencil into the green paint of the front door: a little farewell ode, not to his hosts, but to the house itself.[6] For Rimbaud, it seems, almost everything was easier said in verse.

Rimbaud's uncouth behaviour suddenly became easier to understand when a letter arrived from Charleville. It was a message from 'the Mouth of Darkness', as Rimbaud now called his mother. This curiously sexual, astronomical expression is the title of a poem from Victor Hugo's *Les Contemplations* in which 'la Bouche d'Ombre' engulfs the poet in a dark tidal wave of apocalyptic pronouncements. In Mme Rimbaud's letter, Izambard was verbally savaged for conniving in Arthur's 'escape'. He was to send the boy home at once.

Although letters were obviously getting through, the Ardennes was still cut off from the rest of the country, and Rimbaud was digging his heels in. He had a pleasant room with a well-stocked bookcase, and was quickly establishing himself in the local community with an almost anthropological efficiency usually associated with his later years in Africa.

Every day, he went to sit in the bustling, inky offices of a local newspaper, *Le Libéral du Nord*, which Izambard had been asked to edit. In his best handwriting, he copied out fifteen of his poems and left them with Izambard's friend, the twenty-six-year-old Paul Demeny – a feeble poet, as Rimbaud knew from his reading of Demeny's *Les Glaneuses* (1870), but one who had the invaluable merit of being part-owner of a Paris publishing house.[7] In the evenings, Rimbaud joined Izambard and the local defence volunteers and paraded in the square with his broomstick. In an attempt to render himself indispensable, he wrote a letter to the Mayor of Douai on behalf of the volunteers, demanding funds and pointing out that rifles would be more effective than broomsticks:

> We, the undersigned, members of the sedentary National Guard of Douai [. . .] are to vote next Sunday in the municipal elections and will accord our votes only to those who, in word and in deed, show themselves to be devoted to our interests. [Etc.][8]

It was a masterly imitation of a bourgeois letter of complaint, stiff with subordinate clauses and stodgily indignant.

Whenever Rimbaud showed signs of conformity, something dramatic was about to happen. He seemed compelled to redress the balance, to prove that this convivial Rimbaud was an impostor. On 23 September, after attending a local electoral meeting, he wrote up the minutes and sent his account to the printer of *Le Libéral du Nord*, pretending that it came from Izambard.

When Izambard opened his paper on 25 September, he was horrified to see that Rimbaud had bathed the sedate meeting in the red glow of revolution. There was an inappropriate, sneering joviality about his account. Worst of all, a local worthy called M. Jeannin was referred to, twice, as 'Citizen Jeannin' . . . Shades of 1789.

M. Jeannin complained to Izambard: what would the workers at his factory think when they saw their boss described in the local paper as a revolutionary? Was M. Izambard trying to bring them out on strike? Izambard rounded on his little guest: just when the burghers of Douai needed reassuring that the liberals who had gained power were not wild-eyed reincarnations of Robespierre and Marat. Though Izambard says nothing of this in his memoirs, he had a special reason to be irritated with Rimbaud: a damaging report on his 'liberal' tendencies, which explains why he never returned to teach at the Collège de Charleville.[9] To be accused by his pupil of political timidity was infuriating. His home, his reputation and now his job were being expropriated by a fifteen-year-old anarchist.

It was, therefore, with a mixture of relief and exasperation that Izambard received another smoking envelope from Mme Rimbaud on 24 September 1870. The police were looking for Arthur, and if the 'little rascal' got himself arrested a second time, 'he needn't bother coming home because I swear on my life I shall never let him in the house again'. Then came the rude part:

> How can the boy be so stupid – he who is usually so quiet and well-behaved? What can have put such a foolish thought into his head? Did someone put him up to it? No, I must not think such a thing. Unhappiness makes one unjust. Please therefore be so kind as to lend the wretched boy ten francs, then kick him out and send him home quick!

After a miserable train journey, Rimbaud arrived back in Charleville, with Izambard, on 27 September. The year before, Mme Rimbaud had moved to a pleasant ground-floor apartment in a new house by the river, with a view of Mount Olympus (now 7 Quai Arthur-Rimbaud, opposite the Rimbaud Museum in the Old Mill). The door opened on to the street, a large hand reached out and grabbed hold of Arthur while the other hand smacked him about the head for some time. Then 'the Mouth of Darkness' spoke: M. Izambard was to blame for everything.[10]

Izambard left Rimbaud to his punishment and went on to visit the battlefield at Sedan. It seems to have made a less painful impression on him than the interview with Mme Rimbaud.

Two days later, Rimbaud wrote a poem on the joys of adolescence, or, more likely, rewrote it – the dates on his manuscripts are nearly always the dates of the copy, not of the original composition, as if each poem was born again with each rewriting.[11]

> Nobody's serious when they're seventeen.
> [. . .]
> A young miss goes by with charming little airs,
> Under the shadow of her father's fearsome collar . . .
>
> And since she finds you enormously naive,
> Tripping along in her little bootees,
> She turns around, with a pert and lively air
> [. . .]
> You're in love. Rented out until the month of August.

This was the sort of image that would help to sell the work of a young poet. Rimbaud was manipulating his future readers like an experienced entertainer. 'Roman', according to most editors, is a delightful depiction of 'early amorous stirrings'; 'the poem of a schoolboy with an inflammable heart'.[12] But the title is also a warning: this is a novel, a romance or a tall story, not a realistic self-portrait. The poet can also be identified with the girl who strolls, suspiciously, under the street-lamp on the public promenade, catching the eye of little boys.[13]

When he was allowed to leave the house, he went to call on Delahaye, who was turning out to be the perfect friend: generous, enthusiastic and gullible. Delahaye's romantic account of Rimbaud's early years shows how effective his deadpan expression could be. The Collège was still closed, and while they smoked their pipes behind hedges in the public park, Rimbaud told him all about his great adventure: he had sold his prize-books and gone to Paris. There, he had been arrested for shouting anti-government slogans and for insulting the policeman who called him 'a snotty-nosed kid'. At the Préfecture – where he had to fend off some vicious homosexuals – the magistrate sent him down for being too sarcastic. The prison chaplain and governor had been shocked by his 'atheistic principles'. If he hadn't spent two weeks in solitary confinement on a bed of damp straw, he would have helped to bring about the revolution and made contact with the literary world. However, he had worked as a journalist in Douai. After that, of course, there could be no question of returning to school. The headmaster could keep his 'brilliant career'. 'Some serious young people', says Delahaye, 'condemned his initiative and declared that he was "going to the bad". To my shame, I confess that I did not share their view. For me, he was quite simply turning into a hero.'

*

TOWARDS THE END of September 1870, the new French Republic was trying to ignore the possibility that France might cease to exist as an independent nation. Paris was under siege and Bismarck was longing to bomb it into submission. The medieval fortress of Mézières across the river was being prepared for battle. Ludicrous posters went up on every street corner, boasting of imaginary victories by non-existent regiments and urging the inhabitants to defend 'their fortunes and their honour'.[14]

To the disgust of brother Frédéric, who swallowed all the propaganda, Arthur refused to volunteer to save his home town or his sisters from the Prussian army. Both sides seemed to him to represent the same vanity and greed. Napoleon III had gone but the bourgeoisie remained. One day soon, a revolution would eradicate all social distinctions and private wealth, including Mme Rimbaud's. The disciple Delahaye was given a lesson in revolutionary socialism, taken from Luke 3: 'Every valley shall be filled, and every mountain and hill shall be brought low; and the crooked shall be made straight, and the rough ways shall be made smooth.'

Rimbaud waited for news of his own impending liberation with mounting impatience. Before returning to Charleville, he had left a message for Izambard's friend, the poet Paul Demeny: 'I shake your hand as violently as I can.' 'I shall write to you. And you'll write to me. Won't you?'[15]

The poems he was hoping Demeny would help him to publish would have been one of the oddest collections of its time and would probably have stimulated the wits of reviewers sufficiently to ensure some damaging reviews. Along with obscenities like the ulcerated Venus in a tin bath, there were frisky little poems in difficult, sing-song metres belonging to a genre that can best be described as cute realism: the courting peasant of 'Les Reparties de Nina' or, in 'Les Effarés', the little round bottoms of urchins poking through their trousers as they watch a baker pound his dough and thrust it into the oven's 'warm hole' – a virtuoso piece which leaves the smell of bread in the mind's nostril though smells are never mentioned.

There was also a clutch of political poems that seemed to have been written for a very different audience – the literate, proletarian reader-ship that Rimbaud assumed to exist when he examined the obscene cartoons in the republican press. In 'Rages de Césars', he gloated over the defeated Emperor, exhausted after 'twenty years of orgy'. A sonnet titled 'Le Mal' illustrated the anarchists' dictum, 'God is Evil':

> While the machine-guns' red spittle
> Whistles all day long through the boundless blue sky [. . .]
> While a horrendous insanity pulverizes
> A million men into a steaming mass [. . .]
>
> There is a God [. . .]
> Who nods off to the lullaby of hosannas,
>
> And awakes when mothers, scrunched up
> In anguish, weeping under old black bonnets,
> Give him the penny they wrapped in their handkerchief!

There are no theoretical texts from this period to tell us what Rimbaud might have written as an introduction to this hotch-potch of poems. However, Delahaye remembered Rimbaud praising the 'honesty' of works like *Madame Bovary* and *Hard Times*. Realism, in Rimbaud's view, was 'not pessimism, for pessimists are half-wits'. The idea was 'to see everything up close, to describe modern life with fearless precision, the way in which it warps the human being', to study every detail of modern society 'in order to hasten its destruction'[16] – a great unmasking that would also tear away the face.

There was something quite studious about Rimbaud's anarchism. His carefully imitated insults would appeal to the community of fearless revolutionaries just as his Latin verse had won his teachers' admiration. When he copied out 'Morts de Quatre-vingt-douze', he redated it '3 September 1870' – the eve of the new Republic – and added the phrase, 'Written at Mazas'. Readers would naturally assume that Arthur Rimbaud had been incarcerated for his political convictions.

But there was also a more pervasive anarchism in his poetry. It can be seen in everything he was writing, not just the overtly republican verse: the recovery of repressed experience (his own or that of society's *misérables*), the commandeering of old metaphors for new purposes. Even the rustic romance of 'Les Reparties de Nina' shows troublesome images erupting in the simple narrative like mole-hills on a lawn. The sentimental commonplace of children's bedtime and the revolutionary cliché, 'drunk with blood' – normally applied to tyrants – form an unusual alliance:

> [. . .] I'd squeeze
> Your body, like a little girl being put to bed,
> Drunk with the blood
>
> That flows, blue, beneath your white,
> Rose-tinted skin.

The chemical reactions that took place in the poem between words and realities were beginning to suggest the possibility of a gigantic, dangerous experiment. For now, Rimbaud was happy to enjoy the flashes and effects. The mechanical device of imitative alliteration, for instance, which could make almost anything sound enticing and mysteriously symbolic – '*Et, tout là-bas, / Une vache fientera, fière, / À chaque pas*' – even the soft thump of cow dung dropping in the twilight.

6

Tour de France

'Ah! the life I led as a child: the open road in all weathers,
supernaturally sober, more dispassionate than the best of
beggars, proud to have neither country nor friends. What
stupidity!'

('L'Impossible', *Une Saison en Enfer*)

RIMBAUD HAD been back in Charleville for over a week, but
there was still no word from Demeny. His journalistic experience was going to waste. The weather would be turning cold, and
since Prussia was winning the war, Charleville might be cut off again
at any moment.

On 8 October, Izambard called in to see him on the way back from
Sedan. Another cloud hung over 5 Quai de la Madeleine. Mme
Rimbaud told Izambard that Arthur had gone for a walk – rather a
long walk. He had disappeared up the Meuse valley, apparently to
visit a schoolfriend whose parents ran a café at Fumay, twenty-three
miles to the north. That was a day or two before. He had not been
seen since.[1]

Izambard agreed to root him out in Fumay. If necessary, he was
to 'alert the local authorities and have him brought back by the
gendarmerie'.

Meanwhile, Rimbaud had spent the night with a friend called Léon
Billuart who owed him a favour: Billuart's Latin homework had
recently improved beyond recognition. In the morning, Rimbaud left

with some money, some bars of chocolate and a letter of introduction for Billuart's cousin, an army sergeant at Givet, further up the valley. He passed through Vireux, where he called on another boarder from the Collège de Charleville, and reached the barracks at Givet that evening. The sergeant was out but his room was unlocked. Rimbaud lay down on the bed, slept until dawn, and set off again before the sergeant returned.

He headed now for the Belgian border. Thirty-three miles to the north-west, the father of another schoolfriend, Jules des Essarts, edited an important daily newspaper, the *Journal de Charleroi*. It was known for its progressive views and therefore, Rimbaud supposed, would have work for a belligerent young journalist who could write in any style. With the money from Billuart, he took a train and reached Charleroi at noon, probably at about the time that Izambard was knocking at his door in Charleville. He found the newspaper offices and introduced himself to M. des Essarts.

A Senator in the Belgian parliament, des Essarts was used to seeing exiles arrive from France in a less than seemly condition and invited his son's friend to dinner to discuss his proposal. Dinner, for Rimbaud, was a complex, irritating ritual which interfered with eating. Many of his relationships were destroyed as the result of a dinner invitation. His idea of pleasant company was a negative image of home, and it was important to find out whether a new acquaintance would place table manners before friendship. His inability to engage in smalltalk – sometimes even in talk of any kind – is well attested. This could prove particularly disastrous if an attempt were made to loosen him up with alcohol. (The strongest drink on his mother's table was diluted Charleville beer – never very potent even in its undiluted state.)

All went well until dessert. Then Rimbaud began to talk politics. He seemed to have an opinion on every living politician: one was a 'worthless yokel', another a 'cheating bastard', and so on. This was not the Senator's idea of political debate, and he was not Rimbaud's idea of a republican. When des Essarts called him 'young man', Rimbaud decided to find his accent hilariously Belgian, though we happen to know that it was not. (Rimbaud's own accent was thick and distinctive, with emphatic working-class vowels.) The Senator's daughter was rushed off to bed before she suffered irreparable pollution. The 'young man' was asked to leave and ordered never to write to his friend again. Nothing by Rimbaud has ever been found in the *Journal de Charleroi*.

Rimbaud might have been showing off to his friend, proving that *he* could live perfectly well without a father. He was certainly irritated not to be treated as a potential journalist. For the last ten years, older men had been receiving his work with gratitude and admiration. Senator des Essarts had failed to be impressed. This was the first example of a situation that was to repeat itself several times in Rimbaud's life. The most trivial and fleeting relationships were subjected to the pressure of enormous expectations. When the tiniest defect appeared in the relationship (or in a poem or a whole phase of writing), it would be consigned to the rubbish heap of illusions.

After his eviction, Rimbaud seems to have spent a day or two in Charleroi, sleeping rough. His sonnet, 'Au Cabaret-Vert', describes a nearby carters' tavern in which everything was painted green and where the buxom waitress was like an anti-Mme Rimbaud, with 'enormous tits and twinkling eyes' –

> – She ain't the sort to tremble at a kiss! –
> Laughing, she brought me buttered bread,
> And heated ham on a painted plate –
>
> Pink and white and scented with a clove
> Of garlic – and filled my outsize mug with froth,
> Gilded by a late ray of sun.

This bountiful waitress was identified by an early researcher as a real person, but the ham itself was probably fictitious since Rimbaud told Léon Billuart in a letter that, for supper, he had inhaled the smells of roasting meat that wafted up from 'bourgeois' kitchens; 'and then I went off to nibble a bar of Fumay chocolate by the light of the moon'.

Rimbaud had ruined any chance he might have had of becoming a journalist in Charleroi, but he always set off on his journeys with several goals like spare pairs of shoes. This was his version of the Tour de France (a term originally applied to the educational tour undertaken by young apprentices). He was practising his trade, marking out the miles in sonnets with springy rhythms and rhymes that stuck easily in the mind. His prose texts and free-form poems, by contrast, were composed during largely sedentary periods. These were the 'Bohemian' sonnets that endeared him to later generations of literary vagrants and which seem to lead French poetry out of the library and the furnished room for the first time since François Villon:

MY BOHEMIA

I went on my way, fists in my torn pockets;
My overcoat, too, was turning into an idea.
I walked beneath the sky, Muse! your trusty servant.
Oh! là là! What splendid love affairs I dreamed!

My only pair of trousers had a gaping hole.
– Tom Thumb wrapt in thought, I scattered rhymes
Along the road. I stayed at the sign of the Great Bear.
– My stars made a soft swishing in the sky.

And I listened to them, sitting by the roadside,
On those fine September evenings when I felt drops
Of dew on my brow like an invigorating wine;

When, rhyming in the midst of fantastical shadows,
Like lyres, I tugged the elastic laces
Of my wounded shoes, a foot close to my heart!

The road poems that commemorate Rimbaud's Belgian expedition are not a simple travelogue. 'For eight days', one of them begins, 'I'd been shredding my boots / On the stones of the road. I entered Charleroi' (which he entered by train, three days after leaving Charleville). Another is dated 'En wagon [in a railway carriage], 7 October 1870': 'In winter, we'll travel in a little pink carriage / With blue cushions' – a description which, interestingly, corresponds to the décor of a first-class Northern Railway compartment.[2]

The familiar Ardennes landscape – the wooded hills, the broad folds of the Meuse, the slate quarries of Fumay, the ruined citadel of Givet – is quite absent. Rimbaud was not celebrating his native Ardennes for the benefit of future tourists; he was celebrating his departure.

The affecting nature of these sonnets, which were anthologized for decades as the acceptable face of Arthur Rimbaud, owes very little to the picturesque and a great deal to subliminal suggestions. To analyse them is to witness at first hand the transformation that took place in Rimbaud at the dinner-table. The hole in the trousers, the scattering of rhymes, the petticoats of the covering sky, the acrobatic operation at the end of the poem – a slight tilt of the wrist and Rimbaud's chocolate-box image suddenly turns obscene. To anyone who had recently been at school, the first line of 'Ma Bohème' would be clearly ambiguous. An imaginative rule insisted that holes in trouser pockets be scrupulously darned in order to prevent surreptitious masturbation. Like Baudelaire thirty years before, Rimbaud was using the schoolboy genre of the dirty-poem-in-disguise to re-energize Romanticism. These were poems that would not simply record but re-create the intellectual excitement that produced them.

By now, somewhere to the south-east, Izambard was homing in. From Fumay, he had gone to Vireux, where he learned that Rimbaud had been heading for Charleroi; but by the time he reached Charleroi, Rimbaud had disappeared. M. des Essarts – 'very welcoming but perhaps a trifle solemn' – recounted the unfortunate dinner. The little ruffian had gone, and good riddance. He could be anywhere. Izambard gave up and continued his journey to Brussels, where he had been intending to pay a surprise visit to his friend, Paul Durand.

Strangely, Durand was expecting him. A 'very kind and sweet' little fellow, covered in mud and dust, had just spent two nights with him and his mother. Rimbaud must have heard Izambard talking about his intended visit and memorized the name and address. He appeared to have walked all the way from Charleroi (thirty-four miles). Durand had urged him to stay, but 'he declared that he had to tour Belgium for his education and that he could manage quite well on his own'. Reluctantly, the boy had accepted some money and set off, scrubbed and elegant, in a brand-new suit of clothes.

A week later, Izambard returned to Douai to find the aunts in a flap: the train from Brussels had brought an unexpected visitor. While they spoke, a young 'dandy' in a silk cravat appeared – 'blindingly' attractive, according to Izambard. 'It's me', he said. 'I'm back.'

It appears in retrospect that Rimbaud had planned his journey like an explorer. He had lined his route in advance with staging-posts where the natives were presumed to be friendly – Fumay, Vireux, Charleroi, Brussels and Douai. He had slept rough and worn out his shoes quite enough for the purposes of 'education', but he had also luxuriated in beds and trains, and contrived to have an unwitting relief party (Izambard) follow at a safe distance.

*

Now, IN THE comfort of Douai, he organized his harvest: seven sonnets that would join the other poems he had deposited with Demeny two weeks before. Apart from the Bohemian poems, there was a description of a coloured print of a conquering Napoleon III that Rimbaud had seen in a window at Charleroi – old imperial propaganda, to which he added the cartoon character Boquillon, offering his buttocks to the Emperor. (Implication: Napoleon III had buggered up the French army.) There was also a sonnet on an old sideboard which sounds like a flimsy relative of the scent- and memory-impregnated wardrobes in Baudelaire's *Les Fleurs du Mal*. Finally, a gently shocking cameo of a young soldier 'sleeping' peacefully in a leafy dale: 'On the right side of his body there are two red holes'.

Izambard perceptively says of these sonnets (ignoring the defaced Napoleon) that 'they had the cheek to be charming'. He noticed that after every argument with his mother, Rimbaud became more scatological than ever. Each '*merde!*' represented a slap in the face. The Bohemian sonnets of October 1870 were the happy, holiday Rimbaud who blossomed when 'the Mouth of Darkness' had left the sky; the Rimbaud who breezed into Douai on the direct train, dressed to the nines and planning a glorious career:

> He copied out his poems [. . .] At the slightest mistake, he started again and *demanded* large sheets of school paper. When he had used up a ream, he would come and say, 'I'm out of paper'. He did this several times a day. [. . .] 'Write on the back', suggested one of the aunts. Looking shocked, he retorted, 'When it's for the printer, you never write on both sides.'[3]

Away from his desk, Rimbaud seems to have been in a floppy, unobjectionable state. He allowed Izambard to call him 'pitiful', and there was a tearful, hand-holding episode in his bedroom when Izambard accused him of being heartless: a mother, however monstrous, was still a mother . . . Rimbaud remembered Izambard's 'heartless' as if it had been a useful piece of advice. The word surprised him. A hidden theme ran through his latest poems and seemed to prove that, though he hated his mother, he was full of filial sentiment: 'Nature' is asked to 'cradle' the young soldier, who 'smiles like a sick child'; the story-telling sideboard 'has taken on the kindly air of old people'; the ham and the beer are preceded by two enormous breasts; and the rhymes of 'Ma Bohème' are also, by allusion, the pebbles that the French Tom Thumb drops along the road so that he can find his way home.

Before long, the inevitable letter arrived. This time, Mme Rimbaud demanded that Arthur be returned at tax-payers' expense. Izambard went to arrange the matter at the local police station. The superintendent, struck by Mme Rimbaud's strident letter ('a real *maman-gâteau*', he called her), expressed sympathy and promised that the boy would be treated kindly. Rimbaud promised to be 'good'. 'And', says Izambard, 'he retained his composure. – Perhaps emotions like these were part of his programme of studies.'

Izambard was one of the first to see that Rimbaud's rebellion was a form of intellectual discipline and even, indirectly, a vindication of the French education system. Rimbaud had passionately embraced its principles: its belief that the mind could be shaped by an act of will, its confidence in the power of method. He would soon be confirming his suspicions by reading hyperrationalist philosophers like Helvétius, for whom genius could be acquired by logical steps.[4] Izambard was also right to suspect that Rimbaud's 'programme of studies' involved a degree of self-destruction – the quickest way to gain control over his own destiny.

Having set out from Charleville as an independent apprentice, Rimbaud returned as a weeping child, 'with his little bundle under his arm', in the custody of men in uniform. Izambard would never see him again. When Rimbaud wrote on 2 November 1870, two weeks after his sixteenth birthday, he seemed to have reached a painful decision: he would stick it out in Charleville and, in a manner unspecified, complete his education.

There is a tone in Rimbaud's letter that recalls the grim, ascetic joy of the pupil cramming for examinations. This time, however, he would be following his own curriculum, undertaking the formidable task (as he told Delahaye) of 'demolishing everything and wiping my brain clean', re-creating that hypothetical, pristine state before school, church and mother had filled his head with prejudice.

> I'm dying and decomposing in drivel, dross and drabness. It can't be helped: it's my horrible persistence in worshipping free freedom and a lot of other things. 'Pitiful', isn't it? – I was going to leave again today, and I could have done: I had new clothes. I would have sold my watch, and long live freedom! [. . .] But I'll stay, I'll stay. I didn't promise to, but I'll do it to earn your affection. [. . .]
>
> Your 'heartless'
> A. Rimbaud

Charleville was the same as ever. Even the war was a washout. The Prussians had still not laid siege to Mézières.

> An abominable prurigo of idiocy – such is the mood of the population. You hear some fine things, I can tell you. It's demoralizing.

The last word – '*dissolvant*' – was usually applied to the subversive tracts of revolutionaries who wanted to undermine Society. But that was the view of people who revelled in normality and never listened to their own thoughts and senses. As far as Rimbaud was concerned, Society was undermining *him*.

7

Needful Destruction

'Morality is a weakness of the brain.'

('Alchimie du verbe', *Une Saison en Enfer*)

THE TOWN OF Mézières disappeared on the last day of 1870.
Rimbaud had seen the first sign of the approaching holocaust in November when he was walking with Delahaye in the meadows by the river. A huge gap had opened up in the view. Where once there had been orchards and allotments, there was now an expanse of stubble. The garrison commander had been studying the defence manual. (Trees impeded missiles.)

Paupers were swarming over the ruined landscape, filling baskets with fruit, reminding irate landowners that 'we're a Republic now'.[1] A short distance away, axe-wielding soldiers were warming to their pointless task and had started to fell the ancient lindens that lined the promenade – apparently a part of Charleville that Rimbaud liked:

> The linden-trees smell nice on fine June nights!
> At times the air is so sweet that one closes one's eyes.
> The sound-laden wind – for the town is not far –
> Brings the scent of the vines and the fragrance of beer.

> ('Roman')

Rimbaud managed to stifle his dismay and refocused his mind's eye on a more distant horizon. Delahaye was in for another lesson in revolutionary politics: 'Some demolitions are necessary.' 'There are other old trees that will have to be felled. [. . .] This Society. It will fall to the axe, the pick and the steamroller.' What would happen to Art and Beauty, wondered Delahaye, when everything had been smashed into equality? Rimbaud picked a flower: 'Look. Where could you buy a luxury item or an *objet d'art* more skilfully constructed than this? Even if all our social institutions disappeared, Nature could still offer us millions of jewels.'[2]

He was thinking, not just of Jesus pointing to the lilies of the field and predicting salvation, but also of his plan to purge his brain of 'principles' and 'notions'. Rimbaud had in mind a more shattering redemption: salvation from Christianity and the society it had produced. His poetry would pulverize the world from which it sprang.

As winter drew on, the east wind brought the steady thump of Prussian artillery. Stupidly, the fort of Mézières refused to surrender. On New Year's Eve, Mme Rimbaud locked her children in the house. They sat listening to the shells and incendiaries whistling through the snowstorm and landing on the little town of Mézières. Almost 7,000 were launched in less than ten hours. The bell in the church tower across the river was ringing hours that could not exist.

On the evening of 1 January 1871, Rimbaud managed to slip away and walked up the road to a vantage-point. Mézières was burning. The water had frozen in the pipes and there was nothing to do but watch. In Rimbaud's eyes, it was a pathetic and disappointing sight. It reminded him – if 'reminded' is the correct word – of 'a tortoise in petroleum'.[3]

For several days, Mézières was cordoned off by the Prussians. A Belgian newspaper published lists of the dead. One of the lists included the Delahaye family. On 4 or 5 January, Rimbaud crossed the river and headed for the blackened husk on the horizon. An unusual smell hung over it: half-animal, half-mineral. He was in a state of heightened curiosity, like someone who finds the perfect setting for their thoughts. He imagined how small a handful of dust Ernest Delahaye would make, and noted the evidence that even bombs were on the side of the bourgeoisie: the law courts, the prison and the police station had all survived. However, there was the consolation of knowing that a stray bomb had landed on Charleville and injured his old headmaster.[4]

Une Saison en Enfer presents a gratifying image of Mézières (or of any other civilized settlement) at ground zero: a jubilant wasteland, which bears little resemblance to the 'gentle' Ardennes in which Rimbaud is supposed to have courted his Muse. The optimist among the ruins was seeing the first stage of his social reform programme being put into practice:

> In the cities, the mud suddenly appeared to me red and black, like a mirror when the lamp moves about in the next room, like a treasure in the forest! Good luck, I cried, and saw a sea of flames and smoke in the sky, and, to left and to right, all riches blazing like a billion thunders.

On the pile of rubble that had once been the Delahaye home, he helped some looting soldiers to uncover the entrance to a cellar. No human corpse was found, just some frazzled cats. Suddenly, Delahaye came running up. The whole family had escaped during the firestorm. Delahaye told him of the window panes falling in showers of diamonds, a butcher's carcasses dripping fat on to pots of geraniums: Rimbaud had obviously given him an eye for the farcical and surreal, an aesthetic point of view that worked well as a survival mechanism. But there were aspects of Rimbaud that Delahaye was never able to stomach. His account, thirty-six years later, of a matter-of-fact Rimbaud shrugging off his emotions betrays a certain alarm at Rimbaud's appetite for destruction and loss.

For Rimbaud, the real disaster was that the offices of a local newspaper, the *Progrès des Ardennes*, to which he had recently submitted a satirical piece on a drink-befuddled Bismarck, had been razed to the ground. He had been hoping to silence his mother and avoid school by taking a job at the paper. Now, his work would have to develop underground, without the control of an editor or an audience. When it emerged a few months later, it would look very strange indeed.

*

THERE IS A gap in Rimbaud's meagre correspondence between 2 November 1870, when he told Izambard that he was 'decomposing', and 17 April 1871, when he told Demeny that he was 'condemned [or 'damned'] from the very beginning, and forever'. Condemned to the wet hell of Charleville, for what sins?

The familiar streets and the town slumping back into normality after the bombardment played the same role as regular verse forms in his poetry – a grey backdrop on which his images could explode, like the brimming chamber-pot which he launched from the top of the scaffolded church tower of Mézières, where some stonemasons had left it. Or, in a similar spirit, but reversing the direction of the filth, the message he chalked on to benches in the park: '*Merde à Dieu*' (sometimes reported as '*Mort à Dieu*', which has a more respectable, philosophical ring to it).[5]

He sat at the café on the Place Ducale, voicing opinions for which an adult could have been imprisoned: France was lucky to have been defeated because its chauvinism had been dealt a blow from which it would never recover. Germany, by contrast, was in for fifty years of military dictatorship. He talked to Prussian soldiers in a silly German accent. When he saw some officers relaxing with a drink, he laughed at them until they stopped enjoying themselves. Less daringly, he sneered at passing priests. But even his graffiti failed to produce a response.

The virulence of his new poems – 'Les Assis', 'Accroupissements', 'Oraison du soir', in which the poet's 'evening prayer' consists of urinating on sunflowers (a pun on the type of prayer known as an ejaculation)[6] – probably reflects his disappointment at how hard it was to shock the burghers of Charleville. Things had changed since the days of Baudelaire's bright green hair and tales of munching babies' brains. Baudelaire's poetry had appeared under the smug, economically buoyant Second Empire. Rimbaud's poetry would have to compete with a holocaust.

Because of its more contemplative tone, 'Les Poètes de sept ans' is thought to have been written before Rimbaud became the town hooligan – as if only one tone was available to him at a time. Its technical complexity dates it quite clearly to 1871. Thematically, too, it belongs to this period of frantic stagnation when infantile habits and thoughts returned to infest the adult body.

Lying flat at the foot of a wall and buried in the marl,
He rubbed his reeling eye and stared at visions, [. . .]
                                        He got ideas
From illustrated papers, and gazed, red-faced,
At laughing Señoritas and Signoras. [. . .]
He thought of the fields in heat where the swell
Of luminescence, the healthy scents and gold pubescence
Stir calmly in the depths and take to the air!

With its sensual intelligence and erratic sense of time, 'Les Poètes de sept ans' is one of the few poems that give an insider's view of puberty. At the end of the poem, something strange begins to happen to the syntax. Vast sentences unfurl. The main verbs, which are normally the syntactical hour- and minute-hands of experience, are difficult or impossible to locate. Concatenations of images suggest the existence of a submerged narrative, like an autobiography set in the future:

In the bare, high-ceilinged room, behind the shutters,
Acrid with humidity, and the light turning blue,
He read the novel he was always writing in his mind,
Full of heavy, ochre skies and forests drowned by floods, and

Flowers of flesh unfolded in the starry woods –
Chasms, landslides, routed armies and compassion! –
While the street outside sent up its sounds,
Alone, and lying on sheets of unbleached linen,
With violent presentiments of the sail!

In appearance, too, Rimbaud was a composite of different ages. He still wore his little bowler hat – until he crushed it with his foot, apparently to impress Delahaye. At the end of 1870, he was only five feet four inches tall, but by the end of 1871, he had grown about five inches and walked unevenly, pushing one shoulder in front of the other. Acromegaly (excessive growth, especially of hands and feet) has been diagnosed posthumously – and improbably – though it might be applied metaphorically to his brain. He blushed whenever he met someone new, recoiled at the slightest touch, remained silent for days on end and sometimes burst out giggling like a nervous child.

Delahaye dates the appearance of fair-coloured down on Rimbaud's chin from the summer of 1871. The tales of Rimbaud's active interest in girls are even more thin and wispy. Most of them are blatant attempts by early biographers to cleanse him and, by implication, themselves of the 'stain' of homosexuality. Rimbaud's poems suggest a familiarity with women's bodies that goes far beyond Romantic fiction – and even beyond women's bodies into the exotic vocabulary of medical textbooks. He may well have disposed of his virginity early on – either with a farm girl, a prostitute or, if Rimbaud's café-stories can be believed, a dog. But the only faintly plausible sign that he went courting with romantic ends is Delahaye's account of an incident that occurred early in 1871.

Rimbaud had arranged a rendezvous with a young lady on the Place de la Gare. She turned up in full regalia, accompanied by a tittering maid. The meeting was a total disaster, as he told Delahaye: 'I was as timorous as thirty-six million new-born poodles.' This does sound like one of Rimbaud's multiple images: in the letter of August 1871, he complained that his mother was 'as inflexible as seventy-three lead-helmeted administrations'.

Amazingly, this fiasco has been seen as the cause of Rimbaud's homosexuality, as if, in 1871, having sexual relations with men was a good way to avoid social embarrassment. Anyone who reads Rimbaud's early poems as pages from a diary would have to conclude, from the descriptions of rewarding physical experiences, that the principal beneficiary of his sexual attentions was himself. It would be more useful to note that, in education and upbringing, few Charleville girls in the 1870s would have made a suitable companion. A passage of *Une Saison en Enfer* which shows the influence of socialist feminism serves as a reminder that to contract a relationship with a 'young lady' was to engage in an administrative process akin to finding a job or buying a plot of land:

> 'He said, "I don't love women. Love, as we know, will have to be reinvented. Women today can only desire a secure position. Once they have it, heart and beauty are set aside. All that remains is cold disdain, the food of marriage, in today's world. On the other hand, I see women with the marks of happiness whom I might have turned into

good comrades, but who are instantly consumed by brutes who have all the sensitivity of a stake."'

This unromantic ability to see love as the product of a particular society reflects a methodical approach which makes Rimbaud the most ambitious Cartesian in modern literature: before contracting a relationship, investigate the basis of all relationships; before falling in love, reinvent it.

As Izambard realized when he read Rimbaud's poem 'A la musique', in which a 'dishevelled' young narrator stares unflinchingly at girls in the Place de la Gare, imagining what lies 'beneath the bodice and the flimsy frills', this sort of attitude made for uncomfortable reading. Most editions still print the final stanza of 'A la musique' with Izambard's correction (italicized):

> It takes no time to find the boot and stocking . . .
> I reconstruct their bodies, scorched with lovely fevers.
> They think me strange and whisper to each other . . .
> *And I feel the kisses coming to my lips . . .*[7]

This was Izambard's attempt to pull the poem back into the rut of convention. Rimbaud's original line replaced the passive recipient with an active aggressor: 'And my brutal desires latch on to their lips.'

At the time (July 1870), Rimbaud had accepted Izambard's edulcorated version. By the spring of 1871, he had torn away the 'flimsy frills' of orthodox love poetry and was beyond edulcoration. On paper at least, he was practising his serenades with a vengeance:

> One night, you hailed me as a poet,
>   You blond eyesore.
> Come down and let me whip you
>   In my lap.
>
> I've puked up all your bandoline,*
>   You black-haired eyesore;
> You'd cut the strings of my mandoline
>   With your spiky hair.

---

* 'Gummy substance formerly used for stiffening the hair' (Chambers).

Ugh! my dried-up sputum,
   You red-haired eyesore,
Still infects the gullies
   Of your pudgy breast!

Oh my little lovers,
   How I hate you!
Cover up your ugly udders
   With painful rags!

Rimbaud's anti-love poem can be read as proof of his misogyny, but the primary object of his hate was a certain form of poetry (specifically, a frilly poem on puppy love by Albert Glatigny) and, perhaps, the feelings it had once aroused in him.[8] 'Mes Petites amoureuses' actually implies a more intimate and passionate relationship than any described in French verse since Baudelaire: whipping, vomiting and infecting. Rimbaud was saying farewell to a part of himself and to a section of his potential audience: women who would end up as church-goers and housewives, who offered their bodies, dressed to please, complimented him on his work and had to be told to 'trample' on his feelings – women, in other words, who were quite unlike his mother.

*

THE LONGEST SCHOOL holiday on record came to an end on 15 February 1871. Since the classrooms were still full of mutilated soldiers, the Collège de Charleville reopened in the town theatre. Mme Rimbaud issued another ultimatum: return to school, get a job or leave home. Rimbaud told her that he was 'not cut out for the stage' and threatened to go and live in a derelict sandstone quarry in the woods to the east of Charleville: a place where Nature was slowly eradicating the traces of civilization and where he used to go with Delahaye to smoke a pipe and – an early sign of his interest in natural history – to analyse the contents of owl-droppings. Delahaye was to bring him his daily bread and tobacco and he would live there like a suburban hermit.[9]

Interestingly, Mme Rimbaud relented. It was the first hint of a small change which affected the outward appearance of their relationship so dramatically that it can easily be misinterpreted as a complete volte-face: bullied or indulged, Rimbaud had never wanted for attention. It has also been suggested, by people who knew her, that Mme Rimbaud was not entirely unhappy to have a son who antagonized the whole town.

Ten days later, instead of moving to the woods, Rimbaud sold his watch and bought a third-class ticket to Paris. This time, he was better prepared: he had money in his pocket and an address in the city. On 25 February, he arrived at the Gare de l'Est, found his way to the Rue Bonaparte on the Left Bank, walked into the Librairie Artistique and introduced himself as a friend of the bookshop's part-owner, Paul Demeny.

Rimbaud had come to see his heroes – a band of satirical writers and artists who shot to prominence at the end of the Empire and who now found, under the neurotic Third Republic, that their distorted view of politics was more realistic than ever: Eugène Vermersch, Jules Vallès (both under constant threat of exile) and the poet-cartoonist, André Gill. To Rimbaud, this was the heroic, revolutionary fringe: men who had reached adulthood without losing their sense of humour or their taste for destruction.

Someone at the bookshop gave him the address of André Gill, who had a studio a few streets away on the Boulevard d'Enfer. Rimbaud had often copied Gill's cartoons from the satirical weeklies, *La Lune* and *L'Éclipse*. He drew in pencil, rubbing the paper with a moistened finger 'in order to obtain a more pictorial manner'. Sometimes, he gave the drawings to carters to pay for a ride – undermining the system and manufacturing a trade-item at the same time.[10]

On reaching the Boulevard d'Enfer, he found that Gill was out. Fortunately, the key was in the lock. He opened the door, lay down on a large divan and fell asleep.[11]

According to Gill, he returned to find a small but strangely daunting figure with the face of 'a lugubrious mule'.[12] Asked what he was doing, Rimbaud replied, 'Having a nice dream', to which Gill retorted, 'I, too, have nice dreams, but I have them at home.' Rimbaud explained that he was a poet and that, therefore, it was Gill's duty as an artist to help him stay in Paris. Gill reminded him that Paris had just survived a 132-day siege and was more interested in food than in poetry – or, as a disgusted Rimbaud put it when he next saw Delahaye: 'Paris is nothing but a stomach now.' In any case, according to Gill, literature was a dirty profession, only slightly more agreeable than prostitution and considerably less lucrative.

A poem in Gill's *La Muse à Bibi* (1881) gives some idea of the advice he must have offered Rimbaud – the platitudes that were conventionally meted out to provincial poets: 'Use up your life and your desires / In ephemeral exhilaration. / Drink to the dregs the bitter cup, / And watch your hair turn white. [. . .] Fate holds in store, to reward you for your toil, / The scorn of the exultant fool.' This was quite good advice in the circumstances: Gill himself later poured scorn on Rimbaud and, like some of his colleagues, borrowed aspects of his poetry, but without acknowledging the influence.[13]

Rimbaud was given ten francs and told to go home to his mother. Yet his next letter to Demeny shows that he stayed on in Paris until 10 March. During those two weeks, he seems to have disappeared into the city like an escaped convict. The letter to Demeny suggests that he spent much of his time in bookshops, keeping warm, looking out for writers and catching up with the latest publications. His letter, in fact, is little more than a bibliography – the account of an explorer who ignores exotic landscapes and confines himself to lists of merchandise. Gill was right: Paris was fascinated by its navel. 'Every publisher has his *Siege* or his *Siege Diary*. Sarcey's *Siege* is on its 14th edition. I saw tedious streams of photographs and drawings devoted to the Siege – you can't imagine.'

The most exciting items were the 'admirable *fantaisies*' of Jules Vallès and Eugène Vermersch in the hysterically subversive newspaper, *Le Cri du Peuple*. There were rumblings of revolution in the 'stomach': now that a humiliating peace treaty was being negotiated with Kaiser Wilhelm, the proletariat who had suffered nineteen years of Empire and four months of siege felt betrayed. Vermersch and Vallès wrote their articles in a shrill, acrimonious tone that exactly matched the mood of the poorer quarters. How will the Stock Exchange underwrite the reparations demanded by Bismarck, asked Vermersch. With 'the blood of the people!'

The fact that Rimbaud refers to these violent, histrionic pieces as '*fantaisies*' (a word he also applies to his own poetry) shows that he was primarily interested in the literary fruits of national disaster. This explains why poems like 'L'Orgie parisienne' have proved impossible to pin to a particular square on the calendar.[14] Rimbaud was using political invective for poetic effect, revolutionizing the revolution, mounting his rhetorical firework display with live ammunition.

Biographically, 'L'Orgie parisienne' has the enormous interest of containing the first blurry snapshots of the Paris that entered Rimbaud's eyes, filtered through the lurid panes of *Les Fleurs du Mal*: 'Here is the night of pleasure with deep spasms / Descending into the street. O desolate drinkers, / Drink!' 'What does the whore Paris care / About your bodies and your souls, your poisons and your rags?' It was a city of 'dead palaces' covered in 'planks', a 'stinking ulcer' on the face of Nature.

Contemporary writers agree that post-siege Paris was a horribly drab sight: every tree had been chopped up for firewood, statues were veiled in black crêpe, Prussian shells had left gaping holes in apartment blocks, and the streets were full of beggars and rubbish; yet, in Rimbaud's 'Orgie parisienne', 'The Poet says unto thee, "Splendid is thy Beauty!"' Rimbaud's sufferings should not be exaggerated. He was on holiday from Charleville, testing his thoughts on new surroundings. He walked through the city as if through a gigantic picture-book, feasting on theatre bills, advertisements, pamphlets and shop signs. He was the only writer of the time who was living the life of a *misérable*. He slept in coal barges on the Seine, competed with dogs for scraps of food, and somehow managed to survive.

He was unlikely to starve as a result of false pride. One day, he told Delahaye, he noticed people laughing at him as he passed. Looking down, he saw the herring he had just bought peeking out of his trouser flap. True or not, this self-portrait as vagrant poet with a fish in his pants shows that he had the cheerful detachment that makes it possible to survive long periods of loneliness. The belittling eye of his mother was a constant companion, just as her scathing remarks crop up in his letters and even in *Une Saison en Enfer*, like salutary reminders of reality: 'more idle than a toad'; 'Art is folly'; 'I am a brute'.

His other main asset was his willingness to cross thresholds and to ignore the concept of private property. Exhaustion and helplessness, he found, gave him a kind of ghostly invulnerability:

> On the roads, on winter nights, without shelter, clothes or food, a voice gripped my frozen heart: 'Weakness or strength: there you are, it's strength. You know neither where you are going nor why. Enter where you will. Answer everything. You won't be murdered any more than if you were a corpse.' In the morning, I had such a lost expression and such a deathly demeanour that the people I met *may not have seen me*.[15]

Rimbaud gave up the struggle on 10 March, slipped through the Prussian lines and headed east along country roads. After two weeks in the city, he was as crafty as a beggar. At each town, he marched into the *mairie*, introduced himself to the mayor as an irregular soldier who had just been discharged, and set off again with a municipal hand-out of money and food.

Six days and 150 miles later, he was back in Charleville with a bad case of bronchitis, only to discover that something momentous had happened in Paris. Government troops had refused to fire on protesting women, workers had seized key positions in the city, two generals had been lynched, and the Government had fled to Versailles. Paris was now an independent people's republic. Elections for a Commune were to be held on 26 March.

The pantomime invective that Rimbaud found so inspiring in anarchist journals like *Le Père Fouettard* ('orator, writer, poet and bottom-smacker') was now the voice of an official administration. Paris had fallen to poets who worked with laws and human beings instead of words. The new Chief of Police was the twenty-four-year-old Raoul Rigault (an old friend of Paul Verlaine). Rigault had the Préfecture's secret file of police informers published in a newspaper, complete with addresses, devised a tribunal in which politically correct children would denounce their parents, removed the word 'Saint' from every street-name in Paris, rounded up priests, and promised to issue a warrant for God's arrest.

For Rimbaud, this sudden transformation of extreme ideology into concrete fact seemed to confirm a suspicion that words might have a direct, controllable influence on reality. Like an alternative town-crier, he spread the news in the streets of Charleville, shouting 'Order is vanquished!' He even composed his own revolutionary Constitution (now lost, or perhaps never written down).[16] Had it been published, Rimbaud might have joined Balzac, Hugo and Zola as one of the Western writers whose works remained available behind the Iron Curtain. Instead of people's representatives, there would be a permanent state of referendum. The family would be abolished, as would 'slave-owning' (i.e. having children). Stone-masons would rank higher than orators. Everyone would have equal access to education, scientific progress would accelerate, and the human race would establish intelligent communication with plants, animals and extraterrestrials. Some truly new forms of poetry would emerge . . .

Rimbaud decided to return to Paris to witness the dawn of the new age.

*

SINCE THE PARIS Commune of 1871 became an inspiration to Marx, Lenin, Mao and the students of May 1968, conservative scholars have sometimes tried to discredit the evidence that Rimbaud had anything to do with what they see as a historical obscenity, arguing, incorrectly, that Rimbaud could not have been in Paris at the time.[17] Left-wing critics, 'rescuing Arthur Rimbaud for a left that is in dire need of him' (Terry Eagleton),[18] have exaggerated his involvement, thereby further discrediting the evidence.

In less controversial circumstances, the evidence that Rimbaud witnessed the Commune would be considered reasonably sound.[19] Verlaine and Delahaye both learned, from Rimbaud himself, that he was in Paris during the Commune. The artist Forain, who was then scraping a living as a sign-painter, claims to have 'loafed about Paris during the Commune' with Rimbaud. An unnamed source in Africa heard Rimbaud say that he had been 'imprisoned' by soldiers of the Commune, and in his native region, he was rumoured to be an ex-Communard (though the word was used in the same vague way as 'Bolshie' half a century later). 'Young Raimbault' is also mentioned in a secret police report of 1873 as having 'belonged, under the Commune, to the Paris irregulars'. Only two people who knew

Rimbaud personally – Izambard and Isabelle – deny that he was in Paris at the time, but this was pure conjecture on their part.

The argument about Rimbaud's political affiliation now has such a long history that the initial terms of the debate have been forgotten. His main idea was to get back to Paris as soon as possible, not to carry a gun or support a regime. The three poems which seem most clearly Communard – 'L'Orgie parisienne', 'Chant de guerre parisien' and 'Les Mains de Jeanne-Marie' – are collages of contemporary allusion, not commemorations or manifestos.[20] To celebrate the spine-crushing, machine-gun-wielding hands of a female Communard (in 'Les Mains de Jeanne-Marie') is not to declare one's voting intentions. The words Rimbaud scribbled in the margin of his 'Chant de guerre parisien' suggest anything but a serious attempt to construct a political analysis: 'What rhymes! Oh, what rhymes!'

If French history were to be reconstructed from the works of Arthur Rimbaud, it would appear as a tail-chasing sequence of incomprehensible explosions. His 'Communard' songs are beautifully constructed barricades in which the elegant furniture of conventional verse is jammed up against the cheap rubbish of the vernacular. The final lesson of these poems seems to be that anything can be made to mean anything.

Once the political situation is seen to have been of secondary importance, Rimbaud's actions fall into a plausible sequence. On 12 April, the Collège de Charleville reopened for full business in its original premises. On the same day – surely not by coincidence – the resurrected *Progrès des Ardennes* took Rimbaud on as a secretary. His job was to edit readers' letters and perhaps to write the occasional article. His prospects were good: a teacher at the Collège de Charleville heard that Rimbaud was shaping up to become a newspaper editor.[21] 'I have appeased the Mouth of Darkness for a time', he told Demeny.

But then, five days later, in the general mood of reactionary panic, the *Progrès des Ardennes* was forced to fold. 'Ordinary life', which Rimbaud claimed to have discarded when he left school, was closing in. However, Delahaye had given him an idea: if he had volunteered for the National Guard, he could probably have stayed on in Paris a little longer.

Rimbaud's wages from the newspaper would have enabled him to take the train at least some of the way to Paris. He would have arrived, towards the end of April 1871, at the delirious height of the Commune. This extraordinary carnival-regime is usually viewed from the far end, through the bloody screen of the '*Semaine Sanglante*' (22–28 May), when French government troops tortured and massacred thousands of peaceful citizens who had been caught up in the 'madness'. But in April, the mood, like the weather, was bright and sunny. The poet Jean Richepin said that he 'never had so much fun': 'He was 18 years old, he had a uniform, some money, lots of women, and freedom in springtime Paris.'[22]

This is also the mood of Rimbaud's accounts to Delahaye. He reached the gates of Paris and introduced himself to a group of Communard guerrillas who thought him a perfect little terrorist and took him to the Caserne de Babylone on the Left Bank. The barracks was being used as a depot for miscellaneous soldiers who might be called upon in an emergency – deserters, unemployed sailors, freeloaders and runaways like Rimbaud. The men were unarmed but received some basic training. They whiled away the hours with manly pursuits. Rimbaud told Delahaye about 'the drunken Zouave [a soldier of the French Algerian army, like Rimbaud's father] who was trying, through a hole in the boards, to piss on the face of a man who was snoring on a straw mattress on the floor below'.

None of this amounts to political *engagement*. It looks more like an example of Rimbaud's search for loose structures and temporary commitments that could serve as a nomadic base for the imagination:

> To whom shall I hire myself? What beast should I worship? What holy image are we attacking? Which hearts shall I break? What lie must I keep? – In what blood shall I walk?[23]

In one sense, Rimbaud had already found his place in society and was unusual only when compared with other writers. Statistically, he was part of a nationwide epidemic, one of tens of thousands of boys who had run away from home and were now thought to constitute a separate class: a vast tribe of vagabonds who lived among respectable people like 'wild animals' and who, 'for a cigar or a glass of brandy, would set fire to all of Paris'.[24] The Commune had formed two battalions with these 'wild animals': the 'Enfants perdus' and the 'Pupilles de la Commune', aged between seven and sixteen. Many of them would be imprisoned or executed in the aftermath.[25]

Rimbaud decided to head for home when the government troops stationed in Versailles began to bomb their own capital city – though not necessarily because he was afraid of being killed. His 'Chant de guerre parisien' joyfully describes the shelling as a springtime invasion of insects – as far as one can tell: the meaning is swamped by the huge, comical rhymes that spatter the rectilinear stanzas like petrol-bombs in the city streets. He seems to have passed through Villers-Cotterêts to the north-east of Paris, which might indicate that he was making for the Ardennes Canal (Mallarmé later heard that Rimbaud sometimes rode with bargemen):[26] it joined the Seine fifteen miles from Paris and eventually passed one mile to the north of Roche before joining the river Meuse near Charleville. Perhaps the new poem he would bring to Paris with him on his next visit was already taking shape:

> As I was descending the impassive rivers,
> Suddenly I felt the haulers let me go:
> Screaming Redskins had taken them for targets
> And nailed them naked to their gaudy poles. [. . .]

Rimbaud is often said to have returned from the Commune disenchanted, depoliticized, and determined to console himself by writing lovely poems. On 13 May, from Charleville, he wrote to his old teacher and enclosed the most disgusting poem Izambard had ever read ('Le Cœur volé'). The Commune had inspired him to pursue his own revolution. A glorious plan had formed. Just like Izambard – back 'in the academic trough' – Rimbaud was going to render himself useful to 'Society', as he explained in his letter:

I'm now making myself as scummy as I can.* Why? I want to be a poet, and I'm working at turning myself into a *Seer*. You won't

---

* *'Je m'encrapule'*: a verb created from *'crapule'* ('scum', 'riff-raff'); applied in 'Le Forgeron', as a perverse eulogy, to the proletariat of the French Revolution.

understand any of this, and I'm almost incapable of explaining it to you. The idea is to reach the unknown by the derangement* of *all the senses*. It involves enormous suffering, but one must be strong and be a born poet. And I've realized that I am a poet. It's really not my fault.

---

* *'Dérèglement'* (from *'règle'*, 'rule') also means 'dissoluteness'. *'Dérégler'* (to upset or unsettle) is normally applied to habits, mechanisms or stomachs.

8

The Seer

'Stat mater dolorosa, dum pendet filius.'

(Rimbaud to Izambard, 13 May 1871:
from John 19:25, via the Catholic liturgy)

THE ABSTRUSE, disjointed and obscene letter that Rimbaud sent to Izambard on 13 May 1871 is one of the sacred texts of modern literature. Like the more substantial letter written two days later, it contained the equation that has often been treated as a poetic $E = mc^2$: *'Je est un autre'* ('I is somebody else').

As far as Izambard could tell, Rimbaud's main purpose in writing was to assert his independence in as irritating a manner as possible. When he wrote his memoirs in 1927, he was still smarting from this 'vicious' letter: 'detestable tomfoolery', 'the *literaturicidal* profession of faith of an emancipated schoolboy'; 'I confess I was taken aback'. Rimbaud had written to his old teacher as if he had a score to settle.

> So you're a teacher again. We owe ourselves to Society, you told me. You're a member of the teaching body. You're in the right rut. I, too, am observing the principle: I'm having myself cynically *kept*. I've been digging up old idiots from school. I give them all the stupid, foul and filthy things I can think of, in actions and in words, and they pay me in beer and whores.*

---

* *'En bocks et en filles'*. To save Rimbaud's virginity, the word *'filles'* (girls or whores)

To give Izambard a flavour of the filth, Rimbaud enclosed a short poem called 'Le Cœur supplicié'.* It was a jaunty little piece in the form of a *triolet* – the tight, disciplined form that was normally reserved for humorous ditties:

> My sad heart slobbers at the poop . . .
> My heart is full of cheap tobacco!
> They're pelting it with spurts of soup,
> My sad heart slobbers at the poop . . .
> Under the sneerings of the troop
>
> [. . .]
>
> I'll have intestinal retchings
> If my sad heart is defiled:
> When their chews are all dried up,
> What shall we do, O stolen heart?

'Le Cœur volé' (the usual title) was such a tangle of puns and themes – seasickness, tobacco-chewing, sodomy and the Sacred Heart – that Rimbaud felt it necessary to add a helpful hint: 'It does not mean nothing.'

For Izambard, the main motif was only too clear: the '*cœur*' (heart) was also the penis, and the poem described the poet's rape by a gang of jeering soldiers. 'Heartless', Izambard had called him. Here was Rimbaud's explanation of what had happened to his heart: it had been soiled with mockery and 'depraved' with 'insults'. When he sat 'encrapulating' himself at the café, he was simply acting out what had already taken place, performing like a cynical prostitute for the 'idiots' who gobbled up his tales of homosexual orgies and believed him when he claimed to have taken every stray dog in Charleville to his bedroom and 'subjected them to the ultimate indignity'.†2

---

has been interpreted as a synonym of '*fillettes*', which in some parts of France means a half-bottle of wine; but there is no evidence that '*filles*' was ever used in this sense.1

* 'The Tortured Heart'. Later, 'Le Cœur volé' ('The Stolen Heart') or 'Le Cœur du pitre' ('The Heart of the Clown').

† The original account by Delahaye has the masculine or indefinite plural, '*chiens*'. Cf. Enid Starkie's damage-limitation version: 'he delighted in enticing *bitches* to his home'.3

Spattered with Rimbaud's obscenities, Izambard not surprisingly missed the intellectual point of the letter. 'Le Cœur volé' was not a simple slice of autobiography. Like his 'confessions' at the café, it was a kind of cleansing operation, 'an antithesis', as Rimbaud later explained, to religious vignettes 'in which Cupids disport themselves and plumed hearts soar'.[4] He was exposing the self-pitying, bleeding heart of Romantic verse as a sham – a prostituted libido that dressed itself up as sacred sentiment and believed its own lies. This is what he meant when he told some acquaintances in Charleville, 'I owe my superiority to the fact that I have no heart.'[5] Obscenity would scrape away these egotistical pretensions and restore a kind of purity.

In the theoretical part of his letter, Rimbaud's target was not Romantic verse but one of the main props of western thought and education. In his view, Descartes was sadly mistaken. His '*Cogito ergo sum*' was incorrect even before it reached its '*ergo*':

> It is wrong to say, 'I think'. One ought to say, 'I am thought'. [. . .]
> I is somebody else.[6]

'*Je est un autre*' is probably the most frequently misunderstood sentence in French literature. Interpretations have ranged from the banal to the fantastic: an allusion to the Romantic commonplace of the split personality; a needlessly obscure way of saying, 'I was a poet and I didn't know it';[7] proof that Rimbaud was schizophrenic; a mysterious formula which passes human understanding.

In the context of the letter, its meaning is almost clear. Rimbaud was making a scientific observation. The identity conveniently labelled 'I' – the indivisible, morally responsible self on which Christianity and Western philosophy are founded – was a fiction, a crude name-tag that presented the human mind as a single lump of consciousness.

The source of this insight was the comparatively simple phenom-enon of introspection – the mind observing itself at work. Writing to Demeny two days later, Rimbaud described the process with a splendid image: the poet was both the audience and the conductor of his own orchestra.

> This much seems obvious to me: I am present at the hatching of my thought. I watch and I listen. A flick of the baton and the symphony stirs in the depths or bounds on to the stage.

There was nothing new about Rimbaud's insight. He might have found similar ideas in the works of Baudelaire or Hippolyte Taine. He differed, however, in the use he intended to make of this insight. In the same mood of demystification that inspired the Communards, he had decided to abolish the constraints of education and morality and to seize control of the means of intellectual production. This was the cause of his excitement. Like motion for Newton, time for Einstein, the weather for Lorenz, something intangible seemed to have been brought within the reach of analysis. In terms that were unavailable to him in 1871, he was considering the possibility of detaching the censorious superego from the endlessly imaginative id.

This abstract scenario is more familiar as the story of Rimbaud's first sixteen years. The places in which he describes his mind at work – attic, cellar, bedroom and latrine – are all places of refuge from his mother, the superego incarnate. '*Je est un autre*' was the motto of a child who had been taught to question his sincerity at every turn. Mme Rimbaud's tyrannical interference had forced him into ever deeper parts of his mind, down to the underground passages where resistance could be organized.

Vital questions were left unanswered: what structure would take the place of the superego? Can the personality survive without a moral code? Is it possible to dispense with upbringing and background and yet retain some effective intelligence?

Rimbaud's provisional answer first appears in the form of a coincidence: the letters to Izambard and Demeny (13 and 15 May 1871) were written immediately before and after his younger sister Isabelle's First Communion (14 May).

The significance of the ceremony, for Rimbaud, is recorded in a poem which used to be considered his most offensive. It still sounds like a peculiar mixture of social anthropology and pornographic anticlericalism. 'Les Premières communions' implies that the Catholic Church exploits the sexual instincts of young girls in order to trap them into marriage and conformity. Communion itself is an initiation rite in which God's priestly pimp introduces the flesh of the holy paedophile into the virgin's mouth. Instead of dwelling on the innocence of the young communicant, Rimbaud fastens on her guilty attraction to Jesus, the crucified exhibitionist in a skimpy loin-cloth who displays himself on church walls. The blood of the Passion is also the blood of menstruation: 'She spent her holy night in the latrines.'

> Vaguely immodest forms of curiosity
> Horrify her dream of chaste, blue things
> That caught itself in the vicinity of celestial tunics,
> And the linen with which Jesus veils his nudity.

This violent engagement with the mystery of Communion can be attributed to relatively trivial causes: adolescent revulsion to sexual realities; a protective attitude towards his little sisters, who seem to have admired the brilliant Arthur as much as they turned their noses up at Frédéric; a desire to emulate his priest-bashing heroes in the socialist press. Some of the attraction of Rimbaud's early work lies not in its originality but in its exaggerated conformity to common aspects of puberty.

Rimbaud's unusual achievement was to put his feelings to a practical use. Having already turned himself into the most academically successful and morally reprehensible pupil in north-eastern France, he was now toying with the idea of reincarnating himself as a nineteenth-century Jesus Christ.

When he likened his 'encrapulation' to the Crucifixion – '*Stat mater dolorosa, dum pendet filius*'* – Izambard took it to be a puerile joke: Arthur Rimbaud as a delinquent Messiah, crucifying himself to spite his mother. Yet this twisting of Gospel phrases reflects a determination to use the life of Christ as a career plan. Just as other poets provided him with negative models for his own poems, Christianity, purged of its rules and superstitions, would provide him with a structure for his intellectual quest.

*

THE DAY AFTER Isabelle's Communion, Rimbaud sent a long letter to Paul Demeny. It took the form of didactic prose interrupted, like a church service, by two 'psalms' and 'a pious hymn' (his poems,

---

* 'The grieving mother stands, while the son hangs [on the Cross].'

'Chant de guerre parisien', 'Mes Petites amoureuses' and 'Accroupissements').

Rimbaud's sermon of 15 May 1871 is commonly referred to as the *Lettre du Voyant* ('Letter of the Seer'). On a first reading, it hardly seems to deserve such a grand title. 'Letter of the Excited Schoolboy' would give a more accurate impression of the torrential arguments and half-digested readings – alchemists, socialists, psychologists and mechanistic philosophers.

The main points appear to be these:

1. The true poet is a 'seer', but a seer who creates new realities and becomes the pioneer of a new race. For this, a special training programme is required:

> The first study of the man who wishes to be a poet is complete knowledge of himself. He searches his mind, inspects it, tries it out and learns to use it. As soon as he knows his mind, he must cultivate it.

'Cultivation' was to consist of tinkering with the mind as God created it, 'to make the soul monstrous': 'Imagine a man planting and cultivating warts on his face.' To the notion of a 'derangement of all the senses', he now added the crucial adjective: '*raisonné*' ('reasoned' or 'rational'). This was not to be a simple hallucinogenic stupor. It was a scientific experiment. Drugs would certainly play a role in the process of sensory derailment, but not yet. Charleville had no opium dens, and hashish, though legal, was a rare commodity.

2. The poet-seer will create a new 'universal language':

> This language will be soul for soul's sake, summing up everything, perfumes, sounds and colours, thought latching on to thought and pulling.

Though it sounds like aesthetics-fiction, this is actually a workable description of the idiom Rimbaud was already developing – the merging of different senses, images spiralling off other images instead of referring back to the controlling 'I': a poetic equivalent of the Copernican revolution.

3. The new age will be an age of unbridled intelligence, reminiscent of a socialist utopia:[8]

These poets will be! When the endless servitude of woman is broken, when she lives for and by herself, man – who until now has been abominable – will release her from her duties and she too will be a poet! She will find the unknown! Will her worlds of thought differ from our own? She will discover strange, unfathomable, repulsive and delicious things. We will take them and understand them.

4. To emphasize the novelty of his scheme, Rimbaud ended with a high-speed, 600-word history of poetry from antiquity to the present. It was a tale of stupidity, sloth and accidental insight. Since the end of the Golden Age, poetry had been nothing but 'rhymed prose, a game, the corpulence and glory of countless idiotic generations'. A complete waste of effort.

The first Romantics were swine to their own pearls: 'seers without really noticing'. The Parnassians had tried to galvanize the ancient corpse of Greek poetry, while Victor Hugo, despite being 'pigheaded', had glimpsed 'the unknown' in his visionary poems and in Les Misérables.

But since inspecting the invisible and listening to the unheard-of is something other than reviving the spirit of dead things, Baudelaire is the first seer, the king of poets, a real God. Even then, the milieu in which he lived was too arty; and the form that is supposed to be his finest feature is stingy. Inventing the unknown calls for new forms.

The history ended with a scrapyard of second-rate poets. Rimbaud divided all the Parnassians into mock categories: 'innocents', 'schoolboys', 'dead men and imbeciles', 'journalists', 'Bohemians', etc. Only two were classified as 'seers' – a forgotten Parnassian called Albert Mérat[9] and Paul Verlaine, 'a true poet'.

For all its insults, the Lettre du Voyant is a gripping piece of literary criticism, a curiously plausible attempt to reconcile the two antagonistic trends of nineteenth-century poetry: the 'bourgeois' belief in endless technological progress and the spiritual aspirations of the Romantics. For Baudelaire, poetry had been a source of consoling illusions. For Rimbaud, these shimmering illusions would one day solidify into social fact. Poetry would no longer simply keep step with reality; 'it will precede it'.

Most of this was lost on Demeny. Rimbaud's ability to enthuse about improbable things smelled of a practical joke. Every surge of seriousness was accompanied by a cheerful irony which shows how disarming he could be, even in the pulpit. The nuggets of precision were swallowed up by glorious Gothic visions of the poet as a Promethean Satan, the Romantic Lucifer whose role is to rescue man from God: 'the great invalid, the great criminal, the great damned, – and the supreme Sage!'

> For he reaches the *unknown*! [. . .] and even if, in panic, he ends up losing the ability to understand his own visions, at least he will have seen them! He may burst as he bounds through amazing, unnamable things – other horrible workers will follow.

Rimbaud's willingness to take his own mind seriously should not be underestimated. He was still trying to resolve the dilemma he had raised in the Ophelia poem: to enter the 'unknown', the poet had to divest himself of personal identity; but without that identity, how could the visions be comprehended? How could 'derangement' be reconciled with 'reason'?

If there was any insincerity in the letter, it lay in the humdrum details. He signed off with a hint that he was about to go and join his brother anarchists in Paris. But since the perimeter defences had been breached by a vindictive government army and since the Commune was obviously doomed, this may simply have been a ruse to extract a swift response from Demeny.[10]

*

RIMBAUD DID NOT leave for Paris. A few days after he wrote his letter, the Commune was wiped out by government troops. It was the bloodiest week in French history: a savage humiliation of the proletariat. Thousands were shot, inexpertly tortured or shipped to the penal colonies without a proper trial. Women carrying bottles in the street were bayoneted by soldiers who had heard of the mythical, bomb-throwing '*pétroleuses*'. More people died during the '*Semaine Sanglante*' than in the Reign of Terror or the Franco-Prussian War.[11]

There is no evidence that Rimbaud was especially upset by the defeat of French socialism. In his letter to Izambard, he had contrasted himself with the 'workers' who were dying in Paris: 'Work now? Never, never. I'm on strike.' The Commune was an example. It proved that the most extraordinary notions could be turned into realities. In daily life, nothing had changed. No people's republic had come to jerk Charleville out of its apathy. The 'lead-helmeted administration' of Mme Rimbaud was still in power.

He now withdrew (as he put it three months later) into his 'loathsome, inept, obstinate and mysterious labour, answering inquiries and crude, malicious remarks with silence, behaving with dignity in my extra-legal position'.

There was no outward sign that Rimbaud was engaged in anything that might be described as 'work'. On weekday mornings, through the refectory windows, boys and teachers saw the former glory of the Collège loping across the square, sending up clouds of black smoke from his clay pipe, waiting for the public library to open. His hair spilled over his collar. Long hair signified artistic pretensions. For Rimbaud, it was an important part of his 'martyrdom'. He was jeered at in town and stoned by peasants in the village where Delahaye now lived, but he refused to take a different route. In the evening, he entertained the 'idiots' at the café. Years later, a civil servant still remembered being subjected to Rimbaud's theory of what to do with '*gêneurs*': men whose principal function in life was to prevent someone more able from taking their job. Solution: torture them slowly to death.

Rimbaud was still hoping to find a sinecure in Paris, but he had antagonized Izambard, and Demeny had turned out to be useless – or almost. When Rimbaud wrote to him on 10 June, he asked for a copy of Demeny's *Les Glaneuses*, 'which I should like to re-read and which I can't possibly buy, since my mother hasn't favoured me with a single brass farthing for the last six months'. The year before, he had told Izambard that he was so desperate for books that he had even re-read *Les Glaneuses*, by Demeny ... The extra copy was obviously destined for the secondhand bookshop.

By the time he wrote to Izambard on 12 July, French poetry had become a commercial traveller's stock-list. Even seers needed money. Rimbaud owed the bookseller 33.25 francs – 'an enormous debt'.*

---

* About £106 or $169 today; in 1871, the price of five poetry books, three Charleville–Paris train tickets or 140 mugs of beer.

His mother might try to use it against him and force him to take a job in Charleville. 'Do you want to hang on to *Les Glaneuses*? The schoolboys of the Ardennes might fork out 3 francs to go pottering about in them there azure skies.'

> I'd know how to convince the grasping hypocrite [the bookseller] that the purchase of such a collection would bring astounding profits. [. . .] I'm certain that I'll find I have the disgraceful effrontery to succeed in this secondhand business. [. . .]
>
> If you have any publications that are unseemly on a teacher's shelves and you happen to notice, don't hesitate. But please be quick!

This 'disgraceful' peddling of other poets' work is an exact, commercial equivalent of what Rimbaud was doing on the page. Few poets ever profited so richly from bad poetry.

A typical example of the blandness against which Rimbaud wrote his own poems can be found, appropriately enough, in Demeny's *Les Glaneuses*. Its influences are all quite obvious and all about thirty years out of date. In Demeny's world, a vague, cosy pleasantness referred to as 'poetry' still exists in the colonies in the form of hummingbirds and 'silvery lakes', but in present-day Douai, it has been 'killed' by 'steam', though the Industrial Revolution has at least supplied some 'realistic' details: dark factories and 'wretched pariahs' (the urban poor). The whole world is out to rob the poet of his innocence, and the fate of 'spotless virgins', who all end up as prostitutes or matrons, is frequently bemoaned. There is no effort at sustained thought, nor any attempt to question assumptions since this might create an inconsistency in the poem.

One of Demeny's favourite themes is the blessed simplicity of the village church, contrasted with the 'unbridled luxury' of Notre-Dame de Paris. The opening of Rimbaud's 'Premières communions' is a custard-pie in Demeny's sweetly smiling face:

> Talk about stupid – those village kirks,
> Where fifteen ugly brats, sliming up the pillars,
> Lisping out the holy blatherings, listen
> To a black grotesque with festering shoes.
> Yet the sun awakes, through the patterns of leaves,
> The old colours in the misshapen windows.

Rimbaud's lines have a didactic energy reminiscent of Courbet. Just as private wealth should be abolished, 'poetry', for Rimbaud, was not the exclusive property of a small number of choice realities. It consisted in the arrangement of realities and in a process of transformation akin to the natural processes that rot the priest's shoes and warp the church windows.

Demeny did nothing to help Rimbaud into print, although, fortunately, he kept all the poems Rimbaud sent him. Seventeen years later, he snootily remembered 'that bizarre creature': 'his early lucubrations seemed curious enough to be worth collecting'.[12]

It never seems to have occurred to Rimbaud that Demeny might have been reluctant to help a rival. Large imaginations sometimes find it difficult to enter small minds. It was too late now in any case. Rimbaud had a new idea, as he told Demeny on 10 June:

> Burn – *it is my wish*, and I think you'll respect my decision as you would a dead man's – burn *all the poems I was stupid enough* to give you during my stay in Douai.

He may of course have meant 'the poems I was stupid enough to give to *you*'. At least one of the poems Demeny was asked to destroy was later sent to Verlaine. But this purification by fire was also a symbolic act: he was killing off his old 'Bohemian' self, the cheery Tom Thumb with his shop-window sonnets and mass-produced images.

Rimbaud's pre-Parisian poems seem to confirm the Law of Recapitulation, according to which young painters had to pass through every preceding stage of their art like embryos re-enacting evolution. The history of world poetry in the 'Seer' letter is also a history of Rimbaud's own apprenticeship: Greek and Latin, 'games and relaxations', medieval and classical French, pseudo-religious snivellings *à la* Musset (associated by Rimbaud with 'seminarists', 'grocer boys' and, probably, with his earlier 'sanctimonious' self); then Victor Hugo, the Parnassians and Baudelaire.

Now he had reached the next stage. The poem he sent to Demeny on 10 June – 'Les Pauvres à l'église' ('Paupers in Church') – is the finest example of what, for a few weeks in the summer of 1871, was Rimbaud's new manner: a blend of Balzacian realism and socialist polemic.

Penned between benches of oak in corners of the church
Which their fetid breath has warmed, their eyes
Turned to the gold-drenched stalls and the choir
Of twenty mouths that bellow out the pious hymns;

Snuffing the smell of wax like fresh-baked bread,
Happy and humbled like beaten curs,
The paupers offer to the squire and master, God,
Their stubborn and pathetic prayers.

The women like to sit there smoothing benches
After the six dark days when God makes them suffer.
They cradle, corkscrewed up in strange pelisses,
Child-like things that nearly cry themselves to death.

The eaters of gruel, their grimy breasts pulled out,
A prayer in their eyes but never on their lips,
Watch a group of local lasses, a shambles,
Processing clumsily, their hats all out of shape.

Outside, cold and hunger, men all down the pub.
Another hour of this, then miseries untold!
Meanwhile, all around, the nasal whine and whisper –
A gathering of old turkey-throated crones:

Those frightened faces are there, and those epileptics
Who made them cross the road the other day,
And, waving their snouts over ancient missals,
The blind who enter courtyards on their mongrels' leash.

Slobbering the creed of cretins and beggars,
Reciting the never-ending moan to Jesus,
Who dreams aloft, all yellowed by the livid pane,
Far from the skinny misers and the pot-bellied rogues,

Far from the smells of flesh and mouldy garments,
A prostrate, morbid farce of gross, repellent gestures;
– And the praying blossoms into choice expressions,
And the mystic words take on an urgent tone,

When, from the nave where the sun is dying, with
Tawdry folds of silk, smiling greenly, the Ladies
From the nicer districts – Jesus! – nursing their livers,
Have their long yellow fingers kissed in the fonts.

That summer, Rimbaud practised several different forms of poetry, then gave them up, as if discarding accidental discoveries made on the way to a greater invention. Two long pieces mentioned in the letter of 15 May – 'Les Amants de Paris' and 'La Mort de Paris' – seem to have been lost for want of a stamp. Others began and ended in the form that his poems often take today: graffiti.

Misleadingly lumped together under the title *Poésies*, Rimbaud's forty surviving poems from January 1870 to September 1871 would ideally be published in volumes of three or four poems, each representing a distinct period. 'Les Pauvres à l'église' for instance would appear with 'Les Assis' – the half-human, half-chair 'sitting ones', supposedly inspired by the Charleville town librarian but applicable to any reluctant service-industry employee – and 'Accroupissements', one of the loveliest descriptions in French poetry of the act of defecation. An *abbé* descends the stairs on a hot night, clutching a white pot, while 'something like a bird moves softly in his bowels'. Around him, the furniture mutates into compromising objective correlatives of the *abbé*'s diseased mind: 'Sideboards have choirboy mouths, / Cracked open by sleep that brims with foul appetites.'

These poems make Rimbaud's Charleville one of the most distinctive regions of the fictional land that includes Balzac's Paris, Proust's Combray and Sartre's Bouville.[13] Rimbaudville has the hallucinatory quality of things that have become too familiar: the dungy warmth of an old dove-cote, the sun that shines like a scoured cauldron, the 'brioche yellows' on paper window-panes, the 'white ghost' of a blouse on a washing-line. Rimbaud used his feelings of disgust as an image-creating drug: rain is 'a lachrymal distillation', darkness 'slobbers on the woods', violets are the 'sugary spittle of black nymphs'.

Victor Hugo's famous description of his linguistic revolution – 'I declared all words free, equal and of age' – matches Rimbaud's poetry more closely than his own. Rimbaud was certainly aware of this, and it is significant that his best satirical poem appears to attack Victor

Hugo.[14] 'L'Homme juste' is a sarcastic reversal of Hugo's 'Ce que dit la Bouche d'Ombre': instead of the Mouth of Darkness appearing to Hugo, Victor Hugo appears to Arthur Rimbaud. This was Hugo the pontificating clown who, according to the anarchist press, had left the Commune in the lurch:

> [. . .]
>
> The Sage remained upstanding on his sturdy loins,
> A golden ray fell on his back. I started
> To sweat. 'Do you want to see the aerolites refulgent?'
> I screamed, 'And listen, standing up, to milky stars
> Hum with menstrual flux, and asteroidal swarms?
>
> Your head is being watched by night-time tricks,
> O Sage! You'd better get indoors. Say your prayers,
> And keep your mouth beneath your sweetly expiated sheet;
> And if a wanderer who's lost should hammer on your door,
> Say, "Brother, hie thee hence! I can't get up without a stick!"'
>
> And the Sage remained erect in the blue-hued
> Horror of lawns when the sun has dropped dead:
> 'So, would you put your kneepads up for sale,
> Old Man? Holy Pilgrim! Celtic Bard!
> Whinger on the Mount of Olives! Hand in a glove of pity!'
>
> [. . .]

This would certainly have been counted as one of the great verse satires of the late nineteenth century if it had been clear what Rimbaud was being satirical about. After several re-readings, some of the phrases – like the 'glove of pity' – turn out to have a scathing accuracy, applicable to any moral VIP who uses charity to keep their conscience and their image clean; yet this is obviously something more than strong opinion. Rimbaud can certainly be described as an anti-imperialist, but when his poems are read in chronological order, a peculiar fact emerges: almost all his attacks on Napoleon III were written *after* the Emperor's disappearance from French politics. Polemic was primarily an excuse for the broad vocabulary and violent images.

Whether or not these poems were 'studies' undertaken as part of

Rimbaud's training programme, they have the same blasphemous spirit as the 'Seer' letters. The poet appears as a Dr Frankenstein of the dictionary, stitching together his mockery of scientific rationalism. The Rimbaldian human being is a repellent piece of animated vegetation, a poxy assemblage of femurs, sinciputs, scapulas and hypogastria, a prey to cephalalgia, clottings, fluxions, rickets, nits and nasal mucus – a monster in the shape of a philosophical question-mark: if Man was made in the image of God, then what must God be like?

With its neologisms and barbarisms, its slang words jarring with the drawing-room syntax, Rimbaud's new idiom was dramatic proof that social distinctions in the new France were as virulent as ever. It was also an expression of his hybrid roots: urban and rural, bourgeois and peasant. Something in these destructive poems suggests a person who was not entirely unhappy to be 'smothered' by Charleville – a poet who was laying claim to his inheritance.

9

Departure

'One can never leave.'

('Mauvais sang', *Une Saison en Enfer*)

As THE END OF summer approached, Mme Rimbaud did her best to make Arthur's life of apparent idleness intolerable. The usual assumption is that he was desperate to leave for Paris; but the nervous letter he sent to Demeny on 28 August 1871 suggests that the boot of Mme Rimbaud should be given most of the credit for launching his career.

So far, he told Demeny,[1] all attempts to condemn him to 'hard labour for life in Charleville' had failed.

> Get a job by such and such a date, she said, or you're out!
> I refused to live like that, without giving my reasons. It would have been pitiful. [. . .]
> But now she's reached a point where she continually hopes for my ill-considered departure – my escape! Indigent and inexperienced, I'd end up in a reformatory, and that would be the last that anyone would hear of me!
> This is the gag of disgust that has been rammed into my mouth.

Mme Rimbaud had decided that Arthur might after all make a living by his pen, at least until he grew up. Any profession was better than none.

The prison door now stood open.

Two weeks before, on 15 August, Rimbaud had re-established contact with literary Paris, but in a manner that was scarcely designed to win friends. The 'imbecile' who had sent a Parnassian poem to Théodore de Banville in May 1870 now offered the 'Master' a long piece entitled 'Ce qu'on dit au poète à propos de fleurs' ('What one says to the poet on the subject of flowers'). He signed it 'Alcide Bava' ('Hercules Drooled'), suggesting an unsavoury infant prodigy.[2] 'Last year, I was only 17!' he lied. 'Have I progressed?'

It was a rhetorical question. The real question was: what did the poem mean? From the first stanza, it sounded like a series of offensive jokes:

> Thus, towards the black azure,
> Where the sea of topaz shimmers,
> In your evening will forever function
> The Lilies, those enemas of ecstasy.

A clue to Rimbaud's intentions can be found in the obnoxious poem he had recently submitted to a local republican newspaper, *Le Nord-Est*. It was supposed to be written by a crusty old monarchist complaining about liberals, but the brush of sarcasm was so broad that it also tarred the editor of the newspaper: 'When I see your readers, you clown, fiddling with your filthy organ in their hands . . .' It was a fine example of insult by exaggerated agreement. The editor had the wit not to accept it.[3]

Rimbaud's ode to Banville was similarly two-faced. At first, the 'I' sounds like a literal-minded philistine: 'Lilies! Lilies! You never see them! Yet in your Verse [. . .] those white flowers always shimmer!' Poets should write instead about important things like potato blight and guano. Agricultural subjects were in fact often treated in verse. Epic poems had been devoted to the beetroot. But Rimbaud was clearly not concerned with agriculture:

> Is a Flower – be it Rosemary
> Or Lily, living or dead – worth
> A sea bird's excrement,
> Or a single tear of candle-wax?

Here the mask begins to slip: this is Arthur Rimbaud disguised as a psychotic bourgeois, dreaming of a very different kind of progress

– the supernatural universe of the seer: 'Find flowers like muzzles, / Drooling gold pomades'. 'Find calyxes filled with Eggs of fire, / Cooking in their oils!' 'Find flowers that are chairs!'

If Rimbaud was still hoping to be fostered by the Parnassians, he was asking for a special role as the poet who would come to sweep out the salons of Victorian verse and incinerate their dusty bouquets: 'Hercules Drooled', the nemesis of the aspidistra. The poem was dated 14 July 1871: Bastille Day. The Commune was over but the revolution lived on. Banville had better look to his laurels.

Two weeks later, threatened with eviction, Rimbaud revised his procedure. Two possibilities came to mind. Either Demeny could help him to find one of those jobs 'which are not too absorbing – because thinking requires large slices of time'. Or – his preference – someone could set him up in Paris and fund his visionary project.

Rimbaud's hours of idleness at the Café Dutherme were about to pay off. One of the café's most conspicuous fixtures was a thirty-four-year-old 'clerk of indirect taxation' at a local sugar refinery, known to his friends as 'the High Priest'. A vast, unflappable man who looked like Holbein's Henry VIII, Charles Bretagne had the sort of oceanic erudition that is rarely channelled into books. He was especially interested in anything that might irritate priests, doctors and university professors – barbaric subjects from beyond the Hadrian's Wall of Academe: magic, alchemy, homoeopathy and telepathy. His latest passion was Arthur Rimbaud.[4]

Usually, the foul-mouthed little genius sat at his table in total silence, puffing at his pipe and scowling. Bretagne and his friend, Léon Deverrière – a cheerful republican who had taught philosophy at Charleville's other school – tried to uncork the magic bottle. They invited him to musical evenings at Bretagne's home, which sometimes ended at the brothel. They plied him with beer, tobacco, books and journals, and allowed him to use their addresses for his correspondence. In exchange, Rimbaud showed them his poems and was even persuaded to recite them.

Rimbaud's flower-like sensitivity to his immediate surroundings is normally associated only with his 'Verlainean' period in 1872, but the appreciative, older audience at the Café Dutherme certainly helped to emphasize his comical, anticlerical bent. His last Charleville poems still bear the faint impression of the chortling faces that first enjoyed them.

In contrast to the fussy Izambard and the unhelpful Demeny, Bretagne was keen to provide Rimbaud with a wider audience. Learning of his predicament, he told him about a Parisian poet he had met at Fampoux, near Arras, in the home of a sugar producer. His name was Paul Verlaine.

This was exciting news. In Rimbaud's catalogue of incompetents, Verlaine was the only living 'seer'. Bretagne offered to add his personal recommendation if Rimbaud decided to write. Moments later, Delahaye was sitting with a mug of beer at the largest table in the Café Dutherme, copying out some of Rimbaud's best poems in roundhand ('because', said Rimbaud, 'it can be read more quickly and looks more like printed text').

Rimbaud then wrote a letter (later destroyed by Verlaine's wife), not in the inscrutably derisive style he had used for Banville, but intimate and autobiographical: he was a devoted admirer of Verlaine's poetry, passionately sick of Charleville, and wished to come to Paris, on whose stony face he had cast himself now three times, only to slither back down into the sea of obscurity. He enclosed five poems – 'Les Effarés', 'Accroupissements', 'Les Douaniers', 'Le Cœur volé' and 'Les Assis' – and waited for a reply.[5]

The blushing novice holding out his begging-bowl to the experienced, older poet is a fairy-tale image. When Rimbaud wrote to Verlaine in early September 1871, he already had a clear picture of his correspondent. The go-between, Bretagne, was often described as a 'shady' character, which used to be a genteel code-word for 'homosexual'.[6] When Rimbaud asked him, 'Is Verlaine the man of his poetry?', and Bretagne replied, 'Yes, perhaps too much so', it is not difficult to guess what was meant.[7] Verlaine's latest poems, *Fêtes galantes*, had a tendentiously over-delicate quality that would now be called camp. Rimbaud had found them 'funny', 'bizarre' and 'adorable'. The earlier *Poèmes saturniens* were full of little hints: a poem on a transvestite which began by rhyming '*hommes*' with '*Sodomes*', or a peculiar, 'inverted' sonnet (tercets on top of quatrains) which implied that rich rhymes were an indicator of sexual preference – 'I still hate pretty women, / Assonant [i.e. poor] rhymes and prudent [male] friends.'[8]

In an age when censorship had sensitized most readers to illicit allusions, a significant rhyme was like a secret handshake. Rimbaud's letter to Verlaine showed that he had been paying attention. The five poems he chose to send him are not simply representative samples of his work. They all have something in common: bottoms and acts of pederasty. The supposedly innocent young poet had put together a highly suggestive anthology for his potential patron.

Three days later, still waiting for a reply, he wrote again with some more poems ('Mes Petites amoureuses', 'Les Premières communions' and 'L'Orgie parisienne') and some background details. He was 'planning to write a long poem, and I cannot work in Charleville'. 'My mother is a widow and extremely devout. She gives me only 10 centimes every Sunday to pay for my pew in church.' Then came what Verlaine later called another 'bizarre piece of information': if Verlaine took care of him, he would be 'less bother [to him] than a Zanetto'. Zanetto was the closest thing on the Parisian stage to a homosexual character: a little wandering musician of sixteen, played by the beautifully androgynous Sarah Bernhardt. In the play, if Zanetto promised to be 'no bother' ('I dine on a piece of fruit and I sleep in a chair'), it was because he hoped to seduce his host.[9]

Rimbaud was obviously flirting with Verlaine; but was this an expression of his personality, a sarcastic imitation of Verlaine or simply an attempt to make himself attractive? Signs that Delahaye and Rimbaud experimented with homosexuality are ambiguous:[10] taken literally, male banter of the time would suggest that heterosexuals were a small minority. Bretagne, on the other hand, as a man with practical experience, might have helped Rimbaud to explore an aspect of himself that was already one of the main themes of his work.

For over a year now, Rimbaud had been depicting authority figures as pederasts and paedophiles. The chairs on which 'Les Assis' squirm in sordid ecstasy are likened to captive toddlers – 'real little darlings in harness'. In *Un Cœur sous une soutane*, a young seminarist is 'sullied' in an unspecified manner by his masturbating superior. This was standard socialist invective, but the theme also occurs without the acrimonious remarks. Izambard, Delahaye and, later, Verlaine all heard Rimbaud reminisce fondly about being pawed by soldiers and

DEPARTURE

policemen. In the sonnet 'Les Douaniers' – a souvenir of tobacco-buying trips across the Belgian border with Delahaye – the poet quivers with excitement at the thought of being frisked by customs-men in the woods: 'Hell to the Delinquents whom his palm has stroked!'[11] Some of his stories at the café were intended to convey the same impression: homosexual men were generally believed to be immoderately fond of animals.[12]

There is no evidence that Rimbaud was 'profoundly disturbed' by the discovery of his sexuality. In fact, there is no evidence at this stage that he was homosexual at all. In the contradictory world of Rimbaud criticism, it is quite acceptable to be awed by his vast imagination and to believe at the same time that his sexual feelings were reducible to a tick on a questionnaire. Hinting at colourful forms of delinquency was part of his 'encrapulation'. It might even be said that it was precisely because he could rely on himself to find the thought of homosexual relations disquieting that he decided to investigate. These mental experiments were another attempt to push the personality off the rails, to annihilate illusions and to celebrate instincts that proved the fragility of a society founded on marriage and procreation.

There is nothing unusual about forbidden thoughts haunting the mind of an adolescent. The only abnormality in Rimbaud is his determination to identify and overcome his own resistance. The 'Seer' letter even suggests that some of these fantasies might form part of the training programme: '*All forms of love*, suffering and madness; he searches himself, exhausts every poison in himself . . .'

*

RIMBAUD WENT TO see Bretagne every day, hoping to find a letter from Verlaine. One day in mid-September, Bretagne handed him an envelope with a Paris postmark.

Verlaine had been on holiday and had just returned to his home in Montmartre to discover some 'lines of truly terrifying beauty' and some 'rather vague' details on their author. Anticipating criticisms that were later made of his own poetry, he advised M. Rimbaud not to disfigure his impeccable verse with neologisms, technical terms and foul language: his poetry was 'vigorous' enough as it was.[13]

Rimbaud agreed: these brash innovations showed a childish lack of confidence. He now had confirmation that he was a true poet. 'You are prodigiously well equipped for battle,' Verlaine told him in his indefinably *louche* style. 'I have as it were the smell of your lycan-thropy.'* M. Rimbaud should expect to hear from him again quite soon.

Verlaine wasted no time in spreading the word: a new star had risen in the east. The author of 'Les Premières communions' was already being talked about in the cafés and studios of Paris. It was generally agreed that the Charleville prodigy should be brought to the capital as soon as possible and offered financial support.

Then came the letter that changed everything – the wind that caught the harbour flags. A special fund had been set up and the Verlaines' maid was preparing the spare bedroom. The red carpet was rolled out for M. Rimbaud of Charleville: 'Come, dear great soul. We await you; we desire you.'[14] The envelope contained a money-order for a one-way ticket to Paris. Rimbaud was to leave from Charleville station the following Sunday.[15]

On the eve of his great departure, he went for a walk with Delahaye. It was a sunny autumn afternoon. They sat down on the edge of a wood and Rimbaud pulled out some sheets of paper. He had written a 100-line poem 'to show to the people in Paris'. The verse was quite regular, but the content was extraordinary. Abruptly, without any rhetorical introduction, a boat recounted its adventures since the massacre of its crew – its astounding visions and its gradual disintegration:

> Sweeter than to children the flesh of bitter apples,
> Green water penetrated my pinewood hull
> And washed me of the blue wine-stains and vomit,
> Scattering my grappling-hook and rudder.
>
> And since then, I have bathed in the Poem
> Of the Sea, infused with stars, lactescent,
> Devouring the verdant skies, where, pale, ecstatic
> Flotsam, sometimes a drowned man pensively descends.

---

* A lycanthrope is a werewolf. The word was applied to self-consciously Gothic forms of Romanticism and especially to French poetry's sheep-in-wolf's-clothing, Petrus Borel 'the Lycanthrope' (1809–59).

In mental time, 'Le Bateau ivre' (September) follows closely on the 'Seer' letter (May): the purification by dissolution, the loosening of the rivets and tackle that bind the personality, visions teetering on the brink of the incomprehensible, and a strange nostalgia for the future, where some mysterious *'Vigueur'* lies dormant in 'starry archipelagos'. There was the same self-irony as in the Bohemian poems of the previous summer, except that now the whole vessel had sprung a leak, not just the poet's trousers.[16]

'Le Bateau ivre' was written with a controlled associative process which recalls a phrase of the 'Seer' letter: 'thought latching on to thought and pulling'. The sense is allowed to leap across synapses formed by coincident sounds and memories of other texts so that the poem appears to write itself as it goes along.

> I saw the low sun, stained with mystic horrors,
> Illuminating with long, violet congealments,
> Like actors of very ancient dramas,
> The waves that roll their shivering shutters far away!
>
> I dreamed of the green night with dazzled snows,
> Kisses climbing slowly to the eyes of the seas,
> The circulation of unheard-of saps
> And the yellow-blue dawn of singing phosphorus!

Rimbaud read quickly and convulsively, 'like a child telling a tale of woe', his voice plunging from a boyish squeak to an adult bass.[17] By the end of the poem, Delahaye was beside himself with excitement. He was imagining the effect his friend would have in Paris: 'You're going to enter the world of letters like a bullet.' Delahaye fully expected to see him 'take over from Victor Hugo'.

Curiously, Rimbaud looked dejected – surely not only, as Delahaye claims, because he was afraid of looking like a bumpkin in the elegant salons of Paris. Rimbaud had just relived a poem which owed its glorious effects to a sense of inevitable defeat.

'Le Bateau ivre' is not the work of a young poet on the verge of a brilliant career, but the vision of a whole life, suspended between its final dissolution and the tiny, twilight world of the past. Rimbaud was about to leave the place that had given him his identity and provided him with most of his themes. This time, when he reached

Paris, no one would be forced to send him home. Policemen and railway inspectors would let him pass unmolested. This silent anxiety – and its unmentionable cause – are the hidden source of the poem's power.

A point made so often that it deserves to appear in a *Dictionary of Received Ideas* of literary criticism is that Rimbaud wrote 'Le Bateau ivre' without having seen the sea. One might just as well be amazed that he managed to write it without having met an inebriated boat. Faced with Rimbaud's storm of images, criticism has performed its collective task with a deceptive single-mindedness. If poems can be judged by the variety of interpretations they excite, then 'Le Bateau ivre' is one of the greatest ever written:

– a parody of various Parnassian poems based on a drifting boat metaphor

– a record of the poet's 'unmooring' from morality

– an allegory of a drunken binge, with the hangover, presumably, in stanza 23: 'Dawns are heartbreaking. / Every moon is atrocious and every sun bitter [. . .] O let my hull burst open, let me go to the sea!'

– an account of the pre-natal 'voyage' from womb to world

– a detailed premonition of Rimbaud's life and death

– an allegory of any human life

– a self-referential poem which describes its own creation

– a parable of the Paris Commune

– an illustration of the occult-based socialism of Éliphas Lévi

– a 'Voyage of the Beagle' which re-enacts the nineteenth century's abandonment of religion for Darwinian relativism

– a historical narrative which traces the passage from market capitalism to a world system.[18]

Most critics agree that all these readings – plausible as they are – leave a sense of unresolved obscurity. This is normally blamed on Rimbaud's lack of skill. Why, for instance, does the drunken boat keep referring to children? Why are all these visions – in contrast to the 'Seer' letter – recounted in the past tense? And why, at the end of the poem, in a sudden shrivelling of the vision, does the boat feel a pang of nostalgia for what seems to be the sad and paltry world of a lonely child?

> If I long for any European water, it is for the black,
> Cold puddle where, as the scented twilight falls,
> A squatting infant, full of sadness, releases
> A boat as frail as a May butterfly.

If Rimbaud is assumed to have written a coherent poem, a different point of view emerges. 'Le Bateau ivre' has always been thought of primarily as the heroic adventure of the child-poet. But, as Rimbaud warned his first academic reader, 'I is somebody else'. For the last eleven years, he had been living with the thought of a father who had disappeared into a vast beyond, a man who had freed himself from family ties and the 'racket' of four infants. While Rimbaud had been constructing a whole shooting-gallery of father-figures – teachers, priests, librarians, politicians and God – his real father had retained a kind of purity. The husband of 'Widow Rimbaud' was, after all, officially dead. (Actually, he was enjoying his retirement in Dijon.)

The miraculous visions of the drunken boat are an anticipated adventure, but they are also the imagined stories of the absent father – 'I would have liked to show the children these dorados / Of the blue wave, these golden fish, these fish that sing . . .' – the stories that were never told and which Rimbaud had replaced with *Robinson Crusoe* and the *Voyages* of Captain Cook, the novels of Jules Verne, Edgar Allan Poe and Victor Hugo, and the tales of explorers in the monthly *Magasin pittoresque*, traces of which have been found, half-dissolved, in 'Le Bateau ivre'.

The seemingly skewed conclusion can now be seen as the perfect ending. This dismal, squatting child, picked out in the third person, is a compelling self-portrait. The boat never says that it *wants* to return to Europe and a wretched childhood. The melancholy boy with his flimsy model of the heroic boat is the only reason the *bateau ivre* would ever want to return home.

*

ON SUNDAY, 24 September 1871, a month before his seventeenth birthday, Rimbaud arrived at Charleville station too early.

By coincidence, this happens to be the date on which Victor Hugo and his family were returning, first-class, from Hugo's 'fourth exile' in Luxembourg.[19] The Hugos left the train to eat lunch in Charleville, unfortunately at noon, shortly after Rimbaud's departure.

Delahaye found his friend in a buoyant mood, staring at the clock. His hair showed traces of a hasty pair of shears. The seemingly endless bolt of slate-blue cloth must have run out at last: his trouser legs now stopped short of his ankles to reveal a pair of blue knitted socks. Bretagne and Deverrière had given him a gold twenty-franc piece for emergencies, but his only luggage was a small bundle of manuscripts, including this poem which he knew to be unique in French literature. To give his departure the appropriate air of melodrama, he told Delahaye that he was travelling incognito and that, as far as his mother was concerned, he had 'gone for a walk in the neighbourhood'.

That morning in Paris, several established poets were musing on that great Balzacian theme: the rosy-cheeked prodigy who arrives in the evil metropolis with his sonnets, his illusions and his ludicrously ambitious career plan. But Arthur Rimbaud of Charleville had already reached one of the later chapters. The 'seer' was practising his magic spells, and the little village world of Parisian literature was about to have its fond illusions shattered beyond repair.

Part Two

(1871–1874)

10

'Nasty Fellows'

'And all that heard him were astonished at his understanding and answers.'

(Luke 2:47)

WHILE THE MORNING train from Charleville was crossing
northern France, a tall, balding figure in a grubby cape left his
father-in-law's home in the Rue Nicolet and set off down the slopes
of Montmartre.

Paul-Marie Verlaine[1] was twenty-seven years old and seemed, at
last, to have reached a plateau of respectability. He had given up his
job, taken up drinking and was in danger of being imprisoned,
deported or even executed for his role in the Commune; but a change
was in the air. It was his favourite time of year – September, 'that
delicious month of sharp, pale mornings'.[2] His young wife, Mathilde,
was heavily pregnant with their first child and he had resolved never
to hit her again.

As he reached the crowded Boulevard Magenta and the enticing
cafés around the two big railway stations, 'lines of truly terrifying
beauty' were trotting through his head, trying to attach themselves to
a face.

Rimbaud's patron had lived in Paris since the age of seven, when
his father retired from the army. Captain Verlaine was a dull Lux-
embourgeois who sometimes verged on the mildly interesting when
he lost his temper: the only show of passion recorded by his son was

the ejection of an unsatisfactory omelette through the dining-room window. Mme Verlaine preferred the company of her two children – both still-born: they sat in her bedroom, curled up in pickling-jars. When Paul-Marie was born in 1844, he was treated with the same doting delicacy, and somehow grew up with a pleasant personality – generous, unconceited and endearingly impish.

At school, he was always keen to be led astray, amusing in conversation and hideous in appearance. His best friend's mother claimed to have mistaken him for 'an orang-utan escaped from the zoo', while a teacher proclaimed him 'the dirtiest pupil, in body and dress, in the Lycée Bonaparte';[3] but everyone, including Verlaine, agreed that he was 'basically good and innocent'.[4]

After making steady downward progress, he breezed miraculously through his baccalauréat in 1862 and signed up to 'study Law', which was the conventional euphemism for taking a year off.

By putting in long hours at the café, Verlaine made friends with most of the Paris avant-garde and especially with the republicans who were soon to mastermind the Commune. He shot to prominence with some technically brilliant poems in the *Parnasse contemporain* and a compassionate analysis of Baudelaire – one of the first studies to treat him as a major literary figure rather than as a satanic *poseur*: the poet of 'modern man, with his sharpened, vibrating senses, his painfully refined spirit, his brain saturated with tobacco, his blood scorched with alcohol'.

Captain Verlaine tried to reform his son without success: house arrest for six months, then a job at the Eagle and Sun insurance company. Finally, in 1864, he was shoehorned into a clerical post at the Hôtel de Ville. His hat arrived punctually every day and hung on its hook while its owner went off to the Café du Gaz.

His first book of verse, *Poèmes saturniens* (1866), was followed by a pseudonymous collection – six pornographic sonnets on lesbian love, from boarding-school to Sappho – and then, in 1869, by the deliberately inconsequential *Fêtes galantes*, as technically and emotionally subtle as Debussy's more famous settings. This collection helped to fix the image from which Verlaine's work still suffers: the tenuous butterfly flitting woozily across a Toytown Paris of pastel skies. Verlaine is generally assumed to have had a sponge-like brain that simply absorbed whatever came its way: a painting, a musical phrase, the mud and clatter of the city streets, muted by alcohol and the cotton-wool which his mother still insisted on stuffing into his ears. Gustave Kahn expressed the common view: 'Mallarmé and Rimbaud thought. Verlaine never did.'[5]

Thought does not always take a theoretical form. Verlaine's metrical machines are as intellectually satisfying as philosophical propositions. He never wrote a bad line of verse. His supposedly demulcent little melodies, like 'Chanson d'automne', do have a strange power to calm a violent class of schoolchildren, but this does not necessarily prove their simple niceness. One of Verlaine's greatest admirers – Pol Pot – was not noted for his gentle disposition. The harmonious mangling of language, the little twinges of dislocated rhyme and metre might also appeal to a sense of savagery, just as they appealed to Rimbaud.

Verlaine was less reliable off the page. His affable personality survived literary success but not bereavement. He lost his father in 1865, then his beloved cousin Élisa. After her funeral near Douai, he was drunk for three days. Rimbaud's friend Bretagne had heard tales of a half-naked poet slobbering despondently in the ditches of the Ardennes. His second education had begun – the alcoholic's curriculum: beer, fortified coffee, Dutch gin, American grog, curaçao and finally the intricate ritual of 'the green hour' (forerunner of the cocktail hour): a lump of sugar was placed in a perforated spoon and suspended over cracked ice and absinthe. Water, drizzled on to the spoon, turned the alcohol emerald-green. It was sipped slowly until the body seemed to float above the table. In France, absinthe had been recognized as a dangerous narcotic only by those who liked to drink it.[6]

Two years before Rimbaud arrived in Paris, Verlaine had resolved to save himself. After an energetic night in the bars and brothels of Arras, he asked the sixteen-year-old half-sister of his friend, Charles de Sivry, to be his wife.[7]

Mathilde Mauté's personality was too faint to distract Verlaine from her 'pink halo of mysterious candour' and her enchanting habit of using her feet to remove her hair-ribbons. She had the mind of a fairy-tale princess: she was afraid of being impregnated by a kiss and believed that her parents' excellent furniture was proof of her social superiority. (She still thought this when writing her memoirs in 1907.)

Verlaine seized on Mathilde as his *planche de salut* on the sea of absinthe. His fourth book of poems, *La Bonne Chanson* (1870), is a record of the period of well-meant lies and best behaviour known as courtship. 'Behind me now / The oblivion one seeks in execrated brews', he wrote, ignoring the fact that alcohol was now one of the tools of his trade. He drank to forget, but he also drank to remember, to drown his happiness in a haze conducive to the writing of poems.

It seems that Mathilde was also supposed to be an escape route from something else – a part of Verlaine's past that was now returning in the morning train from Charleville. His passionate friendship with an 'exquisitely proportioned' young railway employee called Lucien Viotti had ended when Verlaine married Mathilde. Viotti promptly joined the army and died a few months later. Three days before the wedding, another young man turned up at Verlaine's office clutching a copy of his will and a loaded revolver. Next day, summoned by a telegram, Verlaine went to his friend's home to find that he had blown his brains out as a wedding present. For some reason, this ability to inspire violent passion is not normally associated with Verlaine, though the years with Rimbaud are incomprehensible without it.

From now on, Verlaine's life would be punctuated by memorably unpleasant acts which seem to have a lasting, lurid significance, like criminal convictions, but which also typify other lives that were shared with the green parasite.

On the one hand, Verlaine acted in a reasonably heroic fashion. During the Siege of Paris, he manned the ramparts with his rifle and his rheumatism. Under the Commune, he stayed at the Hôtel de Ville to serve as the chief censor of counter-revolutionary newspapers. But absinthe – and a tendency to take refuge in a state of childish panic – replaced the friendly clown with a vicious coward. The metamorphosis always took the same course: joviality; stony silence; anger; psychotic brutality. After a dinner of stewed mushrooms and burnt horsemeat, he punched his pregnant wife. While Paris burned, he sent her into the streets, shut himself in the lavatory and tried to make love to the maid. On a visit to his mother's house, he smashed the pickling-jars and sent his grisly siblings swilling across the floor.

Recently, terrified that his Commune activities would lead to his arrest, he had plucked up the courage to go and live with his father-in-law in the genteel, aspidistra area of Montmartre. As a humourless, poetry-hating man of private means, M. Mauté (or, as he preferred to call himself, Mauté de Fleurville) would provide a safe but irritating haven.

After two or three weeks of in-laws, Verlaine was beginning to crack. Mathilde's priggish personality was proving to be a serious obstacle to his affection. He was in desperate need of a friend who would save him from himself and somehow redeem the two deaths that he now blamed on Mathilde.

*

OVERCOME WITH INDECISION or absinthe, Verlaine began to oscillate between the Gare du Nord and the Gare de l'Est. M. Rimbaud was arriving from the north-east and, it seemed to Verlaine, might arrive at either station. This would explain why one of the great meetings in literature failed to occur in the appropriate setting of a busy railway terminus. It is just as likely – and even more appropriate – that Rimbaud, having just missed Victor Hugo on the west-bound platform of Charleville station, walked straight past Verlaine, unnoticed. After reading sophisticated poems like 'L'Orgie parisienne', Verlaine was expecting a distinguishing feature – a bold cravat or a self-conscious coiffure, and in any case some luggage.

Rimbaud left the Gare de l'Est and set off up the Boulevard Magenta towards the hill of vineyards and windmills where the air was fresh and where it always seemed to be Sunday. He found the house, which masqueraded as a provincial villa in the plush new Rue Nicolet, pushed the iron gates and rang the bell.

Thrilled to be playing host to a great unknown poet, Mathilde and her mother were surprised to find a sturdy-looking peasant boy with thatched hair and a twisted shred of tie. The absence of luggage was noted with suspicion, as were the twangy northern vowels. 'His eyes were blue and rather beautiful', Mathilde remembered, 'but they had a sly expression which, in our indulgence, we mistook for shyness.'[8]

After a painful half-hour, Verlaine returned from the station with his friend, the poet Charles Cros. He was amazed to find a gangly adolescent, fresh from the fields, enduring his trial by tea-cup. Dinner was served. Rimbaud looked bored and uncomfortable but 'did justice to the soup', according to Verlaine: he ate like a railwayman stoking the boiler of a locomotive. Charles Cros, who was later known as one of the inventors of colour photography and the phonograph, peppered the boy with 'scientific' questions: how had he constructed his poems, why had he used this word rather than another? Rimbaud remained stubbornly monosyllabic. His only complete sentence, addressed to a large, soppy dog called Gastineau, was an enigmatic, 'Dogs are liberals.'[9]

Whatever it meant, it was an excellent conversation-stopper: was M. Rimbaud perhaps alluding to the Mautés' liberal affectations and comparing them to fat, lazy scroungers feeding on table-scraps? Early in the evening, after filling the air with industrial pipe-smoke, he claimed to be tired and went up to sleep.

This was not the wild and dangerous city he had discovered on his earlier visits. The bed was soft, and at night, the world outside his window was as silent as Charleville.

*

OVER THE NEXT few days, Mathilde saw very little of her husband. When she did, it was usually late at night and he was always drunk. Later, she blamed everything on the vandal in the spare bedroom, the 'doll-faced' destroyer of domestic bliss;[10] but they seem at first to have been on friendly terms. She was eighteen, Rimbaud was seventeen, and they were both trying to cope with a twenty-seven-year-old dipsomaniac. Rimbaud remembered her telling him one day that her husband was 'so nice when he hasn't been drinking'.[11]

However, he soon found the hospitality oppressive and decided that, as a fellow 'seer', Verlaine should be liberated from his domestic jail. Until now, Rimbaud's plans had been rather vague. Verlaine provided him with a mission. His marriage was a drama in which Rimbaud would play the role of catalyst. A few days after arriving, he began to wear out his welcome. A portrait of an old relative hung in his bedroom, its face disfigured by patches of damp. Rimbaud claimed to find it intolerably sinister and demanded its removal. One day, he was found spread-eagled on the tarmac driveway, soaking up the pale October sun, embarrassingly visible to the neighbours. He seemed to be almost conscientiously careless. Some of Mathilde's favourite trinkets were broken. Objects went missing: a pocket-knife and an old ivory Christ, a gift from her grandmother. In Rimbaud's hands, the Christ was subjected to what Mathilde called an 'ignoble mutilation'.[12]

Trapped in a world of tablecloths and ornaments, Rimbaud was setting up his own Bohemia. He helped Verlaine to spend astonishingly large sums of money, though he was horribly parsimonious with soap, in keeping with the 'Seer' project: 'Imagine a man planting and cultivating warts on his face . . .' Before long, the seer's bedroom upstairs was a little oasis of squalor.

Verlaine was delighted with his new friend. He loosened him up with a tour of the local taverns, describing ever larger orbits, descending the slopes of Montmartre to the gaslit boulevards which tourists were warned to avoid, and eventually reaching the Latin Quarter. No letters survive from this period, but it is not difficult to see why the friendship blossomed. Verlaine was unjudgmental, impossible to antagonize and full of flattering admiration. He made copies of all the poems Rimbaud gave him, thus rescuing them from their author's disdain: Rimbaud had decided once again that everything he had written so far was worthless. He now had in mind a form of free verse.[13] Fifteen years before the *vers libre* made its official appearance in French literature, the idea that poems could be written without rhyme or metre sounded like artistic vandalism.

It is a testament to Verlaine's charm that he persuaded Rimbaud to behave like an ambitious young writer. He introduced him to other poets and announced his forthcoming appearance at a literary dinner. Large numbers of Parnassians were expected to attend. Before the dinner, he took him to the studio of the photographer Étienne Carjat, and induced him to sit for a portrait which Delahaye and Izambard both considered the most lifelike image of Rimbaud at any age. Interestingly, it is also the least well known. Perhaps it was too lifelike.

Verlaine thought that Rimbaud's beauty had escaped the lens: 'A kind of sweetness glimmered and smiled in those cruel, pale-blue eyes and on those powerful red lips with their acrimonious curl.'[14] The slightly pudgy face seems to be poised for a moment at the intersection of several expressions: the face of an actor reluctantly contemplating a role. Mathilde would have added the invisible detail that his hair was swarming with lice. She had discovered the little creatures on Rimbaud's pillow ('I had never seen any before') and was told by her husband that Rimbaud liked to carry them around with him so that he could flick them at priests.[15] 'I can still see myself', he wrote later in *Une Saison en Enfer*, 'my skin gnawed by mud and plague, my hair and armpits full of worms, and even bigger worms in my heart . . .'

The eagerly awaited dinner was held on the first Saturday after Rimbaud's arrival (30 September 1871). Verlaine took him to the Place Saint-Sulpice on the Left Bank. They entered a wine merchant's shop on the corner of the square and climbed to an upper room. A group of well-dressed poets had come for their latest 'Dîner des Vilains Bonshommes' and were curious to meet the author of 'Le Bateau ivre'.

The dinner was a regular feast and poetry-reading which dated back to the première of François Coppée's play, *Le Passant*, in 1869. It had been the first public triumph of the younger Parnassians, a relatively piffling event, but one which gave them a sense of collective identity. A sniffy reviewer had called Coppée's supporters '*vilains bonshommes*' ('nasty fellows'), and they adopted the insult as their banner.

To say they were clutching at a straw would be an exaggeration: the straw itself was illusory. The significant changes in French literature were no longer marked by public events like Hugo's *Hernani* or Murger's *Vie de Bohème*. Two decades of State censorship had herded original writers into avant-garde ghettos. Modern chronologies of the period would be meaningless to most people of the time. How could anyone have known that one of the most important aesthetic texts of the 1870s would consist of a few sheets of notepaper sent by a Charleville schoolboy to his teacher?

The 'Nasty Fellows' were a fairly pleasant group of young men. Their average age was thirty and most of them worked in offices. They had been nurturing their part-time careers, celebrating each other's successes, writing up their 'theories' into press releases. Their poems had none of the precarious flippancy of most avant-gardes. They smacked of the desk-drawer and the filing-cabinet.

For many of the 'Vilains Bonshommes', the appearance of Arthur Rimbaud at their weekly dinner was the first warning shot of middle age. The little peasant in his Sunday best, with his brutal poems and unnerving blue eyes, had the same depressing effect that technologically advanced alien beings are presumed to have on the human race in science fiction. Rimbaud's antisocial behaviour would make it easy for these professional writers to remove him later on from literary history.

One of the poets, Léon Valade, who had been eagerly disseminating Rimbaud's poems in the Latin Quarter, recorded the excitement of first contact. He wrote to a friend on 5 October 1871:

> You really missed out by not attending the latest dinner of the *Affreux Bonshommes* [*sic*]. There, under the auspices of Verlaine, his inventor, and myself, his John the Baptist on the Left Bank, was exhibited a *terrifying* poet of less than eighteen years called Arthur Rimbaud. Big hands, big feet, a truly *childlike* face which might suit a thirteen-year-old, deep blue eyes, wild rather than timid – this is the lad whose imagination, with its amazing powers and depravity, has been fascinating or frightening all our friends. [. . .] D'Hervilly said, 'It's Jesus in the midst of the doctors.' Maître said, 'He's the Devil!', which made me think of a better description: 'Satan in the midst of the doctors.'
>
> I can't give you a life history of our poet. Suffice it to say that he has come from Charleville with the firm intention of never seeing his home or his family again. – Come and read his poems and judge for yourself. Unless this is one of Fate's nasty little tricks, we are witnessing the birth of a *genius*.[16]

Rimbaud does not appear to have obliged the 'doctors' with a recitation, but after a few drinks he had the nerve to tell the most senior poet present, the fifty-year-old Théodore de Banville, that 'it was about time the alexandrine was demolished'[17] (the classical metre that had dominated French poetry for three centuries). Valade remembered the shiver of indignation:

You can imagine how surprised we were by this rebellious outburst, which was followed by a statement of his theories. We listened to him attentively, struck by the contrast between the youthfulness of his face and the maturity of his ideas.

At least one of these theories – 'Inventing the unknown calls for new forms' – would not have been well received. The master, Banville, was publishing his famous *Petit traité de poésie française* in which poets are instructed to confine themselves to existing forms. The shortest chapter of the treatise is devoted to 'Poetic Licence': 'No such thing.' Even less acceptable was Rimbaud's idea that Baudelaire had been prevented from realizing his full potential by the 'arty' milieu in which he lived. This was like suggesting that poets could exist without dinners and poetry readings.

Banville tackled the young genius on the subject of 'Le Bateau ivre': why had M. Rimbaud not made his meaning clear by saying at the start of the poem, '*I am like* a drunken boat'?[18] The peremptory opening – 'As I was descending the impassive rivers' – struck Banville in the same way that sudden scene changes would strike early cinema audiences. Some of Rimbaud's innovations looked suspiciously like mistakes.

Eight months later, Banville was still entertaining the readers of his column in *Le National* with tales of Rimbaud's hilarious cheek:

> M. Arthur Raimbaut [*sic*], a very young little fellow [. . .] whose pretty head stares out from under a wild and inextricable thicket of hair, asked me one day if it wouldn't soon be time to do away with the alexandrine!

Rimbaud's only known reaction to Banville's advice was a terse comment made on the street outside: '*Vieux con!*'[19]

Another 'silly old fool', Verlaine's father-in-law, M. Mauté, was about to return from his hunting holiday. It was feared that he might be tempted to reload his rifle when he found a filthy urchin in his home. As a temporary solution, Banville offered Rimbaud a maid's room in his apartment block at 10 Rue de Buci, between the Odéon and the Seine.

Rimbaud was to move into his garret shortly before 10 October. Curtains and bed linen were supplied by Mme de Banville. Some of the poets had clubbed together to provide 'the nursling of the Muses' with a small allowance: three francs a day.[20] It was enough to live on but not enough to fund a vice. The room had been prepared as if for a special pet: there was a table and a chair, some paper, a bottle of ink and several pens. No doubt the baby poet would soon be hard at work, writing splendid poems and refining his technique.

Rimbaud climbed the servants' staircase to the attic. His first encounter with the community of poets had been disappointing. Banville had failed to grasp the originality of 'Le Bateau ivre' – a poem written especially for 'the people in Paris' and which, in Rimbaud's mind, was already out of date. It seemed that, for these literary bureaucrats, the function of poetry was not to change the nature of reality, but to keep up a steady flow of gossip and dinner invitations.

Rimbaud's timidity made him susceptible to small humiliations. Now that he was here in person, he could no longer hide the humorous discrepancy between his age and his talent, nor his north-ern accent. 'Le Bateau ivre', with its 'screaming Redskins' and 'giant serpents', did after all have a lingering air of the nursery, while its bizarre images might easily be interpreted as crude provincialisms. It was exasperating to be forced into a costume, especially when the costume seemed to fit.

That evening at the Rue de Buci, as the smells of bourgeois dinners wafted up the inner courtyard, cries of indignation were heard. Banville rushed out to investigate. High up under the eaves a boy was peeling off his clothes and flinging them over the roof-tiles. Rimbaud was standing under the red sky of Paris, framed by the mansard, in what Banville aptly described as 'mythological' attire.[21]

11

Savage of the Latin Quarter

'In the abyss of great cities, as in the desert, there is something which fortifies and fashions the heart of man [. . .] when it does not deprave and enfeeble him.'

(Baudelaire, *Un mangeur d'opium*)[1]

A LL COTERIES LIKE to see themselves in the eyes of an outsider. The image supplied by Rimbaud was not very flattering. He made the avant-garde look prudish. The 'Nasty Fellows' retaliated with faint praise. Suddenly, Verlaine's protégé was an ex-genius. The boy was reported to have a certain talent, but he was 'full of his own importance, affecting to despise all men and all things'.[2] André Gill described him as a '*fluxion*' (an inflammation or a gum-boil).[3]

Rimbaud's glorious career had lasted less than three weeks. When Verlaine's brother-in-law returned to Paris in October, eager to meet the future great poet, he found 'a vile, vicious, disgusting, smutty little schoolboy whom everyone is in raptures about'.[4] Rumours began to spread about Rimbaud's sudden departure from Banville's garret, a week after moving in:

> On his first evening there, he went to bed with all his clothes on and his muddy feet *between the sheets*! Next day, he amused himself by smashing all the porcelain – water-jug, basin and chamber-pot. Soon after that, being short of money, he sold the furniture.[5]

This early example of room-trashing was embellished over the years, and there is evidence even now of a thriving oral tradition. The latest version heard during the writing of this biography is that Rimbaud left a calling-card on Banville's pillow in the shape of a human turd.

Rimbaud was certainly capable of questioning the principle of ownership in this way. If property was theft, then hospitality was a sham. For the same reason, he refused to play the traditional Bohemian game of penniless student and heartless rent-collector. There is no sign that he ever paid for accommodation in Paris with his own money. When a friend of Renoir later found a room for him in Montmartre and reported that the landlord 'seems a nice fellow', Rimbaud looked horrified: 'Landlord? You mean I'd have to *pay* for the room? Sod it, then.'[6]

In fact, he and Banville seem to have reached an amicable agreement. Rimbaud had a good excuse for his striptease: 'I couldn't possibly occupy such a clean and virginal room with my old, lice-ridden rags.' After suffering Baudelaire's practical jokes for twenty-five years, Banville was not easily offended. He presented Rimbaud with a fresh suit of clothes and invited him to dine with the family.

The Rue de Buci had been a stop-gap in any case. Verlaine's friend Charles Cros lived in a large laboratory-studio in the squalid heart of the Latin Quarter at 13 Rue Séguier, half-way up an alley that led to the Seine. He shared the studio with a painter of seascapes called Michel de l'Hay and allowed it to be used as a hostel for itinerant artists – the perfect place, it was thought, for Arthur Rimbaud. Mme de Banville had some bed-sheets and a folding metal cot delivered, and Rimbaud moved in towards the middle of October 1871.

Rimbaud's new host had been confined to the fringes of Parnassus because he was thought to be a joker: Cros's surreal ditty on a smoked herring is still one of the best-known poems in the language. But like the Surrealists who admired him, he had a mesmerizing ability to be deadly serious about almost anything. In 1869, he published a scheme for sending messages to the inhabitants of Mars and Venus using a primitive form of laser.[7] Attempts to raise the dead proved inconclusive, but his experiments with alchemy were said to have produced a real ruby – unfortunately not real enough to fund a repeat experiment. He also wrote poems: pearly little landscapes constructed according to precise rules like computer graphics. Similar results would certainly have been obtained with less effort, but the idea was to test new principles, not to create a marketable product.

The questions with which Cros had pestered Rimbaud on his first evening in Paris reflected his latest obsession: the 'principles of cerebral mechanics'. The prodigy from Charleville would be an excellent experimental subject.

The experiment in cohabitation went wrong so quickly and so spectacularly that the lasting significance of Rimbaud's fortnight in the laboratory-studio is easily missed. Both poets were interested in the processes of perception and in the action of chemicals on the brain. Cros became so familiar with psychotropic effects that he was soon toying with the idea of a special drug that would help him 'to make normal thinking more frequent'.[8] A few months after Rimbaud left the studio, Cros began to write hallucinatory prose poems which would not be out of place in an anthology of 1960s psychedelia and which might be mistaken for some of Rimbaud's *Illuminations*.

This brief liaison – which Rimbaud expected to turn into a lasting friendship – unfortunately coincides with a dark period in the history of his work. Between 'Le Bateau ivre' and the lyrics of spring 1872, only three verse poems are known. Delahaye claimed to remember an abortive project called *Photographies du temps passé*, in which French history would have been condensed into a series of highly coloured *tableaux*, but no evidence of this remains, and Delahaye's dates are suspiciously fluid.[9] There are also two short dream sequences in prose titled *Les Déserts de l'amour* that may or may not predate Rimbaud's arrival in Paris. They sound like transcriptions of actual dreams and are probably one of Rimbaud's attempts to 'photograph' difficult mental subjects: the ambiguous excitement of fornicating in 'the family house'; the kissing lip 'like a desperate little wave', then the bodies sprawling on 'sail-cloth', and the fetishistic substitution of the desired object at the crucial moment. Even the dream woman turned into a 'Mouth of Darkness':

I pushed her over into a basket of cushions and sail-cloth in a dark corner. All I remember is her white lace knickers. – Then, O despair, the dividing wall turned vaguely into the shade of the trees, and I sank beneath the loving sadness of the night.

The theme of unattainable or non-existent love is so prevalent in Rimbaud's work that this passage might have been written at any time between 1870 and 1873.

There is, however, enough evidence to reveal a trend in Rimbaud's work which corresponds to Charles Cros's line of scientific inquiry. This trend is rarely associated with Rimbaud because it runs counter to the grand narrative of literary history: partly for pedagogical convenience, French poets of the nineteenth century are habitually described as 'liberating' themselves from the 'constraints' of verse until one day, in the mid-1880s, after filing through the last remaining rule, they go scampering off into the open field of free verse. One so much expects this to be true of Rimbaud and hears it so often said of him that it takes the blunt instrument of statistics to hammer the evidence home.

The fact is that, after the 'Seer' letters, Rimbaud's verse became, not less, but more regular. His rhymes grew dramatically larger – an effect which is impossible to achieve by accident. It was *after* his decision to become a seer that he stopped writing irregular sonnets and adopted the more demanding, traditional form. The rare examples of rule breakage (singulars rhymed with plurals, words straddling the caesura) were relatively superficial – prosodic fashion accessories designed to show that he was a member of the avant-garde.

Rimbaud's regular verse and irregular behaviour were part of the same plan. This was not a regression to the prison cell of tradition; it was another attempt to hack off the ball-and-chain of the personality. To allow a rhyme to determine the meaning of a phrase, an irrational impulse to direct an action or a dream to dictate a poem, was to allow himself to become, momentarily, a different person. This is what Rimbaud had referred to in his letter to Izambard as 'objective poetry': poetry that transcended the individual because it was based on scientific principles.

This systematic approach to life and art made Rimbaud intolerable as a room-mate. His conversation was sporadic and obscene, his manners non-existent. On his first morning in the laboratory, he woke to find that Cros's charlady had performed the Herculean task of bringing a shine to his boots. He pulled them on, hurried down to the street, tramped through the gutters and puddles, and returned to sit on the bed, where he lit his pipe and spat tobacco juice at the offending footwear until it was acceptably disgusting again. The following day, Cros was surprised to catch sight of Rimbaud in a mirror, coming at him with a pointed instrument.[10]

This was something more than the youthful exuberance Delahaye had witnessed in Charleville. One day, in an all-night café on the Place Pigalle called the Rat Mort, Cros returned from the toilet to find that his drink had become strangely active: Rimbaud had borrowed some sulphuric acid from the laboratory.[11] Later, he told Mathilde about another of Rimbaud's 'experiments':

> All three of us were at the Café du Rat Mort – Verlaine, Rimbaud and myself. Rimbaud said, 'Spread your hands out on the table. I want to show you an experiment.'
>
> Thinking it was a joke, we did as he asked. Then he pulled an open penknife from his pocket and cut Verlaine's wrists quite deeply. I was able to withdraw my hands just in time and was not wounded. Verlaine left the café with his sinister friend and was stabbed twice more in the thigh.[12]

Rimbaud's murderous pranks, like his poems, lend themselves to various interpretations. He might have been testing Cros's friendship or even expressing affection in a fashion not unknown in boys who shrink from normal physical contact. For Rimbaud, his sadism was an 'experiment'. Daily life was too slow and unrevealing. Human beings were more interesting in extreme conditions – and not just human beings. On 18 October, at the first night of a play, he was spotted on the boulevard outside the theatre, blowing pipe-smoke up the nostrils of a cab-horse.[13]

The idea that Rimbaud was exercising his sense of humour has not proved popular, though, presumably, if there was something funny about breaking rules, few things could be more amusing than attempted murder with a hint of homosexual passion. The stabbing at the Dead Rat café was the first public performance of one of the great comic duos of literature.

From a cultural point of view, Rimbaud was making what would now be called a statement. In 1871, acts of imaginative vandalism were inevitably seen as a homage to Baudelaire, the *adulte terrible* of French letters, who was said to have plucked out a cat's whiskers, tried to set fire to the Bois de Boulogne, and had a pair of riding-breeches cut from the hide of his dead father.[14] By continuing the tradition, Rimbaud was presenting himself as one of the adolescent monsters that Baudelaire's poems were supposed to have spawned. 'Demoralizing' works like *Les Fleurs du Mal* were commonly thought to have had a direct influence on the Paris Communards.

Cros endured his guest for two weeks. Since Mathilde was about to give birth, Verlaine was spending more time at home and Cros was left to bear the brunt of Rimbaud's antics. One day, taking a dislike to one of Cros's plaster busts, he knocked its nose off with a hammer.[15] On another occasion, Cros noticed that the back numbers of the review, *L'Artiste*, in which his poems had appeared, were missing from the sideboard. He had been intending to gather them together and offer them to a publisher. Rimbaud had used the volumes, which were printed on stiff vellum and adorned with classical engravings, as a source of sturdy toilet-paper.[16]

Despite this concise example of practical criticism, Rimbaud was not thrown out: he left of his own accord. Even after losing his poems to the sewer, Cros continued to collect money for Rimbaud's allowance.[17] However dangerous or infuriating, Rimbaud's company brought huge rewards, none of which could easily be expressed in the form of anecdotes and which, therefore, were later assumed never to have existed.

Verlaine was not alone in finding him 'an exquisite creature'.[18] Several people commented on his engaging mannerisms. He rubbed his eyes with his fists like a drowsy child and blushed whenever he met someone new.[19] He warmed quickly to anyone – like the journalist, Jules Claretie ('a good bloke', said Rimbaud) – who treated him with bonhomie instead of inspecting him like a freak.[20] His conversation was hilariously devoid of received ideas and, despite his shyness, there was an air of unshakeable conviction about him. In Rimbaud's intellectual atmosphere, everything became more interesting. The painter Forain described this rare effect with a splendid image drawn from close, daily knowledge of Rimbaud: 'He stank of genius.'[21]

The most eloquent expression of Rimbaud's charm is his poem 'Les Chercheuses de poux', which probably dates from these early days in Paris. The two 'lice-seekers' have been identified as Izambard's aunts, Mme de Banville and, incredibly, the wife of Victor Hugo, who was not only not in the habit of chewing pink gum but had also been dead for three years. Since Rimbaud appears to have been parodying a poem on the seduction of a young boy by the boastful Parnassian supremo, Catulle Mendès, 'Les Chercheuses de poux' is not necessarily a souvenir of a delousing session.[22] The themes of inflammation, dribbling and the crushing of lice have a provocative triviality which recalls contemporary paintings by Manet and Degas. But the verminous head is not just another repulsive, Realist object deposited on the pillow of Romantic cliché. As in the 'Seer' letters, the poet's brain is a musical instrument waiting to be played.

> When the brow of the child, beset with scarlet storms,
> Implores the white swarm of indistinct dreams,
> Two tall, charming sisters come to his bedside,
> Delicate-fingered and silvery-nailed.
>
> They sit the child down by an open window,
> Where the blue air bathes a flurry of flowers,
> And in his heavy hair in which the dew is falling,
> Their slender fingers stroll with terrible enchantments.
>
> He listens to the song their fearful breath sings,
> Scented with long honey-strands, plant-like and pink,
> And sometimes interrupted by a whistle: saliva
> Caught on the lip or stifled kisses.
>
> He hears their black lashes beating in the perfumed
> Silence, and their soft, electric fingers
> Moving through the haze of indolence, the majestic nails
> Killing with a snap the little insects.
>
> And now the wine of Idleness surges up within,
> A harmonica's sob on the verge of delirium,

> With each slow caress, the child can feel
> The rise and fall of an endless desire to weep.*

This combination of cruel intellect and a yearning for physical affection was rapidly becoming irresistible to Verlaine. Rimbaud gave him the pleasant sense of having all his preconceived notions stripped away. With Rimbaud, drunkenness was an intellectual journey.

Verlaine's description of the second photograph by Carjat gives a suitably intoxicating impression of Rimbaud's appeal. It is all the more remarkable for having been written at a time when Verlaine was keen to deny that there had ever been any impropriety in their relations:

> A kid Casanova [. . .] seems to laugh in those bold nostrils, while the handsome, rugged chin appears to say 'Bugger off' to any illusion that is not the result of the most irrevocable act of will. The superb mop of hair, it seems to me, could only have been rumpled in such a fashion by skilfully arranged pillows, dented by the elbow of a pure, sultanic caprice. And the utterly virile disdain for clothes which are quite superfluous to that literally diabolical beauty![23]

*

AFTER TWO WEEKS in the laboratory, Rimbaud suddenly left without saying goodbye. His disappearance seems at first mysterious, but the chronology supplies an obvious motive.

By now, the 'kid Casanova' was a serious bone of contention in the Verlaine household. In her memoirs, Mathilde describes the first known example of Rimbaud's influence on another writer:

> Since Rimbaud's arrival, Verlaine had been dressing in the most casual manner. He had taken to wearing his horrible scarves and floppy hats again. Sometimes, he went for a whole week without changing his clothes or having his shoes cleaned.

A week before the birth of his first child, it became apparent that Verlaine had transferred his affection. After a dinner at his mother's home, he told Mathilde about a recent conversation with Rimbaud:

---

* The 'harmonica' here is not a mouth organ but a row of glasses of different sizes, played with a wet finger.

VERLAINE: How did you manage to get hold of my books in Charleville when you didn't have any money?

RIMBAUD: I used to take them from a bookshop display and put them back when I'd read them. But then I started to worry that I might get caught, so I took them, read them and sold them.

When Mathilde observed, 'That shows that your friend isn't very honest', Verlaine pulled her out of bed and threw her on to the floor.

A week later, he came home at midnight to find that he had a son. At first, he seemed to be pleased. Mathilde was hoping that little Georges would save the marriage.

It was then that Rimbaud disappeared.

His timing was catastrophically accurate. By disappearing at the critical moment, he was driving himself into the crack that had already appeared in Verlaine's marriage. Effectively, it was an ultimatum: Verlaine would have to choose between respectability and artistic freedom. Rimbaud was offering to save him from the 'arty' milieu that had stunted Baudelaire.

Verlaine had no intention of forsaking home comforts, but he blamed himself for losing his protégé to the big city and set off to look for him. The weather was turning cold and Rimbaud had no money. Even after Baron Haussmann's demolitions, most of the Latin Quarter was still a labyrinth of medieval alleyways. Anyone who wanted to disappear in it could do so quite easily.

A few days later, Verlaine was patrolling the scruffy streets around the Place Maubert when he ran into a grim-faced urchin. His cheeks were hollow, his clothes in tatters, his body crawling with vermin. It was Rimbaud, 'dying of hunger and cold', according to Verlaine. 'He was proposing to walk home to his mother.'[24]

Rimbaud had apparently tried to support himself. He was seen at one point on the Rue de Rivoli, selling key-rings. He also wrote some articles, which he offered to the *Figaro*. The articles were rejected and are known only by their titles: 'Les Nuits blanches', 'Le Bureau des cocardiers' and 'Les Réveilleurs de la nuit'.[25]

The first two may be glimpses of Rimbaud's period of destitution: 'Sleepless Nights' and the unexplained 'Office of *cocardiers*' ('gung-ho soldiers') – perhaps his first contact with army recruitment. The last title – 'Les Réveilleurs de la nuit' – seems to refer to a little-known trade which, like the peddling of key-rings, was then on the verge of extinction. In the poorer areas, human alarm-clocks would rush about in the early hours waking up factory workers for a small fee.[26] Rimbaud was already practising the only literary genre he never abandoned: first-hand accounts of uncharted regions.

After being rediscovered by Verlaine, Rimbaud continued his descent into the Bohemian underworld. He was installed now in even seedier surroundings. The Hôtel des Étrangers stood on the corner of the Rue Racine and the Boulevard Saint-Michel. A vast room on the *entresol* had been rented by a group of mostly unknown artists, writers and musicians. The principal piece of furniture was a piano, at which a cadaverous individual sat in a swirl of hashish smoke, playing indescribable tunes.

The 'Nasty Fellows' were on the fringe of Parnassus. The denizens of the Hôtel des Étrangers were a subversive splinter group that had detached itself from the fringe. Rimbaud described them as 'Parnassian debris'.[27] The name that has earned them a place in cultural history – 'Les Zutistes' – was an insult to the very notion of cultural history.* They were so embedded in the avant-garde that some of them seemed unlikely ever to produce any publishable work at all.

The communal room at the Hôtel des Étrangers was the last outpost of the anarchic spirit that had ruled the city the previous spring. Six months after the horrific 'cleansing' of Paris, everyone – including the Nasty Fellows – was talking about the need for national 'regeneration'. Artists who considered themselves liberal routinely deplored the socialist ideals that were supposed to have caused the carnage and destruction. For the Nasty Fellows, the Commune had been a brief nightmare. The Zutistes were waiting for the second act to begin.

After four weeks of disappointment, Rimbaud seemed at last to have landed in a nutritious medium. The Hôtel des Étrangers was his

---

* From '*zut!*': approximate equivalent of '*merde!*' Defined by Littré in 1875 as a 'very familiar interjection by which one expresses a conviction that attempts to reach a goal are a complete waste of time, that assertions and promises are futile, and especially that one could not care less'.

fourth address in Paris and, so far, the least salubrious. But when Delahaye arrived for a short visit that November, he saw at once that his friend had found a new home. Rimbaud had quite clearly 'gone native'.

12

'Mlle Rimbaut'

'the least intellectual place on Earth'

(Rimbaud to Delahaye, November 1872)[1]

HAVING ARRIVED at Verlaine's home unannounced, Delahaye was relieved to find the famous poet friendly and unpretentious. He had a little speech prepared, the point of which was to discover where Rimbaud was living.

Apparently, this was like asking for the address of an animal. However, that day, Verlaine thought he knew where the 'tiger' had his 'lair'. He led Delahaye back down the hill, swerved in and out of the Café du Delta and jumped on the bus at Pigalle.[2]

Verlaine was full of praise for Delahaye's friend. His only complaint was that Rimbaud had failed to find a girlfriend. In his view, this would have cured him of his 'intercostal rheumatism'. Delahaye listened in excitement, thrilled to be having an 'artistic' conversation.

After crossing the river, they left the bus on the Boulevard Saint-Michel, entered the Hôtel des Étrangers and climbed to the *entresol*. Through the smoke, men with beards came up to shake hands with Verlaine. A grubby form rose sleepily from a bench. It was Rimbaud. He explained that he had been smoking hashish. The prose poem 'Matinée d'ivresse' shows that he later developed a happy relationship with the drug, but his first experience had been disappointing – a few basic hallucinations: 'white moons and black moons chasing one another'.

Like a sensible provincial, Delahaye recommended a breath of fresh air and took his friend for a walk. Rimbaud shook off his stupor and showed him the sights – especially the Panthéon and the pock-marked walls of houses where Communards had been shot. Hashish had not made him eloquent. He smiled at the little craters in the plaster and said, 'Bullets . . . bullets . . . bullets!' The visit seems to have been short and difficult. The speed of experience had carried Rimbaud a long way from Charleville in five weeks. He had shot up on his diet of scraps and alcohol and was now a full head taller than Delahaye. He was clearly quite pleased to have become almost unrecognizable:

> Of course, his chubby cheeks were long gone. Now, on his drawn features and bony face there was a horrible redness around the sky-blue eyes. He had the complexion of a cab-driver. [. . .] Thanks to the bustling city crowd – so tolerant in its indifference – Rimbaud now 'couldn't give a damn' about his appearance. He thought he was quite the thing in his long, light-coloured overcoat, which was twice the size it needed to be. It was in a deplorable state, all crumpled and creased from having been worn continually for 48 or 72 hours. The little bowler-hat that he used to keep so carefully brushed had been replaced by an object in soft felt which has no name in any language.

The street-soiled Artful Dodger seemed to be thriving on his lost illusions. He told Delahaye that the Commune had been reduced to a tiny band of suicidal maniacs and that he was thinking of joining them in a final act of urban terrorism. And what of the 'intellectual paradise' he had hoped to find in Paris? According to Rimbaud, the 'city of light' was a small, polluted settlement of arrogant, vulgar people: 'the least intellectual place on Earth'.

Explorers are often reluctant to reveal all their treasures to visitors from home. In reality, Rimbaud was apparently enjoying himself: the winter of 1871–2 was one of his most productive periods, though the products themselves were shovelled away by early editors like the indiscretions of a prize poodle.

The cadaverous pianist at the Hôtel des Étrangers had become a close friend. Ernest Cabaner[3] had arrived from Perpignan twenty years before to study at the Paris Conservatoire and had never left, claiming to be allergic to the countryside. Now, in his late thirties, Cabaner earned his living by playing the piano for a bar-room audience of soldiers and prostitutes. In his spare time, he collected old shoes which he used as flower-pots. He had long, lank hair and a face like a water-stained wall. Manet painted it in 1880: a frail, Goyaesque figure with lugubrious, droopy eyes. Cabaner seemed to be permanently in the final stages of tuberculosis but survived until 1878 on a diet of milk, honey, rice, kippers and alcohol. Verlaine described him as 'Jesus Christ after ten years of absinthe'.[4]

Famously ignorant of political events, Cabaner was none the less deemed sufficiently louche to be included in the century's largest and least reliable biographical dictionary – the files of the Préfecture de Police: 'Eccentric musician, mad composer', says the report, 'one of the most fervent devotees of the caste' (police jargon for 'enthusiastic homosexual'). He seems to have invited Rimbaud to share his bed. Most of the Zutistes appear to have flirted with homosexuality, at least on paper.[5]

Cabaner and Rimbaud were responsible for dispensing drinks to the Zutistes and buying in the alcohol. This unlicensed activity probably explains why the Cercle Zutique had such a brief and boisterous existence: it seems to have closed some time that winter. Even on the Boulevard Saint-Michel, the sight of a smut-encrusted boy in borrowed clothes and a skeletal alcoholic in a red apron[6] lugging crates of bottles into the Hôtel des Étrangers is unlikely to have passed unnoticed. The fact that the conspicuously unhygienic Rimbaud was also entrusted with the job of rinsing glasses and sweeping the floor suggests that his appointment as barman was a disguised act of charity.

Echoes of Rimbaud's conversation in the den of Zutistes have survived in a little song written for him by Cabaner:

> What are you doing in Paris, O poet,
> Come from Charleville?
> Go home. Here, genius stagnates
> And dies of hunger on the streets. [. . .]

> You left to seek your fortune,
> Impelled by your pernicious fate.
> Ungrateful child, you blame your mother
> For stifling your mind in the cradle.[7]

This quaint little song is like a nursery theme-tune of Rimbaud's life: the bitter rejection of the past, a malevolent 'fate', the eye fastened on a formless future, and, of course, the stalking shadow of Mme Rimbaud. The refrain echoes Rimbaud's usual answer to questions about his plans:

> I'm waiting, I'm waiting, I'm waiting.

The friendship survived until Rimbaud's final disappearance from Paris. Cabaner was like a deranged uncle who could safely be teased and subjected to affectionate acts of violence. Rimbaud, who liked to pare his conversation down to a few slogans and expletives, was sometimes heard to chant, 'Cabaner must be killed!'[8] He almost followed his own advice. That winter, when the pneumonic pianist moved to a freezing hovel, Rimbaud carefully circumcised and removed all his window-panes with a glass-cutter.[9]

This is typical of Rimbaud's precise variations on the clichés of subversion: this was no idle smashing of windows. On another occasion, when Cabaner was out, Rimbaud found his daily glass of milk and neatly ejaculated into it.[10]

The essence of these pranks was to pervert the usual state of affairs while preserving an appearance of normality: the holes that might for a moment be mistaken for polished panes; a slight coagulation of the milk. The watered-down versions of the latter story completely miss the point by having Rimbaud adulterate the milk with urine.

This flexible relationship also had its intellectual moments and produced one of the classics of avant-garde culture: Rimbaud's sonnet, 'Voyelles'.

Cabaner had been teaching Rimbaud the piano by an unconventional method. He believed that each note of the octave corresponded to a particular vowel and colour: 'Once these correlations of sound and colour have been discovered, it will be possible to translate landscapes and medallions into music.'[11]

Keys to universal harmony had a long history in France, from machines for creating smell-symphonies to Baudelaire's 'Correspondances', with its 'perfumes as cool to the touch as children's flesh'. Rimbaud had read widely enough to know several texts on the subject. In his 'Seer' letter, he had imagined a future 'universal language' that could be understood by all the senses at once: an Esperanto of the human body. But since he was already proficient in the art of inducing hallucinations, and since every mind has the ability to perceive things synaesthetically, there is no reason to suppose that he preferred someone else's theory to the evidence of his own brain.

If any single entity were to be given credit for Rimbaud's coloured vowels, it would be the duplicitous 'Green Fairy'. A doctor writing in a Communard newspaper in January 1872 prescribed small doses of absinthe for those who wished to 'illuminate the mind':

> The most curious thing about this transformation of the sensorial apparatus – the phenomenon, at least, that struck me most forcibly in the experiments I conducted on myself – is that all sensations are perceived by all the senses at once. My own impression is that I am breathing sounds and hearing colours, that scents produce a sensation of lightness or of weight, roughness or smoothness, as if I were touching them with my fingers.[12]

Rimbaud's sonnet alludes to this phenomenon, but also, teasingly, to the metaphysical theorizing that went with it:

VOWELS

A black, E white, I red, U green, O blue – vowels,
One day I will recount your latent births:
A – furry black corset of spectacular flies
That thrum around the savage smells;

Gulfs of shade. E – whitenesses of steam and tents,
Proud glaciers' lances, white kings, quivering umbels.
I – purples, expectorated blood, the laugh of lovely lips
In anger or in the ecstasies of penitence.

U – eons, divine vibrations of viridian seas,
The peace of animal-strewn pastures and of furrows
That alchemy imprints on broad studious brows.

O – the final trump of strange and strident sounds,
Silences traversed by Worlds and Angels:
O – Omega, the violet ray of His Eyes!

Although Rimbaud never published his sonnet, 'Voyelles' spread quickly through the Latin Quarter and caused a kind of intellectual gold rush. Long after Rimbaud's disappearance, dozens of po-faced imitators tried to refine the mystical keyboard. These were the early days of science envy. Rimbaud's beautiful sonnet appeared to offer up the simple secret of its creation and still has the power to create a hankering after unattainable precision.

This is the ambiguity that lies at the heart of Rimbaud's work: the ardent search for powerful systems of thought that could be used like magic spells, conducted by an acutely ironic intelligence – a combination that rarely survives adolescence gracefully. Do these tiny mental events correspond to universal truths, or is every mind an island in a sea of mutual ignorance? Rimbaud can hardly have failed to notice, when Cabaner stuck his little pieces of coloured paper on to the piano keys, that these synaesthetic perceptions vary from one individual to the next and can hardly be used as universal blueprints.[13]

His real achievement is to have written a sonnet (significantly set in the future) that induces a state of mind in which the flavour of omniscience is almost tangible. As a result, generations of scholars have spent a great deal of time (in some harrowing cases, years) creeping along the interminable ramifications of Rimbaud's magic pyramid, looking for the key. For some, he was describing an illustrated alphabet, for others, an alchemical recipe – which would mean that he was either considerably more or considerably less intelligent than previously supposed. One influential critic had a vision of Rimbaud's vowels as graphic representations of a woman's body in orgasm (a U-shaped woman with green hair).[14]

Some of Rimbaud's images may correspond to actual memories or impressions: a capital 'A' could suggest the half-folded wings of a fly; French schoolchildren were introduced to the vowel sound 'i' with the word '*rire*' because it forces the mouth to form a laugh.[15] But the most plausible interpretation of the vowel rainbow is Tristan Derème's: the colours and vowels are arranged so as to produce a mellifluous, unobstructed line of sounds – '*A noir, E blanc, I rouge, U vert, O bleu*'. As Verlaine knew, there was no real distinction in poetry between a hoax and a revelation: 'Theoretical exactitude, I feel, was probably a matter of complete indifference to the extremely witty Rimbaud.'[16] 'He couldn't have cared less whether A was black or white.'[17]

The intellectual havoc wreaked by Rimbaud's sonnet is insignificant compared to its effect on the rest of his work. While 'Voyelles' appears with 'Le Bateau ivre' as one of the pinnacles of his career, rising over a vast pilgrim city of critical commentary, his other Zutiste productions have been banished to the suburbs of appendices and '*Oeuvres diverses*', and sometimes banished altogether.

The rediscovery in 1936 of the Zutistes' communal album should count as one of the happiest events of modern literary history. Without it, Rimbaud would appear to have written almost nothing after arriving in Paris.

Zutiste etiquette suited him perfectly: it required contributions to be either sarcastic or obscene, preferably both. The usual victim was the poet François Coppée, who was thought to have sailed off into a sunset of respectability and government funding.[18] Rimbaud and Verlaine had noticed that Coppée's odes to the trivial delights of modern life lent themselves beautifully to lewd interpretations. In later terms, Coppée was an unwitting master of the Freudian slip.

Rimbaud's parodies are dazzling little cameos of street life in their own right, with gorgeous, mouth-filling constructions reminiscent of Baudelaire's early poems. A postilion on the late-night omnibus swings about behind the passengers as he masturbates under his satchel. The poet imagines wiping 'the milky rim' of the white toilet-bowl in the night sky with a grizzled lavatory-brush. On a summer evening, he stands inside one of the poster columns that used to double as urinals,[19] dreaming of the coming winter: 'On summer evenings, under the shop-windows' ardent eye . . .'

The longest of Rimbaud's 'Coppées', notorious for its 'atrocious, steely obscenity',[20] is a Zutiste masterpiece – perhaps the only Zutiste masterpiece. A voyeur in his own memory, a 'cretinous old man' arouses himself with thoughts of his childhood home: his little sister's 'lower lip'; the surprising penis of an ass; the alluring lump in his father's breeches; and his mother, 'whose shift had an acrid smell', 'her bulging loins, where the cloth / Wrinkles up, gave me those hot flushes that no one ever mentions' – 'to say nothing [. . .] of the Bible, the toilets and the maid, / The Holy Virgin and the crucifix . . .'[21]

This concise encyclopedia of neuroses was Rimbaud's alternative view of the family. The quasi-military unit that was supposed to save France from anarchy and moral decay is shown to be a claustrophobic enclave of mismatched human beings, beset by stale sexual fantasies and racked with pointless guilt.

In contrast to this festering hive of incest, homosexuality was free and untamed. It had not been a signatory to the social contract. There wasn't even a word for it in the language.[22] In 1871, the love that dare not speak its name had no name to speak. For Rimbaud, this blank space on the social map was a powerful invitation. Perhaps, by now, he had no choice but to explore.

*

THAT NOVEMBER, THE savages of modern Paris were caught in a small spotlight of publicity. Rimbaud and Verlaine attended the first night of Coppée's new play, *L'Abandonnée*, on 14 November. After a post-performance drink with Rimbaud which lasted until three o'clock in the morning, Verlaine returned to the Rue Nicolet and threatened to kill his wife and child in indirect revenge for Coppée's success. This he hoped to achieve by setting fire to M. Mauté's ammunition cupboard and removing number 14 from the street. The nursemaid fended him off with the fire-tongs.

Next day, Verlaine woke up in his clothes, shook off a mild attack of remorse and set out for the Odéon theatre, where he met Rimbaud.

Even at the moderately Bohemian Odéon, the sight of two ostentatiously scruffy men strolling through the foyer in a loving embrace caused a nervous flurry. For the few who were aware of such things, 'pederasty' was an unspeakable vice of the outer boulevards. Lesbianism was treated as a professional malady of actresses and courtesans, a titillating subject for Salon painters. Male homosexuality was associated with pimps, blackmailers and transvestites who lurked in shrubberies and public toilets. Since the fall of the Empire, unmasculine behaviour of any kind was thought to be profoundly unpatriotic. France, it was felt, had wilted under Prussia, not because of its strutting chauvinism, but because its men were too feminine.

Verlaine's old friend Lepelletier decided to use his gossip column in *Le Peuple souverain* to issue a gentle warning. This was Rimbaud's first appearance in a national newspaper: 'All the Parnassians were there [at the Odéon].' 'Paul Verlaine was arm-in-arm with a charming young lady, Mlle Rimbaut.'[23]

A few days later, Lepelletier invited Verlaine and his 'girlfriend' to dinner to make sure they had learnt their lesson. With Verlaine manning the bottles, Rimbaud overcame his shyness and set about destroying the conversation. He accused Lepelletier (in a phrase which later appealed to the Surrealists)[24] of 'bowing down to corpses' because he had seen him take his hat off to a funeral procession. Lepelletier, who had recently lost his mother, seemed intolerably sanctimonious to Rimbaud. He threatened his host with a steak-knife. 'I rammed him back into his seat', Lepelletier remembered, 'saying as I did so that I had recently been at war and that since I had not been afraid of the Prussians I wasn't going to be intimidated by a little trouble-maker like him.' Rimbaud ended the evening in a cloud of smoke.[25]

This should not be the last word on Rimbaud's social life in Paris. He did make serious attempts to forge a career. The story that Victor Hugo patted him on the head and called him an 'infant Shakespeare' is apocryphal, though Rimbaud's retort may well be genuine: 'That old duffer gets up my nose.'[26] Verlaine was on cordial terms with the Hugos and could easily have taken Rimbaud to one of Hugo's eclectic soirées. Rimbaud did not spend all his time drinking in dives and eating out of dustbins. Edmond Goncourt's *Journal* clearly suggests personal acquaintance or at least a handshake: 'That man [Rimbaud] was perversity incarnate. He left me with the memory of the terrible hand – the hand of Dumollard' (a famous murderer of servant girls).[27]

To Verlaine's dismay, Rimbaud even managed to lose his provincial accent, which suggests a serious concession to the prestige of Paris. He also wrote two poems which are so strangely unobjectionable that they have been probed, without much success, for hidden signs of subversion: 'Tête de faune' – an impeccably Parnassian pastoral – and 'Les Corbeaux', in which an 'army' of crows swirls over a rutted landscape of yellow rivers and ruined hamlets. 'The fields of France where the recent dead lie sleeping' appears to be a patriotic allusion to the soldiers who died for the fatherland. 'Les Corbeaux' was published, without Rimbaud's knowledge, in a Parisian review in September 1872. It was the only poem by Rimbaud to be published in France between 1870 and 1882.*

Proof of Rimbaud's attempt to appear respectable can be found in the second photograph by Carjat, which was probably taken in December. The hair has recovered from the comb and the tie is about to escape from its knot, but the face has learned how to cooperate with a camera. A faraway look has been obtained. This stagey portrait, which Izambard and Delahaye both thought less lifelike than the October photograph, is now the face most often associated with Rimbaud.

This is a picture of Rimbaud pretending to be a poet. Critics, like parents, do not always prefer the most realistic image of their darling. The puffy little face of the October photograph stares straight back at the lens and looks far too young to have written a masterpiece like 'Le Bateau ivre'. In the December photograph, the diverted eyes allow the fantasy to slip past their radar: 'His eyes are stars', drooled Jean Cocteau in 1919. 'He looks like an angel – a materialization.'[29]

A comparison of the two photographs reveals a surprising detail: the jacket and the waistcoat (hiding a dubious white shirt) are identical. Rimbaud must have kept his best suit relatively intact. When one of the Zutistes, a journalist called Henri Mercier, gave him some money for clothes, Rimbaud went to the Marché du Temple and bought a blue suit with a velvet collar.[30] Unwearable at the Hôtel des Étrangers, this was the costume of a young poet who wanted to please.

---

* These inoffensive poems have been anthologized and admired so often that one hesitates to point out that they may not be entirely the work of Rimbaud. Rimbaud denied having written 'Les Corbeaux'. Without revealing its source, Verlaine first published 'Tête de faune' in the section of Les Poètes maudits devoted to his own poetry. The manuscripts have never come to light. Some features of the poems are common in Verlaine's work but otherwise unknown in Rimbaud's.[28]

Smug pedants like Lepelletier did not encourage him to pursue this course. Rimbaud's reputation as a catastrophic dinner guest was spreading. Eye-witness descriptions seem to strip him of all the desirable credentials: he was neither entirely male nor entirely middle-class. To Lepelletier, 'he looked like a boy on the run from a reformatory'.[31] Mallarmé's recollection of his only sighting of Rimbaud is a beautifully neurotic summary of his supposed defects, written with the kid gloves of convoluted syntax. A social mutant had escaped from a Zola novel:

> There was something defiantly or perversely emphatic about him, reminiscent of a working girl, specifically a laundress, because of vast hands, red with sores – the result of passing from hot to cold – hands which, in a boy, would have indicated more terrible professions. I learned that these hands had autographed some fine lines, all unpublished. The mouth, sulky and derisive, recited not one.[32]

These hefty hands made a terrific impression on anyone who saw them. The Belgian judge who sentenced Verlaine in 1873 identified them with an expert eye as 'the hands of a strangler'.[33] These were not the delicate appendages from which elegant verses flow. For Mallarmé, Rimbaud was the sort of attractive hooligan who could (and did) do serious damage to French literature.

Rimbaud now began to consolidate his reputation. With an unerring lack of tact, he presented himself as a combination of the two most repulsive characters known to 1870s France: a homosexual and an anarchist. Politically, he was now so far to the left that he was rebelling against the Commune. He berated it for its culpable reticence: it had stupidly failed to obliterate French culture by torching the Bibliothèque Nationale and the Louvre. In his view (expressed by a squeamishly obscure Delahaye), 'the truly efficacious and definitive revolutionary act would have been to present humanity with the irreparable removal of the thing that constitutes its most precious and most pernicious source of pride'[34] – by which he appears to have meant the penis. The only real cure for bourgeois capitalism was comprehensive castration.

As if to indicate the way forward for the human race, Rimbaud boasted publicly of his homosexual relations. One day, the poet

Maurice Rollinat saw him enter a café. He let his head fall on to the marble table-top and began to describe his latest doings in a loud voice: 'I'm completely shagged out. X . . . fucked me all night long, and now I can't keep my shit in.'[35] (This may not be true but it is medically plausible.)

Similar revelations were overheard by the novelist Alphonse Daudet. Rimbaud was complaining about Verlaine: 'He can satisfy himself on me as much as he likes. But he wants *me* to practise on *him*! Not on your life! He's far too filthy. And he's got horrible skin!'[36]

Something like a joint statement was issued by Rimbaud and Verlaine. It took the form of a sonnet: 'Sonnet du trou du cul'. The quatrains, by Verlaine, are on top, Rimbaud's tercets underneath. Like 'Voyelles', the 'Arsehole Sonnet' was widely disseminated in the Latin Quarter but, unlike 'Voyelles', was not released for general delectation until much later.[37] It was omitted from the 1962 Pléiade edition of Verlaine's 'complete' poems on the grounds of 'deliberate obscenity'. (Most of his other obscenities were evidently deemed accidental.)

> Dark and wrinkled like a violet carnation,
> Humbly crouched amid the moss, it breathes,
> Still moist with love that descends the gentle slope
> Of white buttocks to its embroidered edge.
>
> Filaments like tears of milk have wept
> Under the savage wind that drives them off
> Through little clots of russet earth
> To disappear where inclination led them.
>
> Oft did my dream suck at its vent;
> My soul, envious of physical coitus, made it
> Its musky dripstone and its nest of sobs.
>
> 'Tis the swooning conch, the fondling flute,
> The tube from which the heavenly praline drops,
> A female Canaan cocooned in muggy air.

The two complementary techniques are nicely combined: Verlaine lingers over his landscape image, while Rimbaud rushes through a series of concentric images, looking for the little jolts of strangeness that will send the poem into a different orbit. Verlaine's images are mostly physical, Rimbaud's spiritual and synaesthetic. The effect in both cases is to deride poetic convention. If, for example, the sonnet was sufficiently beautiful, did this mean that Rimbaud had 'immortalized' his partner's anus?

The '*trou du cul*', in fact, performs the same function as Rimbaud's coloured vowels: a conduit for new forms of expression. An anthology on the theme of Art and Beauty might give this sonnet an important place, after the carcass of Baudelaire's 'Une Charogne' – the logical finale of the long, Romantic adventure: art emancipated from its subject matter.

*

Rimbaud and Verlaine were able to gauge their declining popularity towards the end of the year.

The painter Henri Fantin-Latour[38] specialized in group portraits, though he preferred to wrestle with the personality of flower arrangements. He had been hoping to compose a 'Homage to Baudelaire' for the 1872 Salon, but the first-division poets were unavailable and he had to make do with what Edmond Goncourt snootily described as 'tavern geniuses'.[39]

In 'Coin de table', Verlaine and Rimbaud sit dreamily at the end of the table, already half-ostracized: a wispy Verlaine with his egg-shell head, and a lap-dog Rimbaud with rag-doll fingers. His hair has grown since the Carjat photograph. To judge by Fantin's comments, the figure is heavily idealized: 'I was even forced to make them wash their hands!'[40]

While Verlaine used the sittings as an excuse to miss dinner at home,[41] Rimbaud sat only once. He broke his silence – which Fantin interpreted as contempt – only to start 'a political discussion which almost turned nasty'.[42] Albert Mérat refused to be painted into the company of 'pimps and thieves'.[43] He was replaced, like a modern-day Daphne, with a vase of flowers.

The web of male camaraderie was unable to cope with heavy sexual tension. The sharpest comment on Rimbaud's disruptive influence is the gouache painted by Fantin on the same occasion. Blatantly feminized and softened up by comparison with the Carjat photograph, Rimbaud sits demurely under a storm of hair, smiling a sweet, cruel smile, wrapped in a shapeless mass of black cloth.

In 1871, this shapeless mass had a particular connotation. It looked like one of those voluminous, proletarian smocks in which anarchists hid their ticking time-bombs.

13

Dogs

'I found the celebrities of painting and modern poetry derisory.'

('Alchimie du verbe', *Une Saison en Enfer*)

W HEN THE Cercle Zutique closed or was closed down, Rimbaud moved in with Verlaine's friend, the painter Jean-Louis Forain.[1]

At nineteen, Forain already had a long career behind him. After abandoning the École des Beaux-Arts out of boredom, he was discovered in the Louvre by the sculptor Carpeaux, who gave him a job, then dismissed him, unfairly, for breaking a statue. Disowned by his father, Forain slept under bridges, joined the Commune's fire brigade, and studied caricature with André Gill. Too resourceful to be a starving artist, he turned his hand to shop-signs, advertisements, decorative fans and, eventually, cartoons for the illustrated papers. He also practised on the walls of the Latin Quarter. Some of his later caricatures, which were admired by Picasso, suggest a misanthropic Daumier with a solid grounding in classical art and graffiti. He would have made an excellent illustrator for Rimbaud's satirical verse.

Their friendship thrived on cheerful antagonism. Rimbaud called Forain 'a young dog' because he was always chasing after skirts. Forain thought that Rimbaud resembled a dog because of his 'big, gangly body' and, presumably, because he spoke 'only when he was angry'.[2] The scratchy lines of Forain's café-table sketches record the cut-and-thrust of conversation like gramophone needles. In one, Rimbaud peers down like a homicidal Cupid, over the caption, '*Qui s'y frotte s'y pique*' (approximately, 'Don't feed – he bites'). In another, Rimbaud is depicted as a country bumpkin in the big city, trussed up like an organ-grinder's monkey, with huge, flipper hands and the posture of someone who is used to lifting heavy weights.

Throughout that winter, Rimbaud followed Forain on his expeditions to the Louvre, because 'we were poor and the Louvre was heated'. While Forain copied old masters, Rimbaud stood at the window and stared at the moving pictures outside on the Rue de Rivoli.[3]

This would have made a splendid allegorical tableau of nineteenth-century art between Romanticism and Modernity: Rimbaud with his back to the Rembrandts, gazing through the window-frames of the Louvre. In his view, Forain was wasting his time with paint. Flat canvas and oils could not compete with the three-dimensional kaleidoscope of reality.[4] This was probably the point Rimbaud was trying to make one day at the Café du Rat Mort when, having spared himself a visit to the toilet, he created paintings on the table with the powerful impasto of human excrement.[5]

The following prophetic tirade is reported by Forain – the first artist, before Cézanne and Picasso, to recognize Rimbaud's insults as a manifesto of modern art:

> We shall tear painting away from its old copying habits and give it sovereignty. The material world will be nothing but a means for evoking aesthetic impressions. Painters will no longer replicate objects. Emotions will be created with lines, colours and patterns taken from the physical world, simplified and tamed.[6]

Similar ideas are now dispensed in the same galleries where Rimbaud slouched about, sneering at the paint. At the time, this notion of an abstract, independent art was only slightly more acceptable than the idea of blowing up the Louvre. Rimbaud wanted to turn the tiny shop of recommended models into a vast, open-air flea-market:

> For a long time I had boasted of being thoroughly familiar with all possible landscapes, and I found the celebrities of painting and modern poetry derisory.

DOGS

I liked idiotic pictures, decorative lintels, theatre sets, fairground
backdrops, shop-signs, popular prints [. . .]

This passage from *Une Saison en Enfer* is practically all that remains
of a body of art criticism that might have rivalled Baudelaire's.
Rimbaud's aesthetic universe was expanding so quickly that there was
no time to make a map of it. The inability to retain the same mind
for long enough to complete a coherent work of art usually ceases to
be a problem at the end of adolescence. For Rimbaud, it was part of
the creative process. Instead of waiting for his mind to slow to the
pace of tradition, he was redefining the work of art. The Industrial
Revolution had finally reached literature: 'Poetry will no longer keep
step with action. It will *precede* it.'

The alliance of the painter and the poet who despised painting was
strong enough to survive their depressing accommodation and Rimbaud's inconvenient habits. On 8 January 1872, they moved into sordid
lodgings on the southern edge of the Latin Quarter. The building
stood on the corner of the Rue Campagne-Première and the Boulevard
d'Enfer (now Boulevard Raspail). It was demolished in the 1930s,
though similar tenements have survived behind iron railings in the
cobbled Passage d'Enfer a few feet away. The site of Rimbaud's home
is marked by a *lycée technique* and the Raspail Métro station. Downstairs
were a bread-and-wine shop and a garage for the cab-drivers who lived
in the building. Across the road lay the section of the Montparnasse
Cemetery that was set aside for unclaimed bodies. The horse and dog
markets on the boulevard ensured that the cafés were always open and
that funeral processions were often interrupted by drunkards.[7]

Rimbaud and Forain lived in a large attic with sloping ceilings,
'full of dirty daylight and the sounds of spiders', according to
Verlaine.[8] A few pieces of furniture accentuated its nudity: a bed-
frame, a mattress covered with horse blankets, a straw chair, a bare
table with a candle in a mustard-pot. The decorations included a red
pencil drawing of two lesbians.

Forain slept on the mattress while Rimbaud took the bed-springs.
'It suited him down to the ground. He actually liked it, he was that
dirty.' 'We had a water-jug the size of a drinking glass. It was almost
too big for him.'[9]

The filth which was so often associated with Rimbaud should be placed in its historical context – an age when weekly bathing was still considered excessive. This was not the faint patina and smell that the word 'filth' conjures up today. After a hundred days in the city, Rimbaud was a semi-stagnant eco-system with its own atmosphere and verminous population.

Rimbaud infested the attic in the 'Rue Campe' for two months. Verlaine called in so often that they were practically living together. A local craftsman who was interviewed in 1936 remembered seeing Verlaine and a very young-looking Rimbaud walking down the street, arm-in-arm. They were almost continually drunk. On one occasion, Rimbaud locked Forain out of the room and refused to open the door.[10]

> Life with Rimbaud was impossible because he guzzled so much absin-the. Verlaine used to come and fetch him and they both sneered at me because I wouldn't go with them.

In later, more respectable days, Forain denied that his two friends were also intoxicated with sex, though a remark reported by Mme Forain suggests that the relationship was not entirely platonic: 'Rimbaud may have romped with homosexuals but he never went all the way.'[11] These shreds of evidence are still sometimes used to defend Rimbaud's 'chastity', but in his poem on the Rue Campagne-Première, Verlaine's fond memory of '*nuits d'Hercules*' and dubious stains on the wall clearly implies unusual acts of sexual prowess.*

*

TO AN OUTSIDE observer, Rimbaud was simply drowning his genius in alcohol. This may be true, but he was also devising a new life for himself and Verlaine that would help to revolutionize poetry and, eventually, sexual morality.

The longest surviving poem from this period – 'Qu'est-ce pour nous, mon cœur . . .' – describes the sweeping out of old ideals in preparation for the new. It was once said to have been written under

---

* Hercules has not always been a symbol of masculinity. Verlaine was alluding to the heroic deflowering of the fifty daughters of Thespius, but also to the period of captivity during which Hercules dressed as a woman.

the influence of absinthe. This at least shows some awareness of Rimbaud's violently dislocated metre. If the story is true, 'Qu'est-ce pour nous . . .' is a powerful argument for the legalization of absinthe. The sense goes tumbling over the ruins of the alexandrine like a torrent over boulders.

> What are they to us, my heart, those sheets of blood
> And cinders, and a thousand murders, and the long cries
> Of rage, sobs from every hell overturning
> Every order; and the Wind still blowing on the rubble?

The commonest dating of this poem – clearly disproved by the decaying carbon-14 of Rimbaud's alexandrines – drags it back to the period of 'Communard inebriation'.[12] But Rimbaud was at least two stages beyond the Commune. The poet of 'Qu'est-ce pour nous . . .' wants to see everything consumed in a global holocaust, including some of the sacred cows of the Commune and even the Communards themselves: 'justice', 'history', 'colonists' and 'peoples'. His dream is that he and his 'romantic' (or 'fanciful') friends will be obliterated in a transcontinental catastrophe that will wipe out the Earth itself: 'Europe, Asia, America, disappear!' Seventy years later, it might have been an ode to the hydrogen bomb.

Unfortunately, this state of total, irreversible anarchy is seen to be a delusion brought on by wishful thinking. No act of the imagination – nor any amount of absinthe – could ever vaporize such a solid Earth. The last line is written in a different metre and stands outside the poem as if in the real world:

> It's nothing. I'm here! I'm still here!

Rimbaud, the poet of drug-induced visions, is more often the poet of the morning after. His new plan – as far as it can be deduced from *Une Saison en Enfer* and Verlaine's letters and poems – lay somewhere between a children's game and a new religion. Verlaine and Rimbaud were to be the holy family of a new faith. Their *culte à deux* would transcend the moral distinctions that had caused humanity and the son of Mme Rimbaud such needless suffering. Rimbaud's later prose poem 'Vagabonds' appears to define the enterprise as a kind of metaphysical therapy: 'I had, in all intellectual sincerity, undertaken to restore him to his primitive state as son of the Sun.'

Rimbaud is still academically separated from the Parnassians; yet he was one of the few French poets who tried to turn their neo-paganism into social reality.[13] His ambition was not to acquire a philosophical trademark for his work but to use his poetry to re-create the Golden Age.

To judge by the letter he sent to Rimbaud later that spring, Verlaine grasped very little but the terminology, and there may at this stage have been little else to grasp. He knew that they were supposed to be undertaking what Rimbaud called a 'martyrdom' and a 'way of the cross', and he was quite happy to humour him if this was the entrance fee to Rimbaud's universe.

For Rimbaud, who mistook Verlaine's infatuation for commit-ment to a shared ideal, their public liaison was not just a smug provocation or another means of 'deranging the senses'. Homosexu-ality was an essential part of the project. In 1871, there was no such thing as 'gay culture', no general prescription for a homosexual lifestyle. The very notion of a 'lifestyle' was peculiar to a few philo-sophical eccentrics, like the utopian socialist, Charles Fourier, who believed that 'omnisexuals' had powers of discernment unavailable to normal people.[14]

Rimbaud's attachment of a particular type of relationship to a social philosophy makes this an important moment in cultural history. However flippant or unfeasible his plans for 'martyrdom' will appear to have been, the drunken lovers of the Rue Campagne-Première did after all become the Adam and Eve of modern homosexuality.

*

THE FIRST STEP was comparatively simple: persuade the apostle Verlaine to leave his wife and child.

By now, the Mautés had begun to fight back. In December, while Verlaine was in Arras collecting a small inheritance, Mathilde and her father examined the accounts. Money was seeping away, and 'that boy' was identified as the drain. Rimbaud would have to be sent away.

The first attempt seems to have consisted of an anonymous letter to Mme Rimbaud. She was informed by a well-wisher that her son was going to the dogs. He was already well known in the neighbour-hood for his drinking sprees and should be summoned back to Charleville before he did anything irreparable. Mme Rimbaud ignored the letter, assuming it to be one of Arthur's face-saving ploys for obtaining the price of a ticket home.[15]

Meanwhile, Verlaine's mother had joined the campaign to salvage her son. She used her connections to arrange a dinner with an important civil servant who was looking for a clerk. On the evening in question, Verlaine failed to appear. Dinner began without him. Forty-five minutes into the meal, a drunkard staggered through the door, moaning about the miseries of married life. The job was offered to someone else.

Every night now, Verlaine was coming home drunk. Once, he tried to set fire to his wife's hair. On 13 January, after complaining that his coffee was cold, he picked up his three-month-old son and hurled him against the wall. M. and Mme Mauté heard the screams from the floor below and ran up to find their daughter being strangled by their son-in-law. The monster escaped and the baby was rescued, apparently unhurt. A doctor was instructed to make a detailed note of the bruises on Mathilde's neck.

After lying low for two days, Verlaine began to send pathetic letters to Mathilde. Eventually, from an undisclosed location in the south of France (Périgueux), she wrote to say that she would come home as soon as 'the cause of all our misfortunes' had been banished for ever. Verlaine refused: how could he prevent Rimbaud from living where he chose?

Mathilde's father now had a petition for legal separation drawn up. It was based on the doctor's report. No mention was made of Rimbaud. At this stage, the idea was simply to frighten Verlaine into behaving decently. Verlaine, however, was terrified of being accused of 'pederasty': private jokes were sometimes quite acceptable, but a public accusation might have severe legal consequences. In a panic, he sent a note to Albert Mérat, threatening him with 'swordsmanlike measures' if he didn't stop gossiping about his relations with Rim-baud: 'Those remarks might fall on stupid ears . . .'[16]

It was now, when Verlaine was about to be driven back into the fold, that Rimbaud committed the most notorious act of his Parisian career. The 'Carjat incident' is often interpreted as a straightforward act of drunken stupidity, but the sequence of events makes it looks suspiciously premeditated.[17]

A 'Vilains Bonshommes' dinner was held on 2 March 1872 at the wine-shop where, five months before, Rimbaud had amazed the *bonshommes* with his brilliant poems and theories.

The meal was over; cognac and coffee had been served. Then came the after-dinner ordeal: poetry readings.

As usual, the most tedious poets took the longest time. Rimbaud bit his tongue and waited for the end. Then a justly forgotten poet called Auguste Creissels stood up and started to recite his 'Sonnet du combat': a pompous attempt at wit which evidently caused its author great satisfaction.

Rimbaud began to add an extra syllable to the end of each line:

> Subject to this law, the uniform tercet – *merde*!
> Stands grave and rigid at its designated post – *merde*!

What happened next is not completely clear, but the general idea is the same in every account. The poet-photographer Étienne Carjat called Rimbaud a 'little toad'. Rimbaud reached behind him, grabbed Verlaine's swordstick and lunged at Carjat across the table, grazing his hand. Rimbaud was disarmed, raised off the floor by the barrel-chested Carjat and dumped in the hall outside. Some accounts say that the attack occurred after Rimbaud's eviction. He lurked patiently in the gloom of the hallway until the readings were over. When Carjat emerged, he jumped out and stabbed him in the stomach.

The unsuccessful murderer was entrusted to Michel de l'Hay, the painter from Cros's laboratory, who helped him back to his hovel in the Rue Campagne-Première.

Carjat seems to have been unscathed, but he was angry enough to destroy the negatives of his two Rimbaud photographs.[18] The other result was that Rimbaud was banned from all future 'Vilains Bonshommes' dinners.

For Rimbaud, this was hardly a disaster, but for Verlaine, who convinced himself that the ban was motivated by jealousy, it was a serious blow – as Rimbaud knew it would be. Since almost all of

Verlaine's friends were 'Vilains Bonshommes', and since Verlaine took Rimbaud's side in the matter, this meant that most of his remaining ties with Paris had now been severed.

At this point, Verlaine seems to have obtained a brief adjournment of his 'martyrdom'. With a drunkard's optimism, he asked for time in which to 'patch up' his marriage and reach the impossible compromise: he would pacify Mathilde *and* follow Rimbaud on his 'way of the cross', whatever it was. Rimbaud was persuaded to leave Paris for a time.

According to Mathilde, who saw a bundle of letters which were later destroyed, Rimbaud was 'irritated to have been sacrificed to *a whim*'.[19] But he may have been quite willing to leave the city. After five months of drunkenness and squalor, the spartan landscape of the Ardennes would be a fresh sheet of paper.

In early March 1872, Rimbaud found himself back at the railway station. As far as the Mautés were concerned, they had seen the last of him.

Rimbaud spent a few days in Arras with some relatives of Verlaine. Nothing is known about his visit. He then returned to Charleville and waited for Verlaine to give the signal.

Since September 1871, Rimbaud had been re-enacting the life of Balzac's 'Great Man of the Provinces in Paris': departure for the city, acclamation, passionate love, public disgrace, homecoming. Unlike Balzac's character, he had no intention of committing suicide. What to most people looked like a trail of destruction was the clearing of new ground. Rimbaud was looking forward to a great experiment that would change the nature of existence or at any rate keep boredom at bay for a season or two.

14

Songs of Innocence

'I came to find my mind's disorder sacred.'

('Alchimie du verbe', *Une Saison en Enfer*)

W HEN RIMBAUD had returned to Charleville, his mother supplied the moral of his season in Paris: 'intellectual work leads
practically nowhere'.[1]

He thought of his coming adventure, sat in the town-centre café
with Delahaye and Bretagne, and told mind-boggling tales of his
life in Paris, In the daytime, he buried himself in the public library
above his old school and worked on some new poems: quaint, airy
little songs that would seem to Verlaine to have been written by a
completely different person.

The Rimbaud who was sending admonitory letters to Verlaine,
care of Forain, sounded like a junior version of Mme Rimbaud. These
'*lettres martyriques*', as Verlaine called them, were later destroyed by
Mathilde, but the thrust of them can be deduced from Verlaine's
replies: Rimbaud suspected him of trying to wriggle out of their
'pact'.

Cowering happily under the verbal thrashing, Verlaine wrote to
thank him on 2 April 1872 for his 'kind letter':

The '*little boy*' accepts the well-deserved spanking, the '*toads' friend*'
retracts everything, and having never abandoned your martyrdom, is

thinking of it, if possible, with even more *fervour* and joy, be assured, Rimbe.

That's right, love me, protect and give confidence. Being very weak, I'm in great need of kindness. [. . .] I won't try to sweeten you up again with my little-boy antics.

Rimbaud could see at a distance that Verlaine was back on the slippery road to respectability. The foolish man even suggested that, when 'Rimbe' returned to Paris, he might care to find a job . . .

The only fragment of Rimbaud's letters deemed quotable by Mathilde in her memoirs refers to this unfortunate proposal:

Work is further from me than my fingernail is from my eye.

Fuck me! [repeated eight times]

You won't stop thinking I'm expensive to feed until you see me actually eating shit.[2]

For Verlaine, these letters were a breath of fresh air. His Bohemian existence had been reduced to a daily aperitif with Forain. Mathilde had returned from the South and the flow of money was stemmed by M. Mauté. The Lloyd Belge company was persuaded to overlook the risk and employed Verlaine as an insurance clerk. He was almost constantly sober. Mathilde had not been set on fire for several days.

With Rimbaud out of the way, Verlaine became more malleable. Mathilde was even able to broach the subject of violent behaviour. Verlaine answered as if she had asked him to explain the workings of a simple machine:

When I go with the little brown-haired [female] pussy-cat [Forain], I am good, because the little brown-haired pussy is very gentle. But when I go with the little fair-haired pussy-cat [Rimbaud], I am bad, because the little fair-haired pussy is ferocious.[3]

This sinister little nursery-rhyme is the only explanation Mathilde was ever offered. Her own analysis, thirty-five years later, was that Rimbaud blamed her for his 'banishment' to Charleville and took revenge by seducing her husband.

Though her chronology is wrong, Mathilde's conviction that Rimbaud was jealous of her may well be accurate, and it certainly reflects a genuine impression. It was after the birth of little Georges that Rimbaud had begun in earnest to wreck the marriage. By abducting the father, he would be re-creating the situation that had darkened his own childhood, running away with a man who had abandoned his wife and child.

The long poem 'Mémoire' probably dates from this period. Set by an arm of the river Meuse in Charleville, it dredges half-remembered scenes out of the sluggish stream with an associative technique that seems to have been invented just for this poem. Rimbaud was writing for an audience that did not yet exist. It is only after a century of modernist literature and cinema that the mind's eye can perform the acrobatic feats that were apparently quite routine for Rimbaud. Even so, 'Mémoire' remains a beautifully difficult poem.

> Clear water; like the salt of childhood tears,
> the assault on the sun of the whiteness of women's bodies;
> the silk, pure lily, in a host, of the banners
> beneath the walls whose defence was entrusted to a maid;
>
> the frolic of angels; – no . . . the golden current moving,
> stirs its grassy arms, black, heavy, above all cool. She
> sinks, with the blue Sky a canopy above her bed, calls
> for curtains: the shade of the hill and the arch. [. . .]

The woman who walks by the river with her children is often said to be Mme Rimbaud, in despair at her husband's departure. The man himself, who heads off over the mountain in the sixth stanza, is identified, with equal conviction on both sides, as Rimbaud or as his father.

These critical disagreements which sputter on for decades usually indicate a resistant ambiguity in the text. The child and man are like synchronic figures in a medieval painting, similar but separate. The adult leaves in a scatter of identities, 'like a thousand white angels parting on the road', but the child remains bogged down in the inscrutable past:

> A toy of this dreary eye of water, I cannot grasp,
> O motionless boat! O too short arms! neither one flower
> nor the other, neither the yellow that importunes me,
> there, nor the friendly blue in the ashen water.

Ah! the dust of the willows that are shaken by a wing!
The roses of the reeds, long since devoured!
My boat, still fixed; and its chain pulled down
to the bed of this rimless eye of water – to what mud?

Like 'Le Bateau ivre', 'Mémoire' is one of Rimbaud's pre-departure poems – a silent room where the traveller sits for a moment, worried about his luggage, trying to piece together a plausible image of the future from fragments of the past. Rimbaud was about to embark on what was effectively a form of married life. The unresolved arguments are the source of the poem's ambiguous charm: how to follow in the footsteps of a father who was associated with home but also with the opposite of home – desertion, irresponsibility and freedom? How was the desperate woman to be consoled if she reserved her love for the man who was no longer there?

Happily, no simple narrative fits the poem. Its biographical signifi-cance lies as much in the structure as in the details. With its remotely corresponding motifs, it replicates the structure of memory itself ('Mémoire' is after all the title) – the interference of past and present, the puzzling obduracy of certain images. Rimbaud never wrote another poem like it. It was as if the act of composition had answered a question or revealed the futility of asking it in the first place: how can the mind detach itself from the 'mud' of its own memory?

The other poems of Rimbaud's temporary 'exile' in his home town are quite different. They were written by the Rimbaud who had already embarked on his adventure, and if they appear to be incom-prehensible according to normal criteria, it is because the poems are not a diary but part of the adventure itself.

Usually published under editors' titles – *Derniers vers*, *Vers nou-veaux* or *Chansons* – these were perhaps the '*Études néantes*'[4] ('Void Studies') that Rimbaud had mentioned to Verlaine: poems purified of any direct message, like musical *études*. When he received the first of them through the post, Verlaine was shocked. The searing obsceni-ties of the earlier Rimbaud had vanished like the trail of a rocket.

M. Rimbaud now changed his tack and worked in the naive (him!), in the very and deliberately over-simple, using only assonances, vague terms, childish or popular expressions. In so doing, he performed

miracles of tenuity, of real blurriness and charm, so slim and spindly
as to be almost inappreciable:

> It's been found again.
> What? – Eternity.
> It's the sea gone off
> With the sun.
>
> [. . .]
>
> Since, from you alone,
> Satin cinders,
> Duty rises,
> Without anyone saying, At last.
>
> There, no hope,
> No rising of the sun.
> Science with patience,
> The suffering is certain.

Since Verlaine retained very little of what Rimbaud told him,
Delahaye is probably a better guide to these anorexic lyrics. The idea,
as explained to him by Rimbaud, was to 'open the senses' and then to
'fix' and set down impressions, however fleeting or illogical.[5] It was a
kind of photographic realism without the kitchen-sinks and statistics.
Rimbaud was claiming a vast new domain for poetry: the mind's full
range of alternative realities. The unnerving spaciousness of the
poems allows a sense of possibilities to invade the mind:

> O seasons, O castles,
> What soul is without fault?
>
> O seasons, O castles!
>
> I made the magical study
> Of Happiness that none can elude.

Rimbaud's own account of these early experiments in *Une Saison
en Enfer* is not as mysterious as it might appear:

> I accustomed myself to simple hallucination: I saw quite plainly a
> mosque in place of a factory, a drummers' school built by angels,
> carriages on the highways of the sky, a drawing-room at the bottom of
> a lake.

This simple form of substitution, perhaps best described as unrealism, is exemplified by the poem 'Larme', with its psychotropic cloudscapes:

> Then the storm changed the sky, until evening.
> There were black lands, lakes and poles,
> Colonnades beneath the blue night, stations.

The next stage was to modify the means of expression: 'Then I explained my magical sophisms with verbal hallucination!'

'Verbal hallucination' was the linguistic equivalent of seeing things: vowels and consonants that come to the ear like musical phrases, words that lose their contours like clouds, so that instead of eating '*boudin noir*' (black sausage), the poet finds himself feeding on '*bouts d'air noir*' (bits of black air).

Rimbaud's view of himself as a realist places him in a small minority among Rimbaud critics. But these were not gratuitous hallucinations. The 'spiritual songs' that fly about 'among the gooseberries' in 'Fêtes de la patience' were not a simple swarm of free-floating signifiers.[6] The defeatism of post-structuralist theory was quite foreign to Rimbaud. If language was inadequate to the task, it should be reinvented.

All of these verbal experiments have an ulterior motive which takes them far beyond the confines of professional literature. In *Une Saison en Enfer*, Rimbaud attaches his songs to a concept which had fascinated him in the works of nineteenth-century illuminists: that behind the stage-set of sensory impressions lies a pure, absolute reality. With astronomic foresight, he compares this reality to the blackness of outer space: 'At last, O happiness, O reason, I drew back the azure from the sky, which is black.'[7] This ultimate truth can be glimpsed only in fleeting moments when the senses are no longer separate from the objects of perception, when the personality evaporates, like 'the gnat intoxicated at the tavern urinal, besotted with the borage, and dissolved by a sunbeam!'

The question is: how can a soluble personality exert control over the means of expression? For this, it was necessary to find a form that could act as a vehicle. Whether or not Rimbaud truly expected this vehicle to transport him to a miraculous new reality, the experiment would be an absorbing test of his poetic skill: how to find exact forms of notation where description seemed impossible.

Rimbaud had stumbled on some promising components for this vehicle in the Charleville public library: ten neglected volumes which contained the complete libretti of the eighteenth-century light opera composer, Charles Favart.

At first sight, Favart's lyrics look far too flimsy to have interested Rimbaud. Idle shepherds and hypersensitive milkmaids drown their vapid sorrows in an endless stream of simple harmony. This was precisely the quality Rimbaud was seeking. Fragments of Favart, already pale with insignificance, re-emerge in Rimbaud's poems, scissored and pasted into a kind of oracular obscurity:

> But! I'll have no more desire,
> He has taken charge of my life.
>
> How should my words be understood?
> He makes them flee and fly!

This sampling technique has no precedent in French poetry, though it obviously has precedents in the human mind. Rimbaud was re-creating the background mutter of sounds and impressions that was supposed to be filtered out by the process of literary composition.

Rimbaud's *chansons* have been used to fill in the poet's blank face in the spring of 1872 with any expression that happens to suit the narrative. In some accounts, he was deliriously happy, in others, deliriously miserable. But the point of this technique was to erase the poet's personality from the poem and to create an anonymous chant: short, liturgical pieces whose purpose was to induce a state of religious contemplation but which also contain explicit reminders of the spiritual goal.[8]

The dominant theme appears in almost everything that Rimbaud wrote in the wilderness of the Ardennes: the first temptation of Christ. Man shall not live by bread (or, in Verlaine's case, by absinthe) alone:

> If I have any *taste* at all,
> It's only for earth and stones.

> Dinn! dinn! dinn! dinn! Let's eat the air,
> The rock, the coals, the iron.

> ME: Enough of these landscapes.
> What's drunkenness, friends?

> I'd just as soon, in fact I'd rather,
> Lie rotting in the pond,
> Beneath the horrible cream,
> By the floating woods.

The stone-munching hermit of these poems is a spiritual alcoholic, 'sapped' by 'the mouthless Hydra' of his thirst, 'tugged along' by his stomach, suffering from dehydration in a world of bitters, wines and rivers of blackcurrant liqueur.

There are several references to his impending 'martyrdom'. In 'L'Éternité', it is said, vaguely, to consist of '*science*' and '*patience*' (etymologically, 'knowledge' and 'suffering'). But these themes are elements of a design in which rhythms and rhymes play an equally important role. Attempts to decipher Rimbaud's hidden messages have concealed his practical achievement. Some of the secret references turn out to be quite humble in any case: the crowing 'Gallic cock' (a reference, obvious at the time, to a triumphant erection), or the violet-eating 'hedge spider' – 'l'araignée *de la haie*' (De-la-haye).[9] Izambard was closer to the truth when he noticed that some of Rimbaud's refrains were adapted from the folk songs he used to sing and which he seems to have collected on his travels:

> Aveine, aveine, aveine,
> Que le beau temps t'amène. [Trad.]

> Ah! Que le temps vienne
> Où les cœurs s'éprennent. [Rimbaud][10]

The songs of the elusive, hallucinating hermit are now among the most commercially successful in the history of poetry. Encouraged, perhaps, by Verlaine's own *chansons*, Rimbaud had repackaged a free resource: the common fund of traditional verse. Having rejected the literary establishment, he was attaching himself now to a far wider community, paring away the sophistication that lies on French poetry in layers as thick as its own history.

Since his death, Rimbaud has been reassimilated by the academy. The unclassical elements of his lyrics – their *'vers impairs'** and assonant rhymes – are described as if they were pedantic experiments or praised, universally, as fine examples of 'subversion'. In fact, the poem thought to be Rimbaud's wildest display of prosodic irregularity – 'Bonne pensée du matin' – has a regular rhythm if the voice is allowed to recite it instead of counting its syllables, while some of his 'incorrect' rhymes are perfectly harmonious when pronounced with what Verlaine called Rimbaud's *'parisiano-ardennais'* accent.[11] Many of these songs could be performed more effectively by Ardennes peasants than by trained actors.

Rimbaud's subversion consisted in rescuing verse poetry from the printed page and returning it to its collective roots. Verlaine might have been less amazed by this poetic volte-face if he had seen that Rimbaud's sarcastic obscenity and folkloric 'naivety' were solutions to the same problem: if literature is a bourgeois institution, how can it be used to convey an anti-bourgeois ideology?[12] Or, from the seer's point of view: how can the language of the Third Republic convey a vision of absolute truth?

A letter arrived from Verlaine towards the end of May: Rimbaud was to take the Paris train the following Saturday. He would be met secretly at the station. Verlaine seemed at last to be ready for the great adventure, though his tone was not what might be expected of an apprentice seer:

> Now, greetings, reunion, joy, waiting for letters, waiting for You. – Me had same dream twice last night: *You, child torturer* ['*martyriseur d'enfant*']. *You all goldez* [*sic* for 'golden']. Funny, eh, Rimbe?[13]

* Lines with odd numbers of syllables, usually said to be a deviation from the 'norm' (lines of eight or twelve syllables).

[162]

15

'The Good Disciple'

'[. . .] the honeymoon
Will pluck their smile and fill the sky
With a thousand bands of copper.'

('Jeune ménage')

IN HIS LAST letter to 'Rimbe', Verlaine had mentioned a trick he was hoping to play on 'a certain gentleman who was not without influence in your 3 months of Ardennes and my 6 months of shit' (a reference to his father-in-law, Mauté). The trick apparently required Rimbaud to look like a decent person, which suggests a double-edged hoax: if Rimbaud could be made acceptable to the Mautés, Verlaine would be able to enjoy him in peace.

Do what possible, at least for a time, to look less terrifying than before: *laundry, polish, comb, simpering smiles*: this necessary if you to take part in tigerish plans. Me too: laundress, body-servant, etc. (if you like).

Rimbaud returned to Paris on 25 May 1872,[1] not as a deceptively elegant young gentleman but as the jealous idol of Verlaine's dreams. Verlaine crumbled instantly. His sonnet, 'Le Bon Disciple', which he wrote for Rimbaud that May, shows that the idea of 'martyrdom' had taken root. The sonnet was never intended for publication. It survived only because a Belgian policeman removed it from Rimbaud's wallet fourteen months later.

I am chosen, I am damned!
A great unknown breath surrounds me.
O terror! *Parce, Domine*!

What hard angel pummels me thus
Between the shoulders while
I fly away to Paradise?

Adorable, malignant fever,
Sweet delirium, tender dread,
I am a martyr and a king,
A falcon I soar and die a swan!

O Jealous One who called me,
Here I am – here's all of me!
Unworthy still, I crawl toward thee!
– Mount my loins and trample!

Verlaine's inverted sonnet is not the flippant ode to anal inter-course it was sometimes thought to be. It could easily have been included with the devout hymns of *Sagesse* which record his conver-sion to Catholicism fifteen months later. In Verlaine's poetry, God and Rimbaud have a strong family resemblance: 'My God, you have wounded me with love / And the wound is quivering still . . .' (a poem later found in the toilet-house at Roche).[2]

The old story of the next two years is that Verlaine plumbed the depths of depravity with Rimbaud and then suddenly saw the light; but he was converted to a religious point of view long before God snatched him up 'like an eagle grabbing a rabbit'.[3] 'Grab hold of me as soon as you get back', he had urged Rimbaud. Rimbaud was his 'great radiant sin', the delicious instrument of divine chastisement.

This was not the sort of martyrdom that Rimbaud had in mind.

*

FOR THE NEXT forty-four days, Rimbaud moved from one board-ing-house to the next like a hunted criminal. He scattered copies of his latest poems among his remaining friends: Verlaine, Forain and a young poet called Jean Richepin, later known for his slang poems on the beggars of Paris. Richepin also acquired – and then lost – Rimbaud's *'cahier d'expressions'*, which the poet had discarded like an old newspaper. Apparently, Rimbaud had filled his notebook with 'uncommon words, pyrotechnic rhymes and outlines of ideas'.[4]

Manuscripts do occasionally resurface when collectors die or receive large tax bills; but Richepin's description of the notebook is precious in itself – evidence of the contradictory Rimbaud who stored up material for his poems and then suddenly liquidated all his assets.

Rimbaud's forty-four days in Paris are unusually well documented thanks to the letter he sent to Delahaye in June. His principal aim was to avoid boredom. He shared his strategy with Delahaye, who was suffering from the stultifying effects of Charleville:

> You might be well advised to do a lot of walking and reading. You certainly shouldn't coop yourself up in offices and homes. Stupefaction should be attained far from places like that. I'm not at all in the business of dispensing balm, but I do believe that there's no consolation to be found in habits when things get pitiful.

In a month and a half, following his own advice, Rimbaud slept in at least three different beds, barely long enough for dust to settle on his suitcase. Wherever possible, he slept on the roof.[5] When he wrote to Delahaye in June from the city of 'Parshit', he was festering in the Hôtel de Cluny, across the street from the Sorbonne. He had a 'pretty' room with a downward view into 'a bottomless courtyard'. 'I drink water all night long, I don't see the dawn, I don't sleep, and I'm stifling.'

Remove the electric toilet, the blue-flower wallpaper and the blocked sink, and this period of Rimbaud's life can be re-created quite easily by the literary tourist. The Hôtel de Cluny itself is now a two-star parvenu, but the blight of renovation has spared several pockets of authentic seediness between the Sorbonne and the Saint-Séverin district by the river.

It was there, a few days later, that a young man from Charleville called Jules Mary saw Rimbaud in a large studio. He had no paper and no pen, and, when asked about his writing, he pointed to an inkwell in which the ink had turned into greenish sludge. Jules Mary treated him to a meal of bread and soup. Rimbaud reciprocated with a bunch of watercress bought on the Place Saint-Michel.[6] The earlier letter to Delahaye suggests that even this was a major concession to etiquette: 'So far, I've managed to avoid the plagues of émigrés from Shitville.'

Like the hermit of his songs, Rimbaud thrived on dissatisfaction. Rage was preferable to boredom, adversity to comfort:

> The heat is not very constant, but when I see that the fine weather is in everyone's interests, and that everyone is a pig, I hate the summer, which does me in whenever it shows itself a little. I'm so thirsty that I think I must have gangrene. The Belgian and Ardennes rivers, and the caverns, that's what I miss.

The exemplary Bohemian was living his days in reverse, writing at night and getting drunk at breakfast-time. His favourite bar ('despite its grudging garçons') was the haunt of 'nameless poets, shirtless scholars and penless journalists', according to Richepin: the 'Académie d'Absinthe' on the Rue Saint-Jacques, so called because instead of forty Academicians, it boasted forty barrels of absinthe.[7] Absinthe was the liquid equivalent of his latest poems – evanescent and unexpectedly brutal. Intoxication with a punch-line:

> It's the most delicate and shimmering of suits – drunkenness by virtue of that sage of glaciers,* *absomphe* – except that, afterwards, you end up sleeping in shit!

Before moving to the Hôtel de Cluny, Rimbaud had occupied a room on the other side of the Boulevard Saint-Michel, in the Rue Monsieur-le-Prince, which snakes up from the Odéon to the Jardin du Luxembourg. Of the three addresses associated with Rimbaud – numbers 22, 41 and 55 – only the Hôtel d'Orient at number 41 (now the murky Hôtel Stella) fits the description in his letter to Delahaye.[9] It was a careful piece of writing that should really be included in all editions of his works:

> Last month [May 1872], my room in the Rue Monsieur-le-Prince looked onto a garden in the Lycée Saint-Louis. There were enormous trees beneath my narrow window. At three in the morning, the candlelight grows dim and all the birds start singing at once in the trees. It's over. No more work. I had to gaze at the trees and the sky,

---

* *'Cette sauge de glaciers'*, perhaps because absinthe is green on cracked ice. (One writer refers to its 'milky sage tint'.)[8]

transfixed by that inexpressible first hour of morning. I could see the school dormitories, completely silent. And already I could hear the delicious, resonant, clattering sound of the carts on the boulevards.

I smoked my hammerhead pipe and spat on the roof-tiles – because my room was a garret. At five o'clock, I'd go down to buy some bread. It was that time of day. Workers are up and about all over the place. Time to get drunk at the wine-shop – time for me, that is. I'd go back to eat and then get into bed at seven in the morning, when the sun brings the woodlice out from under the roof-tiles.

The early morning in summer and the December evenings – that's what I've always found delightful here.

This may be the only relic of Rimbaud's Paris journalism – a colourful 'Scène de la Vie de Bohème' for the *Figaro*, purged of the emblematic *merdes*. It might also support Delahaye's contested claim that Rimbaud was already writing prose poems.[10] 'Aube', in the *Illuminations*, has the same apparent simplicity and a similar theme: the fascination of 'inexpressible' instants and the purity of dawn before hideous, creeping things like woodlice and office workers emerge.

As in some of Baudelaire's prose poems, the paragraphs are like embryonic stanzas. Perhaps, like Baudelaire, Rimbaud discovered his first prose poem by accident, in the draft of a verse poem.

DAWN

I have embraced the summer dawn.

Nothing was stirring yet in front of the palaces.[11] The water was still. The camps of shadows were not leaving the forest road. I walked along, waking up the warm and living breaths, and the precious stones were looking, and the wings rose soundlessly.

The first advance, in the path already filled with cool, pale glints, was a flower that told me its name.

I laughed at the blond wasserfall that tumbled through the firs: at the silvery summit I recognized the goddess.

Then I lifted the veils one by one. In the avenue, by waving my arms. On the plain, where I pointed her out to the cock. In the city she fled among the steeples and the domes, and, running like a beggar on the marble quays, I chased her.

At the top of the road, near a wood of laurels, I surrounded her with her massed veils, and I felt something of her enormous body. Dawn and the child fell down at the bottom of the wood.

On waking, it was noon.

The traces of Baudelaire's 'Crépuscule du matin' might also indicate a real path. Forain had moved to a new studio in the Hôtel Lauzun on the quiet Ile Saint-Louis. Rimbaud certainly visited him there. It was in the Hôtel Lauzun (or Pimodan) that Baudelaire had lived as a young poet and, as Rimbaud knew, attended the meetings of the Club des Hachichins.[12] In the grand salon, with its painted panels and gilded ceilings, Balzac, Gautier and Baudelaire, under the supervision of a doctor, had explored the artificial paradise of opium-tinted hashish.

It is a tantalizing thought that Rimbaud's 'Bonne pensée du matin' might have been written from the same window as Baudelaire's first urban pastorales, with the same unexpectedly bucolic view of Paris in the west, and the same rich salon on the floor below:

> At four in the morning, in summer,
> Love's sleep still lingers.
> Under the groves the dawn evaporates
>   The smells of the evening fête.
>
> But yonder on the vast building-site,
> Toward the sun of the Hesperides,
> In shirtsleeves, the carpenters
>   Are already astir.
>
> In their foaming desert, at peace,
> They prepare the precious panels
> On which the city's wealth
>   Will laugh under false skies.

*

By the end of June, Rimbaud had helped Verlaine to overcome all his good resolutions.

Every morning, the insurance clerk set off for work and never arrived. Mathilde had become so tiresome and her parents so snide that it took several absinthes to restore his good mood.

Mathilde watched her marriage disintegrate again. Her husband was thrashing about with his pocket-knife, demanding 'patience' and 'understanding'. He even tried to puncture Mme Mauté with his swordstick. The ominous glazed look returned. The evil boy could not be far away. A friend of the family had spotted Rimbaud several times, north of the river, in the Passage Jouffroy, where there was a small theatre. Rimbaud might have found a temporary job as a stage-hand or cashier.[13]

On the evening of Sunday, 7 July, Mathilde was 'suffering from a vague cold' (according to Verlaine) or was 'in the grip of a violent headache and a high fever' (according to Mathilde). Verlaine gave her a friendly kiss and went out to buy some medicine.

A few yards down the road, he ran into Rimbaud, who had been about to deliver a letter to the Rue Nicolet. The letter explained that he had seen enough of Paris and had decided that they should leave immediately for Belgium.

Verlaine tried to change his mind:

> 'But my wife is ill. I have to go and get something at the chemist's . . .'
> 'No you don't. Stop going on about your wife. Come on, I told you, we're leaving.'
> So, naturally, I went with him.[14]

Verlaine later blamed his behaviour on Rimbaud's hypnotic powers. In this case, he was probably right. Eleven weeks later, he wrote to Edmond Lepelletier, '*nudus, pauper*, without books or pictures', 'having fled like an improvident Lot from the Gomorrah of the Rue Nicolet, leaving everything behind'.[15]

The overnight train would take them to Arras, where they could stay with Verlaine's relatives before crossing the border to Belgium and freedom.

It was dawn when they arrived in Arras.[16] They left the station, Verlaine tittering like a truant, Rimbaud – 'despite his extraordinary, precocious seriousness' – looking for some 'lugubrious fun'. The shops and cafés were still closed. After a quick tour of the town, they returned to the station buffet for a celebratory aperitif.

At the next table, a man in a straw hat was listening to their conversation. 'I pointed him out to Rimbaud, who began to laugh his silent, muted laugh.' The conversation became more interesting. They talked of burglaries, jailbreaks, and old crones strangled to death. It was a convincing performance. A man stood up and left the buffet . . .

As the two policemen marched Verlaine and Rimbaud through the streets of Arras, a rumour was going about that two famous murderers had just been arrested at the station. Rimbaud's 'way of the cross' might turn out to have consisted of a train-ride and a binge in a station buffet. Verlaine would probably be seen by the examining magistrate as a sleazy civil servant with a history of anarchist activity, a rough-looking, under-age companion and a pair of stained white trousers.

The bogus murderers worked well as a team. At the police station, after winking at Verlaine, Rimbaud began to cry. He was interviewed on his own and impressed the magistrate as a law-abiding young man. Verlaine, meanwhile, protested at their 'arbitrary' arrest and said that, as a native of Metz, he was tempted now to exercise his right to opt for German citizenship. The two policemen were ordered to take the gentlemen back to the station and make certain that they left on the Paris express.

After sharing breakfast and a few drinks with their police escort, Rimbaud and Verlaine settled into a second-class carriage and discussed plan B. They reached Paris in time for dinner, then walked to the Gare de l'Est, where the evening train was about to leave for Charleville.

Meanwhile, M. Mauté was looking for his son-in-law – first, half-hoping, at the Morgue, then at the police station, and finally, bracing himself for sordid revelations, in the cafés of the Latin Quarter. There, he heard 'the most peculiar remarks' and 'the most scandalous suppositions' about Verlaine and his companion.[17] The truth was inescapable: his daughter had married an alcoholic pederast.

One hundred and fifty miles to the north-east, Verlaine and Rimbaud walked as inconspicuously as possible from Charleville station to the home of Charles Bretagne. They drank the next day away and waited for nightfall. After midnight, Bretagne took them to the home of a carter, introduced them as two travelling priests and asked the man to harness up 'the beast of the Apocalypse'.[18]

The plan was to cross the border without falling into the hands of *douaniers*. Verlaine had convinced himself again that he might be arrested as a Communard. It was just as likely now that he would be charged with corrupting a minor.

Two hours before dawn, on 10 July 1872, they abandoned the horse and cart near the village of Pussemange.

After his tobacco expeditions with Delahaye, Rimbaud knew how to avoid the customs patrols. They crept through a wood, crossed the unmarked border and, like lovers reaching Gretna Green, went skipping into Belgium.

16

Fugitives

'completely incomprehensible and repulsive'

(Constable Lombard, report to Préfecture de Police,
1 August 1873)

VERLAINE HAD written practically nothing since the advent of
Rimbaud. Now, as they zigzagged through southern Belgium by
train and on foot, he was flowing with poems again. The 'Paysages
belges' in Verlaine's *Romances sans paroles* should count as one of
Rimbaud's greatest indirect contributions to literature. The little
carriage-window stanzas, with their splotches of landscape and streaks
of light, are a new departure: all inessentials – logic, morals and
luggage – left behind.

> What's this feeling?
> Stations thunder,
> Eyes a-wonder,
> Where's Charleroi?

Rimbaud's Belgian poems intermittently resemble Verlaine's and
there have been many attempts to apportion influence; but the forms
and phrases that passed between them were the shared possessions
and experiences, the happily adjusted habits and felicitous misunder-
standings, even the baby-language of a relationship that was beginning to find its rhythm.[1] Manuscripts from this period show their
handwriting becoming confusingly similar.[2]

Above. The River Meuse at Charleville.

Right. Mme Rimbaud (?), sketched by her son.

Below. The farmhouse at Roche.

Arthur (front row, third from left) at the Institut Rossat in 1864.

Arthur (sitting) and Frédéric on the day
of their First Communion.

5, Quai de la Madeleine
(now 7, Quai Arthur-Rimbaud).

Above. Ernest Delahaye.

Above, right. Georges Izambard.

Right. Arthur's sister Vitalie,
c. 1870.

Below. Mézières after the
Prussian bombardment on
New Year's Eve, 1870.

10 1870-71 — Mézières — L'Église et maisons environnantes
au lendemain du bombardement

Rimbaud in October 1871,
by Carjat.

Rimbaud in December 1871,
by Carjat.

Paul Verlaine, *c.* 1869.

Stéphane Mallarmé.

Above. Théodore de Banville, by Nadar.

Above, right. Charles Cros, by Nadar.

Right. Ernest Cabaner, by Manet.

Edmond Lepelletier.

Mathilde Verlaine after her divorce.

'Coin de table', by Fantin-Latour. (From left to right: Verlaine, Rimbaud,
Pierre Elzéar, Léon Valade, Émile Blémont, Jean Aicard, Ernest d'Hervilly,
Camille Pelletan.)

Rimbaud, by Régamey, shortly
after arriving in London in
September 1872.

Rimbaud and Verlaine in London,
by Régamey.

Rimbaud's poem on
the Imperial Prince,
in Régamey's album.

L'Enfant qui ramassa les balles le Pubère

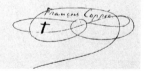

Left. 34, Howland Street.

Above, top. 8, Great (now Royal) College Street

Above. Germain Nouveau.

'Portrait of the Frenchman Arthur Rimbaud, wounded after drinking by his close friend, the French poet Paul Verlaine. From life by Jef Rosman'. Brussels, 1873.

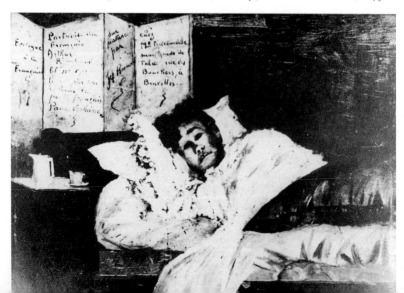

– Juliette, that brings to mind the Henriette,
Charming station on the railway line,
In the heart of a mountain and the depths of an orchard
Where a thousand blue devils dance in the air!

Green bench where the white Irish girl sings
On the guitar in the upper circle of the storm.
Then, from the Guyanan dining-room,
The chattering of children and of cages.

Ducal window that turns my thoughts
To the poison of snails and of box-trees
Sleeping down here in the sun. But oh,
It's too, too beautiful! Let's keep silent.

Rimbaud's language had often changed from one poem to the next. After the crossing of the border, the changes seemed to be occurring from one stanza to the next, or from one line to the next – sometimes even in mid-sentence. No image is allowed to acquire a fixed address in the poem. Whole phrases, stripped of articles, slip past the controls of logic and syntax. Rational links are erased by the speed of association. The only clear theme, ironically, is the impossibility of finding an appropriate language.

But I, Lord! here's my spirit flying,
After the skies glazed red, beneath the
Celestial clouds that run and fly
Over a hundred Solognes as long as a railway.*

Another of Rimbaud's Belgian poems, 'Est-elle aimée? . . .', is known only as two quatrains, which were generally thought to be the whole poem until 1998 when the Rimbaud scholar, Jean-Jacques Lefrère, was allowed to inspect the manuscript for a few seconds by a collector.[3] There were certainly many other poems. Verlaine lamented their loss in 1883: 'That dastardly Rimbaud and I flogged them along with lots of other things to pay for absinthes and cigars!'[4]

After an unknown number of days, they meandered 'vertiginously'[5] up to Brussels and took a room near the Gare du Nord at the Grand

---

* Sologne: region of sand-flats in the Loire.

Hôtel Liégeois. Verlaine introduced Rimbaud to some old acquaintances from the Commune: ambitious intellectuals reduced to menial tasks. This was the atmosphere of defeat and alienation in which Rimbaud thrived – the *tabula rasa* that authorized any kind of revolt. Still primed for the impossible revolution, the exiled Communards were publishing their own newspaper, wistfully titled *La Bombe*.

Rimbaud apparently befriended the smirking Georges Cavalier, known as 'Pipe-en-Bois' because his gnarled features looked like the face on a carved pipe-bowl. 'Pipe-en-Bois' is often presented as an endearing eccentric. As the Commune's Chief Highways Inspector, he was said to have connived in the mining of the Paris sewers and tried to have a park-keeper shot for 'obstructing the revolution'.[6]

It is interesting that Rimbaud managed to 'astonish' these professional terrorists.[7] Verlaine unfortunately fails to say exactly how: perhaps by 'publicly engaging in their amorous affairs' (as a police spy reported). Or perhaps the teenage poet made the Communards look conservative. It has been suggested that Rimbaud wrote his poem 'Qu'est-ce pour nous...' in Brussels as a cruel message for *Bombe* readers:[8] since their cause was doomed in any case, true anarchists should call for the annihilation of the whole planet.

Throughout the two months they spent in Belgium, Verlaine was in at least two minds and sometimes in no mind at all. He agonized over the depraved condition to which Rimbaud had reduced him. A state of permanent holiday had been declared and the new dictator was suspicious of any backsliding. When Verlaine wrote to his mother, he asked her to divide her letters into two: 'one part that can be shown to Rimbaud, the other pertaining to my poor household'.[9] The letter he sent to Mathilde from Brussels was certainly not shown to Rimbaud: 'Don't be sad and don't cry. I'm having a bad dream. I'll come back one day.'

After swilling around in his memory for fourteen years, his honeymoon with Rimbaud shone like a jewel. In '*Laeti et errabundi*', written in 1887, he describes himself and the young 'god' dining 'on public condemnation', countering poverty with 'courage, joy and potatoes', and sampling every form of alcohol:

> The soul in the seventh heaven of delight,
> The body, more humble, on the floor.

Memories of Brussels recorded closer to the time are uniformly wretched: 'Drunkenness unto death, / Black orgy.'[10] It was one thing to hear Rimbaud talk about liberating art when there was dinner on the table. It was something else to be turned into a living experiment in 'derangement'. Parts of *Une Saison en Enfer*, attributed to a 'Foolish Virgin' who has much in common with Verlaine, seem to be snapshots of the Belgian holiday:

> On several nights, when his demon seized me, we rolled about and I wrestled with him! – Often, after dark, when he was drunk, he took up position in streets or in houses, to frighten me to death.

In an attempt to drop anchor in the sea of alcohol, Verlaine wrote again to Mathilde a few days later. This time, he told her that he had gone to Brussels for an unexpectedly sensible reason: he was going to write a history of the Paris Commune.[11] In effect, it was a research trip.

Verlaine's letter had two effects, both disastrous – one for Verlaine, the other for French literature.

First, since Verlaine had asked for some papers, Mathilde took the opportunity to force a desk drawer and discovered Rimbaud's recent correspondence with her husband: 'The letters were so peculiar that I thought they must have been written by a madman.'[12] The whole escapade, she now realized, had been planned in advance.

M. Mauté took the letters, noted their compromising nature and added them to the file for the solicitor. The remaining papers consisted of incomprehensible ramblings (probably poems) and a sealed envelope marked '*La Chasse spirituelle*, by Arthur Rimbaud'. This 'Spiritual Hunt' was almost certainly the extraordinary prose text mentioned by Verlaine: 'full of strange mysticalities and the most acute psychological insights'.[13]

La Chasse spirituelle seems to have joined the rest of the incomprehensible ramblings in the Mautés' rubbish-bin.

Since then, scholars have dreamt of this faceless beauty. It appears in some editions as a title on a blank page and is often described – on no evidence – as Rimbaud's 'greatest work'.[14] In 1949, after being accused of perpetrating an ignorant adaptation of *Une Saison en Enfer*, two student actors published their own *Chasse spirituelle* in the *Mercure de France*. It became an instant bestseller and was authenticated by several scholars, even after the students confessed.

A faint possibility exists that, since *La Chasse spirituelle* was written in prose, M. Mauté mistook it for one of Rimbaud's letters and gave it to the solicitor.[15] A 'five-part poem' bearing the title 'La Chasse spirituelle' *may* have been sold to a collector in 1905 or 1908.[16] These dates correspond roughly to the period in which Mathilde wrote her memoirs (1907–8), when she seems to have had access to Rimbaud's obscene letters. Were these 'destroyed', as she claimed, or sold for profit?[17] If the lost manuscript ever comes to light, it will break all auction records and probably fail to match the dream.

For the time being, there is a small consolation in the fact that, in Verlaine's accounts, Rimbaud's best poems are always the poems that were lost.[18] The fact that he was unable to remember a single word of *La Chasse spirituelle* (including the title) shows that, unlike the rest of Rimbaud's work, this ineffable masterpiece was perfectly forgettable.

The other result of Verlaine's letter was that Mathilde wrote to say that she was coming to Brussels with her mother. Desperation made her ingenious: they would leave the baby with her parents and go and live on the other side of the world on the desolate islands of New Caledonia where Verlaine could interview deported Communards for his book.[19] There was no absinthe in the South Pacific, and Verlaine would be able to stop worrying about deportation since he would be living in a penal colony.

The rescue party arrived in Brussels at dawn on 21 July 1872.[20] Verlaine kept his appointment at 8 a.m. He explained to a mystified Mathilde that his relations with Rimbaud were irredeemably sexual – or, to quote the transcript of the 'Verlaine against Verlaine' case of April 1874: 'details of the most monstrous immorality were revealed to the petitioner'.[21]

True to his self-image as a man with all the autonomy of a 'dead leaf',[22] Verlaine succumbed to mild persuasion. He agreed to meet Mathilde and her mother in a park, an hour before the evening train to Paris.

At 4 p.m., Mathilde and her mother saw a gloomy alcoholic swaying towards them through the park. Verlaine had been saying goodbye to Rimbaud. He followed them to the station, clutching a roasted chicken, lurched on to the train and collapsed into his seat. There was no sign of his evil friend.

Further down the platform, a last passenger jumped aboard and the train pulled out. The other people in the Verlaines' compartment were amused by the sight of an inebriated gentleman pushing his face into a chicken and dismantling it with his teeth. Then he fell into a stupor until the train reached the border at Quiévrain.[23]

Here, all the passengers had to leave the train in order to pass through customs.

Suddenly, in the crowd, Verlaine went missing. The two women searched the station and the customs hall until all the other passengers had reboarded the train. At the last minute, they climbed aboard, scouring the platform from the carriage window.

The guard was slamming the doors shut when they finally caught sight of him. Verlaine was standing on the platform, overcome with fresh resolve. Mme Mauté called to him to hurry up. '"No, I'm staying," he shouted back, and punched his hat down over his eyes.'

As the frantic head of Mme Mauté disappeared in the direction of France, Verlaine was joined on the platform by his friend, still stretching his legs after travelling fifty miles in a toilet.

*

THE BALLAD OF Rimbaud and Verlaine was first written down by Constable Lombard of the 4th Intelligence Brigade, Paris Constabulary. With his admirable blend of forensic report and gaudy melodrama, Constable Lombard deserves his place in history as Rimbaud's first biographer. Apart from a few small errors, the spies had done a good job:

> The action takes place in Brussels.
>
> The Parnassian, Robert Verlaine, had been married for three or four months. [. . .]
>
> The couple were doing quite well, despite the demented antics of Verlaine, whose brain has been unhinged for a long time, when unkind fate brought to Paris a lad – Raimbaud, a native of Charleville, who came all on his own to present his works to the Parnassians.
>
> In morality and talent, this Raimbaud, aged between 15 and 16, was

and is a monster. He can construct poems like no one else, but his works are completely incomprehensible and repulsive.

Verlaine fell in love with Raimbaud, who shared his ardour, and they went off to Belgium to savour their happiness and what follows.

Verlaine had abandoned his wife with unparalleled glee; yet she is said to be very likeable and well-mannered.

The two lovers have been seen in Brussels, publicly engaging in their amorous affairs. A short while ago, Mme Verlaine went to look for her husband to try to bring him back. Verlaine retorted that it was too late, that they could not live together again and that in any case he was no longer his own man. 'Married life is abhorrent to me', he cried. 'We love each other like tigers!' And, so saying, he bared his chest in front of his wife. It was bruised and tattooed with knife wounds administered by his friend Raimbaud. These two creatures were in the habit of fighting and lacerating each other like wild animals just so they could have the pleasure of making up again afterwards.

Discouraged, Mme Verlaine returned to Paris.[24]

Constable Lombard's description of Rimbaud's poetry – 'incomprehensible *and* repulsive' – is a good example of what was to remain the common view until well into the twentieth century: poets were supposed to enlighten their readers, not make them screw their eyes up in puzzlement and disgust. This is almost exactly what Rimbaud had warned Demeny to expect in his 'Seer' letter: 'strange, unfathomable, repulsive and delicious things'.

The coincidence is significant. The voice of a scandalized society was part of the chorus in Rimbaud's head. It would be his great achievement, in *Une Saison en Enfer*, to allow all these voices to have their say. If Constable Lombard had seen the book, he might have found it 'repulsive' but not entirely 'incomprehensible':

I shall gash myself all over. I shall tattoo myself. I want to become as hideous as a Mongol. You'll see, I'll go screaming through the streets.

*

THREE DAYS AFTER the Quiévrain débâcle, Mathilde was in bed with a fever.[25] A letter arrived from Brussels. Verlaine had written to her just after the train left the station. Rimbaud was demanding a sacrifice, and Verlaine promptly obliged. His wife's pet names were used as savage insults:

> Miserable carrot fairy, princess mouse, bug that is waiting for the finger and thumb and the chamber-pot, you've put me through everything now. You might have killed my friend's heart. I'm going back to Rimbaud, if he'll still have me after the way you made me betray him.[26]

Mathilde now stopped hoping for a happy ending and allowed her father to renew the petition for a legal separation. Verlaine's inheritance money – what was left of it – might suddenly be frozen by a court order. Meanwhile, unaware that he had closed the door on married life forever, Verlaine cheered up. He wrote again a few days later: Rimbaud, 'dressed in velvet' (like a worker) was 'making a great impression' in Brussels and would be 'very happy' if Mathilde came and joined them in a *ménage à trois* . . .[27]

Rimbaud was certainly not shown this sad example of alcoholic optimism. He was beginning to tire of Brussels and was in danger of being sent back to his mother again by the police. The city was full of spies. In cafés, men with large ears sat behind newspapers, taking notes. M. Mauté had asked the Belgian Préfecture to trace Verlaine and his companion.

This was a serious development. Since they had crossed the border without passing through customs, their papers were not in order.[28] On 3 August, a note was sent from police headquarters to the Belgian Sûreté. Information was requested on Verlaine, Rimbaud (for once spelt correctly) and an unknown French embezzler called Jules Macagne or Macagno – perhaps a temporary companion. The poste restante office was ordered to supply their addresses.[29]

Filed ominously under 'Criminals and Escaped Convicts', the Verlaine–Rimbaud dossier grew fatter and more interesting by the day. Mme Rimbaud had discovered that Arthur had spent a night in Charleville without coming to see her. After a visit to Charles Bretagne, which left him 'stunned and trembling',[30] she went to the police station and reported Arthur missing.

Since then, strange men had been asking questions at the hotel.

The spy's report dated 6 August 1872 suggests that Rimbaud was either using a false name or staying at a private address:

> Verlaine is lodged at the Hôtel de la Province de Liège in the Rue de Brabant at Saint-Josse-ten-Noode [a suburb of Brussels]. Rimbaud's dwelling place has yet to be ascertained, though it is presumed that he is living with his friend.[31]

A note in red ink was added to the file: Rimbaud was reported to have fought with the irregulars in the Paris Commune. This meant that he was now in almost as much danger as Verlaine. Communards much younger than Rimbaud were still being sent to prison and deported.

Shortly after 6 August, they slipped out of Brussels and continued their erratic tour through northern Belgium: Mechelen, Antwerp and Ghent. Rimbaud never travelled with a Baedeker and showed no interest in any particular category of art or architecture. As for Verlaine, his poem 'Birds in the Night' implies that he was in no condition to have a motive for doing anything: 'I am the Poor Boat running dismasted through the storm'. 'Le Pauvre Navire', he must have noticed, was almost an anagram of 'Paul Verlaine'.

Rimbaud's reasons for leaving Brussels probably had more to do with his 'spiritual hunt' than with nosy policemen. His wanderings were beginning to form a pattern on the map. In Une Saison en Enfer, he describes this period as a voyage to the Cimmerian 'land of darkness and whirlpools': 'By a road of dangers, my weakness led me to the ends of the Earth.' The northern coast of continental Europe was the geographical correlative of a spiritual extreme. The Grail was total enlightenment, and the obstacles were as devious as they usually are in mythological quests: the very act of seeking truth was self-defeating. 'Action is not life, but a way of wasting a kind of strength.'[32]

This vaguely Buddhist dilemma – if enlightenment eludes the conscious mind, how can it be consciously pursued? – is typical of Rimbaud's energetic pessimism, his tendency to embark on a project only when failure was guaranteed by the initial conditions.

No attempt should be made to imagine this quest as the logical consequence of a coherent philosophy. All his notions were provisional. Later, he referred to his ideas as 'the sophisms of madness' –

dogmatic justifications of irrational thought. *Une Saison en Enfer* offers a precise example, perhaps inspired by his reading of the mystic Swedenborg:[33]

> Every being seemed to me to be entitled to several *other* lives. This gentleman doesn't know what he's doing: he is an angel. This family is a litter of puppies. In front of several men, I talked aloud with a moment from one of their other lives. – It was thus that I loved a pig.

This possible allusion to the swinish Verlaine is a reminder that the most effective 'key' to Rimbaud's universe is not a precise knowledge of mystical philosophies but a sense of humour. Verlaine was the ideal side-kick: the whimpering Laurel to Rimbaud's ludicrously ambitious Hardy. Rimbaud probably never 'believed' in the transmigration of souls. He used it as a metaphor for social identity: the human mind reduced by convention to a single persona.

The constant element in Rimbaud's thinking is the notion of 'duty' ('*devoir*'). It might almost be translated as 'job': a voluntary subjugation that allows the multifarious personality to find a purpose and direction.

In *Une Saison en Enfer*, the hysterical Verlaine figure appears to suspect that this 'duty' is not yet attached to any particular end. Having demolished the moral foundations, the seer has yet to start work on the building. He may even turn out to be insolvent: 'Perhaps he has secrets for *changing life*? No, he's just looking for some, I told myself.'

Mme Rimbaud would have recognized the notion of 'duty' as the key to happiness. The core of Rimbaud's thinking is strongly reminiscent of his mother's stoical form of Christianity: stubborn devotion without hope of reward. 'I too have been unhappy', she told Verlaine ten months later.

> I felt my sorrow, without feeling that of others. It was then that I told myself (and every day I see that I am right) that true happiness lies in fulfilling all one's duties, however painful they might be![34]

On Saturday, 7 September 1872, the fugitives reached the coast at Ostend. In the land of mists across the sea, some of Verlaine's Communard friends were living in noble poverty. Money would be a problem and neither of them knew much English. They went to the harbour office and bought two one-way tickets. The ferry was due to sail that evening.

At Ostend, Rimbaud saw the open sea for the first time. It struck him with the symbolic force that any stretch of water carries, however banal the means of transport:

> I had to travel, to dispel the enchantments heaped up on my brain. On the sea, which I loved as though it should have cleansed me of a stain, I saw the rising of the consoling cross. I had been cursed by the rainbow. Happiness was my fate, my remorse, my worm: my life would always be too immense to be devoted to strength and beauty.[35]

On Noah's Ark, the rainbow is the sign of God's covenant with Man. On the cross-Channel ferry, it stood for the religion of Rimbaud's childhood, the salvation from which there was no escape.

If Belgium had been the orgy, England would be the medicinal dawn. The 'rainbow' passage from *Une Saison en Enfer* recalls the moment of ecstatic release when water penetrates the hull of the drunken boat and washes off 'the blue wine-stains and the vomit'. It was a fitting image for the Ostend–Dover ferry that night. The last two months of drunkenness were purged by the sea.

> Almost an island, tossing on my sides the squabbles
> And droppings of yattering, blond-eyed birds,
> I sailed on. [. . .][36]

At dawn, through the mist, grey cliffs appeared.

17

Underworld

'the thick, eternal coal-smoke, – our sylvan shade, our midsummer night!'

('Ville', *Illuminations*)

A FTER LEAVING the ferry, Rimbaud and Verlaine climbed up above the town and walked along the cliff-tops. The sun was shining brightly. France was just a thin mirage on the horizon.

At eight o'clock, they went back down into Dover in search of breakfast. The famous English Sunday lived up to its reputation. Everything was shut.

> It was not until we happened to meet a Frenchman, an interpreter by profession, that we were able, after some real or fictitious difficulties had been raised, to get some eggs and tea by calling ourselves *bona fide* travellers.[1]

After two days' rest and acclimatization, they took the train up to London.[2]

The land called 'Angleterre' was still in large part a figment of Napoleonic propaganda and Caesar's *Gallic War*. 'Perfidious Albion' was a fog-bound Ultima Thule inhabited by prudish eccentrics with no taste in food or clothes, and a genius for selling things, except on Sundays. Since the Great Exhibition of 1851 and the engravings of Gustave Doré (which Rimbaud admired for their compressed narratives),[3] the image had acquired a gleam of modernity and the satanic tinge of industrialization. Britain led the world in labour-saving devices: bathroom appliances and factory children. To cross the Channel was to travel fifty years into the future, as Jules Verne had discovered in 1859: his first attempt at science fiction was an account of a train journey through industrial Britain.

On 10 September 1872, Rimbaud and Verlaine left Charing Cross Station and walked out into the amazing pandemonium of central London. Verlaine tried to describe it with a traffic jam of nouns and adjectives: 'carriages, cabs, buses (filthy), trams, incessant railways on splendid cast-iron bridges, grand and lumbering; unbelievably brutal, loud-mouthed people in the streets'.[4]

The biggest city in the world was a magnificent, hellish sight, impressive in its disappointments, imposing in its seediness: 'Everything is small, skinny and emaciated', wrote Verlaine, 'especially the poor.' 'London is as flat as a black bug': row upon row of horrid, squat houses, 'Gothic' and 'Venetian' schools, dilapidated cafés with black-fingered waiters, and, running through it all, 'a gigantic overflowing toilet' – the river Thames.

Fortunately, the weather was 'superb': 'Imagine a setting sun seen through grey crêpe.'

Their first reaction to London was inevitably defensive. Verlaine claims that both he and Rimbaud found it 'absurd': 'prudish, but with *every vice on offer*, permanently sozzled, despite ridiculous *bills* on drunkenness'. A few days later, he was praising 'the interminable docks' at Woolwich as a sufficient feast for his 'increasingly *modernistic* poetics'.

Rimbaud's English *Illuminations* may not have been written for several months, and the story of his poetic 'follies' in *Une Saison en Enfer* appears to end with the Channel crossing. It would take time to digest this incomprehensible chaos. All that is known for certain is that he was 'delighted and astonished' by London. The next time he saw Paris, it struck him as 'a pretty provincial town'.[5]

They crossed Trafalgar Square and set off up Regent Street, amazed to see hordes of black people ('it seems to have been snowing negroes'). The vast range of the Empire was also represented in shop windows by photographs of Stanley and Livingstone, heroes of the hour. Portraits of the deposed French Emperor only emphasized the sense of strangeness.

That September morning, the painter Félix Régamey, a Communard friend of Verlaine, was sitting in his studio in Langham Street when a knock came at the door:

> It's Verlaine, just arrived from Brussels [. . .]. He is handsome in his own way, and, despite being severely short of clothes, gives no sign of being overwhelmed by misfortune.
>
> We spend some delightful hours together.
>
> But he is not alone. He has with him a silent companion who does not exactly sparkle with elegance either.
>
> It's Rimbaud.[6]

Régamey told his visitors that the Communard refugee, Eugène Vermersch – one of Rimbaud's boyhood heroes – was about to vacate his room in nearby Howland Street. Perhaps they could take over the lease? Then they talked of absent friends, and Verlaine and Rimbaud each inscribed a Coppée parody in Régamey's album.

Rimbaud's first poem in England – 'L'enfant qui ramassa les balles . . .'[7] – seems to be just another piece of beautifully crafted smut, a nostalgic re-creation of the Zutistes' den in the temporary haven of Frenchness; but it contains a vital clue to his state of mind. The subject of the poem is the Imperial Prince who was languishing with his exiled parents at Chislehurst in Kent. Prince Louis is depicted as a budding homosexual: 'His exquisite bust aspires no more to the breaches / Of the Future!' 'His eye is / Deepened by an immense solitude. / "Poor young man, he's probably in the Habit!"'

The implication is that the Prince has abandoned all hope of heterosexual conquest and is now a regular masturbator (popularly and legally considered to be a sign of homosexuality, though there were surely private doubts about this). Above the poem, Rimbaud sketched the Prince as an airborne idiot with an English tie and jughandle ears. The bags under his eyes are the tell-tale signs of self-abuse, while the wings identify him as an angel ('*ange*' was a term for 'homosexual'). An obscene pun on the hollow eye refers to the anal 'carnation' of the 'Sonnet du trou du cul' ('*œil est*', '*œillet*').

This seems a rather inauspicious poem for the first day of Rimbaud's new life in London. Homosexuality is associated with solitude, puerile regression and a degenerate dynasty. His first recorded poem

(1868) had been a Communion ode to the Imperial Prince. In this, his last known poem in regular verse, he returned to the subject as if to compare his own development with the Prince's. It is not uncommon for children and even adults to identify themselves with royalty. Rimbaud's identification was unusually precise: homosexuality, exile in England, and the sad impossibility of emulating a prestigious father.[8]

The Rimbaud who had just arrived in London was an experimental self who saw homosexuality as a path of enlightenment; but there was another Rimbaud for whom it was an admission of defeat. For the time being, neither Rimbaud was inclined to take a tragic view. Life was still a very long Departures board, with a wide choice of destinations.

*

WHILE THEY WAITED for the room in Howland Street to come free, Rimbaud and Verlaine explored their new world. They may have used one of the refugee hostels, which offered communal cooking facilities, books, newspapers and endless political arguments. But since Verlaine had decided not to write a history of the Commune after all, it is just as likely that they went to a hotel.

Verlaine later claimed that his first London adventures with 'the great boy-poet' Arthur Rimbaud were 'of a somewhat frivolous nature, to say the least'.[9] Régamey sketched the foreign tourists: two scruffy disreputables slouching through the city – Verlaine with a cigarette, Rimbaud with a clay pipe – under the leery eye of a London policeman. Before long, they had inspected most of the sights: Hyde Park Corner, the National Gallery, Madame Tussaud's ('*indescribable*'), the theatres with their 'piteously thin' actresses, rowdy audiences and 'a rising smell of feet', the food-stained whores and slobbering boot-blacks, the pubs with their 'pomegranate' interiors and doors on leather hinges that smacked the customer's bottom as he entered and left. They saw the Lord Mayor's parade, the Tower of London, and a terrifying monument to English intrepidity, the Tower Subway: 'a tube sunk fifty metres into the Thames'. 'It stinks, it's hot and it quivers like a suspension bridge, while all around you hear the sound of the enormous volume of water.'[10]

Verlaine's 'frivolous' also refers to the sexual nature of the holiday. Anticipating an attack from the Mautés' solicitor, he was writing up 'a psychological analysis' of 'my very real, very profound and *very persistent* friendship with Rimbaud', he told Lepelletier. 'I won't say *very pure.* – There are limits!'

Homosexuality was a key to the unpublicized parts of the city. Verlaine drooled over the little boys in tight-fitting suits who waited outside public urinals 'to brush you from head to foot for two *sous*': 'I don't know what else they must do to people who know to pay a little extra'. In a similar vein, Rimbaud admired the tiny grooms with their greatcoats and whips.[11] Since English grooms were commonly thought by the French to be sex-toys for aristocrats, this was not an innocent remark.

The tittering sleaze of Verlaine's letters is a complete contrast to Rimbaud's almost abstract poems. It is significant that some contemporary accounts of French travellers to London are reminiscent of the *Illuminations*.[12] The mad perspectives of the *Illuminations* were foreign to French literature but not to nineteenth-century inhabitants of Paddington, Holborn and Southwark: subways, viaducts, raised canals; steam engines passing over streets, mastheads suddenly appearing behind chimney-pots. London was not a city that posed for artists while they sat at a pavement café. It was a challenge to the classically trained mind, confirmation of Rimbaud's insight that, when the depiction exactly matched the appearance, reality itself was surreal.

Every city has its own grammar and syntax. Rimbaud was learning the sentence structure of London and its suburbs. This was not a process that lent itself to picturesque views of dashing horse-guards and public urinals.

*

SHORTLY BEFORE 24 September, they moved into Vermersch's old room at 34 Howland Street. Number 34 was part of an eighteenth-century terrace which had been converted into a hive of furnished rooms and was well on its way to becoming the bleary slum that lingered on until the eve of the Second World War.[13] In the grime of their neighbour's window, a finger had traced the words 'Very dirty'. The inscription was still there at Christmas.

Number 34 Howland Street may be the home which Rimbaud describes ironically in 'Ville' as a 'cottage',[14] nestling in the smog of the urban forest. Figures passing on the street outside enact the little dramas that strike a foreign eye as curiously emblematic:

> [. . .] from my window, I see recent ghosts moving through the thick, eternal coal-smoke, – our sylvan shade, our midsummer night! – new Furies, in front of my cottage which is my homeland and all my heart since everything here resembles this, – Death without tears, our active girl and servant, a desperate Cupid and a pretty Crime whimpering in the mud of the street.

The flaking façade of number 34 used to bear a plaque commemorating Verlaine's (but not Rimbaud's) visit. When the terrace was pulled down in 1938 to make way for a telephone exchange, the plaque disappeared. The site of Rimbaud's first London home is now marked by the glassy prong of the Post Office Tower, which not only has the advantage of being visible at a great distance but is also more in keeping with Rimbaud's vision of the city: 'The official acropolis exaggerates the most colossal conceptions of modern barbarism.' ('Villes')

Now that they had an address – and since Verlaine's money might be cut off at any minute – they started to look for work.

Rimbaud invested ten shillings in a top-hat. Delahaye saw him with it in Charleville a few months later, smoothing the silk with his sleeve and treating it like 'a venerable companion'.[15] One of Régamey's sketches shows Rimbaud slumped on a chair under the black funnel of his hat, a robust human engine at rest, clearly well used to sleeping in awkward places.[16] With the lumpy overcoat and dog-eared boots, the hat completes a rather dubious ensemble: an undertaker's apprentice, or a young thief sporting the spoils of his latest burglary.

With so many refugees in London, the usually dependable market in private tuition was flooded. Like the aristocrats of 1789, the anarchists of 1872 were helping the English bourgeoisie to perfect its French. Instead, they found work writing French business letters for American newspapers.[17] These were probably continental offshoots of the *New York Herald*, which had offices in Langham Place, next door to the future Broadcasting House.

By early October, the drizzle had settled in, and yellow fog added the constant sound of coughing to the roar of traffic. As the shock of foreignness (and perhaps the joys of cohabitation) wore off, they began to look for fresh company.

To the spies who reported to Ministers on both sides of the Channel, the two Frenchmen living at the old address of Eugène Vermersch were denizens of the international socialist underground. This was a reasonable assumption. All their London friends were political exiles; but their only overt political act was to join one of the refugee clubs, the 'Cercle d'Études Sociales', which hoped to reconcile the dynamiters with the desk-bound intellectuals. Under its auspices, Vermersch was giving a series of lectures in a room above the Hibernia Store pub at 6–7 Old Compton Street in Soho.[18]

Verlaine and Rimbaud attended the lecture that was given on 1 November. 'It was much applauded by the very numerous English and French', Verlaine told Lepelletier, 'the majority of whom were of the most distinguished and *least Communard* variety.' He might have been thinking of his elegant friend Lissagaray, who attended the lecture with his secret fiancée, Eleanor Marx.[19] The reporter from *La Liberté*, on the other hand, having perhaps spotted Rimbaud and Verlaine in the audience, told his readers that, for sixpence, they could spend an engrossing evening at the hall in Soho, observing 'the ultra-Communard types who make up nine-tenths of the audience'.[20]

Rimbaud certainly witnessed many political discussions and would have seen Karl Marx several times. Some of the *Illuminations* can be construed as poetic illustrations of *Das Kapital*:[21] the alienated consumers of the modern metropolis, the disinherited masses, the resurrectionary mythology of the Commune and the magic wand of global capitalism. But the political ideology of the *Illuminations* is part of the cosmopolitan landscape, the murmur of a thousand arguments. As social criticism, the *Illuminations* are more Aldous Huxley than George Orwell, more Thatcherite Docklands than Dickensian slums. Even if Rimbaud had shared the political ambitions of his fellow exiles, none of them would have understood his poems anyway.

I am an ephemeral and by no means overly discontented citizen of a metropolis thought to be modern because all known taste has been avoided in the furnishings and exteriors of the houses as well as in the layout of the city. Here, you would be unable to indicate the traces of any monument to superstition. Morality and language have been reduced to their simplest expression, at last! These millions of people who do not need to know each other conduct their education, work and old age in such a similar fashion that their lifespan must be several times shorter than the one that a mad statistic attributes to the continental races.

Like the citizens of 'Ville',[22] Rimbaud was quite happy in Victorian London. He was to return three times in less than two years. There are no tales of horrid pranks and, at least on this first visit, no evidence that he antagonized anybody. Perhaps, with Verlaine, like the narrator of 'Mémoire', he was able to be father and son at the same time. Verlaine was now 'harder at work than ever before': 'entirely given over to poetry, intellectual pursuits, and discussions of a purely literary and serious nature'. A lost drawing by Verlaine showed Rimbaud sitting in a pub, writing the future *Saison en Enfer*.[23] Their home in Howland Street was 'almost a hermitage'.

This was the first time that Rimbaud had shown a strong attachment to a large community. The London he knew in 1872 was the area normally defined as Soho, which, for recent visitors, is likely to conjure up the image of a dense, litter-producing zone on the edge of 'Theatreland'. In 1872, French Soho was one layer of the international village of undissolved foreigners that survived until the early 1980s. It had its own newspapers and institutions, its own fluid class structure. The cultural integrity of the area might explain why Rimbaud and Verlaine at first made such slow progress in English. 'Soho' stretched from Regent's Park and St Pancras in the north to Leicester Square in the south, taking in the British Museum, Tottenham Court Road and the eastern end of Oxford Street. There were French hoteliers, tailors, laundresses, wine-merchants, an ironmonger, a bakery in Carnaby Street and a '*crèmerie parisienne*' run by 'Widow Régamay'. Parisian haircuts were available from M. Toupet, French funerals from M. Héritage. A 'grand café-restaurant français' called 'The Cambridge' offered French newspapers and a 'Parisian dinner' (with a half-bottle of wine) for 2s 6d at the unParisian hours of 1 to 9 p.m. In Frith

Street, an enterprising French newsagent, M. Barjau, helped the refugees to find work and lodgings, then passed their details on to the Metropolitan Police.

French Soho was a more settled form of the sort of ramshackle community of drifters and exiles that Rimbaud later found beyond Suez: a society that was held together, like Rimbaud's poems, by destructive urges. A manifesto written by their friend Vermersch was purchased by Sergeant Greenham of Scotland Yard at the French bookshop in Rathbone Place: 'The hour is come to remember that the lives of tyrants and traitors belong to whomsoever chooses to take them.' He quoted the manifesto in his report as an example of 'the sentiments and intentions of the dangerous men who throng the neighbourhood of Leicester-square.'[24]

Many of these 'dangerous men' were Rimbaud's friends, though the extent of their relations is unknown:[25] Vermersch, Lissagaray, who had defended the last barricade in Paris, Colonel Matuszewicz, a Communard militant, Camille Barrère, the future French ambassador, and Jules Andrieu, who had signed the order to demolish that symbol of Napoleonic imperialism, the Vendôme Column. According to Delahaye, Andrieu was Rimbaud's favourite 'intellectual brother'. A short, shaggy-haired man of thirty-five, Andrieu had been the ringmaster of the republican Parnassians, an encourager and facilitator who realized too late that his own poems were far better than those of his protégés. He and Rimbaud had much in common: a desire to send the snobs of French poetry back to the fields of folklore, an intelligent enthusiasm for works that were quite unlike their own, and a capacity for searing self-criticism that reduced their life's work to a few sturdy fragments. Andrieu's contemporaries hint strongly at homosexuality, which might account for later complications in his friendship with Rimbaud.

Brute research can illuminate Rimbaud's years in Africa in surprising detail. His months in London are irretrievably obscure. There is just enough to suggest that he might almost have forged a literary career for himself in England. In October, Andrieu promised to introduce Verlaine and Rimbaud to his friend Swinburne (there is no record of a meeting) and to an 'astonishing', 'unknown' poet.[26] This was almost certainly Oliver Madox Brown, son of the painter Ford

Madox Brown and brother-in-law of William Rossetti. A few streets and social strata away from Rimbaud in Fitzroy Square, surrounded by his rat and reptile collection, 'Nolly' Brown was being tutored in French and Latin by Jules Andrieu. He was a year younger than Rimbaud, passionately fond of French literature, and hoped to do for London what Balzac had done for Paris. His mildly hallucinatory novel, *The Black Swan* (published in a sanitized form in 1873)[27] suggests a dainty, upper-class English Rimbaud gazing at the foggy, hypochondriacal city through the nursery window.

Here, the unwritten story ends. Just two small facts remain like place-names on a faded map. One is the publication of Rimbaud's early poem, 'Les Effarés', in the middlebrow *Gentleman's Magazine* in January 1878.[28] The discrepancies with the other known versions of the poem are as revealing as a blush: the 'bottoms' have become 'backs', and the masturbatory baker's arm has disappeared. The new title is banal and sentimental: 'Petits Pauvres'. This is Arthur Rimbaud tidied up – perhaps by himself – for a Victorian audience. The poem must have sat in the editorial files for five years, but it shows that someone connected with the magazine (which rarely published poems and was otherwise monolingual) had thought Rimbaud worthy of publication. Camille Barrère and most of the Madox Brown circle were regular contributors to *The Gentleman's Magazine*. Brown Sr was trying to find a publisher for Andrieu's history of the Commune and may have performed a similar service for his young friend.[29]

The other scrap of evidence is a visit which the young Paul Valéry paid to the poet and critic W. E. Henley in 1896.[30] Valéry was shocked to be greeted with a fluent stream of perfect French obscenities. Delighted with the effect of his French, Henley explained that he had known several Communard refugees in London, including Verlaine and Rimbaud.

Solid evidence of Rimbaud's interaction with English writers therefore amounts to this: an edulcorated poem published without his knowledge, and a blast of expletives in the mouth of W. E. Henley.

Rimbaud's only other certified appearance in artistic circles was at the Society of French Artists Exhibition in New Bond Street. Verlaine was delighted to see himself and Rimbaud sitting demurely in Fantin-Latour's 'Coin de table', ironically retitled 'A Few Friends'.[31]

The painting had been bought by 'a moneybags' from the north of England. For the next twenty-six years, the face of Arthur Rimbaud hung, unrecognized, in a Manchester gallery. It was eventually acquired by the Louvre.

*

WHILE THE COMMUNARDS contended with spying, persecution and slander, Verlaine complained of similar treatment from the Mautés. Considering the strain it was under, the Howland Street ménage survived its first London season remarkably well. Any day now, Verlaine might be dragged into court, along with the living proof of his unsuitability as a husband and father. Anonymous letters had been received by both mothers, telling tales of weird depravity.[32] Verlaine detected the long arm of the in-laws:

> All this buggery business that they [the Mautés] have the infamy to reproach me with is simply an attempt to intimidate – i.e. blackmail – with the aim of extracting a larger allowance.

Rimbaud's later distress at losing his London friends shows that he was keen to make a good impression. If he and Verlaine were publicly accused of 'pederasty', and if the case were deemed newsworthy, life would become impossible on both sides of the Channel. It was time to enlist the help of the dark power about which Verlaine had heard so much.

On 14 November, he told Lepelletier: 'Rimbaud recently wrote to his mother to warn her about all the things that were being said and done against us, and I am now in regular correspondence with her.' Nine days later, Mme Rimbaud was 'very vehemently taking charge of the matter'.

The maternal intransigence that Rimbaud had always found so oppressive proved to be a powerful arm in his defence. Leaving the Ardennes for the first time since 1859, Mme Rimbaud took the train to Paris, went to the Rue Nicolet, and asked Mathilde to call her husband home: little Georges would have a father again and Arthur would be saved from public disgrace.

Mathilde condescended to treat 'the good woman' from the

provinces 'politely'. Naturally, she refused to cooperate.[33] Mme Rimbaud now proceeded with her contingency plan, as Verlaine told Lepelletier:

> She thinks that if I stopped living with her son I could *sway* them. [. . .] *I* think that this would give them their *only weapon* – '*They chickened out, therefore they're guilty*'.

Unwittingly prophetic, he went on, 'Rimbaud and I are ready, if need be, to show our arses (virginal) to the whole clique.'

The contingency plan prevailed. In mid-December, Rimbaud left for a short holiday in Charleville, probably of his own accord. Like many inveterate travellers, he was attached to his starting-point by a powerful piece of elastic. Anyone who left home as often as Rimbaud inevitably spent a great deal of time there. In the nine and a half years between his first escapade (1870) and his final departure from Europe (1880), he lived on the farm at Roche or in the house in Charleville for almost five years, rarely missing Christmas.

To those who cherish the image of the blaspheming vagrant who deliberately wrecked his career prospects, this is the unacceptable face of Arthur Rimbaud: an ambitious young writer who repeatedly returned to live with his mother and often induced her to interfere with his life. Rimbaud may have sketched the first drafts of *Une Saison en Enfer* in a London pub, but the writing of this intensely analytical poem would require a more solid work surface:

> I, who claimed to be a magus or an angel, exempt from all morality,
> I've been set back on the ground, with a duty to seek, and rugged
> reality to embrace! – Peasant!

18

Pagan

'. . . completely arseorbed as I am in the contemprostation
of Nature'.

(Rimbaud to Delahaye, May 1873)[1]

RIMBAUD WAS full of London when he returned to Charleville.
Delahaye heard all about it: the 24-hour 'energy', the miraculously viable chaos, the immeasurable stride of the suburbs. Life there
was 'tough' but 'healthy'. Everything was more 'intelligent' and
'logical' than in France. After the frills of Parisian conversation,
Rimbaud had relished the hobnail boot of British humour; and, like
other recent French visitors – Monet, Pissarro and Daubigny – he
loved the fog that bathed the city in unreality. Verlaine's discomfort
was Rimbaud's stimulation: the constant need (as Verlaine complained) 'to overcome a lot of prejudices and habits'.[2]

With Rimbaud temporarily removed, Verlaine became alarmingly
inert. On Christmas Day, some English friends introduced him to
goose 'with apple sauce!' 'Exquisite' though it was, he felt 'very sad'.
On Boxing Day, he wrote to Lepelletier: 'Rimbaud (whom you do
not know – whom only I know) has gone. A horrible void! The others
I don't care about. They're rabble.'

Rimbaud's Christmas holiday ended suddenly. Verlaine had developed a bad case of the sniffles and was sending out invitations to his
funeral. Mme Rimbaud refused to fund Arthur's return journey, but

Mme Verlaine, who had gone to nurse her son in London, sent him fifty francs, care of Delahaye.

By mid-January, Rimbaud was back at Howland Street, beating sense back into the invalid and chaining him to his desk. Verlaine decided that his new book of poems, *Romances sans paroles*, would have to be dedicated to Rimbaud. With a trial looming, a prudently seraphic picture of his companion would do no harm, and anyway, without Rimbaud, the poems would never have been written:

> I am set on the idea of a dedication to Rimbaud, first *as a protestation*, and then because these poems were written when he was there, constantly goading me to write them, and above all as a mark of gratitude for the devotion and affection he has always shown me, especially when I was at death's door.

When the hypochondriac had recovered, Mme Verlaine left him nervously with his friend – the 'surly and spiteful' boy who had already helped her son to spend over 20,000 francs.[3] This would mean that each word in *Romances sans paroles* cost the equivalent of £22. From a literary point of view, it was a bargain.

*

THE NEXT TWO months were among the busiest in Rimbaud's intellectual life. Until now, their English had been a jumble of nouns and phrases culled from schoolbooks and street-signs. Rimbaud instituted a very modern programme of language acquisition.[4] They picked their way through the 'puerile' poems of Edgar Allan Poe, deciphered Swinburne, studied English popular songs,[5] and attempted the impossible task of translating their own poems into English.

Field studies followed the desk work. They asked shopkeepers and barmaids to correct their pronunciation. They attended church services and listened carefully to street preachers. To replenish their brains and exercise their bodies, they went on 'enormous excursions' into the suburbs and the countryside beyond, describing ever larger orbits of the city.

Soon, they were exploring the wilder regions of the language, beyond the *cordon sanitaire* of the dictionary. For poets who found public urinals as interesting as the Houses of Parliament, the comments of prostitutes were as valuable as tea-party conversations. When Verlaine wrote to Rimbaud the following May, he signed off, bilingually: 'I am your *old cunt ever open* or *opened*. (I don't have my irregular verbs with me.)'

Rimbaud read omnivorously, as if he was about to leave for a desert island. Allusions in his later poems suggest a reading list that included Shakespeare and Longfellow, and especially the daily papers. He borrowed books from his London friends, but this resource was soon exhausted. On 25 March, the eighteen-year-old Arthur Rimbaud declared that he was 'not under twenty-one years of age' and obtained a reader's ticket at the British Museum.[6]

He sat for hours in the same fog-filled Reading Room as Karl Marx and Swinburne, studying books that were unobtainable in France, including, perhaps, Communard publications (many of which are still unobtainable in France), and some of the literary and subliterary works mentioned in *Une Saison en Enfer*: 'Church Latin, erotic books with spelling mistakes, novels read by our grandmothers, little children's books'. Unfortunately, he was denied access to the Marquis de Sade, who was safely locked up in the office of the Keeper of Printed Books.

The British Museum was Rimbaud's other London home. Heating, lighting, pens and ink were free, the librarians could speak French and never judged readers by the state of their dress, and a moderately priced restaurant made it possible to survive a ten-hour stretch of reading.

Since the British Museum kept no record of readers' requests, Rimbaud's programme of studies is unknown. Ironically, however, one of the works that might date from this period shows the influence of a book he had no need to consult in a library.

The so-called *Proses évangéliques* are three short prose passages based on episodes in the early ministry of Jesus.[7]

With his anticlerical convictions, Rimbaud might be expected to have twisted the Gospels into a fiendish parody. He is often said to have done so, but the evidence is flimsy. Rimbaud's Jesus is a slightly petulant and 'feminine' young man, and one of his miracles may not be miraculous: the 'strangely steady legs' of the healed cripple suggest that he might have been feigning injury. But if this constitutes an 'anti-Gospel', one would also have to doubt the intentions of Rimbaud's main source, John.

> The light and charming air of Galilee: the inhabitants received him with inquisitive joy: they had seen him, shaken by holy anger, whipping the money-changers and poultry sellers of the temple. A miracle of pale and furious youth, they thought.
>
> [. . .]
>
> Jesus had not yet performed any miracles. At a marriage feast, in a pink and green dining-room, he had spoken a little sharply to the Holy Virgin.

The Bible seems to have served Rimbaud primarily as a stone on which to sharpen his style. The idea was not to mock the Gospels but to retell the story without its moral, to exorcize the ghost of Christianity by translating the text into his own 'pagan' idiom. This is perhaps why his paraphrases are so redolent of Renan's *Vie de Jésus* (1863) and Flaubert's *Hérodias* (1877), which would certainly have been cited as a source if it had been published five years earlier.

The modern biographer of Jesus is a descriptive novelist, sometimes sardonic ('Women and men used to believe in prophets. Now they believe in statesmen'), but more often distracted by 'the infinitely pale reflections' of the pool, the 'magical gleam' of flowers between flagstones, the nobleman's ring-laden hands and balding head, and especially by the chime and clatter of his own language:

> Jesus entered [the 'wash house' at Bethesda] immediately after the noon hour. No one was washing animals or taking them down. The light in the pool was yellow like the last leaves of the vines. The holy master stood against a column and looked at the sons of Sin. The demon was sticking out his tongue in their tongue, and deriding or denying.

Remnants of rewritten Gospel also appear in the slightly later *Saison en Enfer*, parts of which are related to these Biblical passages like a symphony to an *étude*. Jesus is a pretext, in the same way that Rimbaud's 'way of the cross' gave his life a provisional structure. By devoting himself to the charitable cause of renovating Verlaine (or forcing him into a role), he had acquired a kind of intellectual ballast, and it may well be that the *Proses évangéliques* would have allegorized the whole adventure: 'perfidious Samaria' – 'a more rigid observer of its Protestant law than Juda of the ancient tablets' – does sound remarkably like perfidious Albion.[8]

Rimbaud's histrionic relationship with Verlaine enabled him to audition a variety of personae. This might explain why the Gospel project was abandoned. Instead of using Jesus as a persona, why not use himself – or rather, the shady image of himself that had already entered literary history? If 'I' could be 'somebody else', why not the Arthur Rimbaud who was now one of the legendary figures of Bohemian Paris – the foul-mouthed peasant-poet or the little 'Satan in the midst of the doctors'? Like the men who listened to his lurid tales in the cafés of Paris and Charleville, readers would be only too willing to suspend their disbelief.

*

HAVING COMPLETED HIS new poems under the merciless super-vision of Rimbaud, Verlaine decided to creep across the Channel and arrange peace-talks with Mathilde in Belgium. In Paris, he rightly surmised, his name was mud, and since the death of Napoleon III in January, Communards were being rooted out more enthusiastically than ever. Secretly, he was hoping to wrest Mathilde away from her parents and start a new life without Rimbaud.

For several days in a row, Verlaine took his suitcase to Victoria Station and then, mysteriously, returned to Howland Street.[9]

On 3 April, he went back to Victoria Station but this time caught the train to Newhaven and boarded the Dieppe ferry the following morning with an hour to spare. While he waited on deck, he overheard two men talking about Communards and prison cells. In a panic, he disembarked, caught a train to Dover and boarded the *Comtesse de Flandre*, which was sailing for Ostend. A few days later, he was at his aunt's home in Jehonville, twenty-five miles east of Charleville in the Belgian Ardennes.

Verlaine might have been jittery and indecisive but he was also observant. The Paris Préfecture was receiving high-grade intelligence from its London agents:

4 April 1873: Verlaine, a former employee of the Hôtel de Ville before and during the Commune, friend of Vermesh, Andrieux [*sic*] and Co. [. . .] left yesterday for Paris on family business.

8 April 1873: Verlaine [. . .] a member of the Club des Études Sociales, has returned to Paris after going in a conspicuous fashion to Victoria Station and pretending to leave, for several consecutive days.

The details – time of departure and motive – are so precise as to suggest an informant close to home. The landlord at 34 Howland Street was a Frenchman. Apart from this, there is no obvious reason why Verlaine and Rimbaud should have decided to change their lodgings.

Without his '*cher petit*', Rimbaud felt lonely. He, too, left London, but unobserved. For the next week, his movements are unknown, even to the Préfecture de Police.

*

ON 5 APRIL, a small battalion of Rimbauds marched to Charleville station and took the train to Attigny. From there, Frédéric, Vitalie, Isabelle and their mother set off in a carriage across the landscape of poplars and windmills towards the hamlet of Roche – thirteen cottages, no church and a half-incinerated farmhouse. The building had been severely damaged by fire some years before. The masons and carpenters had just left.

Vitalie, who was about to turn fifteen, was keeping a diary:[10]

I barely recognized that big, cold, humid room whose shutters, which had been closed for so long, made it hard to examine. [. . .] Everything was as we had left it three years ago. The upstairs bedrooms and the big loft were still the same. The silent, deserted courtyard was covered with grass. [. . .]

Next day, I arranged all my things as if I were to spend most of my life there.

Despite the influence of old romances, which she must have read secretly at her convent school, Vitalie's prose has the slow tick-tock of a settled existence. Her descriptions of the hamlet are like backdrops for a drama that never begins:

The moon rose nobly from amidst the clouds and cast her silvery mantle o'er the shadows which seemed at that hour to be great giants exploring their property. [. . .] Sometimes, large clouds piled up in the sky like a flock of hurrying sheep. The Queen of the Night, pale and languid, hid far from our eyes. [. . .] The thunder could already be heard grumbling in the distance.

At last, on Good Friday, there was something dramatic to report:

That day was to be a milestone in my life, for it was marked by an event that touched me especially. Without having been as it were forewarned, our happiness was crowned by the arrival of my second brother. I can still see myself, in the room where we usually sat, tidying things away. My mother, my brother and my sister were with me, when a discreet knock came at the door. I went to open it and . . . imagine my surprise when I found myself face to face with Arthur. Once we had recovered from our astonishment, the newcomer explained the object of this occurrence. We were very glad and he was very pleased to see us happy. The day passed in the intimacy of the family and in inspecting the property which Arthur, as it were, hardly knew.

Next Sunday – Easter Day – we attended mass in the chapel at Méry.

The newcomer spent little time 'in the intimacy of the family' and made no further appearance in the diary that year. Lunch and dinner failed to lure him from his room. His younger sister claimed, four decades later, that he lay Chatterton-like on his bed, leaden-hued or blotchy with fever.[11] This sort of behaviour is not unknown in adolescent boys visiting home, but since the legend demands relentless eccentricity, withdrawal symptoms have been diagnosed.[12] Written evidence of substance abuse has been found in an early draft of *Une Saison en Enfer* (a very neatly written draft): 'My entrails are on fire, the violence of the venom twists my limbs and deforms me. I am dying of thirst. I am stifling. I cannot cry out.'

Absinthe had been unavailable in London, and the tale that Rimbaud frequented the Chinese opium dens at Limehouse began as an attempt to explain why some of his poems are so hard to understand, especially when sober.[13]

Une Saison en Enfer is obviously the result of a prolonged effort of will and would not have been dramatically altered by transient chemical changes to the central nervous system. When Rimbaud wrote to Delahaye from Roche on three small sheets of blue paper, the symptoms he described were of a more cerebral nature. Unlike Vitalie, he said nothing of the 'fragrant snow' of fruit blossom or the 'fresh and limpid' stream that dribbled through the hamlet. He sketched himself as a shovel-wielding peasant, crying, 'O Nature, my Mother!', accompanied by a singing dwarf and a talking goose. Widow Rimbaud's son was back from the big city:

> What a fucking bore! These peasants are such 'orrible innercents. The *Mother* [in English] has gone and landed me in a real shithole. I don't know how I'll get out of it, but I will. I miss that atrocious Charlestown, the universe, the Libary, etc . . .*

He 'cheered himself up' with a walk to Vouziers, a small town of '10,000 souls' (including 8,000 billeted Prussian soldiers), cursed the weather ('the sun beats down and it's freezing in the morning'), and worked himself up into a splendid ecstasy of loathing:

> I'm abominably uncomfortable. Not a single book, not a single bar within striking distance, nothing happening in the street. This here French countryside is dreadful.

Rimbaud was thriving on the stony soil. The apostrophe to Mother Nature seems to parody a genuine sentiment. His poetry shows a happy ability to dissolve himself into his natural surroundings; but it was hard to express pantheistic fervour after a hundred years of Nature poems written by men who had never blistered their palms on a pitchfork or trodden in a cow-pat:

> I've got nothing more to say, completely arseorbed as I am in the contemprostation of Nature. I'm yours, O Nature, O my mother!

Rimbaud's rustic, schoolboy idiom has been described as 'infantile', but it did allow him to make an unusually precise link between sexuality and the idea of Mother Nature.

He also had some conventional news for Delahaye:

---

* Charleville, the Café de l'Univers, and the slangily truncated 'Bibliothè'.

But I'm working quite regularly, writing some little stories in prose – overall title: *Livre païen* or *Livre nègre* ['Pagan' or 'Negro Book']. It's stupid and innocent. O innocence! innocence, innocence, innoc . . ., curse it!

[. . .] My fate depends on this book, for which I still have half a dozen atrocious stories to invent. But how can anyone invent atrocities in this place? I'm not sending you any stories, though I've already got three: *it's so expensive!** There you go!

This is almost certainly a description of the future book. In its final form, *Une Saison en Enfer* is divided into nine sections: the three already written and the 'half a dozen' yet to come.

The drafts of three sections have survived, two of them – since paper was scarce at the farmhouse – crammed on to the back of Rimbaud's Gospel adaptations: 'Fausse conversion' (later, 'Nuit de l'enfer'), and two untitled drafts of 'Mauvais sang' and 'Alchimie du verbe'.

When the drafts were published after Rimbaud's death, readers who had pictured him as a human volcano were surprised to discover that *Une Saison en Enfer* was created by a laborious process of accretion and erosion.[14] The finished book has the unmistakable density of a text that has been repeatedly subjected to violent self-criticism. It demands a slower reading speed than almost any other prose work of the time. Ideas are compacted into gem-like obscurity. No word is wasted. This is the style of someone who knew how to pack for long journeys. The drafts as they appear in most editions are the smoothed-out contents of a litter-bin. The following passage was eventually reduced to a single line at the end of 'Alchimie du verbe':

> So weak, that I thought I was no longer bearable in society, except by dint of kindness.
>
> What magic What possible cloister is there for this fine disgust?
> [Prison?] ~~That has p~~ That has all passed away little by little.
> I now hate mystical flights of fancy and stylistic eccentricities.
> Now ~~is there~~ I can say that art is folly. ~~The art of~~ [?] our great poets is as easy · art is folly.
> Hail beauty[15]

---

* '*Ça coûte tant!*': a favourite phrase of Mme Rimbaud.

Rimbaud's famous slogan – '*L'art est une sottise*' ('*faire une sottise*' means 'to do something stupid') – was obliterated by the process it seems to deride. The final version is a practised exit – a sudden slamming of the door that cuts the conversation short:

> That has passed away. These days, I know how to greet beauty.

Rimbaud's 'Pagan Book', on which he would continue to work for several months, could not have had a more appropriate birthplace than the rustic purgatory of Roche. Its narrator appears at first as a confused, philosophizing peasant who believes himself to have been 'damned' by an alien religion. This was not the absinthe-swilling poet, but the son of Mme Rimbaud who sat in the little church at Méry on Easter Day in the fug of his bovine compatriots, watching all his idioms pass before him – novels, philosophies, slogans, idle conversation and, of course, the Bible:

> Why was such faith implanted in my mind? My parents have caused my misfortune, and their own, which doesn't matter much to me! My innocence has been abused. [. . .] I am a slave of my baptism and of my weakness.
>
> [. . .] I think I am in hell, therefore I am.

Rimbaud might have felt that his 'fate' depended on this book, as he told Delahaye, because he was hoping to write himself out of a dilemma: how can freedom be attained by a mind that has been conditioned by its oppressor? But in the letter to Delahaye, 'fate' also seems to have a humbler sense.

One of the sections was to be an anthology of seven of his songs, interspersed with prose, in the manner of his earlier letters to Izambard and Demeny. In the finished book, it serves as an exhibition of Rimbaud's recent work, complete with an analytical catalogue.

Une Saison en Enfer was to be the book that would bring him recognition. No doubt reviewers would be happy to identify this 'pagan' with the poet who had caused such unholy mayhem in Paris:

> One evening, I sat Beauty on my knee. – And I found her bitter. – And I insulted her.
>
> I took up arms against justice.

I fled. O witches, poverty and hatred, it was to you that my treasure was entrusted!

I managed to make all human hope vanish from my mind. To strangle every joy I pounced silently like the savage beast.

The Gauls were the most inept flayers of beasts and burners of grass of their time.

From them, I inherited: idolatry and love of sacrilege; – Oh! and every vice: anger, lust (a magnificent vice, lust), especially deceitfulness and sloth.

I don't understand laws; I have no moral sense; I am a brute.

When *Une Saison en Enfer* was finally reviewed – after its author's death – it was generally supposed that the 'brute' was Arthur Rimbaud. Where else could he have found a model for this self-pitying, suicidal beast?

*

ON 18 MAY, calling himself Rimbaud's 'old sow', Verlaine wrote to his 'little brother' from a café just across the Belgian border at Bouillon. His attempt to mollify Mathilde had failed completely, for reasons which escaped him. He was bored, confused and angry – especially bored. Nothing seemed to be working: 'Forgive this stupid, mucky letter. A bit drunk, writing with a nibless pen, smoking a blocked pipe.'

Rimbaud and Delahaye took the coach to Bouillon several times. Their last meeting was on 24 May. While they sat drinking in the historic hotel where Napoleon III had languished after Sedan, Verlaine revealed that, a few years before, he had decided, on a whim, to take confession and communion. A 'brief period of virtue' had ensued, but the conversion had not lasted.[16]

This is curiously reminiscent of one of the 'stories' Rimbaud was then composing: 'False Conversion'. 'How stupid I'm becoming! O Mary, Holy Virgin. False sentiment, false prayer.' A few weeks later, he would castigate Verlaine for 'persisting in his false sentiments'.

Apparently, Verlaine's irritating tendency to be fooled by his own fantasies had exercised Rimbaud since the previous summer. In

'Chanson de la plus haute tour' – in which half the rhymes are partial anagrams of 'Paul-Marie Verlaine' (part of their private code) – he delivered a similar sermon:

> Oh! the thousand widowhoods
> Of the poor, poor soul
> Who has only the image
> Of Our Lady!
> Whoever heard of praying
> To the Virgin Mary?

That evening, Delahaye returned to Charleville without Rimbaud. The two poets were going back to work in England. They reached Antwerp on the afternoon of 26 May 1873 and boarded the night ferry.

After an 'incredibly beautiful' crossing, they landed at Harwich and journeyed back to London on the Great Eastern Railway, arriving at 6.40 a.m.

It was almost a year since they had run away to Belgium together. The relationship had been surprisingly successful. For Rimbaud, who still had 'half a dozen atrocious stories to invent', its possibilities were far from exhausted. 'Poor Verlaine' was not just a source of money and affection. When he read *Une Saison en Enfer* five months later in prison, Verlaine might have realized that all along he had been living as a half-formed character lives with a novelist. No wonder reality had become so slippery.

'I was a widow [...]. He was almost a child ... His mysterious subtleties had seduced me. I neglected all my human duties in order to follow him. What a life! Real life is absent. We are not in the world. I go wherever he goes. I have to. Often, he loses his temper with me – *me, the poor soul*. The Demon! – He's a Demon, you know, *he isn't a man*.'[17]

19

Household in Hell

'LEÇONS de FRANÇAIS, en français – perfection, finesses – par deux Gentlemen parisiens.'

(*The Daily Telegraph*, 21 June 1873)

THE PAPERS ON SALE that morning at Bishopsgate Station newsstand contained several items that were, or soon would be, of interest to Rimbaud and Verlaine.

In Paris, President Thiers had been forced out of office and replaced with Marshal MacMahon, the exterminator of Communards. Something called 'moral order' was to be restored.

In Spain, another 'outrage' had been committed by the Carlists, whose rebel army was attracting mercenaries from all over Europe.

The Shah of Persia, currently visiting St Petersburg, was due to arrive in London on 18 June.

At home, an Indian wing had been added to the Exhibition at South Kensington, and an electric light had been installed at great expense in the clock tower of the Houses of Parliament.

After the recent late-night frosts, a period of brighter weather was expected.

For the moment, Rimbaud and Verlaine were primarily interested in the teeming miscellany of telegraphic phrases at the back of the papers. The summer rush would not begin for another month and there were still plenty of offers of accommodation. A day or two later, they agreed terms with a Mrs Alexander Smith and moved to 8 Great College Street in Camden Town (since 1940, Royal College Street).[1]

The room was on an upper floor. At the back of the house, an area of sheds, allotments and soot-blackened walls spread eastward in the direction of Islington, interrupted by the no-man's-land of Agar Town. 'Ague Town', as it was often called, had recently been reduced from squalor to devastation by the iron clamp of the Midland and Great Northern Railways. A picturesque scrap of St Pancras village hung on like an old tenant. Next door, the Royal Veterinary College preserved a rare patch of green turf.

Howland Street had had its share of artists and déclassés. In Camden Town, foreign poets were more likely to attract unpleasant remarks. It was a grudgingly apologetic district of costermongers, rag-and-bottle merchants, bird-sellers and pawnbrokers. Verlaine sounded cheerful in his letters but obviously spent as little time there as possible: 'A very gay quarter. You'd think you were in Brussels.'

> It's behind King's Cross, not far from Highgate village. The country-side to the north-west [Hampstead Heath] is admirable. I often go there, when I'm not in the Reading Room of the British Museum.[2]

Wisely, they decided not to wait for the distant day when their English would be fluent and advertised their services in French. Verlaine claims to have placed fifteen advertisements in three news-papers, but several searches by Enid Starkie, V. P. Underwood and the present author have yielded only two:

> LEÇONS de Français, Latin, Littérature, en français, par deux Gentle-men Parisiens; prix modérés. – Verlaine, 8, Great College-st., Camden-town.
>
> (*The Echo*, 11, 12 and 13 June 1873)

Since there was probably little demand for Latin lessons in French, they redrafted the advertisement, omitting 'moderate prices', and appealed instead to the discerning *Telegraph* reader:

> LEÇONS de FRANÇAIS, en français – perfection, finesses – par deux Gentlemen parisiens. – Verlaine, 8, Great College-street, Camden Town.
>
> (*The Daily Telegraph*, 21 June 1873)

Soon, an unknown student of French literature was making his way each day up Great College Street, past the barrows and the donkeys, the dogs and the urchins, to number 8, where two rather shabby 'Parisian gentlemen' – one of whom came from Charleville – were waiting to initiate him into the mysteries of French verse. The lessons were given jointly by Rimbaud and Verlaine. The latter's credentials were displayed in the form of one of his books of poetry. Rather late in the day, he had asked Lepelletier to send a copy from Paris:

> It's for the literature lessons *by a poët*. It's the best reference you can give the maniacs who fork out half a pound (12 fr. 50) for a lesson in versification and poetic 'finesses'.

Time-travel fantasies are a sure sign of unreliability in a historian, but it is hard not to wish for transportation to Camden Town in June 1873 with a ten-shilling note and a tape-recorder. Rimbaud was teaching French versification at a time when he seemed to have abandoned verse poetry altogether. His work in progress, *Une Saison en Enfer*, was written in a style which crackles like a bonfire of literary idioms from the Book of Isaiah to the Victorian penny dreadful, and the seven verse poems it contains are so raggedly versified – or deversified – that they could only have served the unknown student as exercises in spotting deliberate mistakes.

Rimbaud clearly enjoyed the precise simplifications that teaching entailed – the reduction of imaginative activities to their objective components. Once a skill had been learned, its mystery was exorcized and it could either be abandoned or exploited. From one point of view, the final abandonment of poetry would be the logical triumph of good sense over wishful thinking.

The immediate aim of the lessons was purely practical: to pay for tobacco and rent, 'kill boredom', and, for Rimbaud, to create commitments that might attach Verlaine more firmly to England. Rimbaud had declared war on 'indolence'. There were still occasional outings – the Shah of Persia's state visit, French plays in the West End – but in his letters, Verlaine was beginning to sound like a schoolboy in permanent detention: 'For the last two months, I've been doing nothing but English (*grammar and speach*). It's beginning to get on my nerves.'

When he was interrogated by the Belgian police a month later, Rimbaud complained that Verlaine had become 'impossible to live with'. Not only was he bone idle, he had also been misbehaving in an unspecified manner 'with people of our acquaintance'. This was probably a reference to his drinking. Verlaine had adjusted easily to gin and tepid ale and was rarely sober. Since all their London friends were 'skint', they usually met them, not at the pub, but in private homes, where the possibilities for embarrassment were endless.

But when Rimbaud told the police that their sudden departure from London must have made 'an unfortunate impression on our friends', he was alluding to something even more disreputable than drunkenness. A nasty rumour was going about the French Quarter. One day, Camille Barrère received a visit from a tearful Verlaine: 'People are saying I'm a pederast, but I'm not! I'm not!'[3] Inevitably, the rumour reached the ear of international espionage and was relayed to Paris with the usual smattering of scandalous titbits and spelling mistakes:

> A strange sort of liaison exists between [. . .] M. Verlaine and a young man who often goes to Charleville, where he has his family, and who, under the Commune, belonged to the Paris irregulars: young Raimbault.[4]

Since spies are not alone in assuming that anything unusual or illegal must also be destructive, the homosexual antics at number 8 have been identified as the prime cause of the impending disaster. If Mrs Smith had been interviewed in time, she would have remembered hearing scuffles and stifled yelps coming from the floor above. And if she looked through the keyhole, she would have seen her two Parisian gentlemen apparently trying to stab each other with rolled-up towels. The towels were wrapped around long knife-blades so that only the tips protruded, thus preventing fatal or expensive injury. As soon as minor mutilation was achieved, they put the knives away and went out to the pub.[5]

Seen through a keyhole, almost anything has an air of sordid mystery about it. The stabbings acted as an escape-valve and should probably be thought of as a kind of sport rather than as criminal violence. It is a sad relationship in any case that has nothing to hide from the landlady.

The real damage was done by Rimbaud's talent for maintaining a permanent state of crisis. Interviewed in 1938, Camille Barrère remembered that Rimbaud and Verlaine were 'always arguing'. Rimbaud's prose poem 'Vagabonds' in which Verlaine later recognized himself,[6] paints an amusingly sadistic picture of life in a rented room. The lunge of dislocated syntax and the unpredictable vocabulary are a vivid image of Rimbaud's dexterity with the knife.

> Pitiful brother! What atrocious wakes I suffered because of him! 'I didn't have a fervent grasp of the undertaking. I made light of his infirmity. By my fault, we would return to exile and slavery.' He credited me with a very peculiar kind of bad luck and innocence, and gave disturbing reasons.
>
> I answered the satanic teacher with a sneer and eventually reached the window. Away over the countryside, traversed by bands of rare music,[7] I created the ghosts of our future nocturnal luxury.
>
> After this vaguely hygienic distraction, I stretched out on a mattress. And almost every night, no sooner asleep, the poor brother got up, his mouth decomposed, his eyes gouged out – just as he saw himself in his dreams! – and dragged me into the room, howling out his fantasy of idiotic grief.
>
> I had, in all intellectual sincerity, undertaken to restore him to his primitive state as son of the Sun, – and we wandered, nourished by the caverns' wine and the biscuit of the road, I in a hurry to find the place and the formula.

Life with Verlaine was providing Rimbaud with some splendid material for his poetry. For someone who spent so much of his life alone, he obviously revelled in the amateur dramatics of human relationships: the emotional confidence tricks and the self-deception, the humiliations received with gratitude and piously dispensed.

The section of *Une Saison en Enfer* titled 'Délires I', in which a Verlainean 'Foolish Virgin' recounts her life in hell with the 'Infernal Bridegroom', is not a fly-on-the-wall documentary, but it would certainly have lacked its cruel circumstantiality if Rimbaud had never lived with Verlaine. Echoes of Verlaine's poems, conversation and experiences are recognizable enough to make the published text an extremely compromising document.

'I was in his soul as in a palace that has been emptied so as not to see such an ignoble person as oneself.'

'Wretched and frustrated, I sometimes said to him, "I understand you." He shrugged his shoulders.'

'How many hours of the night I lay awake beside his dear, sleeping body, trying to discover why he was so determined to escape from reality.'

'I hungered ever more for his kindness. When he kissed me and embraced me like a friend, it was indeed a heaven, a dark heaven, that I entered and where I wanted to be left, poor, deaf, dumb and blind. I was already getting used to it.'

In contrast to the spineless, masochistic 'Virgin' of *Une Saison en Enfer*, the 'Infernal Bridegroom' is a volatile philanthropist whose only anchor in the real world is the unsavoury activity he refers to as his 'duty':

'In the hovels where we got drunk, he [the 'Infernal Bridegroom'] used to weep at the sight of those around us, the cattle of destitution. He helped drunkards to their feet in the black streets. He had the pity of a spiteful mother for little children. – He went on his way with the pretty manners of a little girl at Sunday school. – He pretended to know about everything: commerce, art, medicine. – I followed him. I have no choice!'

Une Saison en Enfer should not be read as simple autobiography; but it is, like any careful piece of writing, an exercise in self-analysis. Rimbaud was able to observe himself through Verlaine's eyes: a charlatan Messiah who would play the game for as long as his disciple's gullibility allowed.

'Full of emotion, we worked together. But after a penetrating caress, he would say, "How strange everything you have lived through will seem to you when I am no longer there. When you no longer have my arms cradling your neck, nor my heart on which to rest, nor this mouth on your eyes. Because one day I shall have to leave and go far,

far away. And anyway, there are others I must help. It is my duty – though it's not exactly appetizing . . . dear heart . . ."'

For Rimbaud, as for his mother, 'love' was inseparable from the idea of doing good. Every caress and every stab of the knife was a moral lesson. Unlike his mother, he had no rigid system of beliefs by which to interpret his own behaviour.

*

BY THE END of June, the weak disciple was buckling under the strain. The last straw was as trivial as last straws usually are. On Thursday, 3 July, it was Verlaine's turn to do the shopping. He went out and came back with a fish and a bottle of oil.

I was approaching the house when I saw Rimbaud observing me through the open window. For no good reason, he started to snigger. I climbed the stairs anyway and went in. 'Have you any idea how ridiculous you look with your bottle of oil in one hand and your fish in the other?' said Rimbaud. I retaliated, because, I can assure you, I definitely did not look ridiculous.[8]

A fish hit Rimbaud in the face and Verlaine headed for the stairs.

Since Verlaine told this story more than once, with slightly different details, there has been some debate about the identity of the fish: herring or mackerel? In all likelihood, it was a red herring. The later exchange of letters shows that Verlaine had been summoning up the courage to take what was commonly referred to as the coward's way out. He had just enough sense left to realize that he was impossibly confused.

Rimbaud begged him to stay or at least to leave some money.

Verlaine refused and set off without packing his bags.

*

AT ST KATHARINE'S dock, the noon steamer was about to sail for Antwerp.[9] Rimbaud stood on the quayside, signalling to his friend to disembark.

At noon, the ship weighed anchor with Verlaine still on board, and dissolved like a ghost into the yellow fog.

20

'No Serious Motive'?

'Its form is round, its edges contused and torn, its diameter
approximately 5 millimetres.'

(Dr C. Semal, Hôpital Saint-Jean, Brussels, 14 July 1873)

RIMBAUD TRUDGED BACK to Great College Street alone. Verlaine's clothes would fetch enough at the pawnshop to allow
him to stay on for a few days; but what then? On Friday afternoon,
he sat down in the empty room and wrote a letter.

It was the most old-fashioned piece of writing that Rimbaud ever
produced. The scrawl suggests a hasty improvisation, which shows
how easily he wrote in the style traditionally described as 'poetic'.
There were no slang words or expletives. The chiming vowels are a
placatory imitation of Verlaine's tuneful elegies.

London, Friday afternoon

Come back, come back, dear friend, my only friend, come back. I
swear to you I'll be good. My grumpiness was just a joke that I took
too far, and now I'm more sorry than one can say. [. . .] I haven't
stopped crying for two whole days. Come back. Take heart, dear
friend. Nothing is lost. All you have to do is make the return journey.
We shall live here very bravely and patiently. Oh! I beg you. It's for
your own good anyway. [. . .]

Listen only to your kind heart.

Tell me quickly if I'm to join you.
    Yours for life.
        Rimbaud

[. . .] If I am never to see you again, I shall join the navy or the army.
    Oh, come back! My tears return with every hour.

Next morning (Saturday, 5 July 1873), Rimbaud felt better. Verlaine's farewell note had arrived, blotched by tears or spume. Appropriately, it was headed, 'At sea':

My friend,
    I don't know if you'll still be in London when this reaches you, but I wanted to say that you must, *at heart*, understand, *finally*, that I absolutely had to leave, and that this life of violence and *scenes*, the only point of which was to satisfy your whims, simply could not go on buggering me up!
    The only thing is, since I loved you enormously (*Honni soit qui mal y pense*)* I also wanted to confirm that if, within three days, I am not back with my wife, under perfect conditions, I'm going to blow my brains out. 3 days in a hotel and a *rivolvita* don't come cheap, hence my '*stinginess*' just now. You ought to forgive me.
    If, as will *proberly* be the case, I am to go through with this final act of idiocy, I shall at least do it like a brave idiot. – My last thought, my friend, will be for you. [. . .]
    Would you like me to embrace you while I kick the bucket?
        Your poor
        P. Verlaine

The relationship was still performing its old equations. A hysterical Verlaine produced a practical, older Rimbaud. He replied immediately to the poste restante office in Brussels, determined to administer a dose of common sense. As an extra inducement, he added a threat:

Dear friend, I have your letter dated 'At sea'. This time, you're wrong – very wrong. First, there's nothing definite in your letter: your wife will either come or she won't come, in three months, three years

---

* 'Evil be to him who evil thinks' – in case the letter fell into the hands of the police, which it did.

– who knows? As for kicking the bucket, I know you. While you wait for your wife and your death you're going to go flailing about all over the place, bothering a lot of people. You still haven't realized – you, of all people! – that the tantrums were equally bogus on both sides! But it would be you who'd end up in the wrong, because, even after I called you back, you persisted in your false sentiments. Do you think that life will be more pleasant with someone else? *Think about it*! Of course it won't!

You can only be free with me, and since I promise to be very nice in future and deeply regret my share of wrongs, and since I'm finally clear about everything and love you dearly, if you won't come back or if you don't want me to come to you, you're committing a crime, and *you'll regret it for* MANY A LONG YEAR *by losing all your freedom and suffering more atrocious problems* perhaps than any you have known until now. And when you've thought about that, remember what you were before you met me.

Verlaine noted the vague threat, but he was in no condition to be manipulated. He had written to Mathilde to say that he had left Rimbaud for ever and would kill himself if she didn't come to Brussels.[1] The following day, convinced that she would never come, he decided not to kill himself after all. He had met a friend, the painter Auguste Mourot, who advised him to go to the Spanish embassy and volunteer for the army. This struck Verlaine as a sensible solution.*

At the same time, he was feeling guilty about leaving Rimbaud in the lurch and wrote to their friend Colonel Matuszewicz, asking him to go and make sure that Rimbaud was all right. Then he wrote two more suicide notes – one for Lepelletier and one for Rimbaud's mother – and sent a letter to the landlady, Mrs Smith, implying that he was about to return to London.

The suicide note to Mme Rimbaud brought an impressive reply. She wrote with obvious sympathy for a man who had been made miserable by her son, but she also wrote as a Christian. The ancient truths were set out in an axiomatic form that bears comparison

---

* Verlaine is always said to have volunteered for the Carlist rebels in Spain, like Rimbaud in 1875. This would have been unimaginably idiotic, like volunteering for the Sandinistas at a Nicaraguan embassy in the 1970s.

with sections of *Une Saison en Enfer*. How could Verlaine think of killing himself when he had a wife, a child and a 'sainted' mother to protect?

> Killing oneself in such conditions is an act of *infamy*. Society despises the man who dies in such a fashion, and God himself cannot forgive such a great crime and casts him from his bosom.
>
> Monsieur, I do not know in what manner you have disgraced yourself with Arthur, but I have always foreseen that your liaison would not end happily. Why? you might ask. Because whatever has not been sanctioned and approved of by good and decent parents cannot be good for their children. You young people, you scoff and sneer at everything, but the fact remains that we have experience on our side, and whenever you fail to follow our advice, you will be unhappy. As you can see, I am not trying to flatter you. I never flatter those I hold dear.

Both Rimbaud and his mother were at their best when dealing with pusillanimous behaviour. But strong wills tend to create the situations on which they thrive. It was thanks to Rimbaud that Verlaine was writing poetry again and partly because of him that he was about to experience a religious conversion; but it was Rimbaud, too, who had reduced him to his present state.

The final act of the drama began on Monday morning when the landlady showed Rimbaud the letter from Verlaine: apparently, he was about to come back to London. Rimbaud's reply is not well known – probably because it contradicts the legend. Even for Rimbaud, it seems, fear of social embarrassment was almost as powerful as love.

> I have seen the letter you sent to Mme Smith.
>
> You want to come back to London! You don't know how they'd all receive you! And the looks I'd get from Andrieu and the others if they saw me with you again. All the same, I'll be very brave. [. . .]
>
> You will come, won't you? Tell me the truth. You'd be giving a mark of your courage. I hope it's true. You can rely on me. I'll be very well behaved.

Rimbaud wrote this jittery letter at noon and went out to post it. On his return, he found a telegram from Verlaine (7 July 1873).[2]

It was this ten-word message that precipitated the unhappy ending foretold by Mme Rimbaud:

> Volunteer spain come here Hotel liegeois laundry manuscripts if possible

Rimbaud left London as soon as he received the telegram. He took the train from Victoria Station and crossed the Channel by night.

He arrived in Brussels on the morning of Tuesday, 8 July.

*

THERE WAS NOTHING inevitable about the 'tragedy' that is usually referred to as 'the Brussels incident'.[3] The main protagonist, Verlaine, was a spinning weather-vane. He was simultaneously determined to leave for Spain, go back to London, wait in Brussels, have it out with his in-laws, return to Mathilde, get drunk and blow his brains out. He was also keen to recover his books and manuscripts, which Rimbaud had sensibly deposited with Vermersch.

On Tuesday morning, Verlaine had gone to the Spanish embassy with his friend Mourot, only to learn that the Spanish government army did not recruit foreigners. They then returned to the hotel, where Verlaine's mother was waiting.

Meanwhile, Rimbaud had arrived. At this point, Mourot disappeared. He had never met Rimbaud, he later told the police, but 'he inspired me with repulsion'. Like everyone else, Mourot was convinced that Rimbaud had turned Verlaine into his personal milchcow. 'Besides which, ever since Verlaine had been accused in the separation proceedings of having immoral relations with him, I was not eager to see them together.'

Here, the statements given to the Belgian police become slightly muddled. The melodrama that eventually entered literary history is that Verlaine desperately wanted Rimbaud to stay, whereas Rimbaud was cruelly determined to leave. This is a complete reversal of the situation as revealed by the recent exchange of letters.

On Wednesday evening, Verlaine began to drink and must have kept it up all night since he left the hotel at six o'clock the following morning (Thursday, 10 July). For the next thirteen hours, his capacity for rational thought was severely reduced; but there was a passionate consistency about his actions, as if a different kind of logic had taken over.

9 a.m.
In the Galeries Saint-Hubert, Verlaine enters a gunsmith's shop and buys a 7-mm. six-shooter, a patent leather holster and a box of fifty cartridges. The gunsmith shows him how to load the revolver: 'The customer took it away without having mentioned the use to which he intended to put it.'

In a bar in the Rue des Chartreux, Verlaine inserts three bullets in the gun and continues to drink.

Noon
By now, Verlaine, his mother and Rimbaud have moved to the Hôtel de la Ville de Courtrai in the Rue des Brasseurs.[4] Rimbaud and Verlaine share a room: one door leads to the landing, the other into Mme Verlaine's bedroom.

Rimbaud announces his intention to return to Paris. A mail train is due to leave the Gare du Midi at 3.40 p.m. He orders Verlaine's mother to give him twenty francs for the ticket. Verlaine countermands the order.

Noon – 2 p.m.
Rimbaud asks about the gun. Verlaine is unspecific and, according to Rimbaud, 'very overexcited': 'It's for you, for me, for everybody.'

They leave the hotel and go to a café on the Grand-Place. Rimbaud's third statement gives some idea of their conversation:

> It is true that at a certain moment [Verlaine] expressed his intention to go to Paris and attempt a reconciliation with his wife. It is also true that he wanted to stop me going there with him; but he kept changing his mind from one moment to the next and could settle on no particular plan.

The cloud of contradiction begins to assume a recognizable shape. There is little doubt, as the accepted version would have it, that Verlaine wanted to prevent Rimbaud from returning to Paris. But why? In order for this to fit the earlier exchange of letters, one further detail is required.

Rimbaud's circuitous statement shows that the judge was homing in on the missing piece. He had clearly been intrigued by the underlined passage in Rimbaud's letter: 'If you won't come back or if you don't want me to come to you, you're committing a crime, and *you'll regret it for* MANY A LONG YEAR *by losing all your freedom . . .*'

For Rimbaud, blackmail was the obvious solution. Either Verlaine would be forced to go back and live with Rimbaud, in which case his marriage was certainly over; or, if he complained that Rimbaud had threatened to denounce him as a homosexual, his marriage would be over in any case, since Mathilde would have the evidence she needed.

Rimbaud had never allowed conventional morality to ruin a practical arrangement. In his view, he was simply encouraging Verlaine to do what was 'good for him'.

*

THE DISCUSSION CONTINUED in the hotel room. Verlaine locked the door to the landing and sat down in front of it. Rimbaud's account of what happened next is corroborated by the other statements:

> He was still trying to prevent me from carrying out my plan to return to Paris. I remained unshakeable. [. . .] I was standing with my back to the wall on the other side of the room. Then he said, 'This is for you, since you're leaving!' or something like that. He aimed his pistol at me.[5]

A small hole appeared in Rimbaud's left arm just above the wrist. Almost immediately, a second shot was fired. Verlaine had lowered his arm – according to Rimbaud – and the second bullet buried itself in the wall. In fact, given the width of the room (ten feet), Rimbaud's height (about five feet ten inches), the almost horizontal trajectory of the first bullet and the fact that a bullet-hole was discovered twelve inches above the floor, Verlaine must have lowered his arm completely only *after* firing the second shot.

Still clutching the revolver, Verlaine rushed into his mother's room, threw himself on her bed, then pressed the gun into Rimbaud's hands and urged him to pull the trigger.

While Verlaine whimpered with remorse, Mme Verlaine bandaged Rimbaud's wrist. Remarkably, no one came to ask about the noise. At about 5 p.m., they left the hotel and took Rimbaud to the Hôpital Saint-Jean on the other side of town. When the wound had been dressed, they returned to the hotel, where Rimbaud packed his bags.

Mme Verlaine now gave Rimbaud twenty francs and they set off for the station shortly before 8 p.m. Verlaine was still jangling with excitement, begging Rimbaud not to leave for Paris.

As they walked along, Rimbaud noticed that Verlaine was keeping his hand inside his coat. Apparently, no one had thought to disarm him. They came out on to the Place Rouppe, Verlaine ran on ahead, then turned round and seemed to reach for his gun.

Later, a box containing forty-seven cartridges was found. Since two shots had been fired in the hotel, the gun was almost certainly still loaded.[6]

Rimbaud turned and ran until he found a policeman. He told the man what had happened and led him back to the square. Constable Auguste Michel seized the revolver and arrested Verlaine on suspicion of attempted murder.

*

ONCE AGAIN, POLICE records disprove the traditional version of events. (The story is that Rimbaud was shocked to see his friend taken down to the cells. After failing to save him, he returned to Roche, sobbing 'Verlaine! Verlaine!', and wrote *Une Saison en Enfer* as an act of contrition.[7] Years later, according to a well-known fabricator, a crucifix 'surrounded by rays of light' was found deeply etched into Rimbaud's writing desk.)[8]

Rimbaud gave his statement to the unsmiling superintendent. Not surprisingly, he sounded like someone who had just had his would-be murderer arrested:

> For the last year, I have been living with M. Verlaine. We wrote letters for newspapers and gave French lessons. He had become impossible to live with, and I had expressed a desire to return to Paris.

> Four days ago, he left me to come to Brussels and sent a telegram asking me to join him.

There are so many gaps in this account that it can scarcely be described as true. Rimbaud now went on to establish premeditation. As soon as he arrived in Brussels, Verlaine had threatened him, saying: 'Go on, then, leave, and you'll see what happens!' Before firing the two shots, he had repeated his threat: 'I'll teach you to want to leave!'

Rimbaud said nothing of Verlaine's drunken state. In effect, he was sending the father of little Georges Verlaine to prison.

Mme Verlaine was interviewed next and tried to repair the damage: 'For about two years, M. Rimbaud has been living at the expense of my son, who has had reason to complain of his surly and spiteful character.' Verlaine had acted in 'a moment of aberration' and had purchased the revolver simply 'because he intends to travel'.

When Verlaine was interrogated, he made no attempt to exonerate himself, though he did insist that when he reached for his gun on the Place Rouppe, he had been intending to shoot himself, not Rimbaud. Ominously, the question of 'immoral relations' was raised.

Verlaine was locked up with a howling menagerie of drunkards. After a sleepless night and a meal of mashed potato and unidentifiable meat, he was taken to the Prison des Petits Carmes – a former Carmelite convent – to await the trial.

*

THE FOLLOWING MORNING, Rimbaud left the hotel with Mme Verlaine to return to the hospital. His hand had swollen up and he had spent the night in a fever.

This time, the hotel owner, M. Verplaes, was at his desk. Five days later, he was interviewed by the police.

A recent account of Rimbaud's life has the hotelier asking Rimbaud, 'Are you wounded?', to which Rimbaud nobly replies, 'It's nothing.'[9] The original statement gives a different idea of Rimbaud's discretion:

> Rimbaud came down the stairs with his arm in a sling. I asked him what was wrong. He replied that his friend had wounded him with a

pistol shot. Then Mme Verlaine intervened and the conversation was interrupted.

Rimbaud was now quite ill, probably from shock and mild malnutrition. He was to spend the next nine days in hospital.

A police doctor wrote a small essay on his wound (the longest piece of writing devoted to any aspect of Rimbaud until Verlaine's *Poètes maudits* of 1883). The form of the wound was accurately observed to be 'round' and its vertical direction 'from without to within, which is to say from the outer parts to the inner'. 'The swelling and the absence of protuberation caused by a foreign body make ascertainment relative to the presence of a projectile uncertain.' (The doctor couldn't tell whether or not the bullet was still in the arm.) A small projectile was finally extracted on 17 July and preserved as an exhibit for the trial. If it ever emerges from a police archive, it will probably become one of the holiest relics in modern literature.

On 12 July, the pince-nez of Judge Théodore t'Serstevens appeared before Bed 19 of Ward 11 in the Hôpital Saint-Jean. A more detailed statement was obtained. This time, Rimbaud emphasized Verlaine's temporary madness and remorse. The whole statement was less categorical and more faithful to the untidy truth, which was just as well because Rimbaud's belongings were searched and several letters confiscated, along with a copy of Verlaine's sonnet, 'Le Bon Disciple'. This made interesting reading. The accused had apparently asked the plaintiff to 'mount [his] loins and trample' . . .

Even more disturbing was the fact that the judge had obviously seen the other files on Verlaine:

JUDGE T'SERSTEVENS: Does she [Mathilde] not also cite as a grievance your intimacy with Verlaine?
RIMBAUD: Yes. She even accuses us of immoral relations; but I won't even bother to deny such a calumny.

Strictly speaking, 'immoral relations' had no bearing on the case. But judicial curiosity was roused. On 16 July, Verlaine was visited in his cell by Drs Semal and Vleminckx and subjected to a humiliating examination. The doctors' report was presented at the trial as aggravating evidence. It deserves to be quoted as a piece of social history.

- The penis is short and not very voluminous. The glans in particular is small and tapering, becoming increasingly thin towards its outer extremity [. . .]

- The anus can be dilated quite markedly, by a slight parting of the buttocks, to a depth of about one inch. This movement reveals a widened infundibulum, resembling a truncated cone with a concave apex. The folds of the sphincter are without injury and bear no marks . . . Contractability: remains *almost* normal.

- The conclusion to be drawn from this examination is that P. Verlaine bears on his person traces of habitual pederasty, both active and passive. Neither type of trace is sufficiently marked to give grounds for suspecting *inveterate and long-standing* habits; rather, they would indicate fairly recent practices . . .[10]

If there was anything symbolic about 'the Brussels incident', it was this forensic analysis of a poet. After reading the doctors' prose, it is hard to find the 'Sonnet du trou du cul' obscene: 'a violet carnation, / Humbly crouched amid the moss / Still moist with love . . .'

The interpretation of penile anatomy is pure fantasy. The other signs described by Semal and Vleminckx are consistent with anal intercourse, but not categorical, as recent child-abuse cases have shown. Even on its own terms, the report is flawed. The absence of injury would actually suggest 'long-standing' rather than 'fairly recent' habits.

This genital inspection was a worrying development for Rimbaud. There was now enough pseudo-evidence to convict him of 'unnatural practices'. On 18 July, he gave his third statement. This time, he avoided any reference to the passionate nature of their relationship. He could find 'no serious motive' in Verlaine's attack. He reminded the judge that Verlaine had been drinking all morning – 'as indeed he usually does when left to his own devices'.

Next day, 'Arthur Rimbaud, 19 years of age, man of letters, usually residing in Charleville', withdrew his complaint.

For Verlaine, Rimbaud's clemency came too late. On 8 August, he was sentenced to two years in prison and a 200-franc fine. It was the maximum sentence. The widened infundibulum had impressed the jury.[11]

*

RIMBAUD LEFT THE hospital on 19 July. He must have been given more money by Mme Verlaine since he stayed on for a few days above a tobacconist's shop in the Rue des Bouchers where a shop-assistant called Anne Pincemaille rented out part of her flat.[12] By luck, an unknown young artist called Jef Rosman – perhaps another tenant – preserved his woeful image on a mahogany panel: 'Portrait of the Frenchman Arthur Rimbaud, wounded after drinking by his close friend, the French poet Paul Verlaine. From life by Jef Rosman.'

Flattened by a lumpy red quilt and swathed in lacy sheets (Mme Pincemaille was also an embroideress), Rimbaud looks as miserable as a bed-bound athlete, the victim of a sordid boarding-house adventure.

Soon after, he left for Roche. The tale that he was expelled from Belgium, like Victor Hugo in 1871, is untrue.[13] He left of his own free will.

Somewhere along the way, he bought some paper: the 'atrocious stories' of *Une Saison en Enfer* were waiting to be finished and there was never any paper at Roche.

The scar was forming quickly. The last sections of the book were written by someone who was feeling happily posthumous – a poet who had survived two gunshots and perhaps his own upbringing:

> On my hospital bed, the smell of incense came back to me so strongly;
> keeper of the sacred aromatics, confessor, martyr . . .
>> That's my filthy childhood education talking. And what of it! . . .
>> I'll do my twenty years if everyone else is going to.
>> No! No! At the moment, I'm rebelling against death!

In a Belgian prison cell, on a piece of paper that had been used to wrap up cheese, Verlaine was tracing out a poem about his beautiful destroyer: '*Crimen amoris*'. It was written with the poignant limp of the eleven-syllable line.[14] At the Feast of the Seven Sins, the loveliest of the 'adolescent Satans' flies to the top of a tower, declares that Good and Evil do not exist, and is blasted by a thunderbolt.[15]

Rimbaud headed back to the Ardennes under a clear sky. His own treatment of the theme, in 'Matinée d'ivresse', is typically ambiguous: the Tree of Good and Evil – the 'horrid shrub' of *Une Saison en Enfer* – is not destroyed, merely threatened with removal. The poem itself is simply an 'intoxication'. But, pending total enlightenment and a revolution in the nature of reality, hashish – etymologically alluded to in the last word of the poem – is a more than acceptable substitute for frankincense and myrrh:

> This poison will remain in all our veins even when the fanfare turns sour and we're back at the old disharmony. [...] We have been promised that the tree of good and evil will be buried in the darkness, that tyrannical decencies will be deported, that we might introduce our very pure form of love. It began with bouts of nausea and it's ending – since we can't take immediate possession of this eternity – it's ending with a scattering of scents.
>
> [...]
>
> Little night of drunkenness, holy night!, if only for the mask you bestowed on us. Method, we affirm thee! We shall not forget that yesterday you glorified all our ages. We have faith in the poison. We know how to offer up our entire life every day.
>
> The time of the *Assassins* is upon us.

21

Harvest

'– But I've just noticed that my mind is asleep.'

('L'Impossible', *Une Saison en Enfer*)

ACCORDING TO THE Sixth Criminal Court in Brussels, Verlaine had inflicted a wound – a bullet-hole in the left wrist – that rendered Rimbaud 'unfit for work'. Happily, he appears to have been right-handed. As soon as he was back at Roche, he went upstairs to finish his 'atrocious stories'. For the next month, he weeded, pruned and scythed until the drafts were quite transformed and the illusion of confessional autobiography was achieved.

The new title was drily optimistic: *Une Saison en Enfer* – Hell, but just for a season. Apparently, there was life after eternal damnation. To the writers in Paris who were shaking their heads in horror at Verlaine's undoing, it would have suggested a slice of Rimbaud's infernal life.

Rimbaud certainly knew that his book would be read as a savage confession, and that allusions to his misdeeds would be greedily detected.[1] In the opening section, he appears to refer to the shooting ('Very recently, having found myself on the point of croaking my last . . .'), and occasional innuendoes might have worried some of the closet homosexuals among the 'Nasty Fellows': 'the friends of death, the retarded of every sort. – They'd all be damned, if I took revenge!'[2]

Few people would notice, however, that *Une Saison en Enfer* began with quotation marks – « – separating the 'Rimbaud' on the cover from the 'I' in the text. This was the next stage on from the experimental *Déserts de l'amour*. Following the Romantic tradition – Chateaubriand's *René* or Musset's *Confession d'un enfant du siècle* – *Les Déserts de l'amour* had been presented in a foreword as the dreams of a confused but representative adolescent:[3] 'the writings of a young, a very young *man* [. . .] without mother or country', 'fleeing all moral force, like several pitiable young men before him'. 'He had his soul and his heart, all his strength, raised in errors strange and sad.'

The new choice of setting was also a Romantic commonplace. Since the early nineteenth century, the road to Hell had been clogged with poets. 'Hell' was usually a metaphor for the big city and its population of heartless businessmen, prostitutes and book reviewers. The recipe rarely changed. The poet was a hypersensitive young old man who remembered a happy, middle-class childhood and saw his own mishaps and miseries as a crushing condemnation of society. The inscription at the entrance to Dante's Hell, *'Lasciate ogni speranza . . .'*, was invariably used as a title or an epigraph. If the poet was a socialist, hope was embodied by philanthropy and reliable statistics; if a Catholic, by virgins, mothers or miscellaneous symbolic data like the reflection of the sky in a gutter.[4]

Like Baudelaire, who had once thought of publishing his poems under the title *Les Limbes* ('Limbo'), Rimbaud played on the dual identity of Hell: the Christian and the Classical. His title also evokes the underworld adventures of Aeneas, or one of the Parnassians' favourite mythical figures: Persephone, who spent the summer months with her husband Hades, buried in the dark like the seeds of next year's harvest. Persephone's return to the upper world was the autumn sowing – *satio, sationis*, from which 'season' and *'saison'* are derived.

In line with the myth, the fictional time-span of *Une Saison en Enfer* runs from spring ('And the springtime brought me the hideous laugh of the idiot') to autumn ('Autumn already! – but why regret an eternal sun, if we are engaged in the discovery of divine light'). The dates at the end – 'April–August, 1873' – may be more symbolic than historic.

This time, Vitalie did not record her brother's reappearance at Roche, but she did note his absence from the field:

> My brother Arthur did not share in our farm labours. The pen gave him occupation of a sufficiently serious nature to prevent him from joining us in our manual tasks.[5]

Rimbaud wrote his book to the accompaniment of a busy farmyard – the clatter of boots, the clucking of hens, the tut-tutting of Mme Rimbaud. His phrases are not the leisurely propositions of uninterrupted conversation but the cries and grunts of someone who is engaged in physical activity. ('Spiritual combat is as brutal as the battle of men.')

> I detest all trades. Masters and workers, they're all peasants, all ignoble. The hand that wields a pen is just as good as the hand that steers a plough. – What a century of hands! – I'll never get my hand in.

A month later, the two sisters were going out to the orchard and coming back with cheeks like apples to find brother Arthur still hunched over his desk: 'The fruit harvest arrived', wrote Vitalie. 'We all more or less lent a hand.'[6]

> But! who made my tongue so perfidious that it has guided and preserved my slothfulness until now? Without even using my body to earn a living, and more idle than the toad, I have lived everywhere. There isn't a single family in Europe I don't know. – I mean families like mine, which owe everything they possess to the Declaration of the Rights of Man.

Any summary of *Une Saison en Enfer* can easily be contradicted with quotations from the text. None of the ideas are separated from the brain that produced them. The weight of tradition in Rimbaud's range of reference is continually vaporized by the rapid movements of thought. These are not the prefabricated lumps of experience called 'themes', but mental events, apparently described as they occurred.

This gives the text an invigorating, intellectual roughness reminiscent of Montaigne. Other poets seem, by contrast, to talk over themselves, to drown out their own inner voices. As Verlaine had found to his cost, Rimbaud had an exhausting ability to maintain internal disagreements without wrecking the structure. *Une Saison en Enfer* was the product of an entrepreneurial mind that found its stimulation, not in the smug consolidation of success, but in disappointments, dead-ends and even in its own 'stupidity':

> – But I've just noticed that my mind is asleep.
> If it managed to stay awake from now on, we'd soon be at the truth, which perhaps surrounds us with its angels weeping! [. . .] If it had always been wide awake, I'd be sailing by now on the open sea of wisdom! . . .

Une Saison en Enfer should be read first of all without the dubious aid of a description (including this one). Perhaps the ideal pocket edition would contain a ten-word introduction – Rimbaud's retort when his mother asked what it all meant: 'It means what it says, literally and in every sense.'[7] The so-called obscurity of *Une Saison en Enfer* is partly an effect of the critical instruments brought to bear on it.[8] From the very beginning, the impression is one of absolute clarity, even in psychological disarray:

> Once, if I remember correctly, my life was a banquet where every heart was open and every wine flowed free.
> One night, I sat Beauty on my knees. – And I found her bitter. – And I insulted her.
> I took up arms against justice.
> [. . .] I lay down in the mud. I dried myself in the air of crime. And I played fine tricks on madness.
> And the springtime brought me the hideous laugh of the idiot.

The first titled section, 'Mauvais sang', is an overture in which the dilemmas are raised to be agonized over or wished away. A trawl through the past reveals no remedy for rootlessness. The narrator is plagued by the idea of 'salvation', but his 'pagan' soul is denied even the certainty of damnation:

> Priests, teachers, masters, you are wrong to deliver me into the hands of justice. I have never belonged to this race. [. . .] I don't understand laws; I have no moral sense.
> [. . .] I am a beast, a nigger.

Similarly, the future holds little hope. The passages in which Rimbaud appears to recount his own later life take the form of cynical fantasies:

> [. . .] My day is done; I'm leaving Europe. The sea air will burn my lungs; lost climes will tan my hide. [. . .]
>
> I shall return with limbs of steel, a dark skin and a furious eye: my mask will lead people to believe that I belong to a powerful race. I shall have gold: I shall be lazy and brutal. Women take care of those ferocious invalids back from hot countries. I shall be involved in politics. Saved.
>
> For now, I am damned. I detest the fatherland. The best thing would be a good drunken sleep on the beach.

The next sections consider the dilemmas and possible solutions with varying degrees of desperation or flippancy: love is represented by the Foolish Virgin, flailing in her swamp of self-pity; reason is a futile, self-reflecting mirror; scientific progress is 'too slow'; charity is contaminated with pride. The narrator's messianic fantasies are obviously inspired by that 'joker', Satan: 'Come, all of you – even the little children – that I might console you.'

The heart of the book is the splendid 'Alchimie du verbe', in which Rimbaud recounts his poetic experiments of 1872. The enterprise is described from the outset as 'one of my follies', and the poems themselves, which Rimbaud seems to have quoted from memory, are curiously hobbled:[9] syllables have dropped out like stones from an old wall.

The poet's 'verbal alchemy' turns out to have been just another form of self-deception: 'None of the sophisms of madness – the sort of madness that is locked up – was neglected by me. I could repeat them all: I know the system.'

After these seemingly insoluble dilemmas, the end of the book – 'Adieu' – is surprisingly, almost suspiciously optimistic:

> – Sometimes I see in the sky endless beaches covered with white nations in joy. A great golden vessel, above me, waves its multicoloured flags in the morning breezes. I have created every feast, every triumph, every drama. I have tried to invent new flowers, new stars, new forms of flesh, new languages. I thought I was acquiring supernatural powers.

Well! now I have to bury my imagination and my memories! An artist and storyteller of such glorious repute swept away!

It takes a wonderful lack of irony to see this as Rimbaud's farewell to poetry. There is nothing to prove that the narrator will not immediately relapse into self-doubt. From the very beginning, the book is presented as the memoirs of a poet with an unreliable memory, the confessions of a con-man, the self-criticism of a self-deceiver. The echoes of Nero's last words – 'What an artist dies with me!' – do not suggest that 'the open sea of wisdom' has been reached.

Yet the conclusion does appear to correspond closely to the adventure on which Rimbaud was about to embark in his new poems. If absolute truth is unobtainable, the clear perception of untruth is at least an advantage. Meanwhile, the unending, futile struggle of the pagan soul with Christianity is abandoned: 'One must be absolutely modern.' The book which began with a crisis of indecision and lost identity ends with a post-religious affirmation of consciously blind resolve: 'Slaves, let us not curse life.'

It used to be said, with a kind of benevolent gloating, that *Une Saison en Enfer* represents the failure of Rimbaud's 'Seer' project – a warning to those who spurn the benefits of higher education: 'Now he knew that the life he had led had been foolish and wrong, that vice was stupid and so was debauch, that it had all brought him nothing but remorse, regret and ill-health.'[10]

In fact, *Une Saison en Enfer* is a brilliant demonstration of the insight that 'I is somebody else', one of the first modern works of literature to show that experiments with language are also investigations into the self. It brings together, like a particle accelerator, the two repellent forms of thought – the mechanistic and the religious – that gave the 'Seer' letter its exciting implausibility. It is not even certain that Rimbaud's self-critical conclusions discredit the messianic part of the project since this 'quasi holy book'[11] has been responsible for several genuine conversions.

Whatever biography might suggest, Rimbaud's lasting originality does not consist of socially inappropriate behaviour. Other children who felt the lack of a father and doubted the quality of their mother's love have behaved in a similarly colourful fashion. *Une Saison en Enfer* on the other hand is without precedent. Even *post*cedents are hard to find. Fifty years before *Ulysses* and *The Waste Land*, Rimbaud, at the age of eighteen, had invented a linguistic world that can be happily explored for years like the scrapyard of a civilization.

The list of possible influences could occupy almost as much space as the text itself: Isaiah, Job, Ecclesiastes, the Psalms, the Gospels, Revelation; Goethe's *Faust*, and Shakespeare, which Rimbaud had asked Delahaye to obtain for him in cheap editions; the visionary histories of Michelet, the iconoclastic determinism of Taine, the alternative worlds of mystical socialists; fairy stories and melodramas; political and aesthetic slogans; Verlaine's poetry, café conversations, and Mme Rimbaud's home-truths. *Une Saison en Enfer* was a *Fleurs du Mal* without the north and south of Good and Evil, a *Contemplations* without the once-and-for-all philosophy; an autobiography that was also a history of the western mind.[12]

Few poets recover from such a violent harvest.

*

'MY FATE DEPENDS on this book', Rimbaud had told Delahaye. In the absence of a baccalauréat, *Une Saison en Enfer* would be his only professional qualification. As Verlaine had pointed out, a published book was just the thing to impress potential students.

Mme Rimbaud was apparently persuaded. She is said to have saved one of the masterpieces of world literature from oblivion by paying to have it printed. Rimbaud sent his manuscript to a Brussels printer called Jacques Poot. Since Poot & Co. published an important legal journal, Rimbaud might have asked the judge to recommend a printer.

Shortly before or after Rimbaud's nineteenth birthday (20 October 1873), M. Poot wrote to say that the book was ready. Rimbaud left for Brussels and, defying fate, took a room at the hotel where Verlaine had shot him. Then he went to the Rue aux Choux to collect his author's copies.

Rimbaud had ordered an unusually large print-run: 500 copies. Verlaine could have told him that this was far too optimistic. Even with a good reputation, friends on newspapers, a publisher with a shopfront on a boulevard, and a popular subject and style, a poet would be lucky to sell 300.

Rimbaud promised to pay the balance in a few days and walked off with about ten copies.

It was an innocuous-looking slip of a book. There was no title-page, flyleaf or colophon. Almost a third of its fifty-four pages were blank, emphasizing the discrete nature of the nine 'stories' – or, as the opening section calls them, 'these few hideous leaves torn out of my damned man's notebook'.

The title was in red, the author's name – 'A. RIMBAUD' – in black, which gave it a superficial resemblance to Baudelaire's *Fleurs du Mal*. But in the middle of the cover, almost as prominent as the name itself, were the words, 'PRIX: UN FRANC'. Rimbaud's first and only book: printed by Poot & Co. of Cabbage Street in Brussels.

There is always something about a published book that seems to parody its author. The fee paid to Poot evidently did not include proofs. The original edition contains about fifteen mistakes, which Rimbaud, who was so careful with his fair copies, would certainly have spotted: wrong genders, irregular punctuation and typography, and some rogue spellings – *personnne*, *bouilllon*, *puisser* – along with the perversely appropriate typo that always seems to hide until the book is published: '*La dernière innoncence*' ('The final in-nonsense').[13]

The child was orphaned almost as soon as it left the printer's. Rimbaud never returned to pay the balance. Until 1901, when an unopened bundle was discovered in the store-room of M. Poot's successor, the only copies that escaped to the outside world were the few that Rimbaud took away under his arm in October 1873. He deposited one at the prison (the famously gruff inscription, 'à P. Verlaine / A. Rimbaud', is a forgery),[14] then set off for Paris.

The spies, for whom nothing was innocent, reported that Arthur Rimbaud, nineteen years old (his recent birthday had not been forgotten) 'left furtively'.[15]

*

USUALLY, THE DAYS following the publication of a book are rich in information: visits to editors, dedications, reviews and celebratory dinners. All that is known of Rimbaud's launch period is that he was in Paris on 1 November: the money intended for Poot would have enabled him to take the train.[16] He handed out three copies: one to

Forain, another to Raoul Ponchon – a young Zutiste who wrote drinking songs and lived in a 'room' made of crates – and another to Jean Richepin, who had yet to make a name for himself as a poet. Two other copies went to Delahaye and another old school friend, Ernest Millot.

In 1998, a copy came to light containing a strip of paper with Régamey's address on it. Rimbaud may have distributed more copies than we know, but few people were keen to reveal themselves as former friends of a homosexual poet. Raoul Ponchon always denied having received a copy.[17]

Of the seven known recipients of *Une Saison en Enfer*, only one would have been able to publicize it and he was in prison. Until Verlaine's article in *Les Poètes maudits* of 1883, there is no recorded reaction to the book. Since the mistakes are uncorrected in the copies Rimbaud gave to friends, he may not have read it himself.

Une Saison en Enfer was launched into obscurity like a sacrificial object. The later discovery of the unpaid-for copies disproves Isabelle's story that her brother sent the entire print-run up the farm chimney in an act of purification;[18] but the thought was obviously there.

Rimbaud's bashfulness should never be underestimated. Many other works have been annihilated by their authors' modesty. But the most likely explanation is that the finished book was simply not that important to him. He neither foisted it on to literary editors nor buried it completely. Later, he took back the copies he had given to Delahaye and Millot and used them as gifts.

When Millot found him sitting silently with a mug of beer at the Café Dutherme in Charleville and asked about the incident in Brussels, Rimbaud growled: 'Don't stir up that heap of shit. It's too repugnant.'[19] These allergic reactions to the past are often interpreted as a sign that Rimbaud was now disgusted with his homosexual liaison; but his repugnance was not particular. The past was a mausoleum. If the recording of a thought allowed it to be expunged from the brain, then publication was the final flushing away.

> One must be absolutely modern.
> No hymns, now: don't lose the ground that's gained.

Rimbaud's literary life was once thought to end here, with the burning of his books and an unpaid bill. The 'Adieu' that closes *Une Saison en Enfer* was felt to be his farewell to poetry, 'seerhood' and other childish things. The sheer biographical convenience of this scenario makes it deeply suspect. Literary works do not queue up patiently, waiting to write themselves into the chronology. The prose poems of the *Illuminations* overlap *Une Saison en Enfer* at either end. In reality, the 'season in hell' had been the necessary prelude to a new world. God and Verlaine had been left behind, and for a time it seemed as though the anguish for which they provided a focus had also disappeared. At nineteen, Rimbaud was not yet a prisoner of his future.

> Autumn. Our boat raised up into the motionless fogs turns towards the harbour of poverty, the enormous city with its sky stained by fire and mud. [. . .]

> But for now, it's the night before. Let us receive all influxes of vigour and real tenderness. And at dawn, armed with ardent patience, we shall enter the splendid cities.

22

'Métropolitain'

'Travellers rapidly prepared'

(*The Times*, 25 May 1874)

THE CAFÉ TABOUREY, next door to the Odéon theatre, was one of those self-perpetuating establishments where writers went to sit because famous writers had sat there before them. The customers were divided by age and reputation into talkers and listeners, and there was an imperceptible hierarchy in the arrangement of the tables. Among the regulars were Étienne Carjat, who had been attacked by Rimbaud twenty months before, and Rimbaud's former 'John the Baptist on the Left Bank', Léon Valade, who, after announcing the advent of the 'genius' in October 1871, never wrote another word about him.

On 1 November 1873, a shabby young man who looked like 'a peasant athlete' with a 'brick-red face'[1] lumbered into the café and sat down at an empty table. The voices fell to a whisper. This was the fiend who had 'ruined' Verlaine. His mere presence in the Tabourey was an insult to literature.

Only two people tried to talk with him. One was a feeble poet called Alfred Poussin who had come to Paris with his inheritance and was trying to ingratiate himself into the world of letters. Rimbaud scared him off with an expression of 'virile acrimony' which Poussin remembered for the rest of his life.[2]

The other person who tried to start a conversation was instantly befriended.³ The poet Germain Nouveau was a short, stocky Provençal with a handsome face and an agreeable habit of gently contradicting everything that was said in the hope of finding a more interesting angle. He was three years older than Rimbaud. Though he had already spent his small inheritance, he showed no sign of looking for a career.

With Raoul Ponchon and Jean Richepin, who both received copies of *Une Saison en Enfer*, Nouveau belonged to a little group that called itself 'Les Vivants' ('The Living'), in contrast to the mummified Parnassians, or, as Rimbaud appears to call them in *Une Saison en Enfer*, 'the friends of death'.⁴ Nouveau had read the amazing poems that circulated in the Latin Quarter ('Ophélie', 'Les Chercheuses de poux' and perhaps 'Voyelles'), and was one of the first people to imitate Rimbaud's style – which proves that Rimbaud knew, long before he left Europe, that his work had disciples.⁵

Rimbaud refused to discuss poems he had written as a sixteen-year-old. He talked instead about the magical land of mist across the water, where people were more 'intelligent', and where it was practically impossible to be bored. Identifying Nouveau as a replacement for Verlaine, he sold him the idea of a season in England, and Nouveau agreed to join him on his next expedition.

When Jean Richepin heard that Nouveau had met the *homme fatal*, he was worried:

> The energetic, intrepid and brilliant Rimbaud – who was much better known at that time for his adventure with Verlaine than for his works – soon gained an obvious ascendancy over Nouveau. A weak and excitable personality, Nouveau had the nervous temperament of a sensual woman who finds strength irresistible.⁶

Having thus prepared his next adventure, the 'irresistible' Rimbaud returned to Charleville to wait out the winter.

The next five months are a blank. Rimbaud probably worked on the prose poems of the *Illuminations*. He painted his images on the familiar landscape, using grammatical structures that sound as though they might once have carried simple arguments:

You follow the red road to reach the empty inn. The château is for sale; the shutters are hanging off. – The curé must have taken away the key to the church. – Around the park, the caretakers' lodges are uninhabited. The fences are so high that you can see only the rustling tree-tops. There's nothing in there to see anyway.

('Enfance')

I don't miss my old share of divine happiness: the sober air of this bitter countryside feeds my atrocious scepticism in a very active fashion. But since this scepticism can no longer be put to use, and since in any case I'm dedicated to a new disturbance, I'm waiting to become a very nasty sort of madman.

('Vies')

This was the no-man's-land between philosophies. The church is locked, the holy feast is over, and 'Satan' is looking for a job. Both passages have the distinctive tone of 'patience' and waiting that gives Rimbaud's images their peculiar imminence. In a revealing correction to the drafts of *Une Saison en Enfer*, he had replaced 'ruining an insatiety of life' with 'ruining a kind of strength', as if 'insatiety' and 'strength' were the same thing, or as if mere appetite were sustenance enough.

Mme Rimbaud had told Verlaine in her letter that 'a man who saw all his wishes granted and all his desires satisfied would certainly not be happy'. Lessons learned in childhood, however cruel, are always a consolation. Rimbaud followed his mother's precept so tenaciously that large parts of his life look like a quest for unhappiness and frustration. For the next five years, he would return to Charleville or Roche every winter. 'I fear the winter because it's the season of comfort', he had written in *Une Saison en Enfer*. But in his mother's home, there was little danger that he would lapse into comfort or see all his desires satisfied.

*

AT THIS POINT, Rimbaud's life divides into two possible paths, with a question-mark at the junction: was he still writing anything at all, or was *Une Saison en Enfer* his last work?

The order in which *Une Saison en Enfer* and the *Illuminations* were written is the object of one of the longest running debates in French literary studies,[7] and it is only fair to say that a small number of Rimbaud scholars still believe that Rimbaud (rather than the 'I' of his poems) stopped writing in August 1873.* After reading *Une Saison en Enfer* as an agile leap into silence and interpreting Rimbaud's poems as the punctual diary of his present thoughts, it is hard to reconcile the mind to a slow and thorny descent, even if it is more interesting in the long run.

It now seems clear however that many (perhaps most) of the prose poems that were eventually published without Rimbaud's knowledge in 1886 under the title *Illuminations* were written after *Une Saison en Enfer*. The shaky hand of graphology has assigned a variety of dates to the surviving manuscripts of the *Illuminations*, but most scholars agree that two sections are in the hand of Germain Nouveau, who did not live with Rimbaud until 1874.

The evidence of the poems themselves is compelling but impossible to hammer into solid proof. Traces of advanced English might suggest 1874. A preoccupation with mathematical arts and the sudden absence of Catholic terminology are consistent with the new, post-Christian Rimbaud.[8]

Since Rimbaud's first experiments with prose poetry date back to 1871 or 1872, it is reasonable to assume that forerunners of the *Illuminations* and even some complete poems predate *Une Saison en Enfer*, but that the process that led him to abandon poetry altogether lasted several years. Rome was not demolished in a day. There are other texts besides *Une Saison en Enfer* that can be construed as farewells to poetry: 'Départ' and 'Solde' in the *Illuminations*, or, for that matter, 'Le Bateau ivre'. Rimbaud had been giving up different kinds of writing ever since he began to write.

A moment's reflection will reveal the implausibility of the older view: Rimbaud decides to give up poetry and then spends several months perfecting the text (*Une Saison en Enfer*) in which he explains that he is going to give it up. He was not noted for his long farewells.

Even short farewells were unusual. Towards the end of March 1874, the little group of 'Vivants' noticed that one of their number

* See p. 492, n. 7 for a brief summary of the argument.

was missing. Rimbaud had been seen in Paris but had disappeared again immediately. Meanwhile, Germain Nouveau was nowhere to be found, which was odd because his papers were still in his room and his key had not been handed in. Richepin feared the worst:

> This hasty departure, with precious papers left behind in a hotel room, looked very much like an abduction. We felt that nothing good would come of it. Exposed as he was to the direct influence of Rimbaud in a foreign land, with nothing to counteract the influence, we thought that Nouveau was done for.[9]

There was no news until 27 March. Then a letter arrived with a London postmark. Nouveau had been spirited across the Channel:

> My dear Richepin,
>   I left Paris when I least expected and am now, as you see, with Rimbaud. [. . .] We have rented a *room* [in English] in Stampfort street [*sic*], in a family where the young gentleman, knowing a little French, converses with us for an hour every day so that he can improve his French and I can learn a few words. Rimbaud is also going to work on his English. He knows just enough for our common needs.[10]

Rimbaud had continued his descent through the layers of London housing – from the shabby gentility of Howland Street to the black din of Stamford Street. The Stephens family lived three minutes from Waterloo Station, between a pub and a dramatic agent's office. Stamford Street was close to the river and sometimes in it: a day or two after Rimbaud and Nouveau arrived, the houses at the rear, in Commercial Road, were standing under seven feet of foul-smelling Thames water.[11]

Number 178 disappeared altogether fifty years ago, and the encyclopedic ribbon of little shops and workrooms has long since become a bland segment of the A3200; but the buildings opposite have survived. The shop that Rimbaud would have seen on leaving the house is now a French restaurant.

The Phileas Fogg view of Rimbaud has him occupying a room at the top of the house, facing north, so that he can enjoy the Thames-side panorama: the ornate bridges, the new Embankment, and St Paul's Cathedral rising over the East End.[12] But even if Rimbaud and

Nouveau lived upstairs, they would have been peering through the smoke at the backs of warehouses and factories. It is just as likely that they lived in the basement, with a scullery maid's view of shoes, skirts, dogs and carriage-wheels.

One of Rimbaud's *Illuminations* is a hallucinatory vision of the sort of half-buried, sunless cellar that was common throughout the city, including Stamford Street – a Journey to the Centre of the Earth in a London basement. In some of his poems, he seems to have used English rhymes ('eclogues – clogs', 'corridors – gauze', etc.) to produce unexpected images. He would certainly have noticed the suggestive similarity of 'room' and 'tomb':

> Let this tomb be rent to me at last, whitewashed, with the cement-lines in relief – a long way under ground.

> I lean my elbows on the table, the lamp casts a brilliant light on these newspapers that I'm a fool to re-read, these books devoid of interest. –

> At an enormous distance above my subterranean living-room the houses take root, the mists assemble. The mud is red or black. Monstrous city, endless night!

> Lower down are drains. On either side, nothing but the thickness of the globe. Perhaps chasms of blue sky, wells of fire. It may be on these planes that moons and comets, seas and fables are encountered.

> In hours of bitterness I imagine balls of sapphire and of metal. I am master of the silence. Why would something like a basement-window be blanching in the angle of the vault?[13]

The passage from vision back to reality is typical of the *Illuminations*. This is the new practicality promised in *Une Saison en Enfer*. Without God, life has no automatic meaning or moral foundation. The poles of *Une Saison en Enfer* were the pillars of the old world: 'Theology is serious: hell is certainly *down* – and heaven is up.' In the *Illuminations*, where 'good' and 'evil' appear only once in their theological sense, any orientation is possible: floods subside upwards, landscapes are two-dimensional, distances in space and time are interchangeable.

Before Rimbaud, it can usually be assumed that the poet is standing up or sitting down, square to the world like a surveyor's level. In the

Illuminations, relativity complicates the picture. Random, habit-shattering patterns volatilize the urban landscape.

> Grey crystal skies. A bizarre pattern of bridges, some straight, others arched, others yet descending or cutting across the first at oblique angles, and these shapes renewing themselves in the other illuminated circuits of the canal, but all so light and long that the banks, loaded with domes, drop and dwindle. Some of these bridges still support hovels. Others carry masts, signals, flimsy parapets. Minor chords intersect and run away; cords climb from the riverbanks. One can just make out a red waistcoat, perhaps other costumes and musical instruments. Are they popular songs, odds and ends of stately concerts, remnants of public hymns? The water is grey and blue, as broad as an arm of the sea. – A ray of white light, falling from the top of the sky, annihilates this comedy.[14]

Germain Nouveau had yet to enter this futurist world of chance connections where nothing lasts long enough to mirror a personality. He was still in Victorian London. His first impressions were horrible: a smell of musk and coal-smoke in the air, stony-faced people in the street, a permanent solar eclipse.[15]

The new disciple was in need of enlightenment. Rimbaud instructed him in the art of living on a shoestring.[16] He showed him where the biggest 'gingerbeers' were served and the French fish-and-chip shop where fourpence bought a towering plate of fried food. He took him to museums, the music-hall and the virtual-reality dome of the Crystal Palace, which Rimbaud is thought to have used as a kind of image-shop for the *Illuminations*.[17] They walked for hours until they were lost, as Nouveau complained in his letter to Richepin: 'There's no end to these bridges.' They also travelled on the world's first underground (though still mostly overground) railway – alluded to in the title and whizzing images of 'Métropolitain':

> From the asphalt desert, fleeing in a straight line, with the sheets of fog spaced out in horrible stripes in the sky that bends backwards, retreats and descends, composed of the most sinister smoke that the mourning Ocean can make – helmets, wheels, barges and rumps.

In contrast to Verlaine, Nouveau was unmarried, cheerful and easy to control. On the other hand, he was not rich.

Soon after arriving,[18] Rimbaud had talked to a man in a pub who told him that a box factory in Holborn was hiring workers. The unlikely name of the employer – L. W. R. Drycup – has consigned this significant event to the apocrypha of Rimbaud's life. Its unreality was apparently confirmed in 1956 when, in a bogus show of erudition, a critic claimed that there were 'very few box factories' in Holborn.[19]

In fact, the inhabitants of 1870s Holborn were surrounded by paper and cardboard – Holborn was also one of the centres of the printing trade. The story is therefore quite plausible, and there was no reason for early biographers to invent these details since they were of no particular interest to their French readers. In 1874, there were eight firms in the area that might have hired Rimbaud and Nouveau – to pull one name out of the hat: Charles Sarpy, 'fancy box maker', of 160 High Holborn.

The owner was not necessarily the manager. 'Drycup' is presumably the name Dracup, pronounced with a London accent or deformed by a pun: perhaps Mr Dracup was an enemy of the tea-break or a member of the Temperance movement.

The apprentice box-makers would have set off in the early morning, heading east along Stamford Street, past the tobacconist's, the ladies' school, the coffee rooms at number 53 and the Unitarian chapel next door; then a row of windowless, rat-infested tenements known locally as 'the Haunted Houses',[20] across the new Blackfriars Bridge to the rubble-strewn district that had recently been impaled by the Holborn Viaduct.

At the factory, the new workers were presented with a pile of cardboard, a pair of scissors and a pot of glue. The idea was to turn the cardboard into hat-boxes. They seem to have stuck it out for a month. By the end of April, they had earned just enough to pay what they owed the manufacturer for spoiled materials and left the factory no richer than before.

Rimbaud's stint as a factory worker was at least a linguistic education. Many of the phrases in his English vocabulary lists appear in no known dictionary and are obviously the fruits of impromptu conversations, muddled and half-erased like an old recording. This is as close as we can come to hearing the former Commune sympathizer wrestling with the tyranny of a production-line:

How many times do you attend a week
They average . . . apiece
Have you allowed for the waste
See if aught be wanting
What a helpless being
You will account for that sum . . . with all speed
Address yourself to your business at once
The mind cannot advert to two things at once

Help yourself to anything you like
He helped himself to the best bit
They make themselves at home everywhere
Speak out, i do not take hints
A huge eater
This cheese is all alive
You must learn to abstain from these indulgences

Since Rimbaud's mind was well able to advert to at least two things at once, he went to the British Museum on Saturday 4 April to renew his reader's ticket.[21] Nouveau applied at the same time. When they signed the register, they each gave themselves an extra Christian name:

Jean Nicolas *Joseph* Arthur Rimbaud
Marie Bernard Germain Nouveau

The infernal bridegroom had returned with a new virgin.

This private joke in the register of the British Museum is the last, flippant souvenir of Rimbaud's 'way of the cross', unless one counts the fact that Nouveau, like Verlaine, underwent a religious crisis shortly after leaving Rimbaud. Whether this was an effect of living with someone who made everything look like the key to a great mystery, or a reflection of Rimbaud's choice of friends is hard to say.

*

THIS TIME, THE household dissolved after only two months.

On leaving the factory, they resorted to the simpler expedient of teaching, where evidence of ineptitude was less conspicuous than a bungled hat-box. They used the down-market *Echo* to find conversation partners and *The Times* to advertise for pupils.[22]

[245]

Until now, there was no evidence that Rimbaud and Nouveau tried to teach at all. Delahaye said that they did, but his account has been questioned, despite the fact that he remained in touch with both men for several years. An advertisement in *The Times* has the right date and also matches Delahaye's claim that they signed up with an agency:

> Parisian French, with all its finesses and niceties by Mons. J. Lafont and two Parisian Graduates. Special instruction for acquiring facility in French conversation. Travellers rapidly prepared. 16, Brook street, Hanover-square.
>
> (*The Times*, 25 May 1874)

Rimbaud's ability to 'prepare travellers rapidly' was well known to Verlaine, Nouveau and, later, a team of African explorers. He may also have worked briefly in a school. Delahaye claimed that Rimbaud was dismissed for puncturing the drum that was used to summon pupils. Since drums were not generally used for such a purpose, this story, too, has been questioned.[23] But perhaps, like Jules Andrieu, he found work as a French teacher in a military school. 'A une raison' in the *Illuminations* might even be an echo of the poet on playground duty:

> A tap of your finger on the drum releases all the sounds and begins the new harmony.
> [. . .]
> 'Change our lots, destroy all scourges, beginning with time', these children sing to you. 'Nurture wherever you like the substance of our fortunes and our wishes', they beg you.

After the end of May, there is no further trace of the partnership that was supposed to prolong the dream of productive cohabitation. Germain Nouveau left Rimbaud in early June, apparently without acrimony but with no intention of returning.

Before he left, he helped Rimbaud to copy out some of his *Illuminations* and saw the distant future of French poetry. But Rimbaud had become an impediment. Nouveau had been sending poems to Parisian reviews. The poems were published, but the moral constabulary wagged a minatory finger: Rimbaud was seen as a contagious disease.[24] Verlaine's *Romances sans paroles* had just appeared, and though the dedication to Rimbaud had been removed, this record of one of the most fruitful exchanges in French poetry had only one review and no buyers. When the third volume of the *Parnasse contemporain* anthology was prepared in 1875, Verlaine was excluded from this self-congratulatory monument on the grounds that he was 'unworthy'. For the next year and a half, in Nouveau's private letters, Rimbaud would be referred to, prudently, as 'Thing'.

Even in London, in the marginal community to which Rimbaud had attached himself, the belligerent morality that destroyed Oscar Wilde twenty-one years later was already aroused. The once affable Andrieu, who was a friend of Swinburne and, it seems, quite openly effeminate, 'received Rimbaud with ill humour and was even quite brutal with him': Rimbaud was told never to come back. This rude eviction left him 'surprised and distraught'. He had obviously been right to worry about 'the looks I'd get from Andrieu and the others'.[25]

Rimbaud now found himself with no job, an atrocious reputation and a collection of poems that no one would read. The next time he appeared in the crowd of hopefuls at the back of *The Times*, he was on his own. He had changed his tack: teaching was secondary now to companionship and escape.

> A French gentleman (25), most respectably connected, of superior education, possessing a French diploma, thorough English, and extensive general knowledge, wishes EMPLOYMENT as PRIVATE SECRETARY, Travelling Companion, or Tutor. Excellent references. Address A. R., 25, Langham-street, W.
>
> (*The Times*, 8 June 1874)[26]

'He pretended to know about everything', the Foolish Virgin of *Une Saison en Enfer* had said. Rimbaud was embellishing his qualifications. He lied about his age, his diploma and his English. Number 25 Langham Street was a handsome building called Holbein Mansion, a few doors down from Félix Régamey, who had seen the silent poet arrive in London almost two years before.[27] The rooms of this unknown friend or agent would be a suitable setting for someone who was supposed to be 'most respectably connected'.

In order to acquire the 'thorough English' he was offering, he placed an advertisement in *The Echo*:

> A young Parisian – speaks *passablement* – requires conversations with
> English gentlemen; his own lodgings, p.m. preferred. – Rimbaud, 40
> London-st., Fitzroy-sq., W.
>
> *(The Echo, 9, 10 and 11 June 1874)*[28]

Rimbaud had left his room in Waterloo and returned to the
neighbourhood of his first London home. Number 40 London Street
stood almost directly behind the Howland Street house, at the other
end of Cleveland Mews. It was a more expensive district and the
room must have been even more cramped than usual.[29]

No one came looking for a tutor or a travelling companion, let
alone a private secretary. Towards the end of June, Rimbaud fell ill,
this time seriously enough to be admitted to a hospital.[30]

Once again, the point of inertia described in 'Mémoire' had been
reached: the boat held fast by the current and the anchor-chain. In
early July, he sent a sorry letter to Charleville. Could his mother
please come to London? . . .

The spinning images of the *Illuminations* induce a state of mental
flux reminiscent of mild fever. How must Rimbaud's mind have
behaved when he was ill? In an inert body, a powerful imagination is
not necessarily a consolation. Even the more joyful *Illuminations*
sometimes congeal into a kind of apocalyptic despondency.

> The paths are steep. The hillocks are covered with broom. The air
> is motionless. How far away the birds and springs are! It can only be
> the end of the world, ahead of time.[31]

The female figures that appear in Rimbaud's prose poems are
associated with affection, but also with a cowardly salvation.[32] Comfort is seen as a shameful narcotic; but self-inflicted torment is a bitter
alternative without the hope of divine reward.

> Can it be that She will obtain a pardon for my continually dashed
> ambitions, – that a comfortable end will make up for the ages of
> indigence, – that one day of success will close our eyes to the shame
> of our fatal ineptitude?
> [. . .]
> That accidents of scientific magic and movements of social fraternity
> will be cherished as a progressive restitution of original innocence? . . .

But the Vampire who makes us behave commands that we amuse ourselves with whatever she leaves us, or else be more entertaining.

To travel on to the wounds, through the wearisome air and the sea; to the torments, through the silence of the murderous waters and the air; to the tortures that laugh in the atrocious swell of their silence.[33]

*

A FEW DAYS later, a letter arrived from France. Mme Rimbaud was on her way.

Soon, everything would be back to normal.

Part Three

(1874–1880)

23

Pigeons

'How slowly time passes when Arthur isn't there!'

(Diary of Vitalie Rimbaud, 9 July 1874)

RIMBAUD FELT MORE like himself on the morning of 6 July 1874. He arrived at the deafening cathedral of Charing Cross Station with plenty of time to spare. After hiring a porter, he went to the platform and waited for the 10.10 boat-train from Dover.

The letter he had written from his sick-bed (summarized in his sister's diary) was a kind of covenant: he was ready to start again as a 'respectably connected' young gentleman. His mother would stay with him in London until he found a job. She was to bring her best clothes in case he needed her to act as 'a recommendation of worthiness'. As soon as she agreed to come, he had sent a detailed itinerary, explaining exactly what to do at each stage: where to change money, when to check the luggage, what to notice en route.

He found a clean and quiet boarding-house near St Pancras in the modestly genteel Argyle Square, next door to a girls' school.[1] The rooms were spacious and well appointed and looked on to a grassy square. The whole house, to Vitalie's amazement, was under carpet, even the corridors and the stairways. Rimbaud had already moved in. For the first time in his life, he would be in charge of his family. A blistering programme of sight-seeing was planned.

The next three weeks of Rimbaud's life are recorded in his sister

Vitalie's diary.[2] Her remarks are sometimes said to be unrevealing because she simply regurgitated what she heard from other people. This is precisely what makes her account so valuable. It also explains why the diary is one of the most heavily censored documents in the history of Rimbaud biography. For anyone who reveres Rimbaud as a martyr of adolescent revolt, the family holiday of July 1874 is almost obscene in its normality.

*

AT TEN PAST ten, Rimbaud rushed to save his mother and sister from the glut of travellers. He was clearly delighted to see them but disappointed to learn that Isabelle had been left at the convent. He looked 'thin and pale', according to Vitalie, 'but he is much better, and his great joy at seeing us will hasten his complete recovery'.

Though they were still queasy from the crossing and befuddled by the noise and smoke and the size of everything ('Charing Cross is at least twelve times bigger than Charleville station'), Arthur led them to the hotel on foot, dodging traffic, pointing out the sights, 'so as to allow us, he said, to have a quick look around and make contact with London'.

Two miles later, they staggered into the boarding-house at 12 Argyle Square. While the women revived themselves with emergency rations from home, Arthur went to see what had happened to the luggage.

> When the trunk arrived, Arthur helped to bring it up. After placing it in our room, he sat on top of it, laughing. He looked happier than I had seen him for ages; and, as he sat on the trunk, he said, with a great sigh of relief, 'Here you are at last! I hope you're going to stay.' [. . .] He was examining Mama's face with happy, shining eyes.
>
> Now that Mama had been reassured about the trunk, we decided, despite our tiredness, to see a few more streets. Arthur showed us some splendid shops. We lingered in front of them rather too long for his liking; then he took us to a magnificent park. Two hours later, we returned to the hotel, exhausted.

For the next three weeks, Mme Rimbaud and Vitalie saw monuments and curiosities until they were literally sick. Rimbaud was stocked with anecdotal and statistical information on everything: the Tower, St Paul's, the Bank of England, the Subway, the Metropolitan Railway, the Albert Memorial, the Horse Guards, the parks with their preachers and flocks of sheep, and all the secret places he had discovered since September 1872. They visited some unknown English friends – perhaps tutees or conversation partners – who spoke a little French and had advised Rimbaud 'to go to the country or the seaside to recover completely'. He even took them to the docks and pointed out the Antwerp ferry, presumably without mentioning the tearful scene when Verlaine had left for Brussels.

The *Illuminations*, which seem so far removed from common reality, have an invisible core of erudition and personal experience. Rimbaud's high-speed tours of London, like his long afternoons in the British Museum, are symptoms of the encyclopedic urge that poetry had failed to satisfy. Mme Rimbaud and Vitalie were in the hands of a tour guide whose ultimate aim was omniscience.

Since objective reality has had a bad name in French literary criticism for the last fifty years, Rimbaud's desire to record and replicate is easily overlooked.[3] But like James Joyce, he had a powerful onomatopoeic imagination, a passion for devising exact verbal equivalents. Some of his phrases, like skilful photographs, are more vivid than the reality itself: '*Bavardage des enfants et des cages . . .*'; '*Un cheval détale sur le turf suburbain . . .*'*

The other unfashionable aspect of Rimbaud's poetry that the London holiday brought to light was its didactic enthusiasm. He was determined that Vitalie should open her mind to alien customs and discover beauty where she expected not to find it: 'What business would we have going to a sermon in English?' she wondered. 'We returned to our rooms in pensive mood: I was troubled by that Protestant service.' 'How those Protestants seem to pray with modesty and piety! It's a great shame they aren't Catholics.' Like an attentive tutor, he helped her to overcome her testiness: 'I was longing to treat myself to an ice. Arthur, who is so kind, anticipated my desire.'

---

* 'Chattering of children and of (bird-)cages'; 'A horse takes off on the suburban turf'.[4]

Unfortunately, Arthur 'walked too fast' and was 'never tired'. He seemed to live on a different time-scale. It was obviously a relief when he announced that he would have to leave them to their own devices. He gave Vitalie a crash course in English pronunciation and an emergency vocabulary list – gooseberries, strawberries and milk: 'The way I repeat after him makes him laugh and then makes him impatient.' 'How slowly time passes when Arthur isn't there!' she observed when her brother had left for the British Museum.

The original object of the visit was to see him settled into a job. The agency passed on a few offers, but none was acceptable. On 16 July, Arthur asked his mother to put on her grey silk dress and her lace wrap so that she could vouch for his respectability at an interview. Nothing came of it. Vitalie was growing desperate: 'The sooner he finds a job, the sooner we can return to France.'

On 18 July, 'Arthur went again to order some advertisements and to find another agent.' Until now, only one advertisement had been found: in *The Times* of 28 July, a 'French professor' offered to teach 'French, German, and Spanish', which surely exceeds even Rimbaud's capacity for bluffing. A more likely advertisement – the only one that fits all the known details – appeared on 20 July 1874:

> Lessons in French, for two or three hours each day, given in exchange for board and residence. No salary required. Speaks English. Large town preferred, but not London. Address French, care of Frederick May and Son, Advertising Agents, 160, Piccadilly.

This is the first real sign that Rimbaud was either tired of London or curious to see another part of the country. His breakneck tour was a farewell to the city that had been his intellectual sparring-partner as much as Paul Verlaine.

On 23 July, Mme Rimbaud was ready to leave. He begged her to stay a little longer. She gave him one more week to find a job.

At last, on Wednesday, 29 July, a 'sombre and nervous' Arthur returned from the agency to announce that he was to leave in the morning. There was a flurry of last-minute shopping while Vitalie made adjustments to his coat and trousers.

> Thursday 30: Arthur was unable to leave today because the laundress has not returned his shirts.

Friday 31, 7.30 a.m.: Arthur left at half-past four. He was sad.

This was the closing scene of Rimbaud's London adventure: a tearful mother and a walk through the streets at dawn with a suitcase full of manuscripts and laundered shirts.

*

RIMBAUD'S DESTINATION IS usually identified, with varying degrees of confidence, as the seaside resort of Scarborough, 300 miles north of London, because he mentions Scarborough in a prose poem, 'Promontoire': 'the circular façades of "Royals" or "Grands" of Scarbro' or of Brooklyn'.

This conclusion was reached by a deductive method commonly used to convict innocent people. Its refutation can be found in one of the numbered cells at the back of this book.[5]

There is no evidence whatsoever that Rimbaud visited Scarborough or, for that matter, Brooklyn. Guide-books should now be corrected accordingly. However, since poems travel without maps or timetables, and since 'Promontoire' sounds like a dream digest of a thousand holiday brochures, there may be more reason than ever now to make a Rimbaldian pilgrimage to Scarborough, to read the poem on the esplanade and view through his eyes a scene he never saw.

The known facts account for Rimbaud's movements quite satisfactorily. An advertisement in *The Times* shows that, three months later, he was living at 165 King's Road in the small industrial town of Reading, forty miles west of London. Enid Starkie identified this as the address of a Frenchman, Camille Le Clair, 'Professor of the French language and literature'.[6]

As a result of 'increased engagements', M. Le Clair had opened a new language school on 25 July. He would have found M. Rimbaud through the London agency and hired him for the start of the new term. As Enid Starkie pointed out, if Rimbaud was supposed to have been in Reading on 30 July, and intended to catch the first train from Paddington at six o'clock the following morning, he did not leave too early.

M. Le Clair received his pupils in an immodest, three-storey

Georgian mansion called Montpellier House (now converted into flats). It stood in the nicer part of Reading, though not far from Reading Gaol. Almost nothing is known about Rimbaud's period of provincial gentility. Now that Scarborough has disappeared from the map, it is tempting to replace it with the more plausible fantasy of a trip to neighbouring Oxford. While Rimbaud was teaching French in Reading, a young Irishman was enjoying his first days in Oxford as an undergraduate. Oscar Wilde was at the dawn of his literary career, Rimbaud almost at the end of his, though they were born just four days apart.

In Reading, Rimbaud probably continued to work on the *Illuminations* since he was ready to publish them seven months later. Corrections to the manuscript suggest a gradual invasion of foreignness:[7] English has infiltrated the vocabulary (steerage, Embankments, brick, pier, spunk, etc.), the syntax, and even the images. To learn a new language is to return to the nursery, where words are strange, half-tamed creatures. Rimbaud took full advantage of the effect. 'Snowflakes', literally translated, produced '*éclats de neige*' (splinters, sparkles or shouts of snow). 'Cards' are played at the bottom of a 'pool'. Phrases that sound odd in French become normal when translated directly into English: 'to whistle for [the storm]', 'places of worship', 'love feasts', 'old flames', etc.[8]

The title of the whole collection is a cross-Channel pun, according to Delahaye and Verlaine: flashes of insight or divine illumination, festive lighting or fireworks, coloured plates or illuminated panels in a manuscript.[9] Verlaine's transliteration suggests that the title should really be pronounced as the English word, but with a French accent: '*Illuminécheunes*'.[10]

Remarkably, some of the paper-work of this linguistic import–export business has survived. Rimbaud's English word-lists (inconclusively dated by Bouillane de Lacoste to July–December 1874)[11] are a repository of terms culled from advertisements, conversations and even dictionaries. One notorious section has produced the startling suggestion that Rimbaud had taken up pigeon-flying as a hobby:

> Pigeons: homing – working – fantails
> pearl-eyed tumbler –

shortfaced – performing tumblers
trumpeters – squeakers
blue, red turbits – Jacobins
baldpates – pearl eyes, – tumbles well
high flying performing tumblers
splashed – rough legged
grouse limbed
black buglers
saddle back
over thirty tail feathers[12]

If Rimbaud was expecting to find a practical use for these terms, one would have to suppose, from the other parts of the lists, that he was also intending to play cricket and rugby, take up dress-making and open a pet-shop.

These are not conventional vocabulary lists. Nothing in Rimbaud's life suggests that he ever needed to say 'high-shouldered canaries' or 'insertion for petticoat'. The fact that Rimbaud, who hated luggage, held on to these lists even after he left England shows that they had a purpose beyond their literal meaning.

There are two possibilities. In the *Illuminations*, foreign words like 'Scarbro'', 'turf', 'desperadoes', 'Bottom' and 'wasserfall' are used partly as notes in a musical phrase. Even if he had given up poetry, as some believe, he was still collecting words for their poetic value.

The other possibility is that he was beginning to compile a French–English dictionary. To judge by the lists, it would have dwarfed anything that was available at the time. Whatever their function, the English word-lists are one of the monuments to impossible ambitions that litter this mysterious zone between the completed works and the silent desert.

*

AFTER THREE MONTHS in Reading, Rimbaud was trying to migrate. The 'A.R.' who placed an advertisement in *The Times* of 7 and 9 November 1874 is known to be Rimbaud because two drafts of the advertisement were found among his papers.[13] His English was still on the seemingly endless plateau of unidiomatic accuracy familiar to all persistent language learners. Rimbaud's phrase, 'excellent

entertaining linguistic ability' was corrected by an unknown hand –
perhaps M. Le Clair's – to 'social & entertaining in conversation'.
The final version suggests that he was hoping to find a replacement
for Nouveau:

> A PARISIAN (20), of high literary and linguistic attainments,
> excellent conversation, will be glad to ACCOMPANY a GENTLE-
> MAN (artists preferred), or a family wishing to travel in southern or
> eastern countries. Good references. – A.R., No. 165, King's-road,
> Reading.

Was this the *bateau ivre* yearning, with the last leaves of a Reading
autumn, for the skies beyond Europe? At the British Museum, he had
encouraged his sister to admire the relics of Theodoros II, Emperor
of Abyssinia.[14] But there is no other trace of Rimbaud's interest in
Africa at this stage, and 'southern or eastern countries' is rather
vague. The mention of 'artists' may be an early sign that he was
planning a kind of travel book – a project which crops up in various
forms for the rest of his life and which may even have been at the
origin of the urban *Illuminations*.

The most revealing part of the advertisement is its date: two weeks
after Rimbaud's twentieth birthday. Since the defeat by Prussia,
conscription had been extended to the entire male population of
France between the ages of twenty and forty. Rimbaud was now
eligible for military service. His mother had gone to Charleville town
hall to have him exempted on the grounds that his brother had
enlisted in the regular army for five years, but he was still liable to be
called up for periods of basic training.

Fear of conscription is the cloud that comes to sit on Rimbaud's
horizon when the fire and brimstone of Christianity have disappeared.
It brought with it the same sense of unfulfilled duty and undeserved
chastisement. The neurotic nature of this fear is vividly demonstrated
by the fact that Rimbaud volunteered for several other armed forces,
all of them considerably less cushy than the French army: Communards, Carlists, Dutch Colonials and the United States Navy.

This obsession with impending repatriation would be his only
official tie to home. It was almost an act of love. His mother, as he
knew, was haunted by the memory of Captain Rimbaud leaving for

the last time to join his regiment in 1860. Even in old age, the sight of a uniform would remind her of the moment when her 'happiness' walked off.[15] Her son would enact the scene many times over before he finally flew away.

Rimbaud never stopped rewriting his father's story. In the years to come, he would sometimes borrow parts of the Captain's life when giving official details: his birthplace and his regiment, the 47th, from which he would claim to have 'deserted'. This adopted story gives his life a circular structure that is mirrored in his poetry: a meticulous progression towards childhood, when words were not heavy with preordained significance, and when the future was a blank page.

This submerged narrative gives even the most fragmented *Illuminations* a dramatic design. But the story itself could never be reconstructed from these phrases. Perhaps this new, worldly idiom was not after all a means of obtaining 'complete knowledge of himself', as the seer had written, but an attempt to prevent language from becoming a vehicle for self-discovery.

> I am the scholar in the dark armchair. The branches and the rain cast themselves against the library window.

> I am the walker on the high road through the dwarf woods. The sound of the locks covers my footsteps. For a long time I can see the melancholy gold wash of the sunset.

> I'd happily be the child abandoned on the jetty that has left for the open sea, the little valet following the avenue whose brow touches the sky.[16]

24

Philomath

'Every harmonic and architectural possibility will start to
move around your seat.'

('Jeunesse', *Illuminations*)

RIMBAUD ARRIVED HOME unexpectedly in the snow and the
ice on 29 December 1874.[1] No artist or travelling family had
answered his advertisement. His future now depended on his
mother's good will, or, as he hoped she would see it, on her ability to
spot a good investment.

As the old year ended, Rimbaud seemed to be turning over a new
leaf. He now wanted to do something practical and precise: commerce, industry or engineering. The more languages he knew, the
better his prospects would be. After English, in order of usefulness,
came German. To learn German and acquaint himself with German
customs, he would obviously have to go and live in Germany . . .

Mme Rimbaud allowed herself to be convinced. Arthur had been
impressively competent in London and had even shown that he could
hold down a proper job for several months.

On 13 February 1875, Rimbaud left for Stuttgart with his trunk
and a small 'advance' on future earnings. At this point, his traces are
smudged. He either studied German in a Stuttgart language school
or tutored a doctor's children, perhaps both. He may have lived in
the home of a prominent art historian, Wilhelm Lübke, or, according
to some recently rediscovered memoirs, at 137 Neckarstrasse, which

was the home of a policeman called Wagner. The only certainty is that he did not live in the house that now bears a commemorative plaque.[2]

When he was interviewed in 1909, Albrecht Wagner claimed to remember a dependable young man who 'spoke distinguished French, approximate English and abominable German'.[3] For Rimbaud, Stuttgart was just a staging-post. As soon as he arrived, he was planning to leave. In the new German Empire, young Frenchmen were not treated with much respect. On 5 March, he wrote to Delahaye in the surging style that suggests an escapologist struggling with his ropes:

> I've only got one week of Wagner left, and I regret this money paying for hate, and all this time being frittered away for nothing. On the 15th I'll have an *Ein freundliches Zimmer* somewhere, and I'm thrashing my way through the language so frantically that I'll have finished in two months, if not before.
>
> Everything here is rather inferior, with one egxeption: Riessling [*sic*], of vich I am draining ein glass in front of ze slopes ver it vas born, to your imperpetuous health. It's sunning and it's freezing. What a bore.

The 'Wagner' of Rimbaud's letter has been identified as a street or as a reference to a week-long festival of Wagner's music. The original letter suggests a different reading. An obscene doodle in the left-hand margin shows a little man leaving a carriage and entering a tall house, above the caption, '*WAGNER VERDAMMT IN EWIGKEIT*'* (Rimbaud's only known German sentence). Underneath, a naked corpse, also labelled 'Wagner', hangs from a noose with a bottle of Riesling inserted in its rectum. Evidently, Rimbaud was dissatisfied with his landlord.[4]

Below the signature, the town of Stuttgart has been invaded by Riesling bottles and self-supporting male genitalia. It looks like the wall of a public urinal. Compared to the inscrutable detachment of the *Illuminations*, this back-slapping, bar-stool idiom that he used with Delahaye sounds as stilted as a school reunion.

The main point of the letter was to tell Delahaye about the recent visit of an ex-convict. Because of 'good conduct' and his religious

* 'Wagner damned for all eternity.'

conversion, Verlaine had been released from prison in January: God had absolved him of all his sins. Still in a cloud of incense, he wrote to Rimbaud, care of Delahaye, with an ambitious proposal: 'Let us love one another in Jesus.'[5]

Rimbaud took Verlaine's conversion as seriously as he had taken his suicide threats. In a letter known only from Verlaine's paraphrase, he told him that his conversion had nothing to do with the supernatural. It was simply a 'modification of the same oversensitive individual'. The English word for it was '*rubbish*'.

Whether out of curiosity or indifference, he allowed Delahaye to give his address to Verlaine, and in late February, a gaunt man with a droopy moustache, looking much older than his thirty years, arrived in Stuttgart with his message of hope. Unfortunately, Verlaine had reckoned without the combined effect of Riesling and Rimbaud:

> Verlaine got here the other day, clutching a rosary . . . Three hours later, one had denied one's god and caused the 98 wounds of Our Lord to bleed. He stayed for two and a half days, was very sensible, and, when I remonstrated with him, returned to Paris.

This sodden relapse and orderly exit were the final act of the great drama. Rimbaud and Verlaine never saw each other again.

*

LOVE AFFAIRS ARE not supposed to end with 'sensible' behaviour, and so this limp conclusion was traditionally replaced, as it is in the recent film of Christopher Hampton's play, *Total Eclipse*, with one of Delahaye's little fantasies: in a field by the banks of the Neckar, the drunken poets wrestled under a full moon like angel and devil until Verlaine was left for dead. The hyperinformative Albrecht Wagner gave a slightly different version: Verlaine was discovered by a friend of Herr Wagner with blood dripping from his head, near the 'Uncle Tom's Cabin' restaurant.[6]

None of this appears to be even approximately true. According to Verlaine, Rimbaud was very 'proper' in Stuttgart, 'rummaging about in libraries', 'cluttering up art museums', and copying out lists of German verbs.[7] He even had some elegant visiting-cards printed.

Rimbaud still had plans for Verlaine's money and would not have left him bleeding to death in the Black Forest. The relationship had simply exhausted all its possibilities. For Rimbaud, Verlaine was still the dupe of his own emotions. For Verlaine, the boy-wonder was growing up to be a stodgy hypocrite, religiously observing his atheistic principles like Flaubert's M. Homais. This was not necessarily a false impression. Even in the *Illuminations* there are hints of inverted piety: 'the Temptation of Saint Anthony' is stripped of its 'Saint' and its capital T. Verlaine predicted a sad end: 'By the time he turns thirty, he'll be a nasty and very vulgar bourgeois.'

Something dramatic did happen in Stuttgart, but like so many of Rimbaud's significant acts, it hardly seemed to be an act at all. He handed Verlaine a pile of old papers – miscellaneous drafts, word-lists and 'a series of superb fragments':[8] the prose poems that came to be known as the *Illuminations*. According to Verlaine, he was to pass the poems on to Germain Nouveau so that Nouveau could have them printed in Belgium.

This sort of nonchalance is no more unusual in a writer than instructions for devoted admirers to burn manuscripts. It may be that, since Rimbaud was about to sell his trunk, he was simply trying to save on postage ('2 fr. 75!!!', according to Verlaine's calculation).[9]

Whether or not he wanted to see his poems in print, he had obviously written them as a set. Despite the variety of forms – visions, parables, riddles, isolated phrases, a prose 'sonnet' and the first free-verse poems in French literature[10] – the *Illuminations* have a recognizable stylistic fingerprint: the almost total absence of comparisons and analogies. Every image exists in its own right. Nothing defers to a higher authority.

Rimbaud might even have intended his poems to appear in a particular order.[11] 'Après le déluge', which came first in the original edition, does form the perfect sequel to the theological angst of *Une Saison en Enfer*: 'As soon as the idea of the Flood had subsided . . .' But this is pure speculation. It is not even certain that the forty-one poems are the complete work. Several sticky hands sifted through this 'dodgy pack of cards' before it finally appeared, without Rimbaud's knowledge, in 1886. New poems emerged in the edition of 1895, and there was talk that year in a Belgian review of two other 'beautiful' *Illuminations* – 'Document' and 'Janvier' – which have disappeared so completely that not even forgeries exist.[12]

There is no sign that Rimbaud simply woke up one day and found that his muse had packed her bags. Some of Verlaine's remarks suggest that he might have added other poems after Stuttgart.[13] Even his sister Isabelle, who liked the idea of a sudden abandonment, thought that he must have continued to write.[14]

The *Illuminations* themselves imply a gradual change of terrain rather than a sudden precipice. Few poets, in fact, pursue such a logical course. Ever since the songs of 1872, Rimbaud had been narrowing the gap between experience and expression, squeezing out the memory which orders and interprets and dredges up the old defeats.

This is why Verlaine's sacred mission was a complete waste of time. Rimbaud's refusal to embrace a ready-made morality was not just a smug counter-morality but a serious shedding of profundity, a streamlined practicality of the sort that usually brings far greater rewards in business than in art.

Any form of poetry that was based on a process rather than on a fixed set of principles was bound to fall off the edge of its own world. Rimbaud's ideologically flattened globe, where the old anxieties are replaced with ingenious forms of distraction and self-deception, now looks almost alarmingly familiar. With the *Illuminations*, Romantic poetry enters the world of the airport lounge, the theme park and the third-world resort. The seer had turned into a sightseer.

> On whatever evening, for example, the naive tourist finds himself, removed from our economic horrors, the hand of a master animates the harpsichord of the fields [. . .]
>
> [. . .] a little world, pale and flat, Africa and Occidents, will be constructed. Then a ballet of known nights and oceans, a worthless chemistry, and impossible melodies.
>
> The same bourgeois magic at whichever point the packet sets us down! The most elementary physicist can sense that it is no longer possible to subject oneself to this personal atmosphere, this fog of physical remorse that has only to be noticed to be an affliction.[15]

*

ABOUT TWO WEEKS after Verlaine's visit, Rimbaud moved to the third floor of 2 Marienstrasse, where a tradesman called Duderstadt-Reinöhl lived with his wife. Rimbaud had a large, well-furnished room. From his window, he could see into the barracks of the Foreign Legion across the road. Downstairs, a man sold hydraulic appliances and gas boilers.

On 17 March, Rimbaud wrote home to complain about the cost of living. Board and lodging were too expensive ('these little schemes are never anything but trickery and subjugation'). He was hoping to impress his mother with his frugality and tried not to sound too nebulous:

> Either I'm going to stay another month to get things properly under way, or I'll have advertised for jobs that will entail some expense (travelling, for instance). I hope this sounds moderate and reasonable to you. I'm trying to absorb the local customs by whatever means possible. I'm trying to get all the information I can, though one has to put up with some pretty unpleasant behaviour.

By the end of April, Rimbaud felt that he knew all the German he needed. The slow drip of money from home was calculated to prevent him wandering off, and so he wrote to Verlaine, care of Delahaye, with a sordid business proposition: Verlaine would send him 100 francs to pay for the 'English lessons' Rimbaud had given him in London, and Rimbaud would say nothing about Verlaine's homosexuality.

Verlaine had buried himself in the Lincolnshire countryside and was teaching at a tiny school in the alcohol-free village of Stickney. He ordered Delahaye not to give his address to the 'spoilt child'. 'He's gone and killed the goose that laid the golden eggs.' 'And if he sulks, then let him!'[16]

Since the goose refused to lay another egg, Rimbaud sold his trunk, took the train to the Swiss border and crossed the Alps on foot, probably by the Splügen Pass.[17] The scrap of correspondence in which the poet bound for 'old Italy' claims to have slept in 'a solitary barn' next to an accommodating cow is probably a fake, though its winsome tone has made it a favourite with many readers.

By the time he reached Milan, he was starving and exhausted.

In the centre of the city, alongside the cathedral, was a dilapidated building inhabited mostly by tradesmen. The address appears on one of Rimbaud's visiting-cards: '39, Piazza del Duomo, 3rd floor'. He might have gone to the Caffetteria Messaggi downstairs to ask about a room. The flat on the third floor was the home of a widow – presumably the same woman who, according to Delahaye, took Rimbaud in and looked after him for several weeks.[18]

This merciful woman was finally identified in 1998 by Piero Boragina as the widow of a wine merchant. She had lost her son the year before. Rimbaud, who was often at his most appealing when he was down-and-out, had found another temporary maternal haven. He wrote to Delahaye to ask for his signed copy of *Une Saison en Enfer* and gave it to the widow as a token of gratitude.

Little is known about this hectic period of Rimbaud's life; yet the lack of information is somehow fitting. Episodes flashed past, never to be repeated. He was always on his way to somewhere else.

He did however have a kind of plan, or a set of mutually dependent plans. He had heard that Henri Mercier, the journalist who had once bought him a suit of clothes in Paris, was part owner of a soap factory on one of the Aegean islands.[19] The idea of the famously filthy poet manufacturing cakes of soap in the land of the Muses was an attractive irony. After about a month in Milan, he set off for the port of Leghorn (Livorno), where he found work at the docks as a day-labourer.[20]

Rimbaud was rapidly devising his traveller's strategy. From now on, he would gravitate towards busy international ports, where casual work was usually available and where long, inexpensive journeys could begin. The docks of big cities were a special zone where no single nationality was dominant and where civilization began to dissolve into the sea. It was a pattern that Rimbaud had already traced in his writing: from the street-grids of verse to the cosmopolitan chaos of the *Illuminations*.

The main thread of his wanderings in 1875–6 used to be treated as a joke or as an example of Rimbaud's intellectual megalomania: to learn all the major European languages in as short a time as possible. Since the advent of language laboratories and commercial training techniques, this rapid acquisition of languages should no longer seem extraordinary. It is perhaps more remarkable that the process of learning a single language can be made to last for six or seven years. Several weeks in the home of a friendly Milanese widow and a month unloading ships at Leghorn were more than enough to give Rimbaud – or anyone – a basic working knowledge of Italian.

If this guzzling of practical information had an unrealistic side to it, it lay in the peculiar obsession he had defined for Verlaine as 'philomathy': learning for the sake of learning. Whatever form it took – a new language or a new horizon – the point was to keep up the flow of fresh data.

As the pulse of thoughts slowed and the visions congealed, he might have hoped that this 'philomathic fever' would be a substitute for the poetic imagination.

*

RIMBAUD'S FIRST SPELL as a docker ended shortly before 15 June when he left Leghorn and set off for Siena. He was apparently heading for Brindisi, where a ship could take him to the soap factory.[21]

There were easier routes, but few so picturesque or so athletically pleasing. In his letters to Delahaye, Verlaine had taken to calling Rimbaud 'the man with soles of wind', which sounds like the airy expression of someone who preferred to sit. For Rimbaud, the point was to feel the regular thud of 'rugged reality': 'I'm too dissipated [. . .] My life isn't heavy enough; it flies away and floats far above action.' ('Mauvais sang') In 'Ma Bohème', he had written of his 'wounded shoes' with the compassionate attachment that a long-distance walker feels for his equipment. These were the simple tools that turned the world into a moving spectacle. In less than three months, he hammered out more than 600 miles on some of the most gruelling terrain in southern Europe.

The usual result of these marathons – though this can hardly be attributed to a conscious plan – was that he reduced himself to a state of helpless destitution. Each step took him further from home but closer to dependence. Somewhere between Leghorn and Siena, with the June sun beating down and 'a foot of dust' on the road, he collapsed with sunstroke.[22]

This time, Rimbaud's saviour was the French Consul at Leghorn. The Consulate accounts for 15 June 1875 show that 'Raimbaud [*sic*], Arthur, son of Frédéric and Catherine Cuif, native of Charleville', was put up at the Stella Hotel for two days, given three francs twenty centimes, and sent back to France on a steamship.[23]

On disembarking at Marseille, Rimbaud fell ill again and had to spend several days in hospital. As he lay in bed, he hatched another plan. The Carlists' rebel army had set up recruitment offices along the Mediterranean coast. The mercenaries were trained in France, then smuggled into Spain over the Pyrenees. Since the journey east was turning into a circle, he decided to continue west and add Spanish to his collection of languages.[24]

After leaving the hospital, he found a recruitment office and signed up as a supporter of the Carlist pretender, Don Carlos. In exchange, he would have received a small sum of money and instructions on how to join his regiment.

Most of Rimbaud's letters to Delahaye have been lost, but the substance was preserved by Verlaine in caustic little poems that describe the doings of the drunken 'philomath' in his own foul patois. Having tried to volunteer for the other side in 1872, Verlaine was interested to hear of Rimbaud's latest scheme:

> No more smokes, and the *daromphe*'s* dropped me in the shit.
> How sad. What the fuck'll I do now? I've given it
> A lot of thought. Carlists? Nah – not worth the bother.
> It ain't much fun being machine-gun fodder.

This is probably a fair description of Rimbaud's attitude to the Spanish Civil War. The Carlists were suffering heavy defeats, and mercenaries would certainly be involved in bloody fighting.

Instead of making for the Spanish border, he took his money to the station and caught the train for Paris.

The deserter was coming home.

*

* A humorous form of '*daronne*' (slang for 'mother').

ONE DAY THAT summer, the 'mad composer' Ernest Cabaner returned to find his room in a mess and his little supply of absinthe all used up. The signs were unmistakable: 'That evil cat Rimbaud is back again!'[25]

Rimbaud had returned to the scene of his crimes, apparently to commit some more. A few weeks later, he was boasting to Delahaye, 'in a loud-mouthed manner that's quite astonishing in him, that when he was in Paris he kicked *everybody* up the arse'. Back on familiar territory, with the philomathic mind deprived of fresh data, Rimbaud apparently felt that everyone, including himself, was 'scum'.[26] He seemed to be drinking himself stupid. Even for the few people who were still on tolerable terms with him – Cabaner, Forain, Mercier and Nouveau – 'the mad traveller' was best enjoyed at a distance.

A pencilled address on a rediscovered visiting-card suggests that he took a room at 18 Boulevard Montrouge, just up from the attic he had shared with Forain in 1872.[27] Is this where an artist called Garnier painted the dubious 'Portrait of the Poet Arthur Raimbaut'? It shows a well-dressed young man whose hair (unlike Rimbaud's) is parted on the right and bears two different dates: 1872 and 1873. But a note on the back of the canvas says that it was painted 'opposite the gate of the Montparnasse Cemetery'.[28] Number 18 Boulevard Montrouge faced the main entrance to the cemetery.

It is even possible that Rimbaud, like the young man in the painting, was well dressed. A drawing by Delahaye shows a rather swanky Rimbaud announcing his presence with a snooty prod on the shoulder. He wears a bowler hat, a stiff collar, a figure-enhancing suit and shoes that were not made for walking. Isabelle claims that her brother was tutoring in the town of Maisons-Alfort, south-east of Paris.[29] Rimbaud did see his mother and sisters that summer when they came to consult a specialist for Vitalie, who was wasting away with tubercular synovitis.* But the information that Rimbaud had a teaching post dates from a time (1896) when Isabelle was inventing respectable alternatives for every seedy episode in her brother's life.

The only reliable indication of his activities is a letter from

---

* Synovitis is an inflammation of the synovial membrane, which secretes lubricating fluid in the joints.

Delahaye, warning Verlaine of 'the gadfly''s[30] latest attempt to fund his travels: 'According to him, you're just a skinflint [. . .] He went to your mother's house in Paris. The concierge told him she was away in Belgium.'[31]

Rimbaud completed his first circumambulation towards the end of September. He returned to Charleville for what was to become a regular hibernation. Every Thursday and Sunday, he trekked out to distant cafés with Delahaye. For beer money, he gave German lessons to the son of the family's new landlord at 31 Rue Saint-Barthélemy. The rest of his time was spent recuperating and stocking his memory like an Ark.

This appetite for useful knowledge was beginning to look like a serious addiction. According to three different witnesses, the omnilinguist was already swinging through the remoter branches of the Indo-European tree and had reached the Afro-Asiatic: 'Arabic and a bit of Russian';[32] 'Hindi, Amharic [Ethiopian] and especially Arabic'.[33] A former classmate called Henri Pauffin ran into Rimbaud one day in the woods around Charleville. He was learning Russian from a Greek–Russian dictionary; but since books were an encumbrance, 'he had cut the pages up and stuffed the clippings into his pockets'.[34]

Rimbaud seems to have enjoyed the sort of connective mind that can spin one set of facts – or one language – off another without continually referring back to the central store of knowledge. This raises the disconcerting possibility that the *Illuminations* were more coherent to their creator than they appear to us. Fortunately, aesthetic pleasure can often be derived from a mere impression of complex thought: Einstein's blackboards, Wittgenstein's propositions, Rimbaud's prose poems.

Even if, as Delahaye claimed, 'his inspiration had dried up',[35] this was still the same Rimbaud. His last known artistic activity, which dates from this Charleville winter, shows the same passion for integrated bodies of knowledge that lend themselves to some kind of performance. The difference was that the desire to preserve the results – never very strong in the first place – had left him entirely.

Having returned to Charleville, Rimbaud asked a young church organist called Louis Létrange to teach him the rudiments of music. His interest was primarily theoretical. At first, he practised silently on a keyboard gouged into a table. Later, without telling his mother, he had a piano delivered to the house. The idea was that when the neighbours saw a piano being hoisted up to the Rimbauds' apartment, they would complain that pianos were not allowed in the building. Mme Rimbaud would then insist on having it installed. (The plan worked.)[36]

A drawing by Verlaine, based on Delahaye's report, shows a Liszt-like Rimbaud thumping the keys with piston arms, while his mother and the landlord plug their ears. Caption: '*La musique adoucit les mœurs*' ('Music has a civilizing influence'). According to Létrange, Rimbaud was not concerned with scales or pretty tunes. He was looking for 'new sonorities'.

The richest source of information on these philomathic projects is an extraordinary letter sent to Delahaye, who had taken up a teaching post at Rethel, twenty-five miles away. The letter was dated 14 October.

In the first part of his letter, Rimbaud worried needlessly about military service: 'It seems that the 2nd "portion" of the "contingent" of the "class of 74" is going to be called up on 3 November "followg" or next.' In a crude ditty titled 'Rêve' ('Dream'), he pictured himself at night-time in the barracks with a group of farting soldiers. The soldiers, including Rimbaud, are portrayed as a confabulation of cheeses:

Emanations and explosions.
[...]
The Genius: – 'I'm the Roquefort!
            – 'It'll be the death of us! ....'
            – I'm the Gruyère
                And the Brie! .... etc.

Since Rimbaud's obscure piece of private doggerel is technically his last known verse poem, it has sometimes been hailed as the 'pinnacle' of his literary career, the 'manifesto' of his silence. This surprising opinion might reflect an unusually versatile form of literary sensibility; or it might reflect the prestige of the arch-Surrealist, André Breton. Sneering at Claudel's angelic image of a Catholic

Rimbaud, Breton described the cheese ditty in his *Anthologie de l'humour noir* as Rimbaud's 'poetic and spiritual testament'.[37]

Rimbaud had always associated genius with bad smells and sly fermentations, and there is nothing to suggest that this note to a friend was a formal leave-taking of the visionary dream. By all accounts, Rimbaud's intellectual life at the end of 1875 was as vigorous as ever. The second part of his letter was a philomathic shopping-list. It looked for a moment as though he was going to make his mother's dreams come true and apply for the École Polytechnique:

> A little favour: would you tell me exactly and concisely what the current science 'bachot' [baccalauréat] consists of, the classical and math. part, etc. [...] I especially want precise details since I'd be buying the books quite soon. Military training and 'bachot', you see, would make for two or three enjoyable seasons! To hell with this 'merry toil' in any case. But if you'd just be kind enough to tell me in the bestest way you can ['*le plus mieux possible*'] how one goes about it. [...]
>
> Yours 'to the best of my feeble ability'.

If one takes the view that poets are helpless in the 'real world', this request for '*choses précises*' can be interpreted as proof that Rimbaud had finished with poetry. It may be that he had entered a period of dormancy that would last for a few days or for the rest of his life, but since he had never regarded poetry as the involuntary product of a naturally inspired mind, and since the 'seer' was supposed to be a verbal scientist and 'a multiplier of progress', there was nothing inherently unpoetic about 'precision'. This was 1875, not the dawn of the Romantic age.

Since the chronology is unknown, no firm conclusions can be drawn, but it is remarkable that some of what appear to be the later *Illuminations* show a familiarity with mathematical and musical terms which corresponds to Rimbaud's new interests.[38] 'Nocturne vulgaire' even has the formal circularity of a piano *nocturne*.

> Now the endless inflexion of moments and the infinity of mathematics chase me through this world in which I undergo every civil success,

respected by strange children and enormous affections. – I am dreaming of a war, of might or of right, of quite unforeseen logic.

It's as simple as a musical phrase.

('Guerre')

If there are signs of the coming silence in the letter to Delahaye, they lie in the proliferation of inverted commas. The great verbal inventor was hiding behind other people's language. Poetry had failed to eradicate the sense of shame and profligacy.[39] After all the intoxicating experiments and the deliberate 'derangement', Rimbaud's identity was intact. If Verlaine now saw his lover and his 'muse' as a snickering parasite, he was not alone. The 'demon' of *Une Saison en Enfer* was equally disparaging: '"You'll always be a hyena, etc . . .", cries the demon who crowned me with such pleasant poppies.'

25

Mr Holmes

'I know of no obstacle that surpasses the power of the human mind, except truth.'

(Lautréamont, *Poésies* II)

Two months after his twenty-first birthday, Rimbaud stood at his sister's graveside, still shaken by the sight of her long agony. Vitalie, who was said to have looked 'like Rimbaud as a very beautiful young girl',[1] had finally managed to die of synovitis on 18 December. She was seventeen years old.

Rimbaud had always treated her as a favourite pupil and can hardly have been indifferent to her admiration. Even he needed an audience.

At the funeral, the sudden ageing of the Rimbaud boy was remarked upon by some of mourners. At a distance, it looked as though all his hair had fallen out: a parchment-coloured skull on young shoulders. Rimbaud had recently been experiencing severe headaches. Attributing them, bizarrely, to his thick hair, he persuaded a wigmaker to shave it all off. Verlaine might have interpreted his tonsure as a religious gesture, a sign that he was ready for absolution. He wrote, refusing once again to pay for Rimbaud's 'whoring, boozing and piano lessons':

It greatly saddens me to see you following such an idiotic path – you who are so intelligent and *so ready* (it might amaze you to learn!). I say this precisely because of your disgust with all things and all people, your continual anger at everything – an anger which is fundamentally just, though unaware of its *cause*.

Rimbaud had no such simple antidote to disgust. But the fact that he spent the next four years wandering the world without apparent purpose does not necessarily indicate disarray. It is perfectly possible to have a clear perception of things without knowing what one is doing.

When the nights turned warmer, he packed his bag again. This time, he was going to one of the world's largest cities, Vienna, supposedly to perfect his German, and then to Varna on the Black Sea – hoping, perhaps, that the Bulgarian nationalists were hiring mercenaries. His final destination was Russia, where some unspecified 'industrial collaboration' awaited him.[2]

He reached Vienna in early April. Once again, the route to the east was blocked. He took a cab, fell asleep, and was robbed by the driver. Isabelle later refused to believe that her brother had been too drunk to notice,[3] but it must have been an unusually deep sleep if, as he told Delahaye, he woke up on the pavement with no coat, no hat and no money. His street-map of Vienna, which was obviously of little use to a local cab-driver, survived the robbery and is now at the library in Charleville.

Rimbaud reported the loss of all his money to the Viennese police who, showing a nasty talent for lateral thinking, expelled him as a foreign vagrant.

As he had discovered on his first trip to Paris, legal expulsion was a cheap way to travel. He could simply beg in the streets until the local constabulary arrested him and sent him on to the next territory. He had himself expelled all the way through southern Germany until he reached Strasbourg. From there, he walked the 180 miles back to Charleville.

By now, his body was tuned to long distances, though not always capable of covering them. Like verse or music, walking was a rhythmical skill, a combination of trance and productive activity. Delahaye's description of the athletic pedestrian suggests a special state of existence, a happy delegation of responsibility to blood and muscle:

His long legs calmly took formidable strides; his long, swinging arms marked the very regular movements; his back was straight, his head erect, his eyes stared into the distance. His face wore an expression of resigned defiance, anticipating everything, without anger or trepidation.[4]

It seemed as though every road was bound to return elliptically to the Ardennes until a certain escape velocity had been reached. Traced on a map, Rimbaud's wanderings take the same palindromic form as some of the *Illuminations* – repetitions around a non-existent centre.[5]

After a rapid recuperation in Charleville, he decided to head north. He is known to have left home some time before 18 May, perhaps around the 6th, when, by coincidence, the Collège de Charleville burned to the ground.[6]

Although there was no sign of advance planning, Rimbaud was about to embark on his greatest adventure yet. For many years, it was thought to have been invented by his first biographers for the entertainment of credulous readers. Documentary evidence has since justified all but the most extreme forms of credulity.

In Brussels or another 'Flemish town',[7] he met a recruiting agent for the Dutch Colonial Army. Compared to the Carlist desperadoes, the Dutch Colonial Army was an efficient, modern organization. For the last three years, it had been crushing small revolts that threatened to disrupt the flow of colonial produce from the Dutch East Indies. Large sums of money were invested in the enterprise.

For a casual mercenary, it looked like the next best thing to a Cook's tour. A freelance agent in Brussels was advertising that year in the local press for men aged between twenty-one and thirty-seven who either had 'no job, no family and no money' or who were 'very fond of travelling and curious to see the world'.[8] In this case, 'the world' meant the guerrilla-infested forests of the former sultanate of Achin on the island of Java.

Rimbaud signed up at the Dutch Consulate in Brussels for six years, which was the minimum term. He received a lump sum of 300 florins (about £1,800 or $2,800 today) and a train ticket for Rotterdam, with orders to report to the garrison commander.[9]

Instead of making off with the money, he went to Rotterdam, from where he was transferred to the naval port of Harderwijk. He arrived by train, late on the afternoon of 18 May 1876. His papers were found to be in order and his constitution deemed sufficiently robust for jungle combat.

The Arthur Rimbaud who was so reluctant to perform his military service in France now found himself in a run-down barracks, learning to use a rifle and to follow orders in Dutch. In the documents, the new recruit is erased into almost total anonymity:

> Face: oval
> Forehead: ordinary
> Eyes: blue
> Nose and mouth: ordinary
> Chin: round
> Hair and eyebrows: brown
> No distinctive signs
> Height: 1.77 [5′ 10″]

The latest contingent was scheduled to sail for the Malay Archipelago on 27 May, but the agents had failed to muster a full complement. Since the policing operation had begun in 1873, returning soldiers must have spread the word: Java was a tropical hell.

Rimbaud cooled his heels in Harderwijk from 18 May to 10 June. Most of his comrades-in-arms were mercenaries, ex-convicts and men who no longer had a strong attachment to life. There was also a contingent of Italians who already wanted to go home. Every evening from five to nine-thirty, the local pubs and brothels were crammed with soldiers who suddenly had money to spend. Rimbaud is said to have whiled away the hours with a prostitute called 'Rotte Pietje'. The Dutchman who claims to have rescued him from her pimp found him 'a spoilt, overgrown schoolboy who went mad as soon as he had some gin in him', but he must have enjoyed his company since he stayed with him until the ship sailed.[10]

After a gruelling three weeks of drinking, whoring and basic training, 200 soldiers marched to the beat of a drum to Harderwijk station and boarded the train for Den Helder on the north-west coast.

It was now too late to desert, but Rimbaud had obviously decided to see the other side of the world. Whether in fiction or reality, most Romantic poets eventually turned into bourgeois capitalists. Rimbaud took this theme of stagnating ideals to a ludicrous extreme. The former Communard had joined an imperialist force whose only *raison d'être* was money. No one joined the Dutch Colonial Army out of ideological fervour.

The foggy soul of the actor delights in well-defined roles. Rimbaud had already imagined this one for himself in the prose poem, 'Démocratie'. According to Delahaye, this is the authentic sound of Rimbaud's conversation – the sardonic enthusiasm and a rousing ability to shoot the rapids of his own verbal torrent, wherever it was going. 'Démocratie' obviously prefigures Rimbaud's adventure, but its historical prescience is perhaps more remarkable. This could be the Dutch East Indies in 1876 or Vietnam a century later:

> 'The flag is heading for that loathsome landscape, and our patois muffles the drum.
> 'In the centres, we'll support the most cynical prostitution. We'll massacre logical rebellions.
> 'To those spicy, waterlogged lands! – in the service of the most monstrous industrial or military exploitations.
> 'Farewell to here, or to anywhere. Conscripts of arbitrary will, our philosophy will be ferocious. Ignorant for science, cunning for comfort. Let the turning world drop dead. This is real progress. Forward, march!'

On 10 June, Rimbaud and 225 other recruits left Den Helder on a three-masted steamship, the *Prins van Oranje*. It docked at Southampton the following evening and spent two days taking on supplies. The recruits were given tobacco, pipes, a selection of games and a bar of black soap each. A deserter was fished out of the Solent, and the *Prins van Oranje* set sail for Gibraltar on 13 June.

On 22 June, it reached the Bay of Naples, where the Italians were placed under special observation. For Rimbaud, the first part of the voyage was a preview of coming attractions. Cyprus was seen in the distance, and then, after Suez, the Somali coast, with its hinterland of mysterious empires that not even missionaries had reached. Captains were advised not to drop anchor: local tribes had been known to row out and massacre the sailors.

As the last clouds disappeared, tropical dress was handed out: white linen shirt, blue and white striped trousers, tartan beret. For the officers, this was one of the busiest parts of the voyage. Between 26 June and 2 July, nine men jumped into the Red Sea and swam for shore. At least one was drowned.

After Aden, the ship settled into its ocean routine. The day began at 5 a.m. and was spent on chores, games and deck-chairs. A white awning ran the length of the deck. After lunch, an hour of training relieved the boredom. There was a steady supply of tea and tobacco, and, on Saturdays, a small glass of brandy. Sundays were celebrated with fresh meat and cakes.

Two weeks later, the northern tip of Sumatra was sighted off the port bow. Fifty miles south of the Equator, the *Prins van Oranje* anchored off Padang. The following day (20 July), it steamed past the smouldering peak of Krakatoa into the shallow Java Sea and, forty days after leaving Holland, entered the muddy, yellow waters off Batavia (Jakarta). The thermometer showed 35°C.

Rimbaud's battalion was marched to its temporary barracks – a converted tea factory six miles from the harbour in the Meester Cornelis district. After sweating in the barracks for ten days, a contingent of 160 men – minus a few invalids and deserters – returned to the harbour in horse-drawn trams and boarded a tramp steamer for Samarang. On 2 August, the sunlit haze of the Javanese coast revealed a sweltering mass of shipping. Sailors from all over the world were loading cargoes of tea, coffee, sugar, spices and quinine, or watching the latest batch of unsuspecting mercenaries arrive.

Rimbaud was storing away useful information. He noticed the ships with European flags and may have picked up some scraps of language from the Javanese soldiers. The mysterious word that has tormented commentators in the prose poem 'Dévotion' – '*Baou*' (associated with 'the buzzing, stinking summer grass') – is said by some to be a transliteration of a Malay dialect word for 'stench': 'perhaps one of the first words that the great French poet learnt during his brief stay in Batavia'.[11] But the poem, if not the stench, almost certainly belonged to the past.

In Samarang, the first battalion took the train to Tungtang and from there marched through farms and villages to the cooler air of Salatiga, 2,000 feet above sea level.

A day after arrival (3 August), one of the Frenchmen in Rimbaud's battalion died. Soon, there would be other deaths. Final training began in earnest. Eyes that had grown accustomed to ocean vistas focused on the dark mass of unfamiliar vegetation beyond the camp.

*

WITH ITS IMMIGRANT population of Chinese, Arabs and Europeans, Java was the sort of tropical crossroads where a man in a flannel waistcoat and white trousers, with a sun-baked face and an air of 'resigned defiance', might easily have passed as a colonist, a trader or even as a naturalist-explorer. He would certainly have been safer than a man wearing the blue and orange of the Dutch Army. Deserters were always pursued and sometimes ended their career in front of a firing-squad.

On 15 August, Private Rimbaud failed to attend chapel – perhaps not for the first time. At the evening roll-call, he was still missing. A rapid search of the bunkhouse revealed a pair of *fourragères* with epaulettes, two garrison caps, a greatcoat, two sweaters, two shirts, three ties, two pairs of blue trousers, one pair of underpants, a towel and a wooden trunk; but no weapons and no Rimbaud.[12] A detachment was sent in pursuit.

Enough time had elapsed for Rimbaud to scamper downhill to Tungtang railway station before his absence was noted. But if he tried to take the train, he would have been recaptured instantly. Samarang, where a man could dissolve into the melting-pot of nationalities, was just thirty miles away, but for a deserter, it was inaccessible by any obvious route.

Accounts based on Rimbaud's conversations say that he spent a month wandering through Java, 'gorging himself on new sensations'. This is quite plausible if 'a month' is replaced with 'two weeks'. Isabelle Rimbaud's husband, Berrichon, stupidly cast doubt on the whole episode in his 1897 biography by stating that Rimbaud was forced [. . .] to hide in redoubtable virgin forests where orang-utans [unknown in Java] must have taught him how to live in safety from pouncing tigers and stealthy boa constrictors.[13]

It is perhaps not surprising that Berrichon held the intelligence of orang-utans in such high regard.

Since the island was intensively farmed, food – especially fruit – was more readily available than it had ever been on the road from Paris to Charleville. Besides which, Rimbaud had just received almost thirteen weeks of military training specially adapted to the Javanese interior.

He might have dodged his way back to Samarang through the forests and the hill country, or, logically, headed east for the port of Surabaya. But since Rimbaud had stepped outside the administrative web of the Dutch Colonial Army, he disappears at this point as completely as a Javanese orang-utan.*

*

Among the European sailors who were hoping to leave Samarang that summer was a Scotsman, Captain J. Brown, master of a small sailing-ship of 477 tons called *The Wandering Chief*.[16]

Since leaving South Shields six months before, Captain Brown had had a difficult time of it. A man had fallen overboard and was reported drowned ten weeks later when the ship reached Batavia. In July, while *The Wandering Chief* took on a cargo of sugar in Samarang, the cook and another crew member were dismissed for 'illness'.

Captain Brown now faced a dangerous voyage home. He would be rounding the Cape severely short-handed: two officers, four sailors and a fourteen-year-old cabin boy.

His luck seems to have changed in August. Sifting through the disreputables who hung about the wharves and hotels of Samarang and smaller ports on the Javanese coast, he managed to drum up

* One of Rimbaud's friends in Africa says that he also claimed to have seen Australia. He could only have done so in August 1876. The voyage from Surabaya to Palmerston (Darwin) would have taken at least five days. Although this fits the known chronology, and although one of Rimbaud's word-lists contains a term ('Wagga Wagga berry')[14] that was apparently known only in Australia, no good evidence has been found.[15]

three replacements: a Danish cook, Hans Hanssen; a sailor, John Hingston, who had served as a lieutenant on *The Cleveland*; and a man called Edwin Holmes who claimed to be a former crew member of *The Oseco*.

The dates and details of *The Wandering Chief*'s voyage home match Rimbaud's own accounts so closely that this was almost certainly the ship on which he sailed from Java. Yet, as Enid Starkie discovered, no Rimbaud is listed among the crew members of *The Wandering Chief* nor anywhere else in the General Register of Shipping and Seamen.

It would have been untypically stupid of Rimbaud to use his own name. The Dutch military police would have inspected the lists of ships leaving Java, especially those with Frenchmen on board. Since it seems unlikely that Rimbaud had the necessary skills to pass himself off as a Danish cook, and since a Lieutenant Hingston did indeed leave *The Cleveland* on 6 July, Edwin Holmes begins to look rather suspicious.

His ship, *The Oseco*, had recently been abandoned in the Indian Ocean – a fact that would have been well known in Samarang that summer. But how many people would have known that the name 'Edwin Holmes' never appeared on any list, report or contract relating to *The Oseco* or to any other ship? The mysterious Mr Holmes materialized in the muggy air of Samarang only to vanish four months later when *The Wandering Chief* reached Le Havre.

Equally strange, the list of seamen shows that while the other crew members were to receive eighty-seven francs a month, Mr Holmes was promised only seventy-five francs and, in the end, received even less than the cabin-boy.

Rimbaud's ability to gain the sympathy of men in positions of responsibility is well attested. Whoever he was, Edwin Holmes obviously reached a private, illegal agreement with the Captain: when the new crew members were registered in Samarang on 29 August, the day before *The Wandering Chief* set sail, Holmes, late of *The Oseco*, was set down as having been taken on by Captain Brown on 11 July, three days *before The Oseco* was abandoned and, perhaps more to the point, over a month before Private Rimbaud was reported missing.

*

ST. HELENA, 4th November ... On the 30th Sept. in Lat. 31 S, Lon. 31 E, [*The Wandering Chief*] encountered very heavy weather, with high cross seas, washing away every movable article from the decks and throwing vessel on her beam ends, in which position she remained for 30 hours, with hatches and yardarms in the water; every exertion was made to right her, but finding she would not do so, having then about six feet water in her hold, had to cut away mizzenmast and fore and main topgallantmasts. A quantity of sugar was washed away from the cargo in consequence of the water getting below.[17]

To Rimbaud's delight, the Cape of Good Hope lived up to its reputation. The men of *The Wandering Chief*, who happily blasphemed in fair weather, fell to their knees and prayed. All of Rimbaud's tales, even the *Illuminations*, were rooted in reality, and there is no reason to doubt the story that, when the ship was anchored off St Helena (a fact confirmed by the Captain's report), he tried to swim ashore to see the lonely rock on which Napoleon had lived his last years. 'Luckily, a sailor dived in and dragged him back on board.'[18]

In view of the damage to the vessel and the length of the voyage, it is also quite possible that, as he appears to have told Delahaye, he first set foot in Africa on the Atlantic coast, at Dakar.[19]

Ninety-nine days after leaving Samarang, on 6 December 1876, *The Wandering Chief* docked at Queenstown on the southern coast of Ireland.

The final stages of Rimbaud's journey were probably these: from Queenstown to Cork by train; ferry to Liverpool; then a train to London and across the Channel to Dieppe.[20] From there, he went to Paris, where he was spotted on the Place de la Bastille by a sculptor called Wisseaux, dressed 'as an English sailor' – hence the new nickname used by the Rimbaud gossip network: '*Rimbald le marin*' ('Rinbad the Sailor').[21]

On 9 December, he was back at his mother's home, bearded, weather-beaten and slightly rheumatic.[22] He buried himself with his traveller's images for several weeks. Delahaye did not find out that Rimbaud was still alive until 28 January 1877. He wrote to their friend, Ernest Millot: 'He's back! ... from a little voyage – next to nothing': Brussels to Cork, via Java; then 'Liverpool, Le Havre [*sic*],

Paris and – always – ending up . . . in Charlestown.' 'And it's not over yet. It seems we'll be seeing many more adventures.'[23]

A few critics, sad to see the curtain fall, have sifted through the *Illuminations*, looking for images of these adventures – the hypothetical Batavian 'stench', the circus of 'Parade', a possible view of Stockholm in 'Villes'. But Rimbaud had stopped recording. It seems certain now that his only audience was Delahaye and anyone else who happened to be at the café.

If any poem can be dated to this very late period, it could only be 'Solde', which seems to have been inspired by the classified pages of a newspaper. Rimbaud might have intended it to be the last *Illumination*. It would have made a splendidly ambiguous conclusion. Was this the final clearance sale of a bankrupt seer, or was he going into business under a new name?

> For sale: anarchy for the masses; irrepressible satisfaction for superior amateurs; atrocious deaths for disciples and lovers!
>
> For sale: habitations and migrations, sports, spectaculars and perfect comforts, and the noise, the movement and the future they create!
>
> For sale: arithmetical applications and astonishing harmonic leaps. Unsuspected discoveries and terms – immediate possession.
>
> [. . .]
>
> For sale: the Bodies, the voices, the immense unquestionable opulence, things that will never be sold. The salesmen are not yet sold out! The travellers won't be handing back their commission just yet!

26

John Arthur Rimbaud

'I alone hold the key to this wild parade.'

('Parade', *Illuminations*)

DECEMBER 1876: it had now been almost two years since Rimbaud gave any sign that he was still writing poems.

The question – 'Why did he stop?' has already been asked, if not answered, several times, since it concerns Rimbaud's entire career, not just a hypothetical moment of 'literaturicide'.

Many poets give up writing poetry between collections or even, like Baudelaire, between different parts of the same poem. Some, like Paul Valéry or Matthew Arnold, fall silent for years. Mediocre poets, on the other hand, are frequently unstoppable.

For Rimbaud, poetry had always been the means to an end: winning esteem, causing irritation, changing the nature of reality. Each redefinition of the goal had rendered the old technology obsolete. The prose Rimbaud had shown no more nostalgia for verse than most mathematicians showed for their slide-rules after the invention of the personal computer.

Even if Rimbaud still wanted to write poetry, he may not have had the means to do so. He had never developed the kind of metrical machinery that enabled poets like Hugo or Banville to cope with diminishing mental returns. His latest techniques had all been derived from rapid changes in the mind. Once the relative sludge of adulthood had set in, it may be that poems like the *Illuminations* were literally unthinkable.

In the face of venerable mysteries like Rimbaud's 'silence', it is sometimes useful to cultivate a degree of incuriosity or to reformulate the question: not 'Why did he stop writing poetry?' but 'Why did he keep taking it up?'

Almost every aspect of Rimbaud's life has been plagued by the search for single causes. If the mystery can be reduced to one solution, it lies in a simple coincidence: Rimbaud stopped writing poems at about the same time that he gave up living with other people.

Rimbaud's interest in his own work had survived the realization that the world would not be changed by verbal innovation. It did not survive the failure of all his adult relationships. He had always treated his poems as a form of private communication. He gave his songs to *chansonniers*, his satires to satirists. Without a constant companion, he was writing in a void. This is what it meant to be 'ahead of his time'. In 1876, most of Rimbaud's admirers either were still in the nursery or had yet to be conceived.

When Rimbaud wrote the last *Illuminations*, he might have felt in any case that his poetry had crossed the limits of communicability and turned into a simple waste of energy. He was one of the first French poets to reach the logical end of Romanticism. Purged of clichés and common understandings, poems that were based on individual sensibility rather than on convention were in danger of becoming irredeemably private – at least until they created a readership of their own. Perhaps the words at the end of 'Parade' were not intended as a provocation but as a helpful hint: 'I alone hold the key to this wild parade.'[1]

Ironically, Rimbaud's work had already begun its long journey into the light. In 1878, Verlaine looked again at the *Illuminations* and found some 'charming things' there. He seems to have been planning an edition behind Rimbaud's back. He lent the poems to his brother-in-law, the composer Charles de Sivry.[2] If Mathilde had not placed an embargo on the poems, they might have been set to music by Sivry sixty-one years before Benjamin Britten's *Illuminations*.

For Rimbaud, the original quest continued. After disappearing over the horizon of the page, he was still hungry for adventures.

Twelve years after *Une Saison en Enfer*, in 1885, he would write from Arabia like a new Scheherazade, telling himself stories to stay alive:

> If I had the means to travel without being forced to stay and work for a living, I'd never be seen in the same place for more than two months. The world is very big and full of magnificent lands that would take more than a thousand lives to visit.[3]

*

RIMBAUD HIBERNATED SO effectively in 1876–7 that almost nothing is known of his life, only that he was learning Russian again and thinking of going into commerce, perhaps as an insurance salesman.

This was well within his capabilities: a legal confidence trick requiring an ability to inspire fear of sudden damage. He also thought of joining a group of missionaries.[4] This, too, was more sensible than it might appear: missionary societies often advertised in newspapers and were not always fussy about spiritual credentials. But when springtime opened the door to wandering again, he hit upon a different scheme. It was so perversely appropriate that it seems almost obvious.

Having made his way to northern Germany, he went to work under a borrowed name for a Dutch recruiting agent.[5] In cities along the Upper Rhine, he sat in bars, telling young Prussians about the subsidized cruise to Java – the free tobacco, the magic of Samarang, and, presumably, the eventual escape route.

This was business as Rimbaud understood it: a profitable enterprise with a huge irony built into it. If the Javanese excursion had been a boy's adventure story, this was a black comedy: a Frenchman, feeding from the hand he had just bitten, sending Prussians to possible death on the other side of the world.

It is easy to see why many of Rimbaud's admirers find it 'indecent' to follow him into the badlands of his post-poetic career and proceed directly from 1875 to his death bed, where the 'angel in exile' lies like a handicapped child, unable to escape or contradict. 'Let us not read the African Rimbaud's letters to his family,' urges Yves Bonnefoy.

'Let us not try to find out whether the poet who wanted one day to "steal fire", sold one thing rather than another.'[6]

But was Rimbaud only Rimbaud when he wrote? And is admiration incompatible with knowledge? As Baudelaire liked to point out, poetry itself is a confidence trick. The twenty-two-year-old who enticed soldiers into the Dutch Colonial Army was not such a distant relative of the eighteen-year-old who sold to future generations the most incredible metaphysical fantasies, so successfully that some enthusiasts are still waiting for the poet to return with the final instructions.

After recruiting a dozen soldiers, Rimbaud collected his commission from the agent and went to Hamburg, where he lost it all in a casino.

At this point, with the sheet wiped clean again, Rimbaud suddenly appears in the first person. The existence of a genuine Rimbaud manuscript in this Empty Quarter of his life seems an extraordinary stroke of luck, even if there is something about the document that freezes the smile of recognition.

On 14 May 1877, he was in Bremen – the main port for emigrants to the United States[7] – writing to the American Consul. His languages had fused slightly, but the message was clear enough.

Bremen, the 14 May 77

The untersigned Arthur Rimbaud – Born in Charleville (France) – Aged 23 – 5 ft 6. height [*sic*] – Good healthy, – Late a teacher of sciences and languages – Recently deserted from the 47° Regiment of the French army, – Actually in Bremen without any means, the French Consul refusing any Relief, –

Would like to know on which conditions he could conclude an immediate engagement in the American navy.

Speaks and writes English, German, French, Italian and Spanish.

Has been four months as a sailor in a Scotch bark, from Java to Queenstown, from August to December 76.

Would be very honoured and grateful to receive an answer.

John Arthur Rimbaud[8]

This peculiar job application sounds like the work of Poe's 'Imp of the Perverse'. Only United States citizens could enlist in the

American navy and so the application would have failed in any case. But why deliberately wreck his chances by describing himself as a deserter?

The oddest detail of this self-defeating application is a clue to what might be called its logic. The 47th Regiment of the French army was the regiment to which Rimbaud's father had belonged from 1852 until his retirement in 1864.

Like the homesick *bateau ivre*, 'John Arthur Rimbaud' is another fleeting incarnation of the fantasy Captain Rimbaud: the soldier who finally deserted and came home.

These inconsequential acts seem strange only because they occur outside the benign asylum of poetry. Rimbaud had left the page without changing his clothes. The fantastic curriculum vitae of *Une Saison en Enfer* and the chaotic identity parade of the *Illuminations* belong to the same story: the search for a missing person who never existed.

*

A MONTH LATER, in Hamburg, the former 'teacher of sciences and languages' was sitting in a little booth, selling tickets for Loisset's Circus.[9] He might also have worked as an interpreter. Those who contend that 'Parade' refers to Rimbaud's time under the Big Top might have pointed to the last line as the interpreter's private joke – 'I alone hold the key to this wild parade' – but the Cirque Loisset would never have soiled its sawdust with the squalid fairground crew of 'Parade', 'with terrifying voices and a few dangerous tricks; they are sent into town for some rough trade, festooned in repulsive finery'. The Loissets had been touring Europe like a travelling court for several generations. Their sequined acrobats were wooed by princes, and the discipline was tighter than in the Dutch Colonial Army.[10]

Rimbaud stayed with the circus for a few weeks, saw Copenhagen and Stockholm, then deserted. His name appears twice in the register of aliens at Stockholm for June 1877, once as an 'agent' and once as a 'seaman';[11] but these were probably ideas rather than jobs. Once again, he was destitute.

Fortunately, the French Consul in Stockholm proved to be more amenable than his colleague in Bremen. The young man who had run away from the circus was put on a ship for Le Havre and eventually reached Charleville on foot.[12]

Until the Rimbaud sale at Drouot's in 1998, the next three months were a complete blank. The rediscovered interview notes of Rimbaud's first biographer show that in the autumn of 1877, he was back in Marseille. He was seen there by Henri Mercier (the man who was supposed to own a soap factory). Rimbaud had reached a low ebb, though his spirits were incongruously high:

> On the way back from Italy, Mercier met A.R. in Marseille in a state of utter destitution. Claimed to be living by theft and doing something even worse with a cynical Capuchin. Lived in a monastery. Mercier offered him 5 francs. Rimbaud said, '5 francs never come amiss', took the money and ran off.[13]

This is a suspiciously rich slice of life – a catch-all cameo of Arthur Rimbaud as beggar, bugger, blasphemer and thief; but it does match a drawing in one of Delahaye's letters to Verlaine – 'Le Capucin folâtre' ('The Frisky Capuchin')[14] – and it fits one other piece of the puzzle. Fearing the approach of winter, Rimbaud had set his sights on Alexandria, which the Suez Canal had turned into a thriving international job exchange.

Rimbaud's body let him down again. He fell ill during the crossing. A doctor diagnosed 'gastric fever, with inflammation and wearing of the stomach walls caused by the ribs rubbing against the abdomen as a result of excessive walking'.[15]

This unusual affliction might have been invented by Rimbaud. The idea that walking wears the stomach thin would be quite at home among the paradoxes of his *chansons*: even the arrangement of internal organs is self-defeating. The world of Rimbaud's body showed no evidence of a benevolent Creator: ribs protrude inwardly, hair causes headaches, eating causes hunger.

The feverish passenger was dropped off on the coast of Italy at Civitavecchia and went straight to hospital – his fifth hospital in five years. When his stomach had recovered, he visited Rome, and then, towards the end of 1877, returned to the Ardennes via Nice (perhaps)[16] and Marseille, full of images that would never be divulged.

I'll keep quiet: poets and visionaries would be jealous. I'm a thousand times richer than they. Let's lock it all away like the ocean.[17]

In the last three years, Rimbaud had spent about fifteen months at home and about twenty-one at sea or on the road. He had visited thirteen different countries – excluding coastlines seen from the deck of a ship – and travelled over 32,000 miles. He already had more than enough material for his anecdotage. He had worked as a pedlar, an editorial assistant, barman, farm labourer, language teacher, private tutor, factory worker, docker, mercenary, sailor, tout, cashier and interpreter, and he was about to add a few more jobs to the list. On almost every occasion, he had done something for which he was not previously qualified.

Though he lacked the most ordinary qualification of all – the baccalauréat – he had a working knowledge of five languages, had seen more sights and experienced more interesting intoxications than an English lord on the Grand Tour, published a book, been arrested in three countries and repatriated from three others. The most he had ever earned from his writing had been a free subscription to a magazine, but he had left behind a body of work that would one day open up new regions of the mind to poetic explorers. He had begged, been to jail, committed approximately twelve imprisonable offences with impunity, and survived war, revolution, illness, a gunshot wound, his own family and the Cape of Good Hope. He had been on intimate terms with some of the most remarkable writers and political thinkers of the age.

The Arthur Rimbaud who eventually washed up on the shores of East Africa was not a helpless innocent.

*

FOR THE NEXT eleven months, the story of Rimbaud's life is an aerial pursuit over dense vegetation. The reconnaissance photographs sometimes reveal the image of a moving figure, composed of a few bits of data, but some of the images may not even be Rimbaud. One account has him charging about 'all over Switzerland'[18] at a time when he was seen in Paris.* Once, he was said to have worked as a

* On two other Rimbauds, see note 19. The Rimbaud who carved his name on the

bank clerk.[20] On another occasion, 'the man with soles of wind' sold bootlaces.[21] Apart from the following snippets, the chronology is just a small bundle of file-cards labelled 'before September 1879'.

WINTER 1877–8. Mme Rimbaud had bought a house in the village of Saint-Laurent, two miles east of Charleville. In this 'studious retreat', Rimbaud buried himself in textbooks and, with philomathic fervour, memorized the principles of algebra and geometry, mechanics and engineering.[22]

APRIL 1878. Delahaye wrote to Verlaine: 'It's a fact that Rimbe was seen in Paris. A friend of mine spotted him in the Latin Quarter towards Easter.'[23]

SUMMER 1878: Rimbaud works on his mother's farm at Roche and is mistaken by some of the locals for an itinerant labourer. Delahaye witnessed 'his strength, courage and endurance, and the instant skill that he drew from his sharp-eyed, versatile intelligence'.[24]

AUTUMN 1878: Delahaye to Verlaine: 'The "man with soles of wind" has decidedly vanished into thin air. Not a peep.'[25]

*

JUST BEFORE RIMBAUD comes reliably into view again, the trail divides. The following two sequences of events are equally plausible:

A. In Hamburg, an enterprising young Frenchman, recently employed on a farm, introduces himself to some merchants and is entrusted with an errand. He is to proceed to Genoa and from there to Alexandria. This proves to be a poor bargain: the passage to Egypt (about £40) soaks up all the profit.

B. In Charleville, Arthur invents a story for his mother about some Hamburg merchants who want him to go to Alexandria. After arriving

Temple of Luxor was probably a Napoleonic soldier. The other Rimbaud, a looter of shipwrecks, can be identified as a J. B. (Jean-Baptiste?) Rimbaud.[19]

in Genoa, he tells her that 'a passage to Egypt costs a fortune, and so there's no profit'. In other words, she should still expect him to ask for money.[26]

The one certainty is that Rimbaud went to Genoa towards the end of 1878. His hair-raising route is known from the magnificent letter he sent on 17 November 1878 to his 'Dear friends' (his mother and sister, referred to as acquaintances rather than as blood relations).

He left home on his twenty-fourth birthday (20 October 1878) and headed east, intending to tackle the fearsome St Gotthard Pass (or, in Rimbaud's desanctified form: 'the Gotthard').

On either side of Rimbaud's crossing of the Alps, there is an intriguing sequence of events. The day before he wrote his letter, his father died in Dijon at the age of sixty-two. Rimbaud's twenty-nine-day journey, most of which was completed by mail-coach and train, could easily have included a detour south to Dijon.

Whether or not he saw his father again before he died, it is curious that when Rimbaud wrote to his mother in December, asking for a reference, he instructed her to sign as a married woman – 'Épouse Rimbaud' – despite the fact that she had been calling herself 'Widow Rimbaud' for the last eighteen years.

The known itinerary is this: Rimbaud left the coach at the foot of the snowbound pass, near the mouth of the unfinished St Gotthard Tunnel, and set off into the mountains on foot with a small group of other travellers. The first part of his account describes the ascent. It was apparently intended as a geography lesson for his sister. Rimbaud had a teacherly eye for the seemingly obvious detail:

> People who are unaccustomed to the sight of mountains learn that a mountain may have peaks, but that a peak is not a mountain. Thus, the summit of the Gotthard covers an area of several kilometres.

This unexpectedly memorable observation – the Alps are blunt – is a glimpse of the philomath revelling in his demystified world: the satisfying obduracy of physical fact and the inaccuracy of Romantic engravings.

Gradually, the facts gain an almost vindictive momentum:

No more shadows above, below or on either side, despite the enormous objects all about. No more road, precipices, gorge or sky: nothing but white to dream, to touch, to see or not to see, since it's impossible to look up from the white botheration that one supposes to be the middle of the path. It's impossible to raise your head in such a biting wind with your eyelashes and moustache turned to stalactites, your ears lacerated and your neck swollen up. Without the shadow that one is oneself, and without the telegraph poles that mark the hypothetical road, one would be as confused as a sparrow in an oven. [. . .]

[. . .] You wander off course, sink into the snow up to your ribs, then up to your armpits . . . A pale shadow behind a cutting: it's the Gotthard hostel, a civil and medical establishment – an ugly hulk of pinewood and stones; a small steeple. At the sound of the bell, a shifty-looking young man comes to the door. You climb to a dirty, low-ceilinged room where you are treated, by right, to bread and cheese, soup and drink. You see the lovely big yellow dogs that everyone has heard about. Soon the stragglers come in off the mountain, half dead. In the evening there are thirty of us. After the meal, we are each allocated a hard mattress with inadequate blankets. At night, the hosts can be heard giving vent, in sacred hymns, to their satisfaction at having spent another day robbing the governments that subsidize their shack.

[. . .] This morning, in the sun, the mountain is marvellous: the wind has gone, and it's all downhill, taking shortcuts, with leaps and mile-long tumbles that bring you to Airolo, the other end of the tunnel, where the road looks alpine again, circular and obstructed, but descending.

This splendid, rumbling avalanche of a letter deserves to appear in any anthology of Romantic mountaineering – preferably as an epilogue. The intimations of transcendence that are supposed to elevate the poet's soul above the path of tribulation are smothered. Human beings are cut off at the armpits. Divine assistance takes the form of a monastic scam. This is Nature without saints and angels, cluttered with 'enormous objects' (usually called mountains); a world of vexations and ludicrous extremes.

Rimbaud's crossing of the Alps is like an open-air *Illumination*, written for an unliterary audience. This is the same godless universe in which a kind of absolute can be attained at the expense of the personality, where the writer himself is just a 'shadow' in the homi-cidal whiteness.

As the seasons passed, Rimbaud's writing would gradually strip itself bare to reveal the obsessions underneath. This carefully written page re-enacts the seasonal drama of the last eight years. In Act I, the traveller leaves the road and is reduced to a state of helplessness. Act II brings the 'free hospitality', the regimentation and the bogus charity. Finally, after a night of loathing and impatience, the joy of fresh departure.

Until now, the drama had always ended with a return to Act I. When Rimbaud sailed from Genoa on the evening of 18 November 1878,[27] lying on the deck under a blanket and a cloudy Mediterranean sky, he might have hoped that the new continent would bring a different ending.

27

Explosive

'Behold [. . .] a flock of white doves, carrying in their beaks
garlands of scented flowers that Venus had plucked in the
gardens of Cyprus.'

> (Rimbaud, Latin composition, regional examination,
> 6 November 1868)

WITHIN A FORTNIGHT, the consulates and hotel bars of
Alexandria turned up three possibilities: 'a big farming concern
about 25 miles from Alexandria', 'the Anglo-Egyptian Customs', and
a company of French contractors on Cyprus. Thinking in seasons, as
usual, Rimbaud was hoping to find 'a good job to last the winter'.

When he wrote in December 1878 to ask his mother for a
testimonial, there was a hint of trepidation. It was the first time he
had applied for a salaried position. Bureaucrats were consigning his
life to printed forms.

> Be sure not to say that I only stayed at Roche for a while, because
> they'd ask more questions and I'd never hear the end of it. Also, it
> would make the people from the farming company think that I was
> capable of directing works.
>
> [. . .] Soon I'll send you details and descriptions of Alexandria and
> Egyptian life. No time today.

On Rimbaud's accelerated time-scale, the farming company was a
distant prospect: they would not be hiring 'for a few weeks'. Instead,

he discussed terms with 'an obliging and talented' French engineer and sailed for Cyprus, where he was to work for the E. Jean & Thial Fils construction company as an interpreter.

Britain had taken over the administration of Cyprus from the Ottoman Empire a few months before and was turning the island into another bastion on the route to India. Great works were planned, as Rimbaud told his mother: 'Railways, forts, barracks, hospitals, harbours, canals, etc. are going to be built.'

This was the Empire whose 'logic' and 'energy' Rimbaud had admired in London. Perhaps, one day soon, he would have his own piece of the frontier – a new Roche, warmed by the Mediterranean sun. 'On 1 March', he told his mother, 'they are going to allocate plots of land costing only the registry fee.'

Rimbaud reached Cyprus on 16 December 1878 and met his new employers in the shabby little town of Larnaca. 'Interpreting' turned out to be a euphemism. He was to take charge of a stone quarry, sixteen miles to the east at a place called Potamos. He would be responsible for food, equipment, wages and time-keeping, and would submit regular reports to the company.

There were few traces of modern civilization in Larnaca, which still lacked a harbour. By the time Rimbaud reached the village of Xylophagou, the modern world had vanished altogether. From there, it was another hour on foot to the worksite.[1]

Rimbaud's letters to his mother and sister are often as bleak as tourist brochures are rosy. This – and the island's later incarnation as a holiday resort – have led some to suspect him of exaggerating the hardship. But his picture of south-eastern Cyprus in 1878 was quite accurate. In the first five months of British rule, eighty soldiers had died of malaria. Typhoid was common. Later, there would be droughts and locusts.[2]

There's nothing here but a chaos of rocks, the river and the sea. There's only one house. No soil, no gardens, not a single tree. In summer, the temperature is 80 degrees. At the moment, it's often 50. This is the winter. Sometimes it rains. We eat poultry, hens, etc. All the Europeans have been ill, except me. [. . .] Three or four have died.

Rimbaud's spare, excarnated style has been interpreted as a sign of despondency. There were certainly moments of anxiety and self-pity. At the end of his letter, he asked for news of home and gave his mother an opportunity to show that he was needed or missed: 'Would you prefer that I came back?' But for a few months, he blossomed in his 'desert' like a cactus.

After stock-piling languages for six years, he was well able to communicate with the motley workforce of Greeks, Syrians, Maltese, Cypriots, and an impoverished Orthodox priest. He quickly mastered the essential bluffing techniques that teaching manuals rarely mention:

DELAHAYE: How did you manage to be a foreman when you knew nothing about the work?
RIMBAUD: Easy. I watched them doing what they did, and then I told them what they had to do. And they took me very seriously.[3]

One day, when the entire workforce was drunk, he discovered that the cashbox from which he was supposed to pay their wages had been raided. According to Delahaye,

Without becoming flustered, he sought out the wretches, told each one individually of his disappointment, explained his own liability in the matter, and pointed out the harm they were doing to their comrades. In the end, he won them over. Most of them, once they had sobered up, hastened to return the money.[4]

In Cyprus, Rimbaud had an image of himself that was closer to other people's perception of him than to his own inherited loathing: an unusually capable and intrepid twenty-four-year-old in charge of a volatile crew of foreign navvies. The new foreman had an air of precocious authority and compelling indifference. He was quick-witted, physically courageous and pleasantly unpedantic. Under Rimbaud's jurisdiction, Potamos was one of the noisiest stretches of coast on the Mediterranean. To keep the workers happy, he allowed needlessly large amounts of explosive to be used. A few resounding detonations of blasting powder had an excellent effect on morale.[5]

This is a rare image of an almost happy Rimbaud: the poet of the

Illuminations, fishing in the river, sleeping on the beach, and blowing up the landscape.

However, since the workers were employed by the day, it was difficult to maintain a stable régime. In April, as a result of 'quarrels with the workers', he asked the company to supply him with arms. In a letter home, he wondered what had happened to 'the tent and the dagger' he had ordered from Paris eight weeks before.[6] Even the most proficient manager was likely to find himself in awkward situations.

By now, the fleas and mosquitoes were hard at work. The heat was a constant punishment. A fever forced him to leave the island at the end of May 1879, but he was intending to return as soon as possible. At Larnaca, his employers gave him a testimonial. Rimbaud showed it to Delahaye that summer with more pride than he had ever shown in his published work: 'We have always been very satisfied with [M. Arthur Rimbaud's] services and he is free of any obligation to the company.'

Most of Rimbaud's own manuscripts have disappeared, but the testimonial from the quarry company has survived.

*

AT ROCHE, RIMBAUD'S fever was diagnosed as typhoid. This was a serious setback. After helping out on the farm, he left again for Marseille, but was too ill to continue. He had the strange idea that this fever, picked up 15 degrees to the south, was the result of the clammy, northern weather. 'We cultivate the fog! We eat fever with our watery vegetables . . .'[7] He told Delahaye that his constitution was changing. His body had already migrated: 'I need warm countries now, the shores of the Mediterranean at the very least . . .'[8]

Cyprus seems to have loosened the elastic that attached him to the Ardennes. Delahaye was slightly awed when he called at the farm. Rimbaud had a swarthy complexion, slab-like cheeks, and 'a deep, low-pitched voice, full of calm energy'. He found his friend at harvest-time, rhythmically heaving the sheaves of wheat overhead to his mother, who formed the haystack. According to Isabelle, he sang songs in Greek and Arabic that were all the more 'ravishingly harmonious' for being incomprehensible.[9]

That evening, Delahaye joined the family for dinner. Mme Rimbaud urged Arthur to serve his friend – a curious custom, in the traveller's view. He laughed: 'I don't like to serve or to be served.'[10] When they went for a walk, Delahaye, still the poet's straight man, romantically admired the pretty patchwork of fields. Rimbaud examined the landscape and saw a scene of needless waste, a textbook image of institutionalized stupidity.

> It would be better to have less variety and more control. There are too many landowners. The use of machinery is limited, not to say impossible because the plots are small and scattered. Individual farmers lack the means to develop the land by fertilizing it, rotating crops, and so on. They are unable to do things on a large scale. They have to work harder for smaller profits. The so-called 'great advance of 1789' – the division of property – is a scourge.[11]

Delahaye relates this scene to the good old days, when the intellectual terrorist of Charleville was drafting his Communist manifesto; but there is nothing to suggest that Rimbaud had in mind a socialist collective. His comments could easily be mistaken for a passage from Balzac's *Les Paysans*. For Rimbaud, as for Balzac, it was the Revolution that had ruined the countryside. The future – Rimbaud's future – now lay with imperial capitalism.

Sensing perhaps that this would be his last opportunity, Delahaye finally asked the big question: 'So! No more literature, then?'

Rimbaud's expression seems to have given Delahaye some difficulty, and he later admitted that he failed to understand the answer:

> He shook his head, laughed a little laugh – half-amused, half-irritated – as if I had asked him, 'Do you still play with a hoop?' Then he answered simply, '*Je ne m'occupe plus de ça.*' ('I have nothing to do with *that* any more.')[12]

Oracles are often reluctant to be interviewed and usually take advantage of any imprecision in the question. 'Literature' was not the same as 'writing'. It was used to refer to 'the world of letters', 'the community of writers'. Verlaine treated it as the antonym of 'poetry'. Later, on the rare occasions when Rimbaud alluded to his past, his disgust was nearly always directed against the sordid life he had led as a poet, not against the poetry itself. The answer he gave Delahaye is significantly reminiscent of a phrase in the letter of October 1875, referring, not to his poems, but to Verlaine: '*Je n'ai plus d'activité à me donner de ce côté-là à présent*'. – No outstanding business in that department.

Without being asked, he gave a similar reply one evening that summer in Charleville. He had gone to town to order a suit. After instructing the tailor to send the bill to his mother, he went to the café and met some old school friends. A huge distance lay between them: the tanned colonial with his long legs thrust under the table, resting like an athlete who knows how to conserve energy; his friends, with their fancy canes, bowler hats and little pot-bellies, pregnant with respectability.

Ernest Millot was congratulating Louis Pierquin on his acquisition of some books published by Lemerre. (Lemerre was the publisher of the Parnassians, whose display Rimbaud had greedily inspected on his second trip to Paris.) Hearing this, Rimbaud broke his silence:

> 'Buying books – especially books like those – is completely idiotic. You've got a block on your shoulders that ought to take the place of every book. The only thing books are good for is sitting on shelves and hiding the flaking plaster of old walls!'
>
> For the rest of the evening, he was unusually jolly – exuberantly so. At 11 o'clock, he left us – forever.[13]

*

RIMBAUD'S RETURN TO the south, in the spring of 1880, did not begin well. Despite his complaints about northern swamp fever, he had become quite affectionately bound to the farm, like a bird to its annual nest – a bird that flew north in winter. In his next letter (May 1880), he asked for news of 'Le père Michel' (a servant) and another farmyard fixture called 'Cotaîche' (a horse). His combative remark about books might have been a cry of poetic freedom, but it could just as well have been the comment of a farmer for whom books are an idler's excuse.

It was clear by now that Rimbaud would never be given a free rein on the farm. Instituting a matrilineal tradition, Mme Rimbaud had decided that Isabelle would take over. The mother of Arthur

Rimbaud is not usually allowed to change in biographies of her son, except at the very end. But the days of sending policemen after the runaway were long gone. Vitalie Rimbaud had been twenty-nine when Arthur was born. Now she was fifty-four, and anxious to provide herself with a predictable future. Frédéric had turned out to be a waster, and it was time that Arthur went and made something of himself. His question, 'Would you prefer that I came back?' had obviously been answered in the negative.

Rimbaud reached Alexandria in March 1880, failed to find work, and sailed again for Cyprus at the end of April. The construction company had folded, but his references were so good that the British authorities gave him the job of supervising the building of the new Governor's summer residence (or 'palace', as Rimbaud called it) on the summit of Mount Troodos.[14]

For most of May, he was alone in a wood cabin 6,400 feet above sea-level with a British engineer, in the middle of a pine forest. Despite the 'healthy' air, he was suffering from palpitations. Heat was no longer a problem:

At this altitude, it is, and will be for another month, unpleasantly cold. It rains and hails, and the wind is strong enough to blow you over. I've had to buy a mattress, blankets, overcoat, boots, etc., etc.

As soon as the first gang of fifty workers arrived on 22 May, he began to look to the next job. He wrote to ask his mother for two books: *Le Livre de poche du Charpentier* (*The Carpenter's Handbook*) and an exhaustive, illustrated guide to sawmills. Where Delahaye might have seen a dark, romantic forest, Rimbaud saw timber.

His lapidary phrases, lists, underlinings and etceteras were a sign of mounting impatience. He was exasperated by his mysterious illness, unhappy with his British colleague, and angry about everything – the need to travel everywhere on horseback, the cost of food, the belligerent wind, and the time it would take for the books to arrive. Amazingly, when he wrote home on Sunday, 23 May, he raised the dreaded spectre of military service. He had decided to go and settle the matter with the French Consul (who happened to have been a close friend of the young Baudelaire), 'and let things take their course'. It was almost as if he wanted to be repatriated.

On 4 June, he wrote again to say that the weather had improved and that he was intending to leave in a few days 'for a freestone and lime company, where I hope to earn some money'.

It was then, while he hesitated between Europe and Africa, that the obscure catastrophe occurred.

*

SHORTLY BEFORE 17 June 1880, the 'Clerk of Works employed in Superintendence'[15] was making his way down Mount Troodos, moving quickly and stealthily through the forest.

The nearest port was Limassol, twenty-seven miles away. As he reached the foothills, the temperature was rising. Down in the bay, a ship was making sail for Egypt.

Instead of waiting for the regular steamer, he rowed out and boarded the ship. It sailed with the Clerk of Works on board – another transient European, keeping himself to himself.

For a long time, after the coast of Cyprus had disappeared from view, the summit of Mount Troodos remained on the horizon.

*

TWICE IN THE next four months, Rimbaud gave contradictory explanations for his sudden departure:[16] 'arguments with the paymaster general and the engineer'; the 'company' (in this case, the British Empire) 'ceased operations'. Years later, in Africa, where murky pasts were commonplace, the word was that Rimbaud had 'committed some kind of misdemeanour on a Greek island'.

The Italian trader, Ottorino Rosa, who rode with Rimbaud on long expeditions at the end of the 1880s, heard him talk about his time in Cyprus as a part of his troubled past:

> Disgusted with the 'Bohemian' life he was leading, he had expatriated himself in 1880 and ended up in Cyprus as the employee of a construction company. He had only just arrived when an unfortunate work accident, which cost a native his life, forced him to flee in haste on a sailing-ship bound for Egypt.

Rosa's other account is more specific:

There [on Cyprus], he had the misfortune, when throwing a stone, to strike a native worker on the temple, killing him instantly. In fear, he took refuge on a ship that was about to sail.

This is a more plausible and reliable explanation than Rimbaud's muddled half-truths. Rosa, who was generally defensive of Rimbaud – an 'eccentric' but 'honourable' man – was writing private memoirs, not preparing a sensational account for publication.

This accidental killing is not an isolated incident. Rimbaud's years in Africa are punctuated by sudden eruptions of rage and peculiar violence. He might have been fortunate only to face a charge of manslaughter.

It is possible, of course, to imagine the poet sailing for the Arabian deserts in 1880, hungry for the picturesque unknown, filling his lungs with warm sea air under the flapping sheets of an Egyptian felucca. It is also possible to read his poems as a guide to his future life – postcards sent before the holiday. But which of the many Rimbauds should be singled out as the real one – the nabob returning with 'limbs of steel, a dark skin and a furious eye', the drunken sleeper on the beach, or the witless, dancing Negro waiting for the white man to disembark with his Bibles and guns?

If that great metaphor of a life, 'Le Bateau ivre' – written in the waiting-room of Rimbaud's youth – still haunted his memory nine years on, it could only have sounded like the voice of derision. Some voices were too familiar ever to be silenced.

> I've seen archipelagos of stars! and islands
> Whose delirious skies lie open to the wanderer:
> Are these the fathomless nights where you sleep and are in exile,
> Million golden birds, O future strength?

Part Four

(1880–1891)

28

Empires

'Ship me somewheres east of Suez, where the best is
                                        like the worst,
Where there aren't no Ten commandments, an' a man
                                        can raise a thirst'

(Rudyard Kipling, 'Mandalay')[1]

T HERE WERE FEW worse places to be an unemployed drifter, and few so full of promise. In 1880, the Red Sea was the empty heart of two Empires: the British, which owned the entrance and the exit – the Suez Canal and Aden; and the French, with its toe-hold on the African coast across the Bab el Mandeb strait. The French answer to Aden was a strip of barren shore in the Gulf of Tadjoura: a clutch of mud huts with almost no perceptible vegetation and a tiny garrison of feverish soldiers. The colony of Obock was constantly besieged by Danakil (or Afar) tribesmen whose great aim in life was to kill a 'rabid dog' (as white men were known).

Six months after Rimbaud arrived in the region, the French Government warned settlers not to expect any encouragement or protection. Obock was simply a coal station on the route to Indo-China. For the same reason, Aden was a dependency of the British Raj in India. The Red Sea was just beginning to attract interest in its own right. Long before it had any reason to do so, Whitehall suspected the French of trying to forge an east–west route to the Nile Basin – the first stage, supposedly, of a 3,500-mile road that would eventually join the Gulf of Aden to French possessions on the Atlantic. The British, meanwhile, were dreaming of a transcontinental highway that would run like a pump along the north–south axis from Egypt to South Africa.

Abyssinia lay at the hypothetical crossroads. It was one of the few parts of known Africa that had yet to come under European domination. The fabled land of Prester John seemed to be the source of several commodities that were vital to European economies, especially coffee. It was a seductive blank on the map that had men in offices 4,000 miles away sketching out new empires or dreading expensive foreign policy disasters. Italy had already laid claim to Assab (now in Eritrea) in the name of a steamship company. Later, Spain and Russia would declare an interest.

This was the volatile and alluring region that Rimbaud came to know more intimately than almost any other European: a mysterious void in which practically anything – tales of a great river, a packing crate on a shore seen from a passing ship – could send tremors of excitement through the foreign ministries of several countries. The idea that Rimbaud vanished into almost meaningless solitude should be dismissed immediately. Dangerously unmotivated by greed or personal glory, he was about to make his home at the intersection of several empires.

*

FOR TWO MONTHS, Rimbaud 'wandered the Red Sea' in growing desperation. With the first sprinkling of European capital, a few tough traders had sprouted on the edge of the Sudanese and Arabian deserts, but no one was hiring workers. This was imperial capitalism in a tenuous, bacterial state. Its only function was to siphon off a tiny share of the trade that had linked East Africa with the Arabian peninsula since Old Testament times.

In June, he saw Jeddah, with its panoramic population, bound for Baghdad and the Middle East – slaves captured in unrecorded wars in parts of Africa that no European had seen. He crossed the Red Sea to Suakin, the end of the caravan routes that drained the Sudan of gold and ivory, and then to Massawa, 300 miles further south – a once flourishing port that was now in the hands of the rickety

Egyptian Empire and close to collapse: the hinterland was held by the Abyssinian Emperor Yohannes, whose predecessor's remains Rimbaud had seen at the British Museum.

A blank 'etc.' in Rimbaud's list of places suggests an exhaustive search for work. He recrossed the Sea to the Ottoman port of Hodeidah, a devastated, treeless place, surprisingly alive with trade: pearls, spices, tobacco, coffee and slaves.

At Hodeidah, Rimbaud fell ill, perhaps from the after-effects of typhoid. He had no more money, no apparent hope of work, no friends, and a death on his conscience. His face looked like a mask of leather. Someone who saw him that October remembered a 'strangely precocious' young man whose hair had turned quite grey.[2] None of the eye-witness accounts of Rimbaud in Africa mentions his famous blue eyes.

At last, his luck changed. At Hodeidah, a Frenchman called Trébuchet took him to the hospital. M. Trébuchet worked for one of the four French companies that were operating in the region. He told Rimbaud about an ambitious young man from Lyon, almost exactly Rimbaud's age, who had gone to Aden two months before to set up a coffee export business. Alfred Bardey had just set off for the interior but had left a retired Colonel in charge. The Colonel was a friend of M. Trébuchet. When Rimbaud had recovered, Trébuchet gave him a letter of recommendation and put him on a ship for Aden.

Rimbaud passed through the Bab el Mandeb ('the Gate of Tears') for the second time in his life towards the middle of August 1880.

*

AT STEAMER POINT, under the jagged skyline of volcanic rock, the open arms of the bay revealed a long smile of white buildings: arcades on the ground floor, verandahs above. A vast sign, visible from the ship, proclaimed one of these buildings to be the 'GRAND HÔTEL DE L'UNIVERS'. Originally named 'Hôtel Suel' by its owner, Jules Suel, it now declared its infinite superiority over its neighbour, the relatively modest Hôtel de l'Europe.

Rimbaud was rowed ashore to the 'Bender', where trophies from the vast African hinterland were sold to travellers and whetted the appetite of explorers: silver and amber necklaces, spears and swords, ostrich eggs and animal skins, priced according to size: 3 rupees for a monkey, 8 for a panther and 15 for a zebra. Sometimes, human skulls were brought back from distant conquests, but there were no recommended prices for these in the official Aden Handbook.

The owner of 'the Universe' was a large, lively man in colonial white cotton and pith helmet who seemed to thrive in conditions that made other Europeans dissolve in their own sweat. There were few pies in which M. Suel did not have a finger. His hotel was an information exchange and a source of capital for trading ventures that would have been illegal if legislation had been able to keep up with colonial enterprise.

The last Frenchman to stay at 'the Universe' had been an energetic young man called Henri Lucereau. He had just left on a government-funded mission to find the source of what he believed to be an important tributary of the Blue Nile: the Sobat. (The Sobat is an affluent of the White Nile, 350 miles further west.) Having heard the tales of explorers who fell prey to hostile tribes, suffered horrible mutilations and were left for the hyenas or forced to drink boiling water, Lucereau had provided himself with a phial of strychnine. This was standard equipment for African explorers.

The convenient M. Suel happened to be the brother-in-law of the coffee exporters' associate, Colonel Dubar. He directed Rimbaud to the carriages that plied the five miles of stony plain between Steamer Point and Aden: one rupee if the buggy was drawn by a horse, then progressively cheaper as speed and comfort diminished – camels, donkeys and finally human beings ('coolies : 3 annas', according to the Handbook).

The dirt road ran past small mountains of coal, crates of merchandise waiting to be shipped abroad or carried into Aden, a Somali village of straw huts, and then, through the traffic jam of caravans, up a steep slope to the Main Pass Gate into Aden: a white city of dust and noise.

The lists of commodities that passed through the British port give a misleading impression of the place: coffee, spices, scented oils and a huge variety of gums and resins – Arabic and Persian, rosin, frankincense and myrrh, benjamin and olibanum. The overall effect was an intolerable stench, a cacophony of smells to which the goats and sheep, living or cooked, made an important contribution.

On the advice of M. Suel, Alfred Bardey had rented an important-looking building in the centre of town. It stood opposite a minaret and the courthouse: six white arches supporting a wide verandah. Large, square blinds shielded the offices and living quarters.

Colonel Dubar put the new man to work immediately. Rimbaud was to supervise the sorting and packing process and maintain discipline in the 'harem'. The coffee arrived from Africa in bales. It was weighed, paid for and unwrapped by Hindu women, many of them wives of Indian soldiers in the British army. They squatted on the stone floor under the cool arcades. The beans were sorted, the husks set aside for local consumption, then weighed again and packed into tight bales with a double layer of palm-matting and rough local cloth. Rimbaud was paid a small, probationary wage of five or six francs a day. It included board, lodging, laundry and the use of a company horse and carriage.

When Alfred Bardey returned from his exploratory mission, he found the new foreman hard at work: 'a strapping fellow with an intelligent, energetic look about him'. Although M. Rimbaud rarely spoke, Bardey managed to discover that he was a native of Dôle (Captain Rimbaud's birthplace) and had recently managed a stone quarry on Cyprus. 'He accompanies his explanations with short, sharp little gestures with his right hand and *à contre-temps*' ('off the beat'). This curious observation of Rimbaud's syncopated gesturing matches Bardey's later descriptions of him – a man whose body was never in complete agreement with his mind, who often left things unsaid and dismissed what he did say.

Bardey was instantly impressed with the new man's competence. Rimbaud gave orders in Arabic and earned the respect of his workers. They called him '*Karani*', which means 'the Wicked One', but is roughly equivalent to 'the Boss'.

Rimbaud might have been expected to enjoy his new home. The weather was a total contrast to northern France. He had always complained of tasteless, watery stews and 'French vegetables, / Snarling, consumptive and ridiculous, / Amongst which the bellies of basset hounds / Navigate peacefully at twilight'.[3] According to

Delahaye, Rimbaud preferred the glistening, resistant pulp of charred steak, the vivid red of cherries.[4] In Aden, spiced dishes were sold in the streets with roasted coffee. The markets were full of watermelons, bananas, limes and unknown fruits from Abyssinia. He should at least have found some sensual consolation. He wrote home on 25 August 1880:

> Aden is a horrible rock, without a single blade of grass or a single drop of fresh water. [. . .] The constant temperature of a very cool and ventilated office, night and day, is 35°C. Everything is very expensive, and so on. But there's nothing to be done about it: I'm like a prisoner here.

Over the months and years, Rimbaud would hammer away at his themes, adding new details, perfecting his rage, until the melody returned like the *fortissimo* passage of a hellish *Bolero*:

> You have no idea what it's like here. There isn't a single tree, not even a withered one, not a single blade of grass, patch of earth or drop of fresh water. Aden is the crater of an extinct volcano, the bottom of which is filled with sea-sand. There's absolutely nothing to see or touch except lava and sand which are incapable of producing the tiniest scrap of vegetation. The environs are an absolutely arid desert of sand. Here, however, the walls of the crater prevent the air from entering, and we roast at the bottom of this hole as if in a limekiln.[5]

This apocalyptic weather report should not be confused with dismay. This was the voice of an invalid whose anxieties have finally been quelled by the utter certainty of death. For Rimbaud, no snowdrift was deep enough nor any desert sufficiently stifling. His style brings to mind the Somali warriors who added ash to the coffee they chewed on long treks to give it 'bite'. The black lava of Aden was the ideal backdrop for Rimbaud's caustic sense of humour. 'Aden, as everyone acknowledges', he told his mother and sister on 22 September, 'is the most boring place in the world, after the place where you live, that is.'

His real complaint was his inferior status – not something that had troubled him much before. But now this waste of talent was beginning to look like confirmation of his failure. In September, he was already planning his escape:

> Since I'm the only employee in Aden with any intelligence, if, at the end of my second month here, on 16 October, they don't give me two hundred francs a month, plus expenses, I'm going. I'd rather leave than be exploited. [. . .] I'd probably go to Zanzibar, where there's work to be had.

But instead of sailing on down the African coast, he remained in Aden. Listening to Bardey's discussions with Colonel Dubar, Rimbaud glimpsed the possibility of an ideal life: wandering the world and receiving a salary for doing so. In August, frustrated by endless, incomprehensible tales, Bardey had set off to find out for himself where the coffee came from. Until then, its origins had been a complete mystery: 'Mocha' was simply the name of the Red Sea port from where it first reached Europe in the seventeenth century. The Arab traders had told him of a land called Barr-Adjam (*Terra Incognita*). It was said to lie somewhere to the south-west, on the other side of the Somali desert.

Shortly after news of his death reached Aden, Bardey had returned with exciting news: he had rediscovered the 'Forbidden City' of Harar, 200 miles inland. Although the Egyptians had taken the city in 1875 and killed its ruler, only one European had seen Harar since Richard Burton's daring expedition of 1855.[6]

Rimbaud had read explorers' tales as a schoolboy and would certainly have known the famous account in which Burton described his entry, disguised as a Muslim trader, into 'the ancient metropolis of a once mighty race':

> I doubt not there are many who ignore the fact that in Eastern Africa, scarcely three hundred miles distant from Aden, there is a counterpart of ill-famed Timbuctoo in the Far West. The more adventurous Abyssinian travellers [. . .] attempted Harar, but attempted it in vain. The bigoted ruler and barbarous people threatened death to the Infidel who ventured within their walls.[7]

Rimbaud begged his employer to let him go. Having seen Rimbaud work in the warehouse, Bardey agreed. His associate, Pinchard, had remained in Harar with the blessing of the Egyptian Governor to establish a trading-post. Money, cotton fabrics and other trade items would be required. Rimbaud was to lead the caravan.

Suddenly, the metallic sky of Aden looked almost benign. Rimbaud signed a nine-year contract with Bardey on 10 November 1880. He would receive 150 rupees a month (about 100 francs more than he had hoped for) and – a potential gold-mine – a one-per-cent share in all profits on the Harar agency. He wrote to tell his 'dear friends' that he was about to be completely cut off from civilization: Harar was a city without roads or postal service. 'It goes without saying that one cannot go there unarmed and that one risks leaving one's skin in the hands of the Gallas – though it's not really a serious danger.' After the 'hell' of Aden, it would be a rest cure: 'Because of its altitude, the region is very healthy and cool.'

He asked his mother to order twenty-seven books for him on various subjects: carpentry, metallurgy, tanning, candle-making, mining, deep-sea diving, telegraphy, agricultural machinery, artesian wells and steamships. It was the reading-list of someone who was planning to start their own country. More will be said of this book ordering later. For now, it should be pointed out – since this list has sometimes been quoted as evidence of insanity – that, as his letter makes clear, Rimbaud was ordering books for the whole company. Besides which, no one who has lived in a remote part of East Africa will find it odd that an entrepreneurial spirit like Rimbaud should take an interest in agricultural hydraulics or telegraphy. He did, however, lay particular emphasis on *The Tanner's Manual*. It seems that he was already thinking of expanding the operation.

Rimbaud set off from Aden in mid-November with a young Greek employee called Constantin Righas. They were to sail to Zeila on the Somali coast and then try to recover a few mangy camels that had been left by Bardey with some native porters, most of whom had probably died in the latest smallpox epidemic.

The cooperation of a sinister figure called Abou-Bekr had been obtained in a manner unspecified by Bardey. Abou-Bekr, Pasha of Zeila and Tadjoura, controlled all the slave routes (and therefore all the trade) from the coast to the interior, and had eleven sons to help him. Abyssinia was not a good place for merchants – or even missionaries – who wanted to keep a clean conscience and come back alive.

On 23 November, after 160 miles on an Arab dhow, Rimbaud saw the vivid yellow shoreline of Zeila. Its whitewashed houses and minaret seemed to rise directly out of the blue-black sea. He formed his caravan quickly and set off on horseback into the unknown.

Meanwhile, Alfred Bardey had left for Paris to present his findings at the Geographical Society. In Lyon, he received a telegram from Aden, dated 1 December: '*Lucereau assassiné Itou.*' The young explorer had been slaughtered in September by warriors from the Itou tribe. It is not known whether he had been able to take his strychnine.

Lucereau had perished at a place called Warabeili, 500 miles from the river he had set out to find, but just fifteen miles from Harar.

By the time the news reached Aden, it was too late to warn Rimbaud.

29

The Unknown

'[. . .] lands that until now have been inaccessible to white men.'

(Rimbaud to his mother and sister, 16 April 1881)

A TRAVELLER IN a hostile desert allows the monotony to evacuate his mind of all but the essentials. Rimbaud's only account of his first caravan into Africa is a bone picked clean by vultures: 'Twenty days on horseback across the Somali desert'. He said nothing of the nomad encampments, the songs of his guides and porters, the depredations of hyenas or the vital luxuries of the oasis. Most of the missing detail is supplied by Alfred Bardey's account of the same route.

Two weeks after leaving Zeila, the camels climbed above the vast Somali plain into the cloud forests and the black mountain passes. At 3,000 feet, it was almost chilly. Figures appeared on the skyline and disappeared. In this part of East Africa, European travellers never arrived anywhere unexpected.

The mountains gave way to a grassy plateau grazed by herds of zebu. The Chercher highlands were semi-arid but seemed almost miraculously lush after the sulphurous desert. This balmy region was often called 'the Switzerland of Africa'.[1] The red soil supported haphazard, unrotated plots of vegetables, coffee, bananas, tobacco, saffron, an inferior cotton and the mildly intoxicating leaves of qat. There were groves of orange, lemon and almond trees, mostly uncultivated. The staple food was durra (a kind of sorghum). When the durra crop failed, there was famine.

The Issa guides returned to the coast and were replaced by local tribesmen. They passed through the first Galla villages: thatched, conical huts topped with an earthenware pot or an ostrich egg to keep out evil spirits. Women sat outside the huts making ghee or spinning cotton. When they spotted the white man at the head of the caravan, they came up to inspect him, untucking his clothes to see whether he was white all over.

Harar appeared suddenly at the top of a slope, two miles to the south: a reddish mass on an elongated hill.

From a distance, the Forbidden City was two stumpy grey minarets and some scraggy sycamores on a base of sloping 'gardens' (roughly cultivated fields). Grubby, red-ochre walls surrounded it, apparently unrepaired since the Middle Ages. This was not the shimmering line of whitewashed stone that East African explorers came to expect. For some, the sense of relief created a beautiful mirage that would later be preserved as a fairy-tale engraving; but the accounts of most visitors show the strain of concealed disappointment. Richard Burton was typically abrupt: 'Many would have grudged exposing three lives to win so paltry a prize.'[2]

Rimbaud showed his papers to the Egyptian guards and led his caravan into the city through the Bab el Ftouh ('Gate of Triumph').

Harar was a pandemonium of market traders, craftsmen, beggars, lepers, watchful Egyptian soldiers, and young slaves disguised as travellers (since, by Anglo-Egyptian agreement, the trade had officially ceased to exist). Many of the slaves were still recovering from castration.

Rimbaud passed through the inquisitive crowd, catching phrases of unknown languages, buffeted by the smells of an African market – mouth-watering odours that opened the nostrils only to fill them with the sickly stench of sugar cane, excrement and putrefying flesh.

Harar's 30,000 inhabitants lived in squat, flat-terraced houses of mud and stone, interspersed with conical huts that seemed to have walked in from the countryside. The streets were simply the spaces between the houses, rutted by torrents from the surrounding hills. Street-cleaning was left to the hyenas.

There were two schools which taught Arabic and an embryonic hospital, but the Egyptian administration had no lasting hold. At six o'clock every evening, the gates were closed. Harar was a silent, fearful place at night, besieged by wild animals and, in times of famine, raiders from the surrounding villages.

Rimbaud was welcomed by Bardey's associate, Pinchard, a battle-hardened veteran of Algeria who would have become Rimbaud's closest collaborator and even his co-author if malaria had not forced him to leave for Egypt. They may have stayed at first in a rudimentary house near the central market, but before long an Egyptian-style 'palace' near the main mosque was placed at the company's disposal by the Governor. It was one of the few buildings of more than one storey.

The 'House of Raouf Pasha', once occupied by the Egyptian conqueror of Harar, was a domestic fortress in the centre of the town. The single door opened on to a courtyard. A crude stone staircase led to the upper storey. Beyond lay a little herb and vegetable garden, an open kitchen and a reception room lined with benches covered in red cushions. Shutters had been improvised with dismantled packing-crates. Little red birds fluttered about under the rooves of mud and reeds. Rimbaud and his Greek colleague took the rooms on the first floor with windows looking on to the main square. Flat, grey ants swarmed along the roof-beams.[3]

Rimbaud's first description of Harar, in a letter dated 13 December, is so bald that it says more about him than about his new home. By now, the annihilatory 'etc.' was one of his key words:

> The commercial produce of the region is coffee, ivory, hides, etc. This is a highland region but it is not infertile. The climate is cool but not unhealthy. All European merchandise is imported, by camel. There is a lot to be done in the region.

This was his first message home from what was effectively another planet. Modern astronauts sound poetic by comparison. He elaborated, slightly, two months later:

> You shouldn't think that this region is entirely uncivilized. We have the army, artillery and cavalry (Egyptian), and their administration. It's all exactly the same as in Europe, except that they're a pack of dogs

and bandits. [. . .] The only major trade is the pelts of animals that are milked while they're alive and then flayed. Then there's coffee, ivory and gold; scents, incense, musk, etc. Unfortunately, we're 240 miles [actually 200] from the sea and transport is too expensive.

Rimbaud was writing to please his mother. The sentences are as short and repetitive as entries in a ledger. Syntax is a simple nuisance. There was not the slightest whiff of 'literature'. If poetry had been an intoxication, this was the diet of a recovering alcoholic.

*

RIMBAUD WAS MUCH closer to home in Harar than in Aden. Each letter created a new link. Although the Mayor of Charleville was unlikely to send a warrant officer across the Somali desert, Rimbaud kept reminding his mother of his military duty, asking her to make detailed enquiries. Since his living expenses were paid by the company, he was able to send large sums of money to be invested in France – 2,550 francs by mid-January. His mother was to buy him a commercial directory and 'stuff half a pound of sugar-beet seeds' into the package. Brother Frédéric was to root through 'the Arab papers' left by the late Captain Rimbaud: relics of his years in Algeria. Rimbaud remembered seeing a collection of songs in Arabic and 'a notebook titled *Jokes, puns, etc.*' – a mere teaching aid, of course . . . They were not to suspect him of sentimentality: 'But just send it all as wrapping-paper, because it's not worth the postage.'

The sugar-beet and his father's papers would establish a psychological trade route between the Ardennes and the Horn of Africa. Seeds from Roche would sprout in the red soil of Harar, and his father's linguistic labours would bear fruit in the form of his son's commercial activities.

In the rare moments when he was not preparing a caravan for the coast or bartering with traders from the interior, Rimbaud sat at his table, drinking buttery tea or chewing qat leaves, which had an effect similar to that of coffee, recreating the dark, dependable shadow of the '*Bouche d'Ombre*'. He administered his own reprimands and tried to show that he knew how to suffer for the sake of profit: 'If you think that I'm living like a prince, I am quite certain that I'm living in a very stupid and irritating fashion.'

> Anyway, let's hope we can enjoy a few years of true repose in this life; and it's a good thing that this life is the only one and that it's obvious that it is, since it's impossible to imagine another life more tedious than this!

Until the arrival of other Europeans in Harar, these desolate letters home are practically our only source of information on the life of Rimbaud's mind. This effectively places us in stationary orbit above his dark side: the secure rock-bottom of absolute pessimism.

On the brighter side, new landscapes were dawning. Business was brisk and interesting. There were new languages to be learnt, new markets to develop, and a few Greek and Armenian traders to be driven out of business by efficient competition. When Bardey returned to Harar in April with a Catholic bishop, Rimbaud was clearly delighted to have a new target for his sarcasm: 'He'll probably be the only Catholic in the region.'

Since he first began to wander in 1870, Rimbaud had never stayed in the same place for more than six or seven months. He lived in Harar, or used it as a base, for a whole year. As a kind of mental insurance policy, he kept threatening to leave for Zanzibar or the Great Lakes. He even asked his mother to tell him when work began on the Panama Canal; but these were to remain imaginary escape routes. Harar had all the fascination of small-town life but with the added charm of exoticism and routine atrocity: primitive tribes, ostriches stotting across the square, lepers and slaves, and wild animals – usually leopards and hyenas – to be chased out of town at daybreak with a lantern and a rifle.

Whatever Rimbaud's letters might suggest, he was not living like a hermit. In April, Bardey noticed 'the incontestable signs of syphilis in his mouth'. Since the first symptoms appear within a month, he must have contracted the disease in Harar, which confirms his claim that it did not lack the basic amenities of 'civilization'. According to Bardey, 'he took the greatest care not to pass the illness on to us by eating or drinking utensils'. It did not prevent him from enjoying the company of several other women.

The grim profiteer, seething with frustration and self-pity, is one of Rimbaud's most successful fictions. The complete picture is so far from the traditional image of failure that it calls for some explanation. In some cases, simple ignorance of nineteenth-century Abyssinia is to blame, combined with an indiscriminate use of unreliable versions of Rimbaud's letters. It is also worth mentioning the fact that the only explorers who are credited with their discoveries are those who boast about them loudly and in the right places. But perhaps the main reason Rimbaud's achievements have been ignored is that abject misery was felt to be the proper reward for someone who abandoned the profession to which his critics also belong.

The first sign that Rimbaud was fully engaged with his new world appears in a letter written in January. He and Pinchard had ordered a camera and some developing equipment from Lyon.[4] They wanted to take photographs of the region and its inhabitants for a book on unknown Abyssinia. They also sent off for a naturalist's kit, as Rimbaud explained in his letter:

> I shall be able to send you some birds and animals that have not yet been seen in Europe. I already have a few curiosities and I'm waiting for an opportunity to send them.

Why this should be interpreted as a poet's childish fantasy, and why Rimbaud's collaborator, Pinchard, is never accused of similar stupidity, is a mystery. Abyssinia was rich in unidentified species. Rimbaud would certainly have seen the crooked horns of the mountain nyala – unknown to the outside world until 1919: it was the last large mammal to be named by zoologists. The Highlands also sheltered healthy populations of Simien jackals and their favourite prey, the giant molerat, both unknown in Europe. Rimbaud's birds might have included Rouget's rail, the raucous wattled ibis and the white-eyed gull – a creature first spotted by the *bateau ivre*: 'tossing on my sides the quarrels and droppings of yattering, blond-eyed birds'.

It is hard to imagine what Mme Rimbaud might have done with a wattled ibis or a giant molerat, but at least they would have proved that Arthur was up to something serious.

Special derision has been reserved for Rimbaud's requests for books and instruments. A month after arriving in Harar, he was sending off another of his supposedly demented lists of desiderata to a manufacturer of precision instruments in Paris. ('What was this devil of a man thinking of?' asks a recent French biographer.)[5]

> I should like complete details on the best manufacturers, in France or elsewhere, of mathematical, optical, astronomical, electrical, meteorological, pneumatic, mechanical, hydraulic and mineralogical instruments. I am not interested in surgical instruments. [. . .] I have also been asked to obtain manufacturers' catalogues of mechanical toys [not, as one translator has it, 'sports equipment'], fireworks, conjuring tricks, working models, miniature constructions, etc.

Any Rimbaud biographer who finds this sort of exhaustive planning ridiculous cannot be trusted to have undertaken proper research. This is what Enid Starkie had to say about Rimbaud's surge of enterprise:

> With his usual impulsive eagerness and his customary lack of a sense of proportion, he imagined that he would be able to master all the crafts, in a short space of time, from popular treatises. [. . .] It is pathetic to see these puerile efforts at self-instruction on the part of a man of twenty-six, who at school had carried all before him and then, in a fit of arrogance, had despised scholastic learning and had decided that all book knowledge was worthless. [. . .] Now, regretting his past waywardness, he turned, like a gullible reader of advertisements, to the most popular and most inefficient form of instruction.[6]

Many of Rimbaud's critics have a professional interest in believing that skills and information can be acquired only in the form in which they are officially dispensed. But universities do not have a monopoly on knowledge, though they may have patented certain forms of packaging. Even the examinations once administered by Enid Starkie are not proof against a Rimbaldian strategy of prolonged idleness followed by a short spell of intense, cynical cramming.

Rimbaud's furious stocking of information is neither irrational nor particularly unusual. It is not unknown for visitors to certain parts of Africa to be inspired with grandiose schemes of technical and administrative improvement. In Harar, there was a severe shortage of skills: carpenters and masons were scarce, and a visit to the blacksmith meant a three-hour trek through hostile country. Any sort of expertise was worth a fortune. Since 1879, a young Swiss engineer, Alfred Ilg (later a friend of Rimbaud), had been advising King Menelik in the kingdom of Choa, 250 miles west of Harar, and was already laying the foundations of modern Ethiopia.[7] In 1883, an engineer on a French expedition, hoping for trade concessions, astounded the King with a miniature locomotive and steamship.[8] Rimbaud's mechanical toys might have been used as trade items or to turn hostility into curiosity. Bardey had discovered that firecrackers, for instance, were a good initial defence against rampaging natives.

While the readers of *poètes maudits* often identify with the poets themselves, critics and biographers tend to identify with the parents. Rimbaud does not appear to have kept his mother's letters, but it seems clear from his replies that she would have approved of Enid Starkie. Two years later, Rimbaud was still trying to explain himself:

> As for the books, they will be very useful to me in a country where there's no information and where you end up as stupid as an ass if you don't spend a little time going over your studies. The days and especially the nights are very long in Harar. These books will be a pleasant way to pass the time, since, it must be said, there's no public meeting-place in Harar. One is forced to stay indoors all the time. [. . .]
>
> I'm sending a cheque for a hundred francs, which you can cash and then buy me the books listed below. The money spent on the books will not be wasted.

The former glory of the Collège de Charleville was still a shining example of what the imperial education system could achieve.

*

THE SAME CONDESCENSION has wiped Rimbaud off the map of European journeys of discovery, though there are many snide references to his request for a handbook on the theory and practice of exploration: a useful tool for anyone who hoped eventually to publish their findings with proper charts and measurements.

According to Isabelle, who received letters that she later destroyed, her brother went trading and exploring in the surrounding areas and beyond, for periods of 'between a fortnight and a month'.[9] This matches the gaps in his correspondence: a total of 263 days in his first year in Harar.[10]

Exploring was not just an adventurous form of tourism. Shortly before Rimbaud's arrival, the intrepid Pinchard had undertaken a brief camel-buying expedition to the east of Harar. He was captured by the hostile Guerri tribe and declared on his return that he 'wouldn't do it again for 100,000 francs'. The Egyptians never left the city with fewer than 2,000 soldiers. When Bardey planned a short expedition, the Egyptian Governor warned his porters: 'You'll pay for your journey with your blood.'

Rimbaud's first expedition seems to have taken him into Aroussi and Itou territory to the west of Harar, in the direction of the Awash river, along the route taken by the luckless Lucereau. He was forced to turn back, perhaps by illness, tribal war or cautious guides. Sometimes, the means of transport simply disappeared overnight: camels were stolen by raiders, horses were eaten by lions.

The first expedition mentioned by Rimbaud himself was a rather vague 'grand tour in the desert to buy camels'. This was the sort of sensible, commercial motive that would have pleased his mother. The first editor of Rimbaud's letters, who married Isabelle after her brother's death, also liked to think of him as a serious businessman. He therefore deleted some crucial words from Rimbaud's letter of 4 May 1881. Even though an accurate quotation was available, the words (italicized below) always have been omitted, perhaps to preserve the splendid phrase, 'trafficking in the unknown'. The manuscript came to light in 1998. It proves that Rimbaud's motives were not purely mercantile:

> I am intending to leave this town soon to go trafficking *or exploring on my own account* in the unknown. There is a great lake a few days from here, and it's in ivory country.
>
> [. . .] Just in case things turn out badly and I don't come back, please note that I have a sum of 715 rupees [about 1,430 francs] deposited at the Aden branch. You can ask for it if you think it's worth the bother.

This journey into 'the unknown' was probably the same perilous expedition that Rimbaud was inspired to undertake when the French bishop arrived in Harar with five Franciscan monks: 'I might follow them to lands that until now have been inaccessible to white men' (16 April).

Whether or not Rimbaud attempted the journey under the banner of the Catholic Church, this is a significant moment in the history of African exploration. The hunt for ivory and the religious connection suggest that he had heard about the elephant-rich lands to the west, about twenty days from Harar, where ivory was said to be so abundant that it was used to build houses. The 'great lake' would be Lake Zwai (Ziway) at the northern end of the Rift Valley. The inhabitants of its five islands – Coptic Christians and some surviving worshippers of Isis and Osiris – spoke their own language and lived among the ruins of medieval churches. A monastery, which survives to this day, was said to be the final resting-place of the Ark of the Covenant.[11]

Rimbaud's Ark was a stable financial future and a reliable antidote to boredom. His expeditions had nothing to do with personal glory. The charting of 'totally unexplored regions' was a practical extension of the schoolboy's poetic dream, expressed in the 'Seer' letter:

> He reaches the unknown, and even if, in panic, he ends up losing the ability to understand his own visions, at least he will have seen them! He may burst as he bounds through amazing, unnamable things – other horrible workers will follow. They will start on the horizons where the other one collapsed!

Rimbaud's wholehearted commitment to something that might turn out to be nothing is strongly reminiscent of the vague and glorious 'way of the cross', except that the structure was provided now by hides and ivory instead of aesthetics and Verlaine.

Fortunately, a detailed description exists of one of Rimbaud's early expeditions. In May, news reached the agency that a large number of hides had been amassed at a place called Bubassa, a few days to the south. By 11 June, Rimbaud was ready to leave. The camels were loaded up and his colleagues came to see him off. Bardey remembered the scene:

> Just as he was about to set off at the head of his little procession, Rimbaud wrapped a towel around his head as a turban and draped a

red blanket over his usual garment. He was intending to pass himself off as a Muslim. [. . .]

Sharing our amusement at his fancy dress, Rimbaud agreed that the red blanket which orientalized his European costume might attract robbers. But he wanted to be seen as a rich Mohammedan merchant for the sake of company prestige.

Rimbaud's smile breaks through at precisely the moment when he begins to disappear under a new disguise, like the soldier in his tartan beret or the Englishman in his ten-shilling top hat. Rimbaud was taking a holiday from himself. He rode out through the scruffy Bab el Salaam – the south-eastern gate – past the grovelling lepers and the stench of civilized humanity into the unmapped landscape.

He might never have been seen again.

*

AFTER A FEW days, the volcanic terrain turned into open woodland. The grass huts of Bubassa appeared on the edge of a plain. This was the furthest point south that any European had reached.

The creature in the red cape and turban caused huge excitement. He won the protection of the *boko* (the local chief) and set up two markets on either side of the village. Four sturdy warriors were paid to police the markets. 'He was forced several times', says Bardey, 'to intervene with his *gendarmes* in order to break up fights just as the men who were losing were about to suffer the usual mutilation' (castration).

For about a week, Rimbaud did business with the traders, some of whom had come from very distant regions. At night, he slept on the piles of sweaty hides. Then, having revolutionized the village economy, he returned to Harar on 2 July, surprised to be still alive, and spent the next two weeks in bed with a fever.

Rimbaud had seen the edge of the mysterious Ogaden – an unexplored region that was larger than France and Belgium put together. A great river lay somewhere to the south. A new favourite phrase kept appearing in his letters: 'There's a great deal to be done.'

Still convalescing, he wrote home on 22 July, in 'European costume' again. Whatever his mother thought of him now, at least she couldn't say that he was enjoying himself:

> I'm not forgetting you at all. How could I? [. . .] I think of you and only of you. And what could I tell you anyway of my work here, which is already so repellent to me, and of the country, which I abhor, and so on and so forth. What could I say about the things I've attempted with such extraordinary exertions and which have brought me nothing but fever? [. . .] But it can't be helped. I'm used to everything now. I fear nothing.

30

'Poor Arthur'

'All this buttoning and unbuttoning.'

(Anonymous suicide note)

As the coffee harvest began to come in, Rimbaud found himself stuck in Harar for longer periods. His meteorological paranoia returned. At first, he had found the climate 'healthy', then 'unhealthy'. Now it was 'fractious and humid'.

After 'unpleasant arguments with the management and the rest' (two Greeks and a young Harari called Hadj-Afi), he handed in his resignation but showed no sign of leaving. He was planning expeditions, new trading companies, sudden emigrations: 'All I ask of the world is a good climate and suitable, interesting work. I'll find it one day!'

Meanwhile, typhoid and famine brought a daily crowd of beggars to the door. In the morning, the corpses were gathered up and shovelled into a trench. Rimbaud said nothing of this in his letters. He described the changing seasons like a man on a lonely weather-station. 'You're in winter now, and I'm in summer. The rains have stopped. The weather is very good and quite warm. The coffee trees are ripening.'

Despite the 'unpleasant arguments', Bardey was happy to keep him on. Rimbaud was an 'excessively irritable' patient when the fever was on him; he offended several people with his 'mordant wit', and was often 'silent and morose, appearing to shun the company of his fellow man'; but any business that was entrusted to him turned immediately to profit. When he 'brightened up and chatted amiably', he soon had his audience in stitches: 'We naturally found his stories funny – they were always wittily told – though we could never be sure that we wouldn't be treated in the same fashion when he talked to other people.'[1]

Unlike Rimbaud's literary acquaintances, Alfred Bardey judged him as the working member of a small community and inevitably found him 'rather queer' – a disconcertingly brilliant young man whose friendship would have been a source of delight if the different parts of his personality ever learned to live together.

> I attributed his strange behaviour, with some justification, I believe, to a certain disgust with the world, caused by ordeals of which he said nothing, but which his great intelligence had certainly undergone.
> This was the visible side of his personality. Deep down, he was actually quite gentle and obliging. Everyone who knew him and employed him thought him the very spirit of loyalty and probity.
>
> He was especially kind and helpful to those poor expatriates who leave home in the hope of making a quick fortune and who, utterly broken and disappointed, want only to return home as quickly as possible. He was very discreet and generous in his charity: it was probably one of the very few things he did without sneering or proclaiming his disgust.[2]

When Bardey's brother Pierre arrived in Harar, Rimbaud left for Aden. It was not exactly the joyful 'Départ' of the *Illuminations*: 'Departure in new affection and noise!' 'It is unlikely that I shall ever return here', he told his mother.

By 5 January 1882, one of the most successful and promising traders in East Africa was back in the arid crater-bottom of Aden, cursing his employer, growling at the climate, and waiting for the ideal job.

*

WHEN BARDEY RETURNED to Aden in February 1882, he found Rimbaud sitting in the agency, seething with disgust. Rimbaud was quite certain that someone was stealing his money. The 2,504 francs he sent home in January had turned into 2,250 (the result of bank charges and fluctuating exchange rates). Writing to his mother, he blamed the discrepancy on 'those wretches', the Bardey brothers. 'They're skinflints and scoundrels whose only purpose in life is to exploit the exertions of their employees'. The French Consul would hear of it . . . 'Speak correctly in your letters', he warned his mother, after developing a nasty conviction that the 'skinflints' were opening his mail.

When Rimbaud's letters were published after his death, Bardey was disappointed to see that his friend and employee had been slandering him behind his back:

> When he wrote those things, he had just joined us. He had suffered one disillusionment after another and had been living precariously, probably with people who were not entirely commendable. Since he knew nothing about regular living, he formed some rather grotesque suspicions.
>
> He was simply acting out of misanthropy and regret (I know this to be true) at having wasted his life. That is why he spent his time bemoaning his fate and finding everything around him ignoble and disgusting.[3]

Rimbaud was not necessarily suffering from clinical paranoia. For someone who never forgave himself, insulting other people was a form of recreation; and since his mother thought of herself as an island of probity in a sea of kleptomaniacs, she would be more likely to trust his judgment if he accused all his colleagues of theft and deception.

For the next fourteen months, Rimbaud sat in the hot shade of the Aden office, keeping scrupulous accounts, directing the workers, always with one eye on the open door. The rhythm of his daily life can best be heard in a complete reading of the correspondence, with its false departures and repetitions, its relentless practicality and the continual failure to put anything into practice. Each letter seems to be written between one unfinished novel and the next. His mantra – 'I'm leaving' – is a first line or a last, waiting for the rest of the story. This was the same urgent inertia that had given his *chansons* their strange momentum: 'Unwholesome thirst / Darkens my veins'; 'Crying, I saw gold – and couldn't drink.'

12 February 1882: I am not intending to stay in Aden for long [. . .] If I leave – and I intend to do so quite soon – it will be to return to Harar or to go down to Zanzibar.

15 April 1882: A month from now, I shall either be back in Harar or on my way to Zanzibar.

10 July 1882: I shall probably leave for Harar in a month or two.

28 September 1882: I am intending to leave at the end of the year for the African continent – not Harar this time but Choa.

3 November 1882: I'm leaving for Harar in January 1883.

6 January 1883: I'm leaving for Harar at the end of March.

Rimbaud watched the bales of coffee arrive from Africa and sent them on to Europe. He made plans – the same plans – over and over again. He was going to write a book about unknown parts of Africa. The French Geographical Society would fund his explorations. He wrote to Delahaye, calling him 'Alfred' by mistake, and asked for some equipment: a theodolite (or, if that was too expensive, a compass and a sextant), a pocket barometer, a surveyor's line, a geometry kit, some drawing paper, 'a 300-sample mineralogical collection' and ten books, including the explorer's guide, which had still not arrived. This was the last time he wrote to his oldest friend:*

All these things are equally necessary to me. Wrap carefully.
    Details with the next post, which leaves in three days. Meanwhile, make haste.
    Cordial greetings.

Four days later, he wrote home to add a telescope to the list and enclosed a letter for a Paris gunsmith:

I am travelling in Galla territory (East Africa) and am currently training a group of elephant hunters. [. . .]
    Is there a special weapon for elephant-hunting? [. . .]
    What form does the ammunition take – poisoned, explosive?

---

* The inane message to 'Delahuppe', dated May 1885, is not surprisingly a forgery: the postcard on which the message is written dates from 1904 at the earliest.[4]

I would be buying two such weapons for trials – and, perhaps, after testing, half a dozen.

Rimbaud would have seen several tons of ivory plodding about the scrub on his way to Bubassa in the region which is now the Babile Elephant Sanctuary. It was quite logical to want to gain control in this way over the entire supply-chain; but for the time being, the elephants were safe. Six weeks later, Colonel Dubar was writing a letter of recommendation for his 'friend and colleague, Rimbaud' to the French Consul in Zanzibar: 'M. Rimbaud managed our Harar branch (East Africa) to our entire satisfaction.'⁵

Rimbaud did not sail for Zanzibar. Almost immediately, he set his sights on Harar again and then on the distant kingdom of Choa: he would load up a camel with photographic equipment, travel 450 miles into the interior, and turn himself into the Étienne Carjat of Abyssinia. Photography 'is unknown there and it will make me a small fortune in very little time'. Looking even further ahead, he ordered books on railway construction and two manuals on embankments and tunnels.

This period of frantic procrastination lasted for such a long time that Rimbaud might almost be suspected of having found a kind of contentment in Aden. Warped by the gravitational pull of 'the Mouth of Darkness', his letters are misleading. 'I'm slaving away like a donkey in a land for which I have an invincible horror. [. . .] I'm hoping that this life will end before I've had the time to become completely stupid.'

Mme Rimbaud took him at his word: 'poor Arthur'⁶ was frittering away his life in the back of beyond. She decided not to pass his list of expensive toys on to Delahaye, and when Arthur sent money to be invested in a bank, she bought land for him. ('What the hell do you expect me to do with landed property?' he fumed.) If anyone asked about her second son, she told them that he was a language teacher in Arabia.⁷

Sometimes, he hinted that there was an element of playacting in this interminable tale of the wretched son and the reproachful mother: 'I've grown quite accustomed to all sorts of inconveniences, and if I keep complaining, it's just a way I have of harping on about things' (literally, 'singing'). 'I'm not ruined yet', he wrote, after investing 5,000 francs at five per cent interest.

He worked seven days a week and drank nothing but water – 'distilled sea-water' or spring-water that stank of the goatskins in which it was imported. All this was a source of personal pride, stored away against future disappointments and personal failures. He offered up the evidence of his hardships like a prayer.

The books and instruments, which could easily have been ordered through the company's headquarters in Lyon, were partly an attempt to make his mother and sister behave like a family.

> The most depressing thing is that you end your letter by saying that you'll have nothing more to do with my business. This is not a good way to help a man who finds himself a thousand leagues from home, travelling among savage tribes without even a single correspondent in his own country! I would like to think that you will modify your uncharitable intention. If I can't ask my own family to run errands for me, who the devil can I ask?

Bardey was right: in Rimbaud's mind, the last ten years had been wasted, 'wandering the world to no effect'. Now, he was adjusting to the climate of failure. Images and insights earned no interest. He had a new goal. In future, success would be measured by bank statements and a legal contract: 'I'd like to make about fifty thousand francs quickly, in four or five years; and then I'd get married.'

*

IF RIMBAUD'S TEMPERAMENT had allowed, he might have stayed in Aden for years, making plans and saving money.

His departure was hastened by a small international incident, caused by himself.

On Sunday, 28 January 1883, he wrote to the French Vice-Consul in Aden:

> Today, at 11 a.m., the man called Ali Chemmak – a storeman in the company for which I work – having acted in a very insolent manner towards me, I allowed myself to give him a gentle slap.
>
> The coolies who were on duty and various Arab witnesses having taken hold of me in order to leave him free to retaliate, the aforementioned Ali Chemmak hit me in the face, tore my clothes, then grabbed a stick and threatened me with it.

[335]

Since the bystanders intervened, Ali withdrew and left shortly thereafter to lodge a complaint with the municipal police, accusing me of assault and grievous bodily harm. He posted several false witnesses to declare that I had threatened to strike him with a dagger, etc., etc., and other lies intended to inflame the affair to my detriment and to excite the hatred of the natives against me.

Having been summoned to appear in connection with this matter before the municipal police of Aden, I am taking the liberty of alerting M. le Consul de France to the violence and intimidation to which I have been subjected by the natives, and beg his protection in the event that the outcome of the affair should appear to him to advise it.

Even allowing for Rimbaud's extraordinarily stodgy style – a sort of rococo legalese designed to contrast with the brute aggression of the natives – his story is far from clear. This insolent, deceitful Arab was later described by Bardey in rather different terms: 'He was our longest-serving warehouseman and foreman, and very useful to us.' Showing 'solidarity' with Rimbaud, Bardey sacked the man, but at some risk to the company: 'It is not good to have those people against one in an Arab country, commercially speaking, of course.'[8]

Eleven days later, it was decided that Rimbaud should leave Aden. Relations between the natives and the occupying Europeans were often tense, and Rimbaud was probably in danger of being attacked in the street. The only European who would be safer in the Somali desert than in Aden, he was to take over the Harar agency from Pierre Bardey. His contract was renewed on 20 March 1883: 5,000 francs a year, with housing and all expenses paid. Few of his Charleville contemporaries would have been earning as much.

On 22 March, the man who was dreaming of a nest-egg, a good marriage and a salubrious climate sailed for Africa with a load of technical manuals, scientific instruments and a camera. There is nothing to suggest that he had a clear view of his own future. The three hazy photographs that he sent home from Harar in May show a dried-up stick of a man, baked and shrivelled by the sun; a fez on a balding head; a slightly lopsided posture. The face is a mournful smudge of deep shadow. He looks like the inmate of a lunatic asylum.

In two of the photographs – the 'coffee garden' and the rampant banana plantation – he appears to be wearing the makeshift clothes described by Ottorino Rosa: 'He made garments for himself out of white American cotton, and, to simplify things, found ingenious devices for doing away with the tedious use of buttons.'[9]

Life could after all be improved in small ways.

31

Paradise

'And I shall be a fugitive and a vagabond in the earth'.

(Genesis 4:14)

A WEEK AFTER ARRIVING in Harar, Rimbaud wrote home (6 May 1883). It was one of his longest letters – long enough to allow a vision of himself to form that would have to be shaken off like a bad dream. He had been intending to sound happy – 'I'm always better off here than I am in Aden: there's less work and much more air and greenery, etc.' – but as the paragraphs grew longer, the sentences began to trace out the tedious itinerary of button-holes:

Isabelle is quite wrong not to get married if someone serious and educated comes along, someone who has a future. That's how life is, and solitude is a bad thing here on earth. Personally, I regret not being married and having a family. But now I'm condemned to wander, in the service of a distant company, and every day I'm losing my taste for the climate and customs and even the language of Europe. Alas! what's the use of all this to-ing and fro-ing, these exertions and adventures among strange peoples, and these languages one fills one's head with, and these unspeakable ordeals, if one day, a few years from now, I can't rest in a place that's more or less to my liking and find a family, and have at least one son whom I'll spend the rest of my life bringing up in accordance with my own ideas, improving him and equipping him with the most complete education our time has to offer, and whom I'll see become a renowned engineer, a man whose knowledge will make him powerful and rich? But who knows how long I shall live in these mountains? And I could disappear among these tribes without the news of my disappearance ever reaching the outside world.

Writing clearly had a depressing effect on Rimbaud. On the page, his ghosts came back to haunt him: the Europhobe who would fade away like the memory of a mirage; the grizzled colonial who would return like Abel Magwitch to gloat over his prodigy. This was the dream of a self-proclaimed failure: a son to avenge the father, a supereducated success who would redeem every inadequacy and error and turn a wasted life to profit.

Words had long memories. Ten years after *Une Saison en Enfer*, Rimbaud could still conjure up the musty smell of the 'cabbage-green' Bible. His letter was full of the Old Testament: 'It is not good that the man should be alone'; Adam 'begat a son in his own likeness, after his image'; 'I shall be a fugitive and a vagabond in the earth'. When he allowed the pen to siphon up his memories, he was still 'the slave of his baptism'.

In reality, Rimbaud had returned to Harar with new resolve. Now that he was in sole charge of the agency, he set about reforming it with the zeal of a Roman governor. His appetite for 'unspeakable ordeals' was stronger than ever.

This time, he set up a proper household. He hired an intelligent Harari boy of about thirteen years called Djami Wadaï.[1] Like most Europeans in Africa, he also kept a local woman.[2] According to one account, the woman came from the Argoba tribe, which inhabited the country between Harar and Bubassa and was said to be descended from sixteenth-century Portuguese settlers. In southern Abyssinia, female companions were often purchased from a dealer or a parent, usually for practical purposes – cooking, housekeeping, nursing and language-learning.

The languages Rimbaud mentioned so dismissively in his letter as mere intellectual clutter were vital tools for expanding the trading empire and staying alive.[3] Rimbaud is known to have spoken or to have had some working knowledge of Arabic, Amharic (now the official language of Ethiopia), Adarinya (or Harari), Oromo (or Galla) and Somali. He may have spoken Argoba (a close relative of Amharic) and Tigrinya: the Bishop of Harar told Evelyn Waugh that Rimbaud lived at one time with a woman from Tigray. According to an anonymous source who interviewed several of Rimbaud's acquaintances in 1911 and 1913 (and who can now be identified as an expert on Ethiopian languages called Marcel Cohen),[4] he also spoke a language called Kotou. He may have been the first and last European to do so since the language was extinct by 1937. It is no longer listed among the ninety-nine languages and 200 dialects of Ethiopia.

In most cases, a small vocabulary would have sufficed. The explorer Jules Borelli, who travelled with Rimbaud in 1887, was able to construct a list of useful phrases in three Ethiopian languages without much difficulty, though perhaps with Rimbaud's help: 'They struck him with their spears, he is dead', 'Can you see the elephant?', and – an exclamation which can hardly have lent itself to the use of a phrase-book – 'Here comes the rhinoceros: let us flee!'[5]

Rimbaud was now entering one of the most productive and engrossing periods of his life. Under his jurisdiction, the Harar agency became the base for a remarkable series of expeditions that would open up an unknown part of Africa to traders, explorers, political spies and missionaries.

This is by no means apparent if Rimbaud's letters are treated as the only source. Without Alfred Bardey, for example, nothing would be known of Rimbaud's historic trip to Bubassa; and without the Italian explorer, Pietro Sacconi, there would be no record of his three-day journey north, with Sacconi and Righas, to investigate rumours that Menelik, King of Choa, was about to invade Harar.

According to Sacconi, they left at dawn on 13 June 1883 and rode towards the Ahmar Mountains through long, flat valleys dotted with olive trees, mulberry bushes, euphorbias and mimosas. They passed unknown lakes, galloped through hostile Itou-Galla villages, clutching the reins in one hand and a revolver in the other. Eventually, they reached Warabeili where famished refugees were hiding from the genocidal horde of King Menelik. The *boko* showed them the tree where Lucereau had been killed. They took a photograph of it and returned to Harar without stopping to eat or drink, as Sacconi explained:

To travel through the Gallas, the first requisite is speed. We have to
pass like meteors, because, if they are given time to think, we're done
for. Woe betide the traveller who sends someone on ahead![6]

An even more remarkable expedition can only be detected with the
aid of a detailed chronology. Rimbaud appears to have returned to
Harar in the spring of 1883, not from Zeila, but from the French
coal station of Obock.[7] This would mean that he was the first
European to cross the ferocious Danakil region from north to south
without completing the journey as a corpse. The year before, a man
called Arnoux, who had introduced European civilization to the
Kingdom of Choa in the form of guns and brandy, was stabbed to
death at Obock by Danakil tribesmen. The same tribe was responsible
for twenty European deaths between May 1881 and October 1883.
Even in 1927, the region was described by an American explorer as
'*terra incognita*': the north-eastern part 'probably could not be reached
without a force of at least a thousand well-armed men'.[8]

The wanderings of the drunken boat are familiar to most French
schoolchildren, but many of Rimbaud's pioneering journeys are
completely unknown. This is partly due to Abyssinia itself. Until the
late 1930s, maps of southern Ethiopia were hopelessly out of date
even before they were printed: villages disappeared, rivers dried up,
whole tribes were massacred, forced to migrate or sold into slavery
by their neighbours. The descendants of some of the Galla tribes
known to Rimbaud now live in northern Kenya. Some dots and lines
on early European maps were nothing more than stories told by
camel drivers. This is why some scholars who could recite the
numbers and street names of Rimbaud's homes in Charleville have
written about his African adventures without always knowing where
he was.

Rimbaud himself was doubly discreet. He had no interest in
planting flags or naming geographical features, and he was wary of
broadcasting his movements. Since merchants were dependent on the
good will and protection of native slave traders, and since Britain was
ostensibly devoted to eradicating the slave trade, it was important not
to be too precise. Letters were often opened by spies or consular
officials, especially Rimbaud's letters, which were deemed by one

political agent to be 'the most detailed and reliable' to come out of Abyssinia. Even in 1897, Alfred Bardey was reluctant to release some of Rimbaud's documents in case they constituted a security risk.[9]

Rimbaud's commercial interest in the Obock–Harar route is therefore easy to explain. It did not run through British territory. A merchant who had purchased the protection of slave traders and who left from Obock might still be attacked by warriors, but he would not be troubled by the interfering British.

*

Now THAT HIS daily needs were catered to by a servant and a housewife, Rimbaud began to expand the company's sphere of influence. He made a careful study of local fashions and sent precise orders to Aden: '50 tassels of red or green braided wool, to be attached to reins and saddles, among the Gallas and Somalis'; 500 tunics to be cut from 'material of the strength of light sail-cloth, striped longitudinally with red or blue stripes 5 cms wide and 20 cms apart'. 'Will be fashionable in the Galla and Abyssinian tribes.'

Bardey had been interested only in coffee. Rimbaud seemed intent on setting up the Dark Continent's first department store. In addition to the clothes and fashion accessories, he ordered tools, weapons and jewellery to be manufactured from native models.

Unfortunately (as he complained to Bardey), he was forced to work with idiots. When he learned that Bardey's friend and associate Pierre Mazeran was to come to Harar, he offered his professional assessment:

I trust [. . .] that the decision will not be made to exacerbate things by sending an individual who is incapable of doing anything but squandering our investments, getting in our way, making us look ridiculous and ruining us in all sorts of ways. – Personally, we can endure all privations without fear and every setback without impatience, but we cannot bear the company of a lunatic.[10]

Rimbaud was too well organized and confident of his own expertise to tolerate an equal partnership. His instructions were based on first-hand experience and careful calculations. He prided himself on the quality of his merchandise. The coffee that was being sent to the coast by a rival company of three Greek brothers was 'filth scraped off the floors of Harari houses'. Just as his poems had been written against the grain of other poets' work, his business activities were a criticism of other traders' ineptitude.

> The elephant hunter you sent us from Aden [he told Bardey] is prancing about interminably in the gorges of Darimont and will emerge somewhere about here when he's used up your kilos[11] of pork and preserved milk among the Guerris and the Batris.

While Bardey's elephant hunter meandered through the gorges, Rimbaud was ordering steel wolf-traps, training a company of tiger-, leopard- and lion-hunters – 'to whom we have given instructions for the flaying' – and making use of local skills:

> 4 or 5 hours from Harar, there is a forest (Bisédimo) in which wild animals abound. We have alerted the people of the surrounding villages and are having them hunt for us.

As a sideline, he practised his photography ('Everyone wants to have their photograph taken'). He sent a few samples to Bardey – portraits of two employees, a drab and ghostly marketplace, and a dramatic study of a coffee-seller squatting on his animal skins next to two crumbly pillars. Bardey wrote a tentative letter of thanks:

> I would like to be able to acknowledge your thoughtfulness, but you're a rather odd fellow, and I don't know what I could send that you might like. Tell me if you'd be glad of some instruments like a theodolite, a graphometer, etc.

The answer to this would certainly have been 'yes'. Rimbaud was already refining his exploration techniques. Most explorers organized special expeditions with particular aims – a river, a mountain, a lost civilization or fame. Rimbaud set up a kind of exploration agency that could cover large areas in a short space of time. It was a secular version of a religious mission. The missionaries themselves, in fact, were used by Rimbaud to consolidate new markets and keep up the flow of information.

It is not widely known that the poet of 'Les Premières communions' played a seminal role in the history of the Catholic Church in southern Ethiopia. That June, acting on Rimbaud's 'favourable and, indeed, pressing advice', Bishop Taurin sent two French priests to Bubassa: it was the mission's first and, for a long time, only success. (No one was converted, but the priests came back alive.)[12]

Rimbaud was now ready to start work on what might be called his first exploration masterpiece.

Since there was desert to the north and east, and a rampaging native army to the west, he decided to concentrate on the vast Ogaden region to the south, known as 'the Somalis' Paradise', perhaps because of the legend that placed the Garden of Eden in Abyssinia. Rimbaud's right-hand man was Konstantinu Sotiros (or Sotiro) – a loyal, fearless and myopic young Greek who had much in common with Rimbaud: his thirst for precise knowledge (he was once described as 'a geographical dictionary'),[13] his indifference to personal glory, and his ability to pass himself off as an Arab merchant.

In June 1883, Rimbaud sent his colleague on a long and dangerous mission. Sotiro seems to have reached a point about 140 miles south of Harar: two Italians who 'discovered' Bir Gora Abdallah in 1891 were amazed to hear tales of a white man who had passed through rapidly on a horse many years before.[14]

Meanwhile, further west, acting on his own initiative, Pietro Sacconi was heading in roughly the same direction for one of the great unclaimed prizes of African exploration: the river Webi.* (The wavy line that appears on early maps was based only on rumours and guesswork.) Since the Webi was thought, incorrectly, to be part of the Nile system, its discovery would have important political consequences.

Shortly after 11 August, Sotiro was surprised to see three Somali camel-drivers and an Indian cook arriving hot-foot from the west. Sacconi's expedition had met a horrible end: these were the only survivors. When Rimbaud heard the news, he sent a laconic note to Bardey in Marseille: 'M. Sacconi died near the Webi, on 11 August, slaughtered through his own fault and needlessly.'

---

* The Webi Shebele ('Webi' simply means 'river') rises in the northern Rift Valley, crosses the Ogaden in a crook, and flows into the Juba and the Indian Ocean, 1,000 miles from its source, between Mogadishu and Mombasa.

He also wrote, at greater length, to the company offices in Aden, listing the causes of the disaster: ignorant guides, a dangerous route, and M. Sacconi himself – a stubborn, arrogant and stupid man. This stinging obituary might have been a page out of Rimbaud's own Explorer's Handbook:

> He contravened (out of ignorance) the manners, religious customs and rights of the natives. [. . .] He travelled in European clothes and even dressed his camel-drivers as *hostranis* (Christians). He fed himself on hams, swigged alcohol in the sheiks' councils, pressing his own food on his hosts, and conducted his suspicious-looking geodesic surveys, twiddling sextants, etc. all along the route. [. . .]
>
> M. Sacconi bought nothing. His only aim was to reach the Webi, to cover himself in geographical glory.

Having committed the sin of stupidity, the witless Sacconi deserved no sympathy. Rimbaud contrasted him with the admirable Sotiro:

> M. Sotiro stopped at the first place where he thought he might be able to trade his stock. [. . .] Moreover, he travels in Muslim clothes, under the name Adji-Abdallah, and accepts all the natives' political and religious formalities. At the place where he stopped, he became a goal for pilgrims as a *wodad* (scholar) and *shereef* (descendant of the Prophet's companions).

Rimbaud was writing a dramatic fable of the wise man and the fool. He exaggerated Sotiro's triumph in order to blacken Sacconi and underline the moral. In June, two of the Catholic priests – who did not twiddle sextants or swig alcohol – had narrowly escaped death when they ventured into the Ogaden in the direction taken by Sacconi.[15] Good luck – a concept that was quite foreign to Rimbaud – also played a part. Some Ogaden tribes welcomed white men as 'emissaries of God'.[16] Others coped with the shock of an alien civilization more crudely. Further west, the Zenjero tribe, which worshipped a god of iron who had fallen from the sky, sacrificed every tenth foreigner who crossed their invisible frontier.[17]

In fact, Sotiro had been taken prisoner, and, according to Bardey, 'was saved only by his knowledge of the Koran'.[18] Although Rimbaud says nothing of this in his report, he was also saved by Rimbaud.

Writing to the Société de Géographie in November, Bardey explained that 'our agent was set free only after the intervention of an Ogas, or great chief, whom M. Rimbaud sent from Harar to deliver him'.

The implications of this little fact are easily missed. Rimbaud's envoy, Omar Hussein, was a famous warrior and an *ughaz* – a trans-tribal chieftain who interpreted omens and officiated at political events. Omar Hussein was the most powerful *ughaz* in the upper Ogaden. The fact that Rimbaud was able to ask this sorcerer-lord to go and rescue his colleague is an extraordinary testament to his diplomatic skill.

The refusal to adopt contemporary prejudices, which makes the *Illuminations* such an excitingly alien work, also made its author an unusually proficient explorer. Rimbaud's phrase, 'the rights of the natives', is a surprising and provocative concept to find in a French colonial text of 1883.

Sotiro's brief spell as a holy oracle set Rimbaud thinking about new commercial possibilities. Twice before, he had toyed with the idea of attaching himself to missionaries; but Christianity was already proving unpopular in Harar, let alone in the trackless Ogaden. Islam had taken root precisely because it offered no challenge to the old ways.[19]

Rimbaud now revised his original idea. On 7 October 1883, he asked his mother to buy him the Hachette parallel-text translation of the Koran. Since he later thanked her for 'the Korans', she presumably also sent him Captain Rimbaud's manuscript translation.[20] To complete the illusion, Rimbaud had a seal engraved (at an unknown date) with the words: ABDO RINBO (ABDALLAH RIMBAUD), which means 'Rimbaud, servant of God'.[21]

This moment in Rimbaud's life suggests a happy confluence. Abyssinian exploration, like the *Illuminations*, was an enterprise in which success depended on erasing the old, Christian self. Yet, by turning himself into a Koran scholar, he would also be recovering a part of his own past. The son of Captain Rimbaud, the visionary poet and the African trader might after all inhabit the same body.

That December, in his report on the Ogaden, he used the word 'poet' for the first time since leaving Europe: 'There are *wodads* (scholars) in every tribe. They know the Koran and Arab writing and are improvisational poets.'

Ironically, while Rimbaud contemplated a lucrative new use for his literary skills, his old self was making a comeback. Four thousand miles away, in the cafés of the Latin Quarter, poets and journalists, sipping coffee that might have passed through Rimbaud's depot, were beginning to talk again about the little savage who had amazed the Parnassians over a decade before.

Nine beautiful poems, including 'Le Bateau ivre' and 'Voyelles', were published by Verlaine in a Latin Quarter review that October, with some biographical details and an allusion to the poet's mysterious silence:

> If by chance he should happen to see these lines [. . .] let M. Arthur Rimbaud be assured of our complete approbation (but also of our dark dismay) in the face of his abandonment of poetry, provided, as is no doubt the case, that this abandonment, for him, is logical, honest and necessary.

*

RIMBAUD'S *Rapport sur l'Ogadine* is his second major publication after *Une Saison en Enfer*. It is supposed to have been based entirely on Sotiro's oral report, but the Austrian explorer and geographer Philipp Paulitschke noticed that it 'differs on many important points from the account given to me in person by Sotiro'.[22]

Throughout the report, Rimbaud uses the ambiguous 'we', as if determined not to expose himself to admiration. But two Ogaden expeditions are mentioned, and since Sotiro claimed that he made only one journey into the Ogaden,[23] the second expedition was almost certainly undertaken by Rimbaud himself.

The route appears to have followed the Erer river, the course of which is plotted in some detail, through 'the pillaging Somali–Galla tribes' to 'the land of Nokob', where it flows into the Webi.[24] The expedition would have taken about two weeks, which would account for the gap in Rimbaud's correspondence between 7 October and 10 December 1883.

At least one other expedition followed the report. In the section that remained unpublished until 1931, Rimbaud sketched out the short-term plan:

> Omar Hussein has written to us in Harar and is waiting for us to go down with him and all his *goums* [soldiers] to the Webi, just a few days from our first staging-post.
> This is our goal.

On the banks of the Webi, 'where the elephants go to die', 'a ton of ivory' and 'hundreds of dollars' worth of ostrich feathers' could be collected 'in a few weeks'.

> We have therefore decided to create a post on the Webi, and this post will be approximately at the site called Eimeh [Imi], a large, permanent village on the Ogaden bank of the river, eight days from Harar by caravan.

The accepted chronology of East African exploration begins to look rather speculative. A powerful *ughaz* with a small army was ready to take Rimbaud to one of the great unknown African rivers, fourteen months before the James brothers,[25] half-dead with fear and hunger, reached it from Berbera in the north-east.

Whether or not Rimbaud, at the age of twenty-nine, discovered the Webi Shebele, his report on the Ogaden was the first authoritative account of one of the world's largest remaining unexplored regions. It was written as a company report, but Alfred Bardey recognized its importance and sent it to the Société de Géographie, which published it. Rimbaud became quite famous in the Horn of Africa and was later remembered as a writer-explorer by several people who knew nothing of his earlier career.

In his two studies of Harar (Leipzig, 1884 and 1888), Paulitschke hailed it as a landmark: 'He was the first European to report on the Ogaden from personal experience, and his observations are extremely interesting'; 'a very valuable account, despite its dryness'.[26]

Rimbaud would have considered this a compliment. His 'dryness' enabled him to cram more information into less than 2,000 words than some of his contemporaries managed to fit into a book. Despite this, and the opinion of a serious geographer like Paulitschke, the report is often described by literary scholars as 'unprofessional'. This may simply reflect disappointment. Rimbaud's stony concision is a bitter contrast to the flowery, Decadent style that his own poems were helping to foster in France. Anyone who first approached Rimbaud's work through the self-referential delicacies of French verse in the 1870s and 1880s will inevitably find his report as appetizing as a plate of durra.

On its own terms, the *Rapport sur l'Ogadine* is a geographical feast: it details the rivers, tribes, markets and trade routes, the flora and fauna, the general climate and topography of the Ogaden. About two-thirds of the report is devoted to ethnographic information, most of it completely new: some of the tribes mentioned by Rimbaud had never been heard of, let alone seen.[27]

Rimbaud was writing the Genesis of an unknown race, and his Biblical vocabulary lent the report a faintly sardonic tone.

> The Ogadens have rather lengthy legends of their origins. We retained only this, that they all descend originally from Rère Abdallah and Rère Ishay [. . .]. Rère Abdallah had the generations of Rère Hersi and Rère Hammadèn: these are the two principal families of the upper Ogaden.
>
> Rère Ishay begat Rère Ali and Rère Aroun. These *rères* are then subdivided into innumerable secondary families.

The distant sneer that hovers over Rimbaud's Ogaden brings to mind the demystificatory styles of Voltaire, Flaubert or Evelyn Waugh. The simple omission of personal opinion creates a kind of vacuum in the text: this was the expressionless Rimbaud who could make his colleagues laugh hysterically at each other's foibles. Human beings are reduced to their habits. Traditions are an excuse for idleness. The Ogadens described by Rimbaud are close cousins of the Ardennes peasants. His mother, whose 'pastoral toil' he had mentioned in a letter, might have recognized their patriarchal society:

> Their daily occupation is to go and squat in groups under the trees, a short distance from the camp, and, weapons in hand, to conduct interminable deliberations on their various pastoral concerns. Apart from these meetings, and the horse-patrols when animals are being watered or neighbours raided, they are completely inactive. The children and women are left to see to the animals, the manufacture of

household implements, the erection of huts and the despatching of caravans. [. . .]

[. . .] When the spouse of an Ogaden gives birth, the latter abstains from all intercourse with her until the child is capable of walking on its own. Naturally, he marries one or several others in the meantime, but always with the same reserves.

To conclude his picture of humanity as it existed in the Somalis' Paradise, he returned to one of his favourite themes: futile calamity. The Ogadens' unchanging world had been invaded by civilization, with its enlightened intellectuals and, of course, its blundering savages:

M. Sotiro is truly to be congratulated on the wisdom and diplomacy he showed in this circumstance. Whereas our competitors have been hunted, cursed, robbed and killed, and, by their very undoing, have been the cause of terrible tribal wars, we have established ourselves throughout the confederation of the Oughaz and have made ourselves known throughout the Rère Hersi.

*

RIMBAUD WAS UNABLE for the time being to capitalize on his discoveries. The company had made some careless investments in Algeria and Greece. Pending an influx of capital, Bardey was forced to close the agency in Harar.

It was a good time to close in any case. The dervishes of the Mahdi had defeated the Egyptian army in the Sudan. Since the bombing of Alexandria in 1882, Britain had controlled Egyptian affairs and decided that Egypt should abandon its Red Sea possessions. Harar was to be evacuated. Meanwhile, British diplomats were conducting secret talks with Rome: it was hoped that Italy could be induced to act as policeman in Abyssinia until the region was stable again.

In February, Rimbaud prepared a final caravan for the coast. On 1 March, he met the British Resident, Major Hunter, who had come from Aden to organize the evacuation.[28] About ten days later, he left the city and went travelling for six weeks 'in the deserts'.

On returning to that 'horrible hole', Aden, he found a letter from Paris. The Société de Géographie wanted to include him in its series of famous geographers and explorers. Rimbaud was asked for a brief autobiography, a summary of his exploits and a photograph.[29]

He never answered the letter.

When he wrote home on 5 May 1884, he summed up his life so far. This was the only curriculum vitae he had a mind to write:

> Forgive me for recounting all my troubles. But I see that I'm about to turn thirty (half a lifetime!) and I've worn myself out wandering the world, to no effect.

32

Abdo Rinbo

'You can't be a poet in hell.'

('Fausse conversion', manuscript draft of
'Nuit de l'enfer', *Une Saison en Enfer*)

WHEN RIMBAUD REACHED Aden in April 1884, he found
Alfred Bardey with a smile on his face and some unpleasant
news. That Christmas, on the steamer from Marseille, Bardey had
met a journalist who was on his way to cover the war in Indo-China
for *Le Temps*. While they chatted, Bardey happened to mention one
of his French employees – a kind, intelligent, though rather eccentric
young man called Rimbaud.[1]

The journalist, whose name was Paul Bourde, had been a pupil at
the Collège de Charleville with someone called Rimbaud – a young
poet who had made a 'stupefying and precocious début in literature'
twelve years before. But the poet had disappeared and no one knew
what had become of him . . .

Bardey was thrilled to have discovered Rimbaud's little secret. Paul
Bourde could have told him about the poems that had recently been
published by Verlaine, with a picture of Rimbaud based on the
second Carjat photograph. The anthology was reprinted that April,
with chapters on Corbière and Mallarmé, in a book called *Les Poètes
maudits*. The term '*poète maudit*' had originally been applied to any
poor, neglected poet, but was now acquiring connotations of reprehensible decadence.

Verlaine had written about Rimbaud's 'miraculous puberty' with a tantalizing brevity that left plenty of room for conjecture. He compared 'Les Chercheuses de poux' to Racine and 'Les Effarés' to a painting by Goya. The only blot, in Verlaine's opinion – a very beautiful and brilliant blot however – was the blasphemous 'Premières communions', 'whose detestable spirit we vigorously regret'. There were already signs of a Rimbaud cult. The sonnet on coloured vowels was the flavour of the month.

For the last ten years, Verlaine had been struggling with alcoholism, homosexuality and school-children and was trying to revive his literary career. Rimbaud's poems would help him to achieve some critical respect. Wisely, he had failed to notify the author: 'Had we consulted M. Rimbaud (whose address, immensely vague in any case, is unknown to us), he would probably have advised us not to undertake this work.'

'Advised' is a splendid understatement. When Bardey handed Rimbaud a 'friendly and allusive' note from M. Bourde, 'far from being flattered, he got angry and made a grunting noise', reminiscent, apparently, of a wild boar.[2] And that, according to most accounts, was that:

> He would never allow me to mention his former literary works. Sometimes I asked him why he didn't take it up again. All I ever got were the usual replies: 'absurd, ridiculous, disgusting, etc.'[3]

Rimbaud's reaction to the news that his old self was not only alive but launching a career of its own is usually quoted as one histrionic outburst: 'Absurd, ridiculous, disgusting!' Replacing an 'etc.' with an exclamation mark might seem a small matter, but these subtle alterations have a cumulative effect. The upside-down pyramid of the Rimbaud legend is built on such tiny things.

In fact, Rimbaud was uncomfortably ambiguous about his exposure. On the one hand, he had even more reason than most people to fear an eye-witness of his adolescence. Rumours of depravity would not be good for business. The same thought had obviously occurred to Frédéric Rimbaud, who was now a bus-driver in Attigny: perhaps after discovering that his colonial brother was in the news, he seems to have considered blackmail as a means of funding his marriage. Mme Rimbaud wrote to warn Arthur. He replied on 7 October:

> What you tell me about Frédéric is very annoying and might do a great deal of harm to us all. I would find it quite embarrassing for instance if people knew that I had a joker like that for a brother. It doesn't surprise me anyway: we've always known that he's a complete idiot, and we always marvelled at the thickness of his skull.
>
> [. . .] My money is too hard earned for me to make a gift of it to a bedouin like that, who, I'm quite certain, is in a better financial condition than I.

Whatever Frédéric might say, he had an excellent reputation. True, there had been some 'unhappy moments' in the past, 'but I have never tried to live at the expense of other people or by disreputable means'.

This nervous lie appears to confirm Bardey's claim that Rimbaud was more apprehensive about malicious gossip than ashamed of his writing. Once, he alluded vaguely to his time in London as 'a period of drunkenness'. He had known writers and artists in the Paris Latin Quarter, 'but no musicians' (perhaps a private allusion to the 'mad composer', Cabaner), but he had 'seen quite enough of those fellows'.[4] All the same, Bardey had the impression that Rimbaud intended to return to literature once he had 'amassed a sufficient fortune'.[5] According to Bardey's housekeeper, he 'wrote a great deal' and was composing some '*beaux ouvrages*'[6] – a term which suggests an illustrated book.

There is good evidence that Rimbaud kept notes of all his journeys[7] and, although the book on Abyssinia was always in abeyance, he very nearly decided to finish it when he heard that Bishop Taurin was writing a study of Harar: 'I'll cut the ground from under Monsignor's feet!'[8]

It is curious in any case that Rimbaud now began to refer, in almost all his letters, to a possible return to France. This endlessly deferred homecoming was another dream to populate the distant future: the magical moment when the required sum of money would have been amassed. Of course, it had to be presented as a futile hope in case optimism set in and made him responsible for his failure: 'in

France, I'd be a stranger and would find no work' (5 May 1884); 'I'd be seen as an old man and only widows would want me!' (29 May); 'I'd be completely forgotten and would have to start all over again!' (10 September)

As Rimbaud settled in for another long spell in Aden, he appeared to have attained something like an ideal mode of existence. He had an ever-expanding future and a philosophy to protect him from it: instead of yearning for freedom, he seemed to aspire to a state of 'slavery'. This was the sort of self-exonerating fatalism that might have been expressed by any peasant on his mother's farm: 'Since I'm earning my living here, and since every man is a slave of this wretched fate, it might as well be here as anywhere else'. 'Like the Muslims, I know that what will be, will be'.

The supposed evidence for Rimbaud's conversion to Islam is as convincing as his towel-turban: 'As the Muslims say, It is written! – That's life. It's no laughing matter!'

*

IF RIMBAUD'S LETTERS were a simple record of his mental state, his year and a half in Aden (April 1884 to November 1885) would have been a period of uninterrupted misery. One of Bardey's agents, Charles Cotton, reported on 7 May that 'Rimbaud looks very unhappy at having nothing to do';[9] but even after the company had recouped its losses and reappointed him in June, he was still seething with disgruntlement.

He had to work like a 'slave' from 7 a.m. to 5 p.m. There was no weather, just a climate – two seasons that left nothing to the imagination: a rainless winter and 'the hottest summer in the whole world!' Life was 'prohibitively expensive' and 'intolerably boring'. According to him, there were no libraries and no newspapers. (In fact, the Aden office kept a small collection of serious and humorous papers, as well as some discarded novels, which Rimbaud never read.)[10] For company, there was a simple choice: 'savages or imbeciles'.

Five miles across the crater, the Europeans at Steamer Point were a small tribe of 'idiotic business employees who squander their salaries on billiards and then curse the place when they leave'. Rimbaud called them *'licheurs de petits verres'* ('boozers').[11] It was the sort of comment that might have been made by a local Muslim. He was quite happy for people to think that he had gone native and worshipped Allah.

This was orientalism as Rimbaud had always understood it: an allergic reaction to the West. Half a century after Hugo's *Orientales*, the exotic trappings of Romantic poetry – ivory, animal skins and incense – were sums of money in Rimbaud's account books. The *Illuminations* were not so far away: 'I don't miss my old share of divine happiness: the sober air of this bitter countryside feeds my atrocious scepticism in a very active fashion.'

On the bright side, he had managed to 'scrape together' over 16,000 francs by the end of 1885,[12] but no one could be trusted with the money: 'You're forced to lug your nest egg about with you and never let it out of your sight.' Money would soon be useless anyway. One year in Aden was like 'four years' (5 May 1884) or 'five years' (14 April 1885) anywhere else. Even if he had enough life left over to return to France and live in idle luxury, an irreversible mutation had occurred. He was stranded like a cactus in the desert: 'People who have lived here for a few years can no longer spend the winter in Europe: they'd drop dead instantly with some pneumonic infection.'

In April 1885, he developed 'gastric fever' – perhaps a symptom of his syphilis. A month later, the whole of Aden seemed to have it:

> We're in the steambaths of springtime. Skins are dripping, stomachs turning sour, brains becoming muddled, business is rotten, the news is bad.

When Evelyn Waugh visited Aden in 1931, he was almost disappointed not to find the spectacularly awful place of Rimbaud's letters: 'a climate notoriously corrosive of all intellect and initiative; a landscape barren of any growing or living thing; a community full of placid self-esteem'.[13] Like Baudelaire among the Belgians, Rimbaud could still be lyrical about the horribly prosaic. Aden and his venereal muse inspired him to new heights of loathing. His springtime blues even have the same lunging rhythms as parts of *Une Saison en Enfer*:

Enough! here's the punishment. – *Forward march*!

Ah! Lungs are burning, temples throbbing! darkness swirls in my
eyes, under this sun!

('Mauvais sang')

Just in case his mother managed to detect a hint of colonial
comfort, he reminded her that the dried-up crater-bottom was also
part of his inner landscape: 'Don't go thinking now that I'm having
an easy time of it. In fact, I've always noticed that it's impossible to
live more tediously than I do.'

Rimbaud always saved his best prose for the depiction of his
misery. His 'harping on about things'* was the practised moan of a
skilful beggar. Behind the beggar's curtain, in the shade of a cool
room, there was a very different world: old Arab histories, language
books and a writing-desk; a smell of cardamom, cloves and coconut
oil; quiet conversations and European cigarettes.

*

ON 10 AUGUST 1884, while Rimbaud was slaving over the account-
books in Aden, an Abyssinian woman left Harar with the French
Vice-Consul at Zeila. Bishop Taurin made a note in his diary: 'M.
Henri set off with his interpreter, M. Dimitri. An Abyssinian woman,
Mariam, left here by M. Rambaud [*sic*], is going with them to Aden.'[15]

This was almost certainly the Abyssinian woman with whom
Rimbaud had a 'fairly long liaison' from 1884 to 1886.[16] According
to Bardey, he was very fond of her and there were even plans for
marriage – probably the convenient scheme called *ba damouss* by
which the woman was paid a small retainer but had no claim on the
man's property and could easily be divorced.[17]

Mariam would have arrived in Aden towards the end of August, by
which time Rimbaud had rented a house near the office. Before her
arrival, he had been writing home about twice a month. From then
until his departure from Aden, the average interval between letters
was fifty-four days.

* A purely metaphorical harp. As Steve Murphy has shown, Isabelle's famous
drawing of Rimbaud playing the Abyssinian harp is a cheap deception. She traced a
picture of an Abyssinian harpist from a magazine, then grafted her brother's face on
to it.[14]

By extraordinary good luck, the Italian trader, Ottorino Rosa, published a photograph of Rimbaud's companion in his book on Abyssinia in 1913: a young, sturdy-looking woman who had been asked to pose as a typical '*Donna Abissina*'. Apparently, she usually dressed as a European – not that this made any difference to Rosa: 'I might add that I myself, at that time, was keeping her sister. I got rid of her after a few weeks to move to Massawa.'[18]

Bardey's French housekeeper described Rimbaud's companion in a letter of 1897. She had been asked by M. Rimbaud to teach the woman how to sew:[19]

I used to go to M. Rimbaud's home every Sunday after dinner. I was amazed that he allowed me to go and see him. I think I must have been the only person he received. He didn't say very much. He seemed to be very nice to the woman. He wanted to educate her and told me that he wanted to send her to the nuns at the mission, with Father François. [. . .]

The woman herself was very sweet; but she spoke so little French that we couldn't really have a proper chat. She was tall and very thin, with a rather pretty face and quite regular features – not too black. I don't know the Abyssinian race. To my mind she looked quite European. She was a Catholic. I can't remember her name. She had her sister with her for a time. She only went out in the evenings, with M. Rimbaud. She dressed in the European style and their interior was just like a native house. She was very fond of smoking cigarettes.[20]

This was the other side of the diptych: on one panel, the sweating, dyspeptic sinner under a red sky; on the other, a calm Arabian interior inhabited by a white man wearing native dress and an African woman in European clothes.

Rimbaud spent his evenings learning languages, annotating Arab books, preparing his own book on Abyssinia, and studying the political situation. He dressed so casually that the British Resident at Zeila once mistook him for 'a stonemason'.[21] A French trader called Augustin Bernard thought that 'he looked more like some poor Armenian or Greek than a Frenchman'.[22] This would explain the unkind remark of a Frenchwoman who ran a hotel at Obock. In 1886, seeing Rimbaud set off for Choa, she commented that 'Abyssinia won't be getting another shining example of the French race with that one'.[23]

ABDO RINBO

Rimbaud had no illusions about his appearance: 'I won't send you my photograph', he told his mother. 'I'm carefully avoiding any needless expense, and in any case I'm always badly dressed.' Amazingly, he was often seen without a hat.[24] An air of legend was already attaching itself to the second Rimbaud:

> He was famous for having crossed an equatorial desert region with nothing on his head but a Turkish cap, and this was a region into which the Somali natives never venture because, they say, the brain boils, the skull explodes and all who go there never return.[25]

This was how 'Abdo Rinbo' lived for nineteen months in Aden, returning every evening from the office to a woman who was willing to learn, unlike Verlaine, and who allowed him to be silent, unlike his mother. Between 1873 and 1891, only one of Mme Rimbaud's letters has survived. It is dated 10 October 1885. She seems to have taken as her text Genesis 3:16: 'in sorrow thou shalt bring forth children'.

> Your silence is long, and why this silence? Happy are they that have no children, or happy they that do not love them: they are indifferent to all that might befall them. [. . .] Are you so ill that you cannot hold a pen? Or are you no longer in Aden? Have you perhaps gone to the Chinese Empire? [. . .] I say again, Happy, O happy are they that have no children, or that do not love them! They at least have no disappointment to fear, for their heart is closed to all that surrounds them. What's the point in saying any more? Who knows if you'll read this letter? [. . .]
>
> Soon, you are to be called up to do your thirteen days as a soldier: the gendarmes will come here again to fetch you. What can I tell them? If only you had made me your proxy, as you did before, I could have shown the document to the military authorities; but I have asked you for it three times now without receiving anything. Let everything be done then according to God's will! I've done what *I* can.
>
> Yours,
> W[idow] Rimbaud

*

BY THE TIME this maternal lamentation arrived, Rimbaud was on the other side of the Gulf of Aden in the village of Tadjoura: 'a few mosques and palm-trees', and an Egyptian fort 'where six French soldiers snooze under the orders of a sergeant'.

The tectonic plate had slipped again. When he read Rimbaud's letters in their published form, Bardey was surprised to learn that there had been 'a violent discussion with those vile peasants [Bardey & Co.] who wanted to condemn me to hard labour for life': 'I've done those people a lot of favours, and they've always tried to do me out of something. Anyway, they can go to hell. They gave me a good testimonial for five years.'*

This was the sound of Rimbaud breaking with the past. He seemed unable to make a fresh start without reneging on a contract. His mistreatment by 'those vile peasants' was pure fantasy. The 'violent discussion' had been a result, not the cause of Rimbaud's desertion. Bardey had simply reproached him for failing to give the mandatory three months' notice: 'I found out from someone else and two days before he left.' 'I did nothing to stop him. I might just as well have tried to stop a shooting star.'[27]

An escape route had presented itself in the form of a successfully devious French trader. Pierre Labatut[28] had arrived in the Kingdom of Choa about seven years before in search of sudden wealth. King Menelik was eager to encourage European traders – especially those bearing arms – and had given Labatut some land in his grass-hut capital, Ankober.

Since then, Labatut had lived with his Abyssinian wife, ten slaves and five or six mules in a rubbish heap of unsold merchandise and dismantled caravans. It was the home of a chronic optimist. Most of Labatut's schemes ended up as incredible tales in which he was the hero, but his gun-running expeditions had been a real success. Labatut's Remingtons had helped to turn the wandering village that Menelik called his army into a formidable modern force with the power to depopulate entire regions in a few weeks.

In 1881, Labatut had invited Alfred Bardey to join him in an arms

---

* Translated from the manuscript version. The insults that appear in all editions were inserted (perhaps from a lost letter) by the first editor, Berrichon: 'They thought I was going to spend the rest of my life with them just to make them happy. [...] I told them to go to hell – them and their advantages, and their trade, and their horrid company, and their filthy town!', etc.[26]

deal. Bardey had refused, pointing out that life was already dangerous enough for Europeans and natives without gunpowder and bullets. Hearing that Rimbaud had joined forces with this seedy adventurer, he warned him not to waste his time and money, but Rimbaud had already decided that gun-running was the key to a life of leisurely globe-trotting. The Kingdom of Choa would be a foretaste of the life to come. He wrote home with the good news:

> Between here [Tadjoura] and Choa there are about fifty days on horseback through burning deserts. But in Abyssinia the climate is delightful. It is neither hot nor cold, the population is Christian and hospitable, life is easy, and it's a very pleasant resting place for those who have spent a few years slogging their guts out on the incandescent shores of the Red Sea.

A brief hell followed by a just reward. If everything went according to plan, he would return with a large profit and use the surplus to buy more guns in France. 'Which means that you may very well receive a visit from me towards the end of summer 1886.'

Even after he was forced to change his expected date of return to the autumn and then the winter of 1886, he was confident that this was not just another false dawn. Soon, he would have enough money to overpower his 'wretched fate', and then, wealthy and victorious, he would leave 'these unhappy lands' forever.

33

Guns for Africa

'One is born a poet and one dies a businessman.'

(Romanian proverb)[1]

O N THE 'CURSED SHORES' of Tadjoura, in the sweltering mid-winter, Rimbaud began to organize his caravan. Labatut had stayed behind in Aden, partly to arrange for the shipping of rifles and supplies, but also to avoid a violent death. In September, one of his caravans had been attacked and Labatut had killed an Issa-Somali warrior. He was now a marked man in a region the size of Belgium. Rimbaud would have to make the journey alone.

In January 1886, crates containing 2,040 rifles and 60,000 Remington cartridges were unloaded at Tadjoura. But there was little hope of leaving before April. Tadjoura, which had just been made a French protectorate (the cheapest form of government) was a parasitic community which lived by procrastination. The 'mad dog' Europeans were detained for as long as it took to exhaust their bakshish. 'During the formation of a caravan', wrote Rimbaud, 'the entire population [1,300] lives off the caravan for the three, six or even ten months of unavoidable delay'.

None of this dented his confidence. Thieving and scrounging had been factored into the estimates, and there was nothing unexpected about the lack of urgency. There are, once again, some huge adjustments to be made to the tragic tale that appears in every account of

Rimbaud's life: fuming with frustration, the ex-poet sits on the edge of a desert like a shrivelled fruit on the last branch of a dying tree, gambling his life and fortune on a heap of rusting rifles, impatient to embark on the adventure 'that will ruin him financially, physically and psychologically'.[2]

Without the sly alterations made by the first editor of Rimbaud's letters, this fantasy might never have taken root. Rimbaud's description of Tadjoura, for instance, in a letter dated 3 December 1885, was given a very different tone by the simple omission of a short phrase (italicized below):

The local business is the slave trade.

[. . .] Ever since the English admiral Hewett forced Emperor John of Tigré [Tigray] to sign a treaty abolishing the slave trade – which is the only native business that can be said to flourish – the natives have been the enemies of the Europeans. But under the French protectorate, no attempt is made to hinder the trade, *and it's better that way.*

This was the steely practicality that would see him through the desert. No one could travel without the cooperation of the slave traders.[3] Human merchandise was the base of the economy and the reason why trade routes existed. Most caravans – including European caravans – arrived at their destinations with far more people than when they set out. Guides and camel-drivers spent their wages on slaves, usually children, purchased in batches of up to a thousand.[4] The Europeans themselves were often urged to accept slaves as payment and often took them for the sake of good business relations.

Rimbaud's own paperwork shows that some of his camels were supplied by the Abou-Bekr family – the 'redoubtable' Abyssinian Mafia, which Rimbaud himself ostentatiously denounced in an official letter to the French Consul at Aden: 'The most dangerous enemies of Europeans in all these circumstances are the Abou-Bekrs.'[5] This is supposed to prove that Rimbaud kept his hands miraculously clean – as if, having identified the 'bandits' without whom it was impossible to trade, he then decided to do without them.

The other Europeans who were waiting to leave Tadjoura that year camped outside the village under the only clump of palm-trees.

They slept among their camels and merchandise, fingering their revolvers, watching out for robbers, hyenas and young warriors who hoped to prove their manhood by killing a white man. Rimbaud took up residence in Tadjoura itself, which shows not only that he was able to trust his native guards but also that he had the confidence of the local Sultan – one of the region's biggest slave tycoons.[6]

However long it took and whatever compromises it entailed, the journey would be worth the wait. The guns, as Rimbaud told his mother, were 'old percussion rifles declared unfit for service forty years ago'. In Europe, they were worth seven or eight francs each. In Choa, he hoped to sell them for forty francs a piece. King Menelik had already paid an advance, and although Rimbaud had sunk all his disposable assets in the affair, a string was securely attached: 'I have arranged things so that I can recover my capital at any time.' One of the backers was Jules Suel, owner of the Grand Hôtel de l'Univers, who never risked his money on hopeless ventures.

Rimbaud actually became more optimistic as the days passed. In October 1885, he had been looking forward to a profit of 7,000–8,000 francs. In January 1886, he was anticipating 10,000 francs (about £30,000 today). In Choa, he would load up with gold, ivory and musk, which could be sold on the Aden market for 'a profit of about 50 per cent'. His travelling arsenal also included a general store: tools, parasols, raisins for producing a kind of Communion wine (a detail that would have delighted the editor of *La Vogue*, which published Rimbaud's 'Premières communions' that April), and 'camping equipment' for Menelik's army – metal plates for durra pancakes, pots and goblets that fitted one inside the other like Russian dolls.

Naturally, the news from the desert was horrific. In February, a Frenchman called Pierre Barral, travelling with his wife and a large caravan, was ambushed by 500 Danakil warriors. Ominously, some of the bandits carried rifles, though these were unfortunately not used in the final killing. Wading through the unidentifiable carnage, the search party was led to the shattered loom of Mme Barral's corpse by a single gold tooth glinting in the sun.[7]

Rimbaud knew that he might end up as a smile in the desert, but he had his eyes fastened on the distant Shangri-la beyond the

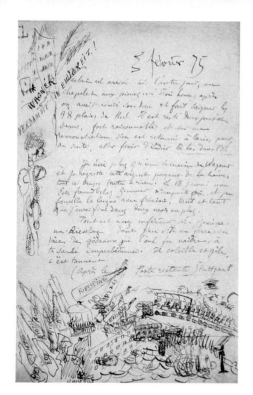

Left. Rimbaud's letter to Delahaye from Stuttgart, 5 March 1875 (incorrectly dated 5 February by Rimbaud).

Below. The *Prins van Oranje*, on which Rimbaud sailed to Java.

Above. 'Le nouveau
Juif errant', by
Delahaye, 1876.

Left. 'Les Voyages
forment la jûnesse',
by Verlaine, 1876.

Right. Alfred Bardey.

Below. La Maison Bardey
at Aden.

Above, left and right.
Rimbaud in Harar, 1883.

Left. Coffee merchant in Harar,
by Rimbaud.

Makonnen,
Governor of Harar.

Menelik II,
Emperor of Ethiopia.

Danakil
warriors.

Left. Rimbaud's companion from
1884 to 1886, by Ottorino Rosa.

Rimbaud's house in Harar from 1888,
by Ottorino Rosa.

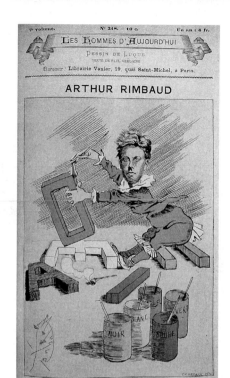

Right. The poet of 'Voyelles', by Luque, 1888.

Below. Verlaine at the Café François Ier, *c.* 1890, by Dornac.

Above. Rimbaud's trunk, now at the Rimbaud Museum in Charleville.

Left. Rimbaud's sister Isabelle, late 1890s.

mountains. Once across the Awash river, all his troubles would be over:

> I hope to take refuge, a few months from now, in the mountains of
> Abyssinia, which is the Switzerland of Africa, where there is no winter
> and no summer: perpetual springtime and greenery, and a life of liberty
> at no cost!

In Choa, life would be free, in both senses of the word. Rimbaud had seen too many paradises come and go to take his hopes too seriously. This businessman's Eden sounds like an almost cheerful self-parody – another 'Adieu' at the end of a Season in Hell.

> But why regret an eternal sun, if we are embarked on the discovery of
> divine light, – far from the people who die with the changing seasons?

*

IN APRIL, THE caravan was finally ready to leave. Then some bad news came from Aden: France had signed a treaty with Britain, banning the import of arms.

Rimbaud and Labatut sent a vigorous letter of protest to the French Foreign Minister, care of the French Resident at Obock. The letter was obviously written by Rimbaud. After complaining that permission had been obtained several times over, he refuted the arguments on which the treaty was based. No weapon would fall into native hands (in fact, 276 of Rimbaud's rifles would end up in the hands of Danakil warriors), and there was 'no correlation between the import of arms and the export of slaves': 'No one would dare suggest that a European has ever sold, bought, transported or helped to transport a single slave.' This was true only in a very special sense.

He then estimated the net profit at 258,000 francs (a huge exaggeration) and instructed the French Government to consider itself 'our debtor for this sum while the present ban remains in force'.

After the stick came a carrot of imperial proportions. If the ban remained in force, the French colony of Obock would be cut off from the interior. While Obock withered away, Britain and Italy would make a fortune on the routes from Zeila and Assab. By obstructing agents of colonial expansion like Rimbaud and Labatut, 'the government of the French nation, which we have honourably and courageously represented in these regions', was throwing away an empire.

Rimbaud was playing on imperial greed. Like most traders, he despised the interfering civil servants who stuck pins in maps and knew nothing of life in the colonies. 'I do believe', he wrote in 1884, 'that no country has a more inept colonial policy than France. England [. . .] at least has serious interests and important prospects, but France is the only power that knows how to fritter away its money in impossible places.'

In his letter to the Minister, Rimbaud only appeared to be criticizing French policy. He knew that the treaty was bogus and that Britain and France routinely suspected one another of paying natives to assassinate their soldiers and diplomats. He also knew that the Minister would privately agree with everything he said. France tacitly tolerated any kind of trade, signing philanthropic treaties and hoping all along that men like Rimbaud would help it to forge a route from the Red Sea to the Nile Basin, wherever that was.

The Resident at Obock had already been sending telegrams to Paris, urging exactly the kind of expedition that Rimbaud had planned: 'If possible send cannon, revolver, crate cartridges, King Menelik, excellent effect, especially current situation.'[8] Rimbaud was simply encouraging the Government to take advantage of its main weapon: hypocrisy.

The Resident urged the Minister to concede. Permission was granted secretly in June. The men could proceed to Choa 'at their own risk'. In the eyes of the British, who had already noted 'a large consignment of arms' at Tadjoura, Rimbaud was little more than a privateer.

*

JUST WHEN THE way was clear, another obstacle arose. Labatut was diagnosed with throat cancer and returned to France for treatment. The date of departure was put back again. The high tide of heat was coming in from the Gulf. Rimbaud watched the mercury rise with grim satisfaction: 'I am well', he told his mother on 9 July, 'as well as one can be here in summer, when it's 50 and 55°C in the shade'.

Fortunately, Rimbaud's letters are not our only view of his year-long wait at Tadjoura. Seen through other eyes, he looks quite different. According to Ugo Ferrandi, who was travelling with the Italian trader-journalist, Augusto Franzoj, Rimbaud was the life and soul of the oasis. 'A tall, scrawny man with hair already turning white above the temples', he went visiting his fellow traders like a parish vicar doing the rounds.[9]

Rimbaud was now well known in the Horn of Africa as the Ogaden explorer and as 'a first-rate Arabist'. With Ferrandi, he talked about geography and gave him 'some concise, clear notes on Tadjoura', which Ferrandi subsequently lost. With Franzoj, 'there were long literary discussions about the Romantics and the Decadents'.[10]

No trace of these literary discussions has survived, but since Franzoj had just arrived from Europe, it is quite possible that one of these 'Decadents' was Rimbaud himself. 'Voyelles' had just been published in an Italian Sunday paper,[11] and, more importantly, Mathilde had finally released the manuscript of the *Illuminations*. Rimbaud's prose poems, mixed up with some verse, had been appearing fortnightly in *La Vogue* (13 May–21 June 1886), attributed to 'the late Arthur Rimbaud'.

There was some doubt about Rimbaud's present condition: he was rumoured to be either dead, selling pigs in the north of France, recruiting for the Dutch foreign legion, or ruling a tribe in Africa. When the *Illuminations* were published that year as a book in a print-run of 200 copies, Verlaine's short preface revealed that M. Rimbaud, 'who was born of a good bourgeois family', was 'travelling in Asia, where he is engaged in artistic works'.

Almost no one bought the book, but there were some reviews, including a long piece by Félix Fénéon in the first issue of a new journal called *Le Symboliste*: 'Rimbaud floats like a mythical shadow over the Symbolists', it said. 'Le Bateau ivre' was interpreted as a Symbolist masterpiece, written fifteen years before the movement existed: its images had a symbolic quality without appearing to symbolize anything in particular, like the icons of a religion that never existed. There were generous quotations from the prose poems – 'images of distant civilizations from a bygone epic or an indus-trial future' – and the *Illuminations* were declared, in the modern,

Decadent style, to be an *œuvre* that 'stands outside all literature and is probably superior to all'.

The *Illuminations* had begun their long journey into the literary mainstream. Meanwhile, 'the late Arthur Rimbaud' was dispensing wisdom of a different sort. He had some illuminating tips for Ferrandi. To reduce the clinging irritation of clothes, he wore baggy trousers and a roomy jacket in khaki-grey.

> When he felt the need to urinate, he squatted like the natives, which led them to believe that he was partly Muslim, and, seeing that I already knew something of Islamic ways, he advised me to do the same.[12]

Rimbaud's standing in the village community probably had more to do with his knowledge of Arabic than with his personal hygiene. His socializing was not confined to the Europeans. 'In his hut, he gave the native dignitaries veritable conferences on the Koran.'[13]

Rimbaud had not been wasting his time in Aden. This was the first sign of a hobby that was to have some surprising and dangerous results. The dust-covered man with the raw-meat complexion who could read and explicate holy scripture must have amazed the Tadjourians as much as Verlaine's protégé had dazzled the Parnassians in 1871. In both cases, Rimbaud's prestige depended on a delicate misunderstanding. The Koran according to Rimbaud was not a source of higher truths. According to Ferrandi, 'he was able to interpret it to serve his own ends'. With a workforce of procrastinating layabouts, the holy Prophet might prove to be a powerful ally.

*

BY SEPTEMBER, RIMBAUD badly needed divine assistance. His latest plan had been to tag along with the experienced explorer and gun-runner, Paul Soleillet. On 9 September, Soleillet was walking down a street in Aden when he collapsed with a heart attack and died.

A week later, Rimbaud received a gruesomely efficient letter from Jules Suel. His partner Labatut was still dying of cancer but had suffered a slight improvement. This was good news: 'You'll have enough time to liquidate everything without being bothered by the heirs, who will probably only learn of the death from here.' Suel was referring to Labatut's native family. Since Labatut had spent seven prolific years in Choa, his heirs might turn out to be innumerable. Financial complications could be avoided if news of the death were somehow delayed ...

Suel took the opportunity to send on Labatut's 'effects': 'There's not much left, but you'll have some clothes for the road: some new and some old.' For Rimbaud, words – and even the clothes of a dead man – had long since lost their superstitious power. In a world where chains of cause and effect were brutally obvious, there was little room for irrational conjecture.

But was this fierce pragmatism simply the triumph of the rational, atheistic intellect? Before leaving Tadjoura, Rimbaud performed one of his characteristic, acrimonious farewells. Franzoj seems to have interceded on Mariam's behalf. Rimbaud wrote to him in September:

> Please excuse me, but I've dismissed that woman once and for all.
> I'll give her a few thalers* and she can leave on the dhow at Rasali [a headland just up from Tadjoura] for Obock, where she can go where she pleases.
> I've seen quite enough of that masquerade.[14]

Bardey claims that Rimbaud's companion (if it was the same woman) was 'decently repatriated',[15] and it may be that Rimbaud was simply playing to his audience or trying to purge himself of sentiment before the ordeal; but the coincidence of departure and righteous rejection suggests the old pattern. *Une Saison en Enfer* had ended with a very similar dismissal:

> What was I saying about a friendly hand! A fine advantage is that I can laugh at those old mendacious love affairs, and strike with shame those lying couples.

The key word in Rimbaud's letter is 'masquerade': the woman who dressed as a European was just another cruel semblance of love,

---

* The Maria Theresa dollar or thaler ($) was the principal currency of Abyssinia: a large silver coin worth approximately 4.5 francs or 2.25 rupees (about £14 or $22 today).

another blue-eyed Mme Rimbaud. If truth was unattainable, at least its opposite could be repudiated and destroyed.

*

IN EARLY DECEMBER 1886, three weeks after nine French sailors were massacred across the Gulf of Tadjoura at Ambado, Rimbaud set off with thirty-four servants and about fifty camels towards the black volcanic mountains. A mule trotted along beside him, with a double-barrelled shotgun strapped to the harness. Rimbaud preferred to walk, to feel the hot desert beneath his feet. He was expecting the expedition to last 'at least a year'.

Reports of his death might turn out to have been only slightly premature. The *Illuminations* had come to an abrupt end in July. An erratum instructed readers of *La Vogue* to replace the words 'To be continued' with 'End':

> Here, indeed – and alas – ends the complete publication of the work of the ambiguous and glorious deceased.

34

Horror

'Man hopes to spend three quarters of his life suffering in order to spend the last quarter taking his ease. Usually, he dies of poverty without knowing how far along he is with his plan!'

(Rimbaud to his mother and sister, 6 January 1886)

R IMBAUD'S CARAVAN sidled down the coast to Sagallo, then turned inland across the volcanic plateau.

Thirty-eight miles from Tadjoura, he found himself on the surface of a different planet: a waste of black rocks that made the camels lose their footing. 'Caravans descend to the salt lake by appalling routes that recall the presumed horror of lunar landscapes.'[1] Far below, Lake Assal – the lowest point in Africa – was a sheet of intense blue with a belt of dazzling white: the bottom of an ancient sea, trapped long ago by mountains.

Between Lake Assal and the high pastures of Herer, 162 miles to the south, lay 'the most horrible landscapes on this side of Africa': a desert of salt; a desert of sand and seashells; then a vast, ironstone oven.[2] The caravan picked its way along the dried-up beds of ancient torrents, past strange tumuli and burial chambers in limestone cliffs. Stone Age shepherds came out of nowhere to peer at the white man with his mule. This was Issa territory. Even the Danakil warriors avoided it. Whenever grass huts appeared on the horizon, expendable members of the expedition – usually women and old men – were sent on ahead.

Rimbaud left no record of the trivial irritations. His terse reports echo his style of command: 'His orders were crisp and precise. His tone, without being brutal, was strangely emphatic.'[3] Almost all the details of this murderous route come from the coffee-table account of the French explorer, Jules Borelli, who had set out from Sagallo eight months before: dust-storms, ailing camels, marauding zebras, the nightly din of hyenas and camel-drivers' dirges, the routine killing of prowlers, and the vast mirage-lakes that had the native guides rushing off to nowhere.

For Rimbaud, this horrendous journey was like the story of his life or of any human life: the triumph of matter over mind. The disappointments were gratifyingly huge. The precious salt of Lake Assal could only be extracted at great expense, and the French company that proposed to mine it was 'a swindle'. A month later, as he watched the camels splash easily across the river Awash into the zone of Choan control, he thought of the grand scheme to use the river as a trading artery:

> On reaching the Awash, one recalls with stupefaction the canalization plans of certain travellers. Poor Soleillet was having a special craft constructed at Nantes for precisely that purpose! The Awash is a tortuous rivulet, blocked every step of the way by trees and rocks. I crossed it at several points, several hundred kilometres apart, and it is patently impossible to sail down it, even in times of flood. Moreover, for its entire course, it runs through forests and deserts which are far from the trading centres and unconnected to any route.

Rimbaud's notes exude a bitter admiration for the land that so effortlessly crushed the Europeans' pretensions. 'Poor Soleillet' and the other heroes of colonial expansion were pathetic visionaries, fooled by their own dreams, like the Charleville seer, building boats for rivers that existed only in the mind.

After several days of grassland and gentle hills, the caravan entered the kingdom of Choa at a village called Farré. Another nasty surprise was in store. Somehow, the word of Labatut's death had flown across the mountains and the desert. The King's *hazage* (chief steward) greeted Rimbaud with the news that Labatut had died owing him an 'immense' sum of money. 'He appeared to be asking me for the entire caravan as security.' Still the master of surreal juxtaposition, Rimbaud fobbed the man off with an eyeglass and some laxative pills, then set off for the mountain stronghold of Ankober, thirteen miles to the south-west.

This was not the best way in which to ingratiate himself with his customers. Foreign traders were treated as honoured guests of the King and maintained free of charge during their stay in Choa. If the *hazage* seemed to want to commandeer the caravan, it was probably for the perfectly innocent reason that imported goods were always impounded at Farré, then sent to Ankober to be examined by royal agents.[4]

It would be reasonable to suppose that Rimbaud's barnstorming approach was the result of frustration: he had just lost a year of his life to procrastinating swindlers, his hair was turning white, and he had seen the sun set over the desert sixty times without knowing whether he would see the dawn. On the other hand, his belligerence might have been a deliberate ploy. A show of self-confidence would underline his strong position. He knew that King Menelik was desperate for weapons and keen to encourage arms-dealers.[5] He also knew – as he led his mule along the narrow mountain passes towards the denuded, hut-covered hill of Ankober – that he had arrived in Choa at a critical moment in its history. His antique rifles were the life-blood of a new nation.[6]

*

AT FARRÉ, HE had learnt that Menelik was away on a campaign. This was a significant piece of news. Until then, the centre of power had been in the north, with the British-backed Emperor, Yohannes IV. Technically, Menelik was the Emperor's vassal, but the vassal had a daring dream: he claimed direct descent from Menelik I, the fabled son of Solomon and the Queen of Sheba, who was said to have founded the nation in the tenth century BC.

Menelik's latest swathe of devastation seemed at first to be a simple intensification of tribal warfare. Since physical labour was considered dishonourable, large numbers of slaves had to be harvested at regular intervals from ever more distant regions. But behind the display of savage destruction, Menelik was carving out his own Solomonic empire to the south and east.

Rimbaud was the first European to realize what was happening to Abyssinia. He pointed to the rise of an Abyssinian nationalism, inspired by intelligently manipulated legends (something that was supposed to be beyond the capability of Africans). He predicted the ultimate victory of Menelik and was almost alone in viewing him as an independent force. Rimbaud and the King had much in common: 'This is not to say that he isn't happy to hear what the [European] diplomats have to say: he'll pocket whatever he can get out of them.'

The man Rimbaud was about to meet was now one of the most powerful native leaders in Africa. While Rimbaud was crossing the desert, Menelik had been acquiring the city of Harar: the first step to winning a port for his landlocked empire. With the Egyptian evacuation in 1884, Harar had fallen into the hands of a blundering Muslim despot. The Emir Abdullahi had succeeded in paralysing all trade, except, of course, the slave trade. He had massacred an Italian expedition which he mistook for the advance guard of an Italian army, and sentenced Bishop Taurin to death as a spy. (He was saved by the Emir's mother.)

Challenged by Menelik, the Emir stupidly chose to fight outside the city walls. In the words of Rimbaud's crisp chronicle, Abdullahi's 'three thousand warriors were cut to pieces and crushed in the wink of an eye by the warriors of the King of Choa'. Six thousand testicles were harvested as trophies and a new regime was installed.

The importance of European arms to King Menelik's grand design is demonstrated by the fact that he took time off from the killing to send Rimbaud a personal letter (3 February 1887):

> How are you? I, by the grace of God, am well. [. . .] Five days will suffice for me to see the merchandise. You will then be able to leave.

*

IN THE CAPITAL, Jules Borelli had been expecting a foreign visitor. Weeks before, from the heights of Ankober, lights had been seen glinting in the Adar plain to the east. Since the natives never lit fires at night, this was almost certainly a European caravan. On 9 February, he recorded its arrival:

M. Rimbaud, a French trader, arrived from Tadjoura [on 6 February] with his caravan. He has had a troublesome time of it. The same old story: misconduct, greed and treachery from the men; harassment and surprise attacks from the Adals; lack of water; the camel-drivers taking advantage ...

Our compatriot has lived in Harar. He knows Arabic and speaks Amharic and Oromo. He is indefatigable. His aptitude for languages, his strong will and unfailing patience place him in the ranks of accomplished travellers.[7]

This respectful portrait of Rimbaud, by a man who was jealous of his own reputation, is a significant contrast to the accepted image: the gun-running ex-poet, shamelessly cheated by that 'crafty devil', the King of Choa; 'lost and bewildered' among grasping natives; a victim of his own trusting nature.

Rimbaud's first act at Ankober showed nothing of the sort. 'Irritated by the impertinent demands' of the camel-drivers, who were asking for a bonus payment (a customary arrangement), he snatched away their contract and tore it up in front of them. The bonus was eventually paid by the royal *hazage* and, according to Rimbaud's report to the French Consul at Aden, was used to buy slaves which were sent to the coast with other European caravans 'and all died en route'.

A more serious threat to profits now presented itself. With the help of a disreputable French cavalry officer called Hénon who had washed up in Choa several years before,[8] Labatut's widow sued Rimbaud for what she claimed was her rightful inheritance. Surprisingly – and despite what most secondhand accounts suggest – Rimbaud won the case: 'After odious discussions, in which I sometimes had the upper hand and sometimes not, the *hazage* gave me an order of distraint on the homes of the deceased.'

Rimbaud now seized the initiative. Armed with his order of distraint, he went to the widow's 'shack' and found a receipt for some ivory which proved that Labatut did indeed owe the *hazage* 300 thalers. Unfortunately, Labatut's money and possessions had already been squirrelled away by the widow. 'All I found were some old underpants, which the widow snatched away with tears of fire, a few bullet moulds and a dozen pregnant slaves, which I left.' He did however confiscate Labatut's animals and various 'effects', which he later sold for $97.

What happened next is so shocking to anyone who values literary labour that almost every account either misrepresents it or omits it altogether. Rimbaud's own account, written for the Aden Consul, is quite clear:

> Labatut had been writing his *Memoirs*. I gathered up 34 volumes of them, in 34 notebooks, at the widow's home, and, despite the latter's imprecations, committed them to the flames. This, it was explained to me, was a great misfortune, because some title deeds were interleaved with these confessions which, after a cursory perusal, had seemed to me to be unworthy of serious inspection.

The burning of Labatut's notebooks was also unfortunate because, as a historian of East Africa has pointed out, the memoirs of Pierre Labatut would have been a uniquely important document in the history of modern Ethiopia.[9] Labatut himself was destroyed by cancer, but his posthumous existence was snuffed out by Arthur Rimbaud.

The sneering term, 'confessions', suggests the kind of self-deceiving literature that Rimbaud had ridiculed in his 'Seer' letter. Another pitiful ego was consigned to the void. If a masterpiece like *Une Saison en Enfer* had been obliterated, why should the ramblings of an 'idiot' like Labatut survive? All sentiment was to be expunged. Labatut's 'filthy bitch' (as Rimbaud called the widow) appears in his account as a savage caricature of loyalty and affection, the grieving wife, clinging to her husband's underpants.

By now, Labatut's creditors were coming thick and fast. One of the King's generals came to call and 'sat down to drink my *tedj*':*

> At the sight of a mule munching the grass, the cry would be, 'That's the mule I gave to Labatut!' [. . .] I sent the noble brigand packing with the words, 'Go to the king!', which means much the same as, 'Go to hell!'

Rimbaud does appear to have settled some genuine debts: 'Since those poor people were always in good faith, I allowed myself to be

---

* A fermented drink made (usually) with honey, bitter herbs and bark.

swayed and paid up.' He even paid wages to the widows of servants who had died on the road from Tadjoura.

> However, the news of my virtuous doings spread far and wide, and there rose up, from hither and yon, a whole series, a whole gang, a whole horde of Labatut's creditors, with tales to make the blood run cold. This effected a change in my benevolent disposition, and I decided to hurry on down to Choa. As I recall, on the morning of my departure, when I was already trotting off to the north-north-east, I saw a delegate of the wife of a friend of Labatut suddenly rise up out of a bush, demanding a sum of 19 thalers in the name of the Virgin Mary; and, further on, a creature in a sheepskin cloak leapt down from the top of an outcrop to ask if I had paid his brother the 12 thalers that Labatut had borrowed, etc. I called to these people that they were too late!

After hurrying across the mountains, Rimbaud swung round to the south-west on to what is now the main road north from Addis Ababa. In Choan territory, the journey was less harrowing. Anyone who failed to supply a royal caravan with food was imprisoned and punished.

Three days later, on 7 April 1887, he marched into Menelik's new capital.

Entotto was a bald hill occupied by hundreds of mud huts dotted about among the stumps of what had once been a magnificent cedar forest. At the top of the hill, enclosed by three concentric stockades, stood Menelik's thatched palace. Entotto was home to several thousand Abyssinians and a handful of Europeans – some wandering wrecks, like the alcoholic French labourer who begged a pair of shoes from Rimbaud, and some adventurous young professionals, like the Swiss engineer, King Menelik's chief foreign adviser, Alfred Ilg.

Rimbaud settled in to wait for the King. A few days later, Menelik's return was announced by the ear-splitting wail of Egyptian trumpets, stolen from Harar, 'followed by the King's army and his booty, which included two Krupp cannons, each one carried by eighty men'.

Menelik conducted his business in front of a lurid portrait of himself flanked by two lions. He sat on a divan, draped in a black silk burnous, surrounded by cushions and courtiers. Negotiations were swift and successful – not that this is evident from Rimbaud's report to the French Consul:

> Menelik seized all the merchandise and forced me to let him have it at a reduced rate, forbidding me to sell it retail and threatening to send it back to the coast at my expense! He gave me a lump sum of 14,000 thalers for the whole caravan. [. . .]
>
> Dogged by the gang of Labatut's so-called creditors, whose side was always taken by the King, [. . .] I was afraid of being stripped completely bare and decided to leave Choa.

To Rimbaud's irritation, further sums were deducted by the King: $2,500 (thalers) for outstanding camel rent and wages that had been paid by the *hazage*, and $3,000 to cover Labatut's debts. (This was eventually reduced with the help of Alfred Ilg to $2,100.) Rimbaud was given a bill for about $9,000 payable at Harar, which he intended to visit on the way back. Though he later complained (but in very different circumstances) of this unreliable method of payment,[10] it can hardly have been a surprise: he knew that there was no cash in Choa. In any case, as he himself admitted, he eventually obtained his money without much delay.

In Menelik, Rimbaud had met his match in haggling and tactical procrastination; but the whole affair could only be described as disastrous if Rimbaud had been hoping to pocket his dead partner's share of the proceeds. Menelik paid a good price for the rifles (about thirty-two francs each), which, according to Rimbaud himself, would otherwise have been bound for the scrap heap. It was quite normal to request a discount on such a large consignment, especially since an advance had been paid many months before. (Rimbaud somehow forgot to mention the advance in his later reports and never specified the amount.)

Even without plotting a tedious course through the labyrinthine accounts (tedious only in the telling), there is enough straightforward information to arouse suspicion. If, as Rimbaud claimed, King Menelik 'robbed' him, why, for example, did he agree to run errands for him and continue to do business with him after the expedition to Choa?

Europeans in Choa were plagued by grasping fingers and were

expected to sell whatever they had with them. Jules Borelli had been driven to distraction by 'these insatiable beggars', though, in terms of the local economy, most of the deals he describes were more than fair: a female slave (worth up to $80 in Harar) for a Remington rifle (worth about $18). With seven years' experience of trading in Abyssinia, Rimbaud had obviously prepared for this potentially ruinous bartering by bringing extra merchandise like the parasols – a favourite item with Menelik's Queen, Taitou.

The contradictions in Rimbaud's accounts are a result of his refusal to accept responsibility for Labatut's debts. This is why he presented himself as a puppet in the hands of King Menelik. He knew that the French Consul, who was to act as arbitrator, would be convinced by his portrayal of the King as an Abyssinian Fagin backed by an army of thieves and castrators. He can hardly have known that his racist caricature would remain convincing for the next hundred years.

Three weeks after arriving in Entotto, Rimbaud was ready to leave. Then a last-minute obstacle arose, as he explained in a style which recalls the scenario of a silent movie:

The day before I left Entotto [. . .] I saw behind me in the mountains the helmet of M. Hénon, who, having learned of my departure, had speedily covered the 120 kilometres from Ankober to Entotto, and, behind him, the burnous of the frantic widow, snaking along the precipices.

The allegations of Labatut's widow were heard in the privacy of the palace. After a few hours, the verdict was proclaimed:

The monarch declared that he had been a friend of the said Labatut and that he wished to extend his friendship to his descendants. As proof, he promptly dispossessed the widow of the lands he had given to Labatut!

This directly contradicts Rimbaud's later claim that the King always took the side of Labatut's heirs. By allowing Menelik to deduct $2,100 for what may well have been a fictitious debt, Rimbaud had effectively paid a bribe and saved himself a lot of money. As he observed in his report to the Consul, 'the King always has other people silenced when he has been paid himself'.

*

HIS FORCEFUL APPROACH to arms-dealing apparently vindicated, Rimbaud set off on 1 May 1887 with Jules Borelli on one of the historic journeys of East African exploration. Though the journey was Rimbaud's idea, he later allowed Borelli to take the credit. This was the route that would be used by Alfred Ilg's engineering masterpiece, the first Abyssinian railway, originally intended to run from Djibouti to the White Nile. (It ends at Addis Ababa.)

For three weeks, they plodded east, through lands recently subdued by Menelik. To the south, they saw the cradle of Menelik's future capital, Addis Ababa ('New Flower'), and the alluring chasm of the Rift Valley, which led by unknown routes to the great African lakes. They passed through rich pastureland and forests of euphorbia and mimosa, flattened to a width of ten metres by the Choan army. Borelli, who was considered a harmless lunatic by the natives, shot elephants and crocodiles and 'twiddled sextants'. Rimbaud took notes, but relied on his native experience: 'The altitude of the Mindjar plain must be 1,800 metres (I deduce the altitude from the type of vegetation).'

Thanks to King Menelik, the route was practically deserted. Terrified guides had to be taken prisoner. At Chelenko, the ground was crunchy underfoot. This was the site of Abdullahi's catastrophe. Human remains lay everywhere. Borelli was able to add to his skull collection.

Few arms dealers ever have the opportunity to examine the effects of their merchandise at such close quarters. But Rimbaud looked beyond the skeletons and, for once, saw a sunny colonial future: 'These regions, which are very healthy and very fertile, are the only parts of East Africa that are suited to European colonization.' One or two phrases in his account have a poetic sound, though they relapse immediately into blunt notation: 'Day 14. 20 kilometres, Herna. Splendid valleys crowned with forests in whose shade we walk. Coffee trees.'

The irony would not have escaped him. By pioneering an east–

west route from the Red Sea to the Nile Basin, Rimbaud found himself at the avant-garde of an empire that was driven by notions and sentiments utterly opposed to his own: wounded patriotism, armchair exoticism and white supremacy. The punchline of this epic joke was that, having increased Menelik's arsenal by one twelfth (by his own reckoning), Rimbaud was making a significant contribution to the first defeat of a European nation in open battle by an African army (Menelik's defeat of Italy at Adwa in 1896).

He reached Harar, ahead of Borelli, on 21 May 1887. Both Rimbaud and Borelli described the town as 'a cesspit'. The indigenous population had either fled from the Choan army or lay rotting in the streets. A mosque had been demolished and coffee trees uprooted. Rimbaud was received by the new Governor, a beautiful, ambitious young man called Makonnen, a cousin of Menelik. His son, the future Emperor Haile Selassie, was born in Harar four years later.

Some of Labatut's creditors had caught up with Rimbaud and were 'pestering' him for payment. To fend off the most persistent, he left $866 with Makonnen and, after 'considerable costs and difficulties', had Menelik's bill converted to drafts payable by merchants on the Red Sea.

After collecting his servant, Djami,[11] he left for Aden and was back by 27 July 1887, nineteen months after leaving for Tadjoura.

Rimbaud now launched a swift and skilful tidying-up operation. He paid off the owner of the Grand Hôtel de l'Univers with a bill for $4,000, then wrote to the French Consul. This was an important letter, since the Consul would be asked to adjudicate in any dispute.

Rimbaud had a wretched tale to tell. 'I have emerged from the deal with a 60 per cent loss on my capital, not to mention 21 months of atrocious exertions spent liquidating this wretched affair.' If this were true, Rimbaud would have been left with a pitiful 6,000 francs.

Mme Rimbaud was given a different version:

I was forced to pay my partner's debts twice over [. . .] I'm back with the 15,000 I started out with after exhausting myself in a horrible fashion for almost two years. I have no luck! (23 August 1887)

What little money he still had was tied up: his 'dear Mama' would have to 'lend' him 500 francs from the money he had previously sent home.

Three days later, he told Alfred Bardey that he had *less* than he started out with; and in October, obviously forgetting his earlier letter, he told his mother the same story: 'I've come out of it poorer than I was before.'

If, as is generally supposed, this sad failure was the real Arthur Rimbaud, who was the Rimbaud who returned to Aden that summer to go on holiday with his manservant to Cairo, there to deposit 16,000 francs (about £48,000 today) in the Crédit Lyonnais at 4 per cent interest? And who was the 'suspicious-looking' individual who was arrested in Massawa that August without a passport, brought before the Consul and found to be carrying two bills worth $7,500 (about £105,000)?[12]

Such an enormous sum of money would have ruined the picture he was trying to paint. But no one had to know about his spectacular success – neither the Consul, nor Mme Rimbaud, nor especially Labatut's creditors.

When he wrote to his mother in August, even the relatively small amount he admitted to owning was depicted as the burden of a sinner in Hell. Rimbaud had abandoned poetry, but not fiction:

Picture this to yourself: I'm continually carrying about 16,000 and a few 100 gold francs in my belt. It weighs eight kilos and it's giving me dysentery.

But I can't go to Europe – for many reasons: first, I'd die in winter; second, I've grown too accustomed to a life of wandering at no expense; and finally, I have no job.

I am thus to spend the rest of my days wandering about in exhaustion and hardship, with nothing to look forward to but dying in harness.

It was almost a shame that there was no audience to applaud the performance.

35

Profit

'Madagascar, where it's possible to save money'

(Rimbaud to his mother and sister, 25 August 1887)

THE FRENCH CONSUL at Massawa to the French Vice-Consul at Aden, 5 August 1887:

Monsieur le Consul,

A certain Raimbeaux, who claims to be a trader in Harar and Aden, arrived at Massawa yesterday on the weekly mailboat from Aden.

This Frenchman, who is tall and thin, with grey eyes and a moustache that is almost fair, but small, was brought to me by the *carabinieri* [customs police]. M. Raimbeaux has no passport and was unable to offer proof of his identity. [. . .]

I should be grateful, Monsieur le Consul, if you could inform me about this individual whose behaviour is somewhat suspicious. This Raimbeau is in possession of a bill for 5,000 thalers payable at sight within five days by M. Lucardi, and another bill for 2,500 thalers payable by an Indian merchant at Massawa.[1]

Rimbaud was travelling as if frontiers had ceased to exist, or as if, once again, he was hoping to be looked after by a government official. On the other hand, since one of Labatut's creditors was trying to track him down in Aden and would obviously try the Consulate, he may have decided to obtain his passport at a safe distance.[2]

The Massawa Consul's reaction to the grey-eyed wanderer was

typical: mistrust followed by esteem. A week later, the Consul wrote
to a friend at the Cairo Court of Appeal, warmly recommending 'M.
Rimbaud Arthur',

> a very honourable Frenchman, a trader-explorer in Choa and Harar.
> He knows the region perfectly and has lived there for more than nine
> [*sic* for seven] years.
>   M. Rimbaud is on his way to Egypt to recover a little from his long
> exertions. He will be able to give you news of the brother of Borelli
> Bey, whom he met in Choa.[3]

Once his identity had been confirmed, a passport was obtained
from Aden. Rimbaud cashed at least one of his bills,[4] then continued
up the Red Sea, returning along the route he had taken, in sickness
and despair, seven years before.

At Suez, the French Consul was similarly charmed. He mentioned
Rimbaud in his next report to the French Foreign Minister as 'one of
the men of great worth and honour who represent France in Choa'[5]
– which meant that Rimbaud had successfully sold arms to Menelik
despite the British ban. From Suez, he went to Cairo and took a
room at the Hôtel d'Europe.

On 22 August 1887, an important Cairo newspaper, *Le Bosphore
égyptien*, which was edited by Jules Borelli's brother Octave,
announced the arrival from Choa 'a few days ago' of 'M. Raimbaud,
the French traveller and businessman'.

He must have started writing as soon as he reached the hotel. On
25 and 27 August, *Le Bosphore égyptien* published a long account by
Rimbaud of his recent expedition. It contained vital information on
the hopeless Lake Assal project, the disappointing river Awash,
Menelik's trail of destruction and the surge of patriotism in Abyssinia.
It also revealed the existence of an excellent new route from Choa to
the coast.[6]

There was more accurate detail and analysis in Rimbaud's report
than in several years' worth of diplomatic despatches. It helped to
shape French policy and thus the modern history of East Africa.
Emphasizing the futile horror of the Tadjoura route, Rimbaud
redirected attention to a stretch of coast known as Djibouti, 'until
now entirely deserted'. Tadjoura was a waste of time, but Djibouti

had water and was much closer to Harar and the new route to Choa. A warehouse and a barracks should be built immediately, although, of course, traders should be left to their own devices: 'It goes without saying that it should remain a free port if the aim is to compete with Zeila.'[7]

This brisk report was not the work of a broken man. The trader of uncertain nationality who sat at a writing-desk in a ventilated hotel with a manservant to see to his needs, charming the compatriots whose help he might require, had hidden reserves in more than one sense.

At the very least, Rimbaud was carrying $7,500 (thalers), after paying $4,000 to the owner of 'the Universe' and $866 to one of Labatut's creditors. He also claimed to have $600 in cash and to be owed $5,800 by Labatut's estate. In his note to Bardey on trade in Choa, the phrase, 'I left the ivory' suggests that, as originally intended, Rimbaud returned with musk and gold. It is unlikely that he wasted the long journey back to Aden by returning empty-handed. According to his calculations, the musk and the gold would have made a fifty per cent profit in Aden.[8]

Rimbaud's earnings from the expedition to Choa would therefore have amounted to $18,766 or about 84,500 francs. His *minimum* profit can be estimated at 33,750 francs (about £100,000 today). This would represent a total net profit of 225 per cent on his original investment. The actual total might have been 62,550 francs, excluding any proceeds from imported merchandise. It would otherwise be difficult to explain how he was able to saunter up the Red Sea, deposit 16,000 francs in a savings bank, spend seven weeks with his servant in a Cairo hotel, and remain unemployed for the next fifty days.

The accounts Rimbaud was ordered to submit to the Aden Consul that November are a dance of the veils, ending with a provocative pirouette and a speedy exit: 'I have the honour to declare to Monsieur le Consul that I refuse henceforth to respond in any fashion to any demand concerning the aforementioned affair.'

Even without subjecting Rimbaud's creative book-keeping to the indignity of a pocket-calculator, it is possible to develop firm suspicions. First, despite repeated demands over the next three years, Rimbaud never produced any documents to support his claim that he, and not Labatut's heirs and creditors, was out of pocket. Second, his muddled accounting was surely the result of wilful ineptitude. A French businessman who knew Rimbaud in Aden and worked for twenty-five years with 'a large number of Arab, Black and White traders', considered him 'by a very long chalk the best of the lot for clear and accurate accounting'.[9]

No matter how the sums are calculated, Rimbaud always comes out ahead. Not only was the Choan expedition not a failure, it was more profitable than he had hoped.* Labatut's death had been a stroke of good luck. This was not the Rimbaud of biographical legend but the Rimbaud whom Borelli had seen at work – an 'embittered' man but not one of life's victims:

> It was very interesting to watch him when, after concluding a deal, he sent his man away with a derisive look on his face and then, half-laughing, he would wink at me in an amusing fashion.[11]

Rimbaud exaggerated the heat of the sun, the stinginess of his employers and his own incompetence – why not also his financial hardship? The only real mystery is this: why has Rimbaud's tale of woe been accepted as the truth? Why, when the whole shape and meaning of his life in Africa depend on it, has the biography of his money never been properly pieced together?

Like the tragic tale of Mozart's obscure burial,[12] Rimbaud's fictitious failure in Choa is part of an edifying fable that makes the absurdity of his end more bearable. It turns the sudden precipice into the tail of a neat parabola. The hero's transgression – squandering his talent, denying the religion of Art, being too original, etc. – is punished by failure in the material world. His death is cloaked in a comforting logic and attributed, without evidence, to a fate-like agency: usually inherited disease or mysterious bad luck. Fake reports of Rimbaud's death-bed conversion are rightly derided, but the idea

---

* The most successful French businessman in Aden – a multi-millionaire called Antonin Besse, who was given his first job by Alfred Bardey in 1897 – claimed to have made his fortune by following Rimbaud's 'intuitions'.[10] M. Besse later donated large sums to the University of Oxford, which means that it was partly thanks to Rimbaud that the present author was able to study Rimbaud's poetry under J. A. Hiddleston, Besse Fellow in French at Exeter College, Oxford.

of ineluctable decline is accepted in its place. Either way, Rimbaud's
life is used, in spite of his own philosophy, to prove that human
existence is subject to a superior form of administration.

There is, however, something in Rimbaud's behaviour that creates
an impression of inescapable misfortune. His letters to the Aden
Consul have the characteristic tone of self-destruction. The tale of
his smash-and-grab mission to Choa is told with a kind of masochistic
glee that hardly inspires confidence in his integrity – the insulting
of officials, the reckless dispensing of laxatives, the forcible seizure of
underpants and the burning of books.

A few days before his thirty-third birthday, Rimbaud was still
behaving like a criminal courting punishment, a fugitive who longed
for the day of his capture. Only in this sense could the expedition to
Choa be described as a failure.

*

RIMBAUD NURSED HIMSELF in Cairo for seven weeks. He had
rheumatism in the small of his back, his left thigh and knee, and his
right shoulder. This might account for the peculiar lunging motion
noticed by Armand Savouré: 'the left shoulder always far in front of
the right'.[13] But the rheumatism seems to have cleared up. News
of his health is generally sunny until February 1891.

Little is known about Rimbaud's seven-week vacation in Cairo,
except that he found it – or claimed to find it – uncomfortably
expensive and boring. In a passage from what may be a hitherto
unrecognized correspondence with his sister,* he painted a significantly more cheerful picture: Cairo was a 'civilized' place, 'a city that

---

* Isabelle claimed that when her brother wrote home, he often included a separate
letter for her, with personal advice and interesting geographical facts. Though she
refused to allow these 'intimate' letters to be published, select passages were
apparently incorporated into the first edition of Rimbaud's correspondence. This
would explain why some of the phrases which seem to have been inserted by
Berrichon – quite properly omitted from modern editions – have no obvious
hagiographical value. It would also explain how Isabelle knew about certain episodes
for which the published correspondence offers no evidence. These passages should
be retrieved from the litter bin (i.e. from the 1899 edition of the letters) and
considered, tentatively, as fragments of a lost correspondence.

resembles Paris, Nice and the Orient, and where one lives in the European style'.[14]

He filled his time with plans:[15] the Sudan was opening up to trade again; at Massawa, an Italian army was squaring up to Emperor Yohannes and would need the services of an enterprising trader. He thought again of that magical place, Zanzibar, 'from where one can make long journeys into Africa', and of 'Madagascar, where it's possible to save money'. He also mentioned 'China or Japan', but he was probably teasing his mother.

All these plans had one thing in common: a desire to avoid a sedentary life and to be paid for doing so. On 26 August, he asked the Société de Géographie to fund an expedition to a region that was 'very fearsome for Europeans', according to the Society's reply. (Rimbaud's letter has been lost.) He might have been thinking of the unknown lands he had glimpsed on the way back from Choa and of the vast, bottomless lakes that were rumoured to lie to the south.[16]

Unfortunately, he was also thinking of a very large sum of money. The Society regretted that it was unable to fund his journey. But even before he received its reply, he was planning a different kind of expedition. He wrote to the French Consul in Beirut, asking where he could buy four thoroughbred donkey stallions 'in peak condition': King Menelik, he explained, was hoping to create 'a superior race of mules'.

Rimbaud obtained a passport for himself and Djami, and may even have travelled to Beirut and Damascus.[17] The only certainty is that he was back in Aden by 8 October 1887, helping Alfred Bardey with his paperwork.[18]

It was just a temporary solution. When he wrote home on 22 November and again on 15 December, he was 'in good health' and contemplating something far more lucrative and tractable than Syrian asses.

*

LARGE PROFITS, AS he now knew, could be made in the arms trade. He also knew that the French Government was being offered huge incentives to circumvent the arms embargo. The Governor of Harar,

Makonnen, had promised to close the British trade routes if France allowed Remingtons to be imported.[19]

Rimbaud found what looked like the perfect solution. He asked his mother to forward a letter to the local *député*, with a letter to the Minister for the Colonies. He seemed to remember that the *député* owned a steelworks, which was all to the good. The idea was that, instead of importing guns and cartridges, he would import the machinery for making them. This, he told the Minister, would mean new jobs and investment, and it was all in a good cause: Choa was 'a Christian power' and 'a friend of Europe and particularly of France'.

At the same time, he sent reports on Abyssinian affairs to several French newspapers, and a letter to Paul Bourde, the journalist who had met Bardey on the steamer, offering his services as a foreign correspondent.[20]

The two schemes were interrelated. Foreign policy decisions affected trade; but, as his recent conversations with French diplomats had reminded him, these decisions were influenced by the inside knowledge of men like Rimbaud – especially if the information they provided appeared in a newspaper, where it could shape public opinion.

No newspaper article has been found with Rimbaud's name on it; but it is interesting that, towards the end of 1887, the news from Abyssinia in *Le Temps* begins to echo Rimbaud's correspondence. *Le Temps* was treated as the main source of reliable information on the region. Soon, speeches were being made in the Chambre des Députés which appear to support Rimbaud's interests quite directly.[21] By 1890, the *députés* were under the impression that Harar sheltered a whole community of French merchants (Rimbaud was the only one): these brave men, who protected trade and 'upheld in those distant parts France's venerable reputation', should be offered all possible assistance . . .[22]

While Rimbaud waited to hear whether the Minister would allow him to introduce a military-industrial economy into southern Abyssinia, he agreed to undertake a clandestine mission for a Parisian arms dealer called Armand Savouré. His job was to arrange for 225 camels to carry 3,000 rifles and half a million cartridges from the coast to Harar. The French Governor of Obock had agreed to turn a blind eye.

Savouré offered 1,000 francs but Rimbaud argued him up to 2,000. Savouré had obviously been warned about his partner. He was more nervous about Rimbaud than about the natives or the British: 'If you were paid in full, how could I be sure that you wouldn't *stop* at the first obstacle and that I wouldn't lose my 2,000 francs?'

Rimbaud seems to have kept his promise. The Minister refused to allow him to import an arms factory and he still had no permanent job. In any case, Savouré had already prepared the way: he had found a good 'slave route' and arranged for a *boutre* (an Arab sailing-ship) to meet Rimbaud at a quiet spot on the coast.

On 1 February 1888, Rimbaud wrote to Menelik's engineer, Alfred Ilg, who was resting at home in Zurich. He told him that he was about to leave for Harar to investigate the market in gums and resins. As Ilg suspected, gum was only part of the story. (It would have been untypically foolish of Rimbaud to discuss a smuggling operation in a letter that would almost certainly be read by British and Italian spies.)

He left Aden on about 14 February, crossed the Gulf and reached Harar in record time on 25 February. He was back in Aden by 14 March. Alfred Ilg was impressed: 'Everything is full steam ahead with you – an excessively rare thing in that part of Africa.'

For some reason, Rimbaud had been unable to deliver the 225 camels to the coast. The whole spring of 1888, in fact, is one of the murkiest periods of his life in Africa. In this obscurity, a long controversy arose in the 1930s which threatened to ruin Rimbaud's reputation – especially his left-wing credentials – just when his homosexuality and anarchism were being tentatively accepted as part of a respectable, literary enterprise.

On 22 May 1888, the Italian Consul at Aden, Antonio Cecchi, who had met Rimbaud in 1881, sent a report to his Foreign Minister.[23] The report was based on British intelligence. A large slave and ivory caravan had been seen at Ambos on 10 May. It was led by a son of the notorious slave trader, Abou-Bekr, and 'accompanied by the French trader Rembau, one of the cleverest and most active agents of the French Govt in those regions'.

A similar message was sent in June to the British Foreign Office, which already had a note in its files about the earlier gun-smuggling activities of 'a Frenchman named Rambon'.[24]

In 1937, Enid Starkie, who discovered the report, leapt to the conclusion that Rimbaud had been a slave trader, and supported her argument with selective quotations. She also accused the Aden merchant, César Tian, who was about to employ Rimbaud, of operating through the same 'unsavoury channels'.

Using information supplied by the son of César Tian, the Italian critic Mario Matucci exonerated both Tian and Rimbaud in 1962, and continued to do so in several books and articles. The crux of his argument is that Rimbaud, who was in Harar on 3 and 15 May 1888,[25] could not have been at Ambos on 10 May.

The file was then closed. César Tian was not a *négrier* after all. He was a decent, self-respecting arms dealer and political agent. Rimbaud's admirers heaved a sigh of relief and poured scorn on Enid Starkie. Although Matucci himself provided valuable evidence of European collusion with the slave trade, the effect of his refutation has been to concentrate the whole question of Rimbaud's involvement with slavery on this relatively small point and then to flush it all away.

The file should now be reopened. Although Rimbaud never tried to profit directly from the slave trade, it is quite clear that no European could do business in Abyssinia without it. Under Makonnen, Harar was once again one of the busiest slave markets in East Africa. This is why Rimbaud wanted laissez-faire principles to be extended to the slave trade. The two-faced French Governor of Obock had actually advised Rimbaud's partner Savouré to use a slave route 'but not to accompany the caravan so that Frenchmen will not appear to be mixed up in it, because of the English'.[26] In the circumstances, Rimbaud's frequent references to his own 'enslavement' are obviously ironic.

The Cecchi report itself is entirely plausible. Rimbaud may not have been a salaried 'agent of the French Govt', but, like Bishop Taurin, who was eventually awarded the Légion d'Honneur for his services to France, he certainly allowed his information to be used for political ends.

The crucial argument that Rimbaud could not have been at Ambos on 10 May is weakened somewhat by the fact that only one person who has written on the subject (Duncan Forbes in 1979) knew where Ambos was. Everyone else, including Matucci, places it on the coast, as far from Harar as possible. A contemporary Italian work shows that Ambos was fifty kilometres inland on the direct route to Harar.[27] It was there that traders had to choose their final route: British Zeila, French Djibouti, or a lonely stretch of coast where slaves could be loaded up and rifles disembarked.

In the two weeks available, Rimbaud could easily have joined the slave caravan at Ambos on 10 May. In March, he had ridden the 200 miles from the coast to Harar in six days and back again in five. The journey to Ambos was thirty-one miles shorter.

This also fits the likely sequence of events. Savouré wrote from Obock in a controlled rage on 26 April 1888: where were the camels that Rimbaud was supposed to have brought from Harar? Rimbaud seemed to have left his partner in the lurch. But since the two men were on good terms again later that year, Rimbaud must have kept (or tried to keep) his end of the bargain – hence his appearance at Ambos on 10 May.[28]

By then, Rimbaud had decided to return home to Harar, with its highland air, its familiar smells and its low cost of living. There, he could help frantic men like Savouré wear themselves out with risky operations while he collected his commission. The experienced Aden merchant, César Tian, had agreed to make Rimbaud his sole agent in Harar.

Rimbaud already had visions of a vast emporium, 'along the lines of the agency I used to run, but with some improvements and innovations'. He wrote to Alfred Ilg, urging him not to do business with the Greek company in Harar (just 'a gang of snoopers'), 'and we'll be able – you in Choa, with your exceptional experience of people, things and languages, and I in Harar – to organize something that will profit both of us'.

Harar was still recovering from the carnage, and a famine was expected; but for Rimbaud, a new life was beginning. 'I shall therefore be living once again in Africa', he told his mother on 4 April 1888, 'and I won't be seen for a long time'.

36

At Home

'I'm very busy and very bored'
(Rimbaud to his mother and sister, 4 July 1888)

UNLIKE HIS EUROPEAN colleagues, Rimbaud never returned to the old continent for a rest-cure. Harar was the only place for which he felt nostalgic. Only there could he savour his obscurity: 'I shall be the only Frenchman in Harar', he wrote in March 1888, evidently placing the Catholic priests in a separate category.

Though Europeans were now 'invading' the region from every corner, he felt sure that Africa would survive the onslaught of 'civilization':

> Every government has sunk millions (even a few billions, all told) on these cursed, desolate shores where the natives wander for months without food or water in the most horrific climate on earth. And those millions that have been poured into the bellies of the Bedouins [slave traders] have brought nothing but wars and disasters of every sort![1]

'All the same', he added, brightly, 'I might find something to do there.'

A century later, Rimbaud might have submitted similar reports to what he called 'the idiotic Reuter Agency'. His description, in a letter to Alfred Ilg, of Italy's occupation of Massawa – 'they'll fire a few howitzer volleys at the vultures and launch an aerostat beribboned with heroic mottoes' – shows the same taste for barbaric absurdity that had seen him through the Prussian invasion, the Paris Commune, the Javanese forests and the Danakil desert. He would have found plenty to amuse him in modern East Africa. It is easy to imagine Rimbaud drily recounting the Marxist revolution that deposed Makonnen's son, Haile Selassie, in 1974, or the recent annihilation of the only pharmaceutical factory in the Sudan not owned by an American company.

Alfred Ilg threatened to send Rimbaud's account of the Italian invasion to the newspapers 'to give a lot of other people a good laugh'.[2] Savouré even suggested that Rimbaud had been sending ludicrous, contradictory reports to the French press as a practical joke.[3] But most of Rimbaud's comments were unpublishable. Editors would have wanted a more obvious display of sentiment and good intentions, and his brutal conclusions would have been more at home in a meeting of military advisers than in the columns of a newspaper:

> Moral: remain an ally of the negroes or don't touch them at all if you don't possess the capability to crush them completely at the first opportunity.

Rimbaud returned to Harar in the spring of 1888 through 'a succession of cyclones' which promised an excellent coffee crop. Harar's independence had been guaranteed by the Anglo-French accord of February 1888, and although there was famine, a smallpox epidemic, and the constant threat of a Muslim uprising, it was still the best place to trade in East Africa.

Like Hugo on his island in the English Channel, Rimbaud had found his philosophical home: a 'naked room with shutters closed', stinking paupers in the street, and 'his soul a prey to repugnant things'. Small-town life was amusingly pathetic whatever the conti-nent. Although the dogs of Charleville were never seen munching pieces of human corpse, and although most of the Carolopolitans belonged to the same tribe, the view from the Café de l'Univers was not so different. Instead of shopkeepers and bureaucrats, there was an itinerant community of traders and explorers, each with his own little dreams and disasters. Rimbaud's business letters to his main client, Alfred Ilg, were also a gossip column from the frontier:

Antonelli laid out at Lit-Marefia with the pox – Traversi hunting hippopotamus on the Awash – M. Appenzeller repairing the bridge, so they say – Borelli with the King of Djimma – M. Zimmermann waiting for you – Antoine Brémond suckling his babes at Alin Amba – Bidault peregrinating and photographing in the Harar hills – Stéphane the dyer of hides stretched out in the gutter at our doorsteps, etc., etc . . .*

Everything as usual.

Despite his mocking tone, Rimbaud felt a sense of solidarity with men who knew how to make the best of a wretched existence and who understood the beauty of futility and waste. His poet heroes, buttoning up their rhymes against real experience, had been a revolting disappointment. But Africa was full of men like Henry Morton Stanley who 'embarked on their exploits with utterly insufficient means': 'He saw in this an almost heroic disregard for life, which usually ended in a futile sacrifice.'[4]

Rimbaud might even have hoped that his expedition to the south would bring him into contact with Stanley, who reached the shores of Lake Albert in April 1888.

*

ON HIS RETURN to Harar, Rimbaud moved into a flat-roofed, one-storey house about as long as an ostrich's shadow in the late afternoon (to judge by a photograph).[5] It was later used as a post office and then demolished. None of Rimbaud's Harar homes has survived. The 'Arthur Rimbaud House' in present-day Harar was built after his death.

To cope with the increase in trade, he had some sheds erected next-door to the house to serve as a depot.[6] As sole agent of the powerful César Tian, and with other, secret deals on the side, he was confident of being able to crush his few competitors.

---

* Count Pietro Antonelli: explorer and diplomat, accompanied on his 1889 mission to Choa by Dr Leopoldo Traversi. Appenzeller (carpenter) and Zimmermann (engineer) were Swiss colleagues of Ilg. The king of the semi-autonomous land of Djimma (Jima) – a slave and ivory kingdom – was Abba Djifar II (r. 1878–1932). The Brémonds, uncle and nephew, were traders and 'adventurers' (according to a government report). Bidault was a French photographer. Rimbaud called the dyer Stéphane '2nd class Stéphane' to distinguish him from an Armenian trader of the same name.

Although Rimbaud is supposed to have given up arms-trading after the expedition to Choa, several letters and some recently published receipts prove that he continued to handle large consignments of rifles and ammunition for Savouré and a retired sea captain called Éloi Pino.[7] His letters sounded almost cheerful: 'I am doing some rather big deals which leave me some profit.' 'I am glad to be resting or rather refreshing myself after three summers on the coast.'

Rimbaud ran his house like an independent consulate. He forwarded mail, arranged transport and received traders and explorers on their way to Choa or the coast: Ilg, Savouré and Count Teleki, returning from Lake Rudolf (Turkana), which Rimbaud might have claimed for France if the Société de Géographie had funded his expedition.

Jules Borelli also stayed for a few days and discovered that Rimbaud had certain expectations of his guests, regardless of their status. Borelli wrote on 26 July 1888 to thank him for his hospitality:

> Just as I have completely forgotten that, when my mules were all loaded up, you wanted to make me sweep the house out (which I stupidly took amiss), I hope that you will be kind enough to forget the indecorous things I said to you.[8]

The broom must have been in constant use. Rimbaud lived as though he wanted to leave no clues behind, or as if someone was already trying to write his biography. Savouré stayed for a month but had practically nothing to report:

> Quite a good house, with no furniture. I had nothing to sleep on but my portable camp-bed, and for the month I was there, I never found out where he slept. I saw him writing day and night on a badly made table.[9]

Rimbaud's writing consisted of customs declarations, accounts and receipts, and perhaps the long-promised book on Abyssinia, which never appeared. Although his notes on the new route to Choa were published by Geographical Societies in Britain, France, Germany, Austria and Italy,[10] he showed no sign of trying to capitalize on his fame as an explorer.

According to a young Italian labourer called Olivoni, Rimbaud's house was indistinguishable from the home of a well-to-do native: a table with a waxed table-cloth and a smattering of floor-rugs.[11] He was popular for his conversation and his ability to speak several European languages,[12] but he rarely entertained. When he did, he served Turkish coffee and sometimes liqueurs. He may have lengthened the working day by chewing qat leaves, but references to more intellectually engrossing drugs like hashish and opium are all second-hand and suspiciously lurid.[13]

In the warehouse next door, all the requisites for an elegant Abyssinian life were stored in bales and recycled cartridge crates until the necessary quantities had been amassed and they were despatched on camels and mules to be sold in Choa. The house itself was almost empty. The only contents that have survived are a knife, fork and spoon, displayed in the Rimbaud Museum like the icons of a highly specialized cargo cult. These are the big, clanking European implements that can sap the flavour of any dish. There is also a beaten metal cup of the sort that singes the lips, contaminates its contents and suddenly sheds its handle.

Rimbaud's tableware is sometimes used to conjure up a bitter-sweet feeling of pity and awe. But were these the sad belongings of a miserable failure or the rugged utensils of a successful miser? Rimbaud had always lived as though he expected life to make a fool of him at any moment: even material objects were hostages to fortune. When the over-optimistic French trader Brémond tried to build a little palace for himself, 'in keeping with his vast commercial operations and his elegant habits', Rimbaud celebrated its inevitable collapse:

> Apparently, he has already erected something at the place called Djibouti, but it was made of imperfectly petrified sponges, and when the springtime rains fell on the coast, it seems that it swelled up, then deflated and went spilling over the ground.[14]

The main difference between the accounts of those who knew Rimbaud and those who pretended to have known him is that the former never confused his unsociability with unhappiness. 'Behind your forbidding mask of horrible severity', wrote Ilg, 'you hide a sunny disposition that many would have good reason to envy you.'[15]

Two of Rimbaud's Italian acquaintances use the word '*scorza*' (bark or exterior) – 'tough and misanthropic', 'eccentric and rather sullen'[16] – but without suggesting that the interior was any different. Rimbaud was the only European in Harar who never attended Bishop Taurin's Sunday mass, the only trader who paid for his drinks in the Greek bars 'without wishing to avail himself of the communal tokens that were used as currency in the cafés of Harar'.[17]

Most people who were asked to describe Rimbaud after his death had very little to say. Like the grainy photographs that grow fainter every year, the composite portrait has barely enough detail to distinguish him from the other traders:

'Always irritable' but 'very self-controlled'. 'Cordial with everyone but intimate with no one.' 'He was considered a canny businessman, astute and wealthy.' – (Olivoni)[18]

'Very serious and competent.' 'He was sometimes rather gruff, but not so that anyone bore him a grudge.' – (Savouré)[19]

'An honourable and very proud man.' – (Rosa)[20]

'Witty and eloquent, with a truly French talent for conversation.' – (Robecchi Bricchetti)[21]

'A great walker', 'good at accounting'. 'He could suddenly make you split your sides laughing.' – (A. or C. Righas)[22]

'A remarkable trader [...] He had a fine future in front of him.' – (Riès)[23]

'He was always in a hurry and gave the impression that he had business elsewhere.' – (Guigniony)[24]

'A very serious young man who did not go out much.' 'A very, very serious young man, the bishop repeated. He seemed to find this epithet the most satisfactory – very serious and sad.' – (Mgr Jérôme, interviewed by Evelyn Waugh)[25]

Even face to face, the great disappearing act of French literature seemed to have a kind of natural camouflage. According to Leopoldo Traversi, he was so 'uncommunicative' that 'he passed unnoticed among the parcels of hides and the baskets of coffee'.[26]

Rimbaud's tragic aura is a later invention. The image that emerges from his letters in the late 1880s is that of a contented misanthrope. Even the blackest of his self-portraits show an austere admiration for his own excruciating personality:

> I still get very bored. In fact, I've never known anyone who gets as bored as I do. It's a wretched life anyway, don't you think – no family, no intellectual activity, lost among negroes* who try to exploit you and make it impossible to settle business quickly? Forced to speak their gibberish, to eat their filthy food and suffer a thousand aggravations caused by their idleness, treachery and stupidity!
>
> And there's something even sadder than that – it's the fear of gradually turning into an idiot oneself, stranded as one is, far from intelligent company.

The narcissist contracts a marriage that can never be dissolved; but the self from which Rimbaud had failed to free himself in poetry had at least earned his respect. Voluntarily 'lost among negroes', the Dr Livingstone of French literature was understandably reluctant to write his own last chapter.

*

DESPITE ALFRED BARDEY'S account of his chance meeting with Paul Bourde, it is often said that Rimbaud knew nothing of his growing fame in France. Since the rediscovery of a letter once thought to be a forgery, however, there can be no doubt that he was aware of his semi-mythical status.

After a long illness, Paul Bourde had finally answered Rimbaud's letter. Unfortunately, *Le Temps* had decided to do without an Abyssinian correspondent. In any case, Rimbaud had asked for more money than even a British newspaper would pay.[27] However, said Bourde,

> I much regret having missed this opportunity to get back in touch with you. My interest might surprise you. Living so far from us, you probably do not know that, in Paris, for a very small group of writers, you have become a sort of legendary figure – one of those figures whose

---

* The original of this letter (4 August 1888) is unknown. I have omitted the phrase 'whose lot one would like to improve' in line with remarks on p. 412. Without the pious thought, the phrase has the rhythm and sentiments of the real Rimbaud. Otherwise, it sounds like his posthumous editor, Berrichon.

death has been announced but in whose existence a faithful few continue to believe and whose return they obstinately await. Your early efforts, both prose and verse, have been published by some Latin Quarter reviews and even collected in volumes. Some young people (whom I find naive) have tried to base a literary system on your sonnet on the colour of letters. Not knowing what has become of you, the little group that calls you its leader is hoping that you will come back one day to rescue it from its obscurity. I hasten to add, to be perfectly frank, that none of this has any practical significance whatsoever. But (if I might be so bold) through a great deal of incoherence and eccentricity, I was struck by the astonishing virtuosity of these works of early youth.

If he wished, Rimbaud could send some articles to *Le Temps* on Abyssinian politics and reap at least 'a moral profit': 'It would give you a connection that would put you back in touch with civilized life.'[28]

This hugely patronizing message from 'civilization' was unlikely to make Rimbaud rush to the Aden shipping office. Yet he folded the letter away and kept it in his papers.

Was this a pang of regret at lost opportunities or simply efficient record-keeping? Nothing is known of Rimbaud's reaction to the news that his earlier self was alive and well in darkest Paris. Neither is there any sign that he was reconciled to his poetry or even thought about it. (The story that, one evening in Harar, he produced a new ending for 'Le Bateau ivre', featuring bare-breasted, honey-coloured Tahitian women, is valuable only as a test of gullibility.)[29]

Most of his African acquaintances were amazed to learn that Rimbaud had once divulged his innermost thoughts in verse. Constantin Righas, who had known him since 1880, was interviewed in 1905:

Q. Did he ever speak of his friends in France?
A. Never. The only thing he liked in France was his sister [. . .]
Q. But you do know that Rimbaud wrote?
A. Oh yes! – some fine things: reports for the Société de Géographie, and a book on Abyssinia . . .[30]

Rimbaud only once referred to his poems in this late period (if a secondhand account can be trusted): they were nothing but '*rinçures*' ('dishwater' or 'slops') – a thin gruel containing some undigested lumps of Hugo, Gautier and Baudelaire.[31]

Any thirty-four-year-old might have said the same about poems written as a teenager. Even if Rimbaud had cared, he would have found his literary apotheosis a ludicrous embarrassment. In Cairo, he is said to have talked (perhaps with the editor of *Le Bosphore égyptien*) about the future of French literature: 'the Villon–Baudelaire–Verlaine lineage had quickly run out of steam; all the really important work had been done in the novel, as it developed after Balzac and Flaubert'.[32]

He now knew, from Paul Bourde, that his masterpiece was supposed to be 'Voyelles', which could hardly be construed as a contribution to social realism. For the Decadents, the poems of 'the absent Young Master'[33] were exquisite little monsters, admiring themselves in the mirror of their own language. Rimbaud could only have agreed with his conservative critics – with Paul Bourde, for instance, who had quoted 'Voyelles' in *Le Temps* three years before. (He did not mention this article to Rimbaud.)

As soon as a writer feels free to add arbitrary meanings to the fixed sense of a word, he speaks a language that is no longer our own. The inevitable result of this system is gibberish.[34]

*

RIMBAUD'S PRESENT ACTIVITIES could scarcely have been less 'Decadent'. Every object had a price-label and every word its literal meaning.

In response to the 'invasion' of Europeans, he had scaled up his operation. By the end of 1888, most of the foreign trade in southern Abyssinia revolved around Rimbaud. He was an importer and exporter, a prospector and financier, a middle-man for the principal arms importer (Savouré), an agent of the oldest trading firm in Aden (Tian & Co.), and the main supplier of the man who was master-minding King Menelik's new nation (Alfred Ilg).

He offered warehousing and banking facilities, guides, camels and mules, accounting and general expertise. He conducted negotiations with the Harar customs house and changed money for a two per cent commission. (Bardey charged 0.5 per cent and the bank in Aden 0.1 per cent.) Rimbaud set the prices for all the major commodities and caused his competitors many sleepless nights.[35]

His caravans set off for the coast like long, repetitive poems in four-legged stanzas: ivory, hides, coffee, gold (in rings or ingots, 'from very far away'),[36] incense and musk of civet, priced according to the degree of adulteration.

The caravans that headed in the other direction for the river Awash and the interior were like travelling warehouses: Indian cotton and Massachusetts shirting, knitted skirts and tunics, goatskin bags and string necklaces (*matebs*), flannel, merino, velvet, silk and damask ('for mules' caparisons or even shirts'), gold braid ('for saddlery or the clergy'), novelty buttons and pearls – 'the sort the Amharas wear on their paws and round their necks'.[37] (Rimbaud rarely missed an opportunity to confuse human beings with animals.)

Every aspect of Abyssinian life was represented: rice, sugar, butter, salt and flour; tobacco, quinine, oil and candles; scissors and rope; socks and sandals; guns and ammunition. In August 1889, he despatched a twenty-four-camel caravan carrying 4,230 francs' worth of saucepans (with lids), 1,000 tin *wantchas* (conical goblets), 1,000 *birillis* (glass carafes for the Abyssinian mead called *tedj*, in a variety of colours, 'made to my design' and 'not on general sale'), and 701 baking-sheets called *matads*: 'they make very well baked bread in very little time', he assured Ilg,[38] who doubted the marketability of some of Rimbaud's imports, especially the 'rosaries, crucifixes, christs, etc.': 'My dear M. Rimbaud, please be sensible and send me things I can sell.'[39]

Ilg's complaint has been seized upon as evidence that the poet still had his head in the clouds. The fact that Ilg himself had recently imported forty-one chromolithographs, including five Raphael Madonnas and five Jesus Christs, should give pause for thought.[40] Ilg was simply trying to bring the price down. His friendship with Rimbaud was secondary to business. Rimbaud pretended to offer him special discounts while charging the normal price. Ilg pretended to be doing Rimbaud a favour by accepting his merchandise and told his Swiss colleague at the same time: 'Rimbaud is an excellent client, and we'd do well to serve him as quickly and as efficiently as possible.'[41]

Ilg may, however, have been right to question the package that Rimbaud sent to him in July 1889 along with some scissors, rosaries, buttons, pearls and 429 yards of cloth. The strangest item in this travelling bazaar was a bale containing fifteen packets of ruled notepads – more paper than Rimbaud had ever used as a poet, and all of it blank.

In Paris, writers were arguing about the famous vowel sonnet: was it the blueprint of a new form of art or a practical joke? Even for Ilg, it was sometimes hard to tell how serious he was: 'Selling notepads to people who can't write and who don't even know the secret uses of such implements is really asking too much.'[42]

37

'Odious Tyranny'

'Why do you always talk about sickness, death and all sorts
of unpleasant things? Let's not harbour thoughts like that.
We should live as comfortably as possible, as far as our
means allow.'

(Rimbaud to his mother and sister, 10 January 1889)

EARLY IN 1889, Rimbaud sounded almost breezy: 'I'm very well
at the moment, and business is not too bad.' Since his scale of
emotional expression was calibrated on a base of total misery, this
was excellent news. On the same day (25 February), he sent a sunny
report to Jules Borelli in Cairo: 'We have never been so much at
peace, and we're completely unaffected by the so-called political
convulsions of Abyssinia. Our garrison has about a thousand Remingtons.'

Two months later, 'the orgies of Easter Week' had ended, the
town was full of starving refugees, and Emperor Yohannes had died
in battle against the Mahdist rebels in the north, but without disturbing southern Abyssinia. On 18 May, writing to his mother and sister,
Rimbaud described this turning-point in East African history with his
usual sarcastic accuracy. There was no hint in his letter that the death
of Yohannes would have horrific consequences:

Last year, our Menelik rebelled against that dreadful Yohannes, and
they were getting ready to slug it out when the aforementioned

Emperor [Yohannes] took it into his head to go and give the Mahdists
a thrashing at Metema, where he met his end – let the Devil take him!
   Here, we're very much at peace.

The only serious problem was the torrential rain which prevented
the caravans from leaving. But even his complaints sounded jocular:
'No one who comes here is in any danger of ending up a millionaire,
except in fleas, if he gets too close to the natives.'

Rimbaud's ability to remain cheerful about the future is his most
underrated quality. He must have known by now that the metaphorical deluge was on the way. In March 1889, on the death of Yohannes,
Menelik, King of Choa, proclaimed himself *negus negast*, king of
kings, Emperor of all Abyssinia, and set about literally taxing his
population to death and conquering the north. While Harar filled up
with refugees, Governor Makonnen left for Italy: a 'Treaty of Perpet-
ual Peace and Friendship' had been signed by the two countries,
effectively making Italy Abyssinia's protector and justifying its continued occupation of the vaguely defined coastal region in the north-
east of the empire called Eritrea. The Amharic version of the treaty
made it look like a simple offer of assistance.

Rimbaud watched Makonnen leave for the coast like a bumpkin
heading for the city: 'Poor monkey! I can see him from here, puking
in his boots.' It was a prophetic remark. The deputation fell prey to
the champagne reception at Naples and staggered out of its first-class
carriage in Rome to the huge amusement of the Italian press.

With the Governor away, petty despots seized the opportunity to
irritate the *franguis* (foreigners) and line their own pockets. Exorbitant
duties were levied on goods that spent less than a day in the customs
house. While Ilg despaired of selling Rimbaud's pots and pans in
Choa, Rimbaud saw whole months of his life being swallowed up by
futile negotiations. To obtain payment for his clients, he begged,
bribed, threatened and lied to 'the little *choums* [chiefs], who have the
voracity of caymans'. He was repeatedly promised the money, then
refused, and finally, months later, offered three tons of 'filthy' coffee
instead of silver coins.[1]

Despite Rimbaud's insults, this was not simply bureaucratic spite.
Harar was sinking into anarchy. That summer, crops failed, disease

decimated the livestock, and practically all the currency was soaked up by Menelik's army. After taxing the whole town, Menelik forced the Europeans to 'lend' him $4,000 each. The soldiers of the garrison turned into a battalion of truncheon-wielding tax-collectors. Rimbaud wrote to Ilg in September, knowing that his employer Menelik would hear of his complaints:

> We are witnessing something here the like of which has never been seen [. . .] a horrible, odious tyranny that will dishonour the name of the Amharas in general throughout these regions and on every coast for many years to come – and this dishonour will certainly taint the King's name as well.
> For the last month, the townspeople have been sequestered, beaten, dispossessed and imprisoned in an attempt to extort as much of the tax as possible. Every inhabitant has already paid three or four times over.

His only real concern was to settle his accounts; but in October, Makonnen was still away, touring 'the Holy sites', Rimbaud supposed: 'Jerusalem, Bethlehem, Sodom and Gomorrah'. 'We await him here with bills unfurled and a chorus of maledictions', he told Ilg. 'The cash-box is in the hands of Dedjatch Makonnen's slaves, who stand there like rabid guerezas.'*

That Christmas, a caravan was attacked on the road to Zeila and two priests were killed. The British launched a three-month campaign against the local tribes. Trade with the coast came to a complete standstill. Somewhere between Harar and Zeila, in March 1890, twenty of Rimbaud's camels were seen standing in the rain 'in a horrible state', their bundles soaked, unable to proceed to the coast or return to Harar.[2]

Even if letters had been getting through, Rimbaud had nothing to tell his mother and sister: 'I can never find anything interesting to say. [. . .] What's there to write about in deserts populated by stupid negroes, with no roads, postal service or travellers?' The only thing to report was mind-numbing boredom; 'and since that's not

---

* A *dedjatch* or *dedjaz* is a lord or governor (literally, 'commander of the gate'). A guereza is a long-haired Ethiopian monkey.

very entertaining for other people either, one ought to remain silent'.

*

RIMBAUD CAN HARDLY be said to have enjoyed what he called his 'abominable enslavement' at the hands of 'bandits',[3] but at least it allowed him to attain that state of pure sarcasm in which the whole world could be summed up and dismissed with an insult.

Civil chaos was also an opportunity to hone his trading skills. In letters to Ilg, who was impatient for his money, he painted a picture of total anarchy. César Tian was given more cheerful reports in case he withdrew his capital. When Rimbaud finally received some money for Ilg, he delayed sending it so that the accounts submitted to Tian would look more encouraging than they were. Ottorino Rosa's letters to his employer in Aden, Bienenfeld, are a pitiful contrast. He complained that M. Rimbaud always seemed to know exactly when to go to the customs house. The other traders would hear that some coffee or some bullion had arrived, only to find that Rimbaud had already snapped it all up and left them nothing.[4]

The 'alternating erections and deflations'[5] of the crisis of 1889–90 seem to have acted on Rimbaud's spirit like a pair of bellows. This was his finest spell as a *provocateur* since Paris in the early 1870s. For a man who was reputed to live like a hermit,[6] his incursions into Harari society were remarkably extrovert.

The first significant incident dates from the beginning of 1889. The dogs that feasted on the offal in the nearby meat market had been cocking their legs against Rimbaud's coffee bales and pissing on the hides that were left to dry outside the depot. Rimbaud set up a cordon sanitaire by scattering strychnine pellets in the dust. The following day, the Hararis woke to find Abdo Rinbo's house besieged by dead and dying animals: sheep, hyenas, birds of prey, and 2,000 dogs, according to one of the priests (twelve, according to Ilg).[7]

Some local people – prompted, perhaps, by Rimbaud's Greek rivals – became convinced that their lives were at risk from contaminated sheep and threatened to lynch him. An official letter complaining about the 'mad' Frenchman was sent to César Tian, who asked

Bishop Taurin to persuade him to leave for a precautionary holiday in Aden.[8]

'The terror of dogs', as he came to be known, may even have spent a few days in the Harar jail, but he made no attempt to keep a low profile. Between 1889 and 1891, he was more often in trouble with the authorities than at any other time in his life. 'I enjoy a certain amount of esteem because of my humane behaviour', he assured his mother on 25 February 1890, nine days after Rosa had told his employer that 'Rimbaud was beaten up by the soldiers the other day.'[9]

The reason for this particular beating is unknown, but there are several possibilities of which the most likely are dog poisoning and insulting customs officials. 'To get any thalers here in the current state of affairs', he told Ilg, 'I'd have to throttle the cashiers and smash in the cash-boxes, and I hesitate to do that.'

There is also evidence of another beating which might easily have been the final episode of Rimbaud's life. Since 1883, his textual studies had turned into a risky and eccentric pastime. When business was slow, he invited local boys into his courtyard and gave them lessons on the Koran. According to the French Governor of Obock, Léonce Lagarde, Rimbaud had his own interpretations of certain suras and 'tried to impart his views to any Muslim he happened to meet'.[10]

Knowledge of the Koran was an asset to any trader; a fondness for theological debate was not, especially at a time when militant Islam was a lively political force, and in a city that was the hub of Muslim dissemination in southern Abyssinia. The local dervishes were Qādiriya Sufis – a powerful mystical order that would not have taken kindly to an infidel businessman reinterpreting the word of God.

Having already become the Decadents' Messiah in Paris, Rimbaud was beginning to acquire a small following in Harar. Inevitably, he was perceived as a threat. Governor Lagarde received some worrying reports about the independent trader in the south:

One day, somewhere in the environs of Harar, it seems that a group of fanatics set upon him and beat him with sticks. They would have killed him were it not for the fact that Muslims do not kill lunatics.[11]

Beyond Harar, the mere ability to read was enough to endow anyone with religious authority, and the history of Rimbaud's reputation proves that intelligent opinions, expressed in a mysterious fashion, are often received with undue veneration. There might also have been some confusion in the minds of those who considered him 'divinely inspired'[12] with the Lugbara water cult which began to spread from north-western Uganda in 1883. Its leader was a 'man of God' called Rembe.[13] (Rimbaud's name in Amharic is pronounced *re-m(i)-bo*.)

Rimbaud's Koran-teaching is the only confirmed example of an imaginative, literary activity surviving his abandonment of poetry. Seventeen years before, in his Gospel adaptations and *Une Saison en Enfer*, he had rewritten holy scripture and borrowed episodes from the life of Christ for his own personal drama. Perhaps the Koran lessons performed a similar function: reclaiming spiritual ideas from their official purveyors; making an intellectual home for himself in a mode of thought that he had always associated with maternal repression.

At the same time, they helped to create those antagonistic situations in which he seemed to find his own internecine personality more bearable. Rimbaud was now attacking two religions at the same time, defying the Muslim authorities and countermining Catholic propaganda.

The idea of a French money-changer turning the tables on Christ proved to be too much for some of Rimbaud's early admirers. His cordial relations with the Catholic mission in Harar were seen as evidence that, beneath that gruff exterior, Rimbaud was a sinner longing for 'the bosom of the Church'.[14]

He did occasionally give candles and cloth samples to the missionaries, though they had to pay for their rosaries and 'sundry devotional articles'.[15] If he admired the priests at all, it was not for their devotion to a metaphysical fantasy but for their ruthless heroism. The word 'fanatical' – so often appended automatically to 'Muslim' – can fairly be applied to Bishop Taurin and his pastors. These were not the smiling Father Christmases whose pictures hang in vestries. Taurin actively supported the arms trade in exchange for diplomatic favours;[16] he bought slave children to convert them to a semblance of

Christianity,[17] and secretly hoped that he was the man whom God had chosen to spearhead the eradication of Islam, that 'second original sin'.[18] In the circumstances, Rimbaud's lack of religious principles was not necessarily an uncivilized trait.

*

THERE WAS ONE other occasion on which Rimbaud found himself, like the narrator of *Une Saison en Enfer*, 'faced with an exasperated crowd'.

Reports of Rimbaud's homosexuality in Africa and Aden are uniformly dubious and date from a later period, when everyone knew about his adventure with Verlaine. When they were interviewed, men who had known him personally were neither shocked by the question nor particularly defensive; they simply had no evidence to offer.[19] In fact, there is no sign that Rimbaud had any lasting emotional attachment at all after 1886. His servant, Djami, lived with his wife and child in a separate house. Rimbaud left him 3,000 francs in his will; but despite some touching speculation, Djami was never the 'son' Rimbaud had dreamt of educating. He was still 'completely illiterate' in 1891.[20] A woman – or women – were sometimes thought to exist in Rimbaud's back room, but 'the interior of his house remained closed to strangers' eyes'.[21]

The only shaft of daylight is a little story told by the two surviving Righas brothers. It should be said that the Righas brothers were fond of Rimbaud in his lifetime and generally kind to him after his death.

> One day, when Rimbaud was at his home in Harar, an infibulated* girl entered his house. Rimbaud set about things a little too bluntly and, coming up against the aforementioned obstacle, tried to perform the operation himself with a knife. He inflicted a nasty wound on the unfortunate young girl, who started to scream. The local people came running and it almost ended badly.[22]

This horrific incident, which 'almost ended badly', is uncorroborated, though it may be related to an unexplained phrase in one of Rimbaud's letters to Ilg (20 July 1889): 'That Makonnen is intolerable

---

* Infibulation: 'The fastening of the sexual organs with a fibula or clasp'. (OED) Harari women were usually circumcized and infibulated before marriage.

when it comes to paying up! He clings to his "insolvency" like *Méram* to her "virginity" – '

In Paris, *Le Décadent* imagined that Arthur Rimbaud was busy conducting psychological experiments in a pristine environment where 'men are closer to Nature'.[23] This was one of its more accurate fantasies. Rimbaud was in close touch with the savage part of his mind. Unlike later Europhobes, he had never looked for an alternative lifestyle in Africa, simply the bare minimum of society. Despite the size of his business, he had only one permanent employee, Djami. Everyone else was hired in the morning and paid off at dusk. When Rimbaud talked about his life of 'freedom' in Africa, he always defined it, negatively, as an absence of constraints, and always in opposition to his mother's part of the world – a place, in his view, where people sat shivering indoors, watching raindrops on a window-pane.

'One of the priests', he told his mother, in an oddly redundant phrase, 'is a Frenchman, like me'. But Rimbaud had ceased to be a Frenchman long ago. The spectacular splintering of the personality that makes *Une Saison en Enfer* a whole choir of different voices had produced an eerie simplicity. His biographers have sometimes appeared to gather the threads of European civilization about him like policemen escorting a nudist. Rimbaud's poetry is such a memorable application of the cherished injunction 'Know thyself', that it is hard to accept the results of the experiment and to conclude that literature is the guardian of culture only if it never tries to leave the page.

Excuses made for Rimbaud are also excuses made for the colonial enterprise as a whole and, more recently, for the secular evangelism that underlies the academic enterprise. Rimbaud was by no means the worst of the Europeans. He was respected and admired by his colleagues, many of whom were upset to see him leave.[24] On the whole, his treatment of the natives was sensibly fair though not necessarily philanthropic. The fact that he was more successful than his rivals proves that he was generally trusted.

In Rimbaud's eyes, Europeans and natives were all human beings and, therefore, equally deserving of scorn: 'The people of Harar aren't any more stupid or crooked than the white negroes of the so-called civilized countries. [. . .] One simply has to treat them humanely.'*

When Rimbaud asked Ilg in December 1889 to send him 'a very good mule and two boy slaves', Ilg advised his colleague Zimmermann: 'Do as you see fit. I think we could entrust the fate of two poor devils to him with a clear conscience.' (22 January 1890)[29] Ilg's later and better-known reply (23 August 1890) was obviously written in the expectation that other eyes would see it: 'I have never bought any [slaves] and I don't want to start. I quite accept that your intentions are good, but I'd never do it, even for myself.'[30] (Ilg himself is known to have used slaves.)[31]

Rimbaud had enough experience of management to know that cruelty and dishonesty were bad for business. The unanswerable question is this: should behaviour be judged according to anachronistic criteria? Even in the mind of a late-nineteenth-century Abyssinian trader, Rimbaud's determination to turn his misery to profit had the power to shock. At close quarters, those camel-trains that meandered exotically off into the African landscape were a smelly and distressing spectacle. On 8 October 1889, Ilg decided that it was time to talk to Rimbaud about his caravans:

> Every single one has arrived famished and with all the servants in a deplorable state. [. . .] It's not worth saving a few thalers on provisions

---

* This appears to represent Rimbaud's practical approach to what most Europeans considered inferior races, though even this text is questionable. The shrewdly ingratiating Bishop Jarosseau's heart-warming tableaux – Rimbaud bestowing his burnous on a naked, rain-soaked Galla, 'keeping his luminous spirit far above a servile preoccupation with trade goods' – were invented for interviewers half a century later.[25] Rimbaud *may* have been known to the natives as '*la juste balance*' (an accurate pair of scales); but this seems to have been a common courtesy title.[26]

The 'discreet and generous' charity mentioned by Bardey was reserved for his fellow Europeans. All the phrases in Rimbaud's correspondence which suggest good deeds appear in letters for which Berrichon is the only authority (fifty-eight out of ninety-nine letters to his mother and sister from Africa and Arabia): e.g. 'I do a little good when I have the chance, and it's my only pleasure.'[27]

In the absence of the manuscripts, these priggish phrases, which are often used to establish Rimbaud's moral credentials, should be treated with extreme caution. Similarly sanctimonious utterances are known to have been inserted by Berrichon – for example: 'We lead a miserable existence among these negroes' was changed to, 'We lead a miserable *and meritorious* existence among these negroes.'[28]

to have all the servants end up sick and exhausted for months. [. . .] All the donkeys that came from Harar are in a very sorry state. I was forced to put them out to grass on my land to let them recover from their wounds. There's isn't a single one that can be used. You'll tell me it's the fault of the servants, etc., but it's precisely when one knows how the Abyssinians travel that one should take precautions.

Rimbaud retorted two months later. Ilg had allowed himself to be fooled by storytellers:

As for your reproach that I'm causing men and beasts to die of hunger on the road, someone's pulling your leg. Actually, I'm known everywhere for my generosity in such cases. – But that's the gratitude of the natives for you!

38

Opportunities

'From all sides we receive letters craving information on the poet; we are bombarded with questions. Indeed, several of our honourable correspondents are indignant to note that Rimbaud does not yet have a statue in Paris.'

(*Le Décadent*, 1–15 March 1889)

EVEN AT THE HEIGHT of the crisis, with half-eaten bodies in the street and the threat of 'widespread looting', Rimbaud clung to his 'beloved Harar'.[1] His taste in cities had barely changed. In September 1890, *La Plume* published his early poem, 'L'Orgie parisienne'.[2] It might have been an ode to Harar in the first years of the new empire:

> [. . .] though no city has ever been changed
> Into such a stinking ulcer on the face of green Nature,
> The Poet says unto thee, 'Splendid is thy Beauty!'

Despite the bands of starving robbers, Rimbaud often saddled up a horse and trotted out of the city gates with Ottorino Rosa (as Rosa remembered):

We tried to go as far as we could in order to satisfy our curiosity and find out what there was of interest in the region – its topography, its flora and fauna, and relics of ancient times.[3]

This is the last hint that Rimbaud was still planning a book on Abyssinia. His own allusion to these intrepid camping trips makes them sound like a simple discharge of energy, a violent engagement with Mother Nature: 'treks on foot of between 15 and 40 kilometres a day; mad gallops through the steep mountains'.[4]

Rimbaud had decided to ride out the storm. The British blockade ended in March 1890, but trade was slow to recover. Exchange rates were increasingly unfavourable and prices continued to fall. Rimbaud's commodity lists sound like little elegies to change and decay:

– Coffees are floating between 7 and 8. Very sluggish.
– Gums in full retreat.
– Leathers likewise.[5]

In 1885, slashing a knot that could easily have been untied, Rimbaud had left the Bardey company in an inexplicable rage. Now, again, there was the characteristic sound of acrimonious severing. He tried to engineer a quarrel with César Tian so that he could 'liquidate' and start again. Rimbaud was burning his bridges with people still on them. Even allowing for his 'habitual exaggeration',[6] Savouré was 'seriously horrified' by a letter in which Rimbaud accused him of unjustified suspicions. 'I tend to have the opposite fault', Savouré observed. 'Instead of believing, like you, that everyone is a scoundrel, I am too inclined to believe that everyone is honest.'[7]

For all the talk of liquidation and collapse, Rimbaud had no intention of leaving Africa. Aden was still the edge of his commercial universe. When his mother wrote in April 1890, apparently suggesting that both he and Isabelle should marry, Rimbaud replied with one of his nightmarish self-portraits. He was stretched on the rack of Time between the horribly immediate and the impossibly remote:

Alas! I don't have the time to get married or to see anyone else get married. It will be an infinitely long time before I can leave my business here. Once one has started something in these confounded countries, there's no way out.

I am well, but with every minute that passes another hair turns white. It's been going on so long now that I'm afraid I'll soon have a head like a powder-puff. This treachery of the scalp is distressing; but what can one do?

Even when he changed his mind about marriage four months later, he was keen to point out that he was not thinking about a fireside and slippers. His mother was to find him a woman who would follow him in his 'peregrinations':

> When I talked about marriage, it was always with the proviso that I'd remain free to travel and to live abroad, and even to continue living in Africa. I've grown so unaccustomed to the climate of Europe that I'd find it hard to get used to it again. [. . .] The one thing I can't do is lead a sedentary life.

There is no obvious reason why Rimbaud should suddenly have revived his marriage plans after six years. Perhaps it was the 'powder-puff' in the mirror, or a fear of impending loneliness. A French-woman had recently arrived in Harar. The wife of Pietro Felter, an agent for the Bienenfeld company, cooked a European meal for the other traders every Sunday. One such meal had been gratefully devoured – with rude remarks about the Abyssinians' use of rancid butter – three days before Rimbaud wrote to ask about a wife.[8]

Coincidentally, a letter arrived from France. The race to find Arthur Rimbaud was gathering momentum. There had been recent sightings in Aden, Algeria and Morocco, where he was apparently 'preparing for the most extraordinary expedition'.[9] A rumour that Rimbaud was living in the Timbuctoo of East Africa reached the editor of a Marseille literary review called *La France moderne*. He addressed his note to 'Monsieur Arthur Rimbaud, Harar':

> Monsieur and dear Poet,
> I have read some of your beautiful poetry. It goes without saying therefore that I should be happy and proud to see the leader of the decadent and symbolist school contribute to *La France moderne*, which I edit.[10]

Rimbaud seems not to have replied,[11] but he filed the invitation away with the condescending letter from Paul Bourde. It might have increased the sense of urgency. He had told his mother that prospec-tive brides could write to the French Consul in Aden, who would supply excellent references; but if word ever reached the Ardennes that Mme Rimbaud's son was 'the leader of the decadent and symbolist school', his choice of wives would be severely restricted.

Rimbaud was now reading French newspapers quite regularly and certainly knew that his 'slops' were bound for posterity; but there was nothing about his reputation that could have tempted him to return. Since November 1886, gaudy poems falsely attributed to him had been appearing in Le Décadent. For a time, he was better known for these fakes than for his own work.[12] He appeared in a humorous 'glossary of symbolist language', an anthology published by Lemerre, a history of modern French literature, and an international writers' dictionary as a 'poète décadent français'. The prominent Revue indépendante published four of his early poems, and 'Voyelles' was quoted in a book by Maupassant. 'Had he been better able to marry rhyme and reason', he would have appeared as a 'fantaisiste' in Gustave Merlet's Choix de poètes du XIXᵉ siècle. Lurid episodes of his life in the Latin Quarter had been briefly depicted in a roman à clé, in which the Cézanne character hailed him as 'the greatest poet on earth'. 'Those fine young men', Edmond Goncourt noted testily in his journal, 'who are simultaneously prudish and full of admiration for Rimbaud, the pederast assassin'.[13]

Mme and Mlle Rimbaud knew nothing of Arthur's literary fame, and he would never have drawn their attention to it. He only once appeared to allude to the Decadent Rimbaud, though this could just be a coincidence. A journalist had suggested, humorously, in March 1889 that a statue to Rimbaud be erected in the middle of the Great Exhibition[14] – presumably in front of Gustave Eiffel's girders. Two months later, Rimbaud wrote home:

> I'm sorry I can't go and visit the Exhibition this year, but my profits are far too small to allow it [. . .] It will have to be the next Exhibition, and perhaps then I can exhibit the produce of this region and even myself, because anyone who has spent a long time in places like this must, I think, look exceedingly bizarre.

*

IN THE END, neither marriage, fame, falling profits, civil disorder nor the cholera epidemic had anything to do with Rimbaud's decision to leave Harar.

With a sufficiently long-term view, prospects were actually better than ever. Emperor Menelik had finally listened to his ferociously patriotic Empress, Taitou, and admitted to himself that his Italian friends had tricked him. Eritrea was just a foot in the door. Italy, he now realised, was dreaming of a racist empire to rival the British and the French. His own young empire was in danger of being crushed in the Scramble for Africa.

The Italian diplomats were forced to leave the new capital that Alfred Ilg was building in the valley below Entotto. They reached Harar in February 1891. Ottorino Rosa decided to return to Italy with his compatriots and to try his luck again later.

Before leaving Harar, he went for another ride in the hills with Rimbaud.

Rimbaud should have been relatively cheerful. The Italian exodus was good news for the French. Remingtons, Mausers and Martinis would soon be flowing freely through Harar. Even now, adventurers were arriving from Europe to bring gold and ivory from the inexhaustible south.[15] Ilg had some exciting new ventures to propose. A telegraph was to join Addis Ababa to Harar along the route pioneered by Rimbaud. Soon, the railway would follow.[16] Rimbaud was predicting 'a terrible famine' – 'this year, they'll be looking for food as far away as the Zanzibar coast' – but even this could be construed as an opportunity: 'Rice will have to be imported', he observed.

However, Rosa found his riding partner preoccupied. He had a pain in his right knee: a little hammer knocking at the inside of the knee-cap; a sense of something tightening up. It prevented him from sleeping. He suspected rheumatism or arthritis and decided to eradicate the pain by working even harder.

In Harar, Olivoni saw him sitting with his legs crossed, clutching his knee. 'Sometimes, a spasm of pain would pass over his face. He never said anything – never a complaint.'[17] The pain increased steadily like a secure investment. Within a few days, the joint had swollen up and the whole leg looked strange: thicker below the knee than above. Rimbaud changed his diagnosis: it must be varicose veins. Privately, he must have suspected syphilis, though neither diagnosis would have explained the loss of appetite. On 20 February 1891, he asked his mother to send a surgical stocking to fit 'a long and spindly leg, shoe-size 41' (approximately a British 7 or an American 7½): 'The silk ones are the best – the most resilient. I don't think they cost much. Anyway, I'll reimburse you.'

At the end of the letter, for the first time in over five years, he raised the spectre of military service ... The pain was rummaging through his secrets, stirring up the old neuroses. His mother was to let him know if his name was still on a list. Would he be sent to prison for failing to do his duty?

The child who had lost his father to the army was still alive inside him; but as the pain settled in, the faceless recruiting officer of Rimbaud's recurrent nightmare began to assume some more familiar and universal traits: a bureaucratic Grim Reaper with an infallible filing system.

By the second week of March, the 'hammer' had turned into 'a nail driven in from the side'. His whole existence was twisted up around the pain. The lump on his right leg was the result of everything that was wrong with life: 'bad food, unhealthy housing, skimpy clothes, all sorts of worries, constant rage among these negroes whose stupidity is matched only by their deviousness'.

At the end of March, he watched with 'terror' as the whole leg stiffened up within a week. The swelling seemed to turn into solid bone. Practical adjustments would have to be made:

> I set up a bed between my cash-box, my ledgers and a window from where I could keep an eye on my weighing-machine at the far end of the courtyard, and I hired some extra hands to keep the work going.[18]

The 'treachery of the scalp' had given short warning of this wholesale betrayal. When he saw the rigid limb, the Italian doctor, Leopoldo Traversi, urged Rimbaud to leave at once for Europe. There was no point, he felt, in depressing the invalid before his long journey by talking about cancerous tumours.[19]

*

THE ITALIANS LEFT, but Rimbaud lingered on. These extra days were crucial and might have cost him his life. He was determined to liquidate everything, even at a loss. Ilg had been instructed to sell the saucepans and the notepads: 'Let's get it over and done with for goodness' sake!' He even paid a nugatory sum to Labatut's creditors when they had his merchandise impounded. Recognizing a superior manipulator, the French agent of Labatut's widow considered himself 'ingeniously swindled', declared the account closed and sent his cordial greetings.[20]

It was early April before Rimbaud managed to tear himself away. He rented a house in Harar, probably to store unsold goods.[21] He was intending to return quite soon.

He drew a rough sketch for his servants: twelve poles lashed together with an A-frame to support a piece of hide. Sixteen porters were hired to carry the litter to the coast at Zeila, 200 miles away. Camels would take the provisions and Rimbaud's luggage – a small leather trunk containing letters, accounts, his cutlery and some souvenirs for Isabelle: a little box of coral pearls and some phials of perfume.

At six o'clock on the morning of 7 April 1891, Rimbaud left Harar, shrouded in pain. It would take twelve days to reach the coast. Ingloriously, he crossed the hills where, ten years before, his life had suddenly acquired a purpose.

Rimbaud's notes on his journey to the coast sound like a last nail driven into the coffin of Romantic travel writing – more Samuel Beckett than Lord Byron. Isabelle later described this horrific ordeal in her best Sunday-school style: a beloved Dr Livingstone figure, lugged into a half-tone sunset by doting natives. 'Throughout the thirteen days the journey lasted, the tribal chieftains came around him weeping, and begged him to come back soon.'[22] Rimbaud's own account is a dark engraving with tiny flashes of what might have been called poetry if he had still been writing poems.

> The descent from Egon to Ballawa very difficult for the porters, who stumble at every stone, and for me, who almost tip over at every minute. The litter is already half-dislocated and the servants completely exhausted. I try to mount the mule, with the sick leg strapped to its neck. – I am forced to dismount after a few minutes and get back into the litter which had already lagged a kilometre behind.
>
> On arriving at Ballawa, it is raining.
>
> Furious wind all night long.[23]

Since almost nothing else survives, this is said to be the only occasion on which Rimbaud kept a diary; but this was hardly the moment to take up a new hobby. These notes can only have been the work of someone who was so used to recording the day's events and discoveries that habit kept him writing even when pain was pressing on his hand.

The truth is that Rimbaud had been writing all along.[24] His report in *Le Bosphore égyptien* and his notes for the Société de Géographie can hardly have been written from memory. He was obviously familiar with the analgesic properties of the written word. Record-keeping helped him to maintain the iron objectivity that had seen him through deserts, plagues and wars. The bitter question then arises: what happened to his other notes? Was the book on Abyssinia never written, or was it lost, along with his other possessions, in the chaos that was about to engulf Harar?

The progress of the pain can be traced in the handwriting which begins to lose its bearings towards the end. At each stop, a tent was pitched over the litter. To relieve himself, he scrabbled at the soil with his bare hands, then shuffled his body sideways to defecate into the hole.

Storms passed over the desert. At night, the dew was heavy and the temperature fell sharply. On the afternoon of the fourth day, at Wordji, with the caravan far behind, he lay under the rain, unable to move, for sixteen hours. The camels straggled into view at four o'clock on the afternoon of the fifth day.

Even in his corpse-like condition, Rimbaud kept a sharp eye out for trading opportunities – hides and cereals that could be bought on the return journey. He also recorded his servants' wages and misde-meanours: 'At 9½, stop at Arrouina. I am dumped on to the ground on arrival. I impose fines of $4.'

The arrival at Zeila, twelve days after leaving Harar, is not recorded. He was paralysed with pain and exhaustion.

A steamship was about to sail for Aden. The litter was winched aboard and a mattress thrown down on the deck. As the ship steamed out into the Gulf of Aden, Rimbaud lay on his back like a manacled slave, unable to watch the African shoreline disappear.

*

THE BRITISH DOCTOR at the hospital in Aden was not a man to offer false comfort. He gasped at the sight of Rimbaud's knee, incorrectly diagnosed synovitis 'at a very dangerously advanced stage', and recommended amputation. Then, perhaps at Rimbaud's insistence, he decided to wait for a few days to see whether the swelling would subside.[25]

Tubercular synovitis was the disease from which Vitalie Rimbaud had died in torment sixteen years before. Rimbaud, however, denied that heredity had anything to do with it. His was not a family illness, he told Isabelle. He was suffering from his own stupidity and a deficient education system:

> It was I who ruined everything by insisting on walking and working to excess. Why don't they teach medicine at school – at least the minimum it would take to prevent people from doing such stupid things?

Both the doctor and his patient were probably mistaken. The final diagnosis, after surgery, would be cancer. Since Isabelle Rimbaud died in 1917 of a cancerous growth which spread from her knee, the disease might have been hereditary after all.

At this point, Rimbaud was still completely lucid. He discharged himself from hospital and went to spend his six days' respite at the home of César Tian to draw up the final accounts.[26]

Since Tian's successor, Maurice Riès, later burned all of Rimbaud's letters, and since the company refused to answer biographers' queries, alleging the 'politically sensitive' nature of Rimbaud's activities,[27] it is impossible to reconstruct their financial history in detail.

The known fact is this: Rimbaud had arrived in Aden in 1880 with little or no money. He left eleven years later with a bank draft for 37,450 francs (about £115,000 today). According to the tragic myth, this was a pathetically small sum. (A recent biography gives it as 37.45 francs.)[28] According to Rimbaud's fellow traders, it was 'a small fortune'.[29]

This raises another mystery. Despite Isabelle's suspicion that César Tian unfairly withheld some of the money, the accounts appear to be accurate. How, then, is it possible that, having returned from Choa in August 1887 with at least 33,750 francs, Rimbaud left Aden in May

1891 with only a few thousand more (37,450)? Nothing in his correspondence suggests that his three-year partnership with Tian had been so disastrous.

The opportunities for fruitless speculation are endless, but there is just enough reliable information to show that Rimbaud was sitting on a much larger pile of money. First, he had also been trading behind Tian's back,[30] and these lucrative, private deals would obviously not have appeared in the accounts.[31] Second, other sums which are known to have existed never seem to have entered Rimbaud's final calculations: what, for instance, had become of the 16,000 francs deposited in the Crédit Lyonnais in 1887 at 4 per cent interest, or the plots of land that his mother had bought for him in the Ardennes and which had been earning rent since 1882?

The phrase used by the agent of Labatut's widow – 'ingeniously swindled' – should haunt the calculations of anyone who tries to interpret Rimbaud's accounts. Rimbaud had assured his mother that none of his hard-earned profits would end up in the belly of brother Frédéric, 'who never sent me a single letter!'[32] He seems to have had similar thoughts about the rest of the family. His mother continually asked after the state of his finances, even when he was obviously dying. Until the very end, she was extremely anxious to learn the final resting-place of Arthur's money, and to prevent him from reinvesting it abroad.[33]

It is of course possible that, just for once, Rimbaud told his mother the truth about his earnings. On the other hand, it should be remembered that, in his mind, none of this was final. He would soon be back in Africa and would need his capital. Twenty-five years after he decided to become 'a man of private means', money was still the symbol and the guarantee of his independence, a secret fortune to protect him from the world's duplicity and his mother's false love.

There is, realistically, no hope of finding an unknown Rimbaud masterpiece in Africa; but there is still a faint chance that some dark regions of his life will suddenly be illuminated by the discovery of a bank deposit slip.

*

RIMBAUD RETURNED TO the Aden hospital towards the end of April. Six days had passed and there was no improvement. 'I've turned into a skeleton', he told his mother. The doctor persuaded him to make the long journey back to France. Since his condition had apparently been 'very dangerous' six days before, the doctor's lack of urgency was either gross irresponsibility or an early death certificate.

He was forced to wait in Aden for another week: 'All the steamers bound for France are unfortunately full just now, because everyone goes home from the colonies at this time of year.' The hospital was a furnace and his back was raw with bedsores. He wrote to his mother on 30 April, acknowledging receipt of the surgical stockings:

> There's no need to tell you what horrible sufferings I endured on the way. [. . .]
> Better days will come. But it's a wretched reward for so much work and so many hardships and tribulations! Alas! how miserable our life is! [. . .]
> P.S. The stockings are useless. I'll sell them somewhere.

Rimbaud's letter is remarkably similar in tone and content to the message that had come with the stockings. In the latest lamentation from the house of sorrows, Mme Rimbaud, who could reasonably be described as rich, was still playing the poor farmer, wringing her hands over the sodden harvest:

> We are still in winter. It is very cold. The wheat is completely ruined. There's none left, and so there's desolation all around. What's to become of us, no one knows.
> *Au revoir*, Arthur,
> and above all look after yourself and write me a receipt immediately for the parcel I sent.
>
> W[idow] Rimbaud

In the face of such irreconcilable similarities, the reunion would not be easy.

At last, Rimbaud was able to book a passage on a steamship called *L'Amazone*. It sailed from Aden on 7 May 1891.

The voyage lasted thirteen days.

This time, Rimbaud kept no account.

39

'Ferocious Invalid'

'I shall return, with limbs of steel'

('Mauvais sang', *Une Saison en Enfer*)

RIMBAUD WAS ADMITTED to the Hôpital de la Conception in Marseille on 20 May 1891 and placed in a ward on the first floor: 'Raimbaud, Arthur, 36 years, merchant, born in Charleville, in transit.'[1]

The initial diagnosis – '*néoplasme de la cuisse*' – showed that the disease had spread to the thigh.[2] This, and later reports, suggest a type of bone cancer, probably osteosarcoma.[3] Successful treatment still depends on early intervention.

A day after arriving, Rimbaud wrote home. There were signs of confusion in his letter: the wrong day with the wrong date, and the left leg instead of the right – sinister, not dextrous. For the first time in his life, he hinted at a merciful release:

It's bound to go on for a long time, if complications don't make it necessary to sever the leg. Whatever happens, I'll be left crippled. But I doubt that I'll wait. Life has become impossible for me. How unhappy I am! How unhappy I've become!

The following day, a telegram was delivered to the farmhouse at Roche:

Today you or Isabelle come Marseille express train Monday morning my leg will be amputated risk of death serious affairs to settle Arthur Hôpital Conception reply

Mme Rimbaud's answer came that evening:

Am leaving will arrive tomorrow evening courage and patience

Rimbaud still showed no sign of referring his complaint to a higher authority. He did not ask to see a priest. The only ceremony to which he submitted was the ritual of the operating theatre – instead of crucifix and aspergillum: forceps, retractors and drainage tubes; antiseptic solutions and carbolized sponges; a tray for the tourniquet, the knives and the bow-saw.

On Wednesday 27 May, two doctors and two interns performed the irreversible operation.

*

THE SURGERY ITSELF was relatively simple. Thanks to the Crimean and Franco-Prussian wars, the art of amputation had made great progress.[4] Survival rates were high, as a large population of limbless veterans could testify. Isabelle sent an encouraging letter in which she described the very spry and jolly amputee who often lolloped past her window: his wooden leg did not prevent him from being 'the most indefatigable dancer at village fêtes'.

For Rimbaud, amputation was the worst thing that could have happened. In his rancorous relationship with his own body, his size-41 feet had always been the favoured exception: a means of escape and contact with a solid earth – almost little Arthurs in their own right, deserving of comfort and respect:

> [. . .] rhyming in the midst of fantastical shadows,
> Like lyres, I tugged the elastic laces
> Of my wounded shoes, a foot close to my heart!

> ('Ma Bohème')

The stump was horribly short.
Six days later, the bleeding had stopped, and he was able to send a

letter to Governor Makonnen, announcing his return to Harar 'in a few months', 'to trade as before'.

The scar formed quickly, but an older wound festered on. Mme Rimbaud left him on the afternoon of 9 June. 'I was going to leave today', she told Isabelle on the 8th, 'but I was swayed by Arthur's tears'.

Had Rimbaud expected her to enact the scene from *Une Saison en Enfer* – 'Women take care of those ferocious invalids back from hot countries' – and found his mother unresponsive? The only other echo of her bedside visits is a paragraph in his next letter to Isabelle, who was suffering from a vague illness (or so his mother had told him): 'I was very cross when Mama left me. I didn't understand why. But it's better now that she be with you so that she can have you looked after.' The last phrase had a dark lining. He did not say, 'so that she can look after you'.

The reunion had been a renewed separation. He never wrote to his mother again. All subsequent letters were addressed to Isabelle.

*

DURING THE TWO months that he spent in the hospital at Marseille, Rimbaud waged war on his disability with his usual weapon: general despair at the human condition and savage optimism in the details. The doctors had warned him that the pain in his stump might linger for a year, but he would then be able to wear an articulated limb and return to lead a useful life in Africa.

In early July, with the pain as intense as ever and the other leg stiff, perhaps from lack of exercise, he tried out 'a very light wooden leg, varnished and padded, and very well made (price 50 francs)'. He managed to stagger along the arcaded verandah but was forced to turn back at the stairs: 'I inflamed the stump and set the cursed instrument aside'.

Rimbaud's letters to Isabelle should not be seen as a complete record of his mental state. They were part of his plan of recovery. Bouts of what sounds like profound self-pity have an experimental quality. These passages of Romantic prose – among the most conventional that Rimbaud ever wrote – were a rhetorical dive to the depths to generate the salutary reaction:

Whither the treks through the mountains, the horseback rides, the expeditions, the deserts, the rivers and the seas? [. . .] I who had decided to return to France this summer to get married! Farewell marriage, farewell family, farewell future! My life is over. I am nothing but a motionless stump.

An understandable reverence for Rimbaud's suffering has tended to strip these letters of their varied tones and their sense of humour. This was still the objective 'I' that could sit and watch itself from the audience, smiling cruelly – the ironic Rimbaud who, according to his sister, often had the other patients in stitches.

When I walk, I have to keep looking at my single foot and the ends of the crutches. The head and shoulders lean forward and you lurch about like a hunchback. You tremble to see objects and people moving around you in case they knock you over and break your other leg. People snigger when they see you hopping about. When you're sitting down again, your hands are numb, your armpit's sawn in two and you have the face of an idiot. Despair reclaims you, and you sit there like a complete cripple, whimpering and waiting for night to return with never-ending insomnia, and the morning even more dismal than the day before, etc., etc.

To be continued.

I really don't know what to do. All these worries are driving me mad. I never get a minute's sleep.

Anyway, our life is misery, endless misery! So why do we exist?

Send me your news.

Best wishes.

Rimbaud

Affectionate messages came from the sunny south: César Tian, Pietro Felter, who had found work for Rimbaud's servant, Djami, and one of the Greek Righas brothers, who sent an interminable letter in bad French: 'I would rather have had my leg cut off than yours. [. . .] Since you left Harar, I feel as though I've lost the world.'

His old exploring partner Sotiro wrote from Zeila to offer his condolences and to point out that this was a good time to be away from Harar: '50 to 60 people are dying of hunger every day'. 'Moconon [*sic*] has shot a lot of Galla Itous who were eating their brothers and children. There is something strange in the country this year!' Makonnen himself wrote to congratulate him on a successful operation. According to Savouré, the Governor of Harar was deeply affected by the news: 'He said that you were the most honourable of men and that you had often proved to him that you were his *true friend*.'

As the days wore on, there were subtle signs that the operation had not been a complete success. Rimbaud's neuroses were multiplying like germs. He became convinced that the surgeons had used him as a practice dummy. The amputation had been unnecessary:

> If anyone asked for my advice, this is what I'd say. Let them chop you up, split you open and carve you into little pieces, but never let them amputate. If death comes, it will at least be better than life with missing limbs. [. . .] Better to suffer for a year like a soul in torment than to be amputated.

Even with one leg missing, he was terrified of being marched away by the military authorities. The post office might betray him. Isabelle was to write as seldom as possible and only to 'Rimbaud' ('Don't put "Arthur"'). Better still, she should use a different post office. A sick police inspector had been pestering him with tales of draft dodgers and was 'planning to play a trick on me'.

There was no question that Rimbaud would be called up or sent to prison. His military record shows that he had always satisfied all the legal requirements,[5] and it is astonishing that it took his mother and sister so long to clarify the situation.

His real fear was the final conscription. The doctors declared him 'cured' at the end of June, but Rimbaud had learned to recognize his enemy. He lay awake at night, listening out for the thief in the rooms below:

> To tell you the truth, I don't even think I'm cured internally. I'm expecting some sort of explosion . . .

> It's this insomnia that makes me fear that I might have some other illness to undergo. I think with terror of my other leg – it's the only means of support I have left! [. . .] Perhaps I'm destined to become a

cul-de-jatte!* I imagine that the military authorities might then leave me in peace!

Rimbaud decided to leave on 23 July. The doctor had recommended a change and he was desperate to escape in any case. The hospital was swarming with disease: 'smallpox, typhus', and the indestructible virus of boredom. He was to be collected like a trunk at the little country station of Voncq.

When he wrote to Isabelle, he insisted on being placed in the upstairs room at Roche. He would be returning to the birthplace of *Une Saison en Enfer*. Eighteen years on, the character was coming home to see how the vision compared with the reality.

I shall return, with limbs of steel, a dark skin and a furious eye . . .

*

IN ITS FEBRUARY–MARCH 1891 issue, *La France moderne* trumpeted its great discovery:

> This time, we've got him! We know where Arthur Rimbaud is – the great Rimbaud, the true Rimbaud, the Rimbaud of the *Illuminations*.
> This is not some Decadent prank.
> We have found the lair of the famous missing poet.

Rimbaud's African hiding-place had been discovered, but there was no danger that anyone would seek him out in a muddy hamlet in northern France. Delahaye, who worked at the Education Ministry, was living in a Paris suburb with his wife and three daughters. Verlaine – at last enjoying recognition as the grand old *enfant* of French letters – was about to be readmitted to the Hôpital Broussais with a cocktail of complaints: rheumatism, heart disease, diabetes and syphilis. Germain Nouveau had suffered a mystical crisis and emerged from a Paris lunatic asylum that October as an itinerant religious poet.[6] Brother Frédéric was still driving buses two miles away at Attigny, but, having disgraced himself by marrying a pregnant pauper, he was considered not to exist and was left in the dark.

Rimbaud's 'way of the cross' seemed to be ending where it had begun. Roche was green, damp, and seething with old smells. In

* Literally 'a bowl-bottom': a legless cripple.

Rimbaud's African mind, this was the frozen North. He wrote to
Maurice Riès from 'the wolves' lair', attributing the stiffness in his
bones to the midsummer cold and warming to the thought of a
daring new adventure: 'Whenever you like', Riès replied, 'you can
bring all the arms you want to through Djibouti, as long as you say
nothing to attract the attention of the Italians.'[7]

Despite the ominous pain, Rimbaud was still mapping out his
future. The money from arms would allow him to start a family of
his own. According to Isabelle, he had modified his plan: 'Rather
than expose himself to the scorn of a bourgeois daughter, he would
go to an orphanage to find a girl of impeccable antecedents and
education. Failing that, he would marry a Catholic woman of noble
Abyssinian descent.'[8]

It is unlikely that Rimbaud discussed the possibility of giving his
mother half-caste grandchildren. His dictated letters from Roche
have not survived, but his complaints can be deduced from Sotiro's
replies:

> There is nothing like a mother's love! Her blessings will bring you
> luck. I can well believe that you are not used to it. All the same, we
> should heed and respect the mother who always has our best interests
> at heart.

The incompetent local doctor, who informed Rimbaud that he was
suffering from a simple tubercular infection, was more accurate in his
general diagnosis. Whenever Mme Rimbaud showed her face, 'his
features would contract'. 'Her mere presence seemed to cause him
physical discomfort.' 'One day, for no apparent reason, he bluntly
told her to get out.'[9]

However bad the weather or his pain, Rimbaud fled the house
every afternoon in an open carriage: 'He liked to be taken to places
where people gathered in their best clothes on Sundays or on holidays
[. . .] to see how things had changed over the last ten years.'[10] The
explorer was still observing alien customs, wondering if he would
ever see home again.

*

THE TRAGIC CHORUS of local gossips, interviewed in 1922 and the early 1930s:

> You could hear him moaning with pain, raving and cursing into the small hours, or having childish ritornellos played on the Ariston* to calm him down.[12]

> 'What a fuss!' I says to him. 'You'll get over it, at your age.' 'Never!' he says to me. Then he stares into the distance and says nothing, just as if I wasn't there.[13]

> I remember helping Arthur to unbandage his leg in the farmyard when the sun was out. He swore like a pagan and made fun of me because I went to mass.
> [. . .] Make sure and say that his mother and his sister Isabelle were a pair of hypocritical bigots and that everyone in the village said that the Captain and Arthur weren't entirely to blame for leaving home.[14]

*

THAT YEAR, AUTUMN came early. There was a sudden frost, then strong winds bared the branches. It was time to head south again.

Rimbaud had taken a decoction of opium poppies for the pain, but was horrified to learn from Isabelle that he had been pouring out his soul in the delirium. He decided to suffer the pain instead.[15]

The less he seemed able to withstand a long journey, the more he wanted to leave. He felt that the surgeon who had performed the sacrificial act would know how to cure him.[16] In Marseille, he would be close to the sea, ready to sail for Africa as soon as he felt his health returning.

For Isabelle, who had just turned thirty-one, the last month had been an accelerated education. Arthur's tales of Africa and Arabia – told in a strange, 'exquisite' idiom full of 'Oriental expressions'[17] – aroused her literary ambitions, though she still had no idea that Arthur had been a poet. (She was only thirteen when *Une Saison en Enfer* was published, and her mother had certainly never mentioned Arthur's scribblings.) This was the high point of her life. The dark-skinned explorer was the first person she had had to care for. Her

* A small, self-playing reed organ.[11]

mother's apparent indifference shocked her: she seemed to think that Arthur was making a meal of his little accident.[18] But Mme Rimbaud had always found it difficult to express anything other than bitterness or rage. She could hardly have put on an appropriate display when she saw her favourite son leave home for the last time, mutilated and in pain.

*

THE DAY OF departure was set for Sunday, 23 August 1891. Isabelle obtained special permission from her mother to accompany Arthur to Marseille.

He was awake at 3 a.m., in good time for the train that was due to leave at 6.30 from the station two miles away. But the farmhands were sluggish and the horse refused to wake up.

As the carriage trundled along between the dark fields, Rimbaud removed his leather belt to drive the animal on, but when they reached the station, the train had pulled out. They returned to the farmhouse for an awkward encore, then left again at 9.30 for the 12.40 train.

During the two-hour wait at the station, there was a last flicker from the old Rimbaud, the ironic anthropologist of 'Les Assis' and 'A la musique'. The stationmaster had evolved a platitudinous flower-bed at the foot of a chestnut: a dahlia surrounded by dejected asters and a circle of sand. Isabelle unfortunately deemed her brother's comment unrepeatable.[19]

The train arrived. At Amagne, ten miles up the line, Rimbaud was hoisted into the Paris train. Each jolt of the carriage flooded his body with pain. With the stump resting on his burnous and a blanket, he leaned his left elbow on the window-ledge and his right arm on the trunk in front of him in a vain attempt to absorb the shocks.

The weather was warm and sunny. Through the window, they saw yachts on the river and summer dresses in gardens. Soon, the train filled up with families out for a Sunday afternoon. Rimbaud stared at the other passengers with a face hollowed out by fever. He thought of Marseille, where a further operation would certainly be needed.

The suburbs of Paris appeared with the first gloom of evening. At 6.30 p.m., the train pulled into the Gare de l'Est, where great adventures had begun. Acting on a sudden hope, Rimbaud decided that they would go and spend the night in a hotel. Perhaps the surgeons of Paris would know of a cure.

If the plan had been put into effect, he might have seen the bald head and tobacco-stained whiskers of Paul Verlaine swaying towards his hospital bed. But as the cab ran down the boulevards, the rain began to fall and the streets emptied. Rimbaud stared at the shining pavements and the overflowing drains and called to the driver to change course. He was to go straight to the Gare de Lyon. When the sun came up, he wanted to be back in the south.

At that moment, across the river in a quiet street by Saint-Germain-des-Prés, a bundle of poems was sitting on a publisher's desk. They had been written twenty years before by a schoolboy from Charleville. A young journalist called Rodolphe Darzens had been tracking down these marvellous poems ever since reading Verlaine's article on Rimbaud in *Les Poètes maudits*. A complete edition was about to be published, with a biographical preface.

Many of the poems had never been seen by anyone except Izambard and Demeny. A few lurid forgeries like 'Le Limaçon' had crept in from the trendy *Décadent*, but the genuine poems were powerful enough to show that this had been one of the great Romantic imaginations, festering in damp, provincial rooms like an intelligent disease,

> While the street outside sent up its sounds,
> Alone, and lying on sheets of unbleached linen,
> With violent presentiments of the sail!

40

Maritime

'Quick! Are there other lives?'

('Mauvais sang', *Une Saison en Enfer*)

RIMBAUD WAS UNCONSCIOUS when the sun rose over the Rhône Valley. He had eaten nothing since leaving Roche. At the station in Paris, like a Danakil tribesman visiting the land of white-skinned lunatics, he had collapsed with hysterical laughter at the sight of an army uniform. A sleeping potion had been ordered, but it was a long time before it took effect. As the heat of Provence entered the compartment through the wooden shutters, he woke, several times, from nightmares.[1]

Years before, this had been one of the roads to freedom: Lyon, Valence, Orange, Avignon, Arles and finally Marseille, where the ships of the Messageries Maritimes sailed for Suez and the world beyond.

Railway employees lugged Rimbaud out to the station forecourt. Isabelle had him arranged in the back of a cab, which ran them to the hospital a mile away.

Just in case the military authorities were still on his trail, he had himself registered as 'Jean Rimbaud' – some other Rimbaud . . .

The deserter was planning his last escape.

*

THE EVENTS OF the next month are unknown but unmysterious. When Isabelle wrote home on 22 September, her brother was further down the tunnel: black rings around his eyes; continual perspiration; sudden jolts to the heart and head that woke him from his daytime stupor.

Once a week, his shrivelled body was propped up naked on a chair while the bed was made. He lost the use of his right arm. Two weeks later, the left arm was strangely desiccated and 'three-quarters paralysed'. Isabelle kept her mother informed: 'Ever since he regained his senses, he has been in tears. He does not believe that he will be left paralysed (if he lives, that is). Deceived by the doctors, he clings to life and to the hope of getting better.' 'He takes me in his arms, sobbing and crying out as he begs me not to leave him.'

One or two laconic notes came from Roche with the usual news – a sick horse, obstreperous servants – and a request to prevent Arthur from doing anything silly: 'He thinks his 30,000 francs are at Roche', Isabelle assured her mother, 'and I could also tell him that you have invested the money. That would delay things for about a month if he was really determined to get it back.'

On 3 October, as a last resort, the doctors decided to try electricity. The electrodes were fastened to the lifeless arm and produced a spasm, then nothing. A doctor urged Isabelle to stay in Marseille: 'In his condition, it would be cruel to withhold your presence.' She reported the doctor's words to her mother, who wanted her back on the farm.

Friendly letters were still arriving from Africa, and there were visits from Alfred Bardey, who spoke encouragingly about artificial limbs and invited Rimbaud to come and convalesce at his home in the country.[2]

But when the specially ordered leg arrived in its box – after being mistaken for a coffin – Rimbaud stared at it in desperation: '"I shall never wear it", he said. "It's over, it's all over. I can feel that I'm dying."'

*

A BUSY LIFE was beginning for the other Arthur Rimbaud. The *Revue de l'Évolution sociale, scientifique et littéraire* was running a series on 'Poets and Degenerates'. A doctor had offered his expert opinion of the absent poet: he was clearly 'unhinged'.[3] (The diagnosis was based on the fake poems from *Le Décadent*.) But where was the madman now? Rumours were reaching Paris all the time. George Moore, who had seen some 'beautiful' poems with 'strange titles', heard that the author of *Une Saison en Enfer* probably still existed, but in a faraway place:

> He left Europe to immure himself for ever in a Christian convent on the shores of the Red Sea; and where it stands on a rocky promontory, he has been seen digging the soil for the grace of God.[4]

Of all the imaginary Rimbauds, this one was the closest to home. The 'single figure digging in the eastern twilight' also existed in Rimbaud's mind. He watched the sun move across the hospital windows and longed to leave for Nice, Algiers or Aden – even for the bone-strewn shores of Obock. If Isabelle had been willing to follow him abroad, he might have tried to leave.

*

BY 5 OCTOBER, the nurses had stopped changing his sheets. Any movement caused him pain. His left leg was cold, and one of his eyelids had drooped. He had palpitations and constipation. 'At night', Isabelle told their mother, 'he allows himself to become drenched in sweat and restrains himself rather than have recourse to the night nurse.'

Horrible things were happening to him after dark . . .

> He accuses the nurses and even the nuns of abominable things that cannot possibly exist. I tell him that he has probably been dreaming, but he won't be convinced and tells me that I'm a simpleton and a fool.

Rimbaud knew that he would not recover. Isabelle was given cursory instructions and left to administer the treatment. She bathed him and rubbed ointment into his body. At his request, she shaved his head so that the nurses would leave him alone with their scissors. Now and then, she attached the electrodes and tried to galvanize the dead arm.

For all the horror and expense, Isabelle was enjoying a new kind of happiness. Arthur's misfortune had enabled her to escape from home for the first time in her life. His conversation, which ranged from the oracular to the obscene, opened windows on to a wider world. In Marseille, where 'it is always radiantly sunny' and where 'there are avalanches of fruit of every sort', she had the unfamiliar experience of being treated like a grown woman.

> This is the place to come to if one wishes to see and feel oneself being respected and even revered as one deserves. What a difference there is between the refined manners of this place and the wild boorishness of the fine young men of Roche! [. . .] And since I only talk to old men, no one can have anything to say against me.

Rimbaud spent his thirty-seventh birthday in agony. The stump had swollen up and a huge growth appeared between his hip and his stomach. Doctors came to admire it.

The hospital chaplain, according to Isabelle, was more reticent. Seeing the retching and spitting, he decided not to offer Communion 'for fear of an involuntary profanation'.[5] The last rites could not be administered if the patient was going to choke on the body of Christ.

Rimbaud's only consolation was a nightly injection of morphine. In his delirium, he sometimes called his sister Djami. He wanted to leave his servant 3,000 francs and to be carried back to Aden, where the cemetery was close to the sea. Apparently, he abandoned the idea so as not to inconvenience his sister.

This was not an environment in which the truth could flourish. At this point in the correspondence, a letter from Isabelle to her mother sits like a self-deluding cuckoo:

> God be blessed a thousand times! On Sunday I had the greatest joy I could ever experience in this world. He who lies dying at my side is no longer a poor unhappy reprobate but a righteous man, a saint, a martyr, one of the chosen!
>
> [. . .] As the priest was leaving, he said to me, with a strange and troubled expression, 'Your brother has faith, my child [. . .]. Indeed, I have never seen faith of such quality!'
>
> [. . .] And [Arthur] said to me also, bitterly, 'Yea, they say that they believe who merely pretend to have been converted, but it's so that people will read what they write. It's a commercial ploy!'

This surprising letter is dated 28 October 1891, which would mean that Isabelle managed to contain her joy for three days (28 October was a Wednesday).

The passage on Rimbaud's conversion is quite different from any other piece of writing that Isabelle sent to her mother. The tone and style and the reference to hypocritical writers belong to the period following Rimbaud's death. The letter was obviously composed after the event, probably after Isabelle discovered that Arthur had written satanic poems like 'Les Premières communions'.[6] No one was going to say that her sainted brother had been 'a vagabond, a Communard, a swindler, a tout, a Carlist, a rapscallion, a drunkard, a madman and a bandit'[7] – especially not in any paper that was read in the Ardennes. 'Where biography is concerned', she wrote in January 1892, 'I allow only one theme, and that's my own.'[8]

Even if Rimbaud did acknowledge the god who exacted his confession under torture, it would be unwise to name the god in question. Isabelle herself heard him repeat the phrase that the Koran prescribes for such occasions: '*Allah kerim!*' ('Allah is munificent').[9]

It is not unknown for dying people, even in the most appalling condition, to find a sudden peace and to talk with complete clarity just before giving up the ghost. Isabelle might have witnessed such a moment of serenity and interpreted it according to her own wishes. She might even have heard something that sounded faintly Biblical.

When he wakes, he looks through the window at the sun that shines continually in a cloudless sky, and he begins to weep, saying that never again will he see the sun out of doors. 'I shall go under the earth', he told me, 'and you shall walk in the sun!'

*

IN A LIFE so full of silence, Rimbaud's authentic last words are an astonishing relic.

On 9 November 1891, he dictated a letter to Isabelle. It was addressed to an unnamed 'Directeur'. He seems to have been thinking at first of the hospital director, but then, as longing filled the sails, of the director of the steam-ship company that would take him back to Africa.

Time and space had become confused. He was in Aden or Harar, organizing a caravan of ivory. The inventory would have to be drawn up carefully, to make sure that everything that left, arrived. If there were no debts outstanding on his hospital account, he would be free to leave.

He was to sail from a place – or on a ship – called 'Aphinar'. The name appears to be imaginary. Perhaps he was remembering a boat that had once existed, or the Arabic for lighthouse: *al fanār*.[10] But even this light is uncertain. 'Aphinar' was just a word.

Item	1 tusk only
Item	2 tusks
Item	3 tusks
Item	4 tusks
Item	2 tusks

M. le Directeur,

I should like to ask whether I have left anything on your account. I wish to change from this service today. I don't even know its name, but whatever it is, let it be the Aphinar line. All those services are there all over the place and I, crippled and unhappy, can find nothing – any dog in the street could tell you that.

Please therefore send me the tariff of services from Aphinar to Suez. I am completely paralysed, and so I wish to embark in good time. Tell me at what time I must be carried on board.

*

RIMBAUD DIED THE following morning at ten o'clock.

Epilogue

'Perhaps he has secrets for *changing life*?'

('Délires I', *Une Saison en Enfer*)

THE BODY WAS taken back to Paris in an oak coffin, then on to Charleville. It arrived at the station on 14 November.

Mme Rimbaud arranged the funeral as hastily as if it had been a medical emergency. The Abbé Gillet, who had taught Rimbaud twenty-two years before at the Collège de Charleville, was given one hour to prepare the service.

He managed to assemble four cantors, eight choirboys, twenty orphan girls with candles, a beadle, a bell-ringer, an undertaker and a grave-digger. Shortly before 10.30 a.m., the organist who had given Rimbaud a crash course in the rudiments of music in 1875 was rushing through the streets in his best suit, wondering which relative of Mme Rimbaud had died.[1]

It was an expensive, first-class funeral. Nobody came, because no one had been invited and no announcement appeared in the local press.

Rimbaud's body was placed in the family vault. The frilly white tombstone bears only his name, age, date of death and the words, 'Pray for him'. It stands just inside the cemetery gates, at the top of the drab avenue that leads out of town to the west.

Apart from most of his bones, there is nothing of Rimbaud in the

Charleville cemetery. Time is better spent in other ways: drinking at the gaudy Café de l'Univers, in sight of the bust in the Square de la Gare ('where everything is well-behaved, the flowers and the trees'), with its gloriously inapt inscription – 'To Jean-Arthur Rimbaud / His admirers / The State' – and its base of council bedding-plants; buying a copy of his poems at the Rimbaud Museum opposite the house on the Quai de la Madeleine (now Quai Arthur Rimbaud); or learning to recite the poems with a teenage Charleville accent by listening to local high-school students, one in five of whom, according to a 1991 poll of French *lycéens*, identifies with Arthur Rimbaud.[2]

*

RIMBAUD WAS IN the news again the day after his death. The edition of his verse poems called *Le Reliquaire* had been seized by the police on the instructions of Rimbaud's biographer, Rodolphe Darzens. Darzens had been horrified to find that the publisher had taken his notes and cobbled together a ludicrous, gossipy preface.

Enough copies escaped to the outside world to reinforce Rimbaud's reputation as a brutish little vagrant who made himself at home in the murkiest parts of the human mind, just as he wandered into strangers' rooms. The stabbing of Étienne Carjat was recounted in detail, and there was an allusion to 'a little drama' with Verlaine that had taken place in Belgium.

The work itself showed that the prize-winning schoolboy had trampled the flower-beds of French poetry with an expert boot. They were often slangy and obscene, but even the incomprehensible poems had the smell of real experience.

Beyond the avant-garde, most of his poetry was too difficult or violent to be appreciated. The details of his life simply confirmed his eccentricity. The journalists who wrote about the seizure of *Le Reliquaire* gave the impression that Arthur Rimbaud had been far too interesting to be considered a serious poet:

12 November: Rimbaud, who was once described by Victor Hugo as an 'infant Shakespeare', is now 'a slave-trader in Uganda'. (*L'Écho de Paris*)

17 November: 'He was an insufferable contemporary. I knew him. He guzzled his food and had no table manners. [. . .] Timorous people experienced certain anxieties in his presence. [. . .] When we cast his horoscope twenty years ago, we weren't absolutely certain that he wouldn't end up on the scaffold.' (Edmond Lepelletier in *L'Écho de Paris*)

28 November: 'The poet Arthur Rimbaud is thought to be in Paris where he is to have his leg amputated. An extraordinary and mysterious character, this Arthur Rimbaud. His poems have just been published under the title *Le Reliquaire*.' (Anatole France in *L'Univers illustré*)

1 December: 'He is said to be living in Harar, Cape Guardafui, in Africa.' 'Spurning everything but brutal pleasure, wild adventure and a violent life, this strangest of all poets seems to have abandoned poetry.' (Remy de Gourmont in the *Mercure de France*)

1 December: 'Having made a complete recovery, Arthur Rimbaud will be arriving shortly to revise the edition of his works.' (*Entretiens politiques et littéraires*)

6 December: 'The death of Arthur Rimbaud has been announced. [. . .] He died in the harbour at Marseille.' (*L'Écho de Paris*)

6 December: 'It is well known that the poet Arthur Raimbaud is considered by the Symbolists and the Decadents to be one of their most interesting precursors.

   If it is true, as rumour in the Latin Quarter would have it, that he is still alive and ruling over a tribe of negroes in Africa, this incident [the seizure of *Le Reliquaire*] will probably be a matter of extreme indifference to him.' (*Le Monde artiste*)

*

THAT DECEMBER, ISABELLE was distracted from her mourning by an unpleasant article in a local paper. *Le Petit Ardennais* had published some notes on her brother by a certain 'M. D . . .' (Delahaye). They made him sound like the exact opposite of a respectable person: a blasphemer, a terrorist, an insulter of policemen, a forager in rubbish-heaps and a friend of Paul Verlaine.

This was the start of Isabelle's career as Arthur Rimbaud's representative on earth. In 1897, she married one of his first biographers, a wilfully gullible writer called Paterne Berrichon who seems to fall asleep half-way through his own meandering sentences. His real name was Pierre Dufour – which, coincidentally, recalls a passage from *Une Saison en Enfer*:[3]

> 'Can you see that elegant young man, entering the calm and beautiful house? His name is Duval, Dufour, Armand, Maurice, or something like that. A woman has devoted herself to loving that pathetic idiot.'

Together, Isabelle and Berrichon set about re-establishing the 'truth': Rimbaud had repudiated his 'youthful indiscretions' and gone to live in the benighted continent where 'the natives called him the Saint because of his miraculous charity'.[4] There, he had purged himself of all impurity: 'Never was any human life less marked by storms of passion.'[5]

In case anyone thought that Rimbaud had been a half-wild hermit, Isabelle and her husband doctored the letters to show that 'the Saint' had also amassed a very respectable sum of money. No detail was too small to be distorted. In 1887, Rimbaud had complained of having to carry 16,000 francs, weighing eight kilos. Stupidly scrupulous in their deceit, Isabelle and Berrichon scaled up both figures – 40,000 francs and twenty kilos – which means that he would have been staggering about Cairo like a grounded albatross.

When the unclaimed copies of *Une Saison en Enfer* were discovered in Brussels in 1901, Berrichon tried to persuade the man who found them to destroy every copy in order to preserve the fantasy that Rimbaud had committed all his work to the purifying flames.[6]

The devotional biographies and editions produced by Rimbaud's posthumous brother-in-law did a great deal of damage, not only by fooling the credulous but also by convincing sceptics that the truth was simply the opposite of whatever Isabelle and Berrichon had said. René Étiemble, who spent more than thirty years compiling his derisive bibliography, *Le Mythe de Rimbaud*, constructed his own counter-legends: the failed businessman, the slave-trader, the seedy colonial with a taste for 'little boys'. Both sets of legends have proved remarkably durable.

Mme Rimbaud, who did not attend the public inauguration of Arthur's bust in 1901, was closer to the spirit of his work than most of his admirers. As Isabelle explained to Berrichon:

I doubt she has read Arthur's books, and it's just as well if she hasn't, because, considering their style and philosophy, she would hold them in exceptional abhorrence [. . .] and, in a moment of decisive energy, would probably annihilate everything, both work and commentaries.[7]

*

BY THE TIME Mme Rimbaud died in 1907, it was too late to prevent Arthur's work from reaching the open road. A new edition of *Une Saison en Enfer* and the *Illuminations* appeared in 1892, then his *Poésies complètes* in 1895, both with a preface by Verlaine. Practically all of Rimbaud's known writing had appeared before the First World War, with the notable exceptions of *Un Cœur sous une soutane* (1924), the 'Zutiste' poems (1942–61) and his Gospel adaptations (1948). At least one unpublished poem exists in a private collection,[8] although there has been no further news of the suitcase full of manuscripts that was apparently discovered in Dire Dawa, just north of Harar, when Allied troops entered the town in 1942.[9]

For most readers, Rimbaud's poetry remained a curious outpost of late Romanticism until the 1930s; but even after its conscription by academic curricula and Ministers of Culture, it retained its avant-garde aura. An icon to the Beat poets, the students of May 1968, intellectual rock musicians and the gay movement, Rimbaud has done more than any other writer to import Romantic ideals into the distant twentieth century. Romanticism's best bad example – and best-selling poet – became the Lord Byron of modern literature: a seductive role-model whose life and work were seen as complementary parts of the same dangerous experiment.

On the 'cursed, desolate shores' of this century, Rimbaud is still an ambiguous presence – warning his unknown readers of the hell to which 'derangement' inevitably leads, and showing them exactly how to get there.

Appendices

I. Family Tree

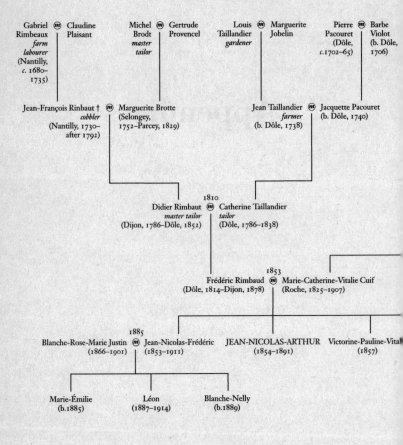

Gabriel ⓜ Claudine
Rimbeaux | Plaisant
farm
labourer
(Nantilly,
c. 1680–
1735)

Michel ⓜ Gertrude
Brodt | Provencel
master
tailor

Louis ⓜ Marguerite
Taillandier | Jobelin
gardener

Pierre ⓜ Barbe
Pacouret | Violot
(Dôle, | (b. Dôle,
*c.*1702–65) | 1706)

Jean-François Rinbaut † ⓜ Marguerite Brotte
cobbler | (Selongey,
(Nantilly, 1730– | 1752–Parcey, 1829)
after 1792)

Jean Taillandier ⓜ Jacquette Pacouret
farmer | (b. Dôle, 1740)
(b. Dôle, 1738)

1810
Didier Rimbaut ⓜ Catherine Taillandier
master tailor | *tailor*
(Dijon, 1786–Dôle, 1852) | (Dôle, 1786–1838)

1853
Frédéric Rimbaud ⓜ Marie-Catherine-Vitalie Cuif
(Dôle, 1814–Dijon, 1878) | (Roche, 1825–1907)

1885
Blanche-Rose-Marie Justin ⓜ Jean-Nicolas-Frédéric   JEAN-NICOLAS-ARTHUR   Victorine-Pauline-Vital
(1866–1901) | (1853–1911)   (1854–1891)   (1857)

Marie-Émilie   Léon   Blanche-Nelly
(b.1885)   (1887–1914)   (b.1889)

APPENDICES

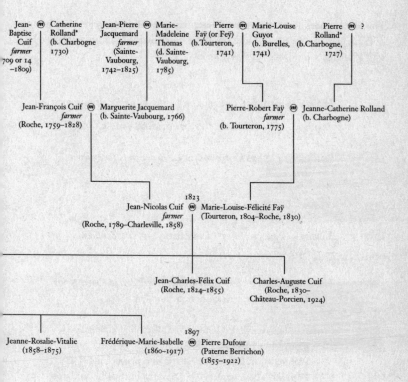

Jean-Baptise Cuif *farmer* 709 or 14 –1809) ⓜ Catherine Rolland* (b. Charbogne 1730)

Jean-Pierre Jacquemard *farmer* (Sainte-Vaubourg, 1742–1825) ⓜ Marie-Madeleine Thomas (d. Sainte-Vaubourg, 1785)

Pierre Faÿ (or Feÿ) (b. Tourteron, 1741) ⓜ Marie-Louise Guyot (b. Burelles, 1741)

Pierre Rolland* (b. Charbogne, 1727) ⓜ ?

Jean-François Cuif *farmer* (Roche, 1759–1828) ⓜ Marguerite Jacquemard (b. Sainte-Vaubourg, 1766)

Pierre-Robert Faÿ *farmer* (b. Tourteron, 1775) ⓜ Jeanne-Catherine Rolland (b. Charbogne)

1823

Jean-Nicolas Cuif *farmer* (Roche, 1789–Charleville, 1858) ⓜ Marie-Louise-Félicité Faÿ (Tourteron, 1804–Roche, 1830)

Jean-Charles-Félix Cuif (Roche, 1824–1855)

Charles-Auguste Cuif (Roche, 1830–Château-Porcien, 1924)

1897

Jeanne-Rosalie-Vitalie (1858–1875)

Frédérique-Marie-Isabelle (1860–1917) ⓜ Pierre Dufour (Paterne Berrichon) (1855–1922)

* Catherine and Pierre Rolland are sister and brother.

† Also written Raimbaud, Rimbaud, Rimbault, Rimbaut and Rimbaux.

Principal sources: Briet (1956 and 1968); Godchot; Henry.

[449]

II. Poems by Rimbaud published in his lifetime

This list excludes Rimbaud's school Latin verse, published in the *Moniteur de l'Enseignement Supérieur*. Only the three items marked * were published with Rimbaud's knowledge and permission.

1870   *January 2* – 'Les Étrennes des orphelins' in *La Revue pour tous*. *

            August 13 – 'Trois baisers' ('Première soirée') in *La Charge*. *

1872   *September 14* – 'Les Corbeaux' in *La Renaissance littéraire et artistique*.

1873   *October* – *Une Saison en Enfer*. *

1878   *January* – 'Petits pauvres' ('Les Effarés') in *The Gentleman's Magazine*.

1882   *June* – 'Les Chercheuses de poux' (two stanzas) in Champsaur, *Dinah Samuel*; new edition, September 1889.

1883   *October* – 'Les Assis', 'Le Bateau ivre', 'Les Chercheuses de poux', 'Les Effarés', 'Oraison du soir', 'Voyelles', and fragments of 'L'Éternité', 'Paris se repeuple' and 'Les Premières communions' in *Lutèce*, published by Verlaine. Collected in *Les Poètes maudits* (April 1884).

1886   *April 11* – 'Les Premières communions' in *La Vogue*.

            May–June – *Les Illuminations* (including some of the *Derniers Vers*) in *La Vogue*. Also published separately.

1888   *June* – 'Le Buffet', 'Le Dormeur du val' and 'Les Effarés' in
        Poètes lyriques français du XIXᵉ siècle (Lemerre anthology).

        October – Verlaine, *Les Poètes maudits*, new edition, with part of
        'Le Cœur du pitre' ('Le Cœur volé') and 'Tête de faune'.

1889   *January–February* – 'A la musique', 'Ma Bohème', 'Le Mal' and
        'Sensation' in *La Revue indépendante*.

1890   *February 8* – 'Le Buffet' and 'Sensation' in *Le Petit Ardennais*.

        March – 'Voyelles' in Maupassant, *La Vie errante*.

        March 15 – 'Au Cabaret vert' in *La Revue d'aujourd'hui*.

        May 15 – 'Le Buffet' and 'Sensation' in *La Plume* (from *Le Petit
        Ardennais*).

        September 15 – 'Paris se repeuple' in *La Plume*.

1891   *November 1* – 'Bal des pendus' and 'Vénus anadyomène' in
        Mercure de France.

        November – *Le Reliquaire* (see pp. 434 and 442).

III. Historical Events

1870   *July 19* – France declares war on Prussia.

         September 1 – Napoleon III surrenders to Bismarck at Sedan.

         September 4 – In Paris, proclamation of Third Republic and
             formation of an emergency Government of National
             Defence.

         September 19 – Siege of Paris begins.

1871   *January 28* – Armistice signed with Prussia.

         February 8–15 – Election of National Assembly with powers to
             negotiate peace with Prussia. Adolphe Thiers President.

         March 26 – Parisians elect their own revolutionary government,
             the Commune.

         May 22–28 – *La Semaine Sanglante*: National Assembly troops
             crush the Commune.

ABYSSINIA* 1872–1897

1872   Yohannes IV Emperor of Ethiopia.

---

* Abyssinia was the foreign name for the Ethiopian Empire, including its semi-independent kingdoms. The most important of these was Choa, the kingdom of Menelik, bordered on the east by the river Awash. Abyssinia therefore excluded the colonies and protectorates on the Red Sea (Obock, Tadjoura, etc.) and Harar, until the city was captured by Menelik in 1887. In his letters, Rimbaud situates Harar tribally ('in the Gallas') or geographically ('East Africa').

1875   Egyptian occupation of Red Sea ports and Harar.

1884   *September* – Egyptian evacuation of Harar begins.

1885   *February* – Italians land at Massawa with plans to colonize
            Abyssinia.

            May – Harar seized by Emir Abdullahi.

1887   *January 8* – Menelik captures Harar; Makonnen appointed
            Governor.

1889   *March 9* – Death of Emperor Yohannes.

            March 25 – Menelik proclaims himself Emperor of Ethiopia
            (crowned 3 November).

            May 2 – Menelik signs 'Treaty of Perpetual Peace and
            Friendship' with Italy (see p. 405).

            October – Italian colony of Eritrea.

1890   *January 26* – Italy occupies Adwa.

1891   Addis Ababa (founded 1887) new capital of Empire.

1896   *March 1* – General Baratieri (Italy) defeated by Menelik at Adwa.

1897   *May 14* – European powers recognize Ethiopia's independence.
            Italy retains Eritrea.

IV. Maps

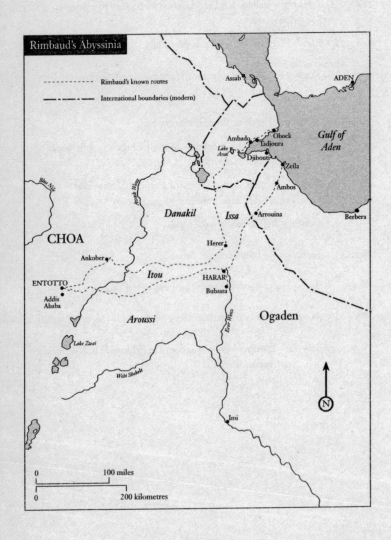

Rimbaud's Abyssinia

- - - - - - - Rimbaud's known routes

— · — · — International boundaries (modern)

ADEN

Assab

Gulf of Aden

Ambado   Obock
Tadjoura
Lake Assal
Djibouti   Zeila

Ambos

Assab Wine

Bleu Nil

Danakil   *Issa*   Arrouina

Berbera

CHOA

Herer

Ankober

Itou   HARAR
Bubassa

ENTOTTO

Addis Ababa

Aroussi   Ogaden

Errer Thess

Lake Zwai

Webi Shebelt

N

Imi

0   100 miles

0   200 kilometres

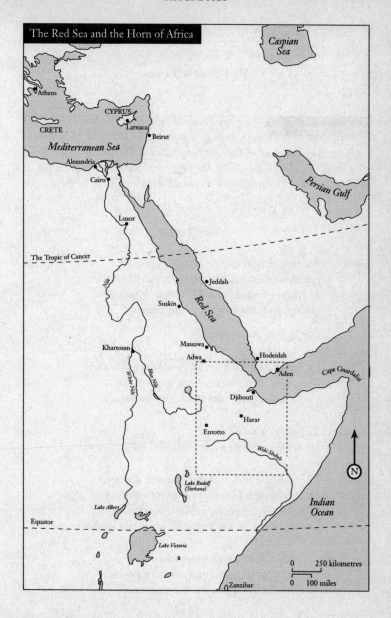

The Red Sea and the Horn of Africa

Caspian Sea

Athens

CYPRUS

CRETE
Larnaca
Beirut

Mediterranean Sea

Alexandria

Cairo

Persian Gulf

Luxor

The Tropic of Cancer

Jeddah

Nile

Suakin

Red Sea

Khartoum

Massawa

Adwa

Hodeidah

Aden

Cape Guardafui

White Nile

Blue Nile

Djibouti

Harar

Entotto

Wabi Shebeli

Lake Rudolf
(Turkana)

Lake Albert

Indian
Ocean

N

Equator

Lake Victoria

0   250 kilometres

0   100 miles

Zanzibar

V. French Texts

This appendix contains the original texts of verse poems by Rimbaud quoted in translation. If space permitted, it would contain all the original texts. I hope that this deficiency will be construed as an encouragement to acquire a copy of Rimbaud's poems ... In the meantime, my own computer file of Rimbaud's complete works can be consulted at www.rimbaud.co.uk.

1. BAD BLOOD

page 6   Madame se tient trop debout dans la prairie
prochaine où neigent les fils du travail; l'ombrelle
aux doigts; foulant l'ombelle; trop fière pour elle;
des enfants lisant dans la verdure fleurie

leur livre de maroquin rouge!

page 7   Et, rendus amoureux par le chant des trombones,
Très naïfs, et fumant des roses, les pioupious
Caressent les bébés pour enjôler les bonnes ...

page 12   Regret des bras épais [. . .]
Or des lunes d'avril au coeur du saint lit!

page 13   Elle veut, elle veut, pourtant, l'âme en détresse,
Le front dans l'oreiller creusé par les cris sourds,
Prolonger les éclairs suprêmes de tendresse,
Et bave ... – L'ombre emplit les maisons et les cours.

page 14   Je songeais à mon père parfois:
Le soir, le jeu de carte et les mots plus grivois,
Le voisin, et moi qu'on écartait, choses vues ...

– Car un père est troublant! – et les choses conçues!...
Son genou, câlineur parfois; son pantalon
Dont mon doigt désirait ouvrir la fente...

2. FILTH

page 16   Ces enfants seuls étaient ses familiers
Qui, chétifs, fronts nus, œil déteignant sur la joue,
Cachant de maigres doigts jaunes et noirs de boue
Sous des habits puant la foire et tout vieillots,
Conversaient avec la douceur des idiots!
Et si, l'ayant surpris à des pitiés immondes,
Sa mère s'effrayait; les tendresses, profondes,
De l'enfant se jetaient sur cet étonnement.
C'était bon. Elle avait le bleu regard, – qui ment!

page 16   – Et, par elle meurtri des poings et des talons,
Remportait la saveur de sa peau dans sa chambre.

page 16   L'été
Surtout, vaincu, stupide, il était entêté
A se renfermer dans la fraîcheur des latrines:
Il pensait là, tranquille et livrant ses narines.

page 17   Dans l'ombre des couloirs aux tentures moisies,
En passant il tirait la langue, les deux poings
A l'aine, et dans ses yeux fermés voyait des points.

page 18   Tout le jour il suait d'obéissance; très
Intelligent; pourtant des tics noirs, quelques traits
Semblaient prouver en lui d'âcres hypocrisies.

page 18   l'enfant
Gêneur, la si sotte bête,
Ne doit cesser un instant

De ruser et d'être traître

Comme un chat des Monts-Rocheux;
D'empuantir toutes sphères!

3. 'PERFECT LITTLE MONSTER'

page 30   Votre cœur l'a compris: – ces enfants sont sans mère.
Plus de mère au logis! – et le père est bien loin! . . .
[. . .]
Les petits sont tout seuls en la maison glacée;
Orphelins de quatre ans, voilà qu'en leur pensée
S'éveille, par degrés, un souvenir riant . . .

4. 'MAD AMBITION'

page 33   Sur l'onde calme et noire où dorment les étoiles
La blanche Ophélia flotte comme un grand lys,
Flotte très lentement, couchée en ses longs voiles . . .
– On entend dans les bois lointains des hallalis.

page 34   Ciel! Amour! Liberté! Quel rêve, ô pauvre Folle!
Tu te fondais à lui comme une neige au feu:
Tes grandes visions étranglaient ta parole
– Et l'Infini terrible effara ton œil bleu!

page 35   Par les soirs bleus d'été, j'irai dans les sentiers,
Picoté par les blés, fouler l'herbe menue:
Rêveur, j'en sentirai la fraîcheur à mes pieds.
Je laisserai le vent baigner ma tête nue.

Je ne parlerai pas, je ne penserai rien:
Mais l'amour infini me montera dans l'âme,
Et j'irai loin, bien loin, comme un bohémien,
Par la Nature, – heureux comme avec une femme.

page *39*   Brune, elle avait seize ans quand on la maria.

. . . . . .

Car elle aime d'amour son fils de dix-sept ans.

5. CONVICTIONS

page *52*   On n'est pas sérieux, quand on a dix-sept ans.

[. . .]

Passe une demoiselle aux petits airs charmants,

Sous l'ombre du faux-col effrayant de son père . . .

Et, comme elle vous trouve immensément naïf,

Tout en faisant trotter ses petites bottines,

Elle se tourne, alerte et d'un mouvement vif . . .

[. . .]

Vous êtes amoureux. Loué jusqu'au mois d'août.

page *54*   Tandis que les crachats rouges de la mitraille

Sifflent tout le jour par l'infini du ciel bleu;

[. . .]

Tandis qu'une folie épouvantable, broie

Et fait de cent milliers d'hommes un tas fumant;

[. . .]

– Il est un Dieu [. . .]

Qui dans le bercement des hosannah s'endort,

Et se réveille, quand des mères, ramassées

Dans l'angoisse, et pleurant sous leur vieux bonnet noir,

Lui donnent un gros sou lié dans leur mouchoir!

page *55*   J'irais, pressant

Ton corps, comme une enfant qu'on couche,

Ivre du sang

Qui coule, bleu, sous ta peau blanche

Aux tons rosés [. . .]

6. Tour de France

page 58 – Celle-là, ce n'est pas un baiser qui l'épeure! –
Rieuse, m'apporta des tartines de beurre,
Du jambon tiède, dans un plat colorié,

Du jambon rose et blanc parfumé d'une gousse
D'ail, – et m'emplit la chope immense, avec sa mousse
Que dorait un rayon de soleil arriéré.

page 59 *Ma Bohème*

Je m'en allais, les poings dans mes poches crevées;
Mon paletot aussi devenait idéal;
J'allais sous le ciel, Muse! et j'étais ton féal;
Oh! là là! que d'amours splendides j'ai rêvées!

Mon unique culotte avait un large trou.
– Petit-Poucet rêveur, j'égrenais dans ma course
Des rimes. Mon auberge était à la Grande-Ourse.
– Mes étoiles au ciel avaient un doux frou-frou

Et je les écoutais, assis au bord des routes,
Ces bons soirs de septembre où je sentais des gouttes
De rosée à mon front, comme un vin de vigueur;

Où, rimant au milieu des ombres fantastiques,
Comme des lyres, je tirais les élastiques
De mes souliers blessés, un pied près de mon cœur!

7. Needful Destruction

page 64 Les tilleuls sentent bon dans les bons soirs de juin!
L'air est parfois si doux, qu'on ferme la paupière;
Le vent chargé de bruits, – la ville n'est pas loin, –
A des parfums de vigne et des parfums de bière . . .

page 68   Gisant au pied d'un mur, enterré dans la marne
Et pour des visions écrasant son œil darne,
[...]
                              – Il s'aidait
De journaux illustrés où, rouge, il regardait
Des Espagnoles rire et des Italiennes.
[...]
– Il rêvait la prairie amoureuse, où des houles
Lumineuses, parfums sains, pubescences d'or
Font leur remuement calme et prennent leur essor!

page 68   Quand, dans la chambre nue aux persiennes closes,
Haute et bleue, âcrement prise d'humidité,
Il lisait son roman sans cesse médité,
Plein de lourds ciels ocreux et de forêts noyées,
De fleurs de chair aux bois sidérals déployées,
Vertige, écroulements, déroutes et pitié!
– Tandis que se faisait la rumeur du quartier,
En bas, – seul, et couché sur des pièces de toile
Écrue, et pressentant violemment la voile!

page 70   J'ai bientôt déniché la bottine, le bas...
– Je reconstruis les corps, brûlé de belles fièvres.
Elles me trouvent drôle et se parlent tout bas...
– Et je sens les baisers qui me viennent aux lèvres...

Or: Et mes désirs brutaux s'accrochent à leurs lèvres...

page 70   Un soir, tu me sacras poète,
        Blond laideron:
Descends ici, que je te fouette
        En mon giron;

J'ai dégueulé ta bandoline,
        Noir laideron;
Tu couperais ma mandoline
        Au fil du front.

Pouah! mes salives desséchées,
    Roux laideron,
Infectent encor les tranchées
    De ton sein rond!

O mes petites amoureuses,
    Que je vous hais!
Plaquez de fouffes douloureuses
    Vos tétons laids!

page 79   Comme je descendais des Fleuves impassibles,
Je ne me sentis plus guidé par les haleurs:
Des Peaux-Rouges criards les avaient pris pour cibles
Les ayant cloués nus aux poteaux de couleurs.

8. The Seer

page 82   Mon triste cœur bave à la poupe,
Mon cœur couvert de caporal:
Ils y lancent des jets de soupe,
Mon triste cœur bave à la poupe:
Sous les quolibets de la troupe

[. . .]

J'aurai des sursauts stomachiques
Moi, si mon cœur est ravalé:
Quand ils auront tari leurs chiques
Comment agir, ô cœur volé?

page 85   Des curiosités vaguement impudiques
Épouvantent le rêve aux chastes bleuités
Qui s'est surpris autour des célestes tuniques,
Du linge dont Jésus voile ses nudités.

page 90   Vraiment, c'est bête, ces églises des villages
Où quinze laids marmots encrassant les piliers

Écoutent, grasseyant les divins babillages,
Un noir grotesque dont fermentent les souliers:
Mais le soleil éveille, à travers les feuillages,
Les vieilles couleurs des vitraux irréguliers.

page 92   Parqués entre des bancs de chêne, aux coins d'église
Qu'attiédit puamment leur souffle, tous leurs yeux
Vers le chœur ruisselant d'orrie et la maîtrise
Aux vingt gueules gueulant les cantiques pieux;

Comme un parfum de pain humant l'odeur de cire,
Heureux, humiliés comme des chiens battus,
Les Pauvres au bon Dieu, le patron et le sire,
Tendent leurs oremus risibles et têtus.

Aux femmes, c'est bien bon de faire des bancs lisses,
Après les six jours noirs où Dieu les fait souffrir!
Elles bercent, tordus dans d'étranges pelisses,
Des espèces d'enfants qui pleurent à mourir.

Leurs seins crasseux dehors, ces mangeuses de soupe,
Une prière aux yeux et ne priant jamais,
Regardent parader mauvaisement un groupe
De gamines avec leurs chapeaux déformés.

Dehors, le froid, la faim, l'homme en ribote:
C'est bon. Encore une heure; après, les maux sans noms!
– Cependant, alentour, geint, nasille, chuchote
Une collection de vieilles à fanons:

Ces effarés y sont et ces épileptiques
Dont on se détournait hier aux carrefours;
Et, fringalant du nez dans des missels antiques,
Ces aveugles qu'un chien introduit dans les cours.

Et tous, bavant la foi mendiante et stupide,
Récitent la complainte infinie à Jésus
Qui rêve en haut, jauni par le vitrail livide,
Loin des maigres mauvais et des méchants pansus,

Loin des senteurs de viande et d'étoffes moisies,
Farce prostrée et sombre aux gestes repoussants;
– Et l'oraison fleurit d'expressions choisies,
Et les mysticités prennent des tons pressants,

Quand, des nefs où périt le soleil, plis de soie
Banals, sourires verts, les Dames des quartiers
Distingués, – ô Jésus! – les malades du foie
Font baiser leurs longs doigts jaunes aux bénitiers.

page 94   Le Juste restait droit sur ses hanches solides:
Un rayon lui dorait l'épaule; des sueurs
Me prirent: 'Tu veux voir rutiler les bolides?
Et, debout, écouter bourdonner les flueurs
D'astres lactés, et les essaims d'astéroïdes?

'Par des farces de nuit ton front est épié,
O Juste! Il faut gagner un toit. Dis ta prière,
La bouche dans ton drap doucement expié;
Et si quelque égaré choque ton ostiaire,
Dis: Frère, va plus loin, je suis estropié!'

Et le Juste restait debout, dans l'épouvante
Bleuâtre des gazons après le soleil mort:
'Alors, mettrais-tu tes genouillères en vente,
O Vieillard? Pèlerin sacré! Barde d'Armor!
Pleureur des Oliviers! Main que la pitié gante!'

9. Departure

page 97   Ainsi, toujours, vers l'azur noir
Où tremble la mer des topazes,
Fonctionneront dans ton soir
Les Lys, ces clystères d'extases!

page 97   – En somme, une Fleur, Romarin
Ou Lys, vive ou morte, vaut-elle

Un excrément d'oiseau marin?
Vaut-elle un seul pleur de chandelle?

page 102   Plus douce qu'aux enfants la chair des pommes sures,
L'eau verte pénétra ma coque de sapin
Et des taches de vins bleus et des vomissures
Me lava, dispersant gouvernail et grappin.

Et dès lors, je me suis baigné dans le Poème
De la Mer, infusé d'astres, et lactescent,
Dévorant les azurs verts; où, flottaison blême
Et ravie, un noyé pensif parfois descend.

page 103   J'ai vu le soleil bas, taché d'horreurs mystiques,
Illuminant de longs figements violets,
Pareils à des acteurs de drames très-antiques
Les flots roulant au loin leurs frissons de volets!

J'ai rêvé la nuit verte aux neiges éblouies,
Baiser montant aux yeux des mers avec lenteurs,
La circulation des sèves inouïes,
Et l'éveil jaune et bleu des phosphores chanteurs!

page 105   Si je désire une eau d'Europe, c'est la flache
Noire et froide où vers le crépuscule embaumé
Un enfant accroupi plein de tristesses, lâche
Un bateau frêle comme un papillon de mai.

11. SAVAGE OF THE LATIN QUARTER

page 126   Quand le front de l'enfant, plein de rouges tourmentes,
Implore l'essaim blanc des rêves indistincts,
Il vient près de son lit deux grandes sœurs charmantes
Avec de frêles doigts aux ongles argentins.

Elles assoient l'enfant devant une croisée
Grande ouverte où l'air bleu baigne un fouillis de fleurs

Et dans ses lourds cheveux où tombe la rosée
Promènent leurs doigts fins, terribles et charmeurs.

Il écoute chanter leurs haleines craintives
Qui fleurent de longs miels végétaux et rosés
Et qu'interrompt parfois un sifflement, salives
Reprises sur la lèvre ou désirs de baisers.

Il entend leurs cils noirs battant sous les silences
Parfumés; et leurs doigts électriques et doux
Font crépiter parmi ses grises indolences
Sous leurs ongles royaux la mort des petits poux.

Voilà que monte en lui le vin de la Paresse,
Soupir d'harmonica qui pourrait délirer;
L'enfant se sent, selon la lenteur des caresses,
Sourdre et mourir sans cesse un désir de pleurer.

12. 'MLLE RIMBAUT'

page 135   *Voyelles*

A noir, E blanc, I rouge, U vert, O bleu: voyelles,
Je dirai quelque jour vos naissances latentes:
A, noir corset velu des mouches éclatantes
Qui bombinent autour des puanteurs cruelles,

Golfes d'ombre; E, candeurs des vapeurs et des tentes,
Lances des glaciers fiers, rois blancs, frissons d'ombelles;
I, pourpres, sang craché, rire des lèvres belles
Dans la colère ou les ivresses pénitentes;

U, cycles, vibrements divins des mers virides,
Paix des pâtis semés d'animaux, paix des rides
Que l'alchimie imprime aux grands fronts studieux;

O, Suprême Clairon plein des strideurs étranges,
Silences traversés des Mondes et des Anges:
– O l'Oméga, rayon violet de Ses Yeux!

page 142 Obscur et froncé comme un œillet violet,
Il respire, humblement tapi parmi la mousse
Humide encor d'amour qui suit la rampe douce
Des fesses blanches jusqu'au bord de son ourlet.

Des filaments pareils à des larmes de lait
Ont pleuré sous l'autan cruel qui les repousse
A travers de petits caillots de marne rousse,
Pour s'aller perdre où la pente les appelait.

Mon rêve s'aboucha souvent à sa ventouse;
Mon âme, du coït matériel jalouse,
En fit son larmier fauve et son nid de sanglots.

C'est l'olive pâmée et la flûte câline,
Le tube d'où descend la céleste praline,
Chanaan féminin dans les moiteurs enclos.

13. Dogs

page 149 Qu'est-ce pour nous, mon cœur, que les nappes de sang
Et de braise, et mille meurtres, et les longs cris
De rage, sanglots de tout enfer renversant
Tout ordre; et l'Aquilon encor sur les débris

page 149 Ce n'est rien! j'y suis! j'y suis toujours.

14. Songs of Innocence

page 156 L'eau claire; comme le sel des larmes d'enfance,
l'assaut au soleil des blancheurs des corps de femmes;
la soie, en foule et de lys pur, des oriflammes
sous les murs dont quelque pucelle eut la défense;

l'ébat des anges; – non . . . le courant d'or en marche,
meut ses bras, noirs, et lourds, et frais surtout, d'herbe. Elle

sombre, ayant le Ciel bleu pour ciel-de-lit, appelle
pour rideaux l'ombre de la colline et de l'arche.

page 156 Jouet de cet œil d'eau morne, je n'y puis prendre,
oh! canot immobile! oh! bras trop courts! ni l'une
ni l'autre fleur: ni la jaune qui m'importune,
là; ni la bleue, amie à l'eau couleur de cendre.

Ah! la poudre des saules qu'une aile secoue!
Les roses des roseaux dès longtemps dévorées!
Mon canot, toujours fixe; et sa chaîne tirée
au fond de cet œil d'eau sans bords, – à quelle boue?

page 158 Elle est retrouvée.
Quoi? – L'Éternité.
C'est la mer allée
Avec le soleil.

[. . .]

Puisque de vous seules,
Braises de satin,
Le Devoir s'exhale
Sans qu'on dise: enfin.

Là pas d'espérance,
Nul orietur.
Science avec patience,
Le supplice est sûr.

page 158 O saisons, ô châteaux
Quelle âme est sans défauts?

O saisons, ô châteaux!

J'ai fait la magique étude
Du Bonheur, que nul n'élude.

page 159 Puis l'orage changea le ciel, jusqu'au soir.

Ce furent des pays noirs, des lacs, des perches,
Des colonnades sous la nuit bleue, des gares.

page 160 Mais! je n'aurai plus d'envie,
Il s'est chargé de ma vie.

Que comprendre à ma parole?
Il fait qu'elle fuie et vole!

page 160 Si j'ai du *goût*, ce n'est guères
Que pour la terre et les pierres.
Dinn! dinn! dinn! dinn! Mangeons l'air,
Le roc, les charbons, le fer.

Moi.   – Plus ces paysages.
Qu'est l'ivresse, Amis?

J'aime autant, mieux, même,
Pourrir dans l'étang,
Sous l'affreuse crème,
Près des bois flottants.

15. 'The Good Disciple'

page 163 [. . .] la lune de miel
Cueillera leur sourire et remplira
De mille bandeaux de cuivre le ciel.

page 168 A quatre heures du matin, l'été,
Le sommeil d'amour dure encore.
Sous les bosquets l'aube évapore
    L'odeur du soir fêté.

Mais là-bas dans l'immense chantier
Vers le soleil des Hespérides,
En bras de chemise, les charpentiers
    Déjà s'agitent.

Dans leur désert de mousse, tranquilles,
Ils préparent les lambris précieux
Où la richesse de la ville
   Rira sous de faux cieux.

16. FUGITIVES

page 173   – La Juliette, ça rappelle l'Henriette,
Charmante station du chemin de fer
Au cœur d'un mont comme au fond d'un verger
Où mille diables bleus dansent dans l'air!

Banc vert où chante au paradis d'orage,
Sur la guitare, la blanche Irlandaise.
Puis de la salle à manger guyanaise
Bavardage des enfants et des cages.

Fenêtre du duc qui fais que je pense
Au poison des escargots et du buis
Qui dort ici-bas au soleil. Et puis
C'est trop beau! trop! Gardons notre silence.

page 173   Mais moi, Seigneur! voici que mon Esprit vole,
Après les cieux glacés de rouge, sous les
Nuages célestes qui courent et volent
Sur cent Solognes longues comme un railway.

page 182   Presque île, ballottant sur mes bords les querelles
Et les fientes d'oiseaux clabaudeurs aux yeux blonds.
Et je voguais [. . .]

17. UNDERWORLD

page 185   Aussi son buste exquis n'aspire pas aux brèches
De l'Avenir! [. . .]
[. . .] Son œil est

Approfondi par quelque immense solitude;
'Pauvre jeune homme, il a sans doute l'Habitude!'

18. Pagan

page 206   Ah! Mille veuvages
De la si pauvre âme
Qui n'a que l'image
De la Notre-Dame!
Est-ce que l'on prie
La Vierge Marie?

24. Philomath

page 273   Émanations, explosions.
[. . .]
Le génie. – 'Je suis le Roquefort!
– 'Ça s'ra not' mort! . . .
– Je suis le Gruyère
Et le Brie! . . . etc.

27. Explosive

page 306   J'ai vu des archipels sidéraux! et des îles
Dont les cieux délirants sont ouverts au vogueur:
– Est-ce en ces nuits sans fonds que tu dors et t'exiles,
Million d'oiseaux d'or, ô future Vigueur? –

38. Opportunities

page 414   [. . .] quoiqu'on n'ait fait jamais d'une cité
Ulcère plus puant à la Nature verte,
Le Poète te dit 'Splendide est ta Beauté!'

39. 'Ferocious Invalid'

page 426   [. . .] rimant au milieu des ombres fantastiques,
Comme des lyres, je tirais les élastiques
De mes souliers blessés, un pied près de mon cœur!

page 434   – Tandis que se faisait la rumeur du quartier,
En bas, – seul, et couché sur des pièces de toile
Écrue, et pressentant violemment la voile!

Notes

Single-name references are to works listed in the bibliography. The following abbreviations are used (for full details, see the bibliography):

AR	Matarasso and Petitfils, *Album Rimbaud*.
ARPV	*Arthur Rimbaud. Paul Verlaine* (Drouot sale).
BH	Bourguignon and Houin, *Vie d'Arthur Rimbaud*.
CPV	*Correspondance de Paul Verlaine*.
D	Delahaye, *Delahaye témoin de Rimbaud*.
DAR	Darzens, 'Arthur Rimbaud. Documents', ed. Lefrère.
EM	Étiemble, *Le Mythe de Rimbaud. Genèse du mythe*.
Iz	Izambard, *Rimbaud tel que je l'ai connu*.
LM	*Lettres manuscrites*, ed. Jeancolas.
MB	Marcenaro and Boragina, *'J'arrive ce matin . . .'*
MV	Mathilde Verlaine, *Mémoires de ma vie*, ed. Pakenham.
OC	*Oeuvres complètes*, ed. Adam.
OV	*Oeuvre – Vie*, ed. Borer.
PBP	Berrichon, *Jean-Arthur Rimbaud. Le Poète*.
PBV	Berrichon, *La Vie de Jean-Arthur Rimbaud*.
PR	Jeancolas, *Passion Rimbaud. L'Album d'une vie*.
Z	Zaghi, *Rimbaud in Africa*.

Pending the new Pléiade edition by André Guyaux, the most useful editions are those by A. Adam (*OC*), S. Bernard (revised by A. Guyaux), F. Eigeldinger and G. Shaeffer, L. Forestier, C. A. Hackett and J.-L. Steinmetz. *OV* is the black pot to the old Pléiade kettle, though its notes and introductions are valuable.

The best scholarly edition is S. Murphy's *Oeuvres complètes* (vol. 1 appeared 1999), accompanied by a volume of facsimiles.

Wherever possible, letters in this biography are translated from facsimiles. On R.'s correspondence, see pp. 360, 387 and 412, and Lefrère–Murphy.

The best translation of R.'s (almost) complete works is still Wallace Fowlie's.

Notes

For iconography, the Pléiade *Album* has been superseded by C. Jeancolas's *Passion Rimbaud* and the catalogue by G. Marcenaro and P. Boragina (MB).

Introduction

1. Camus, 115.
2. *Cahiers* (1899), quoted by J. Robinson-Valéry, in Guyaux, ed. (1993), 276.
3. Martin (1 August 1873).
4. PBP, 289.
5. Sitwell, 39.
6. Rivière, 58.
7. Breton, 1014.
8. Quoted by P. Brunel, in Guyaux, ed. (1993), 331.
9. *Un diagnostic médico-littéraire* (1929): Étiemble (1984), 91.
10. *L'Instabilité mentale à travers la vie et l'œuvre littéraire de Jean-Arthur Rimbaud* (1923): Étiemble–Gauclère, 17.
11. Bockris, 25 and 59.
12. *OC*, 772.
13. Waugh (1938), 5. Waugh himself had hoped to find 'a half-caste son [of R.] keeping a shop in some back street' of Harar: Waugh (1931), 88.
14. Miller, ix.
15. *ARPV* (sale of the Jean Hugues collection, most of which was bought by the Bibliothèque Nationale de France, the Bibliothèque Doucet and the Musée Rimbaud).

1. Bad Blood

1. 'Mauvais sang', *Une Saison en Enfer*. On R.'s real ancestors: Henry.
2. This was the derivation known in R.'s day. A more likely origin is 'Rimbaldi', from '*ragin*' (counsel) and '*bald*' (bold) (Dauzat). Cf. Bodenham, 16–17; Coulon (1929), 23–5. In Provence, the curfew was the '*casso-rimbaud*' (Mistral).
3. 'Mauvais sang', *Une Saison en Enfer*.
4. 'Mauvais sang', *Une Saison en Enfer*.
5. On Mme R.: Briet (1968); Lalande (1987). On the farmhouse: Lefranc (1949).
6. Mijolla.
7. *OC*, 802.
8. *OC*, 799–800; cf. Pierquin's caricatural version (150).
9. On Captain R.: BH, 53 and 205–6; Bodenham; Coulon (1929), 28–31; Godchot, I, 3–39; Kacimi-El Hassani; Petitfils (1974).

10. PBP, 13; Godchot, I, 9.
11. Marriage contract: *PR*, 14. R. estimated his mother's annual income, *c.* 1870, at 6,000–8,000 francs (D, 30 n.).
12. Not, as often stated, 5 p.m. Birth certificate: *PR*, 7.
13. PBP, 18.
14. PBP, 18–19.
15. Goffin, 42 (from Mme R.'s charlady).
16. *OC*, 787–8.
17. Godchot, I, 59–60.
18. *OC*, 797.
19. PBP, 20–21.
20. Lalande (1987), 55.
21. D, 30.
22. J.-L. Delattre, *Le Déséquilibre mentale d'Arthur Rimbaud* (1928), quoted in EM, 171 and Plessen, 8. Also known as '*fugue*' and '*automatisme ambulatoire*' (Hacking).
23. *OC*, 807.
24. J. Bourguignon, interviewed by Petitfils (1974), 9.
25. *PR*, 16; Briet (1956), 111.
26. Labarrière: Mouquet (1933), 96.
27. Briet (1956), 11; Goffin, 40.
28. See *OC*, 810.
29. 'Les Remembrances du vieillard idiot'.

2. FILTH

1. Delahaye (1919), 82–3; Mouret, 82–3.
2. Robinet (1964); Petitfils (1982), 31.
3. 'Honte'.
4. Pierquin, 145–6.
5. Mouret, 82–3; DAR, 723.
6. Robinet (1974), 854–6.
7. Robinet (1974), 856.
8. D, 67 and 275; Delahaye (1919), 81.
9. Poncelet to Berrichon: Briet (1956), 41; Murphy (1988).
10. Méléra (1946), 103 (letter from Isabelle; also *OC*, 732). On Speke and Grant: Mary; Mille, 23–4; Pakenham (1989). Mary is unreliable. See Delahaye (1995), 107; Mouret, 71.
11. *OC*, 1027; Ruff, 8: cf. Briet, ed. (1956). Facsimile: MB, 41–3.
12. *PR*, 19.
13. D, 66.
14. Verlaine (October 1895), 969.

15. D, 273.
16. D, 279.
17. D, 71.

3. 'PERFECT LITTLE MONSTER'

1. Iz, 54.
2. *Un Cœur sous une soutane*, ed. Murphy, 20.
3. Méléra (1930). Identification with Prince: Guyaux (1981, 1982); Murphy (1991), 57–75.
4. Cf. Aeneid, VI, 883.
5. *OC*, 1033.
6. Errard.
7. BH, 59; Iz, 23.
8. D, 31–2.
9. PBP, 37–41 (from Abbé Morigny). On R.'s prizes: Godchot, I, 87–9; Taute.
10. Bonnefoy, 28.
11. Letter of 6 November 1869: *PR*, 29; Robinet (1974), 858.
12. Iz, 41; Robinet; *Un Cœur . . .* , ed. Murphy, 68–72.
13. BH, 63.
14. BH, 63; also D, 71.

4. 'MAD AMBITION'

1. Iz, 40; D, 278.
2. Iz, 54 and 61.
3. Iz, 40.
4. Iz, 63.
5. Iz, 23–4.
6. Friedrich, 82.
7. Izambard to Coulon: Mouret, 76. On connotations of '*cœur*': S. Murphy's edition, 93–5.
8. Mouquet (1933, 1946).
9. Fontaine, 9; EM, 34.
10. Tucker.
11. D, 37.
12. Izambard (59–60) says that the book was *Notre-Dame de Paris*.
13. D, 277–8.
14. D, 32–3.
15. D, 176–7; Goffin, 22–3.

16. D, 71.
17. *Oeuvres complètes* (1946), 629–30. Later titled 'Première soirée'.
18. Given to Izambard on the eve of the declaration of war (i.e. 18 July: cf. Iz, 63).

5. CONVICTIONS

1. Ross, 58. See 'Brune, elle avait . . .', 'Les Reparties de Nina', 'Roman' and both letters to Banville.
2. *PR*, 45.
3. D, 177.
4. Cook, 82.
5. Larousse.
6. The poem was overpainted before Izambard thought to copy it down.
7. Petitfils (1979). Demeny bibliography in Murphy (January–April 1991), 78 n. 1.
8. Incorrect in *OC*; copied by *OV*. Facsimile: *AR*, 53.
9. Robinet (1974), 858.
10. Iz, 32; DAR, 739 n. 29 (interview notes): 'Art. Rimb. at home behaved like a real hooligan – when [Izambard] took him back to his mother – she upbraided him as if he had . . . abducted her son and she knew already about Rimbaud's inclinations. [. . .] Mme Rimbaud is crude and insulting – treating her son harshly (hard-hearted, bony and very pi) – Rimbaud aggressive, angry, furious.'
11. Confirmed by Iz, 101–2.
12. *OC*, 866; *OV*, 1019; Petitfils (1982), 75.
13. Mijolla.
14. *AR*, 66.
15. Brunel, 46, dates the note to R.'s second visit; but it appears with 'Soleil et Chair' in the first set of poems. On the poems: Brunel, 39–60; Murphy (January–April 1991).
16. D, 80–1.

6. TOUR DE FRANCE

1. On R.'s tour: BH, 67–9 (from Billuart – cf. PBV, 54–6); Ginter (from Marius des Essarts, nephew of R.'s friend); Goffin, 17–21; Iz, 71–5.
2. Larousse, quoted by Murphy (1990), 133–4.
3. Iz, 74.
4. In *De l'esprit* (1758).

7. NEEDFUL DESTRUCTION

1. D, 84–9.
2. D, 88.
3. D, 97.
4. D, 97–8.
5. D, 273.
6. Cornulier (1988), 50.
7. Restored by A. Guyaux: *Oeuvres* (1991).
8. '*Amoureuses*' ('lovers') also means 'the girls I loved': Cornulier (1998), 22. The Baudelairian 'Sœurs de charité', dated June 1871, suggests a similar dissatisfaction: 'O Woman, heap of entrails, soft pity . . .'
9. D, 102–3.
10. Arnoult, 539; D, 109.
11. PBV, 61 and PBP, 96; BH, 73–4; Champsaur, 278–9; Coulon (1923), 107–8; D, 35, 152, 304–6, 310; Delahaye (1919), 137; DAR, 729; Mallarmé, 11; Verlaine (1888), 800.
12. Porché, 171.
13. Gill, 63. For R.'s influence: 35, and Demeny's *Les Visions* (1873): 'Les Voyants', 'Vision d'Ophélie', etc.
14. See Murphy (April 1985). Continued disagreement suggests that R. conflated different episodes: the bourgeoisie returning after the surrender; the Commune and its eradication.
15. 'Mauvais sang', *Une Saison en Enfer*.
16. D, 38 and 182–5.
17. The *termini ab quo* and *ad quem* are R.'s letters of 17 April and 13 May – easily enough time for a long visit.
18. In Ross, xiii.
19. Detailed discussion in D, 304–22. See also DAR, 740 n. 32; Errard, 78; Graaf (1956), 633 n. 5; Gregh, 294; Martin (26 June 1873); Verlaine (1888), 800 and letter of 20 November 1872. Rickword's elimination of the Commune episode (176) is based on Izambard's supposition.
20. On 'Communard' poems: Chambers, 66–7.
21. Iz, 226.
22. Gregh, 294 n. 1.
23. 'Mauvais sang', *Une Saison en Enfer*.
24. T. Homberg, *Études sur le vagabondage* (1880): Ross, 57–8.
25. Lissagaray, 327; Noël ('Pupilles').
26. Mallarmé, 11; Lefrère–Pakenham (1990), 21.

8. THE SEER

1. See R., *Lettres du Voyant*, 121–2.
2. D, 197.
3. Starkie (1961), 86.
4. Letter to Demeny, 10 June 1871. The ambiguity is lost in some translations – e.g. the selection published by Gay Sunshine in 1979: *A Lover's Cock and Other Gay Poems* by Rimbaud and Verlaine.
5. D, 182–3.
6. The pun – '*on me pense / panse*' – refers to the idea of being kept like a mistress or a pet. Applied to domestic animals, '*panser*' means to groom, feed or pamper.
7. R., *Oeuvres* (1991), 548–9.
8. R. probably knew Michelet's *La Sorcière*, in which women (witches and seers) are depicted as Promethean visionaries (139–40).
9. R.'s admiration for Mérat is often said to be misplaced: *OV*, 1059; Houston (1963), 34; *Oeuvres*, ed. Bernard, 554 n. 26; Hackett (1992), based on later editions. Mérat's hallucinations and skewed perspectives are well worth exploring: e.g. 'Paysage', 'Chemin de halage', 'La Sensation', 'La Cathédrale [de Rouen]'.
10. R. did not 'believe firmly in the imminent triumph of the Commune' when writing his 'Seer' letter (Ruff, 74). By 15 May, it was common knowledge that the Commune had suffered five major defeats and refused peace terms. R. applies the phrase 'mad [or foolish] anger' to 'the battle of Paris' precisely because victory is unimaginable.
11. Edwards, 340–50; Horne, 418.
12. Demeny to Darzens, 25 October 1887: DAR, 711.
13. On Rimbaud's Charleville: Houston (1963), 53.
14. Reboul (1985); but Hugo is not the only target. For the title, cf. Baudelaire (1975–6), II, 169: Hugo was 'constantly referred to as *le juste*'.

9. DEPARTURE

1. The addressee may not be Demeny. Léon Dierx, cited as a 'talent' in the 'Seer' letter and considered as a possible sponsor by R., is perhaps more likely (D, 39).
2. Alluding to Baudelaire's depiction of the young Banville as a '*petit Hercule*' (*Les Fleurs du Mal*, 1868 ed.)?
3. A satirical 'Lettre du Baron de Petdechèvre' published in *Le Nord-Est* on 16 September 1871 used to be attributed to R. (e.g. EM, 36).
4. D, 39, 132–4, 337; DAR, 725 and 739 n. 24; *Le Bateau ivre*, November

1955; Iz, 83–5; Petitfils (1982), 59–60; Pierquin, 115–16; Verlaine (November 1895), 974.

5. D, 135–7; Verlaine (November 1895), 974.

6. Porché, 151; Verlaine (1962), xxi; (1972), 1178–80.

7. D, 135.

8. 'Marco' and 'Résignation'.

9. Murphy (1991), 73.

10. Chambon (1986), 77–8. Earliest hint of homosexuality: Deverrière to Izambard, 11 November 1870: '*J'ai vu hier la cousine Bête née Raimbaud.*' (Iz, 223)

11. Some critics note that the *douanier* 'confines himself to' [or 'grabs hold of'] the 'charms' that are subject to customs duty (tobacco, etc.). In this view, the stroking palm is engaged on purely official business . . .

12. Thus, the Mons prison chaplain asked Verlaine if he had ever '*been* with animals': Verlaine (1972), 350.

13. D, 136.

14. The phrase takes slightly different forms. This is the earliest, from Delahaye: BH, 80.

15. R. is usually said to have arrived in Paris on 10 September 1871: on 5 October, Valade claims to have had 'three weeks' to consider his opinion. But since Valade had seen the poems from Charleville (Verlaine (November 1895), 974), the 'three weeks' began *before* R. arrived. This matches Mathilde's version: R. stayed for two weeks and left before her father's return (*c.* 10 October). Thus, R. probably arrived on 24 September (a Sunday) and attended the next 'Vilains Bonshommes' dinner (30 September). Valade was therefore referring to the latest dinner, not reporting an urgent piece of news that was twenty-five days old. This also matches the probable dates of R.'s stay with Cros (15–31 October 1871).

16. Frohock, 107.

17. D, 161; Verlaine (November 1895), 974.

18. See editions, and R., *Poésies* (1978), 171; Étiemble (1961), 68–74 and (1984), 91; PBP, 124 (Darwin); Brecht, in Ross, 75 (world system).

19. Hugo, XIII (*Voyages*), 1190.

10. 'NASTY FELLOWS'

1. Biography from Lepelletier (1907), MV, Petitfils (1981), Porché, Verlaine, *Confessions* (1895). The house still stands at number 14 Rue Nicolet.

2. Verlaine, *Confessions* (1895), 541.

3. See also Underwood (1956), 187: 'the ugliest man I have seen in my life' (a teacher in Stickney, 1875).

4. Verlaine, *Confessions* (1895), 444.

5. Kahn (1902), 292.
6. According to Larousse (1866), absinthe aids digestion, circulation and appetite and cures chlorosis. The only harmful effects are headaches, dizziness and blurred vision. 'Very sensitive temperaments' are advised to abstain. Absinthe remained legal in France until after the First World War. For an early indication (1860) of harmful, addictive properties: Champfleury, 105–6.
7. On Mathilde: works quoted in n. 1 above and M. Pakenham's introduction to MV.
8. MV, 140.
9. Verlaine (November 1895), 975.
10. Mathilde, reported in 1912: Porché, 178.
11. Delahaye to M. Coulon, 25 July 1924: Mouret, 63.
12. Verlaine (November 1895), 975; MV, 140 and 159; Mathilde Verlaine, interviewed in 1913: Buisine, 175–6.
13. Verlaine (November 1895), 976.
14. Verlaine (1888), 803.
15. MV, 143.
16. Letters to É. Blémont, 5 October 1871, and J. Claretie, 9 October 1871: Lefrère (1996). Facsimiles: PR, 68–9.
17. Anon. (October 1915), 396; Banville, Le National, 16 May 1872: PR, 84.
18. Godchot, II, 141.
19. D, 186 (from Verlaine).
20. D, 40; Lepelletier (1907), 258; MV, 141. Also in Champsaur, and Cabaner's song (PR, 74–5). See also n. 17 below.
21. Banville, quoted by Mallarmé, 12–13. On Banville's frequent visits from objectionable young poets: Goncourt, II, 270 (25 August 1870).

11. SAVAGE OF THE LATIN QUARTER

1. Baudelaire (1975–6), I, 458.
2. Lepelletier, in L'Écho de Paris, 25 July 1900: Petitfils (1949), 164.
3. ARPV, no. 25; DAR, 729.
4. Charles de Sivry: DAR, 730. Sivry returned to Paris after 18 October 1871: DAR, 740 n. 36.
5. DAR, 730 ('a mirror had the same fate'); Darzens, 143; Richepin (1927), 27.
6. A. Vollard, La Vie et l'œuvre de Pierre-Auguste Renoir (1919): Lefrère (1991), 130–31.
7. Cosmos, August 1869: Cros, 523–4.
8. Cros, 162.
9. D, 41 and 200–201. Delahaye's date for Les Déserts de l'amour (spring

1871) is also doubtful (D, 38). Bouillane de Lacoste dates the handwriting
to 1872 – tentatively supported by Reboul (1991), 51. The 'sad' dreams
and the servant who is also 'a small dog' recall a part of 'Alchimie du
verbe' which seems to refer to the pre-London period. *La Bête nouvelle* (or
La Bête, nouvelle), now lost, might have been another early narrative
project (DAR, 292).

10. L. Marsolleau in Forestier, 99.
11. MV, 165.
12. MV, 165.
13. DAR 731; Darzens, 144.
14. Bandy–Pichois, 149.
15. Goncourt, II, 1244 (18 April 1886).
16. Kahn (1925), 40–41.
17. Cros, 622 (letter to de Pradel [G. Pradelle?], 6 November 1871); Forestier, 97–8 and 100.
18. D, 187.
19. D, 187.
20. D, 40.
21. Lefrère–Pakenham (1990), 25.
22. Murphy (1990), 155–6.
23. Verlaine (1884), 635.
24. PBP, 137 (from Verlaine).
25. DAR, 731; Darzens, 143–4; PBP, 154. 'Les Réveilleurs de la nuit' (Verlaine (1883), 655) was probably part of the same series.
26. Privat d'Anglemont, 71–2.
27. D, 348. On the Zutistes: Pia, ed., *Album zutique*; Murphy (1990), 51–2; M. Pakenham, in *Revue d'Histoire littéraire de la France*, 1964, 135–7; *OV*, 1104–6.

12. 'MLLE RIMBAUT'

1. D, 348.
2. D, 141; Goncourt, I, 970 (30 May 1863). See Cook, 13: 'Ladies should
   [. . .] on no account enter the cafés on the north side of the Boulevards'.
3. Briet (1956), 72–3; D, 193, 196, 348–9; Delahaye (1919), 143–4; *Dictionnaire de biographie française*; Gachet; Lefrère–Pakenham (1994); Petitfils, *Le Bateau ivre*, 1954, 7; Verlaine (1972), 800 and 820; Verlaine (1997), 23–6; allusions to Cabaner's sexuality in *Album zutique*.
4. Some versions add, 'and two weeks in the grave': D, 349; Verlaine (1997), 26.
5. On the ambiguous 'Cercle du doi(g)t partout': DAR, 731 and 741 n. 42; Petitfils (1981), 73.

6. 'Cabaner-cantinière', in *Album zutique*.
7. Facsimile: *PR*, 74–5. R.'s only contribution to the Zutiste conversation recorded in the *Album* is '*Ah, merde!*'
8. DAR, 731 and 741 n. 40; Darzens, 144.
9. Goncourt, II, 1244 (18 April 1886).
10. D, 197.
11. Champsaur; described in a sonnet to 'Rimbald': 'Numbers of the scales, radiating points / Of the hierarchical ring – 1 2, 3 4 5, 6 7 – / Sounds, vowels and colours correspond', etc.: colour facsimile in MB, 96.
12. Anon. (1872): a pro-absinthe tale, quoting Baudelaire's 'Correspondances'.
13. For Victor Hugo, A and I are white, E blue, O red and U black: Hugo, XIV (*Océan*), 210 (1846–7). Anthony Powell (245) associated colours with vowels *and* consonants: 'A, very dark red, almost black; B, very dark brown, almost black', etc. See comparative table in Noulet, 125. Lévi-Strauss (130 and 135) claims that A is most often associated with red, and that R.'s correlations are unconscious, not sensorial.
14. See Étiemble, *Le Sonnet des Voyelles*; Noulet, 117–43.
15. Pape-Carpantier, 149. A common rebus for 'virtue' was a green 'U' (*vert U*). The poem (or fragment), 'L'étoile a pleuré rose . . .' probably dates from the same period.
16. Verlaine (1888), 803.
17. Verlaine to Izambard and Richepin: Arnoult, 164; also Delahaye (1905), 80 n.
18. MV, 90.
19. See M. Pakenham in *OV*, 1128.
20. Arnoult, 161.
21. On 'Les Remembrances . . .': Murphy (1990), 63–7.
22. The usual term was '*pédérastie*', defined by Littré in 1875 with untypical vagueness: '*Vice contre nature.*'
23. *Le Peuple souverain*, 16 November 1871: EM, 37; MV, 143–4.
24. Aragon *et al.*, 254.
25. Lepelletier (1907), 261–2.
26. DAR, 707 and 737 n. 1; Darzens, 143; Anon., *L'Écho de Paris*, 12 November 1891 (EM, 63); D, 40. Hugo seems to have applied the phrase to the wandering poet, Albert Glatigny.
27. Goncourt, II, 1243–4 (18 April 1886): spelt 'Dumolard'.
28. Both poems contain a 'hiatus' – characteristic of Verlaine's poetry but not of R.'s. When Verlaine sent 'Tête de faune' to Charles Morice, he was writing pastiches of other poets. Several significant variants (but only one ms.) suggest that Verlaine continued to make improvements. On other Verlainean elements: Dominicy. See however R.'s Verlainean poem, 'Entends comme brame . . .' (spring 1872?).

29. Cocteau, 16 (7 April 1919).
30. DAR, 731; Darzens, 144. On Mercier: Pakenham (1963).
31. Lepelletier (1907), 30.
32. Mallarmé, 10; Verlaine (1883), 644.
33. A. t'Serstevens, 'Verlaine en prison' (1933): Petitfils (1949), 180.
34. D, 189.
35. Goncourt, II, 1243 (18 April 1886).
36. Goncourt, III, 537 (8 February 1891).
37. Originally inspired by Mérat's sonnets celebrating parts of the female body. The sonnet is usually published under the title *Les Stupra* with two others: 'Les anciens animaux . . .' and 'Nos fesses ne sont pas les leurs . . .'.
38. Abélès; Druick–Hoog.
39. Goncourt, II, 503 (18 March 1872).
40. Arnoult, 161; Godchot, II, 145.
41. MV, 151.
42. PBP, 137; Coulon (1923), 146.
43. Goncourt, II, 503 (18 March 1872).

13. Dogs

1. On Forain: Faxon; Puget.
2. Arnoult, 13 and 166; Lefrère–Pakenham (1990), 21; Porché, 410.
3. Arnoult, 13 and 166–7.
4. Arnoult, 166–7; D, 190; Delahaye (1927), 84 n.; Graaf (1960), 99–100.
5. Charles de Sivry: DAR, 741 n. 46.
6. Arnoult, 167. R.'s influence on late nineteenth-century art is a vast but airy subject. Picasso, for whom '*Il n'y a que Rimbaud!*' (Richardson, 466), would not have known this passage, but he was familiar with the verbal cubism of the *Illuminations*, their simultaneous perspectives, flat planes and conceptual realism. Cézanne – another self-conscious provincial in Paris – was a close friend of Cabaner. He appears, perhaps, in Champsaur's 1882 *roman à clé*, reciting R.'s 'Les Chercheuses de poux' (see p. 417). Renoir knew R. and Verlaine, but not intimately. See Graaf (1960), 85; Lefrère (1991).
7. Lefrère–Pakenham (1990), 20–1 and 24; M. Le Royer, *Le Miroir du monde* (1936): Petitfils (1982), 153. On the location: Caradec; Hillairet, 'Raspail (boulevard)', no. 243; Lefranc (1952).
8. Verlaine, 'Le Poète et la Muse' (1874), *Jadis et Naguère* (on the room in January 1872).
9. Lefrère–Pakenham (1990), 24.
10. DAR, 730.

11. Lefrère–Pakenham (1990), 20, 23 and 25.
12. Berrichon and Delahaye plausibly date the poem from after R.'s arrival in Paris: it contains six *césures enjambantes* and ignores the rule that forbids a mute *e* at the sixth syllable.
13. On R. as a true Parnassian: Watson.
14. Copley, 71. See also Houston (1986), 71.
15. PBP, 183–4.
16. Verlaine (1976), 187.
17. Redated by Pakenham (1985), 44. On the incident: Verlaine (1895), 963–4 (correcting Maurras); DAR, 730; Darzens, 143. Also D, 196; Godchot, II, 159; Lepelletier (1907), 261; Richepin (1927), 26. Looking for a historical event to mark the transition from Parnassians to Symbolists, Madeleine Rudler (29) calls R.'s *merdes* 'the first infant cry of Symbolism'.
18. PBP, 156 n. 1.
19. MV, 164.

14. Songs of Innocence

1. PBP, 187.
2. R.'s letters in MV, 164. On the fate of these mss.: p. 487 n. 17, and cf. DAR, 740 n. 39.
3. MV, 156.
4. Verlaine (October 1895), 971.
5. D, 42, on spring 1872 poems.
6. See Aragon (vii) on 'Fêtes de la patience' and the ability of good poetry to turn anything – even printers' errors – into 'beauties'.
7. R. might have known that high-altitude balloonists had seen a black sky: Goncourt, I, 1135 (January 1865).
8. Parallels between R. and Blake are briefly mentioned in Ahearn, 175 n. The first French translation of Blake was *Le Mariage du ciel et de l'enfer* in 1900.
9. Same rhyme used by G. Nouveau in 'Les Trois épingles'.
10. Iz, 128–9; also Richepin in Arnoult, 94. For the song: Étiemble (1984), 13–17; *PR*, 47.
11. R.'s accent can be deduced from Verlaine's *Vieux Coppées* (see p. 270): Chambon (1983); Lié; Steinmetz, 102 n. Verlaine's transcriptions criticized by Delahaye: D, 233.
12. Sartre, quoted by St. Aubyn, 98.
13. Here, Verlaine added a note: '*Doré* [golden], in English: I forgot that you knew as little English as I.'

15. 'The Good Disciple'

1. Verlaine mentions R.'s '3 months of Ardennes' (from early March) and expects him to return on a Saturday. In June, R. had been in Paris 'last month'. The most likely date of return is therefore Saturday, 25 May 1872.
2. PBV, 105; Isabelle R., 199–200 n. 1, and letter to Berrichon (*OC*, 751). Coulon (1923), 257–60 (Isabelle and Berrichon, interviewed in 1910).
3. 'Il faut m'aimer! . . .', *Sagesse*.
4. Richepin (1927), 26.
5. DAR, 732 and 741 n. 45 (from Sivry).
6. Either Rue Saint-Séverin or Rue des Grands-Degrés (Mary); also Mouret, 71; Pakenham (1989). R. may have lived for a time in the Rue Saint-André-des-Arts (Mercier: DAR, 731).
7. Cazals–Le Rouge, 141–2; Mary; Méric, 88–94; Régamey, 26; Richepin (1872), 111.
8. Sterling Heilig, 'Absinthe Drinking', *Atlanta Constitution*, 19 August 1894: Lanier, 25.
9. On number 22: Lefrère–Pakenham (1990), 21 and 26; Richepin (1927). Number 22 (opposite number 41) housed various artists, including Daumier and Forain. It now bears a plaque to Antonio La Gandara.
10. Delahaye heard some *Illuminations* in 1872 (D, 203). Richepin saw in R.'s '*cahier d'expressions*' 'the wonderful themes of several prose poems that were never published' (thus, not *Illuminations*) (Arnoult, 352–3). The 'List of objects left at the Rue Nicolet' includes 'Ten letters from Rimbaud, containing verse and prose poems': *CPV*, I, 68.
11. R.'s '*au front des*' can be read as an anglicism.
12. E.g. from Gautier's 1868 preface to *Les Fleurs du Mal*.
13. MV, 160. The theatre was the Passe-temps, later a cinema.
14. MV, 161–2; É. Le Brun, reporting a conversation of 1888 in 1924: Coulon (1929), 270. Other incidents: MV, 141–59.
15. Verlaine to Lepelletier, 24 September 1872 (*ARPV*, no. 55; *CPV*, I, 44) – from Revelation 3:17, perhaps via Hugo's *Préface de Cromwell*.
16. Verlaine (1893); Lepelletier (1907), 275–7.
17. MV, 162.
18. Pierquin, 156–7.

16. Fugitives

1. See Brunel, ch. 3.
2. Bouillane de Lacoste, 81.

3. Lefrère (November 1998), 17: the missing first part contains the rhyme, '*tarasques*' – '*fantasques*' and a line repeated later: '*C'est trop beau! c'est trop beau! mais c'est nécessaire*'. R.'s Belgian poems may also include 'Fêtes de la faim' and 'Le loup criait . . .'.

4. Letter dated 17 November 1883: Verlaine (1964), 34.

5. Verlaine to Lepelletier, [July 1872]: *ARPV*, no. 52; *CPV*, I, 37.

6. *Dossier de la Commune*, 169–78; Lefrère (1989); Verlaine (1888), 802.

7. Verlaine (1888), 802.

8. Steinmetz, 147.

9. MV, 166.

10. 'Du fond du grabat', *Sagesse*. See Verlaine's notes (1962), 1129.

11. On this and letters to Mathilde: MV, 162–3.

12. MV, 163–4.

13. Verlaine (1883), 656. *CPV*, I, 68 ('List of objects left at the Rue Nicolet') is the only contemporary mention of the title. Verlaine twice refers to a prose ms.: (1883), 656 and (1888), 800–801. Isabelle R. (154) and Berrichon (PBP, 215) seem to identify it with *La Chasse spirituelle*. Verlaine never called it a masterpiece. He probably mentioned it to P. Burty (n. 16, below) and V. Pica (Morrissette, 31–2). Steinmetz (*OV*, 1041) suggests that Verlaine was referring to *Les Déserts de l'amour*.

14. E.g. Starkie (1961), 194.

15. Petitfils (1949), 134–5.

16. Pascal Pia, in *Carrefour*, 1 June 1949: EM, 326; Morrissette, 42–3. Pia, who forged a R. poem in 1925, was defending his authentication of *La Chasse spirituelle*. Morrissette's *Great Rimbaud Forgery* gives the whole story and the bogus text. Pia claims to have seen this note at the home of Pierre Dufay *c.* 1922. A lost letter from Verlaine to Burty (15 November 1872), suggests that *La Chasse spirituelle* was given to Burty for safekeeping.

17. Mathilde had a suspiciously clear memory of R.'s obscene letters, supposedly destroyed long before. She told Isabelle R. in 1897 that she had destroyed them 'very recently'. This contradicts her published account.

18. On the lost poem, 'Les Veilleurs': Verlaine (1883), 654 ('by far the most beautiful thing M. Arthur Rimbaud ever wrote'). Not to be confused (cf. *OV*) with 'Les Réveilleurs de la nuit'.

19. MV, 167.

20. MV, 166–8; Coulon (1927), 727.

21. Coulon (1927), 727–8.

22. 'Chanson d'automne', *Poèmes saturniens*.

23. Quiévrain incident: MV, 168–9; Delahaye, in Porché, 198.

24. Martin (1 August 1873). Was Verlaine's brother-in-law the main source? The report of 1 August 1873 mentions Sivry and contains a phrase – '*Nous avons des amours de tigres!*' – used by Sivry elsewhere (DAR, 741 n. 48).

25. MV, 169.
26. MV, 170.
27. MV, 171.
28. Postal, 115.
29. Graaf (1956), 627–8. Forensic documents: Postal.
30. PBP, 210. Bretagne left Charleville for ever in September 1872 (DAR, 739 n. 24).
31. This sentence is crossed out and replaced with: 'As for M. Rimbaud, he has not yet been pointed out to my department.' Postal, 118–19.
32. This explains the peculiar logic of 'Le loup criait . . .': 'The wolf cried out beneath the leaves, / Spitting out the fine feathers / Of its poultry feast. / Like him, I am wasting away' (literally, 'consuming myself').
33. See DAR, 731.
34. *OC*, 274.
35. 'Alchimie du verbe', *Une Saison en Enfer*.
36. 'Le Bateau ivre'. 'Almost an island' because '*presque île*' is not '*presqu'île*' (peninsula).

17. Underworld

1. Verlaine (1894), 1085. The only complete text is the English version in the *Fortnightly Review*.
2. R. and Verlaine reached Dover on 8 September. Régamey suggests that they arrived in London on 10 September.
3. Delahaye (1927), 84 n.
4. Verlaine's London observations from *CPV*, I, 41 ff.
5. Delahaye (1905), 109.
6. Régamey, 22.
7. See Murphy (1991), ch. 5.
8. Guyaux (1981), 97.
9. Verlaine (1894), 1085.
10. See n. 4, above.
11. D, 194; Robb (1994), 260–61. R.'s drawing, '*Hune cocher de Londres*': *AR*, 151 and *PR*, 93.
12. Robb (1997), 316–17; D. Scott; Underwood (1976); Vadé.
13. Underwood (1956), 58; (1976), 52 n. 3, 297 and illust. 7.
14. See Verlaine's 'Streets': 'Les cottages jaunes et noirs' of Paddington, which were not cottages.
15. D, 48 and 243; Delahaye (1919), 160–61 n.; Régamey, 23.
16. This Van Gogh-like portrait deserves to be better known than the flimsy little R. of Verlaine's famous sketch, dated 'June 1872'. It was drawn from

memory in 1895 and, according to Isabelle R., 'looks like nobody'. See Dufour–Guyaux, 53–4.

17. *CPV*, I, 47 and 50, and R.'s statement, 10 July 1873 (*OC*, 276).
18. On French refugees: Delfau; Murphy (1985).
19. Kapp, 155 ff.
20. Murphy (1985), 56.
21. E.g. Ahearn; Murphy (1981). See also Iz, 139.
22. See Sacchi (1992) on the tendency to restrict autobiographical readings to poems (e.g. not 'Ville') which match the legend.
23. BH, 197. On dating arguments: *Une Saison en Enfer*, ed. Brunel, 177–80. On possible overlapping of verse poems and *Une Saison en Enfer* and general uncertainty about R.'s poetic development: Murphy (1995), 969.
24. Public Record Office, HO 45 9355 29553 (December 1873).
25. D, 44; Verlaine (1888), 802. On Andrieu: Badesco, 321 and 1042–65; Calmettes, 271–4; *Dictionnaire de biographie française*. C. Barrère was co-translating Charles Delescluze's *From Paris to Cayenne* (1872).
26. D, 44.
27. As *Gabriel Denver*. See Ingram and McCarthy.
28. Found by Meyerstein. The name 'Alfred Rimbaud' appears only on the cover. Contributors who might have championed R.: Arthur O'Shaughnessy, William Hardinge, Franz Hüffer (Francis Hueffer), Swinburne, Frederick Wedmore. Before the change of editor in 1873, the magazine was anti-Communard.
29. W. Rossetti, 195 (4 May 1872). See also Swinburne, II, 186–8 (1 October 1872): 'My friend M. Andrieu'.
30. Valéry, 100–101. Henley might have been introduced by Camille Barrère. Albert Barrère was working on a bilingual slang dictionary. Henley later contributed to John S. Farmer's multilingual slang dictionary (1890–1914). See Williamson, 81.
31. *CPV*, 84; Druick–Hoog, 239.
32. *CPV*, 72–3.
33. MV, 172–3. Also PBP, 212–15 (suspiciously detailed). In *CPV*, letter xliv should precede letter xliii (26 December 1872).

18. PAGAN

1. '*la contemplostate de la Nature m'absorculant tout entier*'.
2. D, 206; PBP, 223; *CPV*, 83.
3. *OC*, 277.
4. *CPV*, 306; Underwood (1976), 112 n. 201.
5. See Andrieu, quoting his father's translations of *London's Popular Songs*.

6. 'Nolly' Brown, by contrast, told the truth and was refused a ticket: Ingram, 141–2. On the Reading Room: Vallès, 1305–6.

7. See editions (especially Steinmetz). Brunel calls it a *'contre-évangile'* (190–91). Bibliographies: Duhart and Sacchi (1993). On Renan: Reboul (1994). Facsimiles: Duhart, 86–7.

8. Cf. *'les derniers potagers de Samarie'* in 'Métropolitain'.

9. Police reports: Martin.

10. *OC*, 817–20.

11. Reported in PBP, 228–9.

12. E.g. Bonnefoy, 125–6; Starkie (1961), 264.

13. The opium story has been peddled mostly by anglophone writers, perhaps in patriotic competition with absinthe: Bercovici, 164; Sackville-West, 41; Starkie (1961), 258; Strathern, 11–12; Ullman, 161 (Chinese hashish . . .).

14. See Ruff, 188.

15. Translation based on facsimiles. Editions differ. The known drafts are not necessarily the earliest and may not correspond to the 'Livre païen': see Brunel (1983), 175–221. These are the so-called 'manuscript of *Une Saison en Enfer*', sold at auction in 1998.

16. D, 208.

17. 'Vierge folle', *Une Saison en Enfer*.

19. HOUSEHOLD IN HELL

1. Thomas, 19; Thornbury, V, 323 and 341; Underwood (1956), 128–9. The house bears a plaque and, at the time of writing, R.'s *Illumination*, 'J'ai tendu des cordes . . .', pencilled on to flaking paint.

2. *CPV*, 312–13.

3. Underwood (1956), 116; also 114 and (1976), 136.

4. Martin (26 June 1873).

5. D, 213.

6. Verlaine to Sivry, 9 August 1878: Petitfils (1969), 78.

7. *'Bandes' was* used in the musical sense, e.g. by Verlaine (see Littré). 'No sooner asleep' can be applied to either protagonist.

8. D, 213; Godchot, II, 230 (from Le Brun).

9. Timetable: Underwood (1976), 136–7.

20. 'NO SERIOUS MOTIVE'?

1. MV, 173–4.

2. For the date: *AR*, 167 and *PR*, 111 (facsimiles).

3. Main sources: Dullaert; Graaf (1956); *OC*, 276–84 and 1089–92. Facsimi-

les: Guyaux (1993), Postal and *PR*, 112–14. Verlaine's later accounts (e.g. Retté, 108–9) are fanciful.

4. Demolished in 1979: Guyaux (1992), 85 n. 10.
5. *OC*, 281.
6. Confirmed by arresting officer: Postal, 122.
7. PBP, 278.
8. Berrichon, to the devoutly gullible Claudel in 1914: Claudel (1965), 527.
9. Petitfils (1982), 219.
10. Lalande (1985). The section on penile anatomy is consistent with medical belief in 1873: e.g. A. Tardieu's *Étude médico-légale sur les attentats aux mœurs* (1857; used until the 1920s).
11. 'Immoral relations' were identified as the cause: Martin (21 July 1873); *PR*, 114.
12. Graaf (1956), 632 and (1960), 173.
13. BH, 93; PBV, 94.
14. This rare metre was probably part of a private code: O. Nadal, in Verlaine (1962), 1165.
15. Ms. version: Verlaine (1962), 1161–3. On R.'s copy and doubts about date: Murphy (1994).

21. HARVEST

1. E.g. Delahaye: D, 220. On *Une Saison en Enfer* as an unravelling of historical and rhetorical patterns: Wing.
2. Cf. 'Les Vivants': see p. 238. (Connection made by Berrichon: R., *Ébauches*, 10–11.)
3. See also Delahaye on R.'s Romantic malady: (1927), 170 n.
4. Robb (1993), ch. 10.
5. *OC*, 820.
6. *OC*, 821.
7. Isabelle R., 143.
8. See Bersani, 231.
9. E.g. Bandelier, 161–83. Most critics find the versions in *Une Saison en Enfer* deliberately inferior.
10. Starkie (1961), 297.
11. Bonnefoy, 113.
12. Ross, 101: 'the world-historical prose poem as antiautobiography'.
13. Original text in *OV*.
14. Jottrand, 160. Cf. Bouillane de Lacoste, 109.
15. Graaf (1956), 632; Postal, 117.
16. Godchot, II, 274.
17. *ARPV*, no. 10; DAR, 319 n. 11. On the Régamey copy and Ponchon:

Lefrère (November 1998), 18. Richepin (PBP, 294) claims that R. *sent* the copies to Forain.

18. Jottrand; Losseau; *OC*, 738 and 764 (Isabelle); PBV, 94–5; PBP, 295.
19. Pierquin, 158–9.

22. '*MÉTROPOLITAIN*'

1. D, 221.
2. PBV, 98–9; PBP, 295. (On Poussin: Méric, 83–5.) Isabelle's chronology – R. at Roche from Good Friday to end October 1873 – is clearly wrong: *OC*, 774.
3. D, 221; also 46 and 224 – probably from R. or Nouveau. R. may have known Nouveau as a Zutiste. See also Zissmann (1994), 124.
4. R., *Ébauches*, 10–11; PBP, 294.
5. Nouveau mentions 'Ophélie' (from Banville?), 'Les Chercheuses de poux', and 'Poison perdu', which may not be by R. (see *OC*, 1063–5; Nouveau, 789–93; Zissmann (1987)). A rediscovered ms. of 'Poison perdu' signed 'Arthur Rimbaud', in the hand of Raoul Ponchon, casts doubt on the attribution to Nouveau: *ARPV*, no. 18.
6. Richepin, 27–8.
7. See especially Guyaux (1985), 13–74, and, below, p. 265. Verlaine, who saw Rimbaud almost daily until July 1873, claimed that the *Illuminations* were written 'between 1873 and 1875'. Verlaine was often hazy about dates, but these years were unforgettable: in 1873, he was imprisoned; in 1875, he saw R. for the last time. See also p. 495 n. 13.

   The poems which the narrator of *Une Saison en Enfer* repudiates as acts of 'folly' are all in verse: no *Illumination* is mentioned.

   Even if Rimbaud was simply copying out poems which already existed, it is unlikely that he gave up poetry, then laboured over an 8,000-word fair copy of the *Illuminations*, improving the poems as he went along.

   Bouillane de Lacoste's graphological findings are not conclusive, but they did, significantly, bring a new maturity and realism to Rimbaud studies. See, however, Smith (1964, 1965) for a cautionary tale of graphological incompetence.

   For a very late dating (1878), based on dubious autobiographical allusions: A. Adam.
8. Except in 'Vagabonds' and 'Matinée d'ivresse', which are the only two poems that Verlaine might have seen.
9. Richepin, 30.
10. Nouveau, 817–19.
11. 'The Inundation in Lambeth', *The Daily Telegraph*, 24 March 1874. Commercial Road is now Upper Ground.

12. Underwood (1976), 144.
13. 'Enfance V', *Illuminations*.
14. 'Les Ponts', *Illuminations*.
15. Cf. Delacroix (49): 'The daylight [is] always as on the day of a solar eclipse'.
16. Nouveau, 817–19 and 827.
17. Underwood (1976), 71–8.
18. This fits the known details: R. and Nouveau reach London shortly before 26 March 1874 and work at the factory for a month (Vérane, 57–8). They first advertise in *The Echo* of 29 April. Underwood (1976), 144, supposes that the British Museum register shows that they were still unemployed; but the application date was a Saturday.
19. Underwood (1956), 175. On Drycup: D, 46 and 223; Vérane, 57–8.
20. Thornbury, VI, 382.
21. R. had not necessarily lost or destroyed his ticket. Tickets were valid for six months.
22. Underwood (1976), illust. 54.
23. Underwood (1976), 147.
24. Petitfils (1982), 236.
25. Delahaye (D, 44) places this scene 'towards the end of 1873', when R. was in France. On Andrieu's 'feminine tendencies': Calmettes, 274.
26. Underwood (1976), illust. 54.
27. Régamey probably lived at 16 Langham Street: Lefrère (November 1998), 18.
28. Underwood (1976), illust. 54.
29. Now Maple Street. Number 40 London Street became 25 Maple Street then disappeared: Underwood (1976), 297.
30. Verlaine (1888), 802. No record has been found.
31. 'Enfance IV', *Illuminations*.
32. Tales of R.'s English girlfriends are pious fabrications (PBP, 241, based on two *Illuminations*): in 'Ouvriers', 'my wife', and in 'Bottom', a wealthy 'Madame'. Even Isabelle repudiated these tales (*OC*, 756).
33. 'Angoisse', *Illuminations*.

23. PIGEONS

1. Later a home for nurses at Great Ormond Street Hospital; now the European Hotel.
2. Full text in *Oeuvres complètes*, ed. Forestier. Isabelle *may* have tampered with the text, but the passages on R. are confirmed by Vitalie's letters: *OC*, 285–96.

3. Objective reality still has a bad name in some editions – e.g. Forestier: 'Without wishing to lapse into realist referents', etc. (516 n. 3)

4. 'Bruxelles' and 'Jeunesse'. Also: 'Les Assis' (*'Tels qu'au fil des glaïeuls le vol des libellules'*); 'Le Bateau ivre' (*'Où les serpents géants dévorés des punaises / Choient . . .'*); 'Ornières' (*'au grand galop de vingt chevaux de cirque tachetés'*).

5. Reduced to its most convincing elements, the argument is this. In 'Promontoire', R. mentions 'the circular façades of the "Royals" or "Grands" of Scarbro' or of Brooklyn'. Scarborough had hotels of this name with circular façades. Underwood thought that the spelling Scarbro' was found only in Scarborough. R. left so early that he must have been going a long way – perhaps to Scotland (BH, 101; D, 226). Scarborough is on the way to Scotland – if one changes trains at York – hence New York, hence Brooklyn, and so on . . .

   In fact, newspapers known to R. carried almost daily advertisements for the hotels of Scarbro' – often with this spelling and sometimes with illustrations. The Grand Hotel, described as 'the largest in England', was almost as familiar at one time as the Crystal Palace and Brooklyn Bridge. (No one has yet claimed that R. visited Brooklyn.)

   If R. did go to Scarborough, 'Promontoire' would be the only *Illumination* in which he labelled his vision with its geographical name.

6. Starkie (1961), 451–4.

7. Guyaux (1985), 47.

8. Also, at the end of 'Métropolitain', *'l'étude des astres – le ciel'*, from 'the star-studded (studied) sky'? A similar use of Spanish has been detected in the works of Lautréamont: Lefrère, *Isidore Ducasse*, 75–6.

9. Delahaye (1905), 108; Verlaine (1886), 631. See Littré; OED. Verlaine claimed that 'coloured plates' was the sub-title. The title appears nowhere in R.'s hand.

10. Verlaine to Sivry, 27 October 1878: Petitfils (1969), 78.

11. Bouillane de Lacoste, 27 (dating English lists to July–December 1874). Chadwick makes a good case for dating them late 1872 to early 1873. Cf. Underwood (1976), 275–6 (after July 1873 to early 1875?).

12. Facsimile: Bouillane de Lacoste, 119.

13. Dufour–Guyaux, 27; Underwood (1976), illust. 54. The corrections to R.'s original and the rewritten version appear to be in the same hand.

14. A military trophy masquerading as an ethnographic exhibit: to persuade Queen Victoria to help him eradicate Islam, Theodoros had taken British hostages and was defeated by Napier's army at Mekdela in 1868.

15. *OC*, 810.

16. 'Enfance IV', *Illuminations*.

24. PHILOMATH

1. Vitalie's diary: *OC*, 834.
2. On R. in Stuttgart: PBV, 17–18; Beurard-Valdoye; BH, 101–2 (from Verlaine); Graaf (1960), 229–30; Isabelle R. (*OC*, 715–16). Letters in *OC*, 296–8.
3. Beurard-Valdoye.
4. Murphy (September 1991) emphasizes the significance of the doodle.
5. D, 47.
6. D, 227–9; PBV, 17–18; Beurard-Valdoye.
7. Verlaine (1887), 802.
8. Verlaine (1883), 656.
9. Thus, about 95 g.: Ruff, 200.
10. C. Scott, 181.
11. The usual published order is that of *La Vogue*; but Fénéon (574) may have arranged the pages himself. Defence of first known order: Osmond, ed., *Illuminations*, 11–16.
12. Louis Fière, in *Stella*, 1895: Lefrère (1991), 136. Fière is known to have had the poems in his possession: *Mercure de France*, 16 May 1914, 441–2.
13. According to Verlaine, the *Illuminations* were written 'during journeys in Belgium as well as in England and in all of Germany'. Since Verlaine alludes to his own trip to Stuttgart as 'a bit of Germany', 'all of Germany' suggests a later stage of R.'s wanderings: (1886), 631 and (1972), 765.
14. Isabelle R., 137 and 149.
15. 'Soir historique', *Illuminations*.
16. D, 230.
17. The letter of 17 November 1878 suggests knowledge of this route: *OC*, 304; Graaf (1960), 232.
18. On R. in Milan (in addition to BH, D, DAR and PBV): Petralia (1954); Verlaine (1888), 802. Photographs of the building in MB, 158–9.
19. BH, 103; D, 48; DAR, 734; Darzens, 145.
20. PBV, 109; Delahaye (1905), 173. Gosse specifies Leghorn. Marseille and Alexandria are also possible, but London is unlikely, after the strikes of the 1860s.
21. See above, n. 19, and PBV, 107.
22. D, 48.
23. *Le Bateau ivre*, 11 May 1949.
24. PBV, 110; D, 243–5; DAR, 734; Darzens, 145; Maurras (R. seen in Marseille by Raoul Gineste); Nouveau, 827. The papers kept by Verlaine include a list of conjugated Spanish verbs.
25. A. Vollard, *La Vie et l'oeuvre* . . . : Lefrère (1991), 131. According to

Nouveau (letter to Verlaine, 17 August 1875), R. lived with Mercier and Cabaner.

26. D, 247–8.
27. *ARPV*, no. 8; DAR, 731. This must postdate Stuttgart, where the cards were printed. The only other possibility is Easter 1878, when R. was seen in Paris; but did he keep the cards for three years? Number 18 was the address of a maker of optical and photographic instruments.
28. The note was probably added later. See Dufour–Guyaux, 57–8; Lefranc (1952). On the even less likely Manets: M. Pakenham in P. Adam (1989), 33–4; Dufour–Guyaux, 59–60; Fénéon, 572.
29. BH, 103 and 213 n. 18 (using unpublished letter from Isabelle); also *OC*, 774 (letter to Berrichon), and Vitalie's 'Mémorial': Petitfils (1982), 255.
30. '*Oestre*': see Chambon (1986).
31. D, 247.
32. D, 48.
33. BH, 104.
34. BH, 107.
35. D, 241 (letter to Verlaine).
36. D, 48–9; Létrange; Pierquin, 146–7 (but dated to infancy); Vaillant (1930), 79–80.
37. Breton, 1014. Unironic analysis by Richter. Demystified by Murphy (1989).
38. E.g. 'Génie', 'Solde', 'Guerre', 'Jeunesse' and 'Nocturne vulgaire', which were not written on the same paper as the 'London' *Illuminations*.
39. See Murphy (1989).

25. MR HOLMES

1. D, 49.
2. On R. in Vienna: D, 49, 153–7, 250; Nouveau, 841; Verlaine's 'Dargnières nouvelles' (Verlaine (1962), 299). Also (less plausibly) PBV, 113–14; BH, 107 (incorrect chronology); DAR, 734; Darzens, 145.
3. *OC*, 716 and 759 (not a cab-driver, but 'an individual who had tagged along').
4. Delahaye (often quoted, but unidentified, e.g. Steinmetz, 243).
5. Little (1983), 27; Plessen, 284.
6. Petitfils (1982), 266.
7. PBV, 117; D, 153.
8. Graaf (1960), 263 and 281 n. 24.
9. On Java voyage: Marmelstein; Van Dam; also Graaf (1960) and Steinmetz, 435–6 and 471 (radio programme by J. Degives and F. Suasso).
10. Hare, 106.

11. De Jong. See Hackett (1989). Little (1984) associates it with 'bahou' (1660 English equivalent: 'a turd in your teeth!').
12. Marmelstein, 501. (R.'s clothes were sold and the proceeds given to the Salatiga orphanage.)
13. PBV, 118.
14. Chadwick, 37 n.; Underwood (1976), 326–7.
15. Rosa; Z, 835.
16. Starkie (1961), 341–3; Underwood (1976), 202–15; D, 253–5.
17. Lloyds of London: Underwood (1976), 204 n. 8.
18. BH, 107.
19. D, 233 and 256; Underwood (1976), 207.
20. Underwood (1976), 205–6.
21. Arnoult, 487; D, 255.
22. PBV, 120.
23. *OC*, 302.

26. JOHN ARTHUR RIMBAUD

1. Similarly, the uninterpretable 'Barbare' may allude to 1 Corinthians 14:11: 'if I know not the meaning of the voice, I shall be unto him that speaketh a barbarian, and he that speaketh shall be a barbarian unto me.' 'H', on the other hand, seems to be a riddle with an answer. (The current favourite is masturbation.)
2. Petitfils (1969), 77–8.
3. *OC*, 397.
4. D, 50 and 252–3.
5. BH, 108; PBV, 121–2; DAR, 734. See 'Conditions' in *PR*, 128.
6. Bonnefoy, 169.
7. *PR*, 134.
8. Mercilessly red-penned by Underwood (1976), 217, most of whose corrections are inaccurate or pedantic. 'Actually' for 'at present' is acceptable in 1877. R. corrected 'Mai' to 'May' and 'Scoth' to 'Scotch'. Facsimiles: *AR*, 227 and *PR*, 135.
9. PBV, 122; BH, 108; D, 51, 153, 156, 235 and 257; DAR, 734; Darzens, 145. R. may have crossed the Arctic Circle. Isabelle claimed that he worked in a Swedish saw-mill, not in a circus (BH, 108), probably remembering later requests for saw-mill manuals: *OC*, 311 and 318.
10. Domino, 130 and 146; Thétard.
11. *PR*, 134.
12. No proof of repatriation has been found, but there is good secondary evidence: BH, 108; D, 156 and 257.
13. DAR, 742 n. 51.

/

14. Carré (1949), 56 (caption: 'It's either true or it ain't').
15. BH, 109.
16. See p. 388.
17. 'Nuit de l'Enfer', *Une Saison en Enfer*.
18. BH, 109 (from Isabelle).
19. Late in 1878, a shipping company employee called Rimbaud was at Cape Guardafui, plundering a wreck. (Carré (1931), 232–4; Guillemin (1953).) R. spent about seventeen days in Alexandria, looking for a job. Guardafui is over 2,000 miles from Alexandria. J. B. Rimbaud is listed in Hunter's 'Commercial and General Directory' of Aden (70).

    In 1949, the name 'RIMBAUD' was found on a column of the Temple of Luxor, about nine feet above the ground (after the later excavations). This caused great excitement. R. had been in Egypt all along, in search of 'ancient wisdom' . . . (T. Briant, J. Cocteau and H. Stierlin in EM, 314 and 349; Borer (1983–4), 453–5 and (1984), 371–2 n. 24.) The Temple – 'near Alexandria', according to E. Starkie (1961), 345 – was 400 miles away. R. could have seen Luxor in the autumn of 1887, but the style of the inscription suggests an earlier date – perhaps a soldier on Napoleon's expedition (1798–1801) and perhaps even R.'s great-grandfather, Jean-François, who disappeared one Sunday morning in 1792 after an argument with his wife, wearing a waistcoat, trousers and a night-cap (Henry, 29 and 32).

20. Delahaye (1905), 189.
21. Hare, 107.
22. BH, 109; D, 52.
23. D, 258.
24. Delahaye (1927), 175 n.
25. D, 259.
26. *OC*, 303; PBV, 124.
27. Not 19 November, as R. writes. For dates, timetables and weather: MB, 160–3.

27. EXPLOSIVE

1. Identified by R. Milliex, 80–4.
2. Anon. (1878); Milliex, 77.
3. D, 259.
4. BH, 113.
5. D, 259; Delahaye (1905), 179; Milliex, 81.
6. Undated note. R.'s second stay lasted about seven weeks. It took six weeks to send a letter and receive a reply. The arrival of the tent and dagger had

been announced 'a fortnight ago'. The note therefore dates from R.'s first stay.

7. 'L'Impossible', *Une Saison en Enfer*.
8. D, 261. Details of last meeting: D, 52 and 260–2.
9. BH, 114 (from Isabelle R.). Misattributed by Graaf to Mallarmé and repeated without reference by Borer: Graaf (1960), 328 and 332 n. 32; Borer (1983–4), 394.
10. D, 22.
11. D, 183.
12. D, 261.
13. BH, 109; D, 262. Pierquin's date (August 1878) is unlikely.
14. A plaque, placed by the British Governor in 1948, reads: 'ARTHUR RIMBAUD POÈTE ET GÉNIE FRANÇAIS AU MÉPRIS DE SA RENOMMÉE CONTRIBUA DE SES PROPRES MAINS À LA CONSTRUCTION DE CETTE MAISON MDCCCLXXXI' *sic*): *AR*, 237 and Milliex (78), who wonders whether this is the right building.
15. *Cyprus Gazette*, 19 November 1881: EM, 480.
16. *OC*, 313 (17 August 1880); *OC*, 716 (letter from Isabelle: cf. PBV, 142 and BH, 124); Bardey (1969), 36; Rosa (1993), 833 and 835; Murphy (1987) (Righas).

28. EMPIRES

1. Alluded to by A. Billy. I have favoured contemporary spellings of Abyssinian place-names. Divergent modern equivalents are given in the index.
2. Bardey: Vaillant (1930), 16. All Bardey quotations from Bardey (1939, 1969, 1981); letters and interviews in BH, PBV and Vaillant (1930), 16–41.
3. 'Ce qu'on dit au poète à propos de fleurs'.
4. Delahaye (1927), 99 n.
5. 28 September 1885: *OC*, 402.
6. G. M. Giulietti reached Harar in October 1879 with a native and three mules. He was killed near Lake Afrera in 1881.
7. Burton, I, 1.

29. THE UNKNOWN

1. Borer (1983–4), 253.
2. Burton, I, 201.
3. Unless otherwise indicated, all details from Bardey.
4. Pinchard's letter in Bardey (1969), 18.

5. Steinmetz, 298.
6. Starkie (1961), 353.
7. Biography of Ilg: Keller.
8. Briet (1956), 174–5; Z, 526.
9. *OC*, 776. On R.'s unknown expeditions, see especially Forbes (1979).
10. Excluding sixty-seven days travelling to and from Bubassa and convalescing.
11. Cohen, 80.

30. 'POOR ARTHUR'

1. Bardey (1939), 21.
2. Bardey (1939), 21 and 14.
3. Bardey (1939), 29 and 25.
4. Gribaudo, 103 and 106.
5. *OC*, 347.
6. Mme R. to Delahaye in 1881: D, 356.
7. Bibliothèque Nationale, 60: 'trois terres' (1880); Godchot, I, 62–3: 'une parcelle de 37 ares 70 ca' (1882). Mme R. described R. as a 'professeur' (*PR*, 97 and 165), perhaps because teachers were excused military service. The letter in which R. oddly approves of his mother's investment is suspect: only Berrichon's version is known (12 February 1882).
8. Bardey (1939), 31–2.
9. Rosa, 832.

31. PARADISE

1. Isabelle, in *OC*, 723–4 and 746.
2. Rosa, 835 ('a Galla woman'); Errard, 80 ('an Argoba woman'); Guigniony (re 1890–91); Waugh (1931), 88 (a woman from Tigray). See also, below, pp. 357–8. Later rumours (from two separate sources) that R. kept 'a small harem' may reflect linguistic rather than sexual ambitions: Mille, 25; Olivoni, 850.
3. Borelli, 200; A. Bernard in Méléra (1946), 158; Errard, 77; U. Ferrandi (Petralia (1960), no. 14); Olivoni, 847; Righas brothers (Segalen (1906), 491). 'Kotou' appears neither in Bender, Cohen, nor Conti Rossini (1937).
4. Described as a civil servant and a linguist who spent eighteen years in Somalia (Errard, 75). Cohen wrote several books and articles on Amharic between 1915 and 1956.
5. Lists in *Éthiopie méridionale*.

6. 'Nei Galla', *L'Esploratore* (Milan), September 1883: Petralia (1960), no. 4; Z, 503–4.

7. Errard, 77 (based partly on memoirs of French hoteliers at Obock). The British Foreign Office reported a French carpenter and cook at Obock in January 1883: Starkie (1937), 46. R. may have returned to Danakil territory in 1884 since he reached Aden 'after travelling for six weeks in the deserts'. Letters of September–October 1884 suggest first-hand knowledge of Obock: *OC*, 391–2.

8. Baum, 96–7.

9. Nerazzini to his Foreign Minister, 14 February 1890 (Z, 843); Bardey (1939), 15.

10. Probably '*aliéné*' (the word is crossed out).

11. '*Votris Kys*': perhaps a transliteration of approximate Amharic.

12. Bernoville, 99 and 101. See also 105: 'Bubassa is a plain, with Babbo [a small village] in the middle.'

13. Count Salimbeni in 1892: Zaghi, ed.

14. Z, 517. Sacconi died two days west of Sotiro, probably near El Fud: Baudi di Vesme, R. and Bishop Taurin in BH, 167–8; *OC*, 368; Z, 510–18 and 709. Neither Sotiro nor R. is mentioned in Mori's history of Ethiopian exploration.

15. Bernoville, 96.

16. Borelli, 124 (on territory of Sheik Hussein).

17. Conti Rossini (1913), 489.

18. Letter to Société de Géographie, 24 November 1883: the Webi was explored on R.'s initiative. Bardey later downplayed R.'s achievements in reaction to Berrichon's exaggerations.

19. Nerazzini (who knew R.); Trimingham, 14–15.

20. Isabelle R., letter to BH: *OC*, 814. (This would explain why she failed to find the translation at home.)

21. *AR*, 254; Bibliothèque Nationale, 59; *PR*, 197.

22. Forbes (1979), 38.

23. Bardey (1969), 52.

24. This is the Ennya route mentioned in R.'s report and letter (*OC*, 373 and 376).

25. See James.

26. Z, 511; BH, 169. See also Olivoni, 849.

27. Bardey to Société de Géographie, 10 January [1884]: *PR*, 164.

28. Bishop Taurin: Z, 709.

29. *OC*, 382.

32. ABDO RINBO

1. Interview with Bardey: Vaillant (1930), 31–2. R. and Bardey were in Aden together, 23–25 April 1884. The article in *Le Symboliste* of 22–29 October 1886 proves that Bardey knew about R.'s past: Pakenham (1973), 145.
2. Vaillant (1930), 32.
3. Bardey (1939), 19.
4. Vaillant (1930), 36. R. *may* have received a letter from Verlaine and replied, 'Leave me alone!' (Vaillant (1930), 39). There is no evidence for this in Verlaine.
5. Bardey (1939), 20.
6. PBV, 159.
7. See p. 421; BH, 174 and 221 n. 4; Ferrandi, quoted p. 367.
8. Vaillant (1930), 36.
9. Bardey (1969), 50.
10. Bardey (1939), 25, 30 and 32.
11. Vaillant (1930), 34.
12. Based on letters of which the ms. is known.
13. Waugh (1931), 109.
14. The scribbly African scenes are also bogus: Murphy (November 1990).
15. Taurin's diary: Foucher, 94; Voellmy (1992), 305.
16. Bardey (1939), 16 ff.
17. Provost, 154.
18. Herling Croce, 6 and 14–15.
19. Bardey (1939), 18.
20. PBV, 158–9.
21. Rosa, 835.
22. A. Bernard in Méléra (1946), 155.
23. Errard, 78.
24. A. Bernard in Méléra (1946), 155; G. Ferrand in Claudel (1968), 238; letters from U. Ferrandi (see n. 12 below); Guigniony, 315–16.
25. R., *Lettres*, 18.
26. Facsimile: *PR*, 168.
27. Bardey (1939), 22–3.
28. On Labatut: Bardey (1939, 1969); Borelli, 3; Cecchi, II, 606; Antonelli, Bianchi and Soleillet in Z, 328.

33. GUNS FOR AFRICA

1. Quoted by J.-J. Lefrère, *Isidore Ducasse*, 520.
2. Petitfils in Bardey (1969), 54.

3. Z, 385–410. See also Brémond (14 September 1883) in Briet (1956): 'the Zeila route is open to our caravans only with the consent of the Abou-Bekr family'. Bishop Taurin bought slaves: Z, 434. Lagarde (letter to Ministre de la Marine, 29 May 1886) confirms R.'s remarks on trade in Tadjoura.

4. E.g. reports to French Foreign Minister by Capts Latour (1886) and Hénon (1888): Z, 394 and 396–7.

5. Abou-Bekr died in November 1885 but left eleven sons.

6. Hénon to Minister Flourens: Briet (1956), 178.

7. Z, 335–6.

8. Briet (1956), 156.

9. Letters to E. M. Gray (1913) and O. Schanzer (1923): Emanuelli and Z, 841–2. See also Lionel Faurot, *Voyage au Golfe de Tajoura* (1886).

10. Emanuelli.

11. By V. Pica, in *Il Pungolo della domenica*, 20 September 1885: Guyaux, ed. (1993), 412.

12. U. Ferrandi, in Emanuelli.

13. *Ibid.*

14. R.'s letter to Franzoj should be redated September 1886. The note on ivory (*OC*, 424) should also be redated. After May 1885, Radouan was no longer 'governor of Harar'.

15. Bardey (1939), 18.

34. HORROR

1. From R.'s letter to *Le Bosphore égyptien*, 20 August 1887: *OC*, 430–40. Other passages on the journey to Choa from R.'s accounts to the Aden Consul (*OC*, 427–8, 452–6 and 461–7) and letter to Bardey (*OC*, 444–8).

2. Cf. Thesiger, 185: 'no one has ever crossed from Dikil to Lake Assal.' R. passed a few miles west of what was later Dikil.

3. Errard, 79.

4. Thiersch, 51.

5. Briet (1956), 180 and Z, 310 (Menelik to President Carnot, 30 February 1887).

6. See Winstanley in 1881: 'It would be difficult to say at what period of decay a weapon is considered to be untrustworthy or useless by the Abyssinian, and the ingenious and complicated methods resorted to to keep the most worn-out arms on the combatant list are many and perilous.' (II, 210)

7. Borelli, 200–201.

8. Briet (1956), 174.

9. Z, 753.

10. See n. 4 below.
11. Djami's name appears on the passport for Beirut.
12. The following have expressed doubts about R.'s losses: Starkie (1961), 376; Fongaro (1966); Forbes (1979), 72 and 77–8.

35. PROFIT

1. Facsimile: *PR*, 183 (editions should be corrected).
2. A. Deschamps to Aden Consul, 28 October 1887: *OC*, 451.
3. *OC*, 429.
4. R. states clearly that he converted his bills. This is confirmed by the Massawa Consul. On *later* problems, see letters of 26 August and 20 December 1889. R.'s complaints about money quickly dried up long before he found another job.
5. Lucien Labosse, 15 November 1887: Briet (1956), 144–5.
6. On the new route, see also Dehérain, 38–9; Provost, 151.
7. Stressing the importance of Djibouti in 1889, Du Paty de Clam referred the Société de Géographie to a person (R.?) 'who has lived in the region for a long time': Z, 97.
8. Despite his claim, R. did take money to Choa, and Borelli's journal (221) shows that R. returned with a caravan: 'Tonight, four men left me. [. . .] M. Rimbaud is experiencing the same difficulties', etc.
9. A. Bernard in Méléra (1946), 157; also M. Riès in 1938 (Z, 550). R. scaled up his earlier calculations (see notes in *LM*, II, 189 and IV, 450).
10. Soupault, 181. Footman (4) says that Besse arrived in Aden in 1899 but mistakes Riès for Tian.
11. PBV, 183–4; Carré (1926), 218–20.
12. See Hamilton, 21–7.
13. Savouré (3 April 1930).
14. See Isabelle to Berrichon in 1896 (*OC*, 779); Méléra (1931), 252 and (1946), 122. But would R. have described the 'temperature' in Cairo as 'mild and cool'?
15. R. may also have applied for a government grant. A. d'Abbadie was in Aden just before R. left for Choa and asked for a copy of Abbadie's Amharic dictionary. In August 1885, Abbadie suggested that the Foreign Minister send to Obock or Tadjoura 'an agent whose only mission would be to learn the Amharic idiom'. This agent (R.?) would travel as a trader and exercise 'a kind of occult diplomacy' (Briet (1956), 142).
16. Forbes (1979), 83. But cf. BH, 174 and 188: Bardey specifies Lakes Stefanie and Rudolf, incorrectly supposing that they were already known to cartographers.
17. Isabelle to Berrichon: *OC*, 777. Passport: *PR*, 183.

18. Vaillant (1930), 27.

19. Makonnen to Lagarde, 1 November 1887: Briet (1956), 187.

20. Bibliothèque Nationale, 96; Guillemin (1954); PBV, 203.

21. See Voellmy (1994), 143; Z, 633. Writers on Abyssinia in *Le Temps*:
Lefrère (1990), 76 n. 11.

22. C. Rossetti, 62–4 (April 1890).

23. Matucci (1962), ch. 4. Italian and British reports, 109–11. 'Remban' in
the English version.

24. Vice-Consul Moss (Zeila) to political agent at Aden, 14 November 1887.

25. Perhaps also 4 May: Borelli to R., 26 July 1888 (*OC*, 497). On R.'s
journey to Harar, via Berbera: Emanuelli (Ferrandi's diary).

26. Matucci (1962), 73.

27. Bardone, 41; Forbes (1979), 92 (45 kms).

28. Perhaps related to the fact that R. was granted permission to import arms
on 2 May 1888. (It was withdrawn again on 15 May.) See also previously
unknown letters in *LM*, IV, 456–7.

36. AT HOME

1. *OC*, 476–7.

2. Ilg to R., 19 February 1888.

3. Savouré to Ilg, 13 February 1888.

4. Olivoni, 851.

5. Rosa, 6 and 17. According to a late and dubious source, R. owned a little
hut on a hill above Harar where he read in the afternoon: Father Émile
Foucher, in Marsden-Smedley, 53.

6. Olivoni, 849.

7. *LM*, IV, 462–503.

8. *OC*, 500; also Borelli, 406, on R.'s 'cordial hospitality'.

9. Savouré (3 April 1930).

10. Lefrère (1990), 60 and 78; Z, 535–6.

11. Olivoni, 846.

12. Emanuelli (on Schanzer).

13. Errard, 79–80.

14. *OC*, 558.

15. Ilg to R., 19 February 1888: *OC*, 482–3.

16. Rosa, 833; L. Traversi to C. Zaghi, 23 December 1931: Z, 875.

17. Olivoni, 847.

18. Olivoni, 845–53.

19. Savouré (12 April 1897).

20. Rosa, 835.

21. Robecchi Bricchetti: Petralia (1960), no. 17.

Notes

22. Segalen (1906, 1950).
23. M. Riès to É. Deschamps, 15 March 1929: *OC*, 815–16.
24. Guigniony.
25. Waugh (1931), 87–8.
26. L. Traversi to C. Zaghi, 2 February 1932: Z, 875.
27. 4,500 francs a month according to Bourde.
28. 29 February 1888: facsimile in *PR*, 188.
29. Graaf (1960), 317–18 (C. Bourdet in 1911).
30. Segalen (1906), 492.
31. Billy; also *Le Figaro littéraire*, 24 December 1940.
32. Zech, 87–8 (with a dubious reference to R. tutoring for a family known to Bardey). Zaghi (737) suggests O. Borelli.
33. *Le Décadent*, 15–31 May 1888.
34. Bourde, 19.
35. E.g. Ilg to R., 30 March 1889; Savouré to R., 16 June 1889; Rosa to Bienenfeld, 17 June 1889 and 18 April 1890 (*OC*, 529 and 547; Z, 583 and 585).
36. *OC*, 502.
37. *OC*, 559 and 556. Coincidentally, Ferdinand Brunetière wondered in 1887 whether R. was now selling flannel and felting: Mendès, 252.
38. *OC*, 554 and 565.
39. *OC*, 580.
40. Voellmy (1984), 70.
41. Ilg to Zimmermann, 22 May 1889: Voellmy (1984), 71. Cf. R. to Ilg, 3 May 1889: *OC*, 540. Despite the argument over unsold pots, Ilg offered R. a new deal as late as January 1891.
42. *OC*, 581.

37. 'Odious Tyranny'

1. Receipt: *OC*, 321 (should be redated 1889).
2. Rosa to Bienenfeld, 28 March 1890: Z, 585.
3. *OC*, 601 and 582.
4. Rosa, letters dated 18 and 21 April 1890: Z, 585.
5. *OC*, 587.
6. A. Bernard in Méléra (1946), 155.
7. Ilg to Appenzeller, 18 January 1889: R., *Correspondance*, 180–1 n. 2; Arnoult, 490 n. 53; Guigniony; letters from L. Brémond, Savouré and R.: *OC*, 515, 532 and 652. One of Menelik's officers, Grazmatch Banti, dubbed 'the defender of dogs' by R., claimed to have lost some hounds: *OC*, 652.
8. Foucher, 92.

[506]

9. Rosa to Bienenfeld, 16 (or 1?) February 1890: Z, 475 and 584.
10. H. d'Acremont, in *Revue hebdomadaire*, 27 August 1932: conversation with Lagarde (Chauvel, 228). Also Isabelle R., 89; Tharaud, 196.
11. Chauvel, 228.
12. Isabelle R., 89; Méléra (1946).
13. Middleton; Trimingham.
14. On 'Saint Rimbaud': Étiemble (1961), 133–54.
15. Foucher, 93. On Taurin's business with R.: Giusto.
16. Z, 295.
17. Z, 434 (from Taurin's diary).
18. Bernoville, 94 and 103.
19. E.g. gossip from André Malraux (Étiemble (1961), 222), and the ramblings of an unknown Capuchin in 1949: R. 'openly practised homosexuality with Somalis and Issas' (in whose societies overt homosexuality was unknown): Guillemin (September 1953), 71. The word 'Menahins', used by Ilg in connection with R. in May 1888, does not refer to 'rough trade' ('Melahin'), as once supposed. 'Menahin' was a Harari term for musk of civet (Voellmy (1992), 303).
20. Isabelle to Aden Consul (quoting R.), 19 February 1892: *OC*, 724.
21. Olivoni, 846.
22. Murphy (1987). On D. Righas, see p. 428 and *OC*, 686; also A. Righas to Isabelle: *OC*, 686 and 725.
23. L. Villatte in *Le Décadent*, 1–15 January 1889: *Oeuvres complètes*, ed. Forestier, 565–6 n.
24. E.g. letter from M. Riès in *OC*, 815–16.
25. Provost, 158; Jarosseau: letters (1936 and 1939) to Starkie (1937), 153 and A. Tian (Matucci (1962), 118–19); Guiheneuf; described as shrewd and ingratiating by Marcus (1987), 2. Jarosseau's memory improved with age; his earlier statements are more vague: Chauvel, 226–8; Tharaud, 195–6.
26. 'Notes de l'éditeur', *Poésies complètes* (1895); Tharaud, 196. The Dankali called Sahle Selassie 'a fine balance of gold': Pankhurst, 89.
27. 25 February 1890.
28. 18 May 1889. On R.'s concept of negritude: Ferguson.
29. R., *Correspondance*, 164–5 n. 2.
30. *OC*, 638.
31. Z, 430.

38. OPPORTUNITIES

1. R. to Ilg, 7 September 1889; Ilg to R., 16 June 1889.
2. Published as 'Paris se repeuple'.
3. Rosa, 832–3.

4. R. to Isabelle, 15 July 1891: *OC*, 688.
5. R. to Ilg, 1 March 1890.
6. Savouré to R., 4 May 1890.
7. Savouré to R., 10 December 1889.
8. Nerazzini to his wife, 7 August 1890: Z, 680.
9. L. Villatte (see above, p. 507 n. 23); P. Valéry (Borer (1983–4), 234–5); *La Wallonie*, 1889 (Lefrère (1991), 135).
10. *OC*, 634. On Gavoty: Lefrère (1990), 72–4.
11. The article in *La France moderne*, 19 February 1891, does not suggest personal contact (see p. 416). The letter in F. Caradec's *Catalogue d'autographes rares et curieux* (Éditions du Limon, 1998), in which R. promises a poem, is a hoax. In December 1889, Savouré announced the arrival of 'a charming young lad', Georges Richard, who 'has, I think, some friends who were once yours'. Richard broke his arm at Obock and may not have reached Harar. His friends are unknown. See Lefrère (1990), 69 and 71.
12. Deffoux–Dufay, II, 16.
13. P. Adam (1888); *Poètes lyriques français du XIXe siècle* (Lemerre, 1888); V. Jeanroy-Félix, *Nouvelle Histoire de la littérature française . . .* (1889) (Guyaux, ed. (1993), 415); A. de Gubernatis, *Dictionnaire international des écrivains du jour* (Lefrère (1991), 130); Maupassant, *La Vie errante* (1890); Merlet, 450; Champsaur; Goncourt, III, 212 (6 January 1889).
14. L. Villatte in *La Revue indépendante*, 1–15 March 1889.
15. Salimbeni, 334 (12 March 1891, quoting R.).
16. Ilg to R., 30 January 1891. Voellmy (1984), 71, suggests the telegraph. See also *OC*, 694 (Ilg's discovery of a coal-mine).
17. Olivoni, 852. On the tale that R. died after being pricked by a mimosa thorn: Borer (October 1984), 13 and 15 n. 16.
18. R. to Isabelle, 15 July 1891: *OC*, 688.
19. Conversation with C. Zaghi in 1932: Z, 757.
20. See Ilg to R., 15 March 1891: *OC*, 658.
21. Bought or rented: Orsi, 17; Z, 675.
22. Letter to L. Pierquin, 17 December 1892: *OC*, 737; see also *OC*, 752.
23. R.'s log is incomplete in *OC* and *OV*. Facsimile in MB, 232–3.
24. See R., *Lettres*, 33–4, and, above, p. 502 n. 7.
25. *OC*, 662.
26. Z, 861–79.
27. R., *Lettres*, 25 n. 1; Billy; M. Riès in *OC*, 1210; Tian (1947, 1954).
28. Petitfils (1982), 367. The shrinking of R.'s profits is also a reaction to Berrichon's hyperbole. Ironically, some of the inflated figures are probably closer to the truth. According to Méléra (1931), 252, Isabelle knew that R. lied to their mother about his earnings and was trying to restore the true figures.

29. Savouré (3 April 1930); M. Riès to É. Deschamps (*OC*, 816); Z, 592: more than double Rosa's earnings in the same period (1880–91).

30. E.g. R. to Ilg, 20 November 1890, and C. Tian to Isabelle R., 6 March 1892.

31. E.g. one of Savouré's arms consignments would have earned R. 3,600 francs and a year's worth of moneychanging 3,416 francs' commission. See *LM*, III, 218–97.

32. *OC*, 509.

33. *OC*, 707.

39. 'FEROCIOUS INVALID'

1. 'Billet de salle': *PR*, 206.

2. *Ibid.*

3. '*Un cancer généralisé*': Hospital Director to R. Darzens, 11 December 1891 (*ARPV*, no. 32); PBV, 253; '*Ostéo sarcome*': M. Riès to É. Deschamps (*OC*, 816). R. talked of a '*maladie des os*'. See Lefrère (1987).

4. See MacCormac.

5. R.'s military record: *PR*, 96–7.

6. Amprimoz, 125–7.

7. M. Riès to É. Deschamps (*OC*, 816), and to R., 3 and 8 September 1891: Z, 775 and Petitfils (1982), 386.

8. Isabelle R., 105–6.

9. Dr Beaudier: Goffin, 46–7; Vaillant (1933).

10. Isabelle R., 105. Dr Émile Baudoin's sighting of R. in Charleville on 31 July 1891, 'dragging his leg a little', is obviously suspect (Baudoin).

11. Sadie.

12. Arnoult, 17; also Goffin, 39.

13. Arnoult, 17.

14. Goffin, 40.

15. Isabelle R., 108–9.

16. Isabelle R., 111.

17. Isabelle R., 108.

18. See Isabelle's letters to Mme R. from Marseille: *OC*, 698–700.

19. Isabelle R., 114.

40. MARITIME

1. Details mostly from Isabelle R. and letters in *OC*.

2. Vaillant (1930), 41.

3. Émile Laurent: EM, 56–7.

4. Moore, 114–15.
5. *OC*, 705.
6. See letter to L. Pierquin, 11 January 1893: Morrissette, 12.
7. *OC*, 772.
8. *OC*, 721.
9. *OC*, 754 and 768 (in 1896).
10. Forbes (1989): *al fanār* is pronounced *affanār*. Berrichon (informed by Isabelle?) claims that R. died at 2 p.m.: PBV, 253.

EPILOGUE

1. *PR*, 211; Pierquin, 149–50; Vaillant (1930), 81. Funeral details: *PR*, 211.
2. Fowlie, 2 (*Le Globe* in 1991).
3. Coincidence pointed out by editors of Iz (1946), 176 n. 1.
4. *OC*, 731.
5. *OC*, 754.
6. Jottrand; Losseau – asked to destroy the copies by future Prime Minister Barthou, whose own copy would have been devalued (DAR, 319).
7. Isabelle R. to Berrichon, 25 August 1896: *OC*, 761.
8. See above, p. 487 n. 3.
9. EM, 293–6; Z, 728–9. Dire Dawa came later, with the railway; but it did have a large European community, and R. almost certainly left some papers behind.

Select Bibliography

(Unless otherwise indicated, the place of publication is either London or Paris.)

PS = *Parade sauvage*
PSB = *Parade sauvage. Bulletin*

Abélès, Luce. *Fantin-Latour: Coin de table. Verlaine, Rimbaud et les Vilains Bonshommes*. Réunion des Musées Nationaux, 1987.
Adam, Antoine. 'L'Énigme des *Illuminations*'. *Revue des Sciences Humaines*, 1950, 221–45.
[Adam, Paul]. 'Jacques Plowert'. *Petit glossaire pour servir à l'intelligence des auteurs décadents et symbolistes*. Vanier, 1888.
[Adam, Paul]. *Symbolistes et Décadents*. Ed. M. Pakenham. U. of Exeter, 1989.
Ahearn, Edward. 'Blake, Rimbaud, Marx: d'"Après le déluge" à "Soir historique"'. In *Rimbaud, cent ans après*, 170–79.
Album zutique. 2 vols. Ed. P. Pia. Cercle du Livre précieux, 1962.
Amprimoz, Alexandre. *Germain Nouveau dit Humilis: étude biographique*. Chapel Hill: U. of N. Carolina, 1983.
Andrieu, Jules. *L'Amour en chansons. Chants de tous les pays*. Taride, 1876.
Andrzejewski, B. W., *et al.*, eds. *Literatures in African Languages*. Cambridge U. P.; Warsaw: Wiedza Powszechna, 1985.
Anon. 'Maladie de cœur. Nouvelle'. *Vermersch-Journal* (London), 6 January 1872, 2–3.
Anon. *Aperçu rapide sur l'île de Chypre*. Montpellier: Boehm, 1878.
Anon. 'Varia'. *Mercure de France*, 1 August 1915, 815.
Anon. 'Petite chronique rimbaldienne'. *Mercure de France*, 1 October 1915, 395–6.
Aragon, Louis. '*Arma virumque cano*'. In *Les Yeux d'Elsa*. Horizon – La France libre, 1943.
Aragon, L. *et al.* 'Permettez!' (23 October 1927). In Maurice Nadeau. *Histoire du surréalisme*. Club des Éditeurs, 1958, 252–7.

Arnoult, Pierre. *Rimbaud.* New ed. Albin Michel, 1955.

Arthur Rimbaud. Paul Verlaine. Manuscrits et lettres autographes. Documents. Éditions originales. Succession Jean Hugues. Drouot, 20 March 1998.

Auden, W. H. 'Rimbaud' (December 1938). In *Collected Poems.* Ed. E. Mendelson. Faber & Faber, 1991.

Badesco, Luc. *La Génération poétique de 1860.* 2 vols. Nizet, 1971.

Bandelier, Danielle. *Se dire et se taire: l'écriture d'"Une Saison en Enfer' d'Arthur Rimbaud.* Neuchâtel: La Baconnière, 1988.

Bandy, W. T. and Claude Pichois, eds. *Baudelaire devant ses contemporains.* New ed. Klincksieck, 1995.

Banville, Théodore de. *Petit traité de poésie française.* 1872; Fasquelle, 1899.

Bardey, Alfred. 'Nouveaux documents sur Rimbaud'. Ed. H. de Bouillane de Lacoste and H. Matarasso. *Mercure de France,* 15 May 1939, 5–38.

Bardey, A. 'Souvenirs inédits d'Alfred Bardey'. Ed. P. Petitfils. *Études rimbaldiennes,* 1 (1969), 27–54.

Bardey, A. *Barr-Adjam, souvenirs d'Afrique orientale, 1880–1887.* Ed. J. Tubiana. CNRS, 1981.

Bardone, Rinaldo. *L'Abissinia e i paesi limitrofi. Dizionario corografico, storico, statistico ed etnografico dell'Etiopia.* Florence: Le Monnier, 1888.

Barrère, Albert. *Argot and Slang. A new French and English Dictionary of the Cant Words, Quaint expressions, slang terms and flash phrases used in the high and low life of old and new Paris.* 1887; New ed. Whittaker, 1889.

[Barrère, Camille]. *The Story of the Commune. By a Communalist.* Chapman & Hall, 1871.

Baudelaire, Charles. *Les Paradis artificiels.* Précédé de *La Pipe d'opium, Le Hachich, Le Club des Hachichins* par Théophile Gautier. Ed. C. Pichois. Folio, 1972.

Baudelaire, C. *Oeuvres complètes.* 2 vols. Ed. C. Pichois. Pléiade, 1975–6.

Baudoin, Dr Émile. 'Le Dernier voyage de Rimbaud à Charleville'. *La Grive,* April 1949, 1–2.

Baum, James E. *Savage Abyssinia.* New York: Sears, 1927.

Beckett, Samuel. *Drunken Boat. A Translation of Arthur Rimbaud's Poem Le Bateau ivre.* Eds. J. Knowlson and F. Leakey. Reading: Whiteknights Press, 1976.

Bender, M. L., *et al.,* eds. *Language in Ethiopia.* Oxford U. P., 1976.

Bercovici, Konrad. *Savage Prodigal.* New York: Beechhurst Press, 1948.

Bernard, Oliver, tr. *Arthur Rimbaud. Collected Poems.* Penguin, 1962; rev. ed. 1997.

Bernoville, Gaëtan. *Monseigneur Jarosseau et la Mission des Gallas.* Albin Michel, 1950.

Berrichon, Paterne. *La Vie de Jean-Arthur Rimbaud.* Mercure de France, 1897. Rpt: New York: AMS, 1980.

Berrichon, P. *Jean-Arthur Rimbaud. Le Poète (1854–1873). Poèmes, lettres et documents inédits.* Mercure de France, 1912.

Berrichon, P. 'Versions inédites d'*Illuminations*'. *Mercure de France*, 1 May 1914, 28–35.

Bersani, Leo. 'Rimbaud's Simplicity'. In *A Future for Astyanax. Character and Desire in Literature*. Boston and Toronto: Little, Brown and Co., 1976.

Beurard-Valdoye, Patrick. 'Verlaine–Rimbaud. La Rencontre de "Stuttgarce": du nouveau'. *Revue Verlaine*, 5 (1997), 100–107.

Bibliothèque Nationale. *Arthur Rimbaud. Exposition organisée pour le centième anniversaire de sa naissance*. Bibliothèque Nationale, 1954.

Billy, André. 'Les Propos du samedi'. *Le Figaro littéraire*, 9 June 1962.

Bivort, Olivier and André Guyaux. 'Pour une bibliographie des *Illuminations*'. In *Rimbaud, cent ans après*, 163–9.

Bivort, O. and Steve Murphy. *Rimbaud. Publications autour d'un centenaire*. Turin: Rosenberg & Sellier, 1994.

Bockris, Victor. *Patti Smith*. Fourth Estate, 1998.

Bodenham, Charles Henry L. *Rimbaud et son père. Les Clés d'une énigme*. Les Belles Lettres, 1992.

Bonnefoy, Yves. *Rimbaud par lui-même*. 1961; Seuil, 'Écrivains de toujours', 1994.

Borelli, Jules. *Éthiopie méridionale. Journal de mon voyage aux pays amhara, oromo et sidama, septembre 1885 à novembre 1888*. Librairies-Imprimeurs Réunies, 1890.

Borer, Alain. *Un sieur Rimbaud se disant négociant*. Lachenal et Ritter, 1983 and 1984. With P. Soupault and A. Aeschbacher.

Borer, A. *Rimbaud en Abyssinie*. Seuil, 1984.

Borer, A. 'La Part de Shiva'. *PS*, 1 (October 1984), 4–15.

Bouillane de Lacoste, Henry de. *Rimbaud et le problème des Illuminations*. Mercure de France, 1949.

Bourde, Paul. 'Les Poètes décadents'. *Le Temps*, 6 August 1885. In Jean Moréas. *Les Premières armes du symbolisme*. Ed. M. Pakenham. U. of Exeter, 1973, 9–22.

Bourguignon Jean and Charles Houin. *Vie d'Arthur Rimbaud*. 1896–1901. Ed. M. Drouin. Payot, 1991.

Breton, André. *Anthologie de l'humour noir*. 1940. In *Oeuvres complètes*. Ed. M. Bonnet. Vol. II. Pléiade, 1992.

Briet, Suzanne. *Rimbaud notre prochain*. Nouvelles Éditions Latines, 1956.

Briet, S. *Madame Rimbaud: essai de biographie, suivi de la correspondance de Vitalie Rimbaud-Cuif*. Minard, 1968.

Britten, Benjamin. *Les Illuminations* (1939). New Symphony Orchestra of London. Eugene Goossens. Decca, 1967.

Brunel, Pierre. *Rimbaud, projets et réalisations*. Geneva: Slatkine, 1983.

Buisine, Alain. *Paul Verlaine: histoire d'un corps*. Tallandier, 1995.

Burton, Captain Sir Richard F. *First Footsteps in East Africa; or, An Exploration of Harar*. 2 vols. Longman, 1856.

Butor, Michel. *Improvisations sur Rimbaud*. Éditions de la Différence, 1989.

Calmettes, Fernand. *Leconte de Lisle et ses amis*. Librairies-Imprimeries Réunies, [1902].

Camus, Albert. *L'Homme révolté*. Gallimard, NRF, 1951.

Caradec, François. 'Devant la porte du cimetière du Sud'. *PS*, 6 (June 1989), 97–101.

Carré, Jean-Marie. *La Vie aventureuse de Jean-Arthur Rimbaud*. New ed. Plon, 1926.

Carré, J.-M. *Lettres de la vie littéraire d'Arthur Rimbaud (1870–1875)*. 5th ed. Gallimard, NRF, 1931.

Carré, J.-M., ed. *Autour de Verlaine et de Rimbaud. Dessins inédits de Paul Verlaine, de Germain Nouveau et d'Ernest Delahaye*. Gallimard, NRF, 1949.

Cazals, F.-A. and Gustave Le Rouge. *Les Derniers jours de Paul Verlaine*. New ed. Mercure de France, 1923.

Cecchi, Antonio. *Da Zeila alle frontiere del Caffa*. 3 vols. Rome: Ermanno Loescher & Co., 1885–7.

Chadwick, Charles. 'The Dating of Rimbaud's Word Lists'. *French Studies*, 1969, 35–7.

Chambers, Ross. 'Réflexions sur l'inspiration communarde de Rimbaud'. *Arthur Rimbaud* 2 (Minard, 1973), 63–80.

Chambon, Jean-Pierre. 'Quelques remarques sur la prononciation de Rimbaud'. *Circeto*, 1 (October 1983), 6–12.

Chambon, J.-P. 'Les Sobriquets de Delahaye'. *PSB*, 2 (January 1986), 69–81.

Champfleury. *La Mascarade de la vie parisienne*. Librairie Nouvelle, Bourdilliat, 1860.

Champsaur, Félicien. *Dinah Samuel*. Ollendorff, 1882; 1889 (Preface: 'Le Modernisme'). Extracts in Guyaux, ed. (1993), 65–7.

Chauvel, Jean. *L'Aventure terrestre de Jean Arthur Rimbaud*. Seghers, 1971.

Claudel, Paul. 'Un dernier salut à Arthur Rimbaud'. In *Oeuvres en prose*. Ed. J. Petit and C. Galpérine. Pléiade, 1965.

Claudel, P. *Journal*. Ed. F. Varillon and J. Petit. Vol. I. Pléiade, 1968.

Cocteau, Jean. *Carte blanche. Articles parus dans 'Paris-Midi'*. La Sirène, 1920.

Cohen, Marcel. *Études d'éthiopien méridional*. Librairie orientaliste Paul Geuthner, 1931.

Cohen, Marcel (?), *see* Errard.

Conti Rossini, Carlo. 'Hamites and East Africa'. *Encyclopaedia of Religion and Ethics*. Vol. VI. Edinburgh: T. & T. Clark, 1913. 486–92.

Conti Rossini, C. *Etiopia e genti di Etiopia*. Florence: Bemporad, 1937.

Cook, Thomas and Son. *Cook's Guide to Paris*. New ed. Simpkin, Marshall & Co., 1882.

Copley, Antony. *Sexual Moralities in France, 1780–1980*. London and New York: Routledge, 1989.

Cornulier, Benoît de. 'L'Ange urine'. *PS*, 5 (July 1988), 50–3.

Cornulier, B. de. 'Le Violon enragé d'Arthur pour ses "Petites amoureuses"'. *PS*, 15 (November 1998), 19–32.

Coulon, Marcel. *Le Problème de Rimbaud, poète maudit*. Nîmes: Gomès, 1923.

Coulon, M. 'Le Divorce de Verlaine'. *Mercure de France*, 1 February 1927, 724–8.

Coulon, M. *La Vie de Rimbaud et de son Oeuvre*. Mercure de France, 1929.

Cros, Charles and Tristan Corbière. *Oeuvres complètes*. Ed. L. Forestier and P.-O. Walzer. Pléiade, 1970.

Darzens, Rodolphe. Preface, Rimbaud, *Reliquaire. Poésies*. Genonceaux, 1891. Rpt. *Cahiers du Collège de 'Pataphysique*, 17–18 (15 haha 82 EP) [October 1954], 137–45. [On this and the following, see p. 442.]

Darzens, R. 'Arthur Rimbaud. Documents, proses et poësies inédits'. Paris, 1891–2. In Lefrère (1998).

Dauzat, Albert. *Dictionnaire étymologique des noms de famille et prénoms de France*. Larousse, 1951.

Deffoux, Léon and Pierre Dufay. *Anthologie du pastiche*. Crès, 1926.

Dehérain, Henri. *Figures coloniales françaises et étrangères*. Société d'Éditions géographiques, maritimes et coloniales, 1931.

De Jong, M. 'Deux petits problèmes rimbaldiens'. *Neophilologus*, 1962, 281–3.

Delacroix, Eugène. 'Letters from England or on English Art'. Tr. E. Roditi. *London Magazine*, February–March 1993, 48–66.

Delahaye, Ernest. *Rimbaud*. Revue littéraire de Paris et de Champagne, 1905.

Delahaye, E. *Verlaine*. Messein, 1919.

Delahaye, E. *Rimbaud, l'artiste et l'être moral*. Messein, 1923; 1947.

Delahaye, E. *Souvenirs familiers à propos de Rimbaud, Verlaine, Germain Nouveau*. Messein, 1925.

Delahaye, E. *Les 'Illuminations' et 'Une Saison en Enfer' de Rimbaud*. Messein, 1927; 1949.

Delahaye, E. *Delahaye témoin de Rimbaud*. Ed. F. Eigeldinger and A. Gendre. Neuchâtel: La Baconnière, 1974.

Delahaye, E. 'Lettres d'Ernest Delahaye à Jean-Paul Vaillant'. Ed. S. Murphy. *PS*, 12 (December 1995), 98–118.

Delfau, Gérard. *Jules Vallès. L'Exil à Londres (1871–1880)*. Paris and Montréal: Bordas, 1971.

Demeny, Paul. *Les Glaneuses, poésies*. Librairie Artistique, 1870.

Demeny, P. *La Sœur du Fédéré. Poème. Mai 1871*. Librairie Artistique, 1871.

Demeny, P. *Les Visions*. Lemerre, 1873.

Dictionnaire de Biographie française. Letouzey et Ané, 1929–.

Dominicy, Marc. 'Tête de faune ou les règles d'une exception'. *PS*, 15 (November 1998), 109–88.

[Domino, Signor]. *Der Cirkus und die Cirkuswelt*. Berlin: Fischer, 1888.

Doré, Gustave and Blanchard Jerrold. *London: A Pilgrimage*. Ed. M. Rose. 1872; New York: Dover, 1970.

Le Dossier de la Commune devant les Conseils de Guerre. Librairie des Bibliophiles, 1871.

Druick, Douglas and Michel Hoog. *Fantin-Latour*. Ottawa: National Gallery of Canada, 1983.

Dufour, Hélène and André Guyaux. *Arthur Rimbaud. Portraits, dessins, manuscrits*. Réunion des Musées Nationaux, 1991.

Duhart, Remy. 'Le Fac-similé des proses dites "évangéliques"'. *PS*, 11 (December 1994), 84–7.

Dullaert, Maurice. *L'Affaire Verlaine*. Messein, 1930. N. p.

Edwards, Stewart. *The Paris Commune. 1871*. 1971; New York: Quadrangle, 1977.

Eigeldinger, Frédéric. 'Lettres inédites de Georges Izambard à Ardengo Soffici sur Rimbaud'. *Versants*, 3 (1982), 89 ff.

Emanuelli, Enrico. 'Deux lettres d'Arthur Rimbaud'. *La Table ronde*, January 1950, 179–84.

Errard, Paul. 'Des souvenirs inconnus sur Rimbaud'. Ed. P. Petitfils. *Mercure de France*, 1 January 1955, 66–83. From *Société des Naturalistes et Archéologues du Nord de la Meuse*, 1934. [On interviewer and interviewees, see p. 500, n. 4. (Chapter 31)]

Étiemble, René. *Le Mythe de Rimbaud. Structure du mythe*. New ed. Gallimard, 1961.

Étiemble, R. *Le Mythe de Rimbaud. Genèse du mythe, 1869–1949*. 2nd ed. Gallimard, 1968.

Étiemble, R. *Le Sonnet des Voyelles. De l'audition colorée à la vision érotique*. Gallimard, 1968.

Étiemble, R. *Rimbaud, système solaire ou trou noir?* PUF, 1984.

Étiemble, R. and Yassu Gauclère. *Rimbaud*. New ed. Gallimard, NRF, 1950.

Favart, Charles-Simon. *Théâtre de Favart, ou Recueil des Comédies, Parodies et Opéra-Comiques qu'il a donnés jusqu'à ce jour, avec les Airs, Rondes et Vaudevilles notés dans chaque pièce*. 10 vols. Duchesne, 1763–72.

Faxon, Alicia Craig. *Jean-Louis Forain. A Catalogue Raisonné of the Prints*. New York and London: Garland Publishing, 1982.

Fénéon, Félix. *Oeuvres plus que complètes*. 2 vols. Ed. J. Halperin. Geneva: Droz, 1970.

Ferguson, J. A. '"Noirs inconnus": The Identity and Function of the Negro in Rimbaud's Poetry and Correspondence'. *French Studies*, 1985, 43–58.

Fongaro, Antoine. 'Les Échos verlainiens chez Rimbaud et le problème des "Illuminations"'. *Revue des Sciences Humaines*, 1962, 263–72.

Fongaro, A. Review of M. Matucci, 'La Malchance de Rimbaud'. *Critique*, 1966, 736–48.

Fontaine, André. *Génie de Rimbaud*. Delagrave, 1934.

Footman, David. *Antonin Besse of Aden. The Founder of St Antony's College, Oxford.* Macmillan, in association with St Antony's College, Oxford, 1986.

Forbes, Duncan. *Rimbaud in Ethiopia.* Hythe and Peterhead: Volturna Press, 1979.

Forbes, D. 'La Signification de *Aphinar* dans les dernières paroles de Rimbaud'. *PS*, 6 (June 1989), 144–5.

Forestier, Louis. *Charles Cros, l'homme et l'oeuvre.* Minard, 1969.

Foucher, R. P. Émile. 'Arthur Rimbaud et la mission catholique de Harar'. *Europe*, June–July 1991, 88–97.

Fowlie, Wallace. *Rimbaud and Jim Morrison. The Rebel as Poet.* Duke U. P., 1994.

Fowlie, W., tr. *Rimbaud. Complete Works, Selected Letters.* U. of Chicago Press, 1966.

Friedrich, Hugo. *Structures de la poésie moderne.* Tr. M.-F. Demet. Denoël / Gonthier, 1976.

Frohock, W. M. *Rimbaud's Poetic Practice. Image and Theme in the Major Poems.* Harvard U. P., 1963.

Gachet, Paul. *Cabaner.* Les Beaux-Arts, 1954.

Garad, Abdurahman. *Harar. Wirtschaftsgeschichte eines Emirats im Horn von Afrika (1825–75).* Frankfurt: Lang, 1990.

Gautier, Théophile, *see* Baudelaire (1972).

[Gill, André]. *La Muse à Bibi.* Marpon et Flammarion, 1881.

Ginter, Roland. 'Rimbaud et le *Journal de Charleroi*'. *Arthur Rimbaud 4* (Minard, 1980), 103–6.

Giusto, Jean-Pierre. 'Rimbaud et les missionnaires du Harar'. *Rimbaud vivant*, 1 (1973), 23–6.

Godchot, Colonel. *Arthur Rimbaud ne varietur.* 2 vols. Nice: Chez l'auteur, 1936 and 1937.

Goffin, Robert. *Rimbaud vivant. Documents et témoignages inédits.* Corrêa, 1937.

Goncourt, Edmond and Jules. *Journal. Mémoires de la vie littéraire.* 3 vols. Ed. R. Ricatte. Laffont, 1989.

Gosse, Edmund. 'Rimbaud, Arthur'. In *Encyclopaedia Britannica*, 11th ed. 1911.

[Gourmont, Remy de]. *Mercure de France*, 1 December 1891, 363–4.

Graaf, Daniel A. de. 'Autour du dossier de Bruxelles'. *Mercure de France*, 1 August 1956, 626–34.

Graaf, D. A. de. *Arthur Rimbaud, sa vie, son œuvre.* Assen: Van Gorcum & Co., 1960.

Gregh, Fernand. *L'Age d'or. Souvenirs d'enfance et de jeunesse.* Grasset, 1947.

Gribaudo, Paul. 'A vendre'. *PS*, 3 (April 1986), 103–6.

Guigniony, G.-L. 'En marge du symbolisme'. [Interview by Pierre Ripert.] *Marseille*, July–September 1952.

Guiheneuf, Max. 'Rimbaud et Mgr Jarosseau'. *Mercure de France*, 1 April 1948, 759–60.

Guillemin, Henri. 'Connaissance de Rimbaud'. *Mercure de France*, 1 June 1953, 261–73, and 1 October 1954, 235–47.

Guillemin, H. 'Approche de Rimbaud'. *La Table ronde*, September 1953, 49–73. In *A vrai dire*. Gallimard, NRF, 1956.

Guyaux, André. 'Rimbaud et le Prince Impérial'. *Berenice*, March 1981, 89–97. 'Post-scriptum', *ibid.*, April–August 1982, 143–6.

Guyaux, A. *Poétique du fragment. Essai sur les 'Illuminations' de Rimbaud*. Neuchâtel: La Baconnière, 1985.

Guyaux, A. 'Bruxelles, 10 juillet 1873'. *Arthur Rimbaud ou le voyage poétique. Actes du colloque de Chypre* (1991). Ed. J.-L. Steinmetz. Tallandier, 1992.

Guyaux, A. 'Rimbaud – Biographie'. *Quarante-huit/Quatorze. Conférences du Musée d'Orsay*, no. 5. Réunion des Musées Nationaux, 1993.

Guyaux, A., ed. *Rimbaud*. Éditions de l'Herne, 1993. Incl. A. Guyaux, 'Chronologie de Rimbaud et du rimbaldisme'.

Guyaux, A., *see* Bivort; Dufour.

Hackett, C. A. 'Fumant des roses'. *PS*, 2 (April 1985), 101.

Hackett, C. A. ' "Bau", "Baoe" et "Baou" '. *PS*, 6 (June 1989), 136–8.

Hackett, C. A. 'Rimbaud et Albert Mérat'. *Revue d'Histoire littéraire de la France*, 1992, 994–1002.

Hacking, Ian. *Mad Travellers. Reflections on the Reality of Transient Mental Illnesses*. U. P. of Virginia, 1999.

Hamilton, Richard F. *The Social Misconstruction of Reality. Validity and Verification in the Scholarly Community*. Yale U. P., 1996.

Hampton, Christopher. *Total Eclipse*. Faber & Faber, 1969; 1981.

Hare, Humphrey. *Sketch for a Portrait of Rimbaud*. Brendin Publishing Co., [1958?].

Helvétius, Claude-Adrien. *De l'esprit* (1758). Ed. F. Châtelet. Marabout Université, 1973.

Henry, Gilles. 'L'Ascendance d'Arthur Rimbaud en ligne directe'. *Études rimbaldiennes*, 3 (1972), 21–31.

Hergé [Georges Remi]. *Tintin au Congo*. Tournai: Casterman, 1946.

Herling Croce, Lidia. 'Rimbaud à Chypre, à Aden et au Harar'. *Études rimbaldiennes*, 3 (1972), 9–19.

Hillairet, Jacques. *Dictionnaire historique des rues de Paris*. 6th ed. 2 vols. Éditions de Minuit, 1976.

Horne, Alistair. *The Fall of Paris. The Siege and the Commune 1870–71*. 1965; Papermac, 1997.

Houin, Charles, *see* Bourguignon.

Houston, John Porter. *The Design of Rimbaud's Poetry*. Yale U. P., 1963.

Houston, J. P. *Patterns of Thought in Rimbaud and Mallarmé*. Lexington: French Forum, 1986.

Hugo, Victor. *Oeuvres complètes*. 15 vols. Gen eds. J. Seebacher and G. Rosa. Laffont, 1985–90.

Hunter, Captain F. M. *The Aden Handbook: A Summary of Useful Information Regarding the Settlement. Guide du voyageur à Aden: renseignements et tarifs, et diverses autres indications utiles*. Harrison, 1873.

Ingram, John H. *Oliver Madox Brown. A Biographical Sketch. 1855–1874*. Elliot Stock, 1883.

Izambard, Georges. *Rimbaud tel que je l'ai connu*. Ed. H. de Bouillane de Lacoste and Pierre Izambard. Mercure de France, 1946; 1963.

James, Frank L. and William D. *The Unknown Horn of Africa. An Exploration from Berbera to the Leopard River*. 1888; G. Philip, 1890.

Jeancolas, Claude. *Passion Rimbaud. L'Album d'une vie*. Textuel, 1998.

Jottrand, Charles. 'Le Secret d'Arthur Rimbaud'. In *Rimbaud, cent ans après*, 159–62.

Kacimi-El Hassani, Mohamed. 'Frédéric Rimbaud, chef de bureau arabe'. *Europe*, June–July 1991, 82–7.

Kahn, Gustave. *Silhouettes littéraires*. Montaigne, 1925.

Kahn, G. *Symbolistes et Décadents*. Vanier, 1902.

Kapp, Yvonne. *Eleanor Marx*. Vol. I. 1972; Virago, 1979.

Keller, Conrad. *Alfred Ilg, sein Leben und sein Werken als schweizerischer Kulturbote in Abessinien*. Frauenfeld and Leipzig: Huber, 1918.

Lalande, Françoise. 'L'Examen corporel d'un homme de lettres'. *PS*, 2 (April 1985), 97–8.

Lalande, F. *Madame Rimbaud*. Presses de la Renaissance, 1987.

Lanier, Doris. *Absinthe. The Cocaine of the Nineteenth Century*. Jefferson, NC and London: McFarland, 1995.

Larousse, Pierre. *Grand Dictionnaire universel du XIXe siècle*. 1866–79.

Lefranc, Jules. 'Roche. La Maison Rimbaud'. *Revue palladienne*, 7 (April–May 1949), 345–6.

Lefranc, J. 'Encore Rimbaud', *Revue palladienne*, 17–18 (1952), 260–5.

Lefrère, Jean-Jacques. 'Diagnostic: carcinose généralisée'. *PSB*, 3 (June 1987), 31–6.

Lefrère, J.-J. 'Qui était ce Pipe-en-bois?'. *PS*, 6 (June 1989), 86–91.

Lefrère, J.-J. 'De Paul Soleillet à Georges Richard'. *PSB*, 6 (November 1990), 50–80.

Lefrère, J.-J. 'Quelques "singularités" . . .'. *Berenice*, July 1991, 130–6.

Lefrère, J.-J. 'Quand Rimbaud comparaissait devant les Vilains-Bonshommes'. *La Quinzaine littéraire*, 16–31 March 1996, 17–18.

Lefrère, J.-J. *Isidore Ducasse, auteur des 'Chants de Maldoror, par le comte de Lautréamont'*. Fayard, 1998.

Lefrère, J.-J. *Les Saisons littéraires de Rodolphe Darzens, suivi de Documents sur Arthur Rimbaud*. Fayard, 1998.

Lefrère, J.-J. 'Les Manuscrits d'un poète'. *La Quinzaine littéraire*, 1–15 July 1998, 12–15.

Lefrère, J.-J. 'Rimbaud et Lautréamont en salle des ventes'. *La Quinzaine littéraire*, 16–30 November 1998, 16–18.

Lefrère, J.-J. and Steve Murphy. 'Vers une édition moins fautive de la correspondance de Rimbaud (1875–1891)'. *PS*, 13 (March 1996), 104–26.

Lefrère, J.-J. and Michael Pakenham. 'Rimbaud dans le *Journal* de l'abbé Mugnier'. *PSB*, 6 (November 1990), 20–27.

Lefrère, J.-J. and M. Pakenham. *Cabaner poète au piano*. L'Échoppe, 1994.

Legangneux, Claude. 'Rimbaud in Cyprus'. *Adam*, 244–6 (1954), 16–18.

Lepelletier, Edmond. Article in *L'Écho de Paris*, 17 November 1891.

Lepelletier, E. *Paul Verlaine, sa vie, son œuvre*. Mercure de France, 1907.

Létrange, Ernest. 'Les Leçons de piano'. *La Grive*, October 1954, 31–2.

Lévi-Strauss, Claude. 'Des sons et des couleurs'. In *Regarder écouter lire*. Plon, 1993.

[Lié, satrape]. 'L'Accent ardennais de Rimbaud'. *Cahiers du Collège de 'Pataphysique*, 17–18 (15 haha 82 EP) [October 1954], 147–50.

Lissagaray, Prosper-Olivier. *Histoire de la Commune de 1871* (1876). Ed. J. Maitron. Maspero, 1976. (Tr. by Eleanor Marx Aveling: Reeves and Turner, 1886.)

Little, Roger. *Rimbaud. 'Illuminations'*. Grant & Cutler, 1983.

Little, R. '"Baou"'. *PS*, 1 (October 1984), 54–8.

Losseau, Léon. 'La Légende de la destruction par Rimbaud de l'édition princeps d'*Une Saison en Enfer*'. *Annuaire de la Société des Bibliophiles et Iconophiles de Belgique* (1915). Brussels: Monnom, 1916.

Lübke, Wilhelm. *Grundriss der Kunstgeschichte*. 9th ed. Stuttgart: Ebner & Seubert, 1882.

MacCormac, Sir William. *Surgical Operations*. Part II. *Amputations, Excision of Joints, Operations on Nerves*. Smith, Elder & Co., 1889.

Maitron, Jean. *Dictionnaire biographique du mouvement ouvrier français*. Vol. VIII. Les Éditions Ouvrières, 1970.

Mallarmé, Stéphane. 'Arthur Rimbaud'. *The Chap-Book*, V, 1 (15 May 1896), 8–17.

Mapplethorpe, Robert, *see* Schmidt.

Marcenaro, Giuseppe and Piero Boragina. *'J'arrive ce matin...'. L'Universo poetico di Arthur Rimbaud*. Milan: Electa, 1998.

Marcus, Harold G. *Haile Sellassie I. The Formative Years, 1892–1936*. U. of California Press, 1987.

Marcus, H. G. *A History of Ethiopia*. U. of California Press, 1994.

Marmelstein, J.-W. 'Rimbaud aux Indes néerlandaises'. *Mercure de France*, 15 July 1922, 500–502.

Marsden-Smedley, Philip. *A Far Country. Travels in Ethiopia*. Century, 1990.

Martin, Auguste. *Verlaine et Rimbaud. Documents inédits tirés des Archives de la Préfecture de Police*. Imprimerie Chantenay, 1944. (From *Nouvelle Revue française*, 1 February 1943.)

Mary, Jules. 'Arthur Rimbaud'. *Littérature*, 8 October 1919. Ed. S. Murphy in *PS*, 13 (March 1996), 127–30.

Matarasso, Henri and Pierre Petitfils, eds. *Album Rimbaud. Iconographie*. Pléiade, 1967.

Matucci, Mario. *Le Dernier Visage de Rimbaud en Afrique*. Florence: Edizioni Sansoni Antiquariato; Didier, 1962.

Matucci, M. 'Sur Rimbaud en Abyssinie'. *Berenice*, March 1981, 107–16.

Maurras, Charles. 'Arthur Rimbaud'. *Gazette de France*, 21 July 1901. In *Barbarie et Poésie*. *Oeuvres*, VI. Nouvelle Librairie Nationale; Champion, 1925, 170–78.

McCarthy, Justin. 'Oliver Madox-Brown'. *The Gentleman's Magazine*, February 1876, 161–5.

Méléra, Marguerite-Yerta. 'Nouveaux documents autour de Rimbaud'. *Mercure de France*, 1 April 1930, 44–76.

Méléra, M.-Y. 'Au sujet de Rimbaud'. *Mercure de France*, 1 January 1931, 252–5.

Méléra, M.-Y. *Résonances autour de Rimbaud*. Éditions du Myrte, 1946.

Mendès, Catulle. *Rapport à M. le Ministre de l'Instruction publique et des Beaux-Arts sur le mouvement poétique français de 1867 à 1900*. Imprimerie Nationale, 1902.

Méric, Victor. *A travers la jungle politique et littéraire*. 1st series. Librairie Valois, 1930.

Merlet, Gustave. *Choix de poètes du XIXe siècle*. Armand Colin–Lemerre, n.d.

Meyerstein, E. H. W. 'Rimbaud and the "Gentleman's Magazine"'. *The Times Literary Supplement*, 11 April 1935, 244.

Michelet, Jules. *La Sorcière*. 2nd ed., 1867. Ed. W. Kusters. Nijmegen, 1989.

Middleton, John. *Lugbara Religion*. 1960; Washington: Smithsonian Institution Press, 1987.

Mijolla, Alain de. 'Rimbaud multiple'. In *Rimbaud multiple*, 215–27.

Mille, Pierre. 'Un aspect du "cas Rimbaud"'. *L'Age nouveau*, 1, January 1938, 23–6.

Miller, Henry. *The Time of the Assassins. A Study of Rimbaud*. Neville Spearman, 1956.

Milliex, Roger. 'Le Premier séjour d'Arthur Rimbaud à Chypre'. *Nota Bene*, Spring 1984, 75–87.

Mistral, Frédéric. *Lou Tresor dóu Felibrige ou Dictionnaire Provençal-Français*. Delagrave, 1932.

Mondor, Henri. *Rimbaud ou le génie impatient*. Gallimard, 1955.

Moore, George. 'Two Unknown Poets' (Rimbaud and Laforgue). *Impressions and Opinions*. David Nutt, 1891, 111–21.

Mori, Attilio. 'Storia della conoscenza e dell'esplorazione'. In Reale Società Geografica Italiana. *L'Africa orientale*. Bologna: Zanichelli, 1936, 3–66.

Morrissette, Bruce. *The Great Rimbaud Forgery. The Affair of 'La Chasse spirituelle'. With Unpublished Documents and an Anthology of Rimbaldian Pastiches*. Saint Louis: Washington U., 1956.

Mouquet, Jules. 'Un témoignage tardif sur Rimbaud'. *Mercure de France*, 15 May 1933, 93–105.

Mouquet, J. 'Rimbaud et le *Parnasse contemporain*'. *Bulletin du Bibliophile*, March 1946, 111–22.

Mouret, Daniel, ed. 'Lettres inédites Izambard–Delahaye–Coulon'. *Arthur Rimbaud 1* (Minard, 1972), 43–84.

Munier, Roger. *Aujourd'hui, Rimbaud . . . Enquête*. Archives des Lettres Modernes, 1976.

Murphy, Steve. 'La Re-constitution des voix exilées'. *Berenice*, March 1981, 124–50.

Murphy, S. 'Rimbaud et la Commune'. In *Rimbaud multiple* (1985), 50–65.

Murphy, S. 'L'Orgie versaillaise ou Paris se dépeuple'. *PS*, 2 (April 1985), 28–39.

Murphy, S. 'Des frères Righas à Enid Starkie'. *PSB*, 3 (June 1987), 48–58.

Murphy, S. 'Les Romanciers de sept ans?'. *PSB*, 4 (March 1988), 42.

Murphy, S. 'La Faim des haricots: la lettre de Rimbaud du 14 octobre 1875'. *PS*, 6 (June 1989), 14–54.

Murphy, S. *Le Premier Rimbaud ou l'apprentissage de la subversion*. CNRS; P. U. de Lyon, 1990.

Murphy, S. '"J'ai tous les talents!": Rimbaud harpiste et dessinateur'. *PSB*, 6 (November 1990), 28–49.

Murphy, S. *Rimbaud et la ménagerie impériale*. CNRS; P. U. de Lyon, 1991.

Murphy, S. 'Autour des "Cahiers Demeny" de Rimbaud'. *Studi francesi*, January–April 1991, 78–86.

Murphy, S. '*In vino veritas*? La lettre du 5 mars 1875'. *PS*, 8 (September 1991), 35–45.

Murphy, S. 'Rimbaud copiste de Verlaine: *L'Impénitence finale*'. *PS*, 9 (February 1994), 59–68.

Murphy, S. '*Une Saison en Enfer* et les "Derniers Vers" de Rimbaud: rupture ou continuité?' *Revue d'Histoire littéraire de la France*, 1995, 958–73.

Murphy, S., *see* Bivort; Lefrère; Mary.

Nerazzini, Cesare. *La Conquista mussulmana dell'Etiopia nel secolo XVI. Traduzione d'un manoscritto arabo*. Rome: Forzani, 1891.

Nicholl, Charles. *Somebody Else: Arthur Rimbaud in Africa 1880–91*. Jonathan Cape, 1997.

Noël, Bernard. *Dictionnaire de la Commune*. 2 vols. Flammarion, 1978.

Noulet, Émilie. *Le Premier visage de Rimbaud. Huit poèmes de jeunesse*. Brussels: Palais des Académies, 1953.

Nouveau, Germain and Lautréamont. *Oeuvres complètes*. Ed. P.-O. Walzer. Pléiade, 1970.

Olivoni, Giovanni Battista. [Memoirs of Rimbaud in Harar, recorded by Olivoni's granddaughter.] In Zaghi (1993), 845–53.

Orsi, Augusto. *Arthur Rimbaud, poète et aventurier*. Addis Ababa: Istituto Italiano di Cultura, 1972.

Pakenham, Michael. 'Un ami inconnu de Rimbaud et de Debussy' (Henri Mercier). *Revue des Sciences Humaines*, 1963, 401–10.

Pakenham, M. '"Trouver le lieu et la formule": Rimbaud dans la Bibliothèque de la Pléiade depuis un quart de siècle'. *Arthur Rimbaud* 2 (Minard, 1973), 137–49.

Pakenham, M. 'Les Vilains Bonshommes et Rimbaud'. In *Rimbaud multiple* (1985), 29–49.

Pakenham, M. 'En marge de Rimbaud: un camarade carolopolitain, Jules Mary'. *PS*, 6 (June 1989), 61–6.

Pakenham, M., *see* Lefrère.

Pankhurst, Richard. *The Ethiopians*. Blackwell, 1998.

Pankhurst, R., ed. *Travellers in Ethiopia*. Oxford U. P., 1965.

Pape-Carpantier, Marie. *Manuel de l'instituteur, comprenant l'exposé des principes de la pédagogie*. Hachette, 1869.

Le Parnasse contemporain. Recueil de vers nouveaux. Lemerre, 1866 and 1869.

Petitfils, Pierre. *L'Oeuvre et le visage d'Arthur Rimbaud. Essai de bibliographie et d'iconographie*. Nizet, 1949.

Petitfils, P. 'Les Manuscrits de Rimbaud'. *Études rimbaldiennes*, 2 (1969), 41–157.

Petitfils, P. 'Le Capitaine Rimbaud écrivain'. *Rimbaud vivant*, 1 (1974), 8–16.

Petitfils, P. 'Du côté de Douai: Paul Demeny'. *Rimbaud vivant*, 16 (1979), 4–7.

Petitfils, P. *Verlaine*. Julliard, 1981.

Petitfils, P. *Rimbaud*. Julliard, 1982.

Petralia, Franco. 'Rimbaud in Italia'. *Rivista di letterature moderne*, 1954, 250–62.

Petralia, F. *Bibliographie de Rimbaud en Italie*. Institut Français de Florence. 1960.

Pichois, Claude and Jean Ziegler. *Charles Baudelaire*. New ed. Fayard, 1996.

Pierquin, Louis. 'Souvenirs'. In Carré (1931).

Plessen, Jacques. *Promenade et poésie: l'expérience de la marche et du mouvement dans l'œuvre de Rimbaud*. The Hague and Paris: Mouton, 1967.

Plowert, Jacques, *see* P. Adam.

Porché, François. *Verlaine tel qu'il fut*. Flammarion, 1933.

Postal, Pol. 'A propos du dossier de Bruxelles'. *PS*, 6 (June 1989), 114–24.

Pound, Ezra. *Instigations*. New York: Boni and Liveright, 1920.

Powell, Anthony. *Journals. 1982–1986*. Heinemann, 1995.

Privat d'Anglemont, Alexandre. 'Les Industries inconnues'. *Paris anecdote*. Delahays, 1860.

Provost, André. 'Sur les traces africaines de Rimbaud'. *La Revue de France*, 1 November 1928, 136–62.

Puget, Jean. *La Vie extraordinaire de Forain*. Émile-Paul, 1957.

Reboul, Yves. 'Les Problèmes rimbaldiens traditionnels et le témoignage d'Isabelle Rimbaud'. *Arthur Rimbaud 1* (Minard, 1972), 95–105; *Arthur Rimbaud 3* (Minard, 1976), 83–102.

Reboul, Y. 'A propos de "L'Homme juste"'. *PS*, 2 (April 1985), 44–54.

Reboul, Y. 'Sur la chronologie des "Déserts de l'amour"'. *PS*, 8 (September 1991), 46–52.

Reboul, Y. 'De Renan et des *Proses évangéliques*'. *PS*, 11 (December 1994), 88–94.

Régamey, Félix. *Verlaine dessinateur*. Floury, 1896.

Retté, Alphonse. *Le Symbolisme. Anecdotes et Souvenirs*. Vanier; Messein, 1903.

Richardson, John. *A Life of Picasso*. Vol. I. Pimlico, 1992.

Richepin, Jean. *Les Étapes d'un réfractaire: Jules Vallès*. 1872. Ed. S. Murphy. Seyssel: Champ Vallon, 1993.

Richepin, J. 'Germain Nouveau et Rimbaud. Souvenirs et papiers inédits' (1927). *Dossier Germain Nouveau*. Ed. J. Lovichi and P.-O. Walzer. Neuchâtel: La Baconnière, 1971, 21–41.

Richter, Mario. *Les Deux 'Cimes' de Rimbaud: 'Dévotion' et 'Rêve'*. Geneva: Slatkine, 1986.

Rickword, Edgell. *Rimbaud, the Boy and the Poet*. Heinemann, [1924]; Daimon Press, 1963.

Rimbaud, Arthur. 'Le Cahier des dix ans'. Ed. S. Briet. *La Grive*, April 1956, 1–16.

Rimbaud, A. *Un Cœur sous une soutane*. Ed. S. Murphy. Musée-Bibliothèque Arthur Rimbaud, 1991.

Rimbaud, A. *Correspondance, 1888–1891*. Ed. J. Voellmy. 1965; Gallimard, 1995.

Rimbaud, A. *Ébauches, suivies de la correspondance entre Isabelle Rimbaud et Paterne Berrichon et de Rimbaud en Orient*. Ed. M.-Y. Méléra. 2nd ed. Mercure de France, 1937.

Rimbaud, A. *Illuminations*. Ed. A. Guyaux. Neuchâtel: La Baconnière, 1985.

Rimbaud, A. *Illuminations. Coloured Plates*. Ed. N. Osmond. The Athlone Press, 1976.

Rimbaud, A. *Lettres de Jean-Arthur Rimbaud. Égypte, Arabie, Éthiopie*. Ed. P. Berrichon. Mercure de France, 1899.

Rimbaud, A. *Lettres du Voyant (13 et 15 mai 1871)*. Ed. G. Schaeffer. Incl. M.

Eigeldinger, *La Voyance avant Rimbaud*. Geneva: Droz; Paris: Minard, 1975.

Rimbaud, A. *Les Lettres manuscrites de Rimbaud, d'Europe, d'Afrique et d'Arabie*. 4 cahiers. Ed. C. Jeancolas. Textuel, 1997.

Rimbaud, A. *Oeuvre – Vie. Édition du Centenaire*. Ed. A. Borer, A. Montègre *et al*. Arléa, 1991.

Rimbaud, A. *Oeuvres*. Ed. S. Bernard and A. Guyaux. Garnier, 1987; 1991. [Revision of S. Bernard edition, 1960.]

Rimbaud, A. *Oeuvres*. 3 vols. Ed. J.-L. Steinmetz. Flammarion, GF, 1989.

Rimbaud, A. *Oeuvres complètes*. Ed. R. de Renéville and J. Mouquet. Pléiade, 1946.

Rimbaud, A. *Oeuvres complètes*. Ed. A. Adam. Pléiade, 1972. (1994 printing.)

Rimbaud, A. *Oeuvres complètes. Correspondance*. Ed. L. Forestier. Laffont, 1992.

Rimbaud, A. *Oeuvres poétiques*. Ed. C. A. Hackett. Imprimerie Nationale, 1986.

Rimbaud, A. *Oeuvres complètes*. Vol. I. *Poésies*. Ed. S. Murphy. Champion, 1999. (To be accompanied by a volume of facsimiles.)

Rimbaud, A. *Poésies (1869–1872)*. Ed. F. Eigeldinger and G. Schaeffer. Neuchâtel: La Baconnière, 1981.

Rimbaud, A. *Poésies*. Ed. M. Ruff. Nizet, 1978.

Rimbaud, A. *Une Saison en Enfer*. Ed. P. Brunel. Corti, 1987.

Rimbaud, Isabelle. *Reliques*. 4th ed. Mercure de France, 1921.

Rimbaud, Vitalie. 'Voyage en Angleterre (Journal)', annotated by Isabelle R. In *Oeuvres complètes*, ed. L. Forestier, 391–410. (Contemporary correspondence in *OC*, 285–96.)

Rimbaud, cent ans après. Actes du Colloque du Centenaire de la Mort de Rimbaud. Musée-Bibliothèque Rimbaud, 1992.

Rimbaud multiple. Colloque de Cerisy. Ed. A. Borer, J.-P. Corsetti and S. Murphy. Bedou et Touzot, 1985.

Rimbaud ou 'La Liberté libre'. Colloque de 'Parade sauvage'. Musée-Bibliothèque Rimbaud, 1987.

Ripert, Pierre, *see* Guigniony.

Rivière, Jacques. *Rimbaud. Dossier 1905–1925*. Ed. R. Lefèvre. Gallimard, NRF, 1977.

Robb, Graham. *La Poésie de Baudelaire et la poésie française, 1838–1852*. Aubier, 1993.

Robb, G. *Balzac. A Biography*. London: Picador; New York: Norton, 1994.

Robb, G. *Victor Hugo*. London: Picador, 1997; New York: Norton, 1998.

Robecchi Bricchetti, Luigi. *Nell'Harrar*. Milan: Galli, 1896.

Robinet, René. 'L'Institution Rossat de Charleville et la réforme de l'enseignement par Victor Duruy'. In *Actes du 88e Congrès national des Sociétés savantes (Clermont-Ferrand, 1963)*. Imprimerie Nationale, 1964, 173–80.

Robinet, R. 'Le Collège de Charleville et l'enseignement secondaire dans les

Ardennes de 1854 à 1877'. In *Actes du 95e Congrès national des Sociétés savantes (Reims, 1970)*. Vol. I. Bibliothèque Nationale, 1974, 845–66.

Rosa, Ottorino. *L'Impero del Leone di Giuda. Note sull'Abissinia*. Brescia: Lenghi, 1913. Extracts in Herling Croce and Zaghi (1993).

Rosa, O. [Texts on R. in French and Italian.] See Zaghi (1993), 832–5.

Ross, Kristin. *The Emergence of Social Space. Rimbaud and the Paris Commune*. Basingstoke: Macmillan, 1988.

Rossetti, Carlo. *Storia diplomatica dell'Etiopia durante il regno di Menelik II*. Turin: Società Tipografico–Editrice Nazionale, 1910.

Rossetti, William Michael. *The Diary of W. M. Rossetti, 1870–1873*. Ed. O. Bornand. Oxford: Clarendon Press, 1977.

Rudler, Madeleine. *Parnassiens, Symbolistes et Décadents*. Messein, 1938.

Ruff, Marcel. *Rimbaud*. Hatier, 1968.

Sacchi, Sergio. 'Oblique Rimbaud'. In *Rimbaud, cent ans après* (1992), 210–19.

Sacchi, S. 'Prolégomènes à une autoconscience "rimbaldienne"'. In *Les 'Illuminations': un autre lecteur?* Ed. P. Piret. *Les Lettres romanes*, 1993, 101–34.

Sackville-West, Edward. *The Apology of Arthur Rimbaud. A Dialogue*. The Hogarth Press, 1927.

Sadie, Stanley. *The New Grove Dictionary of Musical Instruments*. Macmillan, 1984.

Salimbeni, Augusto, *see* Zaghi, ed.

Sartre, Jean-Paul. *Saint Genet, comédien et martyr*. Gallimard, NRF, 1952.

Savouré, Armand. Letters to F. Rimbaud, 12 April 1897, and G. Maurevert, 3 April 1930, in *L'Éclaireur de Nice*: facsimiles in Borer (1983–4), 72–6.

Scarfoglio, Edoardo. *Abissinia (1888–1896)*. I. Edizioni Roma, 1936.

Schmidt, Paul, tr. *Arthur Rimbaud. A Season in Hell*. With photographs by Robert Mapplethorpe. 1986; Little, Brown & Co., 1997.

Scott, Clive. *Vers libre. The Emergence of Free Verse in France, 1886–1914*. Oxford: Clarendon Press, 1990.

Scott, David. 'La Ville illustrée dans les *Illuminations* de Rimbaud'. *Revue d'Histoire littéraire de la France*, 1992, 967–81.

Segalen, Victor. 'Les Hors-la-loi. Le Double Rimbaud'. *Mercure de France*, 15 April 1906, 481–501; *Le Double Rimbaud* (Fata Morgana, 1979), incl. 2nd conversation with Constantin Rhigas (*sic*).

Segalen, V. 'Hommage à Gauguin'. In *Lettres de Gauguin à Daniel de Monfreid*. Ed. Mme Joly-Segalen. Falaize, 1950.

Shack, William A. *The Central Ethiopians. Amhara, Tigriña and Related Peoples*. International African Institute, 1974.

Sitwell, Edith. 'Arthur Rimbaud. An Essay'. In *Prose Poems from 'Les Illuminations' of Arthur Rimbaud*. Tr. Helen Rootham. Faber & Faber, 1932.

Smith, F. R. 'Rimbaud's Performances'. *The Times Literary Supplement*, 4 June 1964, 496.

Smith, F. R. 'The Life and Works of Germain Nouveau'. D. Phil. thesis. U. of Oxford, 1965.

Soupault, Philippe. 'Mer rouge'. *Revue de Paris*, May–August 1951. In Borer (1983–4), 163–98.

Speke, Capt. John Hanning. *Les Sources du Nil, journal de voyage*. Tr. E.-D. Forgues. Hachette, 1864.

Speke, Capt. J. H. and Capt. James Grant. *Les Sources du Nil, voyage des capitaines Speke et Grant*. Tr. E.-D. Forgues. Hachette, 1867.

Starkie, Enid. *Arthur Rimbaud in Abyssinia*. Oxford: Clarendon Press, 1937.

Starkie, E. 'Sur les traces de Rimbaud'. *Mercure de France*, 1 May 1947, 83–97.

Starkie, E. *Arthur Rimbaud*. 3rd ed. Faber & Faber, 1961; 1973. [First edition: 1938.]

St Aubyn, F. C. 'Rimbaud and the Third Republic'. *Nineteenth-Century French Studies*, Fall–Winter 1976-7, 94–9.

Steinmetz, Jean-Luc. *Arthur Rimbaud: une question de présence*. Tallandier, 1991.

Strathern, Paul. *A Season in Abyssinia. An Impersonation*. Macmillan, 1972.

Swinburne, A. C. *The Swinburne Letters*. 6 vols. Ed. C. Y. Lang. Yale U. P., 1959–62.

Taute, Stéphane. 'La Scolarité de Rimbaud et ses prix'. *Centre culturel Arthur Rimbaud*, 6 (November 1978).

Tharaud, Jérôme and Jean. *Le Passant d'Éthiopie*. Plon, 1936.

Thesiger, Wilfred. *The Danakil Diary. Journeys Through Abyssinia, 1930–34*. HarperCollins, 1996.

Thétard, Henry. 'Arthur Rimbaud et le cirque'. *Revue des Deux Mondes*, 1 December 1948, 536–44.

Thiersch, Dr H. W. J. *Abyssinia*. Tr. S. Pereira. Nisbet, 1885.

Thomas, Henri. '8 Great College Street'. *Adam*, 244–6 (1954), 19.

[Thornbury, George]. *Old and New London. A Narrative of its History, its People, and its Places*. 6 vols. London, Paris and New York: Cassell, Petter, Galpin & Co., [1879–85].

Tian, André. '40.000 vers inédits'. *Les Nouvelles littéraires*, 13 February 1947. In Borer (1983–4), 366.

Tian, A. 'A propos de Rimbaud'. *Mercure de France*, 1 October 1954, 248–52.

Treharne, Mark, tr. *Arthur Rimbaud. A Season in Hell and Illuminations*. Dent, 1998.

Treich, Léon, ed. *Almanach des lettres françaises et étrangères*. Crès, 1924.

Trimingham, J. Spencer. *Islam in East Africa*. Edinburgh House Press, 1962.

Tucker, George. '"Jésus à Nazareth" (et Rimbaud à Charleville)'. *PS*, 5 (July 1988), 28–37.

Ullman, James Ramsey. *The Day on Fire. A Novel Suggested by the Life of Arthur Rimbaud*. Collins, 1959.

Underwood, V. P. *Verlaine et l'Angleterre*. Nizet, 1956.
Underwood, V. P. *Rimbaud et l'Angleterre*. Nizet, 1976.

Vadé, Yves. 'Le Paysan de Londres'. *Revue d'Histoire littéraire de la France*, 1992, 951–66.
Vaillant, Jean-Paul. *Rimbaud tel qu'il fut, d'après des faits inconnus et avec des lettres inédites*. Le Rouge et le Noir, 1930.
Vaillant, J.-P. 'Le Témoignage du médecin de Rimbaud'. *Bulletin des Amis de Rimbaud*. Supplément à *La Grive*, January 1933, 1.
Valéry, Paul. *Regards sur le monde actuel et autre essais*. New ed. Gallimard, NRF, 1945.
Vallès, Jules. *La Rue à Londres*. In *Oeuvres*. Vol. II. Ed. R. Bellet. Pléiade, 1990.
Van Dam, J. J. M. 'Le Légionnaire Rimbaud'. *De Fakkel* (Jakarta), February 1941.
Vérane, Léon. *Humilis, poète errant*. Grasset, 1929.
Verlaine, Mathilde. ('Ex-Madame Paul Verlaine'). *Mémoires de ma vie*. Ed. F. Porché. Flammarion, 1935. (Typescript, 'Mes années de ménage avec Verlaine', dated 1907–8.) New ed. M. Pakenham. Seyssel: Champ Vallon, 1992.
Verlaine, Paul. 'Arthur Rimbaud', *Lutèce*, 5–12 October 1883; *Les Poètes maudits*, 1884; 1888. In *Oeuvres en prose complètes*. Ed. J. Borel. Pléiade, 1972 (hereafter *OPC*), 643–57.
Verlaine, P. Preface, Rimbaud, *Les Illuminations*. *La Vogue*, 1886; and Rimbaud, *Poèmes. Les Illuminations. Une Saison en enfer*. Vanier, 1892. *OPC*, 631–2.
Verlaine, P. 'Arthur Rimbaud. "1884"'. *Les Hommes d'aujourd'hui*, 318. Vanier, January 1888. *OPC*, 799–804.
Verlaine, P. 'Une ... manquée'. *Le Chat noir*, January–April 1892; and *Mes prisons*. Vanier, 1893. *OPC*, 327–30.
Verlaine, P. 'Notes on England. Myself as a French Master'. *Fortnightly Review*, July 1894. *OPC*, 1085–95.
Verlaine, P. *Confessions*. Publications du *Fin de siècle*, 1895. *OPC*, 441–549.
Verlaine, P. Preface, Rimbaud, *Poésies complètes*. Vanier, 1895. *OPC*, 961–9.
Verlaine, P. 'Arthur Rimbaud'. *The Senate*, October 1895. *OPC*, 969–73.
Verlaine, P. 'Nouvelles Notes sur Rimbaud'. *La Plume*, 15–30 November 1895. *OPC*, 973–6.
Verlaine, P. 'Arthur Rimbaud. Chronique'. *Les Beaux-Arts*, 1 December 1895. *OPC*, 977–80.
Verlaine, P. *Correspondance de Paul Verlaine*. 3 vols. Ed. A. Van Bever. Messein, 1922, 1923, 1929.
Verlaine, P. *Rimbaud raconté par Paul Verlaine*. Ed. J. Mouquet. Mercure de France, 1934.
Verlaine, P. ['Carnet personnel']. Ed. V. P. Underwood. *OPC*, 1113–32.

Verlaine, P. *Lettres inédites de Verlaine à Cazals.* Ed. G. Zayed. Geneva: Droz, 1957.

Verlaine, P. *Oeuvres poétiques complètes.* Ed. Y.-G. Le Dantec and J. Borel. Pléiade, 1962.

Verlaine, P. *Lettres inédites à Charles Morice.* Ed. G. Zayed. Geneva: Droz; Paris, Minard, 1964.

Verlaine, P. *Oeuvres en prose complètes.* Ed. J. Borel. Pléiade, 1972.

Verlaine, P. *Lettres inédites à divers correspondants.* Ed. G. Zayed. Geneva: Droz, 1976.

Verlaine, P. *Nos murailles littéraires.* Ed. M. Pakenham. L'Échoppe, 1997.

Voellmy, Jean. 'Rimbaud, employé d'Alfred Bardey et correspondant d'Ilg'. *PS*, 1 (October 1984), 66–72.

Voellmy, J. 'Rimbaud et Ilg face à l'expansion coloniale de l'Italie'. In *Rimbaud ou 'La Liberté libre'* (1987), 142–50.

Voellmy, J. 'Rimbaud par ceux qui l'ont connu en Arabie et en Afrique'. In *Rimbaud, cent ans après* (1992), 298–306.

Voellmy, J. 'Les Déclarations de Rimbaud confrontées à celles d'autres voyageurs'. *PS*, 11 (December 1994), 137–45.

Warner, Philip. *Kitchener. The Man Behind the Legend.* Hamish Hamilton, 1985.

Watson, Lawrence. 'Rimbaud et le Parnasse'. In *Rimbaud ou 'La Liberté libre'*, 18–29.

Waugh, Evelyn. *Remote People.* Duckworth, 1931; Methuen, 1991.

Waugh, E. *Waugh in Abyssinia.* Longmans, Green and Co., 1936.

Waugh, E. *Scoop. A Novel About Journalists.* 1938; Penguin, 1987.

Williamson, Kennedy. *W. E. Henley. A Memoir.* Harold Shaylor, 1930.

Wing, Nathaniel. 'The Autobiography of Rhetoric: On Reading Rimbaud's *Une Saison en Enfer*'. *French Forum*, January 1984, 42–58.

Winstanley, W. *A Visit to Abyssinia. An Account of Travel in Modern Ethiopia.* 2 vols. Hurst and Blackett, 1881.

Zaghi, Carlo. *Rimbaud in Africa. Con documenti inediti.* Naples: Guida, 1993.

Zaghi, C., ed. *Crispi e Menelich nel Diario inedito del conte Augusto Salimbeni.* Turin: Istituto per la storia del Risorgimento italiano, 1956.

Zech, Paul. *Jean-Arthur Rimbaud. Ein Querschnitt durch sein Leben und Werk.* Berlin: Rudolf Zech, 1947.

Zissmann, Claude. 'Pointes fines et sac d'embrouilles: "Poison perdu"'. In *Rimbaud ou 'La Liberté libre'* (1987), 45–55.

Zissmann, C. *Ce que révèle le manuscrit des 'Illuminations'.* 2 vols. Le Bossu Bitor, 1989.

Zissmann, C. 'Un brelan de maudits'. *PS*, 11 (December 1994), 123–36.

Index

Writings by AR appear directly under title; works by others appear under author's name

ABBREVIATIONS
Ill: *Illuminations*
SE: *Une Saison en Enfer*

Abba Djifar II, King of Jima (*c.* 1861–1932), 395 & n
Abd-el-Kader (1807–83), 28–9
Abdullahi, Emir of Harar, 374, 380
Abou-Bekr family, 363, 390
Abou-Bekr, Ibrahim, Pasha of Zeila and Tadjoura, 316
Abyssinia: position, 310; AR discovers birds and animals in, 323; languages, 339–40; Catholic missionaries in, 343–4, 409–10; Italian intervention in, 350; rise of nationalism in, 373–4, 384, 404; first railway in, 380, 418; and French interests, 389; British blockade (1889–90), 406, 415; *see also* Choa; Harar
'Accroupissements' (AR), 67, 86, 93, 99
Achin (Java), 278
Adar plain (Abyssinia), 374
Addis Ababa (Abyssinia), 377, 380, 418
Aden: on route to Java, 281; AR first stays and works in (1880), 309–17, 422; AR returns to (1882–3), 331–6;

AR stays in (April 1884–November 1885), 352, 355–9; AR visits (1887), 381, 388; Tian & Co. trade in, 401; AR reaches with diseased leg, and leaves (1891), 422, 424
'Adieu' (AR; *SE*), 236
Adwa, battle of (1896), 381
Aegean Sea, 268
Afar *see* Danakil
Agar Town (London), 208
Ahmar Mountains (Abyssinia), 340
Airolo (Switzerland), 296
'A la musique' (AR), 7, 70, 433
Albert, Lake, 396
Album zutique and AR's poems in, xiv, 137, 445
'Alchimie du verbe' (AR; *SE*), 203, 231
Alexander the Great (356–323 BC), 21
Alexandria (Egypt), 292, 294, 298, 304, 350
Algeria, 6, 7, 9, 28, 320–21, 350, 416
Alin Amba (Abyssinia), 395
'Allocution de Sancho Pança à son âne mort' (AR; lost), 42
Alps, 267, 295–7
Amagne (France), 433
'Amants de Paris, Les' (AR; lost), 93
Amazone, L' (ship), 424
Ambado (Abyssinia), 370
Ambos (Abyssinia), 390–92
Andrieu, Jules (1838–84), 191–2, 200, 217, 246–7

'Angoisse' (AR; *Ill*), 248–9
Ankober (Choa), 360, 373–5
Antonelli, Count Pietro (1853–1901),
    395 & n
Antwerp, 180, 206, 213, 255
Appenzeller (carpenter), 395 & n
'Après le déluge' (AR; *Ill*), 265
Arabia, 289, 310, 334, 432
Ardennes: in AR's poetry, 59; *see also*
    Charleville; Roche
Ardennes Canal, 5, 79
Argoba tribe, 339
Arles (France), 435
Arnold, Matthew (1822–88), 287
Arnoux, Pierre (*c.* 1820–82), 341
Aroussi tribe, 326
Arras (France), 99, 111, 150, 153,
    169–70
Arrouina (Abyssinia), 421
Artiste, L' (journal), 125
Assab (Abyssinia), 310, 365
Assal, Lake (Abyssinia), 371–2, 384
'Assis, Les' (AR), 67, 93, 99–100, 433
Attigny (France), 4, 200, 430
'Aube' (AR; *Ill*), 167
'Au Cabaret-Vert' (AR), 58
'A une raison' (AR; *Ill*), 246
Australia, 283n
Avignon, 435
Awash, river (Abyssinia), 326, 365, 372,
    384, 395, 402

Bab el Mandeb strait, 309, 311
Baghdad, 310
'Bal des pendus' (AR), 34
Ballawa (Abyssinia), 420
Balzac, Honoré de (1799–1850), 42, 76,
    92, 93, 106, 153, 168, 192, 401; *Les
    Paysans*, 302
'Bannières de mai' *see* 'Fêtes de la
    patience'
Banville, Marie-Élisabeth de, 118, 126
Banville, Théodore de (1823–91): AR
    reads, 34; AR sends poems and letter
    to, 36–7, 97–9; and AR's poetic
    theories, 117–18; AR stays with in

Paris, 118–21; poetic technique, 287;
    Petit traité de poésie française, 30, 118
Bardey, Alfred (1854–1934): sets up
    business in Aden, 311, 313; describes
    AR, 313, 315, 331, 335; AR signs
    contract with, 316; addresses
    Geographical Society in Paris, 317;
    describes Harar route, 318; notices
    AR's signs of syphilis, 322; uses
    firecrackers as deterrent, 325; on
    AR's preparations for expedition,
    327–8; retains AR's services, 330; AR
    disparages, 332; reads AR's published
    letters, 332, 360; sacks local storeman
    after quarrel with AR, 336; on AR's
    trip to Bubassa, 340; safeguards AR's
    documents, 342; and AR's
    explorations, 343; AR reports death
    of Sacconi to, 344; on Sotiro's
    escape, 345–6; closes Harar agency,
    350; learns of AR's poetic past and
    disappearance, 352–4; and Bourde,
    352, 389, 399; and housekeeper, 358;
    and AR's leaving firm, 360; refuses
    partnership with Labatut in arms
    deals, 360–61; on AR's separating
    from woman companion, 369; and
    AR's losses from gun-running
    expedition, 382; employs Besse,
    386n; AR assists, 388; commission
    rate, 402; on AR's charity, 412n; AR
    leaves company, 415; visits AR in
    Marseille hospital, 436
Bardey, Pierre (b. 1852), 331, 336
Barjau (French newsagent in London),
    190
Barral, Pierre, 364
Barrère, Camille (1851–1940), 191–2,
    210–11
Batavia (Jakarta), 281
'Bateau ivre, Le' (AR): xiii, 102–5, 116,
    118–19, 122, 137, 140, 240, 306,
    323; published, 347; as Symbolist
    poem, 367; spurious ending, 400
Batri tribe, 343
Baudelaire, Charles-Pierre (1821–67):
    influence on AR, 31, 35, 60–61, 74,

Commune and Communards (1871, Paris), 75–9, 88, 112, 132, 145, 174, 175, 180, 189, 193, 210, 244

Comtesse de Flandre (ship), 199

Cook, Captain James (1728–79), 105

Cook, Thomas (1808–92), 47

Cooper, James Fenimore (1789–1851), 20

Copenhagen, 291

Coppée, François (1842–1908), 137, 185; *L'Abandonnée*, 138; *Le Passant*, 116

'Coppées' (AR), 137, 185

'Corbeaux, Les' (AR), 139–40

Corbière, Tristan (1845–75), 352

Cork, 285

Correggio (Antonio Allegri) (c. 1489–1534), 36n

Cotton, Charles, 355

Courbet, Gustave (1819–77), 91

Courrier des Ardennes (newspaper), 43

'Credo in unam' (AR) *see* 'Soleil et chair'

Creissels, Auguste, 152

Cri du Peuple, Le (newspaper), 73

Crimean War, 12, 426

Cros, Charles (1842–88), 114, 121–5

Cuif, Charles-Auguste (AR's uncle) (1830–1924), 6, 9

Cuif, Félix (AR's uncle) (1824–55), 6, 9

Cuif, Jean-Nicolas (Vitalie's father) (1789–1858), 5, 10

Cuif, Vitalie (AR's mother) *see* Rimbaud, Vitalie

Cyprus, 280, 298–301, 304–6

Daily Telegraph, 207, 208

Dakar (Senegal), 285

Damascus, 388

Danakil (Afar) region and tribesmen, 309, 341, 364–5, 371

Dante Alighieri (1265–1321), 228

Darimont (Abyssinia), 343

Darius III (4th c. BC), 21

Darwin (Australia), 283n

Darwin, Charles (1809–82), 104

Darzens, Rodolphe (1865–1939), 434, 442

Daubigny, Charles-François (1817–78), 195

Daudet, Alphonse (1840–97), 142

Daumier, Honoré (1808–79), 145

Debussy, Claude (1862–1918), 110

Décadent, Le (journal), 411, 417, 434, 437

Decadents (French), xi, 367, 401

Defoe, Daniel (1660–1731): *Robinson Crusoe*, 20, 105

Degas, Edgar (1834–1917), 126

Delahaye, Ernest (1853–1930): on AR's early years, 11, 24–5, 40, 53; half-remembers early AR poem, 39; reads *La Lanterne* in Belgium, 41, 171; friendship with AR, 52–3, 71, 101, 154, 272; on AR's literary tastes, 55; and AR's mental purification, 63; survives destruction of Mézières, 64–6; and AR's bowler hat, 68; and AR's early romantic adventure, 69; and AR's second trip to Paris, 73–4; and AR in Paris Commune, 76, 78; suggests AR join National Guard, 77; on AR's bestiality, 82n; lives in outlying village, 89; copies out AR's poems, 99; suggested homosexual practices with AR, 100; AR reads 'Le Bateau ivre' to, 102–3; and AR's September 1871 departure for Paris, 106; on Carjat portraits of AR, 115, 140; on AR *Photographies du temps passé*, 122; and AR's behaviour, 124; visits AR in Paris, 130–32; on AR's revolutionary views, 141; on AR's *Derniers vers*, 158; letters from AR in Paris, 165–6; claims AR writes prose poems in Paris, 167; and AR's top hat, 188; on AR's liking for Andrieu, 191; AR meets on return from London, 195; Mme Verlaine sends money for AR to, 196; and AR's working in Roche, 202–3; and writing of *Une Saison en Enfer*, 204; visits Verlaine in Belgium with AR, 205–6; buys books for AR, 233; receives copy of *Une Saison en Enfer*,

Delahaye, Ernest (*cont.*)
235; on AR's teaching French in London, 246; letter from AR in Stuttgart, 263; teaching post, 263; letters from AR during European travels, 267–70; and AR's return to Paris (1875), 271; drawings of AR, 271, 292; warns Verlaine of AR's begging for funds, 272; and AR's giving up writing, 275; AR tells of being robbed in Vienna, 277; on AR's walking, 277–8; on AR's 'Démocratie', 280; on AR's return home from Java, 285–6; writes to Verlaine, 292, 294; and AR's work in Cyprus, 300–301; and AR's urge to travel south, 301; dines with AR and family, 302; on AR's eating and food, 313–14; final letter from AR requesting equipment for Africa, 333; marriage and family, 430; newspaper account of AR, 443
'Délires I' (AR; *SE*), 211.
'Délires II' *see* 'Alchimie du verbe'
Demeny, Paul (1844–1918): AR sends poems to, 50, 54, 56, 61, 91, 434; and AR's sense of damnation, 67; and AR's second trip to Paris, 72–3; and AR's job on *Progrès des Ardennes*, 77; AR writes to, 83–7, 91, 96, 178, 204; saves AR's poems, 91; AR hopes for help from, 98–9; *Les Glaneuses*, 50, 89–90
'Démocratie' (AR; *Ill*), 280
Den Helder (Holland), 279–80
'Départ' (AR; *Ill*), 240, 331
Derème, Tristan (1889–1941), 136
Derniers vers (*Vers nouveaux*; *Chansons*; AR), 157–62, 292, 332
Descartes, René (1596–1650), 83
Desdouest (Charleville headmaster) (d. 1878), 20, 30, 31, 40, 66
Déserts de l'amour, Les (AR), 122, 228
Deverrière, Léon, 98, 106
'Dévotion' (AR; *Ill*), 281
D'Hervilly, Ernest (1839–1911), 117

Dickens, Charles (1812–70): 189; *Hard Times*, 55
Dieppe, 199, 285
Dijon, 105, 295
Dimitri (interpreter), 357
Dire Dawa (Ethiopia), 445
Djami *see* Wadaï, Djami
Djeddah *see* Jeddah
Djibouti, 380, 384, 392, 397, 431
Djimma *see* Jima
'Document' (AR; lost), 266
Dôle (France), 7, 313
Doré, Gustave (1832–83), 183
'Dormeur du val, Le' (AR), 61, 62
Douai (France), 49–50, 53, 60–61, 90, 111
'Douaniers, Les' (AR), 99, 101
Dover (England), 182–3, 199, 253
Dozon, Auguste (Consul) (1822–91), 304
Drouot: auction of AR mss., xvii, 292
Drycup (Dracup?), L.W.R. (London box factory), 244
Dubar, Colonel F., 311–13, 315, 334
Duchamp, Marcel (1887–1968), 37
Duderstadt-Reinöhl, August, 267
Dufour *see* Berrichon
Dujardin, Élisa (1836–67), 111
Dumollard, Martin (*c.* 1812–62), 139
Durand, Paul, 60
Dutch Colonial Army: AR enlists in, 278–80, 282–3; AR recruits for, 289–90
Dylan, Bob (b. 1941), xiv

Eagleton, Terry, 76
Ecclesiastes, 233
Echo, The (London newspaper), 208, 245, 247–8
Écho de Paris, L', 442–3
'Éclatante victoire de Sarrebruck, L'' (AR), 61
Éclipse, L' (magazine), 72
'Effarés, Les' ('Petits Pauvres'; AR), 54, 99, 192, 353
Egon (Abyssinia), 420

Egypt, 294–5, 298, 305, 310, 320, 350, 384

Eiffel, Gustave (1832–1923), 417

Eimeh *see* Imi

Einstein, Albert (1879–1955), 84, 272

Eliot, T. S. (1888–1965): *The Waste Land*, 233

'Enfance' (AR; *Ill*), 239, 242, 248, 261

'Enfant qui ramassa les balles, L' . . .' (AR), 185

England: AR and Verlaine visit, 182–3, 206; AR visits with Nouveau, 241; *see also* London

Entotto (Choa), 377, 379, 418

Entretiens politiques et littéraires (journal), 443

Erer, river (Abyssinia), 347

Eritrea, 310, 405, 418

Essarts, Jules Bufquin des, 57

Essarts, Xavier Bufquin des (1809–80), 57–8, 60

'Est-elle aimée? . . .' (AR), 173

'Éternité, L" (AR), 158, 161

Ethiopia *see* Abyssinia

Étiemble, René: *Le Mythe de Rimbaud*, 444

'Étrennes des orphelins, Les' (AR), 30–31, 36

Études néantes (AR; ?*Derniers vers*), 157

Fampoux (France), 99

Fantin-Latour, Henri (1836–1904), 143, 192

Farré (Choa), 172–3

'Fausse conversion' *see* 'Nuit de l'enfer'

Favart, Charles (1710–92), 160

Felter, Pietro, 416, 428

Fénéon, Félix (1861–1944), 367

Ferrandi, Ugo (1852–1928), 367–8

'Fêtes de la faim' (AR), 159, 160–61

'Fêtes de la patience' (AR), 159; *see also* 'Chanson de la plus haute tour'; 'Éternité, L"

Figaro (newspaper), 128, 167

Flaubert, Gustave (1821–80), 265, 349, 401; *Hérodias*, 198; *Madame Bovary*, 55, 265

Forain, Jean-Louis (1852–1931): in Paris during Commune with AR, 76; on AR's genius, 125; AR lives with, 145–8; and Verlaine in Paris, 154–5; AR visits in new studio, 168; AR gives copy of *Une Saison en Enfer* to, 235; remains friends with AR, 271

Forain, Mme Jean-Louis, 148

Forbes, Duncan, 392

'Forgeron, Le' (AR), 42, 79n

Fourier, Charles (1772–1837), 150

France, Anatole (1844–1924), 443

France moderne, La (journal), 416, 430

Franco-Prussian War (1870), 41–4, 48, 53, 56, 63, 64–7

François, Father (of Aden), 358

Franzoj, Augusto (1849–1911), 367, 369

Fumay (France), 56, 58–61

Galla (Oromo) tribes, 316, 319, 333, 341, 342, 412n, 428

Garnier, Alfred-Jean: portrait of AR?, 271

Gaspary, E. de (French Vice-Consul at Aden), 335–6, 363, 375–6, 378–82, 383, 385, 387, 416

Gautier, Théophile (1811–72), 168, 401

Gavoty, Laurent de (b. 1853), 416

Genoa, 294–5, 297

Gentleman's Magazine, The, 192

Geographical Societies: AR's notes published by, 396; *see also* Société de Géographie

Germany, 67, 262–5, 267, 277, 289–91, 396

Gespunsart (France), 8

Ghent, 180

Gibraltar, 280

Gill, André (1840–85), 72–3, 120, 145; *La Muse à Bibi*, 73

Gillet, Joseph, Abbé, 441

Ginsberg, Allen (b. 1926), xiv

Givet (France), 57, 59

Glatigny, Albert (1839–73), 71

Godchot, Colonel, 11

Goethe, Johann Wolfgang von (1749–1832): *Faust*, 233

Goncourt, Edmond (1822–96): on Fantin-Latour, 143; on AR's reputation, 417; *Journal*, 139

Gourmont, Remy de (1858–1915), 443

Goya y Lucientes, Francisco José de (1746–1828), 133, 353

Grant, James Augustus (1827–92): *Discovery of the Source of the Nile*, 20

Great Lakes (Africa), 322, 380, 388

Greece, 268, 350

Greenham, Sergeant George, 191

Grenoble, 10

Grisard, Françoise (housekeeper), 358

'Guerre' (AR; *Ill*), 275

Guerri tribe, 326, 343

Guigniony, G.-L., 398

Hadj-Afi (of Harar), 330

Haile Selassie (Ras Tafari), Emperor of Ethiopia (1891–1975), 381, 394

Hamburg, 291, 294

Hampstead (London), 208

Hampton, Christopher: *Total Eclipse*, 264

Hanssen, Hans, 284

Harar: AR first visits and works in (1880–82), 315–16, 319–28, 330; AR's second stay in (1883–4), 336, 338–40, 342–3; Paulitschke reports on, 348; agency closed, 350; Menelik II conquers, 374; AR revisits with Borelli (1887), 381; French interests in, 389; AR plans to import arms into, 390; AR returns to live and trade in (1888–91), 392–7, 401–2, 405–7, 414–15; conditions under Menelik's rule, 405–7; refugees in, 405; AR quits (1891), 420

Harderwijk (Holland), 279

Harwich (England), 206

Haussmann, Georges-Eugène, Baron (1809–91), 128

Hay, Michel de l' (Michel Eudes, aka Pénoutet) (1850–1900), 121, 152

Helvétius, Claude-Adrien (1715–71), 62

Henley, William Ernest (1849–1903), 195

Hénon, Captain, 375, 379

Henri (French Vice-Consul, Zeila), 357

Herer (Abyssinia), 371

Hergé (Georges Remi) (1907–83): Tintin character, xvi

Héritage (undertaker), 190

Herna (Abyssinia), 380

Hewett, Admiral Sir William (1834–88), 363

Hiddleston, J.A., 386n

Highgate (London), 208

Hingston, John, 284

Hodeidah (Arabia), 311

Holbein, Hans (1497–1543), 98

Holborn (London), 187, 244

Holland, 278–80

Holmes, Edwin, 284

'Homme juste, L'' *see* 'Juste restait droit . . . , Le'

'Honte' (AR), 18

Horace (65–8 BC), 28

Hugo, Adèle (*née* Foucher) (1803–68), 126

Hugo, Victor-Marie (1802–85): influence and success, xvi; AR's youthful knowledge of, 25, 33, 34; AR imitates, 31, 35, 37, 91, 401; supposed alliance with Prussians, 45; works published behind Iron Curtain, 76; linguistic revolution, 93; AR satirizes, 94; AR expected to 'take over from', 103; AR reads, 105; in Charleville, 106, 113; supposed congratulation of AR, 139, 442; expelled from Belgium, 225; poetic technique, 287; in Channel Islands, 394; 'Ce que dit la Bouche d'Ombre', 50, 94; *Les Contemplations*, 50, 233; *Hernani*, 116; *Les Misérables*, 40, 47, 87; *Notre-Dame de Paris*, 34; *Les Orientales*, 356

Hunter, Major F.M., 350

Hussein, Omar, 346, 348

Huxley, Aldous (1894–1963), 189

Ilg, Alfred (1854–1916): as adviser to Menelik, 325, 377; negotiates

Ilg, Alfred (*cont.*)
reduction in AR's payment to
Menelik, 378; builds first Abyssinian
railway, 380; AR writes to on
business schemes, 390, 392, 396; AR
sends account of Italian operations in
Abyssinia, 393–4; on AR's
disposition, 397; AR sends supplies
to, 401–3, 405; letters from AR on
conditions in Harar, 406–8, 410; AR
requests mule and slaves from, 412;
on condition of AR's caravans,
412–13; designs Addis Ababa, 418;
sells AR's goods, 419

Illuminations (AR): posthumous
influence, xiv; similarity of Cros's
writings to, 122; London depicted in,
184, 187, 242–3, 255; and Marx's
Das Kapital, 189; and *Une Saison en
Enfer*, 236; dating of, 238–40; style
and qualities, 248, 255, 265–6, 346;
English-language influence on,
258–9; and AR's plans for travel-
book, 260; and AR's fantasizing
about father, 261; detachment, 263;
AR gives manuscript to Verlaine for
Nouveau, 265; inverted piety in, 265;
cosmopolitanism, 268; structure, 272;
mathematical and musical terms in,
274; and AR's wanderings, 278,
285–6, 297, 301, 331, 356; and AR's
ceasing to write poetry, 288; and
identity, 291; publication and
reception, 367–8, 370; Verlaine
writes preface to, 367; posthumous
editions, 445; *see also* individual
sections

Imi (or Eimeh; Abyssinia), 348
Isaiah, 209, 233
Islington (London), 208
Issa tribe, 319, 362, 371
Italy: AR in, 267–70, 292; Adwa defeat
(1896), 381; army in Abyssinia, 388;
occupies Massawa, 393; peace treaty
with Abyssinia, 405; diplomats
expelled from Addis Ababa, 418;
imperial ambitions, 418

Itou tribe, 317, 326, 340, 428
Izambard, Georges (b. 1848): teaches
AR, 33–5, 38, 99; admires AR, 37;
letter from AR's mother, 40, 50–51;
AR reads books from, 42; and AR's
ambitions, 42; letters from AR, 43–4,
48–9, 204; on AR in prison, 47–9; in
Douai with AR, 50–51; AR's mother
blames for son's escape to Paris, 52;
follows AR on travels, 56, 60–62;
final separation from AR, 62; and
AR's 'decomposing', 67; bowdlerizes
AR's verse, 70; denies AR's presence
in Paris during Commune, 77; AR
sends poems to, 79, 434; May 1871
letter and poem from AR, 81–2,
84–5, 88; AR antagonizes, 89; on
AR's homosexual fantasizing, 100; on
Carjat portraits of AR, 115, 140; on
AR's adaptations of folk-songs, 161

Jacquemin-Parlier, Dr E., xv
James, Frank Linsly and William D.,
348
'Janvier' (AR; lost), 266
Japan, 388
Jarosseau, Mgr Élie (1858–1941), 412n
Java, 278–9, 281–3, 289
Jean, E. & Thial Fils construction
company, 299
Jeannin (of Douai), 51
Jeddah, 310
Jehonville (Belgium), 199
Jérôme, Mgr, Bishop of Harar, 340, 398
Jesus Christ, 32, 39, 42, 65, 84–5, 115,
117, 133, 160, 197, 198–9, 402, 409,
438
'Jeune ménage' (AR), 163
'Jeunesse' (AR; *Ill*), 262
Jima (or Djimma; Abyssinia), 395 & n
Job, 233
Jolly (AR's schoolfellow), 27
Journal de Charleroi (newspaper), 57–8
Joyce, James (1882–1941), 255; *Ulysses*,
233
Juba, river, 344n

Jugurtha (d. 104? BC), 28
'Juste restait droit . . . , Le' (AR), 94

Kahn, Gustave (1859–1936), 111
Kenya, 341
Koran, 12, 345, 346, 368, 408–9, 439
Krakatoa, 281

Labatut, Pierre (1842–86): gun-running
    in Abyssinia, 360, 362; protests at
    Anglo-French arms treaty, 365;
    throat cancer, 366, 368; effects and
    creditors, 368, 375–9, 381, 385–6,
    420, 423; AR burns *Memoirs*, 376
Labatut, Mme, 360, 375–6, 379, 420,
    423
Labosse, Lucien (French Vice-Consul at
    Suez), 384
Lacambre, Dr J.H., xv
Lafont, J., 246
Lagarde, Léonce (Governor of Obock)
    (1860–1936), 365, 366, 390, 408
Lanterne, La (newspaper), 41
'Larme' (AR), 159
Larnaca (Cyprus), 299, 301
Le Clair, Camille, 257, 260
Leconte de Lisle (Charles-Marie
    Leconte) (1818–94), 35–6
Lefrère, Jean-Jacques, 173
Leghorn (Italy), 268–70
Le Havre, 285, 292
Lemerre, Alphonse (1838–1912), 303,
    417
Lenin, Vladimir Ilyich (1870–1924), 76
Lepelletier, Edmond (Edmond-Adolphe
    de Bouhelier-Lepelletier)
    (1846–1913): on AR in Paris,
    139–41, 442; Verlaine writes to on
    relations with AR, 169, 187, 195;
    Verlaine writes to on life in London,
    189, 209; Verlaine writes to on AR's
    mother, 193–4; Verlaine's suicide
    note to, 216
Létrange, Louis (1850–1906), 272–3,
    441
'Lettre de Charles d'Orléans à Louis XI'
    (AR), 34

Lettre du Voyant ('Letter of the Seer';
    AR), 86–8, 91, 101, 103–4, 123, 126,
    135, 178, 327
Lévi, Éliphas (Alphonse-Louis
    Constant) (1810–75), 104
Lhéritier (Charleville schoolteacher), 25
Libéral du Nord, Le (newspaper), 50–51
Liberté, La (newspaper), 189
'Limaçon, Le' (forgery), 434
Limassol (Cyprus), 305
Lissagaray, Prosper-Olivier
    (1838–1901), 189, 191
Lit-Marefia (Abyssinia), 395
Liverpool, 285
Livingstone, Dr David (1813–73), 184,
    399, 420
Livorno *see* Leghorn
Livre de poche du Charpentier, Le, 304
'Livre nègre' (AR; ?SE), 203
'Livre païen' (AR; ?SE), 203
Loisset's Circus, 291
Lombard, Constable, 177–8
London: AR and Verlaine in, 183–96,
    206–8; AR and Nouveau in, 241–6;
    AR's illness in, 248–9; AR's mother
    and sister visit AR in, 253–5; AR
    leaves, 256–7; AR passes through,
    285
Longfellow, Henry Wadsworth
    (1807–82), 197
Lorenz, Edward, 84
Louis, Prince Imperial of France
    (1856–79), 27, 185–6
'Loup criait . . . , Le' (AR; 161
Louvre, 141, 145, 146, 193
Lübke, Wilhelm (1826–93), 262
Lucardi (agent), 383
Lucereau, Henri, 312, 316, 326, 340
Lucretius (*c.* 99–55 BC), 39
Lugbara water cult, 409
Lune, La (magazine), 72
Luxor, 294
Lyon, 8, 311, 317, 323, 335, 435

Mabille, Alfred, 29
'Ma Bohème' (AR), 59, 60, 62, 103, 269,
    426

Macagne (or Macagno), Jules, 179
MacMahon, Edmé-Patrice, Comte de (1808–93), 207
Madagascar, 388
Magasin pittoresque, Le (magazine), 105
Mahdi, the (Mohammed Ahmed) (1848–85), 350
Mahdists, 404–5
'Mains de Jeanne-Marie, Les' (AR), 77
Maisons-Alfort, near Paris, 271
Maître, Edmond, 117
Makonnen, Ras (1862–1906): as Governor of Harar, 381, 391; promises to close British trade routes, 389; leaves for Italy and Holy Land, 405–6; AR criticizes, 410; AR writes to after amputation, 427; shoots Galla Itous, 428; writes to AR after amputation, 429
'Mal, Le' (AR), 54
Mallarmé, Stéphane (1842–98), 35, 79, 111, 141, 352
Manet, Édouard (1832–83), 126, 133
Mao Zedong (1893–1976), 76
Marat, Jean-Paul (1743–93), 32
Mariam (AR's female companion in Aden), 357–8, 369
Marseille: AR's 1875 illness in, 270; AR passes through, 292, 301; Bardey in, 344, 352; AR hospitalized in, 425–7, 443; AR returns to, 432, 435–8
Marx, Eleanor (1855–98), 189
Marx, Karl (1818–83), 76, 197; *Das Kapital*, 189
Mary, Jules (1851–1922), 165
Massawa, 310, 358, 382, 383, 388, 393
'Matinée d'ivresse' (AR; *Ill*), 131, 226
Matucci, Mario, 391–2
Matuszewicz, Colonel, 191, 216
Maupassant, Guy de (1850–93), 417
Mauté (de Fleurville), Théodore-Jean (Mathilde Verlaine's father) (1809–87): 113; AR stays in home, 118; Verlaine threatens to burn house, 138; sees AR as drain on Verlaine's finances, 150; rescues daughter, 151; and AR's departure

from Paris, 153; and AR's return to Paris, 163; and Verlaine's homosexual relations with AR, 170, 175–6, 187, 193; attempts to trace Verlaine in Belgium, 179
Mauté (de Fleurville), Mme (Mathilde Verlaine's mother), 151, 153, 169, 176–7, 187, 193
'Mauvais sang' (AR; *SE*), 203, 230, 269
May, Frederick, 256
Mazas prison (Paris), 48, 55
Mazeran, Pierre, 342
Mechelen (Belgium), 180
'Mémoire' (AR), xiv, 6, 12, 156–7, 248
Mendès, Catulle (1842–1909), 126
Menelik I, Emperor of Ethiopia, 373
Menelik II, King of Choa and Emperor of Ethiopia (1844–1913): Ilg advises, 325, 377; prepares to invade Harar, 340; encourages European traders, 360, 373; buys arms, 364, 366, 378–9, 381; AR meets, 377–8; campaigns, 380, 404; breeds mules, 388; reforms, 401; self-proclamation as Emperor, 405; demands money from Europeans in Harar, 406
Mérat, Albert (1840–1909), 87, 143, 151
Mercier, Étienne-Henri (b. 1848), 140, 268, 271, 292
Merciniez, Alexandre (French Consul at Massawa), 382–4
Mercure de France (journal), 175–6, 443
Merlet, Gustave (1828–91): *Choix de poètes du XIXᵉ siècle*, 417
Méry (France), 204
'Mes petites amoureuses' (AR), 70–71, 86, 100
Metema (Abyssinia), 405
'Métropolitain' (AR; *Ill*), 243
Metz, 41, 170
Mézières, 5, 24, 43, 53, 63–7
Michel, Constable Auguste-Joseph (b. c. 1835), 221
Michel, 'le père' (servant), 303
'Michel et Christine' (AR), 173
Michelet, Jules (1798–1874), 233
Milan, 267–8

Millais, Sir John Everett (1829–96), 34
Miller, Henry (1891–1980), xvii
Millot, Ernest, 235, 285, 303
Mindjar plain (Abyssinia), 380
Mitsiwa *see* Massawa
Mocha, 315
Mogadishu, 344n
Mombasa, 344n
Monde artiste, Le (journal), 443
Monet, Claude (1840–1926), 195
Moniteur de l'Enseignement Supérieur (journal), 27–9, 39
Montaigne, Michel Eyquem de (1533–92), 42, 229
Moore, George (1852–1933), 437
Morrison, Jim (1943–71), xiv
'Mort de Paris, La' (AR; lost), 93
'Morts de Quatre-vingt-douze' ('Les Morts de Valmy'; AR), 42, 55
Mourot, Auguste (b. *c.* 1846), 216, 218
Mozart, Wolfgang Amadeus (1756–91), 386
Murger, Henry (1822–61): *La Vie de Bohème*, 116
Murphy, Steve, 357n
Musset, Alfred de (1810–57), 91; *Confession d'un enfant du siècle*, 228

Nantes, 372
Naples, 280, 405
Napoleon I (Bonaparte), Emperor of France (1769–1821), 285
Napoleon III, Emperor of France (1808–73): founds Second Empire, 3; assassination attempt on, 25; in AR's school work, 22, 28; in Franco-Prussian War, 44, 48; defeat and exile, 53–4, 205; AR lampoons, 61, 94; in England, 184; death, 199
Nasr-ed-Din, Shah of Persia (1829–96), 207, 209
'Nasty Fellows' *see* 'Vilains Bonshommes'
National, Le (newspaper), 118
Nero, Roman Emperor (37–68), 232
Newhaven (England), 199
Newton, Sir Isaac (1642–1727), 84

New York Herald, 188
Nice, 292, 388
Nicholl, Charles: *Somebody Else: Arthur Rimbaud in Africa*, xvii
Nile, river, 21, 312, 344, 366, 380, 381
'Nocturne vulgaire' (AR; *Ill*), 274
Nokob (Abyssinia), 347
Nord-Est, Le (newspaper), 97
Nouveau, Germain (1851–1920): AR befriends, 238; and *Illuminations*, 240; with AR in London, 241, 243–6; undergoes religious crises, 245, 430; refers to AR as 'Thing', 247; separates from AR, 260; AR gives *Illuminations* to for printing, 265; maintains relations with AR, 271; as itinerant religious poet, 430
'Nuit de l'enfer' ('Fausse conversion'; AR; *SE*), 203, 205
'Nuits blanches, Les' (AR; lost), 128

Obock (Abyssinia), 309, 341–2, 358, 365–6, 369, 390, 391, 437
Ogaden (Abyssinia), 328, 344–50, 367
Olivoni, Giovanni Battista (1862–1952), 396, 398, 418
'Ophélie' (AR), 33–4, 36, 88, 238
'Oraison du soir' (AR), 67
Orange (France), 435
'Orgie parisienne, L'' *see* 'Paris se repeuple'
Oromo *see* Galla
Orsini, Felice (1819–58), 25
Orwell, George (1903–50), 189
'O saisons, ô châteaux . . .' (AR), 158, 160
Oseco, The (ship), 284
Ostend, 181–2, 199
'Ouvriers' (AR; *Ill*), 15
Oxford, 258, 386n

Padang (Sumatra), 281
Palmerston (Australia) *see* Darwin
Panama Canal, 322
'Parade' (AR; *Ill*), 286, 288, 291
Paris: AR moves between Charleville and, 46, 72–4, 106, 113–14; siege

Paris (*cont.*)
(1870), 53, 72, 112; post-siege
conditions, 74; '*Semaine Sanglante*',
88; AR goes native in, 129–30; AR
disparages, 132; AR's life in, 133–4,
139, 147, 165–7; AR returns to after
European wanderings, 270, 294;
Great Exhibition (1889), 417; passes
through, 433–4; *see also* Commune
and Communards
'Paris se repeuple' ('L'Orgie parisienne';
AR), 74, 77, 100, 113, 414
Parnasse contemporain, Le (anthology),
35, 37–8, 110, 247
Parnassians, 35–7, 87, 91, 98, 116, 150,
177, 191, 303
Pauffin, Henri, 272
Paulitschke, Philipp, 347–8
'Pauvres à l'église, Les' (AR), 91–3
Père fouettard, Le (journal), 75
Pérette (Charleville schoolteacher), 20
Périgueux, 151
Perpignan, 133
Petit Ardennais, Le (newspaper), 443
Petiteville, Vicomte de (French Consul
at Beirut), 388
Petitfils, Pierre, xvii
'Petits Pauvres' *see* 'Effarés, Les'
Peuple souverain, Le (newspaper), 139
Photographies du temps passé (AR;
projected), 122
Picasso, Pablo (1881–1973), xiv, 145
Pierquin, Louis (1856–1928), 303
Pincemaille, Anne, 225
Pinchard, D., 315, 320, 323, 326
Pino, Éloi, 396
Pissarro, Camille (1830–1903), 195
Plume, La (journal), 414
Poe, Edgar Allan (1809–49), 105, 196,
290
Poésies (AR), 93
Poésies complètes (AR), 445
'Poètes de sept ans, Les' (AR), 15–18,
40, 67–8
Poètes maudits, Les: *see under* Verlaine,
Paul-Marie
Pol Pot (Saloth Sar) (1926–98), 111

Poncelet (Charleville school *surveillant*),
20
Ponchon, Raoul (1848–1937), 235, 238
'Ponts, Les' (AR; *Ill*), 243
Poot, Jacques & Co. (printer), 233–4
Potamos (Cyprus), 299–300
Poussin, Alfred, 237
'Premières communions, Les' (AR), 13,
32, 84–5, 90, 100, 102, 343, 353,
364, 439
'Première soirée' ('Trois baisers'; AR),
41, 149, 211
Prester John, 310
Prince Imperial *see* Louis
Prins van Oranje (ship), 280–81
Progrès des Ardennes, Le (newspaper), 66,
77
'Promontoire' (AR; *Ill*), 257
Proses évangéliques (AR), 197–9, 445
Proust, Marcel (1871–1922), xiv, 93
Pussemange (France), 171
Pyrenees, 270

Queenstown (Ireland), 285, 290
'Qu'est-ce pour nous, mon coeur . . .'
(AR), 148–9, 174
Quiévrain (Belgium), 177

Racine, Jean (1639–99), 353
'Rages de Césars' (AR), 54
Raphael (1483–1520), 36n
Rapport sur l'Ogadine (AR), 347–50
Rasali (Abyssinia), 369
Reading (England), 257–60
Red Sea, 281, 309–11, 366, 385
Régamay, Widow, 190
Régamey, Félix (1844–1907), 185–6,
188, 235, 247
Reliquaire, Le (AR), 442–3
Rembe (prophet), 409
'Remembrances du vieillard idiot, Les'
(AR), 14, 137–8
Remi tribe (Gaul), 4
Renan, Ernest (1823–92): *Vie de Jésus*,
198
Renoir, Auguste (1841–1919), 121
'Reparties de Nina, Les' (AR), 54–5

Rethel (France), 273

Reuter Agency, 393

'Rêve' (AR), 273

'Rêvé pour l'hiver' (AR), 59

'Réveilleurs de la nuit, Les' (AR; lost), 128–9

Revue de l'Évolution sociale, scientifique et littéraire, 436

Revue indépendante, La, 417

Revue pour tous, La, 30, 33, 36

Rheims, 5, 21, 23

Richepin, Jean (1849–1926), 78, 164–6, 235, 238, 241, 243

Riès, Maurice, 398, 422, 431

Rigault, Raoul (1846–71), 75

Righas, Athanase, 398, 410

Righas, Constantin, 316, 320, 340, 398, 400, 410

Righas, Dimitri (d. 1891), 428

Rimbaud, Arthur (1854–91): influence, xiii–xiv, 442–4; sister Isabelle protects posthumous reputation, xv, 443–4; ancestry and family background, 3–5; name, 3; birth and baptism (as Jean-Nicolas-Arthur), 8; childhood and upbringing, 11, 15–16, 18–19, 24–5; and father's disappearance, 13–15; schooling, 16–20, 26–7, 29–32, 39, 42; appearance and dress, 18, 24, 68–9, 89, 106, 113–16, 132, 140–41, 144, 271, 276, 279, 301, 311, 336, 358–9, 383; storytelling, 20; juvenilia, 21–4, 30, 34–9, 52, 54–5; sketches, 23–4; precocity, 24–5, 27–8; sends Communion ode to Prince Imperial, 27; writes homework for schoolfellows, 29–30; youthful reading, 34, 42; experimental and innovative verse, 37–9, 55, 91–5, 115, 148–9, 157–62; plagiarism, 39, 43; view of Franco-Prussian War, 41, 43; leaves Charleville for Paris, 44–6; arrested and imprisoned in Paris, 46–8, 53; released and sent to Douai, 49–50; returns to Charleville, 52; revolutionary politics, 53–5, 57;

admires realism, 55; anarchism, 55, 141, 149, 390; travels to Belgium (1870), 56–62; accent, 57, 139, 162; social manners, 57, 141; 'Bohemian' sonnets, 59–61; mental self-discipline, 62–3; sent back to Charleville, 62–3; as town hooligan, 67; in puberty, 68–9, 85; adolescent love-making, 69–71; homosexuality, 69, 100–101, 138–9, 141–2, 148, 150, 185–6, 210, 390, 410; drawing, 72, 263; second trip to Paris (1871), 72–5; and Paris Commune, 75–9; composes revolutionary Constitution, 76; works on *Progrès des Ardennes* newspaper, 77; vagabondage, 79–80, 293–4; 'Je est un autre', 81, 83–4, 105, 232; on poet as seer, 86–8; debts, 89; satirical method, 94–5; September 1871 departure for Paris, 105–6; Kahn on, 111; meets Verlaine in Paris, 113–14; stays with Verlaines, 113–15; portrait photographs, 115, 127, 140, 352; headlice, 116; meets Parnassians, 116–18; poetic theories, 117–18; moves to Banville's home, 118–19, 121; extreme behaviour, 119–21, 123–5, 134, 139, 146; lack of hygiene, 120–21, 147–8; stays with Cros, 121–2, 125; on frustrated love, 122–3; poetic development, 123; charm, 125–6; leaves Verlaine in Paris, 128–9; newspaper articles rejected, 128; with Zutistes, 129, 133, 137; drinking and drug-taking, 131, 135, 148–9, 160, 166, 201, 397; satirizes Coppée, 137–8; painted by Fantin-Latour, 143, 192–3; sketched by Forain, 145–6; on modern art, 146; neo-pagan aims, 149–50, 153; seeks to wreck Verlaine's marriage, 150–51, 155–6; stabs Carjat, 151–2; leaves Paris for Arras and Charleville, 153–4, 157; letters to Verlaine, 154–5; imitates folk-songs, 161–2; returns to Paris to meet Verlaine,

Rimbaud, Arthur (*cont.*)
163–7; Verlaine writes 'Le Bon Disciple' for, 163–4; notebook ('*cahier d'expressions*'), 164–5; prose poems, 167; leaves Paris for Belgium with Verlaine, 169–74, 179; apprehended in Arras, 170; Belgium poems, 172–3; in Constable Lombard's account, 177–8; foreign police dossier on, 179–80, 200, 210; and 'duty' ('*devoir*'), 181; attitude to Verlaine, 181; first travels to England (September 1872), 182–5; life in London, 185–92, 207–11; under police suspicion in London, 189; leaves London for Charleville, 194; returns to London (January 1873), 196; studies English, 196–7, 241, 244–5, 259; Verlaine dedicates *Romances sans paroles* to, 196; reads at British Museum, 197, 245; religious attitudes, 197–8, 409–10; stays with family in Roche, 201–2; returns to England (May 1873), 206–7; teaches French in London, 208–9, 245–6; complains of Verlaine's behaviour, 210; play stabbings with Verlaine, 210–11, 213; Verlaine leaves in London, 213–14; appeals to Verlaine to return, 214–16; and Verlaine's suicide threat, 215–16; follows Verlaine to Brussels, 218–21; shot by Verlaine in Brussels, 220–23, 227, 442; statements on Verlaine arrest, 221–4; denies immoral relations with Verlaine, 223; withdraws complaint against Verlaine, 224; painted by Rosman, 225; leaves Belgium for Roche, 225–6; and idea of Hell, 227–8; writes at Roche, 229; ceases literary writing, 236, 239–40, 272–4, 286–8, 302–3; friendship with Nouveau, 238, 240–41; regular visits to mother's home, 239, 262, 272, 292–3, 301–2; in London with Nouveau (March 1874), 241–6; works in London box factory, 244;

advertises for post of companion, 247–8; illness in London, 248–9; mother and sister Vitalie visit in London, 253–6; leaves London, 256–7; in Reading, 257–9; travels to Stuttgart, 257, 262–5; English word-lists, 259; anxiety over military service, 260, 273–4, 321, 419, 429; Verlaine visits in Stuttgart, 264–7; moves to Italy, 267–8; wanderings in Europe (1875–6), 268–70, 277–8; collapses with sunstroke in Italy, 269–70; 'philomathic' learning and language acquisition, 269, 272, 289; returns to Paris after European wanderings (1875), 270–71; Garnier portrait of, 271; tutoring, 271–2; learns piano, 272–3; shaves off hair, 276; robbed in Vienna, 277; walking, 277–8, 292; enlists in Dutch Colonial Army, 278–80; sails for Dutch East Indies, 280–82; deserts army in Java, 282–3; returns from Java, 284–5; considers career, 289; occasional work and travels in Europe (1876–7), 289–92; works for Dutch recruiting agent, 289–90; asks about joining US navy, 290–91; gastric fever, 292, 356; in Alps, 295–7; works on Cyprus construction projects, 299–301, 304; typhoid fever, 301; on reforming land use, 302; nostalgia for family farm, 303; suffers from palpitations, 304; flees Cyprus, 305–6; arrives at Red Sea, 309–10; first stays in Aden, 311–17; illness in Hodeidah, 311; journey to and first stay in Harar (1880–82), 315–28, 330; requests books and instruments from mother, 316, 324–5; letters home from Harar and Aden, 320–23, 329–30, 332, 334–5, 338, 351, 359, 366–7, 381–2, 388, 404, 406, 424; sends money home from Africa, 321, 331–2, 334, 423; contracts syphilis, 322, 356, 418; and Abyssinian fauna, 323; exploration and expeditions in

Rimbaud, Arthur (*cont.*)
  Abyssinia, 325–8, 334, 340–41,
    344–50, 380–81, 384, 396, 414–15;
    letters published, 326, 360 & n;
    fevers in Abyssinia, 328, 330; Bardey
    on character of, 331; returns to Aden
    from Harar, 331–3; slanders Bardey,
    332; unfulfilled plans to leave Aden,
    332–4; photography, 323, 334, 343;
    investments and savings, 335, 356;
    leaves Aden for Harar after row with
    local, 335–6, 338–9; marriage
    intentions, 335, 338, 415–16, 428,
    431; second stay in Harar (1883–4),
    336, 338–43; keeps local woman in
    Harar, 339–40, 357; knowledge of
    African and Oriental languages,
    339–40, 358, 375; commercial
    activities in Harar, 342–3, 401–2;
    organizes Sotiro's rescue, 346; studies
    and interprets Koran, 346, 368,
    408–9, 439; ignores request from
    Société de Géographie, 350–51;
    leaves Harar, 350, 420; poems
    published in *Les Poètes maudits*,
    352–3; work and life in Aden, 352,
    355–9; legend and reputation, 353,
    399–401, 411, 416–17, 444–5;
    rejects literary past, 353; considers
    book on journeys, 354; defers return
    to France, 354–5; supposed
    conversion to Islam, 355, 439; joined
    by Abyssinian woman in Aden,
    357–8; leaves Bardey, 360; gun-
    running activities in Abyssinia, 361,
    362–8, 370–81, 387, 396, 418; ends
    relationship with native woman, 369;
    described by Borelli, 375; paid by
    Menelik, 378–9; financial results of
    gun-running expedition, 381–2,
    385–6; acquires new passport in
    Massawa, 383–4; carries money, 383,
    385; charms French Consuls, 383–4;
    account of expedition in Abyssinia,
    384–5; in Cairo, 384, 387–8;
    business acumen, 386; supposed
    death-bed conversion, 386–7, 438–9;

  rheumatism in Cairo, 387; arranges
    arms deal with Savouré, 389–90, 392;
    and French foreign policy, 389; sends
    reports on Abyssinia to France, 389,
    400, 421; activities known to British
    Foreign Office, 390–91; suspected of
    slave-trading, 391; settles in Harar
    (1888–90), 392–7, 401–2, 405–7,
    414; comments on European
    activities in Africa, 393–5; character
    and disposition in Africa, 397–9;
    poisons dogs in Harar, 407–8;
    assaulted in Harar, 408; behaviour in
    Harar, 410–13; racial views, 411–12
    & n; European search for, 416; fake
    poems and forgeries, 417, 434;
    diseased leg, 418–21, 424–5; diary,
    421; financial position, 422–3, 444;
    in hospital in Marseille, 425; leg
    amputated, 426–9; ceases to write to
    mother, 427; leaves hospital for
    Roche, 430–31; returns to Marseille
    hospital from Roche, 433–7; physical
    decline, 436–8; dictates final letter to
    Isabelle, 439–40; death and funeral,
    440–42; posthumous publication and
    notoriety, 442–3
Rimbaud, Captain Frédéric (AR's father)
    (1814–78): courtship and marriage,
    7–8; military career, 7, 28, 78, 291;
    marriage relations, 9, 11–12;
    writings, 11–13; leaves wife and
    children, 12–13, 15, 260–61; as
    figure in AR's writings, 12, 22, 24,
    105, 156–7, 261; retirement, 105;
    death, 295; papers, 321; translation of
    Koran, 346; *Correspondance militaire*,
    12; annotated *Grammaire Nationale*,
    13, 30
Rimbaud, Frédéric (AR's brother)
    (1853–1911): birth, 8; and father's
    disappearance, 13; upbringing, 15,
    19; schooling, 16, 19, 24, 29, 31; low
    ambitions, 23; serves in Franco-
    Prussian War, 41, 53; sisters scorn,
    85; travels with family to Roche, 200;
    character, 304, 430; AR asks to

Rimbaud, Frédéric (*cont.*)
search father's papers, 321; threatens AR with blackmail, 353–4; AR excludes from inheritance, 423

Rimbaud, Isabelle (AR's sister) (1860–1917): defends AR's reputation, xv, 443–4; birth, 10; childhood and upbringing, 18–19; on AR's story-telling, 20; denies AR's presence in Paris during Commune, 77; First Communion, 84–5; travels with family to Roche, 200; claims AR burns *Une Saison en Enfer*, 235; not on family visit to AR in London, 254; and AR's giving up writing, 266; on AR's tutoring at Maisons-Alfort, 271; on AR's being robbed in Vienna, 277; letters from AR, 295, 299, 314, 326, 387 & n, 404, 406, 422, 427, 429–30; and AR's singing on return from Cyprus, 301; mother leaves farm to, 303; on AR in Harar, 325–6; marriage, 326, 415, 443; AR counsels marriage to, 338; spurious drawing of AR playing Abyssinian harp, 357n; unaware of AR's literary fame, 417; AR collects souvenirs for, 420; on AR's journey from Harar to coast, 420; death from cancer, 422; and AR's leg amputation, 426–7, 429–30; and AR's marriage plans, 431; accused of bigotry, 432; effect of AR on during convalescence, 432–3; accompanies AR to Marseille, 433–8; claims AR's conversion to faith, 438–9; AR dictates final letter to, 439–40

Rimbaud, J.B., 294n

Rimbaud, Vitalie I (AR's sister) (1857): birth and death, 10

Rimbaud, Vitalie II (AR's sister) (1858–75): birth, 10; childhood and upbringing, 18–19; stays with family in Roche, 200–202; on AR's inactivity in fields at Roche, 229; diary of stay in London, 253–6;

tubercular synovitis, 271, 422; death and burial, 276, 422

Rimbaud, Vitalie (*née* Cuif; AR's mother) (1825–1907): background and character, 4–7, 9, 12–14; homes in Charleville, 5–6, 10, 52; marriage and children, 7–10, 12; runs family farm, 9; evicted by landlord, 10; husband leaves, 12–13, 15, 260–61; and children's upbringing, 15–16, 18–20, 23–8, 40; in AR's juvenilia, 22; relations with AR, 39, 50, 71–2, 74, 84, 89, 96, 100; fears subversive influences on AR, 40–41; and AR's imprisonment in Paris, 48–9; chastises AR on return from Paris, 52; demands AR's return from Douai, 62; in Franco-Prussian War, 65; demands AR return to school or leave home, 71; encourages AR's departure, 96; Mautés complain of AR to, 150–51; condemns intellectual work, 154; and AR's 'Mémoire', 6, 12, 156; reports AR missing, 179; on duty and happiness, 181; AR warns against slander, 193; demands Mathilde recall Verlaine from London, 193; takes family to Roche, 200; replies to Verlaine's letter threatening suicide, 216–17, 239; influence on AR's *Une Saison en Enfer*, 233; pays for printing of *Une Saison en Enfer*, 233; AR revisits after travels, 239, 262, 272, 292–3, 301–2; visits AR in London, 248–9, 253–6; attempts to have AR exempted from military service, 260; and AR's departure for Germany, 262; supports AR's acquisition of piano, 273; AR returns to from Java, 285; buys house at Saint-Laurent, 294; letters from AR on travels, 295, 299, 314, 320–22, 329, 331–2, 334–5, 351, 359, 366–7, 381–2, 388, 404, 406, 424; AR asks for testimonial, 298; passes farm on to Isabelle, 303–4; AR requests books and instruments

Rimbaud, Vitalie (*cont.*)
  for Abyssinia, 316, 321, 324–5,
  334–5; buys land for AR, 334, 423;
  warns AR of brother Frédéric's
  blackmail plans, 344; sends copies of
  Koran to AR, 346; writes to AR in
  Aden, 359; and AR's finances after
  gun-running expedition, 381–2;
  suggests marriage for AR and
  Isabelle, 415–16; unaware of AR's
  literary fame, 417, 445; and AR's
  money, 423, 436; visits AR in
  Marseille hospital, 426–7; effect on
  convalescing AR, 431; local opinion
  of, 432; and AR's suffering, 433; and
  AR's funeral, 441; absent from public
  inauguration of AR's bust (1901),
  444; death, 445
Rivière, Jacques (1886–1925), xv
Robecchi Bricchetti, Luigi (1855–1926),
  398
Robespierre, Maximilien de (1758–94), 32
Roche: AR's mother's early home and
  life in, 5, 9, 13; AR lives in, 9, 194,
  202, 229; AR's sister Vitalie describes
  life at, 200, 229; AR returns to from
  Belgium, 225, 227; AR revisits
  regularly, 239, 301; AR stays in on
  return from Africa, 430–31; *see also*
  Charleville
Rollinat, Maurice (1846–1903), 142
'Roman' (AR), 52, 64
Rome, 292, 405
Rosa, Ottorino (1854–1930), 305–6,
  337, 357–8, 398, 407, 408, 414, 418
Rosman, Jef (André-Marie-Joseph)
  (b. 1853), 225
Rossat, François-Sébastien, 19
Rossetti, William (1829–1919), 192
'Rotte Pietje' (Dutch prostitute), 279
Rotterdam, 278–9
Rudolf (Turkana), Lake, 396
Russia, 277, 310

Sacconi, Pietro (d. 1883), 340, 344–5
Sade, Donatien-Alphonse-François,
  Marquis de (1740–1814), 197

Sagallo (Abyssinia), 371–2
St Gotthard Pass and tunnel, 295–6
St Helena, 285
St John, 198
Saint-Laurent, near Charleville, 294
St Pancras (London), 208
Saint-Quentin (France), 44, 47
Saison en Enfer, Une (AR): qualities, xiv,
  209, 411; on AR's ancestry, 4; on
  influence of vagrants and convicts,
  40; and destruction, 66; and
  feminism, 69; and AR's mother's
  remarks, 74; on AR's worms, 116; on
  art, 147; and AR's aims, 149; on
  experimental verse, 158; allusions to
  Verlaine in Belgium, 175; and
  popular reaction to writings, 178; on
  wanderings in Belgium, 180–81; on
  Verlaine, 181, 206, 211–12; on sea,
  182; writing of, 184, 190, 194, 197,
  202–4, 209, 225, 227; Gospel
  adaptations in, 198; on drug-taking,
  201–2; ideas, structure and content,
  203–5, 228–32, 242; on Good and
  Evil, 225–6; influences and sources,
  233; printed and distributed, 233–6,
  238; Isabelle claims AR burns copies,
  235; as supposed final work, 236,
  239–40; corrections, 239; dating,
  240; on omniscience, 247; theological
  angst, 265; AR gives copy to Italian
  widow, 268; demon in, 275; and
  identity, 291, 430; and AR's miseries
  in Aden, 356; on old love affairs, 369;
  unclaimed copies discovered, 444;
  posthumous editions, 445
Salatiga (Java), 282
Samarang (Java), 281–5, 289
Sappho, 110
Sarcey, Francisque (1827–99), 73
Sarpy, Charles, 244
Sartre, Jean-Paul (1905–80), 93
Savouré, Armand: on AR's gait, 387; AR
  undertakes mission for, 389–92;
  advised to use slave route, 391; on
  AR's reports to newspapers, 394;
  stays with AR in Harar, 396;

Savouré, Armand (*cont.*)
  describes AR, 398; AR acts as
  middleman for, 401; on AR's
  cynicism, 415; reports Makonnen's
  distress at AR's amputation, 429
Scarborough (England), 257–8
Sebdou (Algeria), 7
Sedan, battle of (1870), 44, 48, 205
'Seer letter' (AR) *see Lettre du Voyant*
Sélestat (France), 10
Semal, Dr Charles, 223–4
'Sensation' (AR), 35, 38
Shah of Persia *see* Nasr-ed-Din
Shakespeare, William (1564–1616), 139,
  197, 233, 442; *Hamlet*, 34
Sheba, Queen of, 373
Shebele (Shibeli), river, 344 & n, 345,
  347–8
Shoa (or Shewa) *see* Choa
Siefert, Louisa, 43
Siena, 269
Sitwell, Dame Edith (1887–1964), xv
Sivry, Charles de (1848–1900), 111, 120,
  288
Smith, Mrs Alexander, 208, 210, 216,
  217
Smith, Patti (b. 1946), xv
Sobat, river, 312
Société de Géographie, Paris, 317, 346,
  350, 388, 396, 400, 421
Society of French Artists Exhibition,
  London, 192
Soho (London), 189–91
'Soir historique' (AR; *Ill*), 266
'Solde' (AR; *Ill*), 240, 286
'Soleil et chair' ('*Credo in unam*'; AR),
  36, 38
Soleillet, Paul (1842–86), 368, 372
Solomon, 373
Somali tribes, 312, 314, 342, 344, 359,
  362
'Sonnet du trou du cul' (AR; with
  Verlaine), 142–3, 185, 224
Sophocles (*c.* 496–405 BC), 43
Sotiro (or Sotiros), Konstantinu, 344–7,
  350, 428, 431
Southampton, 280

Spain: Carlist activities, 207, 216, 270
Speke, John Hanning (1827–64):
  Discovery of the Source of the Nile, 20
Splügen Pass, 267
Stanley, Sir Henry Morton (1841–1904),
  184, 395
Starkie, Enid, 82n, 208, 257, 284,
  324–5, 391
Steinmetz, Jean-Luc, xvii
Stéphane (dyer; '2nd class'), 395 & n
Stephens family (London), 241
Stickney (England), 267
Stockholm, 286, 291
Strasbourg, 10, 277
Stupra, Les see 'Sonnet du trou du cul'
Stuttgart, 262–5, 267
Suakin (Sudan), 310
Sudan, 310, 388, 394
Suel, Jules, 311–13, 364, 368–9, 381,
  385
Suez, 280, 292, 309, 384, 435, 440
Sully-Prudhomme (René-François-
  Armand Prudhomme) (1839–1907),
  39
Sumatra, 281
Surabaya (Java), 283 & n
Surrealists, 121, 139, 273
Swedenborg, Emanuel (1688–1772), 181
Swinburne, Algernon Charles
  (1837–1909), 191, 196, 197, 247
Switzerland, 267, 293, 295–7
Symboliste, Le (journal), 367
Syria, 388

Tadjoura (Abyssinia), 271, 309, 359,
  361–4, 366–7, 369, 384
Taine, Hippolyte (1828–93), 84, 233
Taitou Betul, Empress of Menelik II
  (*c.* 1850–1918), 379, 418
Taurin Cahagne, Ludovic, Bishop
  (1826–99), 322, 344, 354, 357, 374,
  391, 398, 408–10
Tchercher *see* Chercher
Teleki, Count Samuel, 396
Temps, Le (newspaper), 352, 389,
  399–401
'Tête de faune' (AR), 139–40

Theodoros (Tewodros) II (Kassa Hailu), Emperor of Ethiopia (1818–68), 260

Thiers, Adolphe (1797–1877), 207

Tian, André, 391

Tian, César: suspected of slave-trading, 391; makes AR sole agent in Harar, 392, 395, 401; AR submits accounts to, 407; AR attempts to engineer quarrel with, 415; AR recuperates at Aden house of, 422; and AR's financial situation, 422–3; sends greetings to AR in Marseille hospital, 428

Tigray (Tigré), 340, 363

Timbuctoo, 315, 416

Times, The (newspaper), 245–7, 256–7, 259

Tintin *see* Hergé

Toupet (coiffeur), 190

Traversi, Dr Leopoldo (b. 1856), 395 & n, 398, 419

Trébuchet (agent in Hodeidah), 311

'Trois baisers' *see* 'Première soirée'

Troodos, Mount (Cyprus), 304–5

t'Serstevens, Judge Théodore, 141, 223

Tucker, George, 39

Tungtang (Java), 282

Turkana *see* Rudolf

Uganda, 409, 442

Underwood, V.P., 208

United States Navy, 260, 290–91

Univers illustré, L', 443

'Vagabonds' (AR; *Ill*), 149, 211

Valade, Léon (1841–84), 117, 237

Valence (France), 435

Valéry, Paul (1871–1945), xiv, 192, 287

Vallès, Jules (1832–85), 72–3

Varna (Bulgaria), 277

'Vénus anadyomène' (AR), 37, 54

Verlaine, Éliza (*née* Dehée; Paul's mother) (1809–86), 110, 174, 196, 218, 219, 221–3, 225

Verlaine, Georges (Paul & Mathilde's son) (1871–1926): born, 128, 155;

father threatens to kill, 138, 151; and father's absence, 193, 222

Verlaine, Mathilde (*née* Mauté; Paul's wife) (1853–1914): destroys letters from AR to Verlaine, 99, 154; marriage relations, 109, 112–14, 128, 151, 168; pregnancy and birth of son, 109, 125, 128; character and manner, 111–13; writes memoirs, 112, 176; AR stays with, 113–15; on AR's headlice, 116; and AR's behaviour, 124; and AR's effect on Verlaine, 127–8; Verlaine threatens to kill, 138; and AR's effect on marriage, 150–51, 155–6, 223; and AR's leaving Paris, 153; and Verlaine's explanation of AR's influence, 155; Verlaine leaves, 169, 178; Verlaine writes to from Belgium, 174–5, 178–9; discovers AR's letters to Verlaine, 175; follows Verlaine to Brussels, 176–7; AR's mother visits, 193; Verlaine seeks reconciliation with, 199, 205, 215–16, 219; embargoes AR's poems, 288; releases manuscript of *Illuminations*, 367

Verlaine, Captain Nicolas-Auguste (Paul's father) (1798–1865), 109–10

Verlaine, Paul-Marie (1844–96): AR's relations with, xvi, xviii, 24, 127, 138–9, 142, 148, 150–51, 154–5, 178, 181, 187, 198–9, 206, 211–13, 217, 410; poetic technique, 43, 44n; friendship with Rigault, 75; and AR in Paris Commune, 76; AR describes as seer, 87, 99; AR writes to, 99–101; poetic style, 99–100, 111; and AR's homosexual fantasizing, 100; praises AR's poetry in reply to letter, 101–2; offers hospitality to AR, 102; background, 109–11; treatment of wife, 109, 112–14, 128, 151; drinking, 111, 114, 148, 168, 175, 210, 218; marriage, 111–12; homosexuality, 112, 138, 142, 148, 150, 187; immoderate behaviour, 112–13; in Siege of Paris and

Verlaine, Paul-Marie (*cont.*)
Commune, 112; AR stays with in Paris, 113–15; on AR's beauty, 115–16; stabbed by AR, 124; and AR's disappearances in Paris, 128–9, 131; birth of son, 128; describes Cabaner, 133; and Coppée's verse, 137; threatens to kill wife and child, 138; and 'Tête de faune', 140n; painted by Fantin-Latour, 143, 192; and AR's attic in Latin Quarter, 147–8; and AR's aims, 149–50; moves to separate from wife, 150–51; and AR's banning from 'Vilains Bonshommes', 152–3; attempts to save marriage, 153; letters from AR ('*lettres martyriques*'), 154; takes job as clerk, 155, 168; receives AR's *Derniers vers*, 157–8; plans to follow AR, 162, 169; on AR's accent, 162; religious conversion, 164, 205, 217, 264; leaves Mathilde and accompanies AR to Belgium, 169–74; arrested in Arras, 170; resumes writing poetry in Belgium, 172; correspondence with mother, 174; writes to Mathilde from Belgium, 174–5, 178–9; eludes Mathilde's rescue attempt in Belgium, 176–7; in Constable Lombard's account, 177–8; police dossier on, 179–80, 199–200; in AR's *Une Saison en Enfer*, 181, 206, 210–11; travels to England (September 1872), 182–5; life in London, 186–90, 192–3, 195–6, 208–10; under police suspicion in London, 189; AR's mother intervenes in attempt to recall from London, 193–4; parents-in-law persecute, 193; AR stimulates to write, 196; studies English, 196–7, 210; returns for attempted reconciliation with Mathilde, 199, 205; returns to England with AR (May 1873), 206–7; teaches in London, 208–9; denies pederasty, 210; play stabbings with AR, 210–11,

213; leaves AR in London and flees to Belgium, 213–18; AR writes to appealing for return, 214–15; threatens suicide, 215–16; writes to AR after separation, 215–18; AR follows to Belgium, 216; letter from AR's mother, 216–17, 239; AR follows to Brussels, 218–21; proposes volunteering for Spain, 218; shoots AR in Brussels, 220–22, 442; arrest, trial and prison sentence, 221–5, 227; medical examination and report on, 223–4; and AR's contradictions, 229–30; influence on AR's *Une Saison en Enfer*, 233; AR ends relations with, 235–6; excluded from *Parnasse contemporain*, 247; final meeting with AR, 264–7; AR attempts to extort money from, 267, 272, 276; teaching in Lincolnshire, 267; and AR's Carlist plans, 270; drawing of AR playing piano, 273; criticizes AR as parasite, 275; reappraises AR's *Illuminations*, 288; letters and drawing from Delahaye, 292, 294; and AR's giving up writing, 303; and AR's exploring in Africa, 327; publishes and writes on AR poems, 347, 352–3; contributes prefaces to posthumous editions of AR's poems, 367, 445; AR on place in literature, 401; ill-health, 430; and AR in Paris, 434; 'Birds in the Night', 180; 'Le Bon Disciple', 163–4, 223; *La Bonne Chanson*, 112; 'Chanson d'automne', 111; '*Crimen amoris*', 225; *Fêtes galantes*, 43, 99, 110; '*Laeti et errabundi*', 174; 'Paysages belges', 172; *Poèmes saturniens*, 99, 110; *Les Poètes maudits*, 140n, 223, 235, 352–3, 434; *Romances sans paroles*, 172, 196, 246; *Sagesse*, 164; 'Sonnet du trou du cul' (with AR), 142–3
Vermersch, Eugène (1845–78), 72–3, 185, 187, 189, 191, 200, 218

Verne, Jules (1828–1905), 20, 105, 184, 242
Verplaes (Brussels hotelier), 222
Versailles, 75, 79
Vers nouveaux (AR) *see Derniers vers*
Vienna, 277
'Vies' (AR; *Ill*), 239
Vietnam, 280
'Vilains Bonshommes' ('Nasty Fellows'; group), 116–17, 120, 129, 152, 227
'Ville' (AR; *Ill*), 188–90
Villers-Cotterêts (France), 79
'Villes' ('L'acropole officielle . . .'; AR; *Ill*), 188, 286
Villon, François (*c.* 1431 – after 1463), 34, 59, 401
Viotti, Lucien (d. 1870), 112
Vireux (France), 57, 61
'Vivants, Les' (group), 238, 240
Vleminckx, Dr, 223–4
Vogue, La (journal), 364, 367, 370
Voltaire (François-Marie Arouet) (1694–1778), 349
Voncq (France), 430
Vouziers (France), 202
'Voyelles' (AR), xiv, 134–7, 142, 238, 347, 367, 401, 403, 417

Wadaï, Djami (*c.* 1870 – *c.* 1892), 339, 381, 388, 410–11, 428, 438

Wagner, Albrecht (b. *c.* 1842), 263–4
Wagner, Richard (1813–83), 263
Wandering Chief, The (ship), 283–5
Warabeili (Abyssinia), 317, 340
Waugh, Evelyn (1903–66), 340, 349, 356, 398; *Scoop*, xvi
Webi Shebele *see* Shebele
Wilde, Oscar (1854–1900), 247, 258
Wilhelm I, German Kaiser (1797–1888), 73
Wisseaux (sculptor), 285
Wittgenstein, Ludwig (1889–1951), 272
Wordji (Abyssinia), 421

Xylophagou (Cyprus), 299

Yohannes IV, Emperor of Abyssinia (r. 1872–89), 311, 363, 373, 388, 404–5

Zanzibar, 315, 322, 333, 334, 388, 418
Zeila (Zayla, Abyssinia), 316–18, 341, 357, 358, 365, 385, 392, 406, 420–21
Zenjero tribe, 345
Zimmermann, Ernest, 395 & n, 412
Zola, Émile (1840–1902), 76, 141
'Zutistes, Les' (group), 129, 133, 137, 145, 185, 235, 445
Zwai (Ziway), Lake, 327